CRITICAL ACCLAIM for
An American Life

"Reagan's first autobiography was called *Where's the Rest of Me?* . . . There is a rest of him . . . and it's more complicated, and more important, than perhaps even he knows."

—*Chicago Tribune*

"This is one of the coolest and toughest and most talented democratic politicians of the century."

—Richard Reeves, *Los Angeles Times*

"A success. . . . Plainly, Reagan was brilliant at recognizing, well before other knowledgeable observers in the West, that Gorbachev represented a new phenomenon in the Soviet Union."

—*Newsday*

"A terrific read . . . a page-turner. . . . It gets to the nitty-gritty of a situation, without becoming entangled in verbiage. This is the most readable presidential autobiography since Harry S. Truman wrote his."

—*South Bend Tribune*

"What makes this an interesting book [are] . . . the glimpses of Reagan as a man. . . . It may be that as historians begin to try to understand Reagan the man, this book may tell them much more than Reagan intended."

—*Palm Beach Post* (West Palm Beach, Florida)

"Simply right, simply Ron. . . . *AN AMERICAN LIFE* is perhaps most important for the insight it provides into the way the former president made decisions."

—*The Detroit News*

RONALD REAGAN
An American Life

POCKET BOOKS

New York   London   Toronto   Sydney   Singapore

Unless otherwise credited, all photos were taken by White House photographers and appear in the book courtesy of the Ronald Reagan Presidential Library.

Photo 1: AP/Wide World Photos; Photo 2: Ronald Reagan Home Preservation Foundation; Photo 3: 1926 *Dixonian;* Photos 5, 7, and 8: Reagan Family Collection; Photo 6: Photo courtesy of *The Dixon Telegraph;* Photos 9 and 10: Gene Trindl/Shooting Star; Photo 11: Michael Evans photo.

POCKET BOOKS, a division of Simon & Schuster Inc.
1230 Avenue of the Americas, New York, NY 10020

Reagan, Ronald.
    An American life / Ronald Reagan.
        p.   cm.
    Originally published: New York : Simon and Schuster, c1990.
    Includes index.
    ISBN: 0-7434-0025-9
    1. Reagan, Ronald.   2. Presidents—United States—Biography.
I. Title.
[E877.A3   1992]
973.927'092—dc20
[B]   91-28704
                                                         CIP

First Pocket Books trade paperback printing January 1992

10   9   8   7   6   5   4   3

POCKET and colophon are registered trademarks of
Simon & Schuster Inc.

Printed in the U.S.A.

To Nancy. She will always be my
First Lady. I cannot imagine life
without her.

Acknowledgments

Presidential memoirs have become somewhat of a tradition recently—a way for a president to tell his story in his own words. And while that is what *An American Life* does, I had a great deal of help, for which I am most appreciative.

First of all, I thank my beloved wife, Nancy. There are really no words to describe what she means to me. Life with her is everything I always hoped it would be.

Robert Lindsey, a talented writer, was with me every step of the way. Bob has a way with words that has rightly earned him a reputation as one of our country's most gifted authors. Even though I am glad to have this book finished, I will miss my conversations with Bob. I'm also grateful to Bob's wife, Sandra, for her tireless work in typing Bob's notes.

The wonderful and thoroughly professional team at Simon and Schuster, under the able leadership of CEO Dick Snyder, were there day and night, always cheerful and always helpful. Editor in chief Michael Korda patiently read every single word time and time again, dotted every *i* and crossed every *t*—no one could ask for a better editor. Charlie Hayward, Alice Mayhew, and Jack McKeown were also of invaluable assistance. And Mort Janklow, my literary agent, who assembled the whole group, played a key role in bringing this book to completion.

The staff in my Los Angeles office worked with me from the very first—researching files, finding photographs, checking facts, jogging memories. Jeanine Chase, Dottie Dellinger, Kerry Geoghan, Cathy Goldberg, Peggy Grande, Jon Hall, Joanne Hildebrand, Selina Jackson, Bernadette Schurz, and Sheri Semon—loyal and competent, they are the best team anyone could field.

Three persons in particular spent considerable time working with me on this book and deserve a special mention: Fred Ryan, my chief of staff, who came with me from the White House, where he skillfully managed my schedule and where he was the architect of one of my proudest achievements—the Office of Private Sector Initiatives; Kathy Osborne, who has been my personal secretary since Sacramento and always knows just what I need (sometimes even before I do!); and Mark Weinberg, my director of public affairs, who for over ten years has articulately and effectively served as my "ambassador" to the press.

The dedicated team at the Ronald Reagan Presidential Foundation—Doris Heller, Robert Higdon, Chuck Jelloian, John Lee, Suzanne Marx, Stefanie Salata, Marilyn Siegel, Pam Trowbridge, and Sandy Warfield—will always have my gratitude for the work they are doing on the presidential library being built in the Simi-Thousand Oaks area of Ventura County.

And finally, I thank the men and women Nancy and I "left behind." The question I am most often asked these days is whether I miss Washington. Although I enjoyed the presidency, I don't miss the job. What I do miss is the people—the good and decent people from every state in the union, from all walks of life, black and white, Christian and Jew, rich and poor, military and civilian, political and civil service, who comprise the executive office of the president of the United States, joined only by the desire to serve their country. They do so with the greatest dedication and distinction. We miss them, we keep them in our hearts, and we will always be grateful to them.

Ronald Reagan

Contents

Part VI
Arms Control:
From Geneva to Reykjavík, Washington to Moscow
545

Epilogue
724

Index
727

Prologue

Nancy and I awoke early on the morning of November 19, 1985, and, at the first glimmer of daylight, we looked out from our bedroom at the long gray expanse of Lake Geneva. There were patches of snow along the edge of the lake and in the gardens of the magnificent lakeside eighteenth-century residence that had been loaned to us for a few days. In the distance we could see the majestic high peaks of the Alps.

The lake was shrouded in mist that gave its rippled surface the look of burnished pewter. Above, the sky was a dull curtain of dark clouds.

It was a dreary, yet strikingly beautiful panorama.

I had looked forward to this day for more than five years. For weeks, I'd been given detailed information about political currents in the Soviet Union, the complexities of nuclear arms control, and the new man in the Kremlin. In my diary the night before, I wrote: "Lord, I hope I'm ready."

Neither Nancy nor I had slept very well since arriving in Geneva three days earlier. During the eight-hour flight from Washington, we tried to adjust to Swiss time by eating meals aboard Air Force One at the same hour Genevans were sitting down to theirs. Doctors said this would help reduce the effects of jet lag. Yet, as each night passed, I slept fitfully.

Perhaps it was jet lag, but I found it difficult not to think about what was ahead of me.

George Shultz told me that if the only thing that came out of this first meeting with Mikhail Gorbachev was an agreement to hold another summit, it would be a success. But I wanted to accomplish more than that.

I believed that if we were ever going to break down the barriers of mistrust that divided our countries, we had to begin by establishing a personal relationship between the leaders of the two most powerful nations on earth.

During the previous five years, I had come to realize there were people in the Kremlin who had a genuine fear of the United States. I wanted to convince Gorbachev that we wanted peace and they had nothing to fear from us. So I had gone to Geneva with a plan.

The Russians were bringing their team of diplomats and arms control experts and we were bringing ours. But I wanted a chance to see Gorbachev alone.

Since Gorbachev had taken office eight months earlier, he and I had quietly exchanged a series of letters that had suggested to me he might be a different sort of Russian than the Soviet leaders we had known before.

That morning, as we shook hands and I looked into his smile, I sensed I had been right and felt a surge of optimism that my plan might work.

As we began our first meeting in the presence of our advisors, Gorbachev and I sat opposite one another. I had told my team what I was going to do.

As our technical experts began to speak, I said to him, "While our people here are discussing the need for arms control, why don't you and I step outside and get some fresh air?"

Gorbachev was out of his chair before I could finish the sentence. We walked together about one hundred yards down a hill to a boathouse along the lakeshore.

As we descended the hill, the air was crisp and very cold. I'd asked members of the White House staff to light a fire in the boathouse before we got there and they had: Only later did I discover they'd built such a rip-roaring fire that it set an ornate wooden mantelpiece above the fireplace ablaze and had to be doused with pitchers of water and then relighted a couple of hours before we arrived.

We sat down beside the blazing hearth, just the two of us and our interpreters, and I told Gorbachev that I thought he and I were in a unique situation at a unique time: "Here you and I are, two men in a room, probably the only two men in the world who could bring about World War III. But by the same token, we may be the only two men in the world who could perhaps bring about peace in the world."

Borrowing a quotation, I continued: "Mr. General Secretary, 'we don't mistrust each other because we are armed; we are armed because we mistrust each other.' It's fine that the two of us and our people are talking about arms reductions, but isn't it also important that you and I should be talking about how we could reduce the mistrust between us?"

In the preceding months I'd thought many times about this first meeting with Gorbachev. Nothing was more important to mankind than assuring its survival and the survival of our planet. Yet for forty years nuclear weapons had kept the world under a shadow of terror. Our dealings with the Soviets—and theirs with us—had been based on a policy known as "mutual assured destruction"— the "MAD" policy, and madness it was. It was the craziest thing I ever heard of: Simply put, it called for each side to keep enough nuclear weapons at the ready to obliterate the other, so that if one attacked, the second had enough bombs left to annihilate its adversary in a matter of minutes. We were a button push away from oblivion.

No one could win a nuclear war—and as I had told Gorbachev in one of my letters to him, one must never be fought.

When I had arrived in the White House in 1981, the fiber of American military muscle was so atrophied that our ability to respond effectively to a Soviet attack was very much in doubt: Fighter planes couldn't fly and warships couldn't sail because there were chronic shortages of spare parts; our best men and women were leaving the military service; the morale of our volunteer army was in a tailspin; our strategic weapons—the missiles and bombers that were the foundations of our deterrent force—hadn't been modernized in a decade, while the Soviet Union had created a war machine that was threatening to eclipse ours at every level.

I wanted to go to the negotiating table and end the madness of the MAD policy, but to do that, I knew America first had to up-grade its military capabilities so that we would be able to negotiate with the Soviets from a position of *strength,* not weakness.

Now, our military might was second to none. In 1981, we under-took a massive program to rebuild our military might while I began an effort—much of it through quiet diplomacy—that I hoped would lead the Russians to the bargaining table.

I knew very well the Soviet Union's record of deceit and its long history of betrayal of international treaties. I had met Gromyko. I had met Brezhnev. I knew every Communist leader since Lenin was committed to the overthrow of democracy and the free enter-prise system. I knew about this strategy of deceit from personal experience: Many years before, I'd gone head to head with Com-munists who were intent on taking over our country and destroying democracy.

I knew there were great differences between our two countries. Yet the stakes were too high for us not to try to find a common ground where we could meet and reduce the risk of Armageddon.

For more than five years, I'd made little progress with my efforts at quiet diplomacy—for one thing, the Soviet leaders kept dying on me. But when we arrived in Geneva, I felt that possibly we had a chance of getting somewhere with the new man in the Kremlin.

As Gorbachev and I talked beside the fire, it was clear he believed completely in the Soviet way of life and accepted a lot of the pro-paganda he'd heard about America: that munitions makers ruled our country, black people were treated like slaves, half our popu-lation slept in the streets.

Yet I also sensed he was willing to listen and that possibly he sensed, as I did, that on both sides of the Iron Curtain there were myths and misconceptions that had contributed to misunderstand-ings and our potentially fatal mistrust of each other.

I knew that he also had strong motives for wanting to end the arms race. The Soviet economy was a basket case, in part because of enormous expenditures on arms. He had to know that the qual-ity of American military technology, after reasserting itself begin-ning in 1981, was now overwhelmingly superior to his. He had to know we could outspend the Soviets on weapons as long as we wanted to.

"We have a choice," I told him. "We can agree to reduce arms—or we can continue the arms race, *which I think you know you can't win.* We won't stand by and let you maintain weapon superiority over us. But together we can try to do something about ending the arms race."

Our meeting beside the glowing hearth went on for an hour and a half, and when it was over, I couldn't help but think something fundamental had changed in the relationship between our countries. Now I knew we had to keep it going. To paraphrase Robert Frost, there would be many miles to go before we sleep.

As we walked up the hill toward the house where our advisors were still meeting, I told Gorbachev: "You know, you've never seen the United States before, never been there. I think you'd enjoy a visit to our country. Why don't we agree we'll have a second summit next year and hold it in the United States? I hereby invite you."

"I accept," Gorbachev replied, then, with hardly a pause, he said: "But you've never seen the Soviet Union." I said, "No," and he said, "Well, then let's hold a third summit in the Soviet Union. You come to Moscow."

"I accept," I said.

Our people couldn't believe it when I told them what had happened. Everything was settled for two more summits. They hadn't dreamed it was possible.

I understood the irony of what happened that morning under the overcast Geneva sky. I had spent much of my life sounding a warning about the threat of Communism to America and the rest of the Free World. Political opponents had called me a saber rattler and a right-wing extremist. I'd called the Soviet Union an "evil empire."

Now, here I was opening negotiations with the Kremlin, and, while doing so, I had extended my hand with warmth and a smile to its highest leader.

Yet I knew I hadn't changed. If anything, the world was changing, and it was changing for the better. The world was approaching the threshold of a new day. We had a chance to make it a safer, better place for now and the twenty-first century.

There was much more to be done, but we had laid a foundation in Geneva.

As Nancy and I flew home to Washington two days later, I had some time to look back on the journey that had taken me to Geneva.

I had to admit that it had been a long journey from Dixon, Illinois, and Davenport, Iowa.

PART ONE

From Dixon to Washington

1

I f I'd gotten the job I wanted at Montgomery Ward, I suppose I would never have left Illinois.

I've often wondered at how lives are shaped by what seem like small and inconsequential events, how an apparently random turn in the road can lead you a long way from where you intended to go —and a long way from wherever you expected to go. For me, the first of these turns occurred in the summer of 1932, in the abyss of the Depression.

They were cheerless, desperate days. I don't think anyone who did not live through the Depression can ever understand how difficult it was. In the words of Franklin D. Roosevelt, "the country was dying by inches." There were millions of people out of work. The unemployment rate across the country was over twenty-six percent. Every day the radio crackled with announcements warning people not to leave home in search of work because, the announcer said, there were no jobs to be found anywhere. There were no jobs, and for many, it seemed as if there was no hope.

In Dixon, the town in northwestern Illinois where I lived, many families had lost their land to crushing debt; the cement plant that provided many of the jobs had closed; on downtown streets there were perpetual clusters of men huddled outside boarded-up shops.

I'd been lucky. In the summer of 1932, I'd been able to work a seventh summer as a lifeguard at nearby Lowell Park and had saved enough money to finance a job-hunting trip. I had a new college diploma that summer and a lot of dreams.

Keeping it secret from my father—I knew he believed those daily announcements and would have said it was a waste of time for me to leave Dixon in search of a job—I hitchhiked to Chicago after the swimming season ended with visions of getting a job as a radio announcer. But all I got was rejection: No one wanted an inexperienced kid, especially during the Depression. And so I had hitchhiked back to Dixon in a storm, my dreams all but smothered by this introduction to reality.

If there was ever a time in my life when my spirits hit bottom, it was probably the day I thumbed my way back to Dixon in the rain, tired, defeated, and broke.

But when I got home, my dad told me he had some good news: The Montgomery Ward Company had just decided to open a store in Dixon and was looking for someone who had been prominent in local high school sports to manage the sporting goods department. The job paid $12.50 a week.

Suddenly, I had a new dream—not one as seductive as my *real* dream, but one that seemed to be more grounded in reality, and for a time late that summer, nothing in the world was as important to me as managing the sporting goods department of the new Montgomery Ward store. I loved sports; I'd lettered in football in high school and college and loved just about every other sport there was. The job offered me the chance not only to help out my family financially at a time it really needed it, but to get started on a life career. Even during the Depression, Montgomery Ward had a reputation as a steady employer and I knew that if I did well in the sporting goods department, promotions would follow.

I told my father I'd run the best sporting goods department Montgomery Ward had ever seen, and when I applied for the job with the manager of the store, I told him the same thing, and then waited for his decision.

His decision several days later was a heartbreaker. He gave the job to a former superstar on our high school basketball team.

I was raised to believe that God has a plan for everyone and that seemingly random twists of fate are all a part of His plan. My mother—a small woman with auburn hair and a sense of optimism that ran as deep as the cosmos—told me that everything in life happened for a purpose. She said all things were part of God's Plan, even the most disheartening setbacks, and in the end, everything worked out for the best. If something went wrong, she said, you didn't let it get you down: You stepped away from it, stepped over it, and moved on. Later on, she added, something good will happen and you'll find yourself thinking—"If I hadn't had that problem back then, then this better thing that *did* happen wouldn't have happened to me."

After I lost the job at Montgomery Ward, I left home again in search of work. Although I didn't know it then, I was beginning a journey that would take me a long way from Dixon and fulfill all my dreams and then some.

My mother, as usual, was right.

I was born February 6, 1911, in a flat above the local bank in Tampico, Illinois. According to family legend, when my father ran up the stairs and looked at his newborn son, he quipped: "He looks like a fat little Dutchman. But who knows, he might grow up to be president some day."

During my mother's pregnancy, my parents had decided to call me Donald. But after one of her sisters beat her to it and named her son Donald, I became Ronald.

I never thought "Ronald" was rugged enough for a young red-blooded American boy and as soon as I could, I asked people to call me "Dutch." That was a nickname that grew out of my father's calling me "the Dutchman" whenever he referred to me.

My delivery, I was told, was a difficult one and my mother was informed that she shouldn't have any more children. So that left four of us—Jack, Nelle, and my brother, Neil, who had been born two years earlier.

My dad—his name was John Edward Reagan but everyone called him Jack—was destined by God, I think, to be a salesman.

His forebears had come to America from County Tipperary by way of England during Ireland's potato famine and he was endowed with the gift of blarney and the charm of a leprechaun. No one I ever met could tell a story better than he could.

He was twenty-nine when I came into his life. Like my mother's, his education had ended after a few years in grade school. He had lost both of his parents to a respiratory illness that people in those days called "consumption" before he was six years old and was brought up by an elderly aunt who raised him a proper Irish Catholic.

Despite the brevity of his formal schooling, Jack had a lot of what people now call "street smarts." Like a lot of Americans whose roots were on the nineteenth-century frontier, he was restless, always ready to pull up stakes and move on in search of a better life for himself and his family.

My dad believed passionately in the rights of the individual and the working man, and he was suspicious of established authority, especially the Republican politicians who ran the Illinois state government, which he considered as corrupt as Tammany Hall.

Among the things he passed on to me were the belief that all men and women, regardless of their color or religion, are created equal and that individuals determine their own destiny; that is, it's largely their own ambition and hard work that determine their fate in life.

Although I think Jack could have sold anything, his specialty was shoes. A large part of his life Jack pursued a singular dream: He wanted to own a shoe store . . . not an ordinary shoe shop, but the best, with the largest inventory in Illinois, outside Chicago.

Nelle Wilson Reagan, my mother, was of Scots-English ancestry.

She met and fell in love with my father shortly after the turn of the century in one of the tiny farm towns that were planted on the Illinois prairie by pioneers as they moved westward across the continent during the nineteenth century. They were married in Fulton, Illinois, about forty miles from Dixon, in 1904.

While my father was a cynic and tended to suspect the worst of people, my mother was the opposite.

She always expected to find the best in people and often did, even among the prisoners at our local jail to whom she frequently brought hot meals.

I learned from my father the value of hard work and ambition, and maybe a little something about telling a story.

From my mother, I learned the value of prayer, how to have dreams and believe I could make them come true.

Although my father's attendance at Catholic Mass was sporadic, my mother seldom missed Sunday services at the Disciples of Christ church in Dixon.

Like Jack, she had a natural and intuitive intelligence that went a long way toward overcoming a shortage of formal schooling. While my father was filled with dreams of making something of himself, she had a drive to help my brother and me make something of ourselves.

My brother and I never knew our grandparents. They had all died before we were born. My father had one brother, but they lived far apart and seldom saw each other. My mother, on the other hand, had five sisters and brothers and it was a very close family; one sister was married to a farmer and they owned a big farm and a country store and we'd visit with them during the heat of the summer; another sister lived in Quincy, Illinois, and sometimes we'd go there for a vacation. Once, we visited another of my mother's sisters who ran a hotel in the Ozark mountains; she had an only son and later, for some reason or other—I don't know what happened—she was no longer managing the hotel and had to move in with us with her son, and we all lived together for a while.

When I was a child, we moved a lot. My father was constantly searching for a better life and I was forever the new kid in school. During one period of four years, I attended four different schools. We moved to wherever my father's ambition took him.

Tampico, the place where I was born, had a population of only 820. There was a short paved main street, a railroad station, two or three churches, and a couple of stores, including the one where my father worked.

When I was a baby, we moved from the flat above the bank into a house facing a park in the center of Tampico that had a Civil War cannon flanked by a pyramid of cannonballs. One of my first memories was of crossing the park with my brother on our way to an ice wagon that had pulled up to the depot.

A pair of toddlers intent on plucking some refreshing shards of ice from the back of the wagon, we crawled over the tracks beneath a huge freight train that had just pulled in. We'd hardly made it when the train pulled out with a hissing burst of steam. Our mother, who had come out on the porch in time to see the escapade, met us in the middle of the park and inflicted the appropriate punishment.

When I was two, we moved to Chicago, where my father had gotten a promising job selling shoes at the Marshall Field's department store. We moved into a small flat near the University of Chicago that was lighted by a single gas jet brought to life with the deposit of a quarter in a slot down the hall.

Jack's job didn't pay as well as he had hoped, and that meant Nelle had to make a soup bone last several days and be creative in other ways with her cooking. On Saturdays, she usually sent my brother to the butcher with a request for some liver (liver wasn't very popular in those days) to feed our family cat—which didn't exist. The liver became our Sunday dinner.

In Chicago I got a serious case of bronchial pneumonia and while I was recuperating one of our neighbors brought me several of his son's lead soldiers. I spent hours standing them up on the bed covers and pushing them back and forth in mock combat. To this day I get a little thrill out of seeing a cabinet full of toy soldiers.

Our stay in Chicago introduced me to a congested urban world of gaslit sidewalks and streets alive with people, carriages, trolley cars, and occasional automobiles. Once, while watching a clanging horse-drawn fire engine race past me with a cloud of steam rising behind it, I decided that it was my intention in life to become a fireman.

After we'd been in Chicago for less than two years, Jack was offered a job at O. T. Johnson's, a big department store in Galesburg 140 miles to the west of Chicago, and we moved again, this time to a completely different world. Instead of noisy streets and crowds of people, it consisted of meadows and caves, trees and streams, and the joys of small-town life. From that time onward, I guess I've always been partial to small towns and the outdoors.

We lived at first in a rented bungalow on the edge of Galesburg, then rented a larger house with a big lawn a block away—and it was there that I began my career as the Great Naturalist.

In the attic of the house, a previous tenant—an anonymous benefactor to whom I owe much—had left behind a huge collection of birds' eggs and butterflies enclosed in glass cases. Mentally appropriating the collections, I escaped for hours at a time into the attic, marveling at the rich colors of the eggs and the intricate and fragile wings of the butterflies. The experience left me with a reverence for the handiwork of God that never left me.

By the time I entered the first grade in Galesburg, I was already a bookworm of sorts. I don't have any recollection of ever learning how to read, but I remember my father coming into the house one day before I'd entered school and finding me on the living room floor with a newspaper in front of me. "What are you doing?" he asked, and I said, "Reading the paper."

Well, I imagine he thought I was being a bit of a smart aleck, so he said, "Okay, read something to me," and I did.

The next thing I knew, he was flying out the front door and from the porch inviting all our neighbors to come over and hear his five-year-old son read.

I suspect I'd learned how to read through a kind of osmosis: My mother always came into our room at bedtime and wedged herself between my brother and me to read us a story. As she read, she followed each line on the page with her finger and we watched. I think I just picked it up that way.

After entering school I discovered I had a pretty good memory. I could pick up something to read and memorize it fairly quickly, a lucky trait that made schoolwork easier for me but sometimes annoyed my brother, who didn't have the same ability.

My dad was happy at first with his job in Galesburg. But my brother and I often heard him telling Nelle that he would soon be doing better. There was a great deal of love between Jack and Nelle, but in Galesburg I began to suspect there was also a mysterious source of conflict between them.

Sometimes, my father suddenly disappeared and didn't come home for days, and sometimes when he did return, my brother and I would hear some pretty fiery arguments through the walls of our house; if we'd come into the room where Jack and Nelle were talking, they'd look at each other pointedly and start talking about something else.

There were other mysteries in our household: Sometimes out of the blue my mother bundled us up and took us to visit one of her sisters and we'd be gone for several days. We loved the unexpected vacations but were mystified by them.

World War I started when we were in Galesburg. Like almost every other American during those years, I was filled with pride every time I heard a band play "Over There" or I thought of our dough-boys crossing the Atlantic on a noble mission to save our friends in Europe. There were some days when everybody in Galesburg dropped whatever they were doing and rushed down to the depot to cheer on a troop train passing through town. The train windows were usually open to the air and the doughboys would be in their khaki uniforms and would wave to us; we waved back and cheered. Once my mother picked me up and gave me a penny, which I gave to a soldier, saying in my small voice, "Good luck." Another time, there was a big show at the school to raise money for the war and the whole family went. My dad—who as a father of two had been rejected for the army—disappeared and surprised us by coming on stage as a snake charmer wearing a wig and a hula skirt.

Not long after I completed the first grade, we moved to Monmouth, a college town not far from Galesburg, where my father took a job at the town's biggest department store. I'll never forget Armistice Day in downtown Monmouth: The streets suddenly filled up with people, bonfires were lighted, and grown-ups and children paraded down the street singing and carrying torches in the air. I was only seven, but old enough to share the hopes of everyone in Monmouth that we had fought "the war to end all wars." I think the realization that some of those boys to whom I'd waved on the troop train later died on European soil made me an isolationist for a long time.

Not long after the war ended, we moved again, this time back to Tampico, where my dad had been offered the job of managing the same H. C. Pitney General Store he was working at when I was born, and we moved into an apartment above the store. The owner, Mr. Pitney, who wasn't so much a merchant as an investor, liked my father and promised that, as soon as he could, he would try to help him become part owner of a shoe store.

After a year or so, we packed up all our belongings and headed for Dixon, where, keeping his promise, Mr. Pitney had decided to open a swank shoe store called the Fashion Boot Shop with Jack as his partner.

It was in Dixon that I really found myself—and discovered why Jack disappeared from home so often.

2

W ITH NEARLY TEN THOUSAND PEOPLE, Dixon was more than ten times larger than Tampico. We arrived there in 1920 when I was nine years old, and to me it was heaven.

Dixon had a busy main street lined with shops, several churches, an elementary and a high school, a public library, a post office, a wire screen factory, a shoe factory, and a cement plant. At the outskirts of town, dairy farms stretched as far as you could see. It was a small universe where I learned standards and values that would guide me for the rest of my life.

Almost everybody knew one another, and because they knew one another, they tended to care about each other. If a family down the street had a crisis—a death or serious illness—a neighbor brought them dinner that night. If a farmer lost his barn to a fire, his friends would pitch in and help him rebuild it. At church, you prayed side by side with your neighbors, and if things were going wrong for them, you prayed for them—and knew they'd pray for you if things went wrong for you.

I grew up observing how the love and common sense of purpose that unites families is one of the most powerful glues on earth and that it can help them overcome the greatest of adversities. I learned that hard work is an essential part of life—that by and large, you don't get something for nothing—and that America was a place that offered unlimited opportunity to those who did work hard. I learned to admire risk takers and entrepreneurs, be they farmers or small merchants, who went to work and took risks to build something for themselves and their children, pushing at the boundaries of their lives to make them better.

I have always wondered at this American marvel, the great energy of the human soul that drives people to better themselves and improve the fortunes of their families and communities. Indeed, I know of no greater force on earth.

I think growing up in a small town is a good foundation for anyone who decides to enter politics. You get to know people as individuals, not as blocs or members of special interest groups. You discover that, despite their differences, most people have a lot in common: Every individual is unique, but we all want freedom and liberty, peace, love and security, a good home, and a chance to worship God in our own way; we all want the chance to get ahead and make our children's lives better than our own. We all want the chance to work at a job of our own choosing and to be fairly rewarded for it and the opportunity to control our own destiny.

The dreams of people may differ, but everyone wants their dreams to come true. Not everybody aspires to be a bank president or a nuclear scientist, but everybody wants to do something with one's life that will give him or her pride and a sense of accomplishment. And America, above all places, gives us the freedom to do that, the freedom to reach out and make our dreams come true.

Later in life I learned that, compared with some of the folks who lived in Dixon, our family was "poor." But I didn't know that when I was growing up. And I never thought of our family as disadvantaged. Only later did the government decide that it had to tell people they were poor.

We always rented our home and never had enough money for luxuries. But I don't remember suffering because of that. Although my mother sometimes took in sewing to supplement my dad's wages and I grew up wearing my brother's clothes and shoes after he'd outgrown them, we always had enough to eat and Nelle was forever finding people who were worse off than we were and going out of her way to help them.

In those days, our main meal—dinner—was at noon and frequently consisted of a dish my mother called "oatmeal meat." She'd cook a batch of oatmeal and mix it with hamburger (I suspect the relative portions of each may have varied according to our current economic status), then serve it with some gravy she'd made while cooking the hamburger.

I remember the first time she brought a plate of oatmeal meat to the table. There was a thick, round patty buried in gravy that I'd never seen before. I bit into it. It was moist and meaty, the most wonderful thing I'd ever eaten. Of course, I didn't realize oatmeal meat was born of poverty.

Nowadays, I bet doctors would say it was healthy for us, too.

Dixon straddles the Rock River, a stretch of blue-green water flanked by wooded hills and limestone cliffs that meanders through the farmland of northwestern Illinois on its way to the Mississippi.

The river, which was often called the "Hudson of the West," was my playground during some of the happiest moments of my life. During the winter, it froze and became a skating rink as wide as two football fields and as long as I wanted to make it. In the summer, I swam and fished in the river and ventured as far as I dared on overnight canoe trips through the Rock River Valley, pretending with playmates to be a nineteenth-century explorer.

In my hand-me-down overalls, I hiked the hills and cliffs above the river, tried (unsuccessfully) to trap muskrats at the river's edge, and played "Cowboys and Indians" on hillsides above the river.

When we first moved to Dixon, we lived on the south side of the river. When we could afford it, we moved across the river to a larger house on the north side. As I look back on those days in Dixon, I think my life was as sweet and idyllic as it could be, as close as I could imagine for a young boy to the world created by Mark Twain in *The Adventures of Tom Sawyer*.

On the eve of the Fourth of July when I was eleven, I managed somehow to obtain some prohibited fireworks, including a particularly powerful variety of firecracker known as a torpedo. As I approached the town bridge that spanned the Rock River one afternoon, I let a torpedo fly against a brick wall next to the bridge. The ensuing blast was appropriately loud, but as I savored it, a car pulled up and the driver ordered me to get inside.

I'd been taught not to get into automobiles with strangers, and refused. When he flashed a police badge, I got in the car. Then I made a second mistake: As we started to drive away, I said, "Twinkle, twinkle little star, who in the hell do you think you are?"

At the police station, I was taken in to see the police chief, who I knew spent a lot of time playing pinochle with my father. Of course, I expected leniency, but he promptly called Jack and told him of my infraction and, friendship or not, Jack had to pay a $14.50 fine, which was big money in those days. The police chief took the ban on fireworks seriously and I guess my smart aleck attitude in the car hadn't helped. It took me a lot of odd jobs to pay off my debt to Jack.

My parents constantly drummed into me the importance of judging people as *individuals*. There was no more grievous sin at our household than a racial slur or other evidence of religious or racial intolerance. A lot of it, I think, was because my dad had learned what discrimination was like firsthand. He'd grown up in an era when some stores still had signs at their door saying, NO DOGS OR IRISHMEN ALLOWED.

When my brother and I were growing up, there were still ugly tumors of racial bigotry in much of America, including the corner of Illinois where we lived.

At our one local movie theater, blacks and whites had to sit apart —the blacks in the balcony. My mother and father urged my brother and me to bring home our black playmates, to consider them equals, and to respect the religious views of our friends, whatever they were. My brother's best friend was black, and when they went to the movies, Neil sat with him in the balcony. My mother always taught us: "Treat thy neighbor as you would want your neighbor to treat you," and "Judge everyone by how they act, not what they are."

Once my father checked into a hotel during a shoe-selling trip and a clerk told him: "You'll like it here, Mr. Reagan, we don't permit a Jew in the place."

My father, who told us the story later, said he looked at the clerk angrily and picked up his suitcase and left. "I'm a Catholic," he said. "If it's come to the point where you won't take Jews, then some day you won't take *me* either."

Because it was the only hotel in town, he spent the night in his car during a winter blizzard and I think it may have led to his first heart attack.

I had my share of fistfights, including some that started only because I was from an Irish Catholic family. In reality, we were a religiously divided family, but some of my classmates seized on the fact that Jack was a Catholic, and in Dixon that made him—and me—something of an outcast. The other boys claimed the basement of his church was filled with rifles for the day when the Pope was going to try to take over the country, and when I told them Jack said this story was baloney, they called him a liar and that led me to engage some of them in hand-to-hand combat on the playground.

Still the Great Naturalist in Dixon, I read everything I could about birds and wildlife of the Rock River Valley. My mother gave me a book, *Northern Lights,* that was based on the lives of the great white wolves of the north and I read it like a textbook, over and over, imagining myself with the wolves in the wild. She had a book containing Robert W. Service's ballad, "The Shooting of Dan McGrew." I reread it so many times that years later, on the occasional nights when I had trouble falling asleep, I'd remember every word and recite it silently to myself until I bore myself into slumber. If I still couldn't sleep, I'd switch to "The Cremation of Sam McGee," and that usually did it.

I'm sure that the fact our family moved so often left a mark on me.

Although I always had lots of playmates, during those first years in Dixon I was a little introverted and probably a little slow in making really close friends. In some ways I think this reluctance to get close to people never left me completely. I've never had trouble making friends, but I've been inclined to hold back a little of myself, reserving it for myself. As I'd done in the attic in Galesburg, I found a lot of enjoyment during those first years in Dixon in solitary ways —reading, studying wildlife, and exploring the local wilderness. I liked to draw cartoons and caricatures, and for a while fancied myself earning a living as an artist. I was a voracious reader and once I found a fictional hero I liked, I would consume everything I could about him. After reading one *Rover Boys* book, for example,

I wouldn't stop until I'd finished all of them. It was the same thing with *Tarzan* and *Frank Merriwell at Yale*. (I also read *Brown of Harvard* but didn't like the hero as well as Merriwell, and for years that made me a little biased against Harvard.)

The books about college life, with exciting stories about Ivy League life and gridiron rivalries, planted in me the first of my dreams (unless you count a four-year-old's aspirations to become a fireman).

My dad had negotiated a deal with Mr. Pitney under which he became part owner of the Fashion Boot Shop in exchange for his management of it. For a long time while we were growing up, it was assumed by everyone in the family that as soon as we got out of high school, Neil and I would go to work at the store and when Jack was ready to retire, we'd take it over.

From time to time, I helped out at the store, but found it boring; besides, those books I'd read about college life had given me my own ideas about the future.

With their casts of characters drawn from rich old Eastern families, the glamorous Ivy League life depicted in the stories was admittedly pretty remote from the reality of my life as a towheaded kid in overalls from a poor family in rural Illinois.

But I read and reread the stories and I began to dream of myself on a college campus, wearing a college jersey, even as a *star* on the football team. My childhood dream was to become like those guys in the books.

All my heroes weren't college football stars. A wonderful book about a devout itinerant Christian—*That Printer of Udell's*—made such an impact on me I decided to join my mother's church, the Disciples of Christ. Although Jack and Nelle were married by a Catholic priest, Nelle assumed responsibility for the spiritual preparation of my brother and me. She first took us to Sunday school, then, when we were older, to the main services, but always said she'd leave it up to us to decide whether we wanted to actually join the church. At twelve, I made my decision and was baptized as a member of the Disciples of Christ.

When Nelle thought Neil and I were old enough to know, she sat us down and explained why my father sometimes disappeared and told us the reason for those sudden unexpected trips from home.

She said Jack had a *sickness* that he couldn't control—an addiction to alcohol. She said he fought it but sometimes lost control and we shouldn't love him any less because of it because it was something he couldn't control. If he ever embarrassed us, she said we should remember how kind and loving he was when he wasn't affected by drink.

When I was eleven, I came home from the YMCA one cold, blustery, winter's night. My mother was gone on one of her sewing jobs and I expected the house to be empty. As I walked up the stairs, I nearly stumbled over a lump near the front door; it was Jack lying in the snow, his arms outstretched, flat on his back.

I leaned over to see what was wrong and smelled whiskey. He had found his way home from a speakeasy and had just passed out right there. For a moment or two, I looked down at him and thought about continuing on into the house and going to bed, as if he weren't there. But I couldn't do it. When I tried to wake him he just snored—loud enough, I suspected, for the whole neighborhood to hear him. So I grabbed a piece of his overcoat, pulled it, and dragged him into the house, then put him to bed and never mentioned the incident to my mother.

Jack wasn't one of those alcoholics who went on a bender after he'd had a run of bad luck or who drowned his sorrows in drink. No, it was prosperity that Jack couldn't stand. When everything was going perfectly, that's when he let go, especially if during a holiday or family get-together that gave him a reason to do it.

At Christmas, there was always a threat hanging over our family. We knew holidays were the most likely time for Jack to jump off the wagon. So I was always torn between looking forward to Christmas and being afraid of its arrival.

Prohibition was in force in those days, and somebody would usually tempt him to go to a speakeasy to celebrate, and when he left we knew he'd come staggering home at dawn—or maybe several days later.

Sometimes he went for a couple of years without a drop, but we never knew when he would suddenly decide to go off the wagon again and we knew that as soon as he touched *one* drink, the problem would start all over again.

Like my mother, I came to dread those days when he'd take the first drink. Although he wasn't the kind of alcoholic who was abusive to his wife or children, he could be pretty surly, and my brother and I heard a lot of cursing from my parents' bedroom when my mother went after him for his drinking.

Still, I always loved and always managed to maintain my respect for Jack, mostly I think because Nelle tried so hard to make it clear he had a *sickness* that he couldn't help and she constantly reminded us of how good he was to us when he wasn't drinking. As I've said, Nelle always looked for and found the goodness in people.

Every summer, a store in Dixon decorated one of its windows with mannequins outfitted with the uniforms of our high school football team and, as I grew up, filling one of those purple and white jerseys became the noblest and most glamorous goal in my life.

Our house overlooked the high school playing field and I spent countless afternoons sitting on an earthen ledge watching and hearing the clash of padded bodies butting up against one another and dreaming of the day when I could put on a uniform and join the combat.

In grade school I wasn't especially good at sports and worried about it. I could run pretty fast, but I was small and spent a lot of time at the bottom of pile-ons in sandlot football games. In baseball, I was forever striking out or suffering the indignity of missing an easy fly ball. I was so lousy at baseball that when our group was choosing up sides for a game, I was always the last kid chosen.

I remember one time when I was in the eighth grade. I was playing second base and a ball was hit straight toward me but I didn't realize it. Everybody was looking at me, expecting me to catch it. I just stood there. The ball landed behind me and everybody said, "Oh, no!"

I hadn't seen it. I didn't know about the ball coming toward me until I heard it drop on the ground. You don't forget things like that.

I didn't know then that there was a reason for my problems. As a result, I had a lot of trouble convincing myself I was good enough to play with the other kids, a deficiency of confidence that's not a small matter when you're growing up in a youthful world dominated by sports and games. I was always the first to think: *I can't make the team. I'm not as good as Jack or Jim or Bill.*

34

My troubles in sports, along with always having been the new kid in school, left me with some insecurities. I suppose it isn't unusual for schoolchildren to suffer feelings of inferiority and lack of self-confidence—I'd be surprised if it wasn't one of the most common afflictions of childhood—but when it's happening to you, it can seem the biggest thing in the world, and for a while it caused me a lot of heartache.

In a town like Dixon during the early 1920s, the silent movie was still a novelty, "talkies" hadn't been invented yet, visits by vaudeville troupes were still rare, and television was something you read about in science fiction stories. People had to rely on themselves for entertainment, and at this, my mother excelled.

She was the star performer of a group in Dixon that staged what we called "readings": Dixonites would memorize dramatic or humorous passages from famous poems, plays, speeches, or books and deliver them in a dramatic fashion before an audience at church or elsewhere.

Whether it was low comedy or high drama, Nelle really threw herself into a part. She loved it. Performing, I think, was her first love.

One day she helped me memorize a short speech and tried to persuade me to present it that evening at a reading, but I resisted. My brother had already given several and had been a hit; in fact, he could sing or dance with the best of 'em and a lot of people in Dixon thought he'd end up in show business. But I was more shy and told my mother I didn't want to do it. Yet I guess there was something competitive enough in me that made me want to try to do as well as my brother and I finally agreed.

Summoning up my courage, I walked up to the stage that night, cleared my throat, and made my theatrical debut. I don't remember what I said, but I'll never forget the response: *People laughed and applauded.*

That was a new experience for me and I liked it. I liked that approval. For a kid suffering childhood pangs of insecurity, the applause was music. I didn't know it then, but, in a way, when I walked off the stage that night, my life had changed.

3

WHEN I WAS THIRTEEN OR FOURTEEN, my father took the family for a Sunday drive through the green countryside bordering Dixon. As usual, my parents sat in the front seat and my brother and I sat in the back.

Nelle had left her eyeglasses in the back seat, and as we approached the gently rolling prairie outside town, I picked up her glasses and put them on.

The next instant, I let out a yelp that almost caused Jack to run off the road. Nobody knew what I was yelling about, but I'd discovered a world I didn't know existed before.

Until then, a tree beside the road looked like a green blob and a billboard was a fuzzy haze. Suddenly I was able to see branches on trees and *leaves* on the branches. There were words as well as pictures on billboards. "Look!" I shouted, pointing to a herd of grazing dairy cows I hadn't seen before.

I was astounded.

By picking up my mother's glasses, I had discovered that I was extremely nearsighted. A new world suddenly opened up to me. The reason I'd been such a lousy baseball player was that I couldn't see a pitch until it was about three feet from me. Now I knew why I'd always been the last kid chosen for the baseball team. And I also knew why I'd always jockeyed to get a desk in the front row at school. I hadn't realized before that the other kids could see the blackboard from the back of the room.

The next day, my eyes were tested by a doctor and I found out how blind I really was and was fitted with my own pair of glasses —thick, black-rimmed monstrosities I despised that soon had my friends calling me "Four Eyes." But I could see and that outweighed the effects of whatever ridicule I had to endure.

In school, I was always among the first in line when it came to participating in sports and other activities, and when someone in town decided that Dixon ought to have a boys' band, I wanted to be a part of it. I didn't play a musical instrument, but I wound up out in front of the band as drum major and felt very special about it.

My most memorable experience with the Dixon boys' band was a strange one.

We were invited to a nearby small town to play in the Decoration Day parade and were assigned to lead the parade just behind the parade marshal and his horse. Down the middle of the street we marched in our fancy white duck pants, bright tunics, and high, beaked hats. At one point, the marshal turned his horse around and rode back down the line of marchers to assure that everybody was in line; well, I kept marching down the street, pumping my baton up and down, in the direction I thought we were supposed to go. But after a few minutes I noticed the music behind me was growing fainter and fainter.

I turned around and discovered I was all alone: The band was gone.

The marshal had ridden back, gotten in front of the band, and had then led the parade down a cross street, but I didn't know it; the band just followed him and turned the corner; I'd kept going straight down the street. When I saw what had happened I started running, crossed several vacant lots and backyards, got in front of the band, and fell into step again.

It wasn't the last time, incidentally, that people have said I some-times march to a different drummer.

As teenagers, Neil and I began calling our parents by their first names. It started one day when Neil, after enlisting my backing, told the folks that since we were such a close family, wasn't it appropriate for the two of us to address them as Jack and Nelle? They were probably a little shocked at first, but they consented to it, and after a while I think they liked the special familiarity it gave the four of us.

In high school, my brother had a teammate on the football team, Winston McReynolds, who was his closest buddy and they were so inseparable the other players began referring to Neil as "Moon" and Winston as "Mushmouth"—the names of the two lead characters in the "Moon Mullins" comic strip.

Neil's nickname stuck and, from then on, about the only person who ever called him Neil was my mother.

When I entered Dixon High School in 1924, I was thirteen and worshiped football more than anything else in the world. I wanted desperately to play for the school team. The fact that my brother was already a star on the team only intensified my resolve.

Although it fielded only a single football team, Dixon High had recently been divided into two campuses on opposite sides of town, the Northside and the Southside campuses.

Our family had just moved to the north side of Dixon. As a freshman, I was assigned to the Northside campus, but Moon decided to remain with his classmates at the Southside school. It was probably fortunate for me that he did. Although he and I were close, he was still my older—and bigger—brother, and we had our share of brotherly fistfights and rivalries. He had always had an outspoken, self-confident personality that was a little like Jack's, which made him a natural leader, and until then I think I probably felt a little under his shadow. On my own at Northside, I knew I wouldn't have to be compared with him.

As the trees in the Rock River Valley began turning gold that fall, I joined a large group of other boys on the grassy field where for years I'd watched my heroes play football, ready to compete for the right to wear a purple and white jersey.

Slowly surveying the crowd of boys who'd come out for football that season, the coach walked down the line, came to me, and looked down: I weighed 108 pounds and stood only five feet, three inches tall.

After a long moment, he said he would see if he had a uniform to fit me.

The next day, the coach said he'd found shoulder pads and a helmet for me, but the school didn't have a regulation pair of pants that were small enough. However—God bless him—somewhere in his attic or some other musty preserve, he'd found an antique pair of football pants with thigh pads made out of bamboo. I'd never seen anything like those pants before, but they fit.

For the next several days I battled as best I could against the bigger boys, but when the day arrived for the coach to announce the team roster, my name wasn't on it. I went home terribly disappointed but determined to make the team during my sophomore year.

When the following summer came, I hadn't grown much larger than I'd been the year before and decided I had to do something fast to build up my muscles for the next season as well as make some money, because I'd decided to start a bank account for my future. With the dual motivation, I got my first job—at thirty-five cents an hour—working with a pick and shovel to help build and remodel houses in and around Dixon.

I learned a lot that summer—how to use my hands, how to lay floors and shingle roofs and work with concrete. I would like to be able to look back on that summer when I was fourteen years old and say I had an unblemished record as a tireless worker, but one incident tarnished the image: At noon one day, as I raised my pick into the air to take another bite out of a stubborn vein of clay, I saw my father approaching our construction site to pick me up for lunch, and at exactly the same moment, the noon whistle blew.

Without moving the pick another inch, I relaxed my wrists, opened my hands, walked out from under the pick, and headed toward Jack.

The pick plunged to earth and stuck in the ground an inch or two from one of my bosses' toes. As Jack and I walked away together, he said: "That was the damnedest exhibition of laziness I've ever seen in my life."

When September arrived, our high school football conference established a new division for smaller players weighing up to 135 pounds and I was elected captain of the team, playing tackle and then guard.

I loved playing on the line: For me, it was probably a marriage made in heaven. It's as fundamental as anything in life—a collision between two bodies, one determined to advance, the other determined to resist; one man against another man, blocking, tackling, breaking through the line.

By my junior year, I had shot up to five feet, ten-and-a-half inches and weighed over 160 pounds. But although I made the varsity, by mid-season I was still warming the bench. Then one Saturday morning, the coach, who had decided he was unhappy with the playing of one of our first-string guards, convened our regular pre-game meeting in the locker room and, reading off the starting team, said—I'll never forget it—*"Right Guard, Reagan."*

Once I got in, I never let the other guy get his position back. The first string job was mine for the rest of the season and during my senior year, when I'd grown even bigger, I was a starter from the beginning.

About my second year in high school, I got one of the best jobs I ever had: I began the first of seven summers working as a lifeguard at Lowell Park, a three-hundred-acre forested sanctuary on the Rock River named for the poet James Russell Lowell, whose family had given the property to the city. I'd taken a course on lifesaving at the YMCA and when an opening for a lifeguard came up, I went to my old employer in the construction business and told him I was going to have to quit.

I worked seven days a week, ten to twelve hours a day, for $15 —later $20—a week and one of the proudest statistics of my life is seventy-seven—the number of people I saved during those seven summers.

Besides swimming and football, I found two other loves while I was at Dixon High. The first was named Margaret, the other was named acting.

About the same time I was entering high school, the elders of our church hired a new minister. On the Sunday that he preached his first sermon, I looked around and spotted three attractive new members of the congregation; they were his daughters.

Perhaps it was love at first sight, I'm not sure. But I was immediately drawn to one of them. Her name was Margaret Cleaver and, like my mother, she was short, pretty, auburn haired, and intelligent. For almost six years of my life I was sure she was going to be my wife. I was very much in love.

One day when I was out with Margaret she brought up Jack's drinking; it was during one of the times when he'd gone off the wagon, and somebody had given her a vivid account of his behavior.

Coming from a very religious, strict family, she was quite upset. Of course, I'd never said anything to her about Jack's problem with alcohol and had tried to keep it a secret.

I tried to tell her what Nelle had told us about Jack's problem, that it was a *sickness,* but she'd never heard anything like that before and didn't buy it.

My heart was just about broken. I thought I was going to lose her.

When I went home, I told my mother about it and said that if I did lose Margaret because of Jack, I didn't know what I'd do, but I'd probably disown him and never speak to him again. Nelle felt terrible for me but asked me again to be patient with Jack.

In the end, Margaret decided that she was willing to accept Jack's drinking rather than break up our romance.

Another newcomer in Dixon that year was a new English teacher, B. J. Frazer, a small man with spectacles almost as thick as mine who taught me things about acting that stayed with me for the rest of my life.

Our English teachers until then had graded student essays solely for spelling and grammar, without any consideration for their content. B. J. Frazer announced he was going to base his grades in part on the originality of our essays. That prodded me to be imaginative with my essays; before long he was asking me to read some of my essays to the class, and when I started getting a few laughs, I began writing them with the intention of entertaining the class. I got more laughs and realized I enjoyed it as much as I had those readings at church. For a teenager still carrying around some old feelings of insecurity, the reaction of my classmates was more music to my ears.

Probably because of this experience and memories of the fun that I'd had giving readings to my mother's group, I tried out for a student play directed by Frazer—and then another. By the time I was a senior, I was so addicted to student theatrical productions that you couldn't keep me out of them.

Prior to Frazer's arrival in Dixon, our high school's dramatic productions had been a little like my mother's readings: Students acted out portions of classic plays or out-of-date melodramas. B. J. Frazer staged complete plays using scripts from recent Broadway hits and he took it all quite seriously. In fact, for a high school English teacher in the middle of rural Illinois, he was amazingly astute about the theater and gave a lot of thought to what acting was all about. He wouldn't order you to memorize your lines and say: "Read it this way. . . ." Instead, he'd teach us that it was important to analyze our characters and think like them in ways that helped us *be that person* while we were on stage.

During a rehearsal, he'd sometimes interrupt gently and say: "What do you think your character means with that line? *Why* do you think he would say that?" Often, his questioning made you realize that you hadn't tried hard enough to get under the skin of your character so you could understand his motivations. After a while, whenever I read a new script, I'd automatically try first to understand what made that particular human being tick by trying to put myself in his place. The process, called empathy, is not bad training for someone who goes into politics (or any other calling). By developing a knack for putting yourself in someone else's shoes, it helps you relate better to others and perhaps understand why they think as they do, even though they come from a background much different from yours.

As I've grown older, perhaps there's always been a little of that small boy inside me who found some reassurance in the applause and approval he first heard at nine or ten. But in high school, I began to lose my old feelings of insecurity; success in the school plays, in football and swimming, being the only guy on the beach with LIFE GUARD on my chest and saving seventy-seven people, being elected student body president, even the fact I could now *see*, did a lot to give me self-confidence. Still, I think there's something about the entertainment world that attracts people who may have had youthful feelings of shyness or insecurity. After I went to Hollywood, some of the most successful people I met—a lot of actors and great comedians like Jack Benny, for example—would just sit quietly, even shyly, at a party while some of the funniest people were writers who took center stage and became the real show-offs. It made me wonder if some entertainers hadn't gravitated to their calling because they'd been a little insecure and the job gave them a chance to be someone they're not, at least for a while.

4

IN THE 1920s, fewer than seven percent of the high school graduates in America went to college, but I was determined to be among them. Jack wasn't offended when I told him I'd set my sights higher than on working at the store, or if he was, he never showed it. I suspect he was proud that one or both of his sons might go to college. But he always told us that, short of a miracle, he wouldn't be able to help us financially. If we wanted a college education, he said we'd have to earn the money to pay for it ourselves.

Moon didn't think it could be done and when he graduated from high school, he got a job at the local cement plant and was soon making almost as much as Jack did. Going to college, he told me, was a waste of time.

But my dream of attending college was firmly planted and I wasn't going to be discouraged easily.

I was drawn to one college in particular. Ever since I could remember, one of Dixon's biggest heroes had been the husky son of one of the ministers who preceded Margaret's father at our church. After starring as a fullback on our high school team, he'd gone to Eureka College and become an even bigger football celebrity there.

My hero worship of Garland Waggoner was boundless and it made me want to follow him to Eureka, a liberal arts college owned by the Disciples of Christ that was located about 110 miles southeast of Dixon.

Although I'd never seen it, Eureka College began to take on an almost mystical allure as my high school years passed. Even repeating its name silently to myself was exciting after a while.

I'd like to be able to recall that my burning desire to go to college was planted first and foremost in a drive to get an education. But at seventeen, I think I was probably more motivated by love for a pretty girl and a love for football.

Going to college offered me the chance to play football for four more years. And my choice of Eureka was fixed in concrete when Margaret told me that she'd decided to follow her two sisters there.

If I was going to do the same thing, though, I had to overcome a big obstacle: I still didn't have enough money for college. Ever since I'd begun working with a pick and shovel, I'd banked just about everything I earned except for the church tithe my mother called "The Lord's Share." I'd saved $400. But it wasn't enough to finance four years at Eureka, where the tuition bill alone was $180 a year and the cost of room and board was almost as much.

When I drove Margaret to Eureka that September to register for her freshman year, I saw the campus for the first time and I was bowled over. It was even lovelier than I'd imagined it would be.

There were five Georgian-style brick buildings arranged around a semicircle with windows framed in white. The buildings were covered with ivy and surrounded by acres of rolling green lawn studded with trees still lush with their summer foliage.

I knew I had to stay. I also knew my only chance of doing that was to get a scholarship. While Margaret registered, I presented myself to Eureka's new president, Bert Wilson, and Ralph McKinzie, the football coach, and tried to impress them with my credentials as a football player and as someone who could win some trophies for Eureka's swim team.

Like many small church-affiliated colleges, Eureka was perpetually insolvent. It didn't have the luxury of giving students a free ride. But, fortunately for me, I was convincing enough to talk them into giving me a Needy Student Scholarship, which covered half my tuition, and they promised me a job that would pay the cost of my meals.

The balance of my tuition and the $2.50 a week it cost for my room, plus books and other expenses, had to come from my savings account.

· · ·

The boyfriend of one of Margaret's sisters introduced me to his fraternity brothers in Tau Kappa Epsilon. I was accepted as a pledge, and moved into the TKE house, where the fraternity gave me a job washing dishes and serving tables in exchange for my meals.

I entered Eureka when I was seventeen. I stood almost six feet one and weighed almost 175 pounds. My hair was in a crew-cut style and parted down the middle like the hero of the comic strip "Harold Teen," and I wore those thick eyeglasses I despised. I had a trunk filled with almost everything I owned and a head full of dreams.

Eureka, of course, is a Greek word that means *I have found it* and it described perfectly the sense of discovery I felt the day I arrived there in the fall of 1928. Eureka was everything I had dreamed it would be and more.

In later life, I visited some of the most famous universities in the world. As governor of California, I presided over a university system regarded as one of the best. But if I had to do it over again, I'd go back to Eureka or another small college like it in a second.

At big universities, relatively few students get involved in extra-curricular activities: They go to class, go to their living quarters, go to the library, then go back to their classes. There may be a lot to be said for those large institutions, but I think too many young people overlook the value of a small college and the tremendous influence that participation in student activities can have during the years from adolescence to adulthood.

If I had gone to one of those larger schools, I think I would have fallen back in the crowd and never discovered things about myself that I did at Eureka. My life would have been different.

There were fewer than 250 students when I was at Eureka, roughly divided between men and women, and everyone knew one another by their first name.

As in a small town, you couldn't remain anonymous at a small college. Everybody was needed. Whether it's the glee club or helping to edit the school yearbook, there's a job for everyone, and everybody gets a chance to shine at something and build their sense of self-confidence. You get to discover things about yourself that you might never learn if you were lost in the crowd of a larger school.

I've been accused of majoring in extracurricular activities at Eureka. Technically, that wasn't true. My major was economics. But it is true I thrived on school activities—although my expectation of sweeping onto the campus and becoming an overnight football sensation was, to say the least, not fulfilled.

Our coach, Mac McKinzie, was a legend at Eureka who as a student had won twelve letters and been the captain of his team in three sports. During one football game, he single-handedly scored all the points and beat our archrival, Bradley Tech, 52–0, and while he was still a student, he was elected assistant coach of the football team and, shortly thereafter, head coach.

Legend or not, I soon reached the conclusion that Mac McKinzie didn't like me. He was not only unimpressed by my high school exploits, he kept me on the bench most of the season and I spent much of my freshman year sulking about it.

While I didn't play much football that fall, I did taste another type of combat—my first taste of politics.

In the autumn of 1928, the stock market crash and the Great Depression were still a year away. But in the Midwest, farmers were already feeling an economic pinch, and Eureka, which drew much of its support from the region, was feeling the impact in the form of smaller donations to its endowment.

To make ends meet, Bert Wilson, the new president, decided to lay off part of the faculty and impose other cuts. His plan was to be implemented during the week that students went home for the Thanksgiving vacation.

When the students and faculty got wind of the plan, resentment spread over the campus like a prairie fire because the cutbacks meant many juniors and seniors wouldn't be able to take classes they needed to graduate.

We were especially angry that Wilson had decided to throw upperclassmen to the wolves without first asking the faculty and students if they had any alternative suggestions for cutting expenses and because we thought he was doing it in an underhanded way—imposing the cuts as a fait accompli while we were away eating our Thanksgiving turkey.

On the Friday afternoon before Thanksgiving, when students usually began their preholiday exodus, no one left the campus. A student committee was formed to consider the possibility of calling a strike and I was elected to represent freshmen on the committee. That Saturday night, our committee waited while trustees met to ratify the president's cutbacks.

When they came out of the meeting, their expressions told us the decision had been made; the ax was going to fall.

A few moments later, the bell in the college chapel began to ring; the bell-rope was pulled by one of our committeemen. At this signal, students, joined by many of our professors, began to march across the campus toward the chapel, and soon it was filled to overflowing.

Because I was a freshman and didn't have the same vested interests in avoiding the faculty cutbacks that upperclassmen did, I was chosen to present our committee's proposal for a strike.

I reviewed how the cutbacks threatened not only the diplomas of upperclassmen but the academic reputation of Eureka; I described how the administration had ignored us when we tried to present alternate ideas for saving money and then planned to pull off the coup in secrecy while we were gone from the college.

Giving that speech—my first—was as exciting as any I ever gave. For the first time in my life, I felt my words reach out and grab an audience, and it was exhilarating. When I'd say something, they'd roar after every sentence, sometimes every word, and after a while, it was as if the audience and I were one. When I called for a vote on the strike, everybody rose to their feet with a thunderous clapping of hands and approved the proposal for a strike by acclamation.

The strike began when we returned after Thanksgiving. Most students refused to go to class, while studying privately in their rooms; most of our professors went to class, marked the missing students present, and then went home.

A week after the strike began, the president resigned, the strike ended, and things returned to normal at Eureka College.

The following summer, I resumed my old lifeguarding job at Lowell Park and at summer's end decided that I'd tolerated Mac McKinzie's lack of appreciation for my gridiron skills long enough.

Most of my savings were gone and I didn't have enough left for another year at Eureka, and I wasn't sure I wanted to go back there.

I don't think it's unusual for college students to wonder at the end of their freshman year whether they'd made the right choice of a college and I guess I was going through that process. Then one of those series of small events began that make you wonder about God's Plan.

I had a high school chum who worked as rodman for a local surveyor and sometimes their work brought them around Lowell Park; my friend knew I was anxious to save some money and that I was a little unsure about my future, so after the park closed for the season he told me he'd decided to quit his job and suggested I apply for it.

When the surveyor heard I was interested in the job, he not only gave it to me but offered to get me a college scholarship the following year. He had attended the University of Wisconsin where he'd lettered on the crew team, and he had seen me at the park and knew I did a lot of rowing. He said that after I'd worked for him a year, he'd help get me an athletic scholarship to Wisconsin for the crew team that would take care of most of my expenses. It was an offer too good to refuse. I decided not to go back to Eureka, save a lot of money over the next year, then go to the University of Wisconsin.

On the eve of Margaret's return to Eureka, we bid a sad goodbye to each other. The next day when I got up, Dixon was being soaked by a rainstorm, which meant our crew couldn't work. It was a damp, dreary day and I had nothing to do. I already missed Margaret and I decided to call her before she left. She and her parents were just leaving to take her to Eureka and asked me if I wanted to go along for the drive since I had nothing to do for the day.

Once I was back on the campus, I was seduced by Eureka all over again. I went to the TKE house and saw all my friends and then looked up Mac McKinzie and was pleasantly surprised he seemed disappointed when I said I'd decided to drop out of school.

When I told him I was broke and couldn't afford another year at Eureka, he promptly went to bat for me; within an hour or two, the college had renewed my Needy Student Scholarship covering half my tuition and agreed to defer the balance of the tuition until after I graduated. As a sophomore, I couldn't get back my old job waiting on tables at the TKE house because that job was reserved for freshmen pledges, but the coach arranged for me to get one of the more pleasant jobs available to a male at Eureka, washing dishes at Lyda's Wood, the girls' dormitory.

There it was, all of a sudden I was back at Eureka again. I've often wondered what might have happened to me if it hadn't been raining that day.

I picked up the phone and told my mother to send my clothes to me, I was going to stay. Then she gave me some news: After three years of shoveling limestone at the cement plant, Moon had shouted "Uncle" and said he wanted to go to college.

I went back to the coach and sold him on my brother's prowess as a football player and, before long, Moon was attending Eureka on a Needy Student Scholarship and holding down my old kitchen job at the TKE house.

Needless to say, it was quite a kick for me being a sophomore and having my freshman older brother waiting on me at the table.

5

A MONTH AFTER MOON'S ARRIVAL at Eureka, the stock market crashed. Looming behind it was the Great Depression. But the enormity of the economic calamity that was about to engulf America wasn't apparent on our campus yet. As classes resumed that fall, most of my attention was divided between Margaret Cleaver, who had accepted my TKE pin, which was tantamount to engagement, and getting my backside off Mac McKinzie's bench.

Despite what I'd interpreted as an eagerness on his part to have me back on the squad, McKinzie relegated me to the fifth string, convincing me that he disliked me as much as ever. He could look at me and make me feel inadequate.

I resolved to block and tackle as hard as I could during practice to catch his eye, and after several weeks he began to pay me an occasional compliment.

On a rainy day in mid-season, we were practicing a new play, a wide sweep around my end of the line, and Mac told me the only way the play could work was for the guard—me—to take down the defensive halfback before he could nail our running back. He asked an assistant coach—one of his former teammates who served as an unpaid volunteer—to play the role of defensive halfback while I demonstrated what I was supposed to do on the play.

We weren't scrimmaging, just running to where our targets were supposed to be. So I asked Mac: "You don't want me to really take him out?" Before he could answer, our volunteer coach said, "Sure, come and try to block me."

The ball was snapped and I took off. Never before or since did I throw such a block. When I hit our ex officio coach he ascended as if he'd been hurled by a shot-putter and seemed to dangle in mid-air for several moments before plummeting to the ground. As I returned to the huddle, he limped off the field while Mac tried to suppress a cough. The next Saturday, I was in the starting lineup and averaged all but two minutes of every game for the remainder of the season and the two seasons that followed it. I owe Mac a lot; he didn't dislike me after all; he just saw some things in an eighteen-year-old kid that needed some correcting.

On one of our out-of-town trips, the team had to stay overnight in Dixon; Mac said I had to stay at the hotel with the rest of the team and so I went with him to a downtown hotel to help us register. The hotel manager said: "I can take everybody but your two colored boys."

"Then, we'll go someplace else," Mac said.

"No hotel in Dixon is going to take colored boys," the manager shot back.

Mac bristled and said all of us would sleep on the bus that night. Then I suggested another solution: "Mac, why don't you tell those two fellows there isn't enough room in the hotel for everybody so we'll have to break up the team; then put me and them in a cab and send us to my house."

Mac gave me a funny look; he'd just had a chance to observe firsthand what the people of Dixon thought of blacks, and I'm sure he had his doubts my parents would think much of the idea. "You're sure you want to do that?" he asked.

I knew my parents well and said yes. We went to my house and I rang the bell and Nelle came to the door and I told her there wasn't enough room for the whole team at the hotel. "Well, come on in," she said, her eyes brightening with a warmth felt by all three of us.

She was absolutely color blind when it came to racial matters; these fellows were just two of my friends. That was the way she and Jack had always raised my brother and me.

· · ·

Like a lot of college students, I did a little experimenting in college. My father had always been a two- or three-pack-a-day smoker and my brother started smoking when he was fifteen. I'd never liked cigarettes, but I was impressed by a flurry of ads in those days in which women said, "I like a man who smokes a pipe." I'd always liked the look of someone smoking a pipe, so I saved up and bought one. But I never inhaled. I just sucked in the smoke, tasted it, and blew it out—and I only did that during the off season, when I wasn't playing football. I obeyed the training rules.

Out of curiosity, I also did some brief experimenting with alcohol while I was at college. It was during Prohibition and a lot of movies depicted illicit drinking as "collegiate" and I guess I was curious about the effects of alcohol. One night Moon and I were visiting two fraternity brothers who worked for a doctor and in return received the free use of an apartment; they had a bottle and started passing it around. Even with all the experience I'd had with Jack's drinking, I didn't know anything about the effect of highballs; so when the bottle came around to me, I'd take a big drink, as if it was a bottle of soda pop. Well, they soon decided I was so blind drunk that they couldn't take me back to the fraternity house in my condition. Inside, I thought I was sober. I'd try to say something intelligent but what came out of my mouth would make Moon and my fraternity brothers fall down laughing. They took me out of town and walked me along a country road, one on each side, trying to make me sober. But it didn't do a lot of good, so they brought me back to the fraternity house and threw me in a shower. They had to smuggle me in, because everyone was in bed asleep. I woke up the next day with a terrible hangover. That was it for me. Although in later years I might have a cocktail before dinner or a glass of wine with dinner, I'd been taught a lesson. I decided if that's what you get for drinking—a sense of helplessness—I didn't want any part of it.

Although my grades were higher than average, my principal academic ambition at Eureka was to maintain the C average I needed to remain eligible for football, swimming, track, and the other school activities I participated in—two years in the student senate, three years as basketball cheerleader, three years as president of the Eureka Boosters Club, two years as yearbook features editor, and, during my last year, student body president and captain and coach of the swim team.

Despite my preoccupation with extracurricular activities, I'm convinced I got a solid liberal arts education at Eureka, especially in economics. It was a major I chose because I thought, one way or another, I'd end up dealing with dollars, if not at my father's store, in some other business.

As 1930 began, the full contours of the Depression were becoming apparent and one of its first casualties was my father's grandest dream.

In Dixon, troubles in the farming economy had begun months before the crash and when the full force of the Depression struck, it hit our town like a cyclone: The price of milk dropped to a level so low that it didn't pay farmers to milk their cows anymore; hundreds of people were out of work; the cement plant slashed its work force, then closed down; one by one, like streetlights flickering off at daybreak, many of the most prestigious stores in Dixon closed.

One of them was the Fashion Boot Shop.

In a city where few people could afford a new pair of shoes, Mr. Pitney, his wealth depleted by the crash, had to close my father's store, and with it Jack's only chance of ever owning his own store.

The Depression had such an oppressive effect that it cast a dreary pall over everything. But there was a small beacon of light amid the misery: Like any shared calamity, the Depression brought people closer together in marvelous ways. There was a spirit of warmth and helpfulness and, yes, kindliness abroad in the land that was inspiring to me as we all clung to the belief that, sooner or later, things would get better.

To make ends meet, my mother got a job as seamstress-clerk at a dress shop for $14 a week and Jack went on the road looking for work; at first they made a little extra income by subletting a portion of our house, but then things got so bad they couldn't even afford the rent on the house and they had to move to an apartment that was the upstairs of a onetime large home. When Moon and I came home, he slept on the couch and I slept on a cot on the upstairs landing.

I'll never forget one Christmas Eve during the Depression.

We'd never been able to afford a really fancy Christmas, but Jack and Nelle always managed to find a small gift for each other and one for Moon and me. When we couldn't afford a Christmas tree, Nelle found enough ribbon and crepe paper to decorate a table or make a cardboard fireplace out of a packing box to give our home a festive feeling. I'll never forget those Christmases when we didn't have much money but our home radiated with a love and warmth that meant a lot more to me than packages wrapped in colored paper.

On this particular Christmas Eve, Moon and I were getting ready to go out when a special delivery letter arrived for Jack. His eyes brightened. He'd recently gotten a job as a traveling shoe salesman —no salary, just commission—and thought the letter might contain a Christmas bonus.

We watched him pull out a sheet of paper from the envelope and waited to hear his good news. "Well, that's a hell of a Christmas present," he said bitterly. "I've been laid off."

After Moon and I returned to Eureka, my mother called me and asked if she could borrow $50. Jack hadn't been able to find work and she couldn't pay the grocery bill. I still had some of my summer lifeguard earnings and was happy to send her $50. She asked me not to tell Jack about it and I never did.

Subsequently, Jack found a job as manager and sole clerk of a chain store shoe outlet near Springfield, two hundred miles from Dixon and Nelle.

During the football season, our team stayed overnight in Springfield, and Moon and I talked Mac into letting us leave the hotel for a few hours to visit him. We found Jack in a run-down neighborhood at the edge of Springfield. His store was a grim, tiny hole-in-the-wall. Although he'd cleaned it up, there wasn't much anybody could have done with the store. There were garish orange advertisements promoting cut-rate shoes plastered on the windows, and the sole piece of furniture was a small wooden bench with iron armrests where his customers were fitted.

When I saw the store I thought of the hours he'd spent when we were boys talking about the grand shoe store he dreamed of opening one day, then remembered the Fashion Boot Shop, the elegant store that, before he lost it, had fulfilled his dream.

My eyes filled and I looked away, not wanting him to see the tears welling up in my eyes.

. . .

Because a lot of Nelle's great sense of religious faith rubbed off on me, I have always prayed a lot; in those days, I prayed things would get better for our country, for our family, and for Dixon. I even prayed before football games.

I was the only player on our first string who'd come to Eureka directly from high school. Most of the other players were more mature and several were quite a bit older than I; after high school, they'd gone into the working world during the Roaring Twenties when jobs were plentiful, then, when the Depression hit, they had entered college rather than sit on their porch, unemployed.

At a chalk-talk before one game, Mac McKinzie asked the team if any of us prayed.

I had never faced a kickoff without a prayer. I didn't pray to win —I didn't expect God to take sides—but I prayed no one would be injured, we'd all do our best and have no regrets no matter how the game came out.

But I was afraid to reveal this to my older and more sophisticated teammates. Then, to my amazement, everyone in the room said that they prayed—and to my surprise, they all said they prayed along the same lines that I did.

That was the last time I was ever reluctant to admit I prayed.

6

EARLY IN 1932, with graduation a few months off, I faced the same question that gnaws at all college seniors: What do I do with the rest of my life?

It's easy to look back now and say the answer had been inside me for a long time. I suppose it had, but I still couldn't say aloud, even to myself, that I wanted to be an actor.

The dream had probably taken root that week of Thanksgiving vacation during my freshman year when we were waiting for the student strike to begin. Margaret's parents took us to see a touring company's production of *Journey's End,* a tragedy set in World War I that focused on the emotions of a weary, emotionally bruised military officer, Captain Stanhope. I was drawn to the stage that night as if it were a magnet, astonished by the magic of an ordinary man convincing an audience that he was someone else.

Once again fate intervened—as if God was carrying out His plan with my name on it. Just as a new teacher with a talent for teaching high school students how to act had arrived in Dixon High just as I got there, Eureka had hired a new English professor who had a deep love—and talent—for teaching dramatics. Her name was Ellen Marie Johnson and she treated acting as seriously as B. J. Frazer.

After taking over as faculty advisor for theater arts after-school activities, she increased the number of student productions and I began trying out for all the plays. One of the plays she staged was

Journey's End, and when I won the part of Captain Stanhope, I was in heaven.

Miss Johnson organized a drama society that allowed students who were interested in dramatics to work together year round instead of just the weeks before a new play was staged. During my junior year, she took it upon herself to get Eureka invited to a prestigious one-act play contest at Northwestern University.

For college actors, the competition was comparable to the Super Bowl. Hundreds of colleges around the country, including all the big schools—Princeton, Yale, and so forth—competed for invitations to bring student actors to the competition. I never learned how Miss Johnson pulled it off, but she wangled an invitation for tiny, 250-student Eureka College, the only school accepted that year that didn't have a full-time dramatic arts department.

For our entry, she selected *Aria da Capo,* a one-act play by Edna St. Vincent Millay that was set in ancient Greece and had an anti-war theme. I played a shepherd strangled before the final curtain by Bud Cole, my football teammate, fraternity brother, and one of my best friends. Death scenes are always pleasant for an actor and I tried to play it to the hilt.

To our delight, Eureka placed second in the competition and while we were relishing this success, it was announced I was one of three performers who had been selected to receive individual acting awards. Afterward, the head of Northwestern's Speech Department, the sponsor of the contest, called me into his office and inquired if I'd ever thought about making acting my career.

I said, "Well, no," and he said, "Well, you should." It was quite a thrill for a young man trying to set the course of his life.

I guess that was the day the acting bug really bit me, although I think it was probably orbiting pretty close to me for a long time before that, even before *Journey's End* and my student plays at Dixon High.

After we moved to Dixon, I fell in love with the movies. I couldn't count the number of hours I spent in the darkness of our only moviehouse with William S. Hart and Tom Mix galloping over the prairie or having my eyes turned misty by the cinematic perils that befell Mary Pickford and Pearl White. And when I was ten or eleven, one of my mother's sisters came to Dixon for a visit and our whole family went out to a silent movie. I don't remember its name, but it featured the adventures of a freckle-faced young boy and I enjoyed it a lot. Afterward, I overheard my aunt talking to my mother about this young star and saying she thought I had the potential to become a child actor. "If he was mine," she said, "I'd take him to Hollywood if I had to walk all the way."

Her remark didn't plant any visions in me—or Nelle—of rushing off to Hollywood. But it did make me feel good and from then on, whenever I went to a movie featuring a young boy, I fantasized about how much fun it would be to act out a part in a movie.

By my senior year at Eureka, my secret dream to be an actor was firmly planted, but I knew that in the middle of Illinois in 1932, I couldn't go around saying, "I want to be an actor."

To say I wanted to be a movie star would have been as eccentric as saying I wanted to go to the moon. Hollywood and Broadway were at least as remote from Dixon as the moon was in 1932. If I *had* told anyone I was setting out to be a movie star, they'd have carted me off to an institution.

But I had an idea. Broadway and Hollywood were a long way from Dixon, but not Chicago, the nation's hub of radio broadcasting.

In those days, commercial broadcasting was beginning to grab the hearts of America. When "Amos and Andy" came on the air, the whole world stopped: If you were at a movie theater, they'd shut off the projector, turn on the lights, and a radio set would be placed on the stage while everybody sat quietly in their seats for a half hour listening to the latest episode.

Radio was magic. It was theater of the mind. It forced you to use your imagination. You'd sit in your living room and be transported to glamorous locales around the world, and eavesdrop on stories of romance and adventure brought to life by a few actors and vivid sound effects transmitted over the radio waves—a squeaking door or a horse galloping across the desert. It's sad that we've now had several generations who've never had a chance to use their imagination in the way we did.

Radio had created a new profession—the sports announcer—as radio's influence grew in America. Broadcasting play-by-play reports of football games, people like Graham McNamee and Ted Husing had become as famous as some Hollywood stars and often they were more famous than the athletes they reported on.

At Eureka, I'd listened to their broadcasts religiously and sometimes, when we were lounging around the TKE house, I'd pick up a broomstick, pretend it was a microphone, and do a mock locker-room interview with one of my fraternity brothers to get some laughs.

After my graduation in June 1932, I went back to Lowell Park for another summer so I could save some money and begin paying back my debt for overdue tuition. There was a summer hotel at the park called The Lodge that attracted well-off families, mostly from Chicago, who returned year after year to spend their vacations in the country. Over the years I'd taught the children of many of the families how to swim and their fathers had often come up to me and said they'd help me get a job after I'd gotten my college diploma. The Depression had changed all that: A lot of people didn't take summer vacations in the summer of 1932 and among those who did, few were in a position to help me get a job.

There was an exception, a Kansas City businessman who told me he had contacts with people in several businesses and asked what line of work I wanted to go into now that I'd graduated from college. I couldn't bring myself to tell him I wanted to go into the world of entertainment. I knew it would have sounded ridiculous. But he pressed me for an answer, putting me on the spot: "You have to tell me what you want to do," he said.

Although I couldn't bring myself to mention acting, I remembered those mock broomstick interviews in the TKE house and said: "I have to tell you, way down deep inside, what I'd really like to be is a radio sports announcer." (I'd seen several movies in which sports announcers played themselves and thought there was a remote possibility the job might lead me into the movies.)

Then I got what turned out to be the best advice I'd ever received. He told me he had no contacts in radio but it might be better for me that he didn't. If he asked a friend to give me a job, he said the friend might do it, but probably feel no obligation to do anything else for me. It was probably better, he said, for me to do things on my own from the beginning. Then came his second piece of advice: He suggested I start knocking on radio station doors, not mention sports announcing, but say I was a believer in this new industry and was willing to take *any* job to break into broadcasting. And he told me not to be discouraged by turndowns; sometimes, he said, salesmen had to knock on 250 doors before making a sale.

At summer's end, the beach closed and I informed my mother that I was going to take his advice. I'd ride along with Moon to Eureka, where he was going to enroll for another year, then hitchhike to Chicago to hunt for a job as a radio announcer.

After driving with Moon to Eureka, I spent several hours with Margaret, whose father had recently been appointed minister of the local Disciples of Christ church. She was packing for a trip to a distant town in rural Illinois where she'd been lucky enough to find a teaching job.

We had a sad parting, but knew that with things getting worse every day, separations were inevitable in the Depression. We both had to take jobs wherever we could find them.

When I went on to Chicago, I met rejection everywhere I went. When I suggested I wanted to become a radio announcer (I never mentioned my real goal of becoming a *sports* announcer), I was practically laughed out the door, usually without even an interview. The only encouragement I got was from the program director of the NBC station in Chicago. A kind woman, she heard my appeal for a job, then told me I was in the wrong place. "In Chicago," she said, "we can't afford to take people without experience. You've got every reason to try for a job in radio, but first go out to what we call 'the sticks.' You'll find someone who'll take you on and give you experience; then one day, you can come to Chicago."

Discouraged, I hitchhiked back to Dixon in the rain. By this time my summer earnings were almost gone and I needed a job of any kind. Then, several days later, after my hopes had soared, I lost the job at Montgomery Ward.

7

AFTER MY DISAPPOINTMENT over the Montgomery Ward job, I confessed to Jack about my unsuccessful job-hunting expedition in Chicago and mentioned the suggestion from the woman at NBC that I try for a job in the sticks.

Jack was a practical man who firmly believed those announcements advising people to stay at home because there weren't any jobs to be found anywhere. He'd been on the road himself and knew from experience how harsh the times were. But he also knew how disappointed I was after losing the job in Dixon and when I blurted out my dream of breaking into radio, I think his heart went out to me. He was a proud, ambitious man whose own dreams had been crushed by the Depression and I think he understood the fire that was burning inside me. I guess it was the same fire—a drive to make something of myself—that had always burned inside him. At that moment I thought again of Jack in that tiny little shoe store in Springfield and my heart went out to him.

He asked me what I knew about radio stations outside Chicago, which was the source of all the programming people in Dixon listened to. Radio was so new that many Midwestern towns still didn't have a commercial station, but I said I knew of two or three in the tri-cities area of Davenport, Moline, and Rock Island along the Illinois-Iowa border. And I said there were several others further to the west.

Jack heard me out and said that if I wanted to test the advice of that woman in Chicago, he was willing to let me borrow the family car so I could go on the road and look for a job in radio.

A couple of days later I got in our third-hand Oldsmobile and headed for the tri-cities, which were on the Mississippi River about seventy-five miles southwest of Dixon.

I started with stations on the Illinois side of the Mississippi but struck out, then crossed the river into Iowa. My first stop was station WOC in Davenport. In those days, the initials of radio stations' call signs usually meant something and WOC meant "World of Chiropractic."

The station had been founded by Colonel B. J. Palmer, proprietor of the Palmer School of Chiropractic, whose optimism and farsightedness about the future of radio had also led him to acquire Station WHO in Des Moines.

I'd learned during my job hunting in Chicago that if you wanted a job as a radio announcer, the person you applied to was the program director.

After finding the campus of the Palmer School of Chiropractic, an office building in downtown Davenport, I took the elevator to the top floor and asked to see the program director. A few seconds later I was shaking hands with a ruddy-faced Scotsman who was balancing himself on a spindly pair of canes.

Peter MacArthur had crossed the Atlantic as a song-and-dance man, a member of Harry Lauder's original vaudeville troupe, and toured America until arthritis nearly crippled him. Suffering terribly, he left the act in Davenport and went to the Palmer School of Chiropractic in hopes of finding relief from the cruel pain in his joints. He never found it, but his background in show business led to the offer of an announcer's job at WOC and later a job as program director. In that part of the country, Pete's Highland burr, as thick as oatmeal, was probably as familiar as the voices of Amos and Andy when he said: "WOC, Davenport—where the West begins, in the state where the tall corn grows."

Pete, whose cheeks had been burnished by the chilly winds of the Highlands until they were the color of copper, listened while I gave my usual pitch about my willingness to take *any* job to get a start in radio.

"Where were you yesterday?" he demanded.

He said he *did* have an opening for an announcer and held auditions for it the day before, after advertising the job for a month over the air.

"The job's filled. Where ye been?" he said as if I were a little backward.

I didn't want to tell him we didn't listen much to WOC in Dixon.

After losing the job at Montgomery Ward the week before, this was too much. In a daze, I left his office and headed for the elevator, shattered by the bad luck. "How the hell," I said as I walked away, quietly, but loud enough for him to hear, "can you get to be a sports announcer if you can't even get a job at a radio station?"

I reached the end of the hall and pushed the elevator button. As the door opened, I heard Pete's canes shuffling toward me, then a raspy voice, as rough as sandpaper. "Hold on, you big bastard," he said.

I turned around and saw him advancing toward me atop his canes, first on one and then the other, and let the elevator descend without me.

"What was that you said about *sports* announcing?" he asked.

I told him I wanted to get a job in radio because eventually I wanted to become a sports announcer.

"De ye know anything about football?"

"I played football for eight years in high school and college. . . . "

"Could ye tell me about a football game and make me *see* it as if I was home listening to the radio?"

"Yes . . . I'm sure I could," I replied with the bravado of youth.

"Come with me," he said.

Pete led me into a studio and stopped me in front of a microphone.

"When the red light goes on," he said, "I'll be in another room listening. Describe an imaginary football game to me and make me *see* it."

My mind raced for something that would impress him. I decided I had to describe a game with high drama and an exciting finish, name names and describe specific plays. The names were the big thing. How could I come up with different names as I described a play?

I decided the answer was to describe one of the games at Eureka in which I'd played; I'd know the plays and the players.

The previous season we'd won a game in the last twenty seconds with a sixty-five-yard touchdown run by quarterback Bud Cole, my fraternity brother who had done me in on the stage at Northwestern. It was as exciting a game as I'd ever played.

As I stood at the microphone, my only rehearsal for that moment had been those imaginary broomstick interviews in the TKE house. Suddenly the red light flashed on. I looked at the microphone and improvised:

"Here we are in the fourth quarter with Western State University leading Eureka College six to nothing. . . .

"Long blue shadows are settling over the field and a chill wind is blowing in through the end of the stadium. . . ."

(We didn't have a stadium, we had bleachers, but I didn't expect him to know the difference.)

I let the teams seesaw across the field for almost fifteen minutes, then began leading up to that final play, an off-tackle smash. When we played that game, I never knew how Bud made it to the goal line. On the play, the right guard—that was I—was supposed to pull out of the line immediately after the ball was snapped, lead our interference through the line, and take down the first defensive player in the secondary.

I missed the linebacker by a mile and don't know to this day how Bud ever got through to make the touchdown. But during the game that I broadcast for Pete MacArthur, a right guard named *Reagan* leveled a block on the linebacker so furiously that it could have killed him.

Bud not only reached the end zone and tied the game, but drop-kicked the point-after-touchdown and won it for Eureka, 7–6. With Eureka's fans cheering, I ended the broadcast, saying: *"We return you now to our main studio. . . ."*

When Pete clumped back into the studio, there was a smile on his face. "Ye did great, ye big SOB," he said. "Be here Saturday, you're broadcasting the Iowa-Minnesota Homecoming game. You'll get $5 and bus fare."

During the next week I read everything I could about the teams and Big Ten football. On Saturday, I took a bus to Davenport, met Pete at WOC, and drove with him to Iowa City along with a staff announcer Pete was obviously keeping in reserve in case I blew my chance.

Once I was on the air, I tried to make the most of my opportunity and chose phrases and adjectives I hoped would give listeners visual images that would make them think they were in the stadium, and I laced my descriptions with background about the players and teams that I hoped would demonstrate that I knew what I was talking about.

When the game was over, Pete said I'd passed the test and that he wanted me to broadcast Iowa's three remaining games of the season for $10 each.

Well, not only could I now call myself a *sports announcer,* I'd gotten a hundred percent raise in a week's time.

For a twenty-one-year-old fresh out of college, broadcasting the Big Ten games was like a dream, and as the end of the season approached, I prayed the people at WOC would offer me a permanent job. But after the final game, Pete told me the station didn't have an opening. He said if something came up, he'd call me, but with the Depression growing worse daily, he sounded as if there wasn't much hope.

Once again, disappointed and frustrated, I headed for home.

Back in Dixon, Jack reminded me that while I'd been talking about forward passes and quarterback sneaks, events a lot more important than football games had been occurring: Franklin D. Roosevelt had been elected the thirty-second president of the United States by a landslide and Jack predicted he would pull America out of its tailspin.

There weren't many Democrats in Dixon and Jack was probably the most outspoken of them, never missing a chance to speak up for the working man or sing the praises of Roosevelt.

I had become a Democrat, by birth, I suppose, and a few months after my twenty-first birthday, I cast my first vote for Roosevelt and the full Democratic ticket. And, like Jack—and millions of other Americans—I soon idolized FDR. He'd entered the White House facing a national emergency as grim as any the country has ever faced and, acting quickly, he had implemented a plan of action to deal with the crisis.

During his Fireside Chats, his strong, gentle, confident voice resonated across the nation with an eloquence that brought comfort and resilience to a nation caught up in a storm and reassured us that we could lick any problem. I will never forget him for that.

With his alphabet soup of federal agencies, FDR in many ways set in motion the forces that later sought to create big government and bring a form of veiled socialism to America. But I think that many people forget Roosevelt ran for president on a platform dedicated to reducing waste and fat in government. He called for cutting federal spending by twenty-five percent, eliminating useless boards and commissions and returning to states and communities powers that had been wrongfully seized by the federal government. If he had not been distracted by war, I think he would have resisted the relentless expansion of the federal government that followed him. One of his sons, Franklin Roosevelt, Jr., often told me that his father had said many times his welfare and relief programs during the Depression were meant only as emergency, stopgap measures to cope with a crisis, not the seeds of what others later tried to turn into a permanent welfare state. Government giveaway programs, FDR said, "destroy the human spirit," and he was right. As smart as he was, though, I suspect even FDR didn't realize that once you created a bureaucracy, it took on a life of its own. It was almost impossible to close down a bureaucracy once it had been created.

After FDR's election, Jack, as one of the few Democrats in town, was appointed to implement some of the new federal relief programs in Dixon. It removed him from the ranks of the unemployed and also gave me my first opportunity to watch government in action.

8

As administrator of federal relief programs, Jack shared a small office in Dixon with the County Supervisor of Poor. Every week, people who had lost their jobs came to the office to pick up sacks of flour, potatoes, and other food and pieces of scrip they could exchange for groceries at stores in town.

Occasionally, I dropped into the office to wait for Jack before we walked home together. I was shocked to see the fathers of many of my schoolmates waiting in line for handouts—men I had known most of my life, who had had jobs I'd thought were as permanent as the city itself.

Jack knew that accepting handouts was tough on the dignity of the men and came up with a plan to help them recover some of it. He began leaving home early in the morning and making rounds of the county, asking if anyone had odd jobs available, then, if they did, persuaded the people to let him find somebody to do the work. The next week when the men came in for their handouts, Jack offered the work he'd found to those who'd been out of work the longest.

I'll never forget the faces of these men when Jack told them their turn had come up for a job: They brightened like a burst of neon, and when they left Dad's office, I swear the men were standing a little taller. They wanted *work*, not handouts.

Not long after that, Jack told several men he had found a week's work for them. They responded to this news with a rustling of feet.

Eventually, one broke the silence and said: "Jack, the last time you got me some work, the people at the relief office took my family off welfare; they said I had a job and even though it was temporary, I wasn't eligible for relief anymore. I just can't afford to take another job."

Later on, thanks again to his party connections, Jack was placed in charge of the Works Progress Administration office in Dixon. The WPA was one of the most productive elements of FDR's alphabet soup of agencies because it put people to work building roads, bridges, and other projects. Like Jack's informal program, it gave men and women a chance to make some money along with the satisfaction of knowing they *earned* it. But just as Jack got the program up and running, there was a decline in the number of people applying for work on the projects. Since he knew there hadn't been a cure for unemployment in Dixon, he began asking questions and discovered the federal welfare workers were telling able-bodied men in Dixon that they shouldn't take the WPA jobs because they were being taken care of and didn't need help from the WPA.

After a while, Jack couldn't get any of his projects going; he couldn't get enough men sprung from the welfare giveaway program. I wasn't sophisticated enough to realize what I learned later: The first rule of a bureaucracy is to protect the bureaucracy. If the people running the welfare program had let their clientele find other ways of making a living, that would have reduced their importance and their budget.

The winter of 1932–1933 was very cold. Like a lot of other people in Dixon, I spent Christmas and New Year's out of work and without prospects. The only job on the horizon was another summer of lifeguarding at Lowell Park. In February, however, I got a telephone call that changed everything: Pete MacArthur said one of WOC's two staff announcers had quit and he offered me his job, starting at $100 a month.

"I'll be there tomorrow," I said.

Nelle had taught me to contribute ten percent of my income to the church and I'd always done so. As soon as I was certain I had the job, I visited our minister and posed a question to him: My brother has another year of college ahead of him, I said, but he is going to have to leave Eureka because he is running out of money; do you think the Lord would consider it a tithe if I sent him $10 a month instead of putting it in the collection plate? The minister, a kind and wise man, thought about the question a moment and said, "I think that would be fine with the Lord."

The day I arrived for work in Davenport, they put me on the air. I was a disc jockey before they invented the term: As staff announcer, I played phonograph records, read commercials, and served as a vocal bridge between our local programming and network broadcasts. I was not an immediate success as a radio announcer, to put it mildly.

Nobody had bothered to give me any instructions on how to be an announcer and I quickly proved it on the air. I stumbled over my words and had a delivery as wooden as a prairie oak. I'd have hated to have to pay for some of those first commercials I read over the air. But what really got me in trouble was a commercial I *didn't* read.

One of my assignments was to present a half-hour program of organ music from a local mortuary; the mortuary provided the organist in exchange for a discreet plug identifying it as the source of the music.

However, the nature of this quid pro quo was never explained to me, and one night I decided I didn't like the idea of following a romantic song like "I Love You Truly" with a veiled commercial for an undertaker, so I omitted the plug.

Understandably, the mortuary was unhappy and complained. After my previous weeks of on-the-air bumbling, the station management decided that it was time for me to find another career.

Then one of those things happened that makes one wonder about God's having a plan for all of us.

My job was given to a young teacher, and the station asked me to help break him in. While I was doing it, I mentioned how I'd been hired and then fired. When he heard the story, he demanded a contract from WOC that would provide him with job security; he didn't want to give up the relative security of teaching and then wind up in the same fix as I. But WOC didn't give contracts to *anyone* and turned him down. He quit the next day and the station manager asked me to stay until they could find someone else.

I agreed to stay on one condition: They had to assign someone to help me improve my on-the-air delivery.

Pete and other friends went to work on me and gave me a crash course on radio announcing, and I began reading over the commercials before airtime and practicing my delivery to get the right rhythm and cadence and give my words more emotion. Whatever I did during those few days worked: After another week or two, the talk at WOC about replacing me stopped.

Then, enter another break for Dutch Reagan.

I'd been in Davenport less than three months when Pete called me to his office and asked: "Do you know anything about track?"

I said, "Hell, yes, I ran the quarter mile and was on a championship relay team."

WHO, our sister station in Des Moines, he said, needed someone to broadcast the Drake Relays, one of the top track meets in the country. I got the assignment.

A few weeks later, the Palmer Company received a permit for a 50,000-watt clear channel station in Des Moines. We were told WOC was closing and all of us were going to WHO.

Until then, both stations had operated only low-power 1,000-watt transmitters with limited range. There were only fifteen 50,000-watt clear channel stations in America at the time and to work at one was the biggest thing in radio. Overnight, WHO became one of the most powerful NBC stations in the country, and because I'd gotten good marks for my reporting on the Drake Relays, I was offered the post of sports announcer.

I spent four years at station WHO in Des Moines and they were among the most pleasant of my life. At twenty-two I'd achieved my dream: I was a sports announcer. If I had stopped there, I believe I would have been happy the rest of my life. I'd accomplished my goal and enjoyed every minute of it. Before long, during the depths of the Depression, I was earning seventy-five dollars a week and gaining the kind of fame in the Midwest that brought in invitations for speaking engagements that provided extra income I could use to help out my parents, whose financial circumstances had gone from bad to worse after Jack's heart troubles left him unable to work.

. . .

After his graduation from Eureka, Moon visited me in Des Moines and he was in the studio one Friday night when I was predicting which football teams would win Saturday's games. When I caught him shaking his head at some of my predictions, I told the audience about it and made him get on the air with me. Pete MacArthur heard us and liked the interplay and it led to a regular Friday night show in which we matched predictions. Later on, Moon became an announcer and program director, beginning a climb up the ladder of broadcasting that made him a director, producer, network executive, and finally vice-president of one of the country's largest advertising agencies.

During my years in Des Moines, I attended an endless number of football games, auto races, track tournaments, and swimming meets and, through the magic of radio, I "covered" hundreds of baseball games played by the Chicago Cubs and the Chicago White Sox without going to the stadium.

In the press box at Wrigley Field or wherever the Cubs were playing, a telegrapher tapped out a report in Morse code after each pitch and each play of the game. In Des Moines, I sat at a microphone across from another telegraph operator with a pair of earphones wrapped around his head.

After each play, he decoded a burst of dots and dashes from the stadium and typed out a few words that described the play and handed it to me through a slot in a sheet of glass separating the studio and the control room. I then described the play as if I'd been in the press box, even though the slip of paper might say only "Out 4 to 3"; four was second base and three was first, so it was a grounder to the second baseman who threw the batter out at first. It had to be done quickly because we weren't the only ones covering the game. Six or seven other stations were also broadcasting Cubs games, most of them live from the press box. Sometimes, people would try to compare my broadcast to the live broadcast, and they told me that I was able to keep up within a half a pitch of the game.

Between pitches and innings, there was usually a lot of dead time that I had to fill with anecdotes and descriptions of the players, the field, and the weather. I wish I could count the number of ways I managed to describe how the rays of the afternoon sun looked as they fell across the rim of Wrigley Field.

One summer's day—and this is a story that I've probably repeated more times in my life than any other—my imagination was tested to its maximum. The Cubs and St. Louis Cardinals were locked in a scoreless ninth-inning tie with Dizzy Dean on the mound and the Cubs' Billy Jurges at bat.

I described Dean winding up and releasing his pitch. Then Curly, our telegraph operator, shook his head and passed me a slip of paper, and I looked for a description of the pitch.

Instead, his note read: *"The wire's gone dead."*

Well, since I had the ball on the way to the plate I had to get it there. Although I could have told our listeners that the wire had gone dead, it would have sent them rushing toward their dials and a competitor. So, I decided to let Jurges foul off the pitch, figuring Western Union would soon fix the problem. To fill in some time, I described a couple of kids in the stands fighting over the foul ball.

When Curly gestured that the wire was still dead, I had Jurges foul off another ball; I slowed Dean down, had him pick up the resin bag and take a sign, shake it off, get another sign, and let him pitch; I said he'd fouled off another one, but this time he'd just missed a home run by only a few inches.

I searched Curly's face for a look of encouragement, but he shook his head.

I described Dean winding up and hurling another pitch; Jurges hit a foul ball, and then another . . . and another. A red-headed kid in the stands retrieved one of the fouls and held up the ball to show off his trophy.

By then I was in much too deep to admit the wire was dead, so I continued to let Jurges foul Dean's pitches, and his string of foul balls went on for almost seven minutes. I don't know how many foul balls there were, but I'm told someone reported the foul-slugging spree as a record to "Ripley's Believe It Or Not" column.

Finally, Curly started typing again and I knew the wire had been restored. Relieved, I grabbed the slip of paper he handed me through the slot and read it: *"Jurges popped out on the first ball pitched."*

For days, people stopped me on the street and asked if Jurges had set a record for foul balls. I'd just say, "Yeah, he was there a long time." I never admitted a thing.

I only broadcast one football game in the same way via remote control and radio's "theater of the mind."

At the time, many of the big universities were suspicious that radio broadcasts of their football games would cut down the sale of tickets at their box office. One, the University of Michigan, refused us permission to cover its game with the University of Iowa, so I was assigned to do it by telegraphic report. The most memorable thing about the game that day was the name of Michigan's center—*Gerald Ford.*

Not all my work in Des Moines was devoted to sports announcing. During the off season, I filled in as a regular announcer, which gave me an opportunity to interview visiting movie stars and other celebrities. One night our guest was evangelist Aimee Semple McPherson, who'd come to Des Moines for a revival meeting not long after she'd been accused of having an extracurricular romantic liaison with one of her followers, paid for with disciples' contributions.

I finished the interview and invited her to tell our listeners about the revival meeting. I took a seat and as I was thinking about the next commercial that I had to read, I heard her sign off and tell the listeners "Good night."

I looked at the clock and saw that there were four minutes to go before our next program. I jumped up to the microphone and twirled my index finger, signaling the engineer to play a phonograph record, and said: "We conclude this interview with the noted evangelist, Aimee Semple McPherson, with a brief interlude of transcribed music. . . . "

The engineer nodded and a song blasted over the studio's loudspeaker. My guest looked at me with fire in her eyes and then turned around and left the studio with her coat standing out behind her in the wind.

The engineer had played the first disk on his stack of records—the Mills Brothers singing "Minnie the Moocher's Wedding Day."

I gained one love, but lost another in Des Moines. It was there I first heard the words, "Nothing is so good for the inside of a man as the outside of a horse."

I think I'd probably first discovered an affinity for horses when I was still lifeguarding at Lowell Park. There was a lodge at the park run by a Danish immigrant who owned a big gray horse and he occasionally rode it down to the bath house; a couple of times, when there weren't any swimmers on the beach, he let me ride it. I didn't know it then, but he was introducing me to one of the joys of my life. In Des Moines, I made some friends who liked to ride and they began inviting me, when we all had a free afternoon, to go to a local stable and rent horses for an hour or so and I enjoyed it very much.

Then, another announcer at WHO, a reserve officer in the army cavalry, told me the Fourteenth Cavalry Regiment based at Fort Des Moines offered young men a chance to obtain a reserve commission through what the War Department called the Citizens Military Training Program. I didn't have a burning desire to be an army officer—I still thought we'd fought the war to end all wars—but it was a deal too good to turn down: In exchange for enlisting in the reserve, the army offered training by some of the best cavalrymen in the country and unlimited use of army horses, all free. Ever since I'd become addicted to Saturday matinees, I'd had an affection for those scenes when a troop of cavalrymen in blue tunics and gold braid, flags raised and bugles blowing, raced across the prairie to rescue beleaguered pioneers.

In Des Moines, I transformed some of the childhood fantasies into reality and discovered a lifelong love for horses and riding. I just fell in love with riding and I began to dream of owning a ranch. As the years passed, there was no place on earth I'd rather be than in a saddle, on the back of a horse.

I had expected to marry Margaret Cleaver since my sophomore year at Dixon High. So had our families and all of our friends. She was the first girl I ever kissed. I had hung my fraternity pin on her and soon after our graduation, I'd given her an engagement ring and we'd agreed to marry as soon as we could afford it. But after Margaret took the teaching job in a remote part of Illinois and I'd moved to Iowa, it became harder and harder for us to see each other. We wrote often, but our get-togethers were few and far between. Then one day, about two years after I'd moved to Des Moines, I opened a letter from her and my fraternity pin and engagement ring tumbled out of it.

Margaret said she'd gone on a European cruise with one of her sisters and met a foreign service officer with whom she had fallen in love.

75

Then one day I got a call from my mother. She said there was an item in the Dixon paper announcing that Margaret Cleaver was engaged and planning to marry within a few weeks.

Nelle, I'm sure, expected me to jump off a roof and she asked my old high school teacher, B. J. Frazer, to contact me and he sent me a wonderful, understanding letter. He said I had a whole life ahead of me and ought to look ahead, not behind me, and in the end things would work out all right.

My mother, of course, repeated her old dictum that everything works out for the best and that every reverse in life carries the seeds of something better in the future.

Margaret's decision shattered me, not so much, I think, because she no longer loved me, but because I no longer had anyone to love.

Still, I knew in my heart that we had grown apart during our long separation and something inside me suggested that things would work out all right; after a while, the pain eased and I began to admit Nelle and B. J. Frazer were right.

9

As ANYONE WHO HAS EVER LIVED in central Iowa knows, winters there can last forever and slip into the heat of summer with barely a nod to spring. After I started broadcasting the Cubs' games, I concocted a plan to escape part of the frigid Iowa winter by offering to accompany the team to its annual spring training camp in California. If you will pay my expenses, I told the people at WHO, I'll go to California and donate my yearly vacation to the cause, and the trip will pay off in color and knowledge about the team I'll be able to use all through the coming season.

The proposal, which they accepted, wasn't as charitable on my part as it seemed: A baseball announcer never gets to take a vacation during the summer, and my plan gave me an all-expense-paid holiday under the California sun, along with a chance to earn some extra money by writing articles for the newspapers back home. Since I also broadcast games of the Chicago White Sox, I could also look in on their spring practice in Pasadena, a few miles from Los Angeles.

The Cubs, owned by the Wrigley chewing gum family, did their spring training on Catalina, a rocky island off the coast of Southern California that was also owned by the family.

My annual trips to Southern California began in 1935. For someone who'd practically cut his teeth on celluloid shoot-'em-ups and carried around fantasies about becoming an actor for years, Catalina was tantalizingly close to Hollywood, but it was also pretty remote. Every week, there were hundreds of young people—from Iowa, Illinois, and just about every other state—who stepped off a train at Union Station in Los Angeles who had exactly the same dream that I did and they got no closer to realizing it than a studio front gate.

A few weeks before my departure for California in 1937, however, something happened that made Hollywood seem a little less remote from Des Moines. Our station had a popular Saturday night barn dance program featuring a terrific group of musicians called the Oklahoma Outlaws. Gene Autry had heard about the group and signed them to appear in one of his singing cowboy movies. The studios in those days were constantly looking for ways to broaden their audience, and the Oklahoma Outlaws had a big following in the Midwest.

That April when I arrived in Los Angeles for my annual ten-day reporting tour, a storm was socking Southern California with a ferocity that probably set back the Chamber of Commerce's promotional efforts at least a year or two. The streets were flooded, high winds were felling the city's towering palm trees like stalks of wheat, and the horizon was ugly and gray.

I decided to play hooky from the Cubs and took a trolley to Republic Studios so I could watch my friends in the Oklahoma Outlaws act out their new, if temporary role as motion picture players. I'd planned to leave for Catalina that evening, but high seas along the twenty-one-mile Catalina channel were forcing boats to turn back, seaplanes were grounded, and the Cubs' hotel on the island was cut off from the town of Avalon by mud slides.

So I checked into the Biltmore Hotel in downtown Los Angeles, which is where the Cubs stayed when they were playing exhibition games with their farm club, the Los Angeles Angels, and that evening I walked downstairs to the Biltmore Bowl, a nightclub on the lower level, to look up a fellow Iowan, Joy Hodges.

Joy, a singer who had once worked for WHO, had come to Los Angeles several years before with hopes of breaking into the movies and had won several small parts while singing at night with a band at the Biltmore. I sent a note to her backstage, and she joined me for dinner between her floor shows.

Joy was a pretty, dark-haired woman with a sweet quality that hadn't been spoiled by her brief exposure to show business. I was looking forward to a pleasant dinner with an attractive girl and I had planned on bringing her up to date on the latest gossip from Des Moines. But my head was still filled with the sights and sounds of my visit to the studio that day. Seeing the actors, the cameras, the lights, and the scenery had only whetted my appetite to be a member of the club. I was starry-eyed and confessed to Joy how much I'd always had a secret yearning to be an actor.

"Take off your glasses," she said.

Studios, Joy added, as if to paraphrase Dorothy Parker, don't make passes at actors who wear glasses. If I wanted to break into the movies, she said the first thing I had to do was "Get rid of those glasses."

Joy said she knew an agent who might be willing to tell me if I had any realistic chances of making it in Hollywood—and be truthful with me if he thought I was wasting my time.

At promptly ten o'clock the next morning, I looked across a big desk at a skin-colored blur, agent Bill Meiklejohn, while trying to project "star quality" (whatever that was).

I'd taken Joy's advice and not worn my glasses to the interview with Meiklejohn; as a result, I could hardly see him during one of the most important interviews of my life.

But, heart pounding and hopelessly nearsighted, I presented a somewhat exaggerated description of my qualifications for movie stardom.

After finishing my pitch, I asked Meiklejohn gingerly if he thought it would be worth it for me to knock on a few doors in Hollywood.

Without a word, he picked up his telephone and dialed Max Arnow, a casting director for Warner Brothers.

"Max," he said, "I have another Robert Taylor sitting in my office."

"God made only one Robert Taylor," Arnow said of Hollywood's reigning male star, loud enough for me to hear his friendly burst of sarcasm.

Nevertheless, Arnow agreed to take a look at me.

My subsequent interview with Arnow was brief and left me with the impression of being appraised like a slab of beef.

I've often wondered what would have happened to me if Max Arnow hadn't liked my voice.

He and Meiklejohn circled me like a pair of hummingbirds, talking about my face, my shoulders, and my height as if I wasn't even in the room.

For some reason, Arnow said he was impressed by my voice. He said it reminded him of the voice of a young stock player Warners had put under contract but, for reasons I can't remember, was giving the studio some kind of difficulty. I guess maybe Arnow thought of me as a kind of replacement for the guy with the voice like mine.

Meiklejohn was apparently a good salesman because he persuaded Arnow to give me a screen test. Arnow handed me a few pages from the script of a Broadway play, *The Philadelphia Story*, told me to memorize them, and return in several days.

At the end of the day, when I finally arrived on Catalina, Cubs Manager Charley Grimm chewed me out for being absent without leave.

I couldn't bring myself to tell him that my mind was somewhere else; it was exploding with visions of a future of which he wouldn't be a part.

I returned to Los Angeles by boat for the screen test and it lasted only a few minutes, just a Warners starlet and me exchanging a few lines from *The Philadelphia Story*.

The next day, Arnow called Meiklejohn and told him he planned to show the test to Jack Warner, the mogul who ran Warner Brothers like a feudal monarchy, as soon as Warner could work it into his schedule.

"They'll call you in a few days at the Biltmore," Meiklejohn said.

"I'm sorry, but I won't be there," I said. "I've got to be on a train tomorrow—I've got to get back to my job in Des Moines; the season opener's coming up in a few days and I've got to broadcast the Cubs' games."

Arnow and Meiklejohn wouldn't believe it when I refused to delay my trip back to Iowa. Although I didn't do it consciously, I think it was probably a good strategic move: Hollywood was accustomed to people knocking down its doors for a job; it wasn't used to somebody saying, "Sorry, I've got to go home now."

Still, as soon as I was on the train and America was rolling past me, I said to myself: *What a damn fool you were.*

But less than forty-eight hours after the train pulled into Des Moines I got a telegram:

WARNERS OFFERS CONTRACT SEVEN YEARS STOP ONE YEAR OPTION STOP STARTING $200 A WEEK STOP WHAT SHALL I DO MEIKLEJOHN

I broke the speed records driving down to the Western Union office and wrote out a reply:

SIGN BEFORE THEY CHANGE THEIR MINDS   DUTCH REAGAN

Although I broadcast Cubs games for another month, my heart wasn't in it. After a lot of sad good-byes to my friends in Des Moines, I packed everything I owned into a Nash convertible that I'd bought recently for $600 and headed for California.

If those months of rejection after my graduation from Eureka were the low point of my life, that trip across the country, with the top of my car open to the wind and the sun shining on my head, was one of the highest of the highs. I was on my way to Hollywood.

After I checked into the Biltmore, George Ward, one of Bill Meiklejohn's assistants, warned me that it might take weeks or months for Warner Brothers to cast me in a movie because it had a large stable of new stock players who'd be competing with me for roles.

He was wrong. I was playing in my first movie within a few days, but not before I'd played a spectator's role in an offscreen drama that might have been called *The Remaking of Dutch Reagan*.

Thank goodness they liked my voice, for whatever reason, because for a while it seemed that was about all they liked about me.

First stop: Makeup.

"The hair has to be changed," Max Arnow told a hairstylist.

The hairstylist looked at me the way a paleontologist might examine a newly discovered but as yet unidentified fossil plucked from a prehistoric riverbed.

"Where did you get that haircut?" she asked me.

"It looks like somebody cut it with bowl number seven," she added, before I could answer.

I still had my Harold Teen haircut—short and parted down the middle.

Then they announced I had another problem: My head was too small.

"Where did you get that coat?" Arnow demanded, giving a fish-eye once-over to a new sport coat I'd purchased solely to impress him. "You can't wear that outfit. The shoulders are too big. *They make your head look too small.*"

Next stop: Wardrobe.

"See what you can do about his head," Arnow told a wardrobe designer.

A tailor stripped off my coat and committed murder on it, slashing the shoulders and ruthlessly whacking away pleats and tucks.

That helped, but it wasn't enough. Arnow said that if I appeared on screen the way that God had made me, I would look out of proportion.

"Your shoulders are too big and your neck is too short for your head," he insisted, not very tactfully, I thought.

There was a lot of foot shuffling and mumbling among the tailors, but no one, as I hoped, came forward and said: "His head looks okay to me."

Everyone looked troubled. Then somebody thought of Jimmy Cagney, one of Warner Brothers' biggest stars. "He's got the same problem, a short neck," the voice said.

Cagney, the wardrobe expert said, had solved his problem by going to a shirtmaker who had succeeded in creating the appearance of a longer neck and a bigger head by designing a special shirt collar for him.

Behind his neck, Cagney's shirts had a normal collar band, but as it encircled his neck it became smaller and narrower, so by the time it reached his chest, there wasn't any collar band at all. The tips of the collar just lay flat on his chest, revealing a few more inches of skin than would have been exposed by an ordinary collar.

"Get the name of Cagney's shirtmaker," someone said urgently.

This was accomplished and I was sent to have some shirts made with a Cagney collar. But when I came back to the studio the experts said my shoulders and chest still appeared to be a little too wide for my head.

Until then, I'd always worn narrow ties and shirts with small collars, whatever was in style at the time. To solve the problem, the wardrobe people instructed me to have all my shirts made with an extra-wide collar with near-horizontal lines and to use a wide Windsor knot when I tied my tie—anything, they said, to fill the gap between my lapels and reduce the appearance of the width of my shoulders.

I have to admit they knew their business. To this day, I wear the kind of shirts they—and Jimmy Cagney's shirtmaker—helped design.

Next stop: Publicity.

The first item on the agenda was a meeting to choose my name.

Max Arnow and several Warner Brothers press agents sat around a table staring at me, making me feel like a mannequin who was supposed to be seen but not heard.

Going through their minds was the question: What name does he *look* like?

Ignoring me, they'd suggest a name, rule it out, then start over again, getting nowhere.

Finally I interrupted and they looked at me as if I'd done something wrong. The mannequin could speak.

I said, "May I point out that I have a lot of name recognition in a large part of the country, particularly in the Middle West, where I've been broadcasting sports. I think a lot of people would recognize my name on theater marquees."

One of them said "Dutch Reagan? You can't put Dutch Reagan on a marquee."

I had never liked my first name and in school and on the radio, I'd always used my nickname. But I made a spot decision that I'd be happier using my real name rather than some moniker dreamed up by a press agent, and so I ventured inquiringly:

"How about Ronald? . . . Ronald Reagan?"

They looked at each other and began repeating it to one another, "Ronald Reagan . . . Ronald Reagan . . . "

"Hey, that's not bad," one said.

Pretty soon you would have thought *they* had thought it up. Everyone began chiming in their agreement.

And so it was decided, then and there, that I could remain Ronald Reagan.

10

IT WAS A FANTASY COME TRUE. On a Monday morning in the first week of June in 1937, I drove my convertible through the gates of the Warner Brothers lot in Burbank, ready for work, and with a hole in my stomach as deep as an oil well. I asked myself, what am *I* doing here? Once again, I felt like the new kid in school.

Here I was, a twenty-six-year-old radio announcer from Iowa suddenly rubbing shoulders with stars like Errol Flynn, Pat O'Brien, and Olivia de Havilland. They were professional actors. It had been five years since *I* had done any acting, and that was in a college play. I wasn't quite an Iowa hayseed. But I'd never been east of Chicago, north of Minneapolis, south of the Ozarks.

When I was introduced to Edward Everett Horton, he said kindly: "Glad to meet you, Reagan. We need some new faces around here. Hope you stick around."

So did I.

I'd learned there was a clause in my contract that allowed Warner Brothers to fire me after six months if they were unhappy with me. So much for the publicity department's announcement Warners had signed me to a "long-term contract."

In a studio screening room my first day, I was shown the test that had led Warners to offer me a contract and I wanted to bury myself under my seat. I was terrible. I hated it. After that I figured I'd be on a train bound for Des Moines in time for Christmas.

I was in the same boat as all the contract players. The studio liked to keep you a little off balance and uncertain how long you'd stay. George Ward tried to console me with an assurance that Warner Brothers usually took longer than six months to evaluate a new contract player, but he wasn't very successful. That evening, he invited me to his home for dinner and afterward we went to the midget auto races at Gilmore Stadium where I glanced up at the lights of the press box and saw a group of reporters and broadcasters enjoying themselves. It hit me for the first time that I was now only a guy in the grandstand, not a member of the working press, and I wondered how long it would be before I was back in the press box.

Hollywood studios in those days churned out two kinds of pictures —A movies, which led a double bill and featured major stars who could attract customers into a theater, and low-budget B movies, which featured newcomers and lesser-known character actors and filled out the second half of the bill. Like other newcomers, I was assigned to the Warner Brothers B Unit.

Besides filling out their double bills, the studios used B pictures a lot like companies in some industries now use their research and development departments. After they'd put new actors or actresses under contract, they'd cast them in a B picture to test the audience reaction to them. If they seemed to click with the audience, based on the fan mail they received and the response to them at sneak previews, they were given more important parts and then slipped into an A movie in a minor role to further test whether they had the potential to be a star.

Maybe it wasn't intentional, but my first role at Warner Brothers sure seemed like typecasting: I was assigned to play a radio announcer in a movie initially called *Inside Story*, then renamed *Love Is on the Air*. It was a typical B movie—made in a hurry and forgettable.

My preparations for the part consisted of a day with a dialogue coach; at least it was a day longer than the preparation I'd had for my radio announcer's job in Davenport. The coach went over the script with me and told me to report for work the next day.

When I woke up the following morning, I wanted to get out of town as quickly as I could. I thought about getting in my car and driving nonstop to Iowa.

Nothing I'd ever experienced—no stage fright before a college show or steeplechase jump or dive from a high platform, nothing I'd been through, had ever produced in me the kind of jitters I felt when I stepped onto Stage Eight at Warner Brothers that morning.

"Kid, don't worry," a veteran character actor who was in my first scene said. "Just take it easy and everything will be all right."

They sponged some makeup on my face, I took my place on the set, the lights went on, and the director, Nick Grinde, said: "Camera . . . Action!"

Suddenly, my jitters were gone. The old character actor had been right. As soon as I heard the director's words, I forgot all about the camera and the lights and the crew and concentrated on delivering my lines in a way that I hoped would make B. J. Frazer proud.

A couple of minutes later, the director said "Cut." To my amazement, he said he was satisfied with the first take. He started setting up to shoot the next scene and I sat down on one of those canvas chairs you see on movie sets (without my name on it) and said silently to myself: *You know, maybe I can make it here.*

Although we finished *Love Is on the Air* in three weeks, it wouldn't be released for four months so I had a long time to worry about whether Warner Brothers was going to renew my option. But they kept me busy. A few days after finishing this picture, I drew an assignment to play a cavalryman (more typecasting) in a picture based on a true story about a wonder horse named Sergeant Murphy that won Britain's Grand National steeplechase race. The *Des Moines Register* had asked me to send reports home about my experiences in Hollywood. After we finished *Sergeant Murphy,* I wrote: "No matter what anyone says or what the future may bring, now I can always insist that I once was an actor.

"If I'd only made one picture it might have been called a fluke. But I've made two now, and that makes me an actor—even if in name only."

Four months later, *Love Is on the Air* was released and I raced around town searching for reviews of my first movie. For the most part, they were kind. The *Hollywood Reporter,* one of the most important trade papers, said "*Love Is on the Air* presents a new leading man, Ronald Reagan, who is a natural, giving one of the best first picture performances Hollywood has offered in many a day."

A few days later, Warner Brothers picked up my option for another six months and gave me a raise.

I called Nelle and Jack and asked them to come to California. Within a few weeks, they were on their way. And in a way, I suppose I was too, although now I faced the same kind of problem I faced during my first year at Eureka College when Mac McKinzie relegated me to the fifth string of the football squad: I had made the team; now I had to make the first string.

11

I N MY FIRST YEAR AND A HALF at Warner Brothers, I made thirteen pictures. Usually, I was in and out of a movie in three or four weeks. You worked from eight in the morning until seven at night.

Between pictures, I went horseback riding in Griffith Park, learned how to body surf in the Pacific Ocean, and tried to keep up with the demands of the studio publicity machine. Press agents were constantly trying to pair me with my leading ladies and new starlets, a fringe benefit to which I usually didn't object, and wherever I went, they assigned a photographer to follow and collect material for the fan magazines. The experience left me with a lifelong distaste for formalized picture-taking sessions.

After we had filmed *Love Is on the Air,* one of our cameramen told me: "Kid, I don't think you should wear makeup.

"There are some people who have complexions that for some reason or other just can't take makeup well and I think you're one of 'em. What I mean is that you can literally see the makeup on your skin."

Before long, he said it was likely I'd be asked to act out a few lines in a screen test for another new contract player and when that happened, he suggested, "Why don't you try doing the scene without wearing makeup? Some people look better without it than with it." We did the test and he was right. I never wore makeup again.

I had always hated my glasses and after moving to Hollywood I enthusiastically became a guinea pig for some of the first pairs of contact lenses available in this country. They were big, rigid, and fit over the whites of your eyes like a pair of football helmets and weren't much fun to wear. Each lens had a little bubble over your cornea that you had to keep filled with a saline solution, and every couple of hours, the solution would turn gray and you'd find yourself blinded until you replaced the fluid. They were difficult to wear but vanity prevailed, although I found out I couldn't use them much in pictures because they had the effect of making me look a little pop-eyed on the screen. So unless I was doing a long shot or a stunt in which I felt I needed good vision more than a good appearance, I didn't use them during filming.

I was proud of some of the B pictures we made, but a lot of them were pretty poor. They were movies the studio didn't want good, they wanted 'em Thursday.

Until I got the part of George Gipp in *Knute Rockne—All American*, I was the Errol Flynn of the B pictures. I usually played a jet-propelled newspaperman who solved more crimes than a polygraph machine. My one unvarying line, which I always snapped into a telephone, was: "Give me the city desk. I've got a story that will crack this town wide open!"

When the studio played you in an A picture, you always hoped it would generate the kind of reviews and fan mail and audience response at previews that would get you promoted out of the B Unit. But there were a lot of disappointments. You'd make an A picture and think you did okay and then find yourself back in the B's, a little frustrated and saying unkind things about the studio's judgment.

When I arrived in Hollywood, actors and actresses had just won a tough five-year battle with studios for the union shop and recognition of the Screen Actors Guild as the exclusive bargaining agent for actors. Like all contract players, I'd had to join the union and wasn't very happy about it. Making me join the union, whether I wanted to or not, I thought, was an infringement on my rights. I guess I also was a little uncertain as to why actors needed to have a union. But as I spoke to some of the older career actors I met at Warners and discovered how much they'd been exploited in the past, I began to change my mind. Major stars had no trouble negotiating good contracts and working conditions for themselves, but that wasn't the case for the supporting players, many of whom had been blacklisted by the studios and deprived of work after they'd tried to form a union.

As far as I was concerned, some of the studio bosses were abusing their power. Throughout my life, I guess there's been one thing that's troubled me more than any other: the abuse of people and the theft of their democratic rights, whether by a totalitarian government, an employer, or anyone else. I probably got it from my father; Jack never bristled more than when he thought working people were being exploited.

Once I'd become a believer in the union, I was appointed to the Screen Actors Guild's board of directors. I wasn't asked; I was drafted to represent the industry's younger contract players.

My first directors' meeting wasn't at all what I expected. I thought the union would be run by the lesser actors who'd been exploited by the studios, but instead a lot of Hollywood's top stars, like Cary Grant and Jimmy Cagney, were on the board. Most were big box-office draws who could easily command huge salaries and didn't need the Guild's help to negotiate their wages. But they enthusiastically gave their time and prestige to assure that lesser players like me got a fair shake. That night I told myself that if I ever became a star, I'd do as much as I could to help the actors and actresses at the bottom of the ladder.

The studios had a vested interest in helping contract players achieve stardom. But we were all captives of their decisions, right or wrong, and they weren't always right. I decided I had to take my career into my own hands—and came up with a plan to marry my new job in Hollywood with my old love for football.

I was fascinated with the life story of Knute Rockne, the legendary Norwegian-born coach at Notre Dame who died in a plane crash in 1931 after revolutionizing the game of football.

Over lunch in the Warner Brothers commissary, I began talking up the idea of a movie based on his life and asked some of our writers for pointers on how to write a screenplay about him. I began working on a script and over lunch one day suggested to Pat O'Brien, a fellow Irishman who had become a good friend, that he'd make the perfect Rockne.

Of course, I'd already cast my own part in the movie: George Gipp, who casually wandered onto Rockne's practice field one day and as his greatest star became almost as legendary as the coach himself before dying two weeks after his final game.

As I continued my work on a screenplay, I never thought about getting paid for it. My reward was the part of George Gipp—the immortal Gipper. Then one day I saw an article in *Variety:* Warner Brothers was going to make a movie based on the life of Knute Rockne starring Pat O'Brien.

When I asked some friends how this had happened they told me I talked too much, that it was a good idea so Warners bought the rights to Rockne's life story. But then they told me Warners had already tested ten actors for the part of Gipp. I ran all the way to the producer's office and asked for a shot at the role. He turned me down because he said I didn't look like the greatest football player of our time. "You mean Gipp has to weigh about two hundred pounds?" I asked. "Would it surprise you that I'm five pounds *heavier* than George Gipp was when he played at Notre Dame?"

He held out for an actor who was a giant. A lot of players don't look like players when they are out of uniform and, yes, some fellows who aren't players look like they are when they put on a football uniform.

I remembered a cameraman who had once told me that the people in the front office believed only what they saw on film. I got in my car and drove home as fast as I could and dug into the trunk I had brought from Dixon. I found a yearbook photo of myself in my college football uniform, raced back to the studio, and put it on the producer's desk.

He studied the picture, looked up at me, and said, "Can I keep this for a while?" I hadn't been home more than an hour when the phone rang. It was a call telling me to be at the studio at eight in the morning to test for the role of George Gipp.

Pat O'Brien volunteered to play Rockne in my test. The next day, the producer called and said: "Reagan, you're playing the Gipper."

A few weeks after we finished filming *Knute Rockne—All American,* I sat in the back row of a small movie theater in Pasadena where Warner Brothers often sneak-previewed its new pictures. Pat was there too, along with a number of studio executives. We were waiting to sample an audience's reaction to the movie for the first time.

As the picture began to unreel in the dark theater, I sensed a glow radiating from the audience like a warm fire. I was in the picture only a few minutes, but it contained a very emotional scene. Just before Gipp died, I said to Rockne: "Some day when things are tough and the breaks are going against the boys, ask them to go in there and win one for the Gipper. I don't know where I'll be but I'll know about it and I'll be happy."

As I spoke these words, men and women in the audience started pulling out their handkerchiefs. Then, from the back to the front of the theater, I heard sniffles, making me wonder if this was the breakthrough I'd been waiting for.

I drove home satisfied with the picture and had barely gotten into bed when the telephone rang. It was someone at the studio, telling me to report for wardrobe fittings early the next morning: "You're playing Custer in *Santa Fe Trail*."

It was an Errol Flynn picture and I was cast in the second lead— not as costar, but one of the two leads in an A picture. At the studio the next day, I thought people were suddenly more friendly to me. Then I went to the wardrobe department and witnessed a scene I'll never forget.

Seamstresses had been working all night making uniforms for me. As I waited to be fitted, I looked over at a rack of uniforms tagged with the word "Custer" and the name of another actor. I watched a wardrobe man come in and gather up the uniforms, toss them like rags in a corner, and replace them on the rack with blue and gold-braided uniforms marked "Custer" with my name on them. I looked at those uniforms piled up on the floor and said to myself: "That can happen to me some day."

The same year I made the Knute Rockne movie, I married Jane Wyman, another contract player at Warners. Our marriage produced two wonderful children, Maureen and Michael, but it didn't work out, and in 1948 we were divorced.

After the Rockne movie, I began to be cast regularly in A pictures in leading roles. I was able to buy a home for my parents, the first anyone in our family had ever owned, and I think I helped Jack, who hadn't been able to work much since the first of his heart attacks, get back some of his pride.

Although I bought the house in their names I knew he would feel uncomfortable about that, so, after talking it over with my mother, I came up with a plan that worked like a charm. I told him I was starting to get more fan mail than I could handle and said: "Look, you don't have to do this if you don't want to, but you could really help me; I've got a heck of a problem with this fan mail, mailing out autographed pictures and so forth; what would you say if I got you a secretary's pass and a regular salary at the studio and you came in every day to pick up the mail, look it over, order the pictures, and so forth."

Well, Jack jumped at it. It was a real job, it gave him self-respect, and he did a great job at it.

One day he showed me a letter from a young woman who had written that she was dying and wanted a photo of me before she did.

I thought it was a story invented by someone who believed that's what it took to get an autographed picture. Jack urged me to sign the picture anyhow and I did. About ten days later, I got a letter from a nurse who told me that the woman, who was named Mary, had died with my picture in her hands and that it had made her very happy to have it.

Jack never said "I told you so."

He kept on handling the fan mail for me until, at the age of fifty-eight, his heart finally gave out and he died in the home in California that he had come to love.

When he died so young, I blamed it at first on his problem with alcohol. Now I think his heart may have finally failed because of smoking. I'd always thought of Jack as a three-pack, one-match-a-day man: In the morning he'd use one match to light his first cigarette of the day, and from then on, he'd light the next one from the old one.

The home he loved in California and his job at the studio may have helped him finally lick the curse that had hounded him so long. I was in the East on an errand for the motion picture industry when my mother called and told me that he had died. During the call, she told of finding Jack one night standing in the house, looking out the window, and he began talking about his drinking and wondering how their lives might have been different if he hadn't been a drinker. Then he told my mother that he had decided he was never going to take another drink, and she said, "Jack, how many times have I heard you say that?"

"Yes," Jack said, "but you've never seen me do this before," and then he disappeared and came back with a big jug of wine he'd hidden from my mother. Then he dumped the wine into the sink and smashed the jug.

She also told me Jack had started going to church again, a Catholic church near the house. As Jimmy Cagney described it once to me, "He'd heard the flutter of the wings."

After I rushed back to California, Nelle told me something else I'll always treasure. Back when the Rockne film was being premiered at Notre Dame, she had told me Jack, as Irish as you could get, wanted to be there, and I invited him to join us on the Warner Brothers train that took us to South Bend for the ceremonies and premiere.

Before he died, Nelle told me, Jack told her what the trip had meant to him: "I was there," he said, "when our son became a star."

Although Jack may have never completely defeated the curse to which he had been a slave, he and my mother had many years of great love together.

She rejoined him twenty-one years later, after years of torment by the illness we now call Alzheimer's disease.

12

As an actor, I guess I spent some of my finest moments in bed —the Gipper's death in *Knute Rockne—All American,* then a scene in *Kings Row,* in which I discovered my legs had been amputated by a sadistic and vindictive surgeon who was angry that I had romanced his daughter.

I started preparing for this scene days before it was filmed. The scene called for me to be unconscious in bed, then awaken, discover my legs were gone, and scream, "Randy [my wife, played by Ann Sheridan], where is the rest of me?" Long before we filmed this scene it was very much on my mind. Would I be semiconscious in my condition and not be able to scream? I wanted to ask doctors what a man in that situation would be like but I never got the chance. Finally, it was the fatal day. When I arrived on the set I found they'd cut a hole in the mattress for my legs and they asked me to get in the bed to see how it felt and looked. When I got under the covers my legs went into the hollowed out section of the mattress. As I lay there looking down the length of the bed, it really looked like my body ended at my hips. From there on, the bed covers were smooth and flat. When they told me I could get up while they lighted the scene, I said, "No, I'll just stay here until you're ready to shoot."

I had experienced a shock at seeing myself with only about two feet of body and I just stayed there looking at where my body ended. The horror didn't ease up. When the camera crew announced they were ready, I whispered to Sam Wood, the director, "No rehearsal—just shoot it." I guess he understood. When he said, "Action," I screamed, "Randy, where is the rest of me?" while I reached with my hands, feeling the covers where my legs should have been.

There was no retake. Sam quietly said: "Print it." I realized I had passed one of the biggest milestones in my career. I still believe *Kings Row* is the finest picture I ever appeared in and it elevated me to the degree of stardom I had dreamed of when I had arrived in Hollywood four years earlier.

Bob Cummings, my costar, must have wondered in later years whether he might be a psychic of some sort: Clear back then on the set of that movie, Bob had a line that he would always use on me: "Someday," he said, "I'm going to vote for this fellow for president."

Kings Row was the only picture I was in for which there was ever any talk of my getting an Academy Award. But that year, Warner Brothers also made *Yankee Doodle Dandy*, with Jimmy Cagney playing George M. Cohan. In those days the studios usually got behind only one picture in the Oscar race, and it picked *Yankee Doodle Dandy*. I've certainly never begrudged Jimmy Cagney for that: It was not only a great picture, but he was great in it. This actor, so much identified in people's minds as a tough guy, had originally begun his career as a dancer and in that picture he was brilliant.

I didn't get an Oscar, but even before *Kings Row* was released, Warners offered me a seven-year contract at a considerable increase in salary over my existing contract, which only had a couple of years to go. It was an indication big things were expected of *Kings Row* and that after its release I might be in a position to ask for more than they were offering me or sit out the old contract and become a free agent.

Negotiations for my new contract were going on when I received a telephone call from my brother on a Sunday morning telling me that the Japanese had bombed Pearl Harbor. Very shortly I started another picture costarring with Errol Flynn. It was called *Desperate Journey* and we played RAF pilots shot down behind the German lines.

My agent at the time was Lew Wasserman, now head of MCA

Inc. He persuaded me to accept the studio's offer, pointing out that I was a reserve officer and soon could be called to active duty, so why not get the added money for whatever time was left? I have to confess I hadn't given a thought to possible active duty, probably because the army had designated me for "Limited Service" because of my poor eyesight.

Thank heaven for Lew. He was a great agent and friend and I was lucky to have him in both capacities. Three months after Pearl Harbor, I received a letter from the War Department. I didn't have to open it to know what it was. Written on the envelope in red ink were the words "Immediate Action," which meant active duty. I was ordered to report in fourteen days to Fort Mason, the port of embarkation in San Francisco.

There were more than fourteen days of filming left on *Desperate Journey*. A lot of rescheduling took place to get my final scenes on film. Long shots and shots of my back were saved for a double after I was gone.

On the morning of the fourteenth day, I reported to Colonel Philip T. Booker—thirty-four years, regular army, a graduate of the Virginia Military Institute. Along with some ROTC cadets from the University of Arizona, I was to serve as liaison officer loading convoys with troops bound for Australia. Our strategy was to build up a force there to prevent Japan from pinning down its flank on Australia and then being able to turn and attack the west coast of the United States.

When my turn came for a physical exam, everything was fine except my vision without glasses. One of the doctors who was administering the test told me after checking my eyes that if they sent me overseas, I'd shoot a general. The other doctor said, "Yes, and you'd miss him." My report read: "Confined to the continental limits, eligible for corps area service command or War Department overhead only." So I was a liaison officer. All of us newcomers were cavalry. Then we discovered the commanding general of Fort Mason was a cavalry officer.

My career in loading ships only lasted a few months, then Colonel Booker called me in and showed me an order transferring me to Army Air Force Intelligence, Los Angeles, California.

At the time, General Hap Arnold was moving toward achieving his dream of creating an independent air force. He'd established the intelligence unit to make air force training films and documentaries, train camera crews, and accompany our planes on combat missions. I was sent to the unit because of my experience in motion pictures.

My first assignment was to recruit technicians and artists from the movie business for the new unit who were ineligible for the draft, and pretty soon, even though I was wearing the bars of a second lieutenant, I was offering majors' insignias to half-million-dollar-a-year movie directors. We also had first call on draftees from the industry.

Our unit took over the Hal Roach film studio in Culver City and a nearby, recently closed school that became our training center for combat camera crews. Before long, the post was being called "Fort Roach"—a completely unofficial title and one, I think, that was not intended to be complimentary.

I wound up as adjutant and personnel officer for the unit. Our combat camera crews went to every war zone in the world and our training films were used throughout the army air corps. In a way, we'd become the Signal Corps for Hap Arnold's new air force.

Our greatest and most unusual achievement was developing a new method for briefing pilots and bombardiers before their bombing missions.

Under the old method, a briefing officer stood in front of a map with a pointer, describing to the crew the route of their mission and the targets of the attack.

Our uniformed special effects magicians took over almost the entire floor of a sound stage and, working from prewar photographs and intelligence reports, created an amazing replica of Tokyo complete with thousands of buildings and its nearby coastline; then they mounted a camera on a movable overhead derrick from which they took motion pictures simulating what flight crews could expect to see as they approached and passed over Tokyo; after each bombing raid, new aerial photos were taken and our replica was updated to show the latest damage inflicted by our planes.

No more map and pointer. The films were airlifted to our bomber bases in the Pacific and replaced the old-fashioned briefings. My job was to narrate the films, identify features by which the pilots could reach their targets, then say "Bombs away" at the appropriate time.

At Fort Roach, I became one of the first Americans to discover the full truth about the horrors of Nazism. One of our jobs was to prepare classified films about the progress of the war to be shown to members of the general staff in Washington. As a result, we handled a lot of classified footage taken by combat cameramen around the world that was never seen by the public.

During the final months of the war, we began receiving secret Signal Corps films showing the liberation of Hitler's death camps and they engraved images on my mind that will be there forever.

I'll never forget one especially. It showed the interior of a huge building. Our troops had just taken over a camp and had entered the building. It was cavernous, like a warehouse. And the floor was covered with bodies. Then, as we watched in horror, one of the bodies rose up on an elbow and a hand reached up—a hand rising out of a sea of bodies, as if it were pleading for help.

There were many other ghastly images: Camp inmates so gaunt and emaciated you wondered how they could possibly still be alive; ditches filled with bodies being bulldozed into the earth; footage of German families brought from nearby villages to see for themselves the unspeakable inhumanity of their countrymen.

One of these films was amazing. The trip to a camp had been ordered by the commander of our troops and as the people left their village, some of them were almost in a festive mood, laughing and enjoying themselves, as if they were on an outing to someplace pleasant they'd never seen before.

Then, you followed the villagers through the camp and the cameramen switched between them and the horrors they were witnessing. Soon their reactions had changed completely: The men began to grow stooped and their faces turned ashen, many of the women began crying, some fainted and others turned away from the camera and began vomiting. They had learned something about their country they had never known before.

When the war ended and Fort Roach closed, I decided to keep a print of one of the films because I remembered that after World War I, there'd been a lot of talk about how Americans had been duped by false propaganda about the enemy, and I thought it might come in handy.

Some years later, a producer and his wife came over for dinner and we started talking about the war and he said, "I really wonder if all that stuff we're hearing about the Germans is true. I don't know if I believe it or not."

"Well, I have a little movie I'd like to show you," I said.

I set up my 16-millimeter projector, put up the screen, and let the story tell itself.

There was one scene in this film that showed a barbed-wire fence. A group of Jews had been trying to escape from a concentration camp and were running toward the fence when they were mowed down by German machine guns. Their bodies were stacked deep along the fence and the hands of some who had almost made it to freedom were still clinging to the fence.

It was a terrible and poignant scene of small, thin fingers desperately gripping rusted strands of barbed wire, in death.

When the film ended, the producer and his wife just sat there in silence with tears in their eyes.

13

AT FORT ROACH I had my first exposure to the peculiar ways of the federal bureaucracy since those days during the Depression when Jack worked on Dixon's relief program. About midway through the war, Congress challenged the military's widespread use of civilian workers, saying it was a drain on the defense industry and the nation's pool of draft-age men. An order went out setting a goal for reducing civilian employees at every post where they were used. It didn't affect us. Although we'd asked for civilian typists to help our writers with their scripts, we were refused because our work was regarded as too secret to employ civilians; often, we learned the identity of the targets planned for future bombing missions long before they occurred, so enormous security precautions had to be imposed at the post. But one day I was visited by two men from Washington. They told me they were checking out our need for civilians. I told them we couldn't have any. They smiled at each other and said, "You'll have 'em."

Sure enough, one day a contingent of fifty civilians arrived and announced they were going to establish a personnel office for the two hundred or so civilian employees that were going to be sent to us.

At the time, we had about twelve hundred military men at the base, and our whole personnel section consisted of eighteen people.

When the new civilian employees began arriving, every one of them was a transfer from another military installation; there'd been a program to reduce the number of civilians assigned to the military; instead, the military ended up with more civilian employees than they'd had before the program started—the bureaucracy had just transferred them from one place to another.

My assignment as the post's adjutant and personnel officer (I ended the war a captain) put me in close contact with the civilian bureaucrats and it didn't take long for me to decide I didn't think much of the inefficiency, empire building, and business-as-usual attitude that existed in wartime under the civil service system. If I suggested that an employee might be expendable, his supervisor would look at me as if I were crazy. He didn't want to *reduce* the size of his department; his salary was based to a large extent on the number of people he supervised. He wanted to increase it, not decrease it.

I discovered it was almost impossible to remove an incompetent or lazy worker and that one of the most popular methods supervisors used in dealing with an incompetent was to transfer him or her out of his department to a higher-paying job in another department.

We had a warehouse filled with cabinets containing old records that had no use or historic value. They were totally obsolete. Well, with a war on, there was a need for the warehouse and the filing cabinets, so a request was sent up through channels requesting permission to destroy the obsolete papers. Back came a reply—*permission granted provided copies are made of each paper destroyed.*

One assignment took me away from Fort Roach for a time. During World War I, Irving Berlin had put on a great Broadway show, *Yip, Yip Yaphank,* in which most of the performers were military personnel and the proceeds went to Army Emergency Relief.

Irving did a reprise during World War II with *This Is the Army.* Warner Brothers offered to film it and give all the proceeds to the same cause. Again, the cast was mainly military and I found myself in a starring role. I'm told the picture earned more than $10 million for Army Relief.

In Hollywood, if a contract player was suspended or absent for other reasons, including military service, a studio added the lost time to the end of his or her contract. The rule meant that when I returned to Hollywood after the war, I would have as much time left on my Warner Brothers contract as I'd had when the war began.

But Olivia de Havilland challenged this procedure in court and won. Her legal victory set a precedent for all of us, and for me it meant that the four years I'd spent in the service would reduce by four years the amount of time left on my Warner Brothers contract; soon I'd be on the open market.

Stallion Road, my first picture after the war, costarred Zachary Scott and Alexis Smith, and it was like a welcome-home gift: The story involved horses, with riding in fox hunts and jumping events in horse shows. I played a veterinarian, Larry Hanrahan, the owner of a black thoroughbred hunter named Tar Baby.

Because of the war, my riding had gotten a little rusty. A few weeks before the filming was to begin, I called Dan Dailey, who was also a reserve officer in the cavalry, and said, "Dan, it's been four years since I've done much riding. Do you happen to know somebody I could get to help me get back in the saddle?" He told me about an Italian count, Nino Pepitone, a former captain in the Italian cavalry, which had been considered the fountainhead of high-quality riding since the turn of the century. I went to see him and discovered that he owned a black thoroughbred mare named Baby. Well, Nino taught me things I'd never known before about jumping and riding, and I fell in love with the horse. Nino had done some bit parts before, and so I persuaded the studio to hire him for a minor role in the picture and also talked it into renting Baby for me to ride in the picture; she was a super horse, and I did my own jumping in the picture, without a double.

Before we'd finished the picture I bought Baby, and not long after that I was able to buy my own ranch—eight acres in the San Fernando Valley—that fulfilled the dream I'd first had back in Des Moines. With Nino's help, I went into business, breeding thoroughbreds and selling them at the yearling sale.

During these early postwar years I found myself becoming increasingly involved with contract negotiations and other activities for the Screen Actors Guild.

As I look back now, I guess I was also beginning a political transformation that was born in an off-screen cauldron of deceit and subversion and a personal journey of discovery that would leave me with a growing distaste for big government.

I didn't realize it, but I'd started on a path that was going to lead me a long way from Hollywood. But that was a long way off and I sure never suspected it at the time.

I was back in pictures and loving it. After Warners brought several successful Broadway plays to the screen and cast me in starring roles, I didn't have much to complain about. But I did wish Jack Warner would think of me on the back of a horse wearing a cowboy hat.

He always wanted to cast me in drawing-room comedies in the kind of parts that might have gone to Cary Grant. I was hungry to do action pictures. I believed the war had given audiences a taste for action—not necessarily more war movies, because they'd had four years of those, but adventure and outdoor pictures, especially westerns. But when I'd ask Jack to put me in a western, he'd cast me in another movie in which I'd wear a gray-flannel suit.

In his defense, it wasn't only Jack Warner who acted like that. That was the way Hollywood operated: If I'd played a sailor in a picture that made a lot of money, I'm sure I would have had to buy a ton of seasick pills because I wouldn't be seeing land for years.

"If you ever *do* let me be in a western," I once told Jack, "you'll probably make me the lawyer from the East."

14

At the end of World War II, I was a New Dealer to the core. I thought government could solve all our postwar problems just as it had ended the Depression and won the war. I didn't trust big business. I thought government, not private companies, should own our big public utilities; if there wasn't enough housing to shelter the American people, I thought government should build it; if we needed better medical care, the answer was socialized medicine.

My brother, meanwhile, had decided to become a Republican. We spent hours arguing—sometimes with pretty strong language —over the future of the country. He complained about the growth of government, claimed Washington was trying to take over everything in the American economy from the railroads to the corner store, and said we couldn't trust our wartime ally, Russia, any longer. I claimed he was just spouting Republican propaganda.

Like a lot of people in my generation, I'd come out of the Depression and a war expecting a better and more equitable world. I really thought we had fought a war to end all wars.

But I didn't like some of the things I saw after VJ Day.

If you wanted to buy a new car, a salesman told you it was available only if you paid a sizable fee under the table. This didn't sit well with those of us who had been in uniform for four or five years. Meanwhile, old patterns of racism were reappearing after four years in which blacks and whites had fought side by side. My own industry, motion pictures, was being ripped apart by a bitter labor dispute. What troubled me most was what I saw as the rise of fascism in our country, the very thing we had fought to obliterate.

Scores of new veterans' groups had sprouted up around the country and were trying to peddle some of the same venom of fascist bigotry that we had just defeated in the war.

In Hollywood, as I've often said, if you don't sing or dance, you end up as an after-dinner speaker. And almost before I knew it, I was speaking out against the rise of neofascism in America.

I joined just about any organization I could find that guaranteed to save the world, like the United World Federalists and American Veterans Committee, which got me with their slogan: "A Citizen First, a Veteran Afterward." I really wanted a better world and I think I thought what I was saying would help bring it about.

One day after giving one of my speeches to the men's club at the Hollywood Beverly Christian Church where I worshiped, our pastor came up to me and said he agreed with what I'd said about the rise of neofascism. But he said: "I think your speech would be even better if you also mentioned that if Communism ever looked like a threat, you'd be just as opposed to it as you are to fascism."

Well, during the war, the Russians had been our allies, and I'd dismissed the people after the war who had started to denounce them as foolish and paranoid.

I told the minister I hadn't given much thought to the threat of Communism but the suggestion seemed like a good one and that I'd begin saying if the day came when it also posed a threat to American values, I'd be just as strongly opposed to it as I was to fascism.

Not long afterward, I was asked to give a speech to a local citizens' organization. I made my usual speech defending American values against the new fascism that seemed to be abroad in the land and was applauded after almost every paragraph. I was a smash. Then I finished up with my new line at the end: "I've talked about the continuing threat of fascism in the postwar world, but there's another 'ism,' Communism, and if I ever find evidence that Communism represents a threat to all that we believe in and stand for, I'll speak out just as harshly against Communism as I have fascism." Then I walked off the stage—to a dead silence.

A few days later, I received a letter from a woman who said she'd been in the audience that night. "I have been disturbed for quite some time," she said, "suspecting there is something sinister happening in that organization that I don't like." Then she added: "I'm sure you noticed the reaction to your last paragraph when you mentioned Communism. I hope you recognize what that means. I think the group is becoming a front for Communists. I just wanted you to know that that settled it for me. I resigned from the organization the next day."

Thanks to my minister and that lady, I began to wake up to the real world and what was going on in my own business, the motion picture industry.

There were then forty-three labor unions in the picture business. A few were independents but most were affiliated with the American Federation of Labor. The Screen Actors Guild was one of the latter, as was the International Association of Theatrical and Stage Employees—better known as the stagehands' union or by its initials, IATSE.

During the absence of so many of us during the war something new had come into being. Some of the unions had gotten together to organize what they called the "Conference of Studio Unions," also known as CSU.

The IATSE had recovered from a prewar crisis in which Chicago mobsters had taken it over and extorted under-the-table payoffs from studio officials while also trying to create an actors' union in opposition to the Screen Actors Guild. This was before my time but I learned about it from the actors who had met the challenge and succeeded in getting the AFL to oust the mobsters.

Now there was another problem. The rump CSU group was run by a man named Herb Sorrell, head of the studio painters' union, who set out with a plan to gain jurisdictional control over a group of workers within an IATSE branch called the Set Erectors. There were only about 350 set erectors in the whole industry but the CSU called a strike demanding that the studios recognize it as their exclusive bargaining agent.

The IATSE told its members to cross the CSU picket lines and war broke out. Naturally, actors and actresses came to the officers of the Guild, asking us what they should do.

At a meeting of Guild directors, I proposed that we try to set up a meeting between the management of the studios, the CSU leaders, and the leaders of IATSE to determine what was going on. The studio executives were a little reluctant at first, but we assured them that the Guild, as a neutral party, would be there to referee and make sure there weren't any shenanigans.

When we held the meeting, it was obvious that the CSU strike was a phony. It wasn't meant to improve the wages and working conditions of its members, but to grab something from another union that was rightfully theirs.

The actors were in a key position: If we refused to cross the CSU picket lines, the industry would be shut down. If we crossed the lines, it could stay open and make movies.

Those of us who had attended the meeting reported to the Guild's Board of Directors that we thought it was not a legitimate strike but a jurisdictional dispute between two unions and recommended that the actors cross the picket lines.

The directors called a meeting of the full membership of the Guild at the Hollywood boxing stadium the following week, at which I was assigned to present our findings and recommend that we cross the lines and keep on working.

Two or three days before the meeting at the fight stadium, I was making a movie on location out at the beach when I was called to a telephone at a nearby oil station. The caller wouldn't identify himself but said that if I made the speech, a squad of people would be waiting for me.

"Your face will never be in pictures again," the voice said.

I reported the call to the director of the picture when I got back on the set, and when we closed for the day and went back to the studio, I was met by officers of the Burbank police force who hung a gun and a shoulder holster under my arm that I wore for the next seven months. They also put a twenty-four-hour guard on my house.

I later found out the plan was to throw acid in my face, which would have indeed ended my career in pictures.

I made the report to our members on schedule and said the CSU strike was a phony. They voted 2,748 to 509 in favor of going through the picket lines.

The gates of the studios soon became a bloody battleground of daily clashes between the people who wanted to work and the strikers and outside agitators brought in to help them. A union of waterfront workers headquartered in San Francisco suspected of having Communist affiliations sent mass pickets to aid the CSU strikers. Homes and cars were bombed and many people were seriously injured on the picket lines; workers trying to drive into a studio would be surrounded by pickets who'd pull open their car door or roll down a window and yank the worker's arm until they broke it, then say, "Go on, go to work, see how much you get done today."

We began traveling to the studios in caravans and rented buses. At midnight actors who were scheduled to work the next day would get a telephone call telling them where to rendezvous with the bus in the morning. One day I arrived at our meeting place and found our bus going up in flames, the target of a fire bombing.

While this was going on, Guild officers continued to meet with strike leaders in the CSU to see if we could help bring about a reasonable settlement. The meetings went on for months on an almost daily basis.

Some days I'd go home after hours of negotiations and think we'd made some progress toward a settlement. But the next morning we'd meet again and the strikers would walk into the room with their lawyers and twenty-seven new demands we'd never discussed before, which they said had to be settled before they'd call off the strike.

In the end, we beat 'em. The strike collapsed in February 1947. The decision by the Guild and several other unions to ignore the picket lines ultimately destroyed not only the strike but the Conference of Studio Unions.

Later, several members of the Communist Party in Hollywood who had been involved in the attempted takeover went public and described in intimate detail how Moscow was trying to take over the picture business. The California Senate Fact-Finding Committee on Un-American Activities, after a lengthy inquiry, confirmed that the strike was part of a Soviet effort to gain control over Hollywood and the content of its films. Although the principal leader of the strike told Congress that he had never been a Communist, investigators produced evidence that they said proved he was a secret member of the party, and a year later, national leaders of his union concluded he had "willfully and knowingly associated with groups subservient to the Communist Party."

American movies occupied seventy percent of all the playing time on the world's movie screens in those first years after World War II, and, as was to become more and more apparent to me, Joseph Stalin had set out to make Hollywood an instrument of propaganda for his program of Soviet expansionism aimed at communizing the world.

So the fight to gain control over Hollywood continued even after the strike. For a long while, I believed the best way to beat the Communists was through the forces of liberal democracy, which had just defeated Hitler's brand of totalitarianism: liberal Democrats believed it is up to the people to decide what is best for them, not—as the Communists, Nazis, and other fascists believed—the few determining what is good for the rest of us.

But I was to discover that a lot of "liberals" just couldn't accept the notion that Moscow had bad intentions or wanted to take over Hollywood and many other American industries through subversion, or that Stalin was a murderous gangster. To them, fighting totalitarianism was "witch hunting" and "red baiting."

15

ONE NIGHT JUST BEFORE BEDTIME, during the strike, there was a knock at my front door. I peeked through a little hole in the door and saw two men holding up the credentials of FBI agents. I opened the door and they asked me if they could come in to ask some questions. I invited them in but inquired what I could possibly know that the FBI didn't know already. One of them answered, "Anybody that the Communists hate as much as they do you must know something that can help us." Well, that got my attention and I asked him what he meant.

He said my name had come up during a meeting of the American Communist Party in downtown Los Angeles a few nights before (of course, this meant someone representing the FBI had been present at the meeting). During the meeting, he said, one of the Party members had said: "What the hell are we going to do about that son-of-a-bitching bastard Reagan?"

They confided in me that FBI investigations had shown the Party was attempting not only to gain control of the Hollywood work force but striving to influence the content of movies through the work of several prominent film writers and actors who were party members or party sympathizers. They asked if they could meet with me periodically to discuss some of the things that were going on in Hollywood. I said of course they could.

Not long after that, I accepted an invitation to fill a vacancy on the board of directors of the Hollywood Independent Citizens

Committee of the Arts, Sciences, and Professions. The group, known to everybody by its initials, HICCASP, had come into being as a support group for President Franklin D. Roosevelt and was a respected and prestigious liberal organization that had attracted some of the best-known names in Hollywood.

Like a number of other groups I had joined, it was pledged to fighting fascism and safeguarding our national freedoms, and I was greatly honored by the invitation to be on its board of directors and looked forward to my first meeting.

There were about sixty board members at the meeting, many of whom I didn't recognize, particularly the members of the executive committee, who were seated at a table facing the board members.

As the meeting got under way, I became slightly annoyed at how it was conducted: An item of business would come up for discussion and one of the officers would say, "Well, there's no need to take this up with the entire board. The executive committee can take care of it." It also bothered me when FDR's son, Jimmy Roosevelt, whom I knew, came under brutal personal attack from a couple of well-known Hollywood writers after he said groups such as ours needed to be vigilant against being used by Communist sympathizers.

Dore Schary, the head of MGM, was sitting next to me and I nudged him and said: "Where are all the people that used to be here, the heads of the other studios and so forth?"

He looked at me and then leaned over and whispered: "Stop by Olivia de Havilland's apartment after the meeting."

Olivia was a member of the executive committee of HICCASP. Ten of us met later that night at her apartment and I was amazed when she and others in the room said they suspected Communists were trying to take over the organization. As we talked over the situation, I turned to her and whispered: "You know, Olivia, I always thought *you* might be one of 'them.' "

She laughed and said, "That's funny. I thought *you* were one of them."

I'd previously decided that as a new board member I should keep my mouth shut and listen to the others. But knowing a little about Communist tactics from my dealings with the FBI, I suggested that we propose a resolution to the executive committee with language that we knew a Communist couldn't accept and have Olivia submit it in the next meeting the following week and see what happened.

We wrote out what was essentially an innocuous declaration of principles ending with a phrase in which HICCASP's executive board reaffirmed its "belief in free enterprise and the Democratic system and repudiates Communism as desirable for the United States."

The next week, we got together while Olivia attended the executive committee meeting. After an hour or so, the phone rang. It was Olivia. "They voted it down," she said.

She joined us later and said she'd been the only one in favor of our resolution.

It was all the proof we needed: HICCASP had become a Communist front organization hiding behind a few well-intentioned Hollywood celebrities to give it credibility.

The next day, the twelve of us resigned, not only from the board, but the entire organization. We were the last front of respectability for HICCASP and within a week it was out of business—but not the people running it.

They erased the name of HICCASP from the office door but put up the title of a new group—it was the same people with the same objectives behind a new front group.

One night after I gave a speech to the Guild in which I said it was essential that Hollywood join together and beat back the Communist attempt to take over the industry, I arrived a few minutes late for a meeting of the board of the veterans' organization I'd joined which was being held in an abandoned store that had been loaned to us for the meeting.

I started walking down the center of the room, looking for an empty seat among the folding chairs that had been set up on both sides of the aisle.

I saw an open seat and turned toward it; although it took me a moment to realize it, something had been planned: As soon as I sat down every member on the board who had been sitting on that side of the aisle got up and moved across to the other side, leaving me to sit alone.

Shortly after that, I learned the group had become another front for the Communist Party in Hollywood.

The Communists gained control of the groups through hard work and good organization—a minority of perhaps one percent moving in, coming to meetings early, and staying late and volunteering to do the hard work for the well-meaning liberals (like me) who were its members.

The strike and the efforts to gain control over HICCASP and other organizations had a profound effect on me. More than anything else, it was the Communists' attempted takeover of Hollywood and its worldwide weekly audience of more than five hundred million people that led me to accept a nomination to serve as president of the Screen Actors Guild and, indirectly at least, set me on the road that would lead me into politics.

One of the best reviews I ever got didn't involve a movie but came from a fellow actor testifying in court. Sterling Hayden, who'd been among those flirting with Communism before later renouncing it, said: "Ronald Reagan was a one-man battalion of opposition" to the attempted Communist takeover of Hollywood during the 1946 strike.

In the end, we stopped the Communists cold in Hollywood, but there was a dark side to the battle; unfortunately, it was a story with victims as well as villains.

Some members of the House Un-American Activities Committee came to Hollywood searching more for personal publicity than they were for Communists. Many fine people were accused wrongly of being Communists simply because they were liberals.

As the news spread of Moscow's attempted takeover of Hollywood, the glamour of the movie business and the people who worked in it made it a popular target for people in politics who wanted publicity for themselves. And some of them abused the powers of their office to get it. I was all for kicking Communists out of Hollywood, but some members of the House Un-American Activities Committee, ignoring standards of truth and fair play, ganged up on innocent people and tried to blacklist them.

Jimmy Cagney and Humphrey Bogart and other good Americans were accused falsely of being Communists. Petitions landed in Hollywood from around the country signed by thousands of people who declared they would not go to a theater if—and they listed dozens of Hollywood stars—certain people were in a movie. The thing had gotten out of hand.

We faced a dilemma: Olivia de Havilland and others with whom I had become close were determined to get rid of the Communists, but we had to protect the people who were innocent. To deal with the problem, we formed an industry council to contact people in the industry who were being threatened with blacklisting—including many who didn't know they were—and said to them: "Look, we can't clear you, but we can help you clear yourself."

We urged them to publicly declare their opposition to Communism and to volunteer to appear before the FBI and the House Un-American Activities Committee—two things no Communist could agree to. We would arrange their meetings and we would vouch for their innocence.

If on the other hand, someone said, "I won't do that," we simply said: "We can't help you."

The system allowed people to clear themselves and it worked, it really worked. The industry and the public accepted our recommendations of innocence.

These were eye-opening years for me. When I'd come back to Warner Brothers after the war, I'd shared the orthodox liberal view that Communists—if there really *were* any—were liberals who were temporarily off track, and whatever they were, they didn't pose much of a threat to me or anyone. I heard whispers that Moscow wanted to infiltrate the world's most powerful medium of entertainment, but I'd passed them off as irrational and emotional red baiting.

Now I knew from firsthand experience how Communists used lies, deceit, violence, or any other tactic that suited them to advance the cause of Soviet expansionism. I knew from the experience of hand-to-hand combat that America faced no more insidious or evil threat than that of Communism.

16

OF THE FIFTY-THREE PICTURES I APPEARED IN, thirty-one were made before the war and twenty-two after the war. In addition to *Kings Row* and *Knute Rockne—All American,* I'm especially proud of several of the postwar pictures, particularly *The Voice of the Turtle, John Loves Mary, The Hasty Heart,* and *The Winning Team,* in which I played the great baseball player, Grover Cleveland Alexander.

But enormous change was coming to Hollywood after the war, and a lot of it wasn't for the good.

When I arrived there in my Nash convertible in 1937, there were seven major studios in Hollywood. Each had a huge production lot dominated by barn-like soundstages where the interior scenes of movies were shot, a make-believe New York City neighborhood, and a western town with false-fronted saloons and a dusty main street for exterior shots. The studios also owned large ranches in the San Fernando Valley where western and outdoor movies were filmed.

In those days Hollywood was run a lot like an old-fashioned candy store: You cooked it in the back and sold it in the front. Each studio had a big stable of contract actors, writers, directors, musicians, and producers who turned out the pictures, and a nationwide chain of theaters where the pictures were exhibited. The studio was like an assembly line that was entrusted to keep a steady stream of pictures flowing to the theaters.

This system turned out many of the best pictures ever made. Each studio was like a big family. You belonged to Warner Brothers or MGM or Paramount and your associates and friends were mostly other performers and writers and directors from your studio. Sometimes we had family fights, but the system gave a solid stability to the picture business. You belonged someplace.

But that all changed after the war. An antitrust suit was brought by a private chain of theaters and as a result the Justice Department issued a series of decrees declaring that the studios could either make pictures or operate theaters—they couldn't do both.

This turned Hollywood inside out overnight. The studios chose to continue producing movies. But no longer could they afford stables of actors and other workers under contract because from now on, they had to make movies purely on the speculation theaters would want to show them.

Because of tax problems, many stars were willing to give up the security of a studio contract and a weekly salary. I was one of them. I was in the ninety-four percent tax bracket, which meant the government took most of what I earned. I'd always thought there was something inherently unfair toward actors in the tax system. I'd seen careers take off like a comet, shine briefly, then burn out almost overnight, but during their brief period of stardom, taxes would have eaten up most of their income and they'd have little left afterward.

Nevertheless, I believe the government's decision to break up the studio system was wrong. It destroyed the stability of the industry under the justification that the studios monopolized the picture business. But they didn't have a monopoly; there was intense competition that worked well for everybody. You had seven companies who were always competing with each other to turn out a better movie than the guy down the street, and if people didn't like a picture, they'd show it by voting with their feet.

Owning the theaters provided a guarantee to the studios that if they guessed wrong on a movie and made it, at least they'd get some of their money back by playing it at their own theaters. This allowed them to take risks on people and stories.

It allowed the public to create real stars—legendary stars with staying power like Clark Gable, Olivia de Havilland, Gary Cooper, Jimmy Stewart, and a lot more.

A star like Judy Garland or Mickey Rooney wasn't born a great star. When a studio spotted people they thought had talent and promise—for instance, a pretty girl in a college play—they'd sign them up for a small salary and send them to classes where they were taught to act and sing and dance. Then they tried to nurture them, bring them up.

The studios knew *they* didn't make stars, the *public* did. But they could tailor movies to showcase an actor's particular talents, allow their talent to develop, and give them the backing of wonderful character actors and actresses who would never become stars. In those days, the great stars were built up over time and their names and faces became as familiar to people as their next of kin. The studio publicity machine saw to that. Every performer had a publicity agent whose responsibility it was to see that you were in the trade papers, the gossip columns, and the movie magazines: It built an image of you. That's what sold the tickets.

As a free lance, I agreed to make one picture a year for three years at Warner Brothers and was also able to make pictures at Paramount, MGM, RKO, and Universal. I finally got to do some westerns. Among them two of my favorites were *The Last Outpost* and *Cattle Queen of Montana,* with Barbara Stanwyck. In *The Last Outpost*, I teamed up with my favorite horse, Baby, the mare I rode and bought during *Stallion Road.*

During the late 1940s, one side effect of the attempted Communist infiltration of our industry was a kind of national backlash against Hollywood. The movie business became a popular target for politicians who attacked it as a hotbed of reds and immoral conduct, and organizations began forming around the country with the declared purpose of censoring the movies.

Like any big group of people, we had our bad apples, but they were in the minority and most of the anti-Hollywood propaganda wasn't true. As president of the Screen Actors Guild, I began speaking out to defend the industry.

At first, I just spoke to others in Hollywood and motion picture theater owners, encouraging them to get together to improve our industry's image and its public relations by speaking out against the critics and columnists who unfairly maligned us. I described how we'd responded to the Communist threat in the industry, pointed out that the life-style of the majority of people in Hollywood was tame, and tried to emphasize how important the movies were to American culture. Pretty soon, I was giving a couple of speeches a week, and as time went on, I was speaking less frequently to others in the industry and more often to groups like the Rotary Club and local Chambers of Commerce.

By now, I guess I was beginning to undergo a political transformation. As I've said, I'd emerged from the war a liberal: Like my father, I mistrusted business and believed government could solve all our country's problems, as it had during the Depression. Only later did I realize it was probably World War II that ended the Depression. I think my political transformation began with my exposure to the business-as-usual attitude of many civil service bureaucrats during the war; then came the attempted Communist take-over of the picture business, which a lot of my liberal friends refused to admit ever happened; next, I had a brief experience living in a country that promised the kind of womb-to-tomb utopian benevolence a lot of these liberal friends wanted to bring to America. In 1949, I spent four months in England filming *The Hasty Heart* while the Labor Party was in power. I saw firsthand how the welfare state sapped incentive to work from many people in a wonderful and dynamic country.

Probably because of my dad's influence and my experiences during the Depression, I had loved the Democratic Party. I agreed with Thomas Jefferson, its founder, who said: "Democrats consider the people as the safest depository of power in the last resort; they cherish them, therefore, and wish to leave in them all the powers to the exercise of which they are competent . . . the equal rights of every man and the happiness of every individual are now acknowledged to be the only legitimate objects of government."

But the party had begun to change drastically in the thirties. Jefferson repeatedly said that the best government was the *smallest* government, that "governments are not the masters of the people, but the servants of the people governed." Abe Lincoln once said, "The principles of Jefferson are the definitions and the axioms of a free society." But during the Depression, the Democrats began to repudiate many of these principles while creating a government that grew ever larger and increasingly demanded the right to regulate and plan the social and economic life of the country and move into arenas best left to private enterprise.

I guess I was beginning to form one of my own principles about government: There probably isn't any undertaking on earth short of assuring the national security that can't be handled more efficiently by the forces of private enterprise than by the federal government.

Our federal bureaucracy expanded relentlessly during the post-war years and, almost always with the best of intentions, it began leading America along the path to a silent form of socialism. Our government wasn't nationalizing the railroads or the banks, but it was confiscating a disproportionate share of the nation's wealth through excessive taxes, and indirectly seizing control of the day-to-day management of our businesses with rules and regulations that often gave Washington bureaucrats the power of life and death over them.

Well, pretty soon my speeches in defense of Hollywood were beginning to take on a new tone. And I received a telephone call that was to change my life and enrich it forever after.

17

THE TELEPHONE CALL WAS from director Mervyn LeRoy, who told me an actress working on one of his pictures needed my help. The young woman, Nancy Davis, was extremely upset because the name of another actress identified as Nancy Davis had appeared on the membership rosters of several Communist front groups and she was receiving notices of their meetings in her mail.

Mervyn said he was sure the young woman had absolutely no interest in left-wing causes, and knowing of the work we had done to clear movie people unfairly accused as Communists, he asked me if I would look into it.

As president of the Screen Actors Guild, I did a little research and found out that there was more than one Nancy Davis connected with show business—in fact there were several—and it took me only a few minutes to establish that Mervyn's Nancy Davis was not the one who belonged to several Communist front groups. I told him to tell her we had cleared her, that she had nothing to worry about.

Pretty soon, Mervyn called back and said his assurances hadn't been enough to satisfy the young lady.

"She's a worrier," he said. "She's still worried that people are going to think she's a Communist. Why don't you give her a call? I think she will take it better from you than from me. Just take her out to dinner and tell her the whole story yourself."

I agreed, and, besides, taking out a young actress under contract to MGM, even sight unseen, didn't seem like a bad idea to me—and I could call it part of my duties as president of the Guild.

To be on the safe side, however, when I called her, I said: "I have an early call in the morning, so I'm afraid we'll have to make it an early evening."

"Fine," Nancy said, "I've got an early call, too. I can't stay out too late either."

She had her pride, too.

We were both lying.

When I picked her up that evening at her apartment, I was standing on two canes a la Pete MacArthur: Several months earlier I'd shattered my right thighbone during a charity softball game and was still hobbling around because of it.

I took her to a restaurant on the Sunset Strip and soon realized that Mervyn hadn't been exaggerating when he'd said she was really steamed up over having been confused with someone else.

Well, I suggested, one solution would be to change her name—actresses did it all the time, I said.

When I said that, Nancy looked at me with her hazel eyes and a sense of logic that made me feel a little ridiculous: *"But Nancy Davis is my name,"* she said.

Pretty soon, we weren't talking any more about her problem, but about her mother, who had been a Broadway actress, and her father, a prominent surgeon, and our lives in general. Although we'd agreed to call it an early night, I didn't want the evening to end, so I said: "Have you ever seen Sophie Tucker? She's singing at Ciro's just down the street. Why don't we go see the first show?"

Well, she'd never heard Sophie Tucker before so we went to Ciro's to catch the first show. Then we stayed for the second show and we got home about three o'clock in the morning. No mention was made of early calls. I invited her to dinner the following night and we went to the Malibu Inn.

After that, we dated occasionally, sometimes with our good friends, Bill and Ardis Holden, but both of us continued to date other people, and now and then our paths would cross while we were out with someone else.

This had been going on for several months when I found myself booked for a speech to the Junior League Convention at the Del

Coronado Hotel in San Diego. I had always looked forward to that trip down the Coast Highway: In those days before freeways, it was my favorite drive, with the blue Pacific on my right and the rolling green hills of California on my left.

I wanted to share the ride with someone and wondered who I should ask to join me. Then it suddenly occurred to me there was really only one person I wanted to share it with—Nancy Davis. I called her and she accepted and said she was a member of the Junior League in Chicago.

Pretty soon, Nancy was the only one I was calling for dates. And one night over dinner as we sat at a table for two, I said, "Let's get married."

She deserved a more romantic proposal than that, but—bless her —she put her hand on mine, looked into my eyes, and said, "Let's." Right after that, I had pictures coming up, so we had to wait two or three months before we could marry.

If the Hollywood press had gotten wind of our plans, they would have stormed the church, so, apologizing to Nancy, I suggested we have a quiet, secret wedding. She agreed and we were married in a touching ceremony in the Little Brown Church in the Valley on March 4, 1952. There were just five of us in an empty church: Nancy and me; Bill Holden, my best man; Ardis, Nancy's matron of honor; and the minister.

After we said "I do," Bill and Ardis took us to their house for dinner where they had a photographer who took our wedding photos. After dinner, we drove to Riverside about seventy miles southeast of Los Angeles, where we stayed overnight before driving on to Phoenix, where Nancy's parents were vacationing.

If ever God gave me evidence that He had a plan for me, it was the night He brought Nancy into my life.

I have spent many hours of my life giving speeches and expressing my opinions. But it is almost impossible for me to express fully how deeply I love Nancy and how much she has filled my life.

Sometimes, I think my life really began when I met Nancy.

From the start, our marriage was like an adolescent's dream of what a marriage should be. It was rich and full from the beginning, and it has gotten more so with each passing day.

Nancy moved into my heart and replaced an emptiness that I'd been trying to ignore for a long time. Coming home to her is like coming out of the cold into a warm, firelit room. I miss her if she just steps out of the room.

After we were married, Nancy asked to be released from her seven-year contract at MGM: Maybe some women can handle a career and a marriage, she said, but she wasn't going to try. She was going to be my wife.

I can sum up our marriage in a line I spoke when I played the great pitcher Grover Cleveland Alexander, a line spoken by him in life to his wife, Aimee: "God must think a lot of me to have given me you."

I thank Him every day for giving me Nancy.

In college I had a philosophy class in which our professor told us that the world was divided into two kinds of people: those who are skeptical of others until the other persons prove themselves, and those who assume that other people are good and decent unless proven otherwise.

I suppose that pretty well describes one of the differences between Jack and Nelle. And maybe it describes a difference between Nancy and me. I can't say which of us has been right more often than the other. I believe, in general, people are inherently good and expect the best of them. Nancy sees the goodness in people but also has an extra instinct that allows her to see flaws if any are there.

She's a nest builder and defender of her own. If you've seen a picture of a bear rearing up on its hind legs when its mate or one of its cubs is in danger, you have a pretty good idea of how Nancy responds to someone whom she thinks is trying to hurt or betray one of hers.

Although I was pleased with several of the pictures that I made as a free lance, there were two or three that I wish I hadn't said yes to —and after a while I began worrying a little about the direction my career and Hollywood in general were taking.

The turmoil set off by the Justice Department's consent decrees was still reverberating through the industry and nobody knew where it was headed. And sometimes it seemed the studios were trying to respond to the crisis by making poorer, not better, pictures.

After Nancy and I talked it over, I decided to begin turning down roles in bad pictures and holding out until something really good came along.

I went for more than a year without making a movie. Although lots of scripts were sent to me, there were not many I liked and I turned down roles that would have earned me more than $500,000. I filled the money gap by doing guest shots on television.

Our first child, Patricia Ann, had been born, and she had added lots of joy to the Reagan household. But financially, they were pretty lean and sometimes difficult times. Before I'd made the decision to say no to film offers I didn't like, we'd bought a home in the Pacific Palisades. I already owned the ranch in the San Fernando Valley where I was breeding thoroughbreds. But there was a hefty mortgage on the house and that ninety-four percent tax rate hadn't left us with a lot of savings.

While turning down bad roles in pictures, I had several options to support the family.

I still couldn't sing or dance, but, with Nancy in the audience every night, I did a nightclub floor show at the Last Frontier Hotel in Las Vegas for two weeks, in which I was an emcee for a group called the Continentals. The audience's reaction was good, the reviews were good, the pay was terrific, and they invited me to come back. But Nancy and I missed our life in California and neither of us thought much of smoke-filled nightclubs, so when the two weeks ended we were glad to go home.

I could have gotten a job on Broadway, which was always looking for Hollywood actors, but Nancy and I were devoted Californians and not interested in a long-term relationship with New York.

There were many offers to star in a television series, but I was firmly against it.

I was sure a television series could be a professional kiss of death to a movie actor: The people who owned movie theaters thought nobody would buy a ticket to see someone they could see at home in their living room for nothing. Besides, most television series expired after two or three years, and from then on, audiences—and producers—tended to think of you only as the character you'd played in the TV series.

In the end, television guest spots not only tided us over financially but led me to one of those unexpected and unplanned turns in the road—the kind that can take you a long way from where you thought you were going.

18

Taft Schreiber, who headed television activities for MCA, knew I was adamant against doing a TV series. But in 1954, he came to me with a proposal: The General Electric Company was in the market for a new television program, and he wanted to propose a weekly dramatic anthology in which I would only act several times a season but serve as the host every week.

I knew that having my face beamed into homes across the country every week risked the kind of overexposure that could be fatal to a movie actor's career. But I liked the idea because it offered me a chance to share in the growing financial prosperity of television while avoiding the kind of typecasting that acting in the same role week after week in a regular series brought with it.

I agreed to do it and thus was born the General Electric Theater, which for eight years at nine o'clock on Sunday nights produced what I think were some of the finest programs to emerge from the period that show business historians now refer to nostalgically as the "Golden Age of Television." Each Sunday, the GE Theater offered a different story with a different cast, and virtually every Oscar winner in Hollywood showed up in one of our plays.

My new job called upon me to play a supporting role in an extraordinary experiment by American industry. Until then, most of America's industrial giants had tended to function under a strong central management within a single geographic region—United

States Steel in Pittsburgh and General Motors in Detroit, for instance. But Ralph Cordiner, General Electric's chairman, a remarkable and foresighted businessman, believed GE would grow more dynamically if he dispersed its manufacturing operations around the country. Smaller divisions headed by strong local managers who had considerable autonomy over their products and manufacturing operations, he thought, ought to be more competitive and more responsive to the marketplace than a large, unwieldy organization dominated by a powerful head office, and I think he was right.

Cordiner implemented his vision on a grand scale, establishing 139 GE plants in thirty-nine states.

In doing so, he recognized that such a sweeping decentralization might cause some morale problems. Managers of GE plants far from the company's New York headquarters, for example, might consider themselves as second-class citizens, forgotten by the home office.

As an adjunct to my job on the television show, he asked me to travel to GE plants around the country as a kind of goodwill ambassador from the home office. Sending the host of the GE Theater to the far-flung plants, he thought, would demonstrate that the New York office cared about company employees no matter where they were and would also help forge a closer link between the plants and the communities where they were located. Local managers were instructed to take me to local events.

At first, all I did was walk the assembly lines at GE plants, or if it didn't interrupt production, I'd speak to them in small groups from a platform set up on the floor of the factories; I'd tell them a little about Hollywood and our show, throw it open to questions, then move on to another plant.

About a year or two after the tours began, the GE representative who always accompanied me told me I was scheduled to speak to a group of company employees who had been working on a local charity fund-raising project. I think everybody expected me to get up and tell a few Hollywood stories as usual and then sit down. But instead, I decided to give a speech about the pride of giving and the importance of doing things without waiting for the government to do it for you. I pointed out that when individuals or private groups were involved in helping the needy, none of the contributions were spent on overhead or administrative costs, unlike government relief programs where $2 was often spent on overhead for every $1 that went to needy people.

When I sat down, my remarks got a huge ovation. As we were driving away from the plant, the man from GE said, "I didn't know you could give speeches." I said, "I have been doing that for quite a while."

Well, that changed everything. From then on, whenever I went to a GE plant, in addition to meeting workers, they'd schedule a speech or two for me to a local organization like the United Fund or Chamber of Commerce; before long, the company began to get requests for me to speak before larger audiences—state conventions of service organizations and groups like the Executives Club in Chicago and the Commonwealth Club in San Francisco.

For eight years I hopscotched around the country by train and automobile for GE and visited every one of its 139 plants, some of them several times. Along the way, I met more than 250,000 employees of GE—not just shaking their hands, but talking to them and listening to what was on their minds.

Looking back now, I realize it wasn't a bad apprenticeship for someone who'd someday enter public life—although, believe me, that was the farthest thing from my mind in those days.

As a radio sports announcer, I had sometimes flown to ball games or other events I was covering in an open-cockpit biplane wearing a leather helmet and goggles, and I'd loved it. But during the early fifties, there was an epidemic of plane crashes that caused something inside me to say it wasn't a safe time for me to go flying. Call it a hunch if you will, but I felt that if I agreed to fly, I'd get in the wrong plane someday. So, I had it written in my contract that GE couldn't ask me to fly.

I knew that someday I'd fly again but I'd know when the time was right. In the meantime, I got to see a lot of the country through the windows of a moving train; I still can't think of a more comfortable way of travel than taking the Super Chief from Los Angeles to Chicago.

Initially, my speeches were only about the picture business, but after a while I began trying to make them a kind of warning to others. This is what had happened in Hollywood; if they weren't careful, people in other occupations might soon find themselves in the same fix as those of us in Hollywood and be denied fair treatment by the government: If it could happen to people in the picture business, I said, it could happen to people in any business.

Well, after I began including these remarks in the speeches, an interesting thing happened: No matter where I was, I'd find people from the audience waiting to talk to me after a speech and they'd all say, "Hey, if you think things are bad in your business, let me tell you what is happening in my business. . . ."

I'd listen and they'd cite examples of government interference and snafus and complain how bureaucrats, through overregulation, were telling them how to run their businesses.

Those GE tours became almost a postgraduate course in political science for me. I was seeing how government really operated and affected people in America, not how it was taught in school.

From hundreds of people in every part of the country, I heard complaints about how the ever-expanding federal government was encroaching on liberties we'd always taken for granted. I heard it so often that after a while I became convinced that some of our fundamental freedoms were in jeopardy because of the emergence of a *permanent government* never envisioned by the framers of the Constitution: a federal bureaucracy that was becoming so powerful it was able to set policy and thwart the desires not only of ordinary citizens, but their elected representatives in Congress.

I'd make a note of what people told me, do some research when I got home, and then include some of the examples in my next speech. Pretty soon I had quite a few. For example, I learned the government had six programs to help poultry growers increase egg production. It also had a seventh program costing almost as much as all the six others to buy up surplus eggs.

As time went on, the portion of my speech about government began to grow longer and I began to shorten the Hollywood part. Pretty soon, it became basically a warning to people about the threat of government. Finally, the Hollywood part just got lost and I was out there beating the bushes for private enterprise.

No government has ever voluntarily reduced itself in size—and that, in a way, became my theme.

I'd emphasize that we as Americans should get together and take back the liberties we were losing; with fewer than sixty percent of the voters turning out at many national elections, it was like hand-ing ourselves over to the enemy. Our whole system of government is based on "We the people," but if we the people don't pay atten-tion to what's going on, we have no right to bellyache or squawk when things go wrong. So I would tell them that, and the place to start was to begin paying more attention to what was going on in their government.

I've always believed that you can't hold an audience by *reading* a speech, but when you're giving three or four or more talks a day, as I was, it's difficult to memorize every word you wanted to say; so, refining a technique I first tried out during my early speech-making days in Hollywood, I developed a shorthand I've used ever since.

I began listing the main points I wanted to make in a speech on four-by-six-inch cards with abbreviations for some words: "That," for example, became "tht," "barren desert" would be "barrn dsrt." Just the letters told me what the word was, and usually other words in a sentence would be so obvious to me when I looked down at the card, I'd remember the rest. I might include three or four words to remind me of a story or joke that I wanted to tell, then I'd ad lib the rest. (Of course, this hasn't done much for my spelling now when I write a note to someone.) Let me take that sentence and show how I'd compress it: ". . . cours ths hsnt don much . . . my splng now whn . . . write . . . note . . . sm one."

Although GE gave me a platform, it left it up to me to decide what to say. As a liberal in my younger days I'd had an inherent suspicion of big business and couldn't believe there wouldn't come a day when the company would begin trying to write my speeches for me. Never once did that happen.

In 1958, our second child, Ron, was born, bringing more joy into our lives. In 1960, after leading the Screen Actors Guild in its first major strike in history in my fifth term as president, I resigned after becoming a partner in a production company, and therefore, from the union's point of view, I was no longer a working stiff but a producer.

Some authors have suggested my work in the Screen Actors Guild fighting the studios hurt my film career, as it had hurt some of the early pioneers in the union, but I've never felt any sour grapes about it. To a newspaper columnist who asked, after the 1960 strike, if I thought the union work had hurt my career, I said, "I think it has hurt some, although certainly not in the way that someone says, 'I'm mad at this guy so I won't use him in my pictures.' In all my years with the union, I've never seen any grudges carried deliberately out of the conference room. Any suffering careerwise definitely isn't retaliatory, although there are a lot of people involved in making a motion picture, and you become typecast in their minds on the basis of what they know about you off the screen. They stop thinking of you as an actor. The image they have of you isn't associated with your last role, but with the guy who sat across the conference table, beefing. And that's death! You develop a sort of aura. People even forget in time how you came to have it. Your name just doesn't come up when parts are being discussed."

I wasn't unhappy, though. In Hollywood, I'd found more than I'd ever expected life to give me. For many, many reasons, these were very happy years for Nancy and me. My income from General Electric had enabled us to build a dream home overlooking the Pacific Ocean that GE stuffed with every imaginable electric gadget. We also bought a 350-acre ranch in the Santa Monica Mountains north of Los Angeles that we loved. And, although GE kept me on the road a lot, there were long stretches of my life during that period when my daily routine focused entirely on my family, our ranch, and a horse.

To my mind, nothing compares with the kinship between man and animal you find on the back of a horse. I'm not sure what it is, but there you are, in charge of an animal with more muscle in its neck than you have in your whole body. From the minute the horse takes its first step, every muscle in your own body begins to respond to it; how much of the experience is physical and how much is mental, I don't know, but there's no better place for me to think than on the top of a horse.

As you rock along a trail to the sound of the hooves and the squeak of leather, with the sun on your head and the smell of the horse and your saddle and the trees around you, things just begin to straighten themselves out. Somehow, it just seems a lot easier to sort out a problem when I'm on a horse.

I did a lot of thinking atop Baby during those pleasant years, and I made some important decisions about my life.

19

I GUESS IT WAS IN 1960, the year Richard Nixon ran against John F. Kennedy for the presidency, that I completed my political journey from liberal Democrat to dedicated Republican.

One day I came home and said to Nancy, "You know, something just dawned on me: All these things I've been saying about government in my speeches (I wasn't just making speeches—I was preaching a sermon), all these things I've been criticizing about government getting too big, well, it just dawned on me that every four years when an election comes along, I go out and support the people who are responsible for the things I'm criticizing."

As a liberal Democrat, I was naturally opposed to Richard Nixon. In 1950, he ran for a seat in the U.S. Senate from California against Congresswoman Helen Gahagan Douglas, the wife of an actor-friend of mine, Melvyn Douglas, and I campaigned against him. Nixon won after a bitter battle that focused on allegations Helen Douglas was a Communist sympathizer. In those days I worked on the campaigns of just about any Democrat who was willing to accept my help. In 1948, I campaigned for Hubert Humphrey and for Harry Truman, and to this day, I think Truman was an outstanding president, with one exception. He had a common sense that helped him get to the root of problems; he stood up to the bureaucrats, and when he had a tough decision to make, he made it. And he wasn't a tax-and-spend Democrat; during the past sixty years, there have been only eight scattered years when the federal budget was in balance and four of those years were under Truman. Looking back, I think he and I were in tune on a lot of things about government and I think if he had lived longer he might have come over to the other side like I did. In my view, the only thing that kept Harry Truman from real greatness was his decision not to completely back General Douglas MacArthur and win the Korean War.

I think, as MacArthur did, that if we as a nation send our soldiers abroad to get shot at, we have a moral responsibility to do *everything* we can to win the war we put them in. I'll never forget one prophetic remark by MacArthur: "If we don't win this war in Korea, we'll have to fight another war—this time in a place called Vietnam." Until then, I had never heard of Vietnam. I only knew about a place called French Indochina. How right he was.

I also greatly admired the man who followed Truman into the White House, Dwight Eisenhower. In 1952, I joined several other Democrats in sending a telegram to Ike urging him to run for president as a Democrat. At the time, he was very reluctant to run at all. But I always suspected he'd have to run; it's always seemed to me that when it comes to the presidency, it's not candidates who make the decision whether to run, it's public opinion—the people make the decision.

When Ike decided to run on the Republican ticket, I decided: If I considered him the best man for the job as a Democrat, he still ought to be my choice. So I campaigned and voted for Ike—my first for a Republican. In 1960, when Nixon was preparing to run against Kennedy for the presidency, I still carried around some bitter feelings from the 1950 Senate campaign. After I mentioned this to Ralph Cordiner, he said, "I think you might be wrong about Nixon."

He said he had just heard Nixon speak to a group of businessmen who had been initially hostile to him, then were won over. Nixon had convinced them he was a solid citizen.

I was such a fan of Ralph Cordiner by then that I decided to reevaluate some of the things that the liberals (including me) had been saying about Nixon. Realizing after that that he wasn't the villain I'd thought him to be, I volunteered to campaign for him against Kennedy. I told Nixon I was going to register as a Republican, but he said I'd be more effective if I campaigned as a Democrat, and so I agreed not to change my party affiliation until after the election.

After hearing about my decision, John Kennedy's father, Joseph Kennedy, who spent a lot of time in Hollywood, asked to see me. He tried to persuade me to change my mind and support his son but I turned him down.

Although I agreed at Nixon's request not to register as a Republican, I was really no longer a Democrat by 1960.

I'd remain a Democrat for another two years, but by 1960 I had completed the process of self-conversion.

After that, the more I learned how some liberal Democrats wanted to rein in the energy of free enterprise and capitalism, create a welfare state, and impose a subtle kind of socialism, the more my view changed.

Upon reflection, I'm not so sure *I* changed as much as the parties changed.

One of the greatest of liberals, Thomas Jefferson, the founder of the Democratic Party, once remarked: "A wise and frugal government, which shall restrain men from injuring one another, shall leave them otherwise free to regulate their own pursuits of industry and improvement and shall not take from the mouth of labor the bread it has earned—this is the sum of good government."

My first vote at the age of twenty-one was for Franklin D. Roosevelt. His platform called for a twenty-five percent cut in federal spending and returning to people in the states and local communities authority and autonomy that had been taken over by the federal government. He also declared: "The federal government must and shall quit this business of relief. Continued dependence upon relief induces a spiritual and moral disintegration fundamentally destructive to the national fiber."

Many of the relief programs FDR instituted during the Depression were necessary measures during an emergency, but I remain convinced that it was never his intention—nor those of many of his liberal supporters—to make giveaway programs that trapped families forever on a treadmill of dependency a permanent feature of our government. "Doing for people what they can, and ought to do for themselves, is a dangerous experiment," the great labor leader Samuel Gompers said. "In the last analysis, the welfare of the workers depends on their own initiative."

The classic "liberal" believed individuals should be masters of their own destiny and the least government is the best government; these are precepts of freedom and self-reliance that are at the root of the American way and the American spirit.

But then came the newfangled "liberals" who rejected these beliefs. They claimed government had a greater wisdom than individuals to determine what was best for the individual and it should engineer our economic and business life according to its goals and values; dictate to states, cities, and towns what their rights and responsibilities were; and take an increasing bite out of the earnings of productive workers and redistribute it to those who are not productive. To them, government was the fount of all wisdom— the bigger government was, the better—and they rejected the principles of Democrats who had gone before them.

"Liberty has never come *from* government," Woodrow Wilson, one of FDR's predecessors and another Democrat, said. "The history of liberty is the history of *limitation* of government's power, not the increase of it."

Somewhere along the line, the liberal Democrats forgot this and changed their party. It was no longer the party of Thomas Jefferson or Woodrow Wilson.

The competitive free enterprise system has given us the greatest standard of living in the world, produced generation after generation of technical wizards who consistently lead the world in invention and innovation, and has provided unlimited opportunities enabling industrious Americans from the most humble of backgrounds to climb to the top of the ladder of success.

By 1960, I realized the real enemy wasn't big business, it was big government.

Following the election that year, I began to get more and more invitations from the Republicans to speak at their dinners and fundraisers and they more or less adopted me as one of their own even though I was still a Democrat. When a lot of the nation's most prominent Democrats got behind socialized medicine, I started speaking out against it. If we didn't head it off, I said, "one of these days you and I are going to spend our sunset years telling our children and our children's children what it once was like in America when men were free."

In 1962, while campaigning for Nixon during his unsuccessful attempt to unseat California's Democratic governor, a tax-and-spend liberal named Edmund G. (Pat) Brown, I made it official: I spoke to a Republican fund-raising event near my home in Pacific Palisades and a woman in the audience stood up in the middle of my speech and asked me: "Have you reregistered as a Republican yet?"

"Well, no, I haven't yet," I said, "but I intend to."

"I'm a registrar," she said, and walked down the center aisle through the audience and placed a registration form in front of me. I signed it and became a Republican, then said to the audience, "Now, where was I?"

20

By the early 1960s, GE was receiving more speaking invitations for me from around the country than I could handle. And, although I was still saying the same things that I'd said for six years during the Eisenhower administration, I was suddenly being called a "right-wing extremist." The liberals just didn't like to hear someone say the growth of government ought to be restrained.

Some of the arrows I was firing into my old political camp seemed to be hitting home. After the Democrats won the White House in 1960, wherever I'd give a speech, in city after city, there'd be a cabinet member or other high official from the Kennedy administration who'd be giving a speech on the same day. In the television business, we used to call that "counter programming," an effort to knock out the competition with a rival show. I don't have any proof they planned it that way, but I don't think it was coincidental.

In 1962, there was a change in management at General Electric that brought an end to my satisfying eight-year relationship with the company. Ralph Cordiner was retiring and the new management asked me, in addition to continuing as host of the GE Theater, to go on the road and become a pitchman for General Electric products—in other words, become a salesman.

I told them that after developing such a following by speaking out about the issues I believed in, I wasn't going to go out and peddle toasters.

They insisted and when I still resisted, they canceled the show.

I realized that appearing on the General Electric Theater for so long probably hadn't endeared me to the people who owned the movie theaters of America. But there was still a part of me that wanted to be a motion picture actor, and in 1964 I made my last picture—*The Killers.*

For the first time in my acting career, I played a villain—and the reaction may have proven that Jack Warner had something when he kept casting me as the good guy in those drawing-room comedies.

The Killers was a remake of a 1946 picture starring Burt Lancaster that was based on an Ernest Hemingway story. I had seen the original picture and hadn't liked it very much because everybody in the script was a villain and there was no one to root for.

When Universal asked me to play a gangster in the remake of *The Killers,* my instinct was to say no. But I'm afraid they took advantage of an actor's ego:

"But you've never played a villain before," they said.

It was a challenge no actor could resist. I said, "Okay, I'll do it."

A lot of people who went to see *The Killers,* I'm told, kept waiting for me to turn out to be a good guy in the end and dispatch the villains in the last reel, because that's how they had always seen me before. But I didn't, and for whatever reason, the picture didn't ring many bells at the box office.

Although my movie career was coming to a close, I was still receiving lots of offers to act as a guest star in television shows. Before long I agreed to do another series, as host—and occasional actor—in "Death Valley Days."

If I wasn't scheduled to act in a show, I'd drive down to the studio from our ranch, spend an hour or so taping an introduction for the next show, then drive home; some days, I didn't even have to get out of my ranch clothes for the filming.

The job left me plenty of time for speeches and Republican activities, and when I was asked to be the cochairman of Barry Goldwater's 1964 presidential campaign in California, I didn't hesitate a moment. I'd met Barry at the home of Nancy's parents in Phoenix several years before and admired him greatly. His book, *The Conscience of a Conservative,* contained a lot of the same points I'd been making in my speeches and I strongly believed the country needed him.

This was the era of the so-called "Great Society." After he followed John Kennedy into the White House, Lyndon Johnson had begun to make most of the tax-and-spend Democrats of the past seem miserly by comparison. I thought we sorely needed Goldwater to reverse the trend. I said I'd do anything I could to get him elected.

While another cochairman managed the day-to-day operations of the campaign, my job was to travel around the state speaking on behalf of Barry and to help him raise campaign funds.

During the summer and fall of 1964, I spoke at many fundraising functions, but, for me, one was more important than all the others: an address late that summer to about eight hundred Republicans at the Coconut Grove, a big nightclub decorated with palm trees at the Ambassador Hotel in Los Angeles.

I gave basically the same talk I'd been giving for years, altering it slightly so that it became a campaign speech for Barry. I recounted the relentless expansion of the federal government, the proliferation of government bureaucrats who were taking control of American business, and criticized liberal Democrats for taking the country down the road to socialism. As usual, I included some examples of Americans whose business or personal lives had been tormented by bureaucrats and cited examples of government waste, including one federal job training program that was costing taxpayers about seventy percent more for each trainee than it would have cost to send them to Harvard.

I said America was at a crossroads: We had the choice of either continuing on this path or fighting to reclaim the liberties being taken from us. It was a speech, I suppose, that, with variations, I'd given hundreds of times before.

After dinner, five or six people from the audience came up to me and asked if I would join them for a few minutes at their table.

The Coconut Grove by then was almost empty. Except for the waiters, who were noisily clearing off dishes and glassware, everyone was gone except this little group, which I later learned included some of the biggest Republican campaign contributors in California, and I sat down with them.

They asked me if I would be willing to repeat the speech I'd just given for Goldwater on national television if they could raise the money to buy airtime for it.

"Sure," I said, "if you think it would do any good."

If we did it, I suggested that instead of repeating my speech in front of a camera in a television studio, it might be more effective if I spoke to an audience in a setting similar to the one in which they'd heard it. They agreed and within a few days had raised enough money to buy a half hour of time on NBC a week before the election. We taped the speech in a big NBC studio in front of an audience of invited Republicans, simulating the kind of gatherings that I'd been speaking to for years.

A few days before the speech was scheduled to go on the air, I got a telephone call from Barry Goldwater. He sounded uneasy and a little uncomfortable.

Some of his advisors, Barry said, wanted him to use the airtime that had been purchased for my speech to rebroadcast a videotape of a meeting he'd had at Gettysburg with Ike Eisenhower.

He said they were afraid my speech, coming so close to the eve of the election, might backfire on him because of references in it to problems with the Social Security system. Social Security, of course, was an issue dear to the hearts of many older voters, and Barry said he had spent almost a year denying Democratic claims that he wanted to do away with it. Some members of his staff, he said, thought my speech would bring up the touchy question all over again and set back their efforts to neutralize the issue.

In the speech, I had strongly supported the concept of Social Security, but I argued that improvements were needed in it—pointing out, for example, that Americans had been deceived regarding the security of their money that was deducted from their paychecks to pay for Social Security benefits. For years we'd all been told that we were contributing to an old-age insurance fund that was being set aside for our retirement years, but, in fact, there was no "fund" at all; it had become a compulsory tax producing revenues Congress could—and did—use for any purpose it wanted, while letting the reserves needed for future benefits fall $298 million in the hole.

"Barry," I said, "I've been making the speech all over the state for quite a while and I have to tell you, it's been very well received, including whatever remarks I've made about Social Security. I just can't cancel the speech and give away the airtime; it's not up to me.

These gentlemen raised the money and bought the airtime. They're the only ones who could cancel or switch it."

"Well," Barry said, "I haven't heard or seen the speech yet; they've got a tape here, so I'll run it and call you back."

Barry was campaigning someplace in the East, Cleveland I think, and my brother, whose advertising agency was working on his campaign, was part of a group that was traveling with him and so he was there when this was all happening.

According to my brother, who told me about it later, Barry hung up after talking with me and then he and the members of his staff sat quietly in his hotel suite while an audiotape of the speech was played.

When it was over, Moon said, Barry looked up at everybody and said, "What the hell's wrong with that?"

Then he called me and said it was fine with him to go ahead with the speech.

Of course, now I was really on edge.

Who was I to tell a presidential candidate what he should or shouldn't do in his campaign?

I'd seen the film showing Barry's meeting with Eisenhower at Gettysburg and didn't think it was all that impressive. But his people were the experts and they said Ike would do him more good than I would.

After Barry's second call, I thought for a while of calling the group who had purchased the airtime and asking them to withdraw my speech. Barry's advisors had shaken my confidence a little. But then I thought back on some of the other times I'd given that speech —it had always gotten a good response—and decided, after some lost sleep, not to ask them to withdraw it.

On the evening of October 27, 1964, Nancy and I went to the home of some friends to watch the broadcast of the speech:

I have spent most of my life as a Democrat. I recently have seen fit to follow another course. . . .

I believe that the issues confronting us cross party lines. Now one side in this campaign has been telling us that the issues of this election are the maintenance of peace and prosperity. The line has been used, "We've never had it so good!" But I have an uncomfortable feeling that this prosperity isn't something upon which we can base our hopes for the future. No nation in history has ever survived a tax burden that reached a third of its national income. Today, thirty-seven cents out of every dollar earned in this country is the tax collector's share, and yet our government continues to spend seventeen million dollars a day more than the government takes in. . . .

This idea that government is beholden to the people, that it has no other source of power except the sovereign people, is still the newest and most unique idea in all the long history of man's relation to man. This is the issue of this election: whether we believe in our capacity for self-government or whether we abandon the American Revolution and confess that a little intellectual elite in a far-distant capital can plan our lives for us better than we can plan them ourselves. You and I are told increasingly that we have to choose between a left or right.

There is only an up or down: up to man's age-old dream—the ultimate in individual freedom consistent with law and order—or down to the ant heap of totalitarianism. And re-gardless of their sincerity, their humanitarian motives, those who would trade our freedom for security have embarked on this downward course. In this vote-harvesting time they use terms like the "Great Society," or as we were told a few days ago by the president, we must accept a "greater government activity in the affairs of the people." But they have been a little more explicit in the past and among themselves. . . .

It was, as I've said, a compilation of a lot of the thoughts I'd been expressing for several years, but if I could summarize in just a few words, I'd say it was a reminder to my listeners of three words that begin the Constitution of the United States: "We the people . . ."

I wound up the speech with these words:

You and I have a rendezvous with destiny. We will preserve for our children this, the last best hope of man on earth, or we will sentence them to take the last step into a thousand years of darkness.

We will keep in mind and remember that Barry Goldwater

has faith in us. He has faith that you and I have the ability and the dignity and the right to make our own decisions and determine our own destiny. . . .

When it was over, the others in the room said I had done well. But I was still nervous about it and, when I went to bed, I was hoping I hadn't let Barry down.

At about midnight, Nancy and I were awakened by a phone call from Washington, where it was 3 A.M. The call was from a member of Barry's campaign team, who told me the Goldwater-for-President campaign switchboard had been lit up constantly since the broadcast.

Thousands of people, he said, had called in pledging support to Barry and the party. After that, Nancy and I both had a good night's sleep.

During the next few days, my speech was played and replayed at fund-raising events and on local television stations around the country and it ultimately raised eight million dollars for Goldwater and the party.

Of course, I didn't know it then, but that speech was one of the most important milestones in my life—another one of those unexpected turns in the road that led me onto a path I never expected to take.

21

THE 1964 PRESIDENTIAL ELECTION, as historians and journalists have amply recorded, was a disaster for our party. Not only was Goldwater swamped under a Lyndon Johnson landslide, the party came out of the election bitterly divided because of a vicious primary battle between Goldwater and Nelson Rockefeller. A lot of liberal Republicans simply refused to support Goldwater against Johnson. The split was especially deep in California, where moderate and conservative factions of the party had already been feuding for years.

After the election, I went back to doing what I'd been doing before it—speaking on national issues and doing my job on "Death Valley Days." The following spring, Holmes Tuttle, a Los Angeles automobile dealer who had been one of the Republican contributors I'd met at the Coconut Grove dinner and who later bought the airtime for my speech for Goldwater, called me and asked if he and several friends might drop by our home in Pacific Palisades.

After I heard what they said, I almost laughed them out of the house. I can't remember my exact words, but I said, in effect: "You're out of your mind."

Tuttle and the other members of his group said they wanted me to run for governor in 1966, when Pat Brown, the liberal Democrat who had beat Nixon for reelection in 1962, was expected to run for a third term.

I'd never given a thought to running for office and I had no interest in it whatsoever. After doing as much research as I had on the operations of government, the last thing I wanted was to become a part of it. I just wanted to keep on making speeches about it.

"I'm an actor, not a politician," I said several times. "I'm in show business."

But they claimed the party was in such shambles following the 1964 election that its survival as a force in California was in doubt and, mentioning my speech for Goldwater, they said they thought I might be the only Republican around who had a chance of beating Brown and bringing the party back together.

Nothing was said, incidentally, about whether I would make a good governor or not. They just said I was the only one who could bring the party together.

I told them that running for governor was out of the question for me, but that I wanted to help the party and made a proposition: Find somebody you think would make a good governor and then I'll campaign for him as hard as I can, the way I campaigned for Barry. "Pick your candidate and I guarantee you I'll campaign for him, whoever it is," I said.

When they left, I hoped I'd put the idea to rest. But they kept coming back, and then the Federated Republican Women's Club sent a delegation to the house urging me to run and I told them I wasn't interested in political office, I was happy in show business.

Nancy had no more interest in my running for governor than I did and she was just as flabbergasted by the idea as I was. We loved our life as it was and didn't want it to change.

We had our children, our friends in Hollywood, our home, our ranch, our privacy; we had a good income and all the opportunities I ever wanted to speak about the issues that concerned me.

I was approaching an age when some of the men I knew were already starting to think about retirement. Although I didn't have any thought of retirement, I had a good job and a good life and, at fifty-four, the last thing I wanted to do was start a new career.

I told Nancy's father, Loyal Davis, who had seen the seamy side of politics in Chicago, about the pressure I was coming under to run for governor and he said I would be crazy to run for office; he said there was no way a man could go into politics without sacrificing his honesty and honor, because no matter how well intentioned he was, a politician was inevitably forced by the realities of political life to compromise.

I said I didn't need any convincing, I wasn't going to run.

The pressure didn't let up. I kept saying no and Holmes Tuttle and his group kept coming back and saying they wouldn't take no for an answer.

It soon got to the point where Nancy and I were beginning to have trouble sleeping at night; the constant emphasis that I was the only guy around who could beat Brown and heal the split in the party put a lot of weight on our shoulders. After a while we'd lie in bed and ask ourselves: *If they're right and things get worse for the party and we could have done something about it, will we ever be able to sleep at night again?*

I finally decided to make an offer to the people who wanted me to run for governor: "Even though I think you're wrong about my being the only Republican who might be able to beat Brown, if you fellows will arrange it for me to go on the road and accept some of the speaking invitations I'm getting from groups around the state, then I'll go out and speak to them and come back in six months, on the last day of 1965, and tell you whether you're right or whether you should be looking for somebody else to run for governor."

I believed that if I continued speaking for six months I'd be able to identify someone whom the people thought would make a good governor, then I'd campaign for him.

Well, my plan worked out that way, but not in the way I expected.

Holmes Tuttle's group hired a California political consulting company headed by Stuart Spencer and William Roberts to look over my speaking invitations and pick out ones they thought would get me around the state, but exclude Republican functions; the idea was to avoid partisan events and speak to ordinary Californians.

Starting roughly July 1, 1965, I drove up and down the length and breadth of California for six months, commuting to luncheon and dinner meetings from San Diego at the southern border all the way to the coastal fishing villages near the Oregon border.

I'd give a speech, then get in my car and drive to the next one, meeting the members of organizations like the Rotary Club, Chamber of Commerce, and United Way.

The speeches had pretty much the same flavor that my speeches had had since the later years on the General Electric plant tours; after the speeches, I'd hear a lot of the same things from members of the audience that I'd heard for years on the GE tours: People were tired of wasteful government programs and welfare chiselers; and they were angry about the constant spiral of taxes and government regulations, arrogant bureaucrats, and public officials who thought all of mankind's problems could be solved by throwing the taxpayers' dollars at them.

Their comments didn't surprise me. By then, I'd come to expect it when I went out to the grass roots of America. But I *was* surprised by something else: No matter where I went, in San Jose or Modesto, Los Angeles or Newport Beach, after I'd give a speech, people would be waiting and they'd come up to me and say, "Why don't you run for governor?"

I'd laugh and give my standard response: "I'm an actor, not a politician," then ask them to suggest someone who was really qualified to be governor. But all I heard were voices of more people chiming in to urge me to run against Brown.

Of course, I wondered at first if this wasn't a setup and if the fellows who were pushing me to run for governor hadn't planted these people in the audience. But pretty soon I realized it was happening too often in too many places to be a setup; these were people with no special interest in politics.

After about three months of this, I returned home one night and said to Nancy, "This isn't working out the way I thought it would. You know, these guys may be right. All these people are telling me after my speeches that I ought to run for governor; this may end up putting us in an awful spot."

Then I'd go out back on the road and give another speech and hear the same things again and I'd come home and Nancy and I would talk about it again. Before long, we were having trouble getting to sleep again; we'd lay in bed and say, "Will we ever be able to live with ourselves if we turn our backs on this and Pat Brown wins a third term?"

When the six months were almost over, I asked her: "How do you say no to all these people?"

If I decided to run, we agreed our life we knew and loved would change dramatically, perhaps forever. But I told Nancy: "I don't think we can run away from it." She agreed.

I called the people who were pressing me to run against Brown and said, "Okay, I'll do it," and on a television broadcast January 4, 1966, I announced my intention to seek the Republican nomination for governor.

22

WHEN PAT BROWN COMMISSIONED a television commercial in which he told a group of small children, "I'm running against an actor, and you know who killed Abe Lincoln, don't you?," I knew he knew he was in trouble.

I won the chance to run against Brown after a Republican primary campaign that was very bitter at times, largely because of the lingering split between conservatives and moderates in the state party.

My principal opponent in the primary was George Christopher, a former mayor of San Francisco who tried simultaneously to portray me as a right-wing extremist and attack me because I'd admitted having been in Communist front groups—without mentioning that I'd resigned and declared war on them as soon as I'd realized what they were.

I was a novice in politics and at times I showed it. At a convention of black Republicans, I made my talk, sat down, and was followed by Christopher, who got up and implied during his speech that I was a racial bigot.

I fumed about it for a moment or two, stood up, and said (some people there say I *shouted*) to Christopher that he was wrong, that I'd never been a bigot and I deeply resented his attack on my integrity. Then I walked off the stage and drove home, leaving a startled audience behind me.

During almost thirty years in Hollywood, I had become accustomed to taking potshots from critics. But I'd grown up in a home where no sin was more grievous than racial bigotry, and I wasn't going to take it from Christopher.

After I got home, two members of my campaign team found me there and convinced me to return to the meeting. I cooled down and was back at the auditorium before the meeting had ended; I got back on the platform and tried to explain how I had been raised and why I took such offense at Christopher's remarks. I think they understood why I had exploded in response to the attack on my integrity. But it was the last time I stalked off a stage during a political debate. That day, I suppose, was all part of my political education.

The personal attacks against me during the primary finally became so heavy that the state Republican chairman, Gaylord Parkinson, postulated what he called the Eleventh Commandment: *Thou shalt not speak ill of any fellow Republican.* It's a rule I followed during that campaign and have ever since.

After beating Christopher in the primary, I had to deal with Brown, whose campaign against me, simply put, asked a question: What is an actor doing seeking an important job like the governorship of California?

As the campaign got under way, Brown seemed confident he'd win his third term in a breeze. He had previously beaten not only Dick Nixon, a former vice-president of the United States, but U.S. Senator William F. Knowland, an Oakland publisher who was another Republican powerhouse in California, and I suspect he thought it would be even easier to knock off this newcomer to politics from Hollywood.

I intended to focus my campaign on issues, but couldn't ignore Brown's attacks that I was unqualified for the job because I was an actor inexperienced as an elected politician. I decided to turn this around and present myself as what I was: an ordinary citizen who wanted to start unraveling the mess politicians were making of our government.

"Sure," I said, "the man who has the job has more experience than anyone else . . . that's why I'm running."

Pat Brown brought Senator Edward Kennedy to California to help him campaign, and he began a speaking trip around the state declaring, "Reagan has never held any political office before and here he is seeking the top spot in the government of California."

He abandoned that theme after my next speech, when I said, "I understand there's a senator from Massachusetts who's come to California and he's concerned that I've never held office prior to seeking this job. Well, you know, come to think of it, the senator from Massachusetts never held *any* job before he became a senator."

Still, I realized that if I didn't handle it right, the "he's only an actor" theme could hurt me. I knew a lot of people had misconceptions about actors: If you're an actor, the only thing you can do is act. . . . Yes, you've played a lot of parts on the screen, but it's only make-believe and that's *all* you can do: pretend. . . . Those who can, do; those who can't, act.

Being an actor who was running for political office wasn't all drawbacks: Many people develop an affection and feelings of friendship for someone they enjoy on the screen, and that could be an advantage for me.

Nevertheless, I knew I had to prove I had more to offer than a familiar face.

One of Brown's favorite ploys was to say, "Reagan is only an actor who memorizes speeches written by other people, just like he memorized the lines that were fed to him by his screenwriters in the movies. Sure, he makes a good speech, but who's *writing* his speeches?"

Well, *I* was writing my speeches. But I couldn't get up and say to an audience, "Hey, I write my own speeches."

We called a meeting and Stu Spencer and Bill Roberts, who were managing the campaign, said that Brown was making so much headway with this that we had to defuse it or else lose the election.

"I've got a suggestion," I said. "From now on, why don't I just say a few words to whatever group I'm with, no matter how big it is, and then just open it up to questions and answers? People might think somebody had written my opening remarks for me, but they'll know it would be impossible for somebody to feed me answers to questions I didn't know about in advance."

The political professionals in our group blanched when I said that.

They were used to hiding candidates, not turning them loose.

I think the idea of a candidate being on his own scared them. *Do you really want to do that?* they asked.

"I think I *have* to do it," I said.

Well, it worked like a charm. From then on, whether the campaign audience was three or three thousand, I'd make a few remarks, then take questions. I hadn't planned it that way, but this turned out to be a wonderful way to learn about the issues that were on people's minds.

At the time, the public universities in California were going up in smoke; rioting students were literally setting fire to them.

Californians were rightfully proud of and dedicated to their great system of higher education—especially the nine campuses of the University of California—and they were upset by what was going on.

After I started the new question-and-answer style of campaigning, I'd make a few introductory remarks and ask for questions and no matter where I was, before I could finish, there'd be people waving their hands and asking: "What are you going to do about these things going on on the college campuses?"

I had to come up with some answers.

I said I thought the students had no business being at the university if they weren't willing to abide by the rules; if they *refused* to obey them, they should go somewhere else.

Whenever I said that, the audience cheered. Californians just didn't like students tearing apart the university system of which they were so proud.

Once I got on the campaign trail, I discovered, a little to my surprise, that I enjoyed campaigning. And I was out to win.

I guess I'd been a competitive fellow since my childhood in Dixon and a political campaign was a competitive game of another sort, except the stakes were higher.

The question of how to deal with rebellious students became one of the central issues of the campaign, but it was just one of many problems troubling California in 1966. Californians paid the highest per capita taxes in the nation; the state's crime rate was the highest in the nation; it had the nation's most wasteful welfare program; it was threatened by increasing problems of air and water pollution. For more than a century, California had been a land of boundless opportunity attracting an ever-growing stream of immigrants from around the country and around the world. Its climate and easygoing lifestyle were part of the reason for its popularity, but perhaps more than other states, California symbolized opportunity: It was a place where people could make a new start—and with hard work, they could *make* it.

While newcomers were still flocking to California, the rate of migration to the state had begun to slow for the first time since the Gold Rush, largely because the pace at which it produced new jobs had begun to decline for the first time since the Depression. More and more businessmen were complaining of overregulation, high taxes, and an "adversarial" attitude toward them by state officials; they were giving up on California, electing to build new plants outside the state, or deciding to pack up and leave the state altogether.

Pat Brown was one of those liberals who thought all the world's problems could be solved by throwing taxpayers' money at them, and in a way, he made the campaign easier for me.

While ducking the real issues that were worrying Californians, he stuck to his one-note campaign of attacks on me as "that Hollywood actor in makeup."

Well, I hadn't worn makeup since I made *Love Is on the Air* in 1937, and one of the biggest laughs I got during the campaign was after the two of us were invited to appear on "Meet the Press." When I arrived for the broadcast, Brown (as well as all the reporters on the panel) was wearing makeup; I was the only one in the room with a bare face.

The climax to Brown's campaign of bad taste was his guilt-through-association commercial late in the campaign comparing me to an actor named John Wilkes Booth—Lincoln's assassin.

On election day I defeated Brown by a margin of fifty-eight percent to forty-two percent.

Until that day, I don't think it had dawned on him that a new wind was blowing in America. Brown and a few journalistic pundits attributed my victory to conservatives and "extremists." In fact, analysis of the election returns showed that most of my support didn't come from right wingers or even conservative Republicans, but from middle-of-the-road voters in both parties.

A lot has been written about college students and other young people who rebelled against society during the 1960s. But there was another, quieter revolution sweeping across the land during the same decade.

It was a rebellion of ordinary people. A generation of middle-class Americans who had worked hard to make something of their lives was growing mistrustful of a government that took an average of thirty-seven cents of every dollar they earned and still plunged deeper into debt every day.

There was a growing sense of helplessness and frustration across the country over a government that was becoming a separate force of its own, a master of the people, not the other way around.

People were growing resentful of bureaucrats whose first mission in life seemed to be protecting their own jobs by keeping expensive programs alive long after their usefulness had expired. They were losing respect for politicians who kept voting for open-ended welfare programs riddled with fraud and inefficiency that kept generation after generation of families dependent on the dole. And they were growing mistrustful of the self-appointed intellectual elite back in Washington who claimed to know better than the people of America did how to run their lives, their businesses, and their communities.

There was unrest in the country and it was spreading across the land like a prairie fire.

23

ON THE NOVEMBER EVENING IN 1966 when I learned I had been elected governor of California, three of our four children—Maureen, Mike, and Ron—joined Nancy and me at a victory celebration. Patti was away at school in Arizona and when we called and told her that I'd won, she started to cry. She was only fourteen, but as a child of the sixties she believed the antiestablishment rhetoric that was popular among members of her generation, and she let me know that she didn't like having a member of the establishment in the family.

In different ways, the election changed the lives of everyone in our family that night.

As funny as it might seem now, when I gave in to the appeals to run for governor, I had never given much thought to the possibility I might win. All the emphasis had been on deciding whether to run and bringing the party back together. I'd figured, "Well, okay, I'll run and help the party with the unity problem, then in November it will all be over."

Well, it wasn't over. I had less than two months to prepare for putting my ideas about government into practice. Nancy started packing for Sacramento and we put the ranch up for sale.

Although I may have been (as the papers put it) a "citizen politician" whom reporters liked to compare to the Jimmy Stewart character in *Mr. Smith Goes to Washington,* I knew that reality often turned out to be a lot more complicated than Hollywood portrayed it, and I knew I had to do some quick homework about my new job before arriving in Sacramento. After years of criticizing government, I was about to stick my head into the lions' den and the lions would be waiting for me.

Friends arranged for a veteran Republican legislator who'd spent years in Sacramento to brief me on the fine points of state government. I knew the basics regarding how laws were enacted in the capitol, but during a period of several days at our home, he told me about political life in Sacramento. We went over the rules and procedures and key players in the legislature, he outlined the budgetary processes and the statutory powers of the governor, and told me some of the things that would be expected of me as governor.

Meanwhile, I made a priority list of the things I wanted to accomplish in Sacramento. At the top of the list was my determination to attract a new kind of civil servant into state government.

During the campaign, I'd promised voters I wouldn't appoint people who *wanted* jobs in government, but go after outstanding people outside government who *didn't* want these jobs but could be persuaded, as I had been, to make a sacrifice and help put government back on course.

As I started forming my cabinet and filling other senior positions, I discovered a great many good people willing to do that, talented executives who believed as I did that the people deserved better from government than what they were getting.

Some of the business leaders who had initially persuaded me to run for governor—Holmes Tuttle, Henry Salvatori, Justin Dart, Leonard Firestone, Cy Rubel, and a handful of others who became known collectively as my "Kitchen Cabinet"—scoured the business world to identify top managers and administrators and then helped me persuade them to come to Sacramento and work for the state at a reduced salary. We brought scores of good people into the top jobs that way.

For me, finding these people and putting them to work was really the beginning of the realization of a dream. After years of preaching about what government should be, I had a chance to practice what I preached.

Shortly after the election, a national meeting of governors was scheduled and in a gesture I appreciated, Pat Brown suggested that

I represent California instead of him because he would be leaving office soon.

At the conference, I got an idea from Governor Jim Rhodes of Ohio that proved priceless to me, not only in Sacramento but later in Washington. In an effort to streamline his state's government, Governor Rhodes told me he had asked a group of top businessmen in Ohio to evaluate the operations of all state agencies and suggest ways to make them more efficient by applying modern business principles. These advisory panels had come back with hundreds of recommendations, he said.

Since I'd never seen a government agency that was run as efficiently or as economically as a well-run business, I thought it was a great idea and unashamedly borrowed it. I called some of the leading business people in California together at a luncheon, told them what I had in mind, and said, I'll leave it up to you. You tell me how we can make our state government work better."

Within a few days, they had put together an executive board to coordinate the project and a committee to raise money for administrative expenses, and then began studying the operations of every agency in the state government.

Meanwhile, I learned that things were even worse for California than I'd thought they were during the campaign. Through accounting sleight of hand, the previous administration had concealed the fact that the state government was *broke*.

One day, after he'd met with members of the outgoing administration, Caspar Weinberger, a San Francisco lawyer who was among the first people we brought from outside government to assist in the transition as director of finance, came to me and said: "The state's spending more than a million dollars a day more than it's taking in and it's been doing that for a year."

The Democrats in Sacramento had known about the mounting deficit for almost a year, but had concealed it by altering bookkeeping procedures that pushed the deficit into the subsequent fiscal year; then, they had gone on spending as extravagantly as always, while avoiding the embarrassment of an election-year tax increase.

Now suddenly the state faced its worst financial crisis since the Depression, and it was up to me, as the new governor, to end it.

In my inauguration speech on January 2, 1967, I informed Californians about the financial mess we had uncovered and promised to do everything I could, as soon as I could, to put the state's financial house back in order.

"We are going to squeeze and cut and trim until we reduce the cost of government," I said. "It won't be easy and it won't be pleasant."

And it wasn't.

24

For a while, it seemed that every morning I walked into the capitol somebody was standing at my desk waiting to tell me about a new problem we hadn't known about before.

It was as if they opened a new drawer at midnight every day and uncovered another crisis.

Cap Weinberger told me the state was facing a deficit of at least $200 million and within two weeks of my inauguration, I had to send a balanced budget to the legislature. Unlike the federal government, California had to have a balanced budget before the fiscal year began each July 1, and the job was up to me.

We imposed a hiring freeze and a ten percent budget cut at all state agencies and did other things we could to slow the hemorrhage of red ink; we sold Pat Brown's state-owned airplane, slashed out-of-state travel by state employees, canceled several construction projects, and stopped buying new automobiles and trucks for the state. But more drastic steps than that were needed, and soon I found myself in an all-out war with the legislature.

Although California's voters had ended eight years of Democratic leadership in the governor's office, they had left the state assembly and state senate in Democratic hands—and the Democrats didn't like a brand-new Republican governor telling them how to spend the taxpayers' money.

With Pat Brown's departure, the most powerful Democrat in Sacramento had become Jesse Unruh, the speaker of the assembly.

Called "Big Daddy" because of his girth and reputation as a political manipulator of the smoke-filled-room variety, Unruh was a classic tax-and-spend liberal. He ruled the assembly with an iron hand and had close ties with the big-spending lobbyists who maneuvered for favors from the legislature. In the past, he had usually gotten his way with Pat Brown.

From my viewpoint, Unruh represented many of the things I thought were wrong with government. From his viewpoint, I must have seemed like an inexperienced and naive alien trying to force my way into what he and his cronies thought of as their private club, with an exclusive franchise for spending the taxpayers' money.

Over time, I gained some grudging respect for Unruh's skills as a legislative tactician—he was good at what he did—but he put partisanship above all else and never took prisoners.

I have often wondered about a paradox in American government: Every four years, voters elect a president and in California a governor, the only officeholders elected by *all* the people; then, the same people in their individual districts turn around and elect a legislature and congress that is often controlled by the opposing party, enabling it to prevent the president or governor from carrying out the things they elected him or her to do.

I know some people think this is good because they consider it as part of our system of checks and balances. Well, if that's the case, why don't we have a Republican legislature more often when we have a Democratic governor? Every ten years, after each census, the boundaries of our electoral districts are redrawn during the reapportionment process. And for most of the past half century, a single party—the Democrats—have been in power and they have used this power to draw the boundaries of electoral districts in such a blatantly partisan fashion that the districts seldom have reflected the real political sentiment in much of the nation. As a result, a lot of the effects of that prairie fire I've mentioned—the quiet revolution in which middle-class Americans have tried to regain control over their government—have been smothered by the outrageous machinations of incumbent legislators.

I don't limit that to Democratic legislators.

Gerrymandering has been around a long time, but with modern computers, it has become a science as well as a political weapon.

Incumbents of both parties are able to hold on to their office—and their power—by drawing the boundaries of electoral districts in ways that assure they will get reelected, circumventing the public will with crazy-quilt borders so convoluted that they make the gerrymandered districts of previous generations seem neat and symmetrical by comparison.

And I'm afraid many Republican incumbents have been all too willing to go along with Democratic reapportionment plans that disenfranchise voters in return for a "safe" district that assures their reelection.

Now that I had to govern California, it occurred to me there was something so basic about doing any job—call it common sense, if you will—that it didn't take a lot of reflection on my part to decide how I was going to approach my new occupation.

First, I had to select the best people I could find for my administration—people whom I could rely on and trust; this we accomplished by going out and recruiting top people from the business world and elsewhere.

Then, I had to set policies and goals I wanted these people to accomplish and to do whatever I could to help them achieve these goals. It seemed like simple, basic, sound management policy to me. It worked for me in Sacramento and it worked for me later in Washington.

I've been criticized for what some people call a "hands off" management style. But I think the criticism has come from people who don't understand how we operated.

I don't believe a chief executive should supervise every detail of what goes on in his organization. The chief executive should set broad policy and general ground rules, tell people what he or she wants them to do, then let them do it; he should make himself (or *her*self) available, so that the members of his team can come to him if there is a problem. If there is, you can work on it together and, if necessary, fine-tune the policies. But I don't think a chief executive should peer constantly over the shoulders of the people who are in charge of a project and tell them every few minutes what to do.

I think that's the cornerstone of good management: Set clear goals and appoint good people to help you achieve them. As long as they are doing what you have in mind, don't interfere, but if somebody drops the ball, intervene and make a change.

Of course, for chief executives to make intelligent decisions and good choices, they have to be well informed about what's going on in their organization and the world around it.

As we began plowing into the problems we found in Sacramento, one of the first things I told the members of my cabinet was that when I had a decision to make, I wanted to hear all sides of the issue, but there was one thing I didn't want to hear: the *"political ramifications"* of my choices.

"The minute you begin saying, 'This is good or bad politically,'" I said, "you start compromising principle. The only consideration I want to hear is whether it is good or bad for the people." I made the same statement at our first cabinet meeting in Washington.

Like a presidential cabinet, the governor's cabinet was composed of specialists—the top people who headed the departments of finance, parks, employment, agriculture, and so forth.

As I later did in Washington, I told the cabinet members that I didn't want them to speak up only on the matters that affected their own departments. They were all my advisors, I said, and I wanted to hear everything that each of them had to say about whatever topic we were considering, whether it involved their department or not, including any reservations they might have about a proposal; this gave me the opportunity to get opinions from a variety of perspectives, not only from the people who might be supporting a certain project or program.

Some people have suggested that both in Sacramento and in Washington my cabinet meetings resembled the meetings of a corporation's board of directors. I suppose that's true, but there was one difference: We never took a vote.

Everyone pitched in and was involved in the give and take of debate, but when the discussion was over, they all knew it was up to me and me alone to make the decision.

I learned a lot during those first few months in Sacramento. I'm sure Jesse Unruh, who wanted to be governor, and other Democratic legislators regarded my arrival in Sacramento as the beginning of a jousting match, with them determined to knock the novice from Hollywood out of the saddle.

It didn't work out that way. But there were plenty of days in those first months when I had to hang on to my saddle pretty tightly.

25

W<small>HEN</small> I <small>ARRIVED IN</small> S<small>ACRAMENTO</small> it had been less than two years since a large portion of Los Angeles had gone up in smoke during the Watts riots. I wanted to understand more about the causes that had led to the rioting, heal the scars it had left, and assure that minorities had the same opportunities as every other Californian did.

To find out what was going on, I decided to visit families who lived in black neighborhoods around the state as well as the large Mexican-American barrio in East Los Angeles. I decided to keep the visits secret from reporters and never told anyone about them: I'd disappear for a few hours, travel incognito to private homes, and talk to the family to learn what was on their minds. Sometimes they invited neighbors or relatives and some of the meetings got so large that we had to move them to a school or neighborhood store-front.

One of the first things I heard was a complaint that blacks weren't being given a fair shot at jobs in state government. I looked into it and confirmed that virtually the only blacks employed by the state were janitors or those working in other menial positions, largely because state civil service tests were slanted against them.

Some blacks just hadn't had the opportunity to get the same kind of schooling as other Californians. They were as capable as anyone else, but the tests were skewed to make it difficult for them to compete on an equal footing with whites for the better jobs, trapping them forever at the bottom of the ladder. We then changed the testing and job evaluation procedures to make sure that, in the future, everyone got an even break.

My visits, incidentally, gave me a new insight on the state bureaucracy. One black man told me he had been trying to help young men from welfare families in his community to find work, and he had taken a half dozen or so to a state employment assistance office to register for jobs.

After they finished and were standing outside the state office, he said he questioned the young men about their applications and learned that two or three of them had not answered a few of the questions on the application forms; so he took them back inside so that they could fill in the blanks.

When they returned to the office, the clerks said they couldn't find the applications.

Since they'd only been gone a few minutes, the man walked over to a wastebasket on a hunch and discovered all of the young men's job applications had been tossed away. When I got back to Sacramento, I made sure that our bureaucrats didn't do that again.

At a meeting in East Los Angeles, several mothers told me that their kids weren't doing well in school, in part because their teachers were ignoring the fact that their native language was Spanish.

One mother told me that because her son had had difficulty in school, his teacher had sent him to a special class for retarded children; luckily, another teacher realized his only problem was difficulty with English, and he was transferred out of the class and eventually graduated from high school with the highest honors. This mother told me she knew of other children who had not been as fortunate as her son. I suggested to the group of mothers that they volunteer to take turns visiting their children's classes to monitor whether their children were having a language problem. They looked at each other, then back at me, and said they'd be delighted to do that, but couldn't because only people with teachers' certificates could participate in classroom functions.

I thought it was ridiculous that a parent couldn't assist in school and arranged for the rule to be changed. Later on, as an outgrowth of this, California became a national pioneer in a program that enlisted the help of parents in the early education of their children.

· · ·

Although our efforts to "squeeze, cut, and trim" reduced the state's rate of spending substantially, we had had only six months to close the deficit before the new fiscal year, and I realized this wasn't going to be long enough to deal with the fiscal mess left by the Brown administration.

We hired a team of independent auditors who documented for the people how bad the mess was, and then I went on television and said I had no choice but to ask for a tax increase.

It was not an enjoyable speech to make. I'd campaigned on a promise to keep the lid on taxes, now I was asking for an increase. But I swallowed hard and said that as soon as I could, I'd make sure we gave the people some of their money back to them.

Over the next eight years, we did just that four times, but that's getting ahead of my story.

26

ONE REPORTER WROTE A STORY describing my first year in Sacramento headlined "The Political Education of Ronald Reagan." I suppose this description of my introduction to political life wasn't far off the mark, although the reporter might have added this was a period of "education" for Nancy, too.

For much of that first year or so, nothing went according to my plan: We kept uncovering problems nobody had told me about before; there was continuing violence on our campuses; Democratic legislators rejected my proposals right and left; moderates and conservatives in my own party couldn't get along; and I made lots of mistakes because of inexperience.

As I remarked during one speech, "Out in California we have a form of on-the-job training: When I got to Sacramento, I felt like an Egyptian tank driver reading a set of Russian instructions. . . . "

Yes, I was learning that it was one thing to preach a sermon about reducing the size of government, another to put it into action when you're fighting a hostile legislature determined to expand it.

In Hollywood, Nancy and I had become used to having critics take shots at us and reading things about ourselves in the papers that weren't true. But what we found in Sacramento made our Hollywood experience seem mild by comparison.

After a while, when I'd get home from the capitol, I'd know exactly where Nancy was—in the bathtub.

I'd smell bath salts at the front door and hear her voice echoing down the hallway from the bathroom.

Her way of dealing with attacks on me was to get in a hot bath and hold an imaginary conversation with whoever had taken after me that day—she'd just talk to the wall and get it off her chest.

I wish I had been able to find as easy a way to deal with attacks on her. In some ways Nancy and I are like one human being: When one of us has a problem, it automatically becomes a problem for the other; an attack on one of us is an attack on both of us. When one suffers, so does the other.

Over the years, I've often felt guilty that so much flak meant for me was aimed at her. When somebody would say something untruthful or nasty about Nancy and I'd get upset about it, people would tell me, "Oh, that's just politics."

Well, I never agreed with that or got used to it. There is no justification for a political opponent or someone in the press to go after a man's wife just because he is in politics.

During those first few months in Sacramento, Nancy began to realize that being the wife of a man in public life could bring with it the unwanted role of serving as a target of potshots meant for him; but it wasn't easy for her, and it never would be. I know it never became any easier for me.

We hadn't been in Sacramento for more than a few months when I came home one day and told Nancy: "I spent thirteen years at Warner Brothers and they couldn't give me an ulcer, but I think I'm getting one now."

I'd felt a sharp pain down in my stomach that wouldn't go away. When I told Nancy's father and brother, who was also a doctor, about it, they agreed it sounded like an ulcer, then my regular physician confirmed the diagnosis.

I'm not sure when I started to get the ulcer; it's possible it started when I first came under that pressure to run for governor, when I couldn't get people to take no for an answer. Whatever its origins, my battles with the legislature, the continuing upheaval on our campuses, and the other problems we ran into during that first year or so contributed a lot to that pain down in my stomach.

I was ashamed for having an ulcer. I'd always regarded an ulcer as evidence of weakness, and now I had one.

I didn't want anybody to know about it and so I kept it a secret from everyone except the family. I certainly didn't want the press saying the Democrats had given me an ulcer. I watched my diet, avoided the inevitable fried chicken, took a daily dose of Maalox, and prayed the ulcer would go away. But as we continued to open drawers and find more problems, the ache in my stomach got worse.

A little over a year later, however, I reached for my bottle of Maalox one morning and something inside me said, "You don't need this anymore." So I put down the bottle and didn't take my medicine that morning. An hour or two later, I had an appointment with a man from Southern California who had a problem he wanted to discuss with the governor. As he was leaving my office, he turned around and said, "Governor, you might like to know that I'm part of a group of people who meet every day and pray for you."

I was taken aback by what he said, but thanked him and said I also put a lot of stock in the power of prayer. Later the same day, another person, this time a man from Northern California, came to see me about a different matter, and as he was leaving, a similar thing happened: He turned around and told me that he met with a group of people who prayed daily for me.

Not long after that, I went to the doctor for my regular checkup. He poked my stomach and did the usual battery of tests. When he was finished, he looked up at me and said it seemed I didn't have an ulcer anymore.

When more test results came in, he said there was no evidence that I had ever had an ulcer. The power of prayer? I don't know, but I'd prayed daily for relief and I can't forget that impulse I had to stop taking my medicine, and then hearing about those prayers other people were saying for me.

Besides our privacy and the ranch, another thing I had to give up after my decision to run for governor was my aversion to flying. Prior to the election, I was still committed to give a few speeches out of the state including a pair in Texas—in El Paso and Fort Worth. I asked the staff to book me on the train from Los Angeles to El Paso and then arrange for a bedroom on a night train from El Paso to Fort Worth that I'd taken previously. They got back to me and said the night train now had only day coaches, no berths.

I decided I didn't want to sit up all night in a coach and then remembered what I'd always told myself: The day would come when something would happen that would make me realize it was time to fly.

The time had come, I decided. I asked the staff to get me a ticket on the train to El Paso and the morning plane from El Paso to Fort Worth. There was a long silence on the other end of the phone. They had never heard me say that before. But I assured them I really meant what I said and they made the arrangements. I picked up my tickets and was driving home when I stopped at a signal on Sunset Boulevard and bought an afternoon paper from a newsboy. As I waited for the light to change, I placed the paper down on the seat beside me and studied the front page: There was a story about an airliner that the day before had lost a wheel on takeoff in El Paso and had had to circle the airport at Fort Worth while it emptied its fuel and emergency crews spread foam on the runway, before making a belly landing. It was the same flight for which I had just picked up a ticket. When I read the story, I remember looking up and saying aloud: "Make up your mind." But I took the plane and got to Fort Worth safely and from then on, there would be lots of airplanes in my life.

Around the same time that my ulcer disappeared, things had started to turn up for me in Sacramento. Our spending cutbacks and the tax increase had begun to put the state's financial house in order; I was learning a little more about how to deal with a hostile legislature; I was learning how valuable the line-item veto, the governor's authority to veto individual items in a budget proposal, can be when you're dealing with an unfriendly legislature; and I was learning probably the most important political lesson of my years in Sacramento: the value of taking my case to the people.

Although the Democrats controlled the legislature, it occurred to me that I had an opportunity to go over their heads. Franklin D. Roosevelt gave me the idea with his Fireside Chats, which made an indelible mark on me during the Depression.

By going on television or radio and telling the people what was going on in Sacramento and what we were trying to do about it, I thought I might be able to get public opinion on my side.

It worked better than I ever dreamed it would.

. . .

During eight years of travels for General Electric and during the campaign for governor, I'd gotten a good idea of what was on the minds of people. They wanted their government to be fair, not waste their money, and intrude as little as possible in their lives. A lot of people in Sacramento had different ideas of what government should be and I told the people that.

I discovered that if you could make the public understand what was going on, they'd do the rest: They'd write letters or call their assemblymen and senators and apply pressure on them. The legislators knew that sooner or later they'd have to face voters again, and as I suspected, there was a limit to how far they'd go in opposing what the folks back home wanted.

During the first year or two in Sacramento, I kept my distance from legislators. Nancy and I had never done much partying in Hollywood—our idea of an exciting evening was to spend it at home with the children—and when we got to Sacramento, we hadn't plunged into the social world there either, causing some of the legislators to regard us as snobs.

There were still some hard feelings toward me left over from the campaign, when I'd gone out of my way to say I thought the professional politicians in Sacramento and I were natural enemies: My loyalty was to the people, not the political establishment, and I had said so fairly pointedly. Although that sentiment never changed, I realized after a while that to accomplish what I wanted to do swimming upstream against a current of opposition legislators, I'd have to do some negotiating with them. And that meant I'd make a truce of sorts with the opposition, meet with them socially, invite them over for a drink, get to know them. I began doing that. And the more time I spent in government, the more I realized that legislators and congressmen were often less responsible for the growth of government and taxes than the "permanent government"—the people in the bureaucracies who were forever trying to enlarge their power and budgets and prolong programs after their need had expired. As I'd learned back in Dixon, the first rule of the bureaucracy is, protect the bureaucracy.

I began to socialize with the legislators, and in more on-the-job training, I also discovered the value of picking up a telephone and calling a legislator to tell him or her why I thought he or she should vote for something I wanted.

Although I may have been a former actor, I knew something about negotiating. As president of the Screen Actors Guild, I'd matched wits with some of the shrewdest negotiators on the planet —people like Jack Warner, Y. Frank Freeman, the president of Paramount, MGM's Louis B. Mayer, and the heads of the other studios.

When I began entering into the give and take of legislative bargaining in Sacramento, a lot of the most radical conservatives who had supported me during the election didn't like it. "Compromise" was a dirty word to them and they wouldn't face the fact that we couldn't get all of what we wanted today. They wanted all or nothing and they wanted it all at once. If you don't get it all, some said, don't take anything.

I'd learned while negotiating union contracts that you seldom got everything you asked for. And I agreed with FDR, who said in 1933: "I have no expectations of making a hit every time I come to bat. What I seek is the highest possible batting average."

If you got seventy-five or eighty percent of what you were asking for, I say, you take it and fight for the rest later, and that's what I told these radical conservatives who never got used to it.

Although the first year or so in Sacramento was hard going for us at times, Nancy and I had learned a lot.

For years, I'd been giving speeches about the problems in government. Now, after being dragged kicking and screaming into public office at a time when the state was facing a real emergency and I was uncovering problems I hadn't even known existed before, I'd been given a chance to do something about them.

As cumbersome as they were, I was at the controls. It was exciting. Suddenly, instead of just trying to rouse people to act, the problems were mine to deal with and it was a lot more fun than just talking about them.

As we finished dinner, Nancy and I agreed my new job made everything we'd ever done before seem as dull as dishwater.

27

Nancy and I learned in Sacramento that one of the inevitable consequences of holding a prominent public office is a degree of personal risk. Death threats and security people become part of your life.

In 1968, after Robert F. Kennedy was assassinated on election night in Los Angeles, Secret Service details were sent from Washington to guard the governors of several states because of reports that foreign agents were plotting to kill other American officials. Shortly after the agents arrived in Sacramento, I had to make a trip to Los Angeles. While I was there, I was curious to see our old ranch near Lake Malibu again. I'd always enjoyed target shooting and while we were there in the wilderness, several of the agents and I decided to do some practice shooting. We set some tin cans up on a log and began firing away. While we were reloading, I mentioned an article I'd recently seen describing techniques for shooting from the hip and one of the agents said, "Oh yeah, we have to do that."

When it was my turn, I went into a low crouch, raised my gun, and shot from the hip.

I've always been a right hander but sometimes I think I was intended to be a southpaw because there are some things I just do automatically with my left hand—like shooting a gun.

Well, in any event, that afternoon I shot from the hip with my left hand, following the method described in the article, and missed the can by a mile. Then one of the Secret Service agents stepped up and pulled his gun from a holster and started shooting from the hip. But he didn't crouch: He just stood completely erect and hit the can with almost every shot.

I said, "Good shooting—but you know, you didn't go into a crouch."

"No, we lose our rating if we crouch," he said.

I said, "What are you talking about—is the article wrong?—It says you're supposed to go into a crouch."

Then the head of the Secret Service detail stepped in and came to the agent's rescue: "Governor, if we are ever shooting at someone, we're between him and his target and we don't crouch."

I looked at these guys, perfect strangers, who had taken a job where, if anyone was shooting at me, they were going to stand up straight between him and me and make themselves a target. I was amazed—and grateful.

During the peak of the rioting on our university campuses, Nancy and I were asleep in bed late one night when I heard a loud noise outside our window that could have only been a gunshot fired very close to the Governor's Mansion. I jumped out of bed and went into the hall and was met by an agent running toward me who shouted: "Stay away from the windows."

The guards outside the Governor's Mansion had discovered two men beneath our window in the act of lighting a Molotov cocktail. When they were spotted, the men had sprinted to a waiting car, although one of the guards got off a shot as they drove away. I don't know what would have happened if the men had succeeded in throwing the gasoline bomb into the house. Nancy, of course, was very upset by the near miss, but I calmed her down, assuring her the two men were gone.

Within a few minutes, there was a large group of reporters at the Governor's Mansion. Still in my robe and pajamas, I went out to explain to them what had happened and said one of the security men had gotten off a warning shot; well, about the third time I said that, the guard spoke up and said: "Governor, we don't fire warning shots. I just missed the bastard."

Not long after that, I went to Modesto, an agricultural town in the lush San Joaquin Valley where local people had put on a successful campaign to raise money for a new medical center and had invited me to speak at the dedication banquet. We were still at the height of the campus rioting and the administration was doing other things that hadn't made me popular, including an effort to reform California's welfare system, and our security people told me they didn't think it was a good time for me to leave Sacramento. But I'd given my word I'd go, and insisted we do so.

When we got to Modesto, there were four different groups of placard-waving people demonstrating outside the building against me. While I was inside giving my speech, I learned later, a citizen reported to the police that a suspicious-acting man had been repeatedly circling the building and stopping every so often to ask people which door I was going to use after the banquet.

This alarmed the police and sheriff's deputies, who couldn't find the man, and a real dragnet was put into action. Finally, someone spotted the man in a car slowly circling the block again and again; the next time he came around, the police pulled him over, yanked him out of the car, and bent him face down over the hood of his car as they frisked him.

He realized pretty quickly what was going on: "No, no, no," he said, "you fellows have it all wrong. I just want to *see* the son of a bitch."

In a country ruled by laws, it seemed to me that nothing was more important than removing politics from the process of choosing judges. During previous administrations in California, governors had often handed out judgeships to friends and cronies like prizes at a company picnic. Not only had this produced a lot of inferior judges, it had placed a number of partisans on the bench who believed that putting on the black robes of a judge gave them a license to rewrite the laws. I wanted judges who would interpret the Constitution, not rewrite it. So I sent out an order setting up a new system to take politics out of the selection of judges: Whenever there was an opening for a judge around the state, we asked lawyers in the community, through their local Bar Association, to appoint a committee to consider eligible candidates and recommend the best available man or woman for the judgeship; at the same time, we asked a citizens' group in the same community to give us their recommendations on the best candidate; third, we asked all the judges sitting in the district to give us their recommendations. Each of the three groups acted independently, unaware of the others' recommendations. Then, all the recommendations were sent to me and assembled in the form of a scoresheet with a point system ranking the top candidate; without exception, I chose the person at the top of the rating. Politics or party membership played no part in the selection.

The system reminded me a little of how All-American football teams are chosen. Although none of the groups knew the others' recommendations, many times the three groups recommended the same candidate. As a result, we got the cream of the crop.

One day in 1968, Cap Weinberger, the state finance director, came to my office to tell me he had been going over the books and that he expected the state to have a budget surplus of more than $100 million the following fiscal year. The surplus was a result of the tax increase I'd signed to close the Brown administration deficit and some of our initial cost-cutting efforts.

Cap said no legislators knew about the projected surplus yet and he asked me if I had any ideas on how I wanted to spend it—whether, for example, I wanted to proceed with projects or programs we'd had to curtail because of the deficit crisis.

"I think you ought to decide now," Cap said, "before the legislature hears about the money and starts thinking of its own ways of spending it."

"I already know what we should do with the money," I said. "Let's give it back to the people, give them a tax rebate."

"It's never been done," Cap said.

"You've never had an actor up here before, either," I said.

The legislature had to approve any refund of money to taxpayers, and if there was one thing I'd learned about government, it was that if there was any loose money lying around, the people in government would find a way to spend it. The worst sin in the bureaucracy was to give money back because it meant the bureaucracy's budget could be reduced the following year. If at the end of the fiscal year they hadn't spent all the money in their budget, there would be a rush to buy new office furniture, take a trip at the taxpayers' expense, or spend the money on something else, just to assure their budget wouldn't be smaller in the future. The idea of *returning* money to taxpayers once it had been collected from them had never come up before.

I knew what would happen if word leaked out about a surplus. Some legislators just wouldn't countenance the notion of giving money back to the people. To them, taxpayers were meant to be fleeced, not fattened.

Before legislators could learn about the extra money, I decided to go on the air and tell Californians about the surplus and suggest that it be returned to them. Since the surplus was expected to equal about ten percent of the revenue normally collected through the state income tax, I suggested the best way to deal with it was for Californians, when they computed their income tax the following year, to send a check for only ninety percent of what they owed.

When the legislators heard that, they went wild. But it was too late; the people knew about the surplus. They wanted it back—and they got it back.

By the spring of 1968, I was really starting to enjoy my new job. The ulcer was gone (no evidence of it ever returned) and I was making some progress on the things I wanted to accomplish. Nancy and I weren't ready for another round of pressure to run for office, but that's what we got. It had started shortly after we came to Sacramento: I'd give a speech and afterward there'd be a cluster of people who'd be waiting to talk to me and they would urge me to run for president. I'd always said I wasn't interested.

Then early in 1968, several leaders of the state Republican party came to see me and said they wanted me to run for the Republican presidential nomination on the California primary ballot the following June as a favorite-son candidate. If I did, he said the party could avert a repeat of the kind of bloody battle between moderates and conservatives that split the party so badly in 1964.

I agreed with them that there were still lots of hard feelings left over from the Goldwater-Rockefeller primary fight and that a heated primary race between the three major candidates in 1968—Richard Nixon, Nelson Rockefeller, and George Romney—would probably reopen the wounds. But running for president was the last thing on my mind. I'd been governor for less than two years and I said it would look ridiculous if I ran for president.

But they countered: "A favorite-son candidate is not the same thing as a *real* candidate. If you enter the primary as a favorite son, the major candidates won't enter the race, so we'll avoid a disas-

trous primary fight; as governor, you'll win the primary, but that only means you'll head the delegation to the convention."

"Okay," I said, "I'll do that, I'll enter my name as a favorite son, but that's all, and only on one condition: that our delegation be representative of all sides in this split, not just one group." They promised to balance the delegation—and they did.

After the word leaked out of my agreement to run as a favorite son in the primary, I began getting calls from Republicans around the country asking me if it was true that my name was going to be placed in nomination as a candidate.

I'd say, "Well, yes, because that goes with being a favorite son, but I'm not *running* for president." Then, they'd say, "That's all we wanted to know; we're going to consider you a real candidate and campaign on that basis."

Then I replied: "I'll have to repudiate you if you do that—I'm not a *real* candidate."

"We know that," they'd say, "but we're going to do it anyway."

As I traveled around the country on the speech circuit that spring, preaching Republicanism and the Eleventh Commandment, I ran into some of these people, repeated what I'd told them on the phone, and declined to let them place my name on state primary ballots. But that still didn't stop it. A lot of top Republicans in California kept telling me I was foolish not to launch an all-out bid for the nomination, but I said I didn't want to run for the presidency and I meant it.

By the time the convention opened in Miami Beach in early August, George Romney had lost his initial momentum and the race had boiled down to a battle between Rockefeller and Nixon, who was completing his great political comeback after the defeats of 1960 and 1962. When I arrived at the convention, I was surprised to learn quite a few delegates had pledged their support to me, but I continued to tell them I wasn't a candidate and didn't want it. But they'd just go away and say I *was* a candidate.

Former Senator William F. Knowland came to me one day when all of this was going on and said he wanted to let me know that the California delegation were planning to issue a unanimous statement declaring that, in their minds, I should be considered a bonafide candidate for the nomination.

"Damn it, Bill," I said, "you know it's not true. I'm going to

have to repudiate them if they do that." He said, "We know that, Ron, but there's so much sentiment for you we think you'll end up as a laughing-stock if somebody doesn't say we are taking you as a serious candidate."

Well, when the balloting took place, I got a sizable number of votes behind Nixon and Rockefeller, but Nixon had the clear majority and so I ran up to the front of the hall and jumped on the platform and asked the chairman for permission to address the convention.

At first, I was turned down because of a procedural rule, but after a minute they agreed to waive the rule and let me speak and I made a motion that the delegates nominate Richard Nixon by acclamation and they did so with a tremendous roar.

Afterward, Rockefeller told me, "You didn't get as many votes as we counted on; we thought you'd stop Nixon for us." I guess he thought I'd take enough votes away from Nixon to give him the nomination on a split.

The next day, Nancy and I left on a restful trip through the Florida Keys aboard a friend's yacht—only the two of us and the crew.

That first night, we slept fourteen hours, and we felt the greatest sense of relief either of us had ever known.

Because I consented to be a favorite-son candidate that year, some people have suggested that I was bitten by the presidential "bug" back in 1968. But it wasn't true. When Nixon was nominated, I was the most relieved person in the world. I knew I wasn't ready to be president.

We spent almost three days on the yacht and we didn't pay any more attention to the convention. We were relaxed and very happy when we got back to California. I knew there was still lots of work to be done in Sacramento.

28

DURING THE PEAK OF UNREST on our college campuses, student leaders from the nine campuses of the University of California asked to see me in Sacramento. I was delighted to see them. During those days, if I'd visited one of their campuses, I'd have started a riot. When I'd been campaigning, I was cheered by students because I was running against an incumbent who was part of the establishment. Now, *I* was the establishment.

When the delegation arrived in the capitol, some were barefoot and several were wearing torn T-shirts; when I entered the room, they sat silently where they were, some sprawled out on the floor. No one stood up. Then their spokesman began:

"Governor, we want to talk to you, but I think you should realize that it's impossible for you to understand us. . . . It's sad, but it's impossible for the members of your generation to understand your own children. . . .

"You weren't raised in a time of instant communications or satellites and computers solving problems in seconds that previously took hours or days or even weeks to solve. You didn't live in an age of space travel and journeys to the moon, of jet travel or high speed electronics. . . ."

While he paused to take a breath, I said:

"You're absolutely right. We didn't have those things when we were your age. We invented them. . . ."

As a seventeen-year-old college freshman, I'd known something about student protests firsthand. But what occurred on California's campuses during the late 1960s didn't bear any resemblance to our placid protest at Eureka College against an administration plan that would have denied dozens of upperclassmen their chance for a college degree.

When it began, perhaps students at the University of California had grounds for grievances against the institution they had entered: Full of dreams and full of ambition, they had been herded into gigantic classes and handed over to a faculty they seldom saw, one that spent most of its time on "research," and turned over its responsibility to teach to inexperienced teaching assistants not much older than the students themselves. The students were given little attention as individuals.

I understood their sense of alienation, but whatever the source of this alienation, it was expropriated by articulate agitators—many of whom had never been inside a college classroom—who then turned it into an ugly force that could not be tolerated.

A great educational institution became paralyzed. In later years, some participants in those revolutionary days have tried to look back on them as heroic and noble.

Whatever it might have been at the beginning, the upheaval that shook so many of our campuses when I was governor wasn't a gallant or idealistic rebellion to right some wrongs: It was violent anarchy; the campuses were literally set afire by rioting mobs in the name of "free speech."

During one eleven-month period, there were eight bombings and attempted bombings at the Berkeley campus of the university alone; during those eleven months, the police confiscated more than two hundred rifles, pistols, and shotguns and nearly a thousand sticks of dynamite and dozens of Molotov cocktails.

There were undoubtedly well-meaning students caught up in the demonstrations who thought they were doing the right thing. They had a right to express their grievances. As Americans, the Constitution guarantees them the right of free expression. But there was nothing noble about those who under the anonymity of a mob injured others, burned, destroyed, and acted like storm troopers on the streets of Berkeley and other college towns.

The vast majority of students at the university only wanted an education. But for months they were robbed of it by the rampaging of a minority; meanwhile, many moderate voices on the faculty were silenced by the intimidation of left-wing professors whose vision of freedom of speech was limited to speech about things they agreed with.

As I've said, I campaigned for the governorship by saying the campus rioters should "Obey the rules or get out," and that was the policy I applied when I became governor.

The state had a responsibility to establish rules of behavior for the students to whom it gave an education, and, as governor, it was my job to enforce them.

One day during the spring of 1969, more than two thousand rioters charged down a street in Berkeley toward a line of policemen and literally trampled them underfoot, sending forty-seven to the hospital. The president of the university called me from the chancellor's office at the Berkeley campus and said he was with the mayor and police chief of the city. They had agreed unanimously, he said, that they could no longer guarantee the safety of citizens in Berkeley and wanted me to send in the National Guard to quell the rioting.

These were stormy times, but I'll never forget one very quiet moment during that period. One day, I arrived at the University of California campus in San Diego for a meeting of the Board of Regents and there was a huge crowd of demonstrators waiting outside.

The security people told me to remain in the car so that they could drive around to a rear entrance of the building away from the demonstrators. Well, I didn't want to do that. I told them I'd walk through the front door of the university administration building as I was supposed to.

It was a long walk, about 150 yards, to the building. On one side was a knoll and on the other side a smaller rise; both areas were packed with demonstrators all the way from the street to the front door of the building, and I had to take that long walk between them by myself.

The protesters had decided to hold a silent demonstration, with not a sound, and everyone just standing and glaring at me as I made the walk; the silence had an effect and pretty soon it began to seem like a very long walk and I was feeling a little uncomfortable. I had almost reached the building when one girl left the crowd and started descending from the knoll, headed right for me, and I thought, Lord, what have they got planned now? As I approached her, she was waiting for me and she held out her hand and I took it. Then her voice broke the stark silence and said: "I just want to tell you, I like everything you're doing as governor."

I'll never forget the sound of her voice rising out of the silent crowd. I was going on into the building, she was going to be left outside with her peers in a crowd with whom she had had the courage to disagree.

In subsequent years, sometimes when I had a decision to make and the easy way out was to go along with the crowd, I have thought about this young woman's demonstration of courage. And I have always felt terrible that afterward I didn't try to learn her name so that I could tell her how much it had meant to me that day.

Once the National Guardsmen restored order on the campuses, no more policemen or other people were attacked by rioters and peace began to be restored to our universities.

Once the campuses were quieter, I could turn back to our efforts to cut costs and try to make government efficient. The teams of business people that I appointed right after the election had conducted in-depth studies of sixty-four state agencies and confirmed what I had suspected: Many were run in such an old-fashioned and inefficient fashion that they wouldn't survive in the real world outside government for more than a few weeks.

Giving of their time month after month, sometimes to the detriment of their own businesses, members of our task forces (who dubbed themselves "Reagan's Raiders" and had cuff links made with a replica of my head on them) helped implement thousands of recommendations to upgrade the efficiency of the state departments.

They saved taxpayers hundreds of millions, possibly billions, of dollars, often simply by incorporating into the state government the most basic modern business practices found in any forward-looking business.

This project, incidentally, taught me something about the psychology of audiences.

As we started to make some headway in trimming costs, I began telling the public about the savings we were making and I learned it can be difficult for many people to envision a hundred million dollars or even one million for that matter.

I'd mention an example of something we'd done that saved several million dollars and would get a glassy stare and polite applause.

But during one speech to a group of business and professional people in San Francisco, I happened to mention that we'd been able to save about $200,000 by sending motorists their annual automobile registration renewal notices several weeks earlier than in the past; postal rates were going up and so we rushed to do our mailing before the increase went into effect. Well, after I said that, the audience came to their feet with a roar of approval. Two hundred thousand dollars they could visualize. Two hundred million, they couldn't.

After discovering that state hiring policies sometimes unintentionally discriminated against minorities, I devoted a lot of time to bringing more blacks and Hispanics into important jobs in the state government. Nevertheless, a myth persisted that I was insensitive to minorities. Once I got a call from several black leaders from the San Francisco Bay Area who said they wanted to talk to me about my "treatment of blacks."

When they arrived in my office, it was clear what was on their minds; there was a look of hostility on their faces and it was evident they were just itching to attack me as a racist. And so, I said:

"Look, are you aware that I've appointed more blacks to executive and policy-making positions in the state government than all the previous governors of California put together?"

One said, "Yes, but why aren't you out there telling people about it? How come you haven't bragged about it?"

Well, I was amazed by the question. "In appointing these people, I just was doing what I thought was right," I said. "I think it would have been cheap politics if I'd gone out and started singing a song about it. Besides, they were the best people for the job; I didn't appoint them just because they were blacks. . . ."

With that, the whole atmosphere of the meeting changed. They said they thought I had been quiet about it because I was fearful of angering my more conservative white supporters.

When we left the room, we left literally with our arms around each other.

As I found myself enjoying my job more, Nancy, as always, gave me a lot of support, but not in the way some of my critics have claimed over the years. She's been subjected to a bum rap.

I know she's been accused of being a kind of "shadow governor" or "shadow president" with some sort of undue influence over me. Well, that's another myth that has no foundation in reality. It's true that I'll sometimes use her as a sounding board, but Nancy has never tried to intervene on matters of policy or affect the important decisions I've had to make. As in any good marriage, I value her opinion and we talk over everything, but she'd be the first to tell you I can be a stubborn fellow when I don't agree with her.

One of the things that has been most helpful to me is Nancy's instinct about people. As I've mentioned, I tend to trust people until they give me reason not to, while she usually focuses a more skeptical eye on people, especially those in a position to harm me. She's a very good judge of people and it's helped me a lot over the years.

In any top position, you risk becoming isolated: People tell you what you want to hear and are reluctant to tell you about somebody who might not be pulling his weight or doing something hurtful to your administration. Not many people close to you are willing to say: *You're wrong.* Nancy has always been there to point out when the emperor—including me—wasn't wearing any clothes. Sometimes people who've been reluctant to tell me about a problem have felt they could go to her and she might pass it on to me; then, alerted, I'd do some digging on my own.

By the end of 1969, I realized I was going to need more time than I had left in my first term to accomplish my goals as governor, and I'd had enough experience—and enjoyment—at it to know I didn't want to stop. I'd tasted briefly what it was like to be governor with a Republican legislature: As a result of some special elections, we had a bare majority in the legislature for one year and passed some forty anticrime measures that until then had been buried in committee. I knew that if I could win a second term, the odds were high I'd be stuck again with a Democratic legislature, but I didn't want to quit before I'd accomplished my most important goal, reforming California's bloated welfare program.

I have never questioned the need to take care of people who, through no fault of their own, can't provide for themselves. The rest of us have to do that. But I am against open-ended welfare programs that invite generation after generation of potentially productive people to remain on the dole; they deprive the able-bodied of the incentive to work and require productive people to support others who are physically and mentally able to work while prolonging an endless cycle of dependency that robs men and women of their dignity. I wanted to see if we couldn't rescue some of those people from what FDR had called the "narcotic" of welfare.

And so in 1970 I decided to run for a second term—but *only* one more term. My opponent was Speaker of the Assembly Jesse Unruh, the tax-and-spend liberal who from the beginning had opposed our reforms tooth and nail. On election day, I was reelected by a margin of fifty-three percent to forty-five percent. I think the people had made it clear that they wanted the reforms to continue.

29

IF CALIFORNIA WERE A NATION, it would have been the seventh-ranking economic power in the world. As governor, I discovered a large industrial state like California has many of the same problems and challenges of any industrialized nation: the challenge of keeping our economy strong and modern and our citizens fully employed; the challenge of expanding opportunity for all people; the challenge of helping businesses compete and prosper without over-regulating them; the challenge of helping those who cannot help themselves; the challenge of assuring that every man, woman, and child can go to sleep safe at night and wake up the next day guaranteed the freedom to better their lives.

Even international relations were important to a state like California. We had more imports and exports coming across our borders than any other state—more than many nations—and foreign markets were vital to our prosperity. Fortunately, I had a chance to get a little experience in dealing with foreign leaders that would help me when I got a different job a few years later.

On four occasions when I was governor, President Nixon sent us abroad to represent him on goodwill missions; I carried a personal message from him to foreign leaders but always managed to do a little salesmanship on behalf of California and its business opportunities.

Nancy and I met the heads of state of eighteen countries in Europe and Asia during four overseas trips and had person-to-person experiences we'll never forget.

In Manila, President Ferdinand Marcos and his wife, Imelda, put us up at Malacañang Palace.

In Australia, I happened to mention during a luncheon speech that Nancy enjoyed working on the Foster Grandparents Program in which older adults volunteer to help retarded or troubled children through bonds of love and support. People in the audience asked Nancy about it and before we'd left the country, they were already establishing a Foster Grandparents Program in Australia.

In Japan, I became the first foreign official other than a head of state to be formally presented to Emperor Hirohito. As our plane approached Tokyo and the city spread out beneath us, I couldn't help but think of the huge model of Tokyo that we'd made secretly during the war.

President Nixon invited Nancy and me to take our children with us on the trips. A government plane similar to Air Force One was made available and Secret Service and government aides went along and took care of everything for us. We never carried much money on those trips. The security people didn't want us going out on the streets shopping or walking up to the front desk of our hotel to pay the bill. They took care of everything and sent us the bills when we got home.

One evening in Paris, our schedule was clear so Nancy and I decided to take Ron to dinner at Maxim's; about midway through the meal, the restaurant's strolling violinist headed our way.

I knew he'd expect a tip and I reached into my pocket to look for a dollar bill, the appropriate tip in those days for a strolling violinist; well, all I found was a $5 bill, a dime, and a penny—it was all the money I'd taken with me from home.

Since $5 was too large a tip I asked Nancy for a dollar; she said she didn't have any cash with her; so then I asked Ron, who was only a kid then, and he said, "Dad, are you kidding?"

I said: "Okay, keep your head down, don't look up, keep on eating and maybe he won't come to our table."

Well, we kept our heads down, but he kept moving in our direction and when he was just a few inches from our table, he began playing, "California, Here I Come."

I reached into my pocket and got the $5 bill and handed it to him.

Well, I was now down to a dime and a penny. A couple of days later, we were in Ireland in the company of a young Irish guide when we passed a tombstone close to where, according to legend, St. Patrick had erected the first cross in Ireland. The tombstone was inscribed, "Remember me as you pass by, for as you are so once was I, but as I am you too will be, so be content to follow me." The sentiment had proven too much for another Irishman who'd scratched on the stone beneath the inscription, "To follow you I am content, I wish I knew which way you went."

The guide showed us a wishing well and suggested we might want to toss in a coin. I reached in my pocket, gave Nancy the dime, and I flipped the penny into the well.

After I got home, I liked to tell people what it was like to travel through Denmark, Belgium, France, Spain, Italy, England, and Ireland on $5.11.

As my second term began, my most important priority was welfare reform. Because of lax eligibility standards, the number of people in California receiving welfare checks had almost quadrupled between 1960 and 1970 to more than two million. With about ten percent of the population, the state had more than sixteen percent of the nation's total welfare recipients; it had become a magnet for able-bodied people from around the country who preferred a handout to a job. During my first term, I appointed a special task force on welfare that concluded that even if we were able to pay off the deficit and solve the financial mess the state had fallen into during the Brown years, welfare expenditures were growing so fast that the state would be bankrupt again soon unless something was done to control the open-ended spending.

The task force tried to reduce waste and fraud and improve efficiency of the welfare program through administrative reform but encountered a brick wall: The last thing that many of the people who supervised the welfare program wanted was to reduce their caseload because it might have threatened their jobs. As always, the first goal of the bureaucracy was to protect the bureaucracy. The study panel concluded that the state needed a top-to-bottom rewriting of its welfare regulations.

The eligibility standards were so lenient they were an invitation to steal. Through computer cross-checking, we discovered thousands of people who were receiving welfare checks at the same time they were gainfully employed, and many people were getting aid who didn't need it. One couple, for example, earned more than one hundred thousand dollars a year between them but had a household helper for their handicapped child, paid for by the taxpayers.

Welfare was taking away the very thing that people needed most —the initiative to provide for themselves. At the same time it was undermining the family: Teenagers from the inner cities, who for various reasons decided they didn't want to live at home anymore, discovered that by getting pregnant—they didn't even have to wait for their baby to be born—they got a welfare check that allowed them to rent their own apartment, and they discovered they could increase their monthly welfare check any time they chose simply by getting pregnant again.

Meanwhile, the father of the child might have a good job and want to live with his family. But he was told his family was better off financially if he walked out on them; if he stayed, they wouldn't get a welfare check.

Not only was the welfare program a tax-financed incentive for immorality that was destroying the family, it was responsible for an endless and malignant cycle of despair in which generation after generation went on the dole and never had any incentive to leave it.

Some of my most conservative supporters tried to pressure me to wage an all-or-nothing battle to virtually eliminate the welfare program; but I believed we should not take aid from the people who really needed and deserved it, the truly impoverished elderly, blind, and disabled. I just wanted to stop the abuses, take people off the welfare rolls who didn't belong there, and try to end the open-ended cycle that had made a monthly welfare check a way of life for too many people.

The Democrats in the legislature agreed with us that welfare costs were headed for the stratosphere but claimed the solution was a huge tax increase—in other words, to keep pouring more money into a bucket that was full of holes.

I'd been in Sacramento long enough by now to know that in order to get genuine welfare reform past the bureaucracy and legislature, we'd have to go to the people, and this time we really put on the pressure.

I went back out, speaking about welfare reform and to urge people to demand that their legislators clean up the mess. We organized committees in all fifty-eight counties of the state to apply pressure on the legislature. Boy, did it work.

One day the liberal Democrat who succeeded Jesse Unruh, Speaker of the Assembly Bob Moretti, came into my office holding his hands in the air as if I had a gun on him and said, "Stop those cards and letters!"

"Sit down," I said. "Look, we're all partners in this. Let's put aside our personal feelings and jointly go to work and see what we can get done."

Over the next week or so, he and I, along with members of our staffs, met almost around the clock to put together a package of welfare reform that cut expenditures by hundreds of millions of dollars a year while raising benefits and providing cost-of-living increases for the *truly* needy in the state.

By tightening eligibility standards and eliminating loopholes, we turned a monthly increase in the welfare caseload of forty thousand to a monthly *decrease* of eight thousand. California was no longer the welfare capital of the country.

We obtained authority from the federal government, which set a lot of the rules regarding welfare, to let us try an experiment in which able-bodied welfare recipients were given a job. We contacted every level of government throughout the state and asked if there were things they would be doing if they had the money and manpower to do it. We got all kinds of affirmative replies—none of them boondoggles. Washington gave us permission to go ahead with the experiment only after President Nixon intervened on our behalf. We took the able-bodied welfare recipients, assigned them to these jobs in return for their welfare grants, and as they learned some job skills, they were moving into jobs in the private sector.

During the 1973–1974 recession, this program got seventy-six thousand people off the welfare rolls and put them into productive jobs. Later, a lot of them wrote and thanked me for the program, saying for the first time in their adult lives they had felt a sense of self-respect because they were doing something in return for their monthly check; the remarks reminded me of the smiles I'd seen on the faces of the men my father helped find jobs during the Depression.

During my second term, I was able to announce a fourth rebate of state taxes to the people—the biggest surplus yet. I'll always remember what happened after I'd announced we wanted to do that. The Democratic leader of the state senate burst into my office and said, "Giving that money back to the people is an unnecessary expenditure of public funds."

In all, largely through property-tax relief, we returned more than $5 billion in taxes to the taxpayers—the people to whom it belonged in the first place.

It's not easy for me to boast, but during the eight years, I think we made the state government less costly, smaller, and more businesslike; we were able to upgrade the quality of people attracted to government and cut the government's growth to a rate at or below the level of California's population growth; we made the bureaucracy more responsive to the public; and we began to return some of the power and taxing authority usurped by the state from local communities back to where they belonged, at the local level.

During the eight years, I used my line-item veto authority 943 times and was never overridden by the legislature. If a bill had something beneficial in it but legislators had voted too much money for it, I could sign the bill but cut spending to a reasonable level, allowing me to set priorities and enabling the state to live within its means. The power of the line-item veto is held by forty-three governors. How I would miss it later in Washington. Presidents don't have a line-item veto.

Although many of my supporters wanted me to run for a third term in 1974, I'd accomplished most of what I'd set out to do and I'd sworn from the beginning that I was going to stop at two terms.

Nancy and I left Sacramento in early 1975. The previous eight years had changed both of us—and we had found a new love.

30

ITS NAME WAS RANCHO DEL CIELO, although it was called Tip Top Ranch the first day we saw it.

After I became governor and taxes forced us to sell our ranch near Lake Malibu, Nancy and I purchased a large piece of land in an isolated rural area north of San Diego, planning to make it our ranch-hideaway once I left office. Although there was no utility service on the property when we bought it, we were assured water and electrical service would be extended there shortly. But as the time approached for us to leave Sacramento, there was still no utility service and we were told none was likely to be provided very soon.

When one of our friends, Bill Wilson, heard about our problem, he said he had heard rumors that a cattle ranch not far from a lemon ranch he owned north of Santa Barbara might be coming on the market and he offered to find out if we could visit it. We'd been at his ranch many times as guests and loved the area, but didn't know what we were getting ourselves in for.

Bill and his wife, Betty, and Nancy and I got in Bill's car and we started driving up a narrow, winding road into the Santa Ynez mountains, a range of granite peaks that rise above the Pacific Ocean a few miles north of Santa Barbara.

The road seemed to go on forever and as we got higher and higher up the mountain, Betty started saying, "Bill, there can't be anything up here that they'd want, why don't you turn around?" But Bill didn't answer and kept on driving.

Although I kept quiet, I was beginning to have the same doubts as Betty: The road was so steep and the area was so primitive I thought, well, maybe somebody's got a house up here they call a ranch, but it sure looks like goat country to me. Where would you ride a horse?

After seven miles of twists and turns, the road straightened out briefly and we were surrounded by a stand of oak trees; then we turned off the road, went through a gate, and started down another narrow road.

Pretty soon, we were passing through another lovely grove of trees and suddenly we emerged on a huge green meadow with rugged hills stretching far beyond it. Across the meadow I saw a tiny house.

I took one look at the view and was ready to buy, even before we reached the house, but Bill kept saying, "Shut up. If you're gonna buy it, don't tell the owner you like it."

The owner was a cattleman named Ray Cornelius. He put us on horses and we took a ride over the place. Well, after that, I was really sold.

The previous Christmas Eve, Ray and his wife had lost their daughter (who by coincidence had been a classmate of Patti's) in an automobile accident; until then, they'd kept the ranch mostly for her to ride on. Now they no longer wanted it, but they were hesitant to sell the ranch because, they told us, they were afraid it would be taken over by someone who wouldn't love it as much or have as much feeling for it as they did.

Nancy and I said we'd bestow all the love in the world on the ranch, and pretty soon, we sold our land near San Diego and with that money bought Tip Top Ranch.

The ranch, which covered 688 acres, was named Tip Top after a mountain peak that marked a dividing point for rainfall in the Santa Ynez range: Rain that fell on one side flowed toward the Pacific Ocean, rain that fell on the other side drained into the Santa Ynez Valley and then found its way to the ocean.

Nancy and I chose another name, Rancho del Cielo, "Ranch in the Sky," for that's what it was.

The tiny plastered adobe house on the ranch had been built in 1872 and it needed lots of work. On two sides, the previous owners had erected a makeshift screened porch with an ugly corrugated aluminum roof and walls made of green plastic siding. It wasn't very pretty, nor was most of the house itself, which hadn't really been lived in full-time for years and was used mostly by overnighting cattlemen.

We tore out the porch, leaving only the concrete floor, and with the help of a contractor, built a big L-shaped room with a fireplace and big windows all around. The house now had about fifteen hundred square feet, not a big house by some standards, but our new addition and the windows, which opened up wonderful views across the meadow, did wonders in giving it a greater sense of spaciousness.

With the help of Barney Barnett, a retired California highway patrolman who'd been our driver and friend in Los Angeles, and another friend, Dennis LeBlanc, we replaced well-weathered asbestos shingles on the roof with a new roof of simulated Spanish tiles on the main house as well as the new addition, giving it all the look of a nineteenth-century Mexican adobe.

Our bedroom was only nine feet by fourteen feet and before long, Nancy was feeling a little claustrophobic, so Barney and I knocked out a wall and expanded it. (My experience remodeling houses as a fourteen-year-old in Dixon never came in handier.) But we didn't stop there. We got the contractor who had rebuilt the porch to turn the bedroom into an even larger room.

From the first day we saw it, Rancho del Cielo cast a spell over us.

No place before or since has ever given Nancy and me the joy and serenity it does.

Rancho del Cielo can make you feel as if you are on a cloud looking down at the world. From the house we look across the meadow at a peak crowned with oak trees and beyond it, mountains that stretch toward the horizon. From some points on the ranch, you can watch boats cruising across the Santa Barbara Channel, then turn your head and see the Santa Ynez Valley unfold like a huge wilderness amphitheater before your eyes.

When we want to take a horseback ride, we have a choice of at least half a dozen trails, and every time we take a ride, we see something different, discover something new about the ranch.

When I was still in the acting business, I'd bred my horse, Baby, with a dapple gray thoroughbred stallion and she produced a dapple gray mare I named Nancy D because I was courting someone by that name. After Baby got up in years, I trained Nancy D and she became a wonderful hunter and jumper; later on, I bred Baby once more and got a beautiful black colt I named Little Man because he was very large.

I lost Nancy D when she was sixteen with an extreme case of gastroenteritis and then I switched to Little Man, the son of Baby.

A friend of ours, a surgeon who also likes to ride, once told me that when he had a really difficult operation ahead of him, he always got up early in the morning and went for a ride and when he was finished, he felt ready for the operation.

Riding has the same kind of effect on me.

Since the day we bought the ranch, if Nancy or I wanted to think something out, there's been no better place to do it than Rancho del Cielo.

As I've said, there's something about the wild scenery and serenity at the ranch and having a horse between my knees that makes it easier to sort out a problem. I think people who haven't tried it might be surprised at how easily your thoughts can come together when you're on the back of a horse riding with nothing else to do but think about a decision that's ahead of you.

During those first months after we left Sacramento, I spent a lot of time on Little Man riding around the ranch thinking about the future.

My health was excellent and even though I was nearly sixty-five, I didn't feel old and I never gave a thought to retiring. I was getting more requests than ever to speak. Nancy was busy with her Foster Grandparents Program; I had a newspaper column and regular radio spot that gave me a chance to continue speaking out about things that concerned me. We had our home in Pacific Palisades; we could see the children often; we were looking forward to fixing up the ranch and spending more time there.

I think we would have been content to spend the rest of our lives that way.

Yet, hardly a day passed when someone didn't call and ask me to make a run for the Republican presidential nomination in 1976.

These weren't only calls from people in California, but from people all over the country—people I'd met over the years on the speech circuit.

Eight years earlier, I'd been dragged kicking and screaming into politics. But now my opinion about holding public office was different.

I didn't automatically turn a deaf ear to the appeals I was receiving. I had changed, probably, I think, because when I'd been governor I'd felt the excitement and satisfaction that comes from being able to bring about change, not just talk about it.

It had been thrilling and fun and I was proud of what we had accomplished. Yet, the longer I had been governor, the more I realized the biggest problems we had regarding big government had to be solved in Washington, which was gradually but inexorably taking power from the states.

It reminded me of something that James Madison said in 1788: "Since the general civilization of mankind, I believe there are more instances of the abridgement of the freedom of the people by gradual and silent encroachment of those in power than by violent and sudden usurpations."

His friend and neighbor, Thomas Jefferson, thought much the same way. "What has destroyed liberty and the rights of men in every government that has ever existed under the sun?" he asked, and then gave an answer: "The generalizing and concentrating of all cares and powers into one body."

As governor, I'd experienced how the federal bureaucracy had its hand in everything and was "concentrating all cares and power into one body." Washington would establish a new program that the states were supposed to administer, then set so many rules and regulations that the state wasn't really administering it—you were just following orders from Washington. Most of these programs could not only be operated more effectively but more economically under our own laws.

The federal government hadn't created the states; the states had created the federal government. Washington, ignoring principles of the Constitution, was trying to turn the states into nothing more than administrative districts of the federal government. And the path to federal control had, to a large extent, become federal aid. From our schools to our farms, Washington bureaucrats were trying to dictate to Americans what they could or could not do, and were portraying bureaucratic control as the price Americans must pay for federal aid administered from Washington. The money came with strings that reached all the way back to the Potomac.

Usually with the best of intentions, Congress passed a new program, appropriated the money for it, then assigned bureaucrats in Washington to disperse the money; almost always, the bureaucrats responded by telling states, cities, counties, and schools *how* to spend this money.

In Madison's words, Washington was usurping power from the states by the "gradual and silent encroachment of those in power."

In ever greater amounts, federal handouts started cascading to states and communities, often for programs they had no need or desire for, but they took the money because it was *there;* it seemed to be "free."

Over time, they became so dependent on the money that, like junkies, they found it all but impossible to break the habit, and only after they were well addicted to it did they learn how pervasive the federal regulations were that came with the money.

As all this was going on, the federal government was taking an ever-increasing share of the nation's total tax revenues and making it more difficult for states and local governments to raise money on their own; as a result, they had to turn even more to the federal government for financial aid and became the captives of a relentless Washington and its multitude of bureaucracies. In return for federal grants, state and local governments surrendered control of their destiny to a faceless bureaucracy in Washington that claimed to know better how to solve the problems of a city or town than the people who lived there. And if local officials or their congressmen ever tried to end a program they didn't like or they thought was unproductive and wasteful, they discovered that the beneficiaries of the program and the bureaucrats who administered it had formed such a tight alliance that it was all but impossible for elected officials to kill it. Once started, a federal program benefiting *any* group or special interest is virtually impossible to end and the costs go on forever.

We had strayed a great distance from our founding fathers' vision of America: They regarded the central government's responsibility as that of providing national security, protecting our democratic freedoms, and limiting the government's intrusion into our lives—in sum, the protection of life, liberty, and the pursuit of happiness. They never envisioned vast agencies in Washington telling our farmers what to plant, our teachers what to teach, our industries what to build. The Constitution they wrote established sovereign states, not administrative districts of the federal government. They believed in keeping government as close as possible to the people; if parents didn't like the way their schools were being run, they could throw out the Board of Education at the next election; but what could they do about the elite bureaucrats in the U.S. Department of Education who sent ultimatums into their children's classrooms regarding curriculum and textbooks?

Of course, I had been disturbed by the expansion of the federal government and its encroachment on our freedoms for a long time, but the problems increased dramatically during the years I was governor with the start of Lyndon Johnson's "Great Society" and "War on Poverty."

Those years were a watershed in the evolution of our central government that I think many historians have not yet paid sufficient attention to.

Between 1965 and 1980, the federal budget jumped to roughly five times what it had been while the federal deficit grew to fifty-three times as much and the amount of money doled out under various federal "entitlement" programs quadrupled to almost $300 billion a year; along the way, a lot of the decision-making authority traditionally exercised at the grass-roots level of America was transported to Washington.

Yet, as you look back on that myriad of new federal programs, it's hard to find any that did much good for the poor or the nation as a whole.

A lot of the money just got lost in the administrative process. Hundreds of billions were spent on poverty programs, and the plight of the poor grew more painful. They had spent billions on programs that made people worse off.

The waste in dollars and cents was small compared with the waste of human potential. It was squandered by the narcotic of giveaway programs that sapped the human spirit, diminished the incentive of people to work, destroyed families, and produced an increase in female and child poverty, deteriorating schools, and disintegrating neighborhoods.

The liberals had had their turn at bat in the 1960s and they had struck out.

As I rode Little Man around Rancho del Cielo during the spring of 1975, I thought a lot about the lost vision of our founding fathers and the importance of recapturing it and the voices from around the country who were pressing me to run for president. And I remembered something I'd said many years before: A candidate doesn't make the decision whether to run for president; the people make it for him.

31

ALTHOUGH I'D ONCE BROADCAST a University of Michigan football game in which he played, I knew Gerald Ford only slightly before he succeeded Richard Nixon in the White House. He offered me a choice of virtually any position I wanted in his cabinet, but I wanted to complete my second term as governor and said I'd prefer to remain in Sacramento.

After he became president, a number of Republican leaders around the country began urging me to challenge Ford for the party nomination in 1976. Running for the presidency wasn't something I had planned on. But, as I've said, I had always believed a candidate doesn't make the decision whether to run for president, the people make it, the people let you know whether you should run for office. And so, I agreed to go after the nomination, but pledged to follow the Eleventh Commandment and I did.

Senator Paul Laxalt of Nevada, whom I'd gotten to know and like while we were governors of neighboring states, agreed to serve as general chairman of the campaign. The team of political professionals led by Stu Spencer and Bill Roberts, who had helped oversee my campaigns for governor, had already agreed to work for Ford, so to manage the campaign, my supporters brought in John Sears, a well-respected Washington lawyer who had worked in the White House during the Nixon years.

For the primary campaign, we decided on a simple and straightforward strategy: Our attacks would be aimed solely at the Democrats and big government, not Gerald Ford.

Our main theme was that I wasn't part of the Washington establishment—I was an outsider—and therefore I offered voters a clear-cut alternative to the Democrats.

The first time I ran for governor, I had had to overcome the argument that I was an actor without any experience in government. My eight years as governor had taken care of that. Now, in a presidential race, I knew we'd have to confront a different stereotype: the bias many Northeasterners held against Californians—the one that says since California is a land of fruit and nuts, it's a great place if you're an orange.

My theme on the campaign stump was familiar to anyone who had heard me speak over the years: It was time to scale back the size of the federal government, reduce taxes and government intrusion in our lives, balance the budget, and return to the people the freedoms usurped from them by the bureaucrats.

As we set off on the campaign trail, I attempted to tell Americans what we had accomplished in California to reduce waste and welfare abuse, and I proposed returning to states and communities direct control over a variety of federal programs such as welfare, aid-to-education, and housing, along with the taxing power to pay for them.

Our first battleground in the campaign was the New Hampshire primary in late February. I should have spent the weekend before the primary barnstorming New Hampshire, but instead John Sears arranged for us to leave the state and fly to Peoria, where I campaigned for the Illinois primary. Only afterward did friends in New Hampshire tell me that by leaving the state on the eve of the election, I'd sent a message to the voters of New Hampshire that I was taking them for granted, that New Hampshire wasn't important to me.

I lost the primary by fewer than 1,500 votes out of 108,000. We lost Florida, then the primary in Illinois, my home state. After three big losses so early in the campaign, the press began writing off my campaign, along with my political future. But once I'd entered the race, I wanted to see it through.

The North Carolina primary was coming up in late March and I had to pull off a victory there in order to remain a credible candidate. I stumped the state day and night and in a last-ditch effort gambled much of our remaining campaign funds to buy a half hour of airtime to present my case shortly before the election.

The gamble worked. The speech generated enough support for me to turn things around and we won North Carolina; this helped us raise the money needed to keep the campaign alive. After that, I won in Texas, Alabama, Georgia, California, and several other states, which set up a confrontation between Ford and me at the convention in Kansas City.

The votes of 1,140 delegates were needed to win the nomination. As the convention approached, the competition for delegates was nip and tuck and I came under pressure, especially from my more conservative supporters, to go on the attack against Ford.

Although I did make it clear I didn't like some things that had happened under his administration, such as the agreement giving away control of the Panama Canal, which Americans had bought and paid for, it wasn't in me to violate the Eleventh Commandment and I refused to attack Ford personally.

When the balloting was over, I had 1,070 votes—70 votes shy of victory—and Ford had 1,187. The nomination was his. I'd come close, but not close enough. It was a big disappointment because I hate to lose. But I'd always known that challenging an incumbent president was going to be difficult.

Ford's people sent signals to me that I could have the vice-presidential nomination if I wanted it, but for months I'd said I wouldn't consider it. I just wasn't interested in being vice-president.

After the balloting, President Ford called me down to the platform. Nancy and I went and I asked the delegates to make the vote unanimous for Ford and pledged my support for him. It was an exciting and unforgettable evening.

32

AFTER GERALD FORD WON THE NOMINATION in Kansas City, I met with the members of the California delegation and said: "Nancy and I are not going back and sit on our rocking chairs and say, 'That's all for us.' "

Nancy was among those in the room that day with tears in her eyes. She had never tried to influence me, one way or the other, whether I should run for president, but I knew she felt a great sadness for me. She knew how much I hated to lose. In her heart, though, I think Nancy may have felt a sense of relief. Now we could go home and get on with the rest of our lives.

But I think we both knew it wouldn't—couldn't—end in Kansas City. After committing ten years of our lives to what we believed in, I just couldn't walk away and say, "I don't care any more."

After the convention, I campaigned in more than twenty states for President Ford and when he lost to Jimmy Carter, I began writing my newspaper column and radio scripts again and continued to speak out for Republicanism and how we had strayed from the visions of our founding fathers. With contributions left over from the campaign, I established an organization called the Citizens for the Republic to focus attention on these concerns.

After Ford's loss, I knew some of my supporters would begin knocking on my door and urge me to run in 1980, and they did. I told them I wasn't going to make a decision yet.

I wasn't the reluctant candidate I'd been in 1965 and 1976.

I wanted to be president. But I really believed that what happened next wasn't up to me, it was up to the people: If there was a real people's movement to get me to run, then I said I'd do it, but I was going to wait and see.

Paul Laxalt asked if he could put together the nucleus of a campaign organization for 1980 in case I decided to run. I told him I wouldn't object, but it wasn't a commitment. He accepted my terms and tirelessly went to work organizing for a campaign that might never take place.

As this was going on, we picked up the threads of our life in Southern California and enjoyed it very much. After the enforced separation of the campaign, we got to see the children more often. Nancy, always the nest builder, never ceased fixing up and redecorating our house in Pacific Palisades and she kept busy with the Foster Grandparents Program. And we had more time than ever for the ranch and more time for travel. On a trip to England, I bumped into Justin Dart, one of the Californians who'd been in my Kitchen Cabinet, and he said he wanted me to meet a friend of his who had recently been elected the first woman to head the British Conservative Party.

I'd planned on spending only a few minutes with Margaret Thatcher but we ended up talking for almost two hours. I liked her immediately—she was warm, feminine, gracious, and intelligent— and it was evident from our first words that we were soul mates when it came to reducing government and expanding economic freedom. At a reception that evening, an Englishman who had heard about our meeting asked me, "What do you think of our Mrs. Thatcher?"

I said I'd been deeply impressed. "I think she'd make a magnificent prime minister."

He looked at me out of the corners of his eyes with a kind of mocking disdain that seemed to suggest the idea was unthinkable: "My dear fellow, a *woman* prime minister?"

"England once had a queen named Victoria who did rather well," I said.

"By jove," he said, "I'd forgotten all about that."

Of course, it never occurred to me that before many years would pass, Margaret and I would be sitting across from each other as the heads of our respective governments.

· · ·

With each passing month of the Carter administration, I became more concerned about the things that were happening—and not happening—in Washington.

Jimmy Carter had run for the presidency on a platform calling for cuts in defense spending and implementation of what the Democrats called "national economic planning." That meant one thing to me: The Democrats wanted to borrow some of the principles of the Soviets' failed five-year plans, with Washington setting national production goals, deciding where people worked, what they would do, where they would live, what they would produce.

The Democratic platform also called for "fairer distribution of wealth, income, and power"—code words that to me meant a confiscation of the earnings of people in our country who worked and produced, and their redistribution to people who didn't.

I'm sure they meant well—liberals usually do—but our economy was one of the great wonders of the world. It didn't need master planners. It worked because it operated on principles of freedom, millions of people going about their daily business and making free decisions how they wanted to work and live, how they wanted to spend their money, while reaping the rewards of their individual labor.

Our country didn't need social engineers or economic master planners. Our economic system is based on the law of supply and demand and the right of individuals to choose their line of work, their manner of living, where they live and how they live—all so long as they do not impose on the right of others to enjoy the same freedoms.

I also thought the administration was a disaster in the arena of national security. While it was cutting back on our military power, we were losing ground to Communism in much of the globe; the morale of our volunteer army was plummeting; our strategic forces were growing obsolete; and nothing was being done to reduce the threat of a nuclear Armageddon that could destroy much of the world in less than a half hour's time.

There were other serious problems: Unemployment, inflation, and interest rates were climbing and it looked as if administration policies would lead the nation into a serious recession.

But perhaps worst of all, it seemed to me that America was losing faith in itself. Almost every day, the president was sending a message to the American people that America had passed its prime, that Americans were going to have to get used to less in the future, that we should not have the same hopes for the future that we once did, and that we had only ourselves to blame for it.

As the months passed and the problems got worse, I received more and more calls urging me to run for president, and I was edging closer to a decision to run in 1980.

George Bush and several friends visited me in Los Angeles and he told me he expected to run for president in 1980. I suspect that he would have liked me to say I wasn't going to run, but I said, "You know, I haven't made a decision yet myself, but I might be doing that, too."

About the same time, fifteen or so of my most conservative backers asked me to meet with them at the Madison Hotel in Washington. They asked me to run for president as an independent third-party candidate.

Their intention was to launch a full-blown national conservative movement with me at the head of it. Some in the group had made the same pitch four years earlier and I'd turned them down. This time, I told them they were out of their minds. I said the bulk of conservatives in America were Republicans and they wouldn't desert the party for a third party. If I was ever going to make progress in accomplishing the things I believed in, it would have to be within the Republican Party. They wouldn't listen to me, and so I walked out on them.

Some of those conservative diehards have never forgiven me for it. (Later, I learned some of them subsequently held a secret meeting at which they almost convinced Alexander Haig to run against me.)

If I decided to run in 1980, I knew I'd have to deal with two issues in particular: I'd have to show the Easterners who were suspicious of *any* Westerner, but especially Californians, I wasn't an extremist and I'd have to deal with the issue of my age.

If I won in 1980, I would turn seventy shortly after Inauguration Day and become the oldest president in history. (Actually, that birthday would be the thirty-first anniversary of my thirty-ninth birthday. When I turned sixty-five, I'd begun joking, like Jack Benny, that subsequent birthdays marked the anniversary of my thirty-ninth birthday.)

The truth is, I felt thirty-nine or younger. I didn't feel any different or any older than the way I'd *always* felt. But I realized it was inevitable that the press would focus attention on my age.

I'd never taken naps or dyed my hair, but that hadn't stopped reporters from suggesting I did. (The rumor about dyeing my hair, incidentally, started when I was governor. My barber told me that after I left his shop people sometimes came in and asked if they could pick up a strand or two of my hair to see if the roots were gray. I'm the first person I know of who was actually happy when gray hair started growing on his head.)

At the time I was moving closer to a commitment to run in 1980, the sense of anger and frustration over taxes and government regulation I'd first seen on those cross-country tours for General Electric was beginning to boil over at the polls.

In 1978, voters in California passed Proposition 13, slashing property taxes and setting off a taxpayers' revolt across the nation. Five years earlier when I was governor, I'd tried to get a similar measure passed, but it was defeated. It had been ahead of its time. Now, people were rebelling, trying to get government off their back and out of their pocketbooks. That prairie fire I've talked about was really spreading across the land, and it shouldn't have surprised anyone.

Between 1960 and the late 1970s, the federal government payroll had jumped from less than $13 billion to more than $70 billion.

Total federal spending had jumped six times to more than $500 billion; the national debt had almost tripled and was approaching the trillion-dollar mark; during the same period, the country's population had increased only about twenty percent.

People were growing tired of having to work four months of every year just to pay their taxes. Taxes kept rising and the only consistency in the system was that once a tax was imposed, it was never rescinded.

At our factories and workshops, high taxes were discouraging investments in plants and equipment, eroding the productivity of American workers—the best in the world—and obsolete and punitive regulations imposed by government were inhibiting and restricting the dynamic energy of the free market.

After a half century that had given them the New Deal and the "Great Society" and produced a government that took an average of forty-five percent of the national wealth, people were just fed up.

33

I ANNOUNCED MY DECISION TO RUN FOR PRESIDENT in a speech at the New York Hilton Hotel on November 13, 1979. Immediately after the speech, we left on a campaign swing to Washington, New Hampshire, Illinois, and other points. I'm told that en-route to La Guardia Airport, the bus carrying the campaign press corps got lost.

Maybe it was an omen, because the campaign itself didn't get off to a very smooth start.

To manage the campaign, we'd brought in most of the same team from 1976, led by Paul Laxalt as national chairman and John Sears as director of day-to-day operations. Mike Deaver, a close and valued assistant since my Sacramento days, came aboard as a political strategist and chief fund-raiser; Lyn Nofziger, another old hand from Sacramento, was press secretary; and Ed Meese agreed to serve as my advisor on key issues of the campaign.

During the weeks leading up to the speech in New York, serious friction developed among the top players on the team. John Sears began asserting a right to exercise absolute control over the campaign and move aside some of the people who had been with me in California. Although I intervened and stopped an attempt to remove Paul Laxalt as the general chairman of the campaign, John replaced Nofziger with his own man, Jim Lake, as press secretary, and brought in a new advisor on issues, Charles Black, after ousting Martin Anderson, another valued advisor from California.

John resented in particular my closeness to Mike Deaver and Ed Meese and began trying to bump them from the campaign staff. By the end of November, after we'd been on the campaign trail only two weeks or so, there was so much tension and bickering that I decided to call the key players together at my house in Pacific Palisades to see if I could smooth things over.

As soon as they got there, Sears, Jim Lake, and Charles Black, in effect, gave me an ultimatum: Mike Deaver had to go. They said he had too much authority and was often working at cross purposes to what they wanted to accomplish in the campaign. This put me in the position of having to choose between Mike and the three of them, but before I could say anything, Mike spoke up:

"Look, if it comes down to a choice between me and John, I don't believe you can afford to lose John, and I'll leave."

With that, Mike stood up and walked out of the living room. He had helped bring John Sears on to the team and believed in his capabilities completely and was willing to sacrifice himself.

I ran after Mike and caught up with him at the front door and tried to persuade him to stay. But he said, "No, Governor, you need John Sears more than you need me."

When I returned to the living room, I was very upset. "Damn it," I said, "you've just driven away someone who's probably a better man than the three of you are."

With Mike gone, the friction on the staff began to subside—for a while—and the campaign began to pick up steam.

When I'd announced my decision to run for the Republican presidential nomination, the field was already crowded; with seven candidates already in the race, it promised to be a *long* campaign.

As I had in 1976, I told my campaign staff that I intended to abide by the Eleventh Commandment: I'd attack only Democrats while trying to let the voters know where I stood.

I figured I would deal with the skepticism that some Northeasterners had about me simply by showing myself to them, answering their questions, and letting them hear what I had to say.

I had never regarded the question of my age as an important or pivotal issue, but I couldn't ignore it, and to show voters and the press that I was as vigorous as anyone, we kept a dawn-till-darkness schedule of campaigning that usually had members of the traveling press corps complaining of fatigue before anyone else;

there were a lot of nights when I'd walk down the darkened aisle of the campaign plane after a day on the stump, and everybody would be asleep but me. (When one of my supporters quipped I was the "oldest and *wisest*" candidate in the race, I didn't mind.)

I learned a lot about how the national press corps covered a presidential campaign. As far as I could tell, when we started out on the campaign trail each morning, the goal of many of the reporters traveling with us was simply to catch me fouling up my speech or to trap me into a minor error about an obscure or inconsequential topic that had nothing to do with the substance of the campaign. Then, satisfied, most would run off in a pack and report the identical story about a minor goof, while ignoring other, important things that were said during the day and neglecting the kind of beneath-the-surface digging that could have shed more light on the campaign and the differences between the various candidates. I thought it was all pretty superficial.

Until 1976, the New Hampshire primary, usually held in mid-February, was considered the first test of a presidential candidate's strength every four years. But that year Jimmy Carter came out of nowhere and made himself a credible candidate by getting a majority of the votes during a one-day canvas of party members held in communities throughout Iowa a few weeks before the New Hampshire primary.

As a result, by 1980, the first battleground in the presidential contest was considered the Iowa caucuses, which were scheduled for January 21.

John Sears said polls indicated I had a comfortable lead in Iowa, where a lot of people still remembered me from my radio days, and so I didn't have to campaign much there. He kept me out of a debate sponsored by the *Des Moines Register and Tribune* that most of the candidates agreed to, and we ended up making only a handful of token appearances there instead of trying to visit all the communities in Iowa where they were going to have those meetings.

Well, as we discovered, it was a big mistake.

George Bush practically lived in Iowa before the caucuses (something I should have done) and he won the caucuses by a narrow margin.

This loss was a real shocker and a big disappointment to me.

Even after all those years in Hollywood, I'd thought of Iowa as my adopted home state. Although a lot of years had gone by since I'd lived there, I considered myself a transplanted Iowan and had really expected to win. But we'd made the mistake of taking Iowa for granted; in a way, it was the 1976 New Hampshire primary all over again.

The day after the caucuses, most of the pundits agreed that by upsetting me George Bush now had the momentum to win the nomination—the "Big Mo," as George called it.

Suddenly for me the New Hampshire primary on February 26 loomed as a do-or-die contest. If Bush could beat me there, I knew —and everybody else on our team knew—it would be extremely difficult to ever get the campaign on a winning track.

The Iowa caucuses reminded me too much of my loss in New Hampshire four years earlier, when I'd left the state on the eve of the primary because of the advice I was ahead in the polls and didn't need to campaign there anymore.

Well, this time, I decided, we weren't going to make the same mistake again. I knew I had relied too much on the advice of Sears instead of my own instincts and had to take more direct control of the campaign.

I brought everybody together and said we were going to work our tails off in New Hampshire—and we did.

Day after day, we traveled the snow-splattered highways of the state from early in the morning to late at night; I'd speak to anyone who was willing to listen to me, then we'd get back in our convoy of cars and buses and drive someplace else and seldom get to bed before midnight.

I think the loss in Iowa had really whipped up my competitive fires, and I didn't want to lose again.

As I've said, I have often wondered at how our lives can turn on what seem like small or inconsequential events, like my losing the job at Montgomery Ward.

That winter, a brief and seemingly small event, one lasting only a few seconds, occurred in a high school gymnasium in Nashua, New Hampshire, and I think it helped take me to the White House.

34

IN THE FINAL DAYS before the election in New Hampshire, I think almost everybody except the other candidates agreed that the primary had settled down to a race between George Bush and myself, with Bush the front runner.

When the *Nashua Telegraph* offered to sponsor a debate between the two of us on the Saturday evening preceding the election, we both accepted. Understandably, this brought howls from the other candidates. In protest, one of them, Senator Bob Dole, complained to the Federal Elections Commission that by financing a debate between only two of the seven candidates, the newspaper was making an illegal campaign contribution to the Bush and Reagan campaigns.

The commission agreed with him. Rather than scrap the scheduled debate, we suggested to the Bush camp that the two of us split the cost of holding it. After the Bush people turned down our proposal, we offered to pay the full cost of the debate—a few thousand dollars—and they accepted.

I thought it had been unfair to exclude from the debate the other candidates, most of whom were also campaigning in New Hampshire that weekend, and since we were now sponsoring and paying for it, I decided to invite them to join the debate; four of the other candidates—Bob Dole, Howard Baker, John Anderson, and Phil Crane (John Connally was campaigning elsewhere)—accepted.

When we walked on to a platform set up for the debate at the Nashua High School gymnasium Saturday night, there was one table, two chairs, and six candidates.

When he spotted the four other candidates, Jim Baker, George Bush's campaign manager, protested and said George would not participate in the debate as long as they were part of it.

Since I had invited them, I couldn't go along with him and exclude the other candidates, so we were at an impasse, a strange, awkward impasse.

George just sat frozen in his chair, not saying anything; I sat in the other chair with the four other candidates standing behind me, looking embarrassed in front of two or three thousand people while being literally told they had to leave.

Unable to understand what was going on, the audience hooted and hollered and urged us to proceed.

I decided I should explain to the crowd what the delay was all about and started to speak.

But as I did, an editor of the Nashua newspaper shouted to the sound man, *"Turn Mr. Reagan's microphone off."*

Well, I didn't like that—we were paying the freight for the debate and he was acting as if his newspaper was still sponsoring it—and so I turned to him, with the microphone still on, and said the first thing that came to my mind: *"I am paying for this microphone, Mr. Breen."*

Well, for some reason my words hit the audience, whose emotions were already worked up, like a sledgehammer. The crowd roared and just went wild.

I may have won the debate, the primary—and the nomination— right there. After the debate, our people told me the gymnasium parking lot was littered with Bush-for-President badges.

During the weeks following the Iowa caucuses when I'd been trying to make a comeback, the bickering, tension, and morale problems on our staff because of John Sears's efforts to exert total control over the campaign had reached a boiling point again.

I thought Sears was smart and talented, but he became angry if I spoke to anyone but him about campaign affairs and he kept pressing me to fire Ed Meese and other people on the staff whom I thought highly of. And I guess I still hadn't forgiven him for what John had done to Mike Deaver, and so as election day approached, I decided enough was enough.

The morale problem and bickering wasn't our campaign's only problem: We had been spending money at such a rate we were in danger of exceeding limits established by federal election laws, which meant we might not have enough left for important primaries later in the spring.

A change was necessary at the top of the campaign staff. I knew I had to do it before the results were in from New Hampshire because if I lost and then fired Sears, people could say I was trying to make him the scapegoat for my loss, and I didn't want that to happen.

So, on the day that New Hampshire voters were going to the polls, I invited John, Jim Lake, and Charles Black to my hotel room and I asked them to resign. They took it well and I think they understood why the changes were necessary.

I had already asked Bill Casey, a former chairman of the Securities and Exchange Commission whom I'd met while campaigning in New York City, to take over as campaign director, straighten out our finances, and assure we didn't run out of money prematurely; Ed Meese became chief of staff in charge of day-to-day campaign operations; and soon Mike Deaver, Lyn Nofziger, and Martin Anderson rejoined our team. Later on, Stu Spencer also became a part of the leadership group.

Several hours after the meeting in the hotel room, the polls closed and I learned I had won the seven-way New Hampshire primary with fifty-one percent of the vote.

In retrospect, this was really the pivotal day of the whole primary campaign for me. From then on, with the management changes we had made, the campaign ran smoothly and the victory in New Hampshire gave us a momentum that helped me win all but a few of the remaining primaries that spring.

Shortly after New Hampshire, all the candidates except George Bush dropped out, and then, near the end of May, he dropped out, too.

In early July, when Nancy and I arrived at the Republican National Convention in Detroit, it appeared I had more than enough delegate votes to win the nomination and the next thing on my agenda was choosing a running mate.

Even before we landed in Detroit, a number of party leaders and members of my own team such as Paul Laxalt had been talking up the possibility of asking Gerald Ford to run with me as the vice-presidential candidate. By the opening day of the convention, the idea had really taken on a momentum and everyone was calling it a "dream ticket."

An ex-president, of course, had never run for vice-president before, but we had been through an unusual time in history, and I said I was in favor of it.

Members of our campaign team began quietly discussing the idea with Ford and some of the people close to him, and for a while it looked like the plan would fly. Then Paul Laxalt and some of the other people in our camp began coming back from the meetings with word there might be some problems with the dream ticket.

Some of Ford's advisors were pushing for him to become a kind of "copresident" with responsibilities in foreign affairs and other areas much broader than those normally assigned a vice-president.

After news of our secret negotiations leaked out, Gerald Ford spoke to Walter Cronkite on CBS and during the interview hinted at some of the things that his people were proposing and said that if the plan went through, he expected to play a significant role with me in making White House decisions; well, as I watched the interview, it really hit me that we had some major problems with the idea: *Wait a minute*, I remember thinking, *this is really two presidents he's talking about.*

The talks continued for a few more hours, but that night Ford came to my suite and said, "Look, this isn't gonna work."

Until this point, I had still thought there might be a way of working something out. Although I never envisioned him sharing in decisions and wouldn't have accepted it if that had been proposed to me, I thought there might be assignments he could handle that would take advantage of his experience and prestige as a former president.

But, when he came to my suite, he took himself out of consideration.

Because he was a former president, he said his advisors believed it would be appropriate for him to take on responsibilities beyond those normally given to a vice-president. But he said he knew from his own experience in the White House the country couldn't operate with two presidents.

For several days, I had expected Ford to be on the ticket and I hadn't given much thought to other candidates; now I had to choose a running mate and time was of the essence. The delegates were waiting for me at the Joe Louis Arena to announce my decision.

The obvious choice was George Bush. We had been through a competitive and sometimes rough primary battle, but I had always liked him personally and had a great respect for his abilities and breadth of experience; and I knew he had a lot of support within the party.

George and Barbara Bush were upstairs in the hotel. A few moments after Gerald Ford left my suite, I called Bush and said:

"George, it seems to me that the fellow who came the closest and got the next most votes for president ought to be the logical choice for vice-president. Will you take it?"

George jumped at it without a moment's hesitation and said he would be pleased to be on the ticket.

"Okay," I said, "I'm going to get in the car and go over to the convention right now and tell the people that you're my choice."

When I announced my decision to the throng of delegates crowded into the arena, they rose to their feet with a tremendous roar. The roof almost came off. As George and I stood there together, it was almost as if we were putting the party back together again. I then asked the delegates to join me in a silent prayer.

Now George and I faced a challenge together: beating Jimmy Carter and Walter Mondale.

35

As the campaign for the presidency got under way late that summer in 1980, Americans for a second year in a row were trying to cope with the ruthless effects of double-digit inflation, which was eating away at their savings, their paychecks, and their way of life like a horde of locusts. Interest rates were over fifteen percent, depriving millions of American families of a chance to buy a home; in countless communities, the unemployment rate, like inflation and interest rates, was in double digits.

Militarily, our nation was seriously in danger of falling behind the Soviet Union at a time a former naval officer was holding the watch as Commander in Chief. The Soviets were modernizing their fleet and their ground and air forces on a massive scale. Yet on any given day, I was told as many as half the ships in our navy couldn't leave port because of a lack of spare parts or crew and half our military aircraft couldn't fly for lack of spare parts; the overwhelming majority of our military enlisted personnel were high school dropouts.

Abroad, the Soviet Union was engaged in a brutal war in Afghanistan and Communism was extending its tentacles deep into Central America and Africa. In Iran, more than fifty Americans had been held captive for almost a year under the regime of a vicious religious despot who had risen to power while an old and loyal ally of the United States had been forced from power and our country had done nothing to help him.

I made a decision not to criticize President Carter regarding Iran. I knew anything I might say could interfere with efforts to free the hostages. Being governor had taught me that sometimes there are things going on that only the top person in the government knows about, and I thought it was best for me to keep quiet; there might be something going on I didn't know about.

But I wasn't happy with the events in Iran. The sudden emergence of fanatic Islamic fundamentalism as a political force in the Middle East was a development that would have posed a difficult challenge to any Western leader concerned with our strategic interests there. It wasn't an easy situation for Carter to deal with, and he couldn't be faulted for the awakening of this dark and fanatical force.

But I felt that by standing by and failing to come up with a viable alternative to deal with the crisis when the Shah of Iran was forced from power in early 1979, the Carter administration had sown the seeds of the foreign policy disaster that would later engulf it.

I was told by officials of the Shah's government that after rioting began in the streets of Teheran in 1979, the Shah's advisors told him if they were allowed to arrest five hundred people—the most corrupt businessmen and officials in the government—the revolutionary fires could be extinguished, and they could head off the revolution.

But people in the American Embassy told the Shah to do nothing, and he didn't. Until the very end, he kept telling his staff, "The United States has always been our friend and it won't let me down now." Well, he took our advice on how to respond to the mobs and when he had to flee his country, the United States didn't even want to let him in for the medical care that he desperately needed. It was terrible treatment for a man who had been our friend and solid ally for more than thirty-five years.

Yes, there had been serious human rights abuses under the Shah. But he had done many good and progressive things for his country; he had brought it into the twentieth century, and in the years preceding his downfall, the Shah had begun to tolerate dissent to his policies and try to stamp out the corruption that was so prevalent in his country that had made it ripe for revolution.

Our government's decision to stand by piously while he was forced from office led to the establishment of a despotic regime in

Teheran that was far more evil and far more tyrannical than the one it replaced. And, as I was to learn through personal experience, it left a legacy of problems that would haunt our country for years to come.

During the summer and fall of 1980, there were many problems facing our nation: the tragic neglect of our military establishment, high unemployment and an ailing economy, the continuing expansion of Communism abroad, the taking of the hostages in Iran.

But to me none was more serious than the fact America had lost faith in itself.

We were told there was a "malaise" in our nation and America was past its prime; we had to get used to less, and the American people were responsible for the problems we faced.

We were told we would have to lower our expectations; America would never again be as prosperous or have as bright a future as it once had.

Well, I disagreed with that.

Yes, we had problems in 1980, a lot of them of our own making in Washington. But I disagreed with those who said that the solution was to give up and be satisfied with less. I saw no national malaise. I found nothing wrong with the American people.

We had to recapture our dreams, our pride in ourselves and our country, and regain that unique sense of destiny and optimism that had always made America different from any other country in the world.

If I could be elected president, I wanted to do what I could to bring about a spiritual revival in America.

I believed—and I intended to make it a theme of my campaign—that America's greatest years were ahead of it, that we had to look at the things that had made it the greatest, richest, and most progressive country on earth in the first place, decide what had gone wrong, and then put it back on course.

In September, Nancy and I rented a lovely home in the Virginia hunt country an hour or so from Washington called Wexford, once owned by Jacqueline Onassis, to serve as our base of operations while I stumped the country in the final weeks of the campaign.

On those rare days when we weren't on the campaign trail, I was able to ride across the lovely green hills and mentally sort out the problems we faced at the time.

Obviously, no one could take the challenge of defeating an incumbent president lightly. Although public opinion polls indicated Americans were fed up with the leadership in the White House, by then I had had enough experience in politics to realize that no one, least of all the candidate, should take anything for granted.

I tried to focus the campaign on the things that had gone wrong in America during the previous four years, especially regarding the economy, and to present my vision of how, working together, we as a people could get our country back on track again and advance it toward the fulfillment of its destiny.

Carter took a low road of personal attacks on my character. Because I said I believed states should be allowed to regain the rights and powers granted to them in the Constitution, he implied I was a racist pandering to Southern voters; because I opposed Senate ratification of the SALT II treaty in the belief it had serious weaknesses that would leave the Soviets with a dangerous preponderance of nuclear weapons—I wanted true arms *reduction*—Carter went around the country suggesting I was a warmonger who, if elected, would destroy the world.

I think the voters saw through these false and often mean-spirited personal attacks; I do know that they made me even more anxious to beat him. Nothing has ever aroused me more than competing against someone who I think isn't fighting fairly.

During the 1976 campaign, Carter had come up with what he called the "misery index" to attack Gerald Ford. He'd added together the rates of inflation and unemployment (it had come to something like twelve percent), called it the misery index, and claimed no man responsible for giving the country a misery index that high had a right to even ask to be president. Well, he didn't mention the misery index in 1980, probably because it was then more than twenty percent.

I was anxious to get Carter into a nationally televised debate, but his people wouldn't go for it. In late September, John Anderson, who was running as an independent candidate, and I had a televised debate in Baltimore but Carter stayed out of it. Stu Spencer said that if we kept challenging him to a debate, sufficient public pressure would eventually build up on him and he would be forced into a debate; but from our point of view, the timing of the debate was critical: The closer it was to election day, the more impact it would have.

When Carter finally agreed to a debate, the date was set for October 28, one week before the election, and we were delighted. The debate went well for me and may have turned on only four little words.

They popped out of my mouth after Carter claimed that I had once opposed Medicare benefits for Social Security recipients.

It wasn't true and I said so:

"There you go again . . . "

I think there was some pent-up anger in me over Carter's claims that I was a racist and warmonger. Just as he'd distorted my view on states' rights and arms control, he had distorted it regarding Medicare, and my response just burst out of me spontaneously.

The audience loved it and I think Carter added to the impact of the words by looking a little sheepish on the television screen.

To me, the finish of the debate was probably more significant: In my closing statement, I asked people if they thought they were better off now than they had been four years earlier. If they were, I said they should vote for my opponent; if not, I said I thought they'd agree with me that it was time for a change.

After a final week of campaigning, Nancy and I returned to Los Angeles for election day and to await the people's decision. It was our tradition to have dinner on election night with a small group of old friends at the home of Earle Jorgensen, who'd been a member of my Kitchen Cabinet in Sacramento, and then drive over to our campaign headquarters to wait out the returns.

Late that afternoon, I was in the shower, getting cleaned up for the evening, when Nancy, who'd already taken her bath and was wrapped in a towel, came into the bathroom and shouted above the drizzle of the shower water that I was wanted on the telephone.

"It's Jimmy Carter," she said.

I turned off the water and got out of the shower and dried off a little, then grabbed an extension phone in the bathroom while Nancy stood beside me.

After listening for a few minutes, I said, "Thank you, Mr. President."

Then I hung up the phone and looked at Nancy and said, "He conceded. He said he wanted to congratulate me."

Instinctively, she gave me a big hug and I hugged her.

The polls in California wouldn't even close for another two hours. But standing in my bathroom with a wrapped towel around me, my hair dripping with water, I had just learned I was going to be the fortieth president of the United States.

PART TWO

The First Year
A New Beginning

This photo of me with my parents and my brother, Neil, was taken in Tampico, the small town in Illinois where I was born. My "Dutch boy" haircut encouraged my father to call me "the Dutchman." I later shortened it to "Dutch."

2

Our first house in Dixon. Years later, when I returned for a visit, I was amazed at how small the rooms were.

The Dixon High School football team—when I was a freshman and still five foot three and just over 108 pounds. I'm the fourth from the left on the bottom row; my brother is third from the right in the last row.

4

The Eureka College swimming team,
which I helped create; I was coach and
captain. The picture below shows me in
the uniform I wore as a lifeguard at Lowell
Park in Dixon, a job I had each summer
for seven years.

4a

In Hollywood. Once I learned Warner Brothers was going to renew my first contract, I asked my parents to join me and I bought them the first house they had ever owned.

6

One of the benefits of my success in Hollywood was being invited, along with my mother, to visit Dixon for the annual Petunia Festival.

This picture was taken in the early fifties, with Nancy, my mother, and Nancy's parents, Dr. and Mrs. Loyal Davis.

The birth of our children, Patti and Ron, brought much joy into our lives.

9

10

Here I am on Nancy D, Baby's daughter, which I named after a
young lady I was dating at the time. The pictures were taken at
our ranch in Malibu, which we subsequently had to sell when I
ran for governor.

12

Nancy and I spent many hours crisscrossing the nation during the 1980 campaign. I was rewarded with a big kiss on inauguration day. Nancy was also at my side when I returned to the White House after being shot in the spring of 1981.

15

The lowest point during my eight years in Washington was the day when 241 Marines lost their lives during the bombing of our Marine barracks in Beirut. One of the things about being president I never got used to was consoling the families of men and women who died in the service of their country, something that was necessary far too many times during my terms in office, including (below) the tragic troop carrier crash in Greenland in 1985 and (above, right) the bombing of the *U.S.S. Stark* in 1987.

17

16

On the fortieth anniversary of the Normandy landing, Nancy and I visited the graves of the thousands of American soldiers who died on D day.

18

Prime Minister Eugenia Charles of Dominica, a truly great lady, was one of the Caribbean leaders who asked us to conduct our successful rescue operation on Grenada.

It was at the Williamsburg economic summit in 1983 that I was asked: "Tell us about the American miracle." Left to right: Prime Minister Pierre Trudeau, President of the Commission of the European Economic Community Gaston Thorn, Chancellor Helmut Kohl, President François Mitterrand, President Ronald Reagan, Prime Minister Yasuhiro Nakasone, Prime Minister Margaret Thatcher, President Allesandro Pertini.

Nancy and I at Rancho del Cielo. I'm proud of the fact that I built the dock we're sitting on and that fence across the pond.

36

SHORTLY BEFORE NOON on January 20, 1981, Nancy and I left Blair House, the Washington guest house for visiting heads of state, and were driven through the gates of the White House and up to the North Portico.

Jimmy and Rosalynn Carter were waiting for us, and a few minutes later, by tradition, he and I got in one car and Nancy and Mrs. Carter got in another for the drive to the inaugural ceremonies.

As we drove up Pennsylvania Avenue, the limousine was very quiet. The president and I were seated side by side. Although he was polite, he said hardly a word to me as we moved slowly toward the Capitol, and I think he hesitated to look me in the face.

Perhaps he felt drained after having been up most of the previous night trying to complete negotiations to free the hostages in Iran. Whatever the reason, the atmosphere in the limousine was as chilly as it had been at the White House a few days before when Nancy and I had gone there to see for the first time the rooms where we would be living. We'd expected the Carters to give us a tour of the family quarters, but they had made a quick exit and turned us over to the White House staff.

At the time, Nancy and I took this as an affront. It seemed rude. But eight years later I think we could sense a little of how President Carter must have felt that day—to have served as president, to have been through the intense highs and lows of the job, to have tried to do what he thought was right, to have had all the farewells and good-bye parties, and then to be forced out of the White House by a vote of the people. . . . It must have been very hard on him. One of the great things about America is how smoothly we transfer presidential power, but after having lived in the White House, and having left it, I can understand how sad it must have been for Jimmy and Rosalynn Carter that day.

For the first time, the inauguration was being held on the west side of the Capitol. When we arrived, tens of thousands of people were already waiting on the Capitol grounds and streaming down the Mall in a great river of humanity. Flags and bunting were everywhere. In the distance above the people was the glittering white column of the Washington Monument and, beyond it, at the far end of the Mall, the Lincoln Memorial sparkled under the overcast sky like a beautiful diamond. Off to one side I could see the soft white dome of the Jefferson Memorial.

Those monuments, all those people—it was an unforgettable sight.

George Bush was sworn in as vice president and then it was my turn. As I took my place, the sun burst through the clouds in an explosion of warmth and light. I felt its heat on my face as I took the oath of office with my hand on my mother's Bible opened to the seventh chapter, fourteenth verse of Second Chronicles: "If my people, which are called by my name, shall humble themselves, and pray, and seek my face, and turn from their wicked ways; then will I hear from heaven, and will forgive their sin, and will heal their land."

Next to these words my mother—God rest her soul—had written: "A most wonderful verse for the healing of the nations."

Because it was on the minds of so many Americans, I devoted a good deal of my inaugural address to the state of our economy:

The economic ills we suffer have come upon us over several decades. They will not go away in days, weeks or months, but they will go away. They will go away because we as Americans have the capacity now, as we've had in the past, to do whatever needs to be done to preserve this last and greatest bastion of freedom. In the present crisis, government is not the solution to our problems; government is the problem. From time to time we've been tempted to believe that society has become too complex to be managed by self-rule, that government by an elite group is superior to government for, by, and of the people. Well, if no one among us is capable of governing himself, then who among us has the capacity to govern someone else? All of us together, in and out of government, must bear the burden . . . it is my intention to curb the size and influence of the federal establishment and to demand recognition of the distinction between the powers granted to the federal government and those reserved to the states or to the people; all of us need to be reminded that the federal government did not create the states, the states created the federal government . . . in the days ahead I will propose removing the roadblocks that have slowed our economy and reduced productivity. Steps will be taken aimed at restoring the balance between the various levels of government.

Progress may be slow, measured in inches and feet, not miles, but we will progress. It is time to reawaken this industrial giant, to get government back within its means, and to lighten our punitive tax burden. And these will be our first priorities, and on these principles there will be no compromise. . . .

My inaugural address ended the ceremonies and we went into the Capitol for lunch with members of Congress and other guests. On the way to lunch, I stopped in a room in the Capitol called the President's Room and performed my first official act as president: I signed an executive order removing price controls on oil and gasoline, my first effort to liberate the economy from excess government regulation.

At lunch, I was able to announce that President Carter's efforts to free the fifty-two Americans held hostage for 444 days in Iran had been successful, and that the plane carrying the hostages had just crossed the border and was no longer in Iranian airspace. Jimmy Carter was already on his way home to Georgia, and my heart went out to him: I wished he had had the chance to make that announcement.

After lunch, we drove back to Pennsylvania Avenue and took our seats on a temporary grandstand that had been set up on the front lawn of the White House. From there we watched the inaugural parade. One of the bands was from Dixon High School, and for a moment or two I had a vision of the school, the main street in Dixon, Lowell Park, the lush cliffs overlooking the Rock River.

Then, with the parade over, Nancy and I headed toward the front door of the White House.

With its iron-grille fence and acres of green lawn, the big white mansion had had a mystical, almost religious aura for me since I was a child. I had first visited there when Harry Truman was president as part of a delegation of motion-picture labor leaders and then had come back when I was governor, when Lyndon Johnson and later Richard Nixon were president. But nothing had prepared me or Nancy for the emotion we felt the first time we entered the White House as its legal residents.

We walked through the front door, entering what's called the State Floor—the section of the White House that is open to public tours—and then the two of us took an elevator to the second floor, to the rooms where we would be living.

When the doors of the elevator closed behind us, we stood in a huge, long hall with a very high ceiling that extended almost the full length of the White House. On the west side of this hall, through an archway, we could see our new living room, and amazingly, our furniture from California was already there, welcoming us with a warm familiarity; it was the first example of the kind of minor miracle we later came to take for granted from the White House staff.

I think it was only then, as Nancy and I walked hand in hand down the great Central Hall, that it hit home that I was president. We'd had the election, the election-night parties, the weeks of planning for my administration, the hours spent choosing a cabinet, then the pomp of the inaugural ceremony. But it was only at this moment that I appreciated the enormity of what had happened to me.

Maybe it was just recognizing our own furniture in the White House that did it. Maybe it had something to do with being reminded of my childhood by the Dixon High marching band. The depth of the emotion we felt at that moment is hard to describe. It packed a wallop that made both of us misty-eyed.

For so long, I had shared the reverence most Americans have for that historic building; back when I was a kid in Dixon, I'd imagined what the private part of the White House must be like; but I had never imagined myself actually living there. Now, we had gone in the front door, gotten on an elevator, and we were here to stay—at least for four years.

If I could do this, I thought, then truly any child in America had an opportunity to do it.

Still walking hand in hand, Nancy and I examined the rooms on the second floor that were to be our new home. We could almost feel the presence of those who had lived here before—Roosevelt, Truman, Eisenhower, Wilson, and others, especially Lincoln, whose bedroom was furnished exactly as it had been during the period when he lived in the White House. In it was a large, oversize wooden bedstead that Lincoln's wife, Mary, was having made for her husband at the time he was assassinated; he'd died without ever returning to the White House. Next to the Lincoln bedroom, with an entrance opposite the grand staircase, was the Treaty Room, its walls lined with historic treaties and documents, including the Emancipation Proclamation. Off the great center hall of the family quarters, on the south side, was the formal living room, a thirty-by-forty-foot oval room opening onto the Truman Balcony.

Even though we were faced with having to get into formal dress for the evening's inaugural festivities, Nancy and I couldn't escape a feeling of unreality as we went from room to room.

Later, I peeked into the Oval Office as its official occupant for the first time. I felt a weight come down on my shoulders, and I said a prayer asking God's help in my new job.

That evening, we almost danced our feet off at ten different inaugural balls held all over the city of Washington. Then Nancy and I spent our first night in the White House.

The next day, the celebrating was over and it was down to work. I had come to Washington with my mind set on a program and I was anxious to get started on it.

37

I DON'T KNOW WHAT I EXPECTED, but my first morning in the Oval Office had a surprising ring of familiarity to it. It reminded me a lot of my job as governor. On my desk was a schedule of appointments for the day; there were meetings with the cabinet, staff, and legislators; and outside my door were Ed Meese, Mike Deaver, and others who had been with me in Sacramento. There was another similarity: Just as I'd come to Sacramento when the state was facing its worst financial crisis in decades, I was arriving in the White House as the country was experiencing what many economists called its greatest economic emergency since the Great Depression.

The most immediate priority was dealing with double-digit inflation, high unemployment, and a prime interest rate of 21.5 percent, the highest since the Civil War.

As I've said, I believed that policies of the federal government reaching back for decades were mostly responsible for the problems. Although I knew we couldn't turn things around overnight, I wanted to begin reversing those mistakes, and now I had a chance to try to do it. With my advisors, I had begun working on an economic recovery plan the first day after the election. The morning after inauguration day, at our first cabinet meeting, and at a meeting the following day of a team of specialists I had appointed to coordinate economic policy, we began the job of implementing the plan.

Its basis was tax reform—reducing federal income tax rates from top to bottom. Simply put, I believed that if we cut tax rates and reduced the proportion of our national wealth that was taken by Washington, the economy would receive a stimulus that would bring down inflation, unemployment, and interest rates, and there would be such an expansion of economic activity that in the end there would be a net increase in the amount of revenue to finance the important functions of government.

Excessive tax *rates* were at the heart of the problem. Back in the fourteenth century, a Muslim philosopher named Ibn Khaldoon wrote something about taxes in ancient Egypt: "At the beginning of the dynasty taxation yields a large revenue from small assessments. At the end of the dynasty, taxation yields a small revenue from large assessments." In other words, when rates were low, the revenue was great; when rates were high, the revenue was low.

During the 1980 campaign, a new term, *supply-side economics,* came into vogue. People said I embraced this theory, and several economists claimed credit for inventing its principles, which they said I had then adopted as the basis for my economic recovery program.

To set the record straight, that wasn't true.

At Eureka College, my major was economics, but I think my own experience with our tax laws in Hollywood probably taught me more about practical economic theory than I ever learned in a classroom or from an economist, and my views on tax reform did not spring from what people called supply-side economics.

At the peak of my career at Warner Bros., I was in the ninety-four percent tax bracket; that meant that after a certain point, I received only six cents of each dollar I earned and the government got the rest. The IRS took such a big chunk of my earnings that after a while I began asking myself whether it was worth it to keep on taking work. Something was wrong with a system like that: When you have to give up such a large percentage of your income in taxes, incentive to work goes down. You don't say, "I've got to do more pictures," you say, "I'm not gonna work for six cents on the dollar." If I decided to do one less picture, that meant other people at the studio in lower tax brackets wouldn't work as much either; the effect filtered down, and there were fewer total jobs available. I remember one scene in the Knute Rockne picture that had only a farmer and a horse in it: Shooting it on location created work for seventy people.

The same principle that affected my thinking applied to people in all tax brackets: The more government takes in taxes, the less incentive people have to work. What coal miner or assembly-line worker jumps at the offer of overtime when he knows Uncle Sam is going to take sixty percent or more of his extra pay?

And the principle applies as well to corporations and small businesses: When government confiscates half or more of their profits, the motivation to maximize profits goes down, and owners and managers make decisions based disproportionately on a desire to avoid taxes; they begin looking for tax shelters and loopholes that contribute nothing to the growth of our economy. Their companies don't grow as fast, they invest less in new plants and equipment, and they hire fewer people.

Any system that penalizes success and accomplishment is wrong. Any system that discourages work, discourages productivity, discourages economic progress, is wrong.

If, on the other hand, you reduce tax rates and allow people to spend or save more of what they earn, they'll be more industrious; they'll have more incentive to work hard, and money they earn will add fuel to the great economic machine that energizes our national progress. The result: more prosperity for all—and more revenue for government.

A few economists call this principle supply-side economics. I just call it common sense.

I have always thought of government as a kind of organism with an insatiable appetite for money, whose natural state is to grow forever unless you do something to starve it. By cutting taxes, I wanted not only to stimulate the economy but to curb the growth of government and reduce its intrusion into the economic life of the country.

By the way, that philosopher, Khaldoon, and I weren't alone in believing lower tax rates result in higher revenues for government. In 1962, President John F. Kennedy said, "Our true choice is not between tax reduction on the one hand and avoidance of large federal deficits on the other; it is increasingly clear that no matter what party is in power, as long as our national security needs keep rising, an economy hampered by restrictive tax rates will never produce enough revenues to balance the budget—just as it will never produce enough jobs or enough profits. In short, the paradoxical truth is that the tax rates are too high today and tax revenues are too low and the soundest way to raise revenues in the long run is to cut rates now."

Fortunately, our party won a majority in the Senate in the 1980 election. But I knew we faced a Democratic majority in the House of Representatives that had a very different view about cutting the tax rates and reducing the role of government.

In Sacramento, I learned through experience that it was important to develop an effective working relationship with my opponents in the legislature, our political disagreements notwithstanding. A few days after the inauguration, I invited Tip O'Neill, the Speaker of the House, over to see me in the White House.

He was full of Irish warmth, a great storyteller, and I liked him. But it was evident he had come to the Oval Office to set me straight on how things operated in Washington.

"You're in the big leagues now," he said.

I felt that my eight years as governor of one of the largest states in the union hadn't exactly been the minor leagues. I told him I thought I'd been in the big leagues for quite a while.

We agreed that since we were going to have to do business with each other, we should try our best to get along. Still, Tip didn't try to hide the fact that he thought I had come to Washington to dismantle everything he believed in—things he and other liberals had spent decades fighting for, starting with the New Deal.

As far as he was concerned, I was the enemy. I guess from his point of view, he was right.

My experience in Sacramento taught me that many liberal legislators believed in their cause with an almost religious zeal and were prepared to play hardball—and other games—to further it. It was no different in Washington. I'd only been in the Oval Office a few days when I became embroiled in a fight in which I had to persuade Congress to raise the ceiling on the national debt. Because of the spending excesses of the past, everyone in Washington knew the ceiling had to be raised—otherwise, the country would be broke and not able to pay its bills. But in an example of the games I later learned they played all the time, many of the Democrats tried to make it appear to the public that the first thing the new guy in the

White House wanted to do after campaigning in favor of cutting the federal deficit was to raise the national debt. It was another example of the Congress flexing its muscles at the new boy in town. With a great show of reluctance, the Democrats finally relented and voted to raise the debt ceiling. Later, I learned a similar scenario played out every year: Congress approved appropriations that sent the federal deficit through the roof, then opposed raising the debt ceiling. They wanted to make the public think it was the Republican president, not Congress, who wanted higher spending.

In Sacramento, the most important lesson I learned was the value of making an end run around the legislature by going directly to the people; on television or radio, I'd lay out the problems we faced and ask their help to persuade the legislators to vote as *they* wanted, not in the way special-interest groups did. As president, I intended to do the same thing. It had worked in Sacramento and I thought it would work in Washington.

In early February, in a national television broadcast, I told the people that solving problems that had accumulated over decades would take time, but that all of us working together could do it: "We must realize there is no quick fix . . . but we cannot delay in implementing an economic program aimed at both reducing tax rates to stimulate productivity and reducing the growth in government spending to reduce unemployment and inflation."

I sent to Congress a bill calling for an across-the-board thirty-percent tax cut over three years. Meanwhile, we launched a program under Vice-President Bush to reduce unnecessary government regulation of the economy. After the broadcast, Tip O'Neill and other tax-and-spenders in Congress let out a howl and I knew we were in for a battle. A few days later, we unveiled a plan to cut billions of federal expenditures by eliminating needless boards, agencies, and programs—a start at reducing the $80 billion budget deficit the federal government faced that year—and the Democrats let out another howl and proposed drastic cuts in defense spending. Well, I was determined to *increase* military spending to reverse the effects of years of neglect of our armed services.

Pentagon leaders told me appalling stories of how the Soviets were gaining on us militarily, both in nuclear and conventional forces; they were spending fifty percent more each year on weapons than we were; meanwhile, in our armed forces, the paychecks were so small that some married enlisted men and women were eligible for welfare benefits; many military personnel were so ashamed of being in the service that as soon as they left their posts, they put on civilian clothes.

I told the Joint Chiefs of Staff that I wanted to do whatever it took to make our men and women proud to wear their uniforms again. I also asked them to tell me what new weapons they needed to achieve military superiority over our potential enemies. I knew reversing the effects of years of neglect would be expensive and difficult. But during the campaign, the people of America had told me nothing mattered more to them than national security. Time and again, when I went around the country calling for a balanced budget, I'd get this question: "But what if it comes down to a choice between national security and the deficit?"

Every time, I answered: "I'd have to come down on the side of national defense." And every time I did, the audience roared. Nobody wanted a second-class army, navy, or air force defending our country.

I wanted a balanced budget. But I also wanted peace through strength. My faith was in those tax reforms, and I believed we could have a balanced budget within two or three years—by 1984 at the latest.

38

A WEEK AFTER THE INAUGURATION, we held a ceremony on the South Lawn of the White House welcoming home the fifty-two hostages who, thank God, had finally been freed from their long captivity in Iran. Also present were relatives of the eight men who had lost their lives during the unsuccessful attempt to rescue the hostages during the previous administration; one courageous couple had lost their only son, and as I looked into their faces I had difficulty finding the words to lessen their terrible sense of grief.

For the rest of the day, I carried around a lump in my throat as big as a mountain. Unfortunately, it would not be the last time I would have to try to console the relatives of men and women who died in the service of our country. That morning, I was introduced to the worst part of my new job.

The Algerian and Swiss go-betweens who represented us during the hostage negotiations with the Iranians said that the final weeks of negotiations had been dominated by a concern among Iranian officials that they would have to do business with the new administration. In the weeks leading up to the inauguration, I had gone out of my way to say some nasty things in public about the Ayatollah Khomeini, hoping it would encourage him to expedite the negotiations before we arrived in Washington. I referred to them at one time as barbarians. Whether this had anything to do with the hostages' release on inauguration day, I don't know, but the job wasn't complete. An American writer had gone to Iran shortly before the hostages were freed and had been arrested upon her arrival in Teheran; she had been charged with being a spy and thrown in jail.

When the other hostages were released, I checked and found out that she wasn't among them, and I asked the State Department to ask the Algerian and Swiss diplomats to do one more errand for us, suggesting that they hint to the Iranians that the new administration would be much more likely to implement the Carter administration agreement to free Iranian funds held in American banks in exchange for the hostages' release if she was freed first. We never said anything about it publicly. Several days later, she was released.

Long before I ever entered the Oval Office, I had adopted a very simple philosophy regarding the question of what we as a nation should do if an American was held captive abroad against his or her will. I believed that whenever one of our citizens, even the least among us, through no fault of his or her own, was denied the right to life, liberty, and the pursuit of happiness, it was up to the rest of us to do everything we could to restore those rights, wherever it took us, anywhere in the world that person was. It was a policy I followed for eight years as president.

During the campaign, I'd been given classified briefings on various problems facing our country internationally, but as president I began to receive much more detailed briefings each morning on the state of the world, and they introduced me to new problems and great opportunities for the country.

I learned the Soviet economy was in even worse shape than I'd realized. I had always believed that, as an economic system, Communism was doomed. Not only was it lacking in the free market incentives that motivated people to work hard and excel—the economic propulsion that had brought such prosperity to America—but history was full of examples showing that any totalitarian state that deprived its people of liberty and freedom of choice was ultimately doomed. The Bolshevik revolution had simply replaced an inherited aristocracy with a self-appointed one, the Soviet leadership, and it, like its predecessor, could not survive against the inherent drive of all men and women to be free.

Now, the economic statistics and intelligence reports I was getting during my daily National Security Council briefings were revealing tangible evidence that Communism as we knew it was approaching the brink of collapse, not only in the Soviet Union but throughout the Eastern bloc. The Soviet economy was being held together with baling wire; it was a basket case, partly because of massive spending on armaments. In Poland and other Eastern-bloc countries, the economies were also a mess, and there were rumblings of nationalistic fervor within the captive Soviet empire.

You had to wonder how long the Soviets could keep their empire intact. If they didn't make some changes, it seemed clear to me that in time Communism would collapse of its own weight, and I wondered how we as a nation could use these cracks in the Soviet system to accelerate the process of collapse.

Responding to the Soviet invasion of Afghanistan, Jimmy Carter had imposed an embargo on the shipment of American grain to the Soviet Union. Although I supported the idea of sending a strong message of disapproval to Moscow, I suspected the embargo had probably hurt our farmers more than it hurt the Russians, because some of our allies had simply come in and filled the breach and supplied the grain that the Soviet Union needed. I was inclined to lift the embargo to help our farmers, but it wasn't an easy decision; I didn't want to send a message that we approved of what the Russians were doing. In theory, expanding trade was supposed to make the Soviets more moderate, but as far as I could tell, it had simply allowed them to spend fewer resources on agriculture and consumer goods and more on armaments.

Lifting the embargo would be a big boost to our farmers and help our economy at a time when it needed help, but should we do it if it helped extend the life of Communism? It was a dilemma I had to deal with during my first months in the White House.

We were also faced by another serious dilemma: How do we stop the advance of Communism in Latin America without making the people of Latin America think Uncle Sam is a bigger threat to them than the Communists?

A few days after the inauguration, our intelligence agents obtained firm and incontrovertible evidence that the Marxist government of Nicaragua was transferring hundreds of tons of Soviet arms from Cuba to rebel groups in El Salvador. Although El Salvador was the immediate target, the evidence showed that the Soviets and Fidel Castro were targeting all of Central America for a Communist takeover. El Salvador and Nicaragua were only a down payment. Honduras, Guatemala, and Costa Rica were next, and then would come Mexico.

The plans had been in the archives of Communism for a long time. I had been told that Lenin once said, "First, we will take Eastern Europe, then we will organize the hordes of Asia . . . then we will move on to Latin America; once we have Latin America, we won't have to take the United States, the last bastion of capitalism, because it will fall into our outstretched hands like overripe fruit."

We had already lost Cuba to Communism. I was determined the Free World was not going to lose Central America or more of the Caribbean to the Communists, but we had to tread softly. In the minds of many people in Latin America, the United States was the "Great Colossus of the North" that in the past had been too willing to send in the marines and interfere with their governments. The prospect of American troops being dispatched across their borders to fight Communism was abhorrent to these people. And after Vietnam, I knew that Americans would be just as reluctant to send their sons to fight in Central America, and I had no intention of asking them to do that.

Besides, I knew that simply sending our troops into Central America wouldn't end the threat of Communist subversion. There were formidable economic and political problems in many of these countries that made them fertile ground for Castro's revolutionary guerrillas, and these problems had to be dealt with. Millions of people in Latin America lived under terrible conditions of bleak poverty, and close to ninety percent of them lived under governments that were virtual dictatorships. Sure, we could send in the troops, but the threat of Communism wouldn't diminish until the people's standard of living was improved and the totalitarian countries of Latin America gave them more freedom.

Franklin D. Roosevelt, John F. Kennedy, and other American presidents had introduced a variety of plans aimed at dealing with the economic, social, and political imbalances that made Latin America so ripe for revolution, but none had succeeded; the Latin American countries always saw the "Great Colossus" coming down from the north with a blueprint to impose on them against their will.

Yet something had to be done. I asked David Rockefeller to see if he could help develop a plan to improve the economies of the Latin countries that they would not construe as another attempt by the "Great Colossus" to tell them what to do.

In the final analysis, I realized that the problems of Latin America would have to be solved by the Latin American countries themselves, but I had believed for many years (in fact I'd opened my 1980 presidential campaign with a speech on the theme) that the largest countries of North America—Canada, Mexico, and the United States—should forge a closer alliance and become more of a power in the world and help with the problems. Not only would it be to our mutual economic benefit—I thought that working together, those of us in North America might be able to help the Latin American countries help themselves.

On my first trip out of the country as president, a get-acquainted meeting in Ottawa with Canadian Prime Minister Pierre Trudeau, I found that he agreed; then President José López Portillo of Mexico said he would work with Venezuela and other Latin American countries to help negotiate an end to the shipment of Communist arms from Cuba into El Salvador. The policy had gotten off to a good start. Through diplomatic channels, I sent word to our friends south of the border: "We'll help you do the things you need to do, but we won't come in and try to do them for you."

39

In the winter of 1981, the automobile industry was suffering more than any other segment of our economy. Car sales had never fully rebounded from the effects of the Arab oil embargo, and showrooms were flooded with unsold cars; Detroit and its suppliers had furloughed thousands of workers around the country and, in the industrial heart of America, countless communities that relied on a healthy auto industry for their economic sustenance were in trouble.

Japan was landing more and more cars on our soil, and many people in Detroit wanted to make the Japanese the scapegoat for all their problems. As a result, strong sentiment was building in Congress and in the capitals of many industrial states to impose quotas on Japanese imports.

I am a free-trader. I firmly opposed import quotas. I believed that the new competition Detroit faced, like all competition, was good for it and good for consumers—a spur that would motivate our auto industry to produce better cars. That's how the free enterprise system works. I believed that once we started down the road to protectionism, there would be no way to turn back, no way of telling where it would end.

I'd learned that during the Great Depression, when Congress passed the Smoot-Hawley Tariff Act. This law imposed the stiffest tariffs in our history in an effort to protect American farmers from foreign imports. But it backfired and ended up hurting the farmers

—and much of American industry—because other nations promptly levied their own tariffs, which resulted in our farmers and manufacturers selling fewer products abroad. The Smoot-Hawley Act touched off an international trade war that prolonged the Depression and brought on a worldwide plague of economic nationalism. I always agreed with FDR when he said in 1933: "The only practicable way to assure American trade of protection against injurious trade barriers in foreign countries is to join with these countries in concerted efforts to reduce excessive trade restrictions and to reestablish commercial relations on a nondiscriminatory basis."

When I was young and a Democrat, the Democratic Party was the party of free trade and the Republicans were the party of high tariffs and protection. Today, it's just the opposite. I've wondered how that happened. Back then, when the Republican Party came up with the Smoot-Hawley tariffs, it was unquestionably the party of big business and wanted to protect our industry, while the Democrats were closer to the working man and wanted free trade; today, it's the Democrats in Congress who do most of the fighting on behalf of protectionist legislation and the Republicans who usually oppose it. I think the change probably came about because, as the labor unions that were affiliated with the Democrats became more powerful and the wages of their members grew higher, they decided that it was in their interest to limit competition from products made by foreign workers.

Although I intended to veto any bill Congress might pass imposing quotas on Japanese cars, I realized the problem wouldn't go away even if I did. The genuine suffering of American workers and their families made this issue intensely charged politically. And the protectionists in Congress had some powerful ammunition on their side: There was plenty of evidence that the Japanese weren't playing fair in the trade arena. They refused to let American farmers sell many U.S. agricultural products in Japan, and they imposed subtle but effective barriers that eliminated many of our other products from the Japanese marketplace: American cigarette companies, for example, could advertise their products *only* in English in Japan.

I believed in free but *fair* trade. I appointed a task force under Secretary of Transportation Drew Lewis to consider how we should deal with the flood of Japanese cars.

. . .

As we were launching our economic recovery program and beginning to lay the foundation for a new foreign policy during those first few weeks of 1981, I continued to discover my day-to-day office routine was surprisingly similar to what it had been during my time as governor, and I realized that governing a large industrial state was a good primary school for future presidents.

As Nancy and I settled into our new routine, she proved once again that, first and foremost, she's a nest-builder.

Because the White House belongs to all the American people, Nancy said it should be the prettiest house in the land, and she set out to make it so. As far as I'm concerned—and thanks to her—it is. She began with the great Central Hall on the second floor that opened up from our living room. When she started out, its spectacular chandeliers shone on drab walls and dull, worn carpeting. It was a beautiful space badly in need of a renovation. The same was true of many other rooms in the White House.

With the help of Ted Graber, an old friend of ours who is a decorator, Nancy set out, as her first project, to recapture the lost beauty of the Central Hall. She saw to it that its floors were sanded and refinished for the first time in thirty years. For the first time in over fifty years, its mahogany doors were stripped and refinished; new carpeting was laid; the walls were painted and some were covered with lovely wallpaper. The result was stunning. Suddenly the drab hall had become a beautifully furnished parlor illuminated by those glittering chandeliers.

That was only the beginning: As time went on, virtually every room in the White House felt the touch of Nancy's good taste and her determination to make it the most beautiful house in America.

She did it at no cost to the taxpayers. She went out and raised contributions from Americans who shared her dream of making the White House beautiful again. Once she got started, members of the White House staff began pitching in. A kind of treasure hunt began: Dipping into their memories, veteran staffers told her about pieces of fine furniture, mirrors, paintings, and so forth that had adorned the White House in years past and were gathering dust in nooks and crannies around Washington; Nancy went looking for them and brought the best back. She found a priceless English antique octagon desk, for example, that had been given to the White House when John F. Kennedy was president and was hidden under a layer of dust in a Quonset hut used by the government as a storage unit.

I'll never forget one night when we were having dinner alone and a butler who had worked in the White House for over thirty years put Nancy's meal down in front of her, then turned slightly and looked down the length of the Central Hall. "It's beginning to look like the White House again," he said very quietly.

Some people in the news media criticized Nancy's work on the White House. I'll never understand why. They gave the impression that she was extravagantly spending a fortune of public funds on unnecessary changes and new furnishings when in fact the furnishings were coming out of storage or being paid for by private contributions, not taxpayers.

A classic example was the new set of state china she ordered for the White House. Although it was frequently necessary at state dinners to serve well over a hundred guests, the staff told Nancy that, because of breakage and souvenir collectors, there weren't enough matching dishes to go around for large groups. As a result they had to use unmatched sets of china whenever there was a sizable group at the White House for dinner. Knowing that the White House needed it, Nancy accepted the gift of a new set of White House china with 4,372 pieces that cost about $200,000. But taxpayers didn't pay a cent for it; it was purchased by the Knapp Foundation and donated to the White House. Yet for some reason, some of Nancy's critics still claim she *bought* the china; it was a bum rap, a backhanded way of getting at me.

One of the rooms in the White House that benefited from Nancy's good taste was the Oval Office, which got some new paint, a new floor, and new carpeting. I did my part by hanging up a picture of Calvin Coolidge in the Cabinet Room.

I'd always thought of Coolidge as one of our most underrated presidents. He wasn't a man with flamboyant looks or style, but he got things done in a quiet way. He came into office after World War I facing a mountain of war debt, but instead of raising taxes, he cut the tax rate and government revenues increased, permitting him to eliminate the wartime debt and proving that the principle mentioned by Ibn Khaldoon about lower tax rates meaning greater tax revenues still worked in the modern world.

. . .

Back when I was governor, I started having the same dream, often night after night: I'd find myself in a big old house that had huge rooms—not always the same house, but always one with huge rooms. Each time somebody would take me for a tour of the house; usually it was up for sale at a bargain price. I'd wander around, walk from room to room, stare up at high ceilings and great staircases and balconies above me. Although the house in my dream might be run-down, I'd see a great potential for it as a place to live, and I'd want to buy it. I guess there was a yen in me for a big house with big rooms, and the dream even spilled into my waking hours. After we bought the land near San Diego for a new ranch when I was governor, I told Nancy I wanted to build a ranch house with one really huge room, a combined living room and dining room. After we discovered that there wasn't any water or electricity available on the land, and we had to sell it, we happily settled for our little adobe ranch house near Santa Barbara, but living in a house with big rooms was always on my mind and I still got the same dream year after year.

Funny thing: Once I moved to Washington, I never had that dream again. Somehow, living in the White House, with its ceilings that reached up to eighteen feet, cured me of my yen to live in a house with big rooms. I guess something inside me said: "You've made it."

40

UNTIL I GOT TO THE WHITE HOUSE, I wrote all of my own speeches. But presidents make so many public appearances and have so many other demands on their schedule that I soon learned there wasn't enough time to write every speech and I would need help from the White House staff. Because I'd always taken pride in my speeches, this didn't sit well with me, but I didn't have much choice.

I continued to write my more important speeches, but much of the time I would sit down with White House speech writers and go over the points I wanted to make during an upcoming talk, and then they would present me with a draft to edit. I gave them copies of talks I'd made in the past so they would understand my style and technique, and I told them some of my rules for speaking: I prefer short sentences; don't use a word with two syllables if a one-syllable word will do; and if you can, use an example. An example is better than a sermon.

Sometimes, speech writers write things that seem very eloquent on paper, but sound convoluted or stilted when you say them to an audience. "Use simple language," I'd say. "Remember, there are people out there sitting and listening, they've got to be able to absorb what I'm saying."

When I was a sports announcer, I learned something about communicating with people I never forgot. I had a group of friends in Des Moines and we all happened to go to the same barber. My friends would sometimes sneak away from their offices or other jobs when I was broadcasting a game and they'd get together at the barbershop to listen to it; after a while, I began to picture these friends down at the shop when I was on the air and, knowing they were there, I'd try to imagine how my words sounded to them and how they were reacting, and I'd adjust accordingly and spoke as if I was speaking personally to them. There was a specific audience out there I could see in my mind, and I sort of aimed my words at them.

After I did that, something funny happened: I started getting mail from people all over the Midwest who told me I sounded as if I was talking directly and personally to *them*.

Over the years I've always remembered that, and when I'm speaking to a crowd—or on television—I try to remember that audiences are made up of individuals and I try to speak as if I am talking to a group of friends . . . not to millions, but to a handful of people in a living room . . . or a barbershop.

I enjoyed trying to make my case to an audience, and have often been amazed at how little the people know about some of the things you believe need correcting. So, I suppose I became a kind of preacher. I'd preach in my speeches about the problems we had and try to get people roused and to say to their neighbors, "Hey, let's do something about this."

My years in show business and the experience of making thousands of speeches over the years probably taught me something about timing and cadence and how to reach an audience. Here's my formula: I usually start with a joke or story to catch the audience's attention; then I tell them what I am going to tell them, I tell them, and then I tell them what I just told them.

I've always found humor is a good way to get an audience's attention, and for years I've been mentally collecting quotes and jokes to use in speeches. In fact, I've told some audience-catchers so often that they should be interred—like the story about a group of Christians who were about to be fed to a pack of lions in the Colosseum before a multitude that had gathered to witness the slaughter. As the hungry lions came charging onto the Colosseum floor, one of the Christians stepped forward and spoke to the lions and suddenly the beasts all lay down on the ground, leaving the Christians unharmed. The crowd was enraged and went wild, and people shouted that they were being cheated. Then the Roman Caesar sent for the man who had spoken to the lions and asked, "What did you say that made them act like that?" The Christian replied, "I just told them that after they ate, there would be speeches."

For some speeches as president, I relied on my old private short-hand using four-by-six inch-cards. But for major speeches I usually used a teleprompter, which rolled the text of my speech across a screen that's not seen by the audience and makes it appear that the speaker is looking directly at them. I always kept a copy of my speech handy in front of me, however, because I knew from experience that sometimes teleprompters went haywire.

I learned a trick with my contact lenses that helped me see not only my notes and the teleprompter but everything else in life. As I've noted, I am very nearsighted in both eyes and started wearing some of the first contact lenses made in America. But a few years ago, I discovered that if I wore only one lens, nature sort of took over and, in effect, gave me bifocals. I wear a contact lens on my left eye but nothing over my right eye; the corrective lens over my left eye gives me 20–20 vision for seeing things over distances, while my right eye takes over at shorter range and allows me to read fine print. Everything is in balance, equalized by nature.

Although I had a few problems when I was president with tele-prompter machines that failed midway through a speech, I always managed to recover because of my rule of always having a written copy of the speech in front of me. However, I once learned that even having a speech in front of me couldn't save me completely from embarrassing mistakes. One cold day, I put on my topcoat and went down to the South Lawn of the White House for a cere-mony marking the start of a formal state visit by the president of Venezuela. When the time came for my opening remarks I took my speech out of my pocket and began to read it and found that if I did read it, I would be welcoming "His Royal Highness, the Grand Duke of Luxembourg."

Stammering a bit, I couldn't imagine why the staff had given me the wrong speech. Then, as I started to ad-lib, I remembered that the last time I had worn that topcoat was the month before, when we'd had a welcoming ceremony for the grand duke and duchess of Luxembourg. The correct speech was in my suit coat pocket, and so I reached in and found it and continued my welcome, albeit somewhat embarrassed.

We got into a routine during our first few months in the White House that lasted for the next eight years. Our day usually began about seven thirty, with Nancy and me having a light breakfast of fruit or juice, bran cereal, and decaffeinated coffee while we read *The New York Times* and *The Washington Post*. I might also have to study some homework left over from the night before. Then, a few minutes before nine, I'd take the elevator from the family quarters down to the ground floor of the White House and walk down the colonnade past the Rose Garden to the Oval Office, which was in the West Wing. Along the way, I passed the White House medical office, where the doctor was usually standing outside waiting to say hello.

At nine, there was a meeting with the vice-president and the top staff people to go over our current agenda and discuss any new problems that might have come up over the previous twenty-four hours. At nine thirty, my national security advisor joined us and briefed us on what had happened overnight in world affairs. The rest of the day was filled with meetings with cabinet members, staff people, foreign visitors, Congressmen, and other people, and sometimes a speech or other event outside the White House.

Especially during the early months, we spent a lot of time discussing appointments to key jobs in the administration. As I had done in California, I told the staff I wanted them to look for the best people we could find who were willing to leave their homes and their secure positions to come to Washington and give the country a hand. When I'd approach somebody about taking a job, I'd often say, "We don't want people who *want* a job in government, we want people of accomplishment who have to be *persuaded* to come to work here."

Lunch was usually a light meal of soup and fruit at my desk or in a small study off the Oval Office; on most Thursdays, lunch was with George Bush, when I brought him up to date on everything that was going on.

About five or so each afternoon—or whenever all the work was done—I went upstairs, peeled down and got into my trunks, then crossed the Central Hall to a guest bedroom that we'd converted into a gym with exercise equipment. I worked out a half hour or so, then took a shower. After that, unless there was a state dinner or other function on the agenda, Nancy and I usually went to the small study next to our bedroom and ate our dinner from portable tables while watching the evening's three network television news shows tape-recorded by the White House staff.

After dinner, we both usually had more paperwork. Although I had not yet thought about writing this book, I decided to keep a daily journal while I was in the White House. This diary became in many ways the core of my recollections of the presidency that are contained in this book. Each night, I'd write a few lines about the day's events, and Nancy would do the same in her diary.

After all our homework was done, we'd go to bed with a novel or another book, or I might pick up a magazine about horses and riding, and we'd drop off to sleep about ten or eleven.

A month or so after the inauguration, we invited Tip O'Neill and his wife and a few other guests to have dinner with us in the family quarters. Nancy had already made a lot of progress in her efforts to renovate the second and third floors, and Tip said, "You know, I have been in and out of this place for twenty-seven years and I have never seen it look as beautiful as this."

It was a warm, pleasant evening, and a good time was had by all. By the time it was over, I was certain Tip and I had worn out Nancy and the other guests by trying to top each other with Irish stories passed on by our fathers. I also thought I'd made a friend. But a day or two later, I picked up a newspaper and read a story in which Tip really lit into me personally because he didn't like the economic recovery program and some of the cuts I proposed in spending.

Some of his remarks were pretty nasty. I was not only surprised but disappointed and also a little hurt. I called him and said, "Tip, I just read in the paper what you said about me yesterday. I thought we had a pretty fine relationship going . . . "

"Ol' buddy," Tip said, "that's politics. After six o'clock we can be friends; but before six, it's politics."

Tip was an old-fashioned pol: He could be sincere and friendly when he wanted to be, but when it came to the things he believed in, he could turn off his charm and friendship like a light switch and become as bloodthirsty as a piranha. He was a politician and a

Democrat to his roots. Until six o'clock, I was the enemy and he never let me forget it. So, after a while, whenever I'd run into him, whatever time it was, I'd say, "Look, Tip, I'm resetting my watch; it's six o'clock."

41

ONE THING I NEVER got comfortable with as president was riding in motorcades. Anytime we drove anywhere, we went in a convoy behind a police escort, and every time we crossed an intersection against the lights and I looked out and saw long lines of cars backed up on the side streets, I felt guilty because I knew how those people in the cars must feel having to wait like that.

How much our motorcade could disrupt traffic really became evident to me when we went to New York City in the middle of March, about two months after the inauguration. After flying from Washington to LaGuardia Airport, we helicoptered around the Statue of Liberty and saw the spectacular skyline of lower Manhattan, landed on a downtown helipad, and then sped through the city in the usual motorcade while the police closed off all the intersections. Ever since the presidential campaign, we'd had police escorts, but something was different about this trip I wasn't prepared for: The streets were lined with crowds of people all the way to the Waldorf Astoria, as if New York were having a holiday parade. Suddenly, I realized I was the parade. As we passed the crowds, people cheered and clapped and I wore out my arms waving back to them. It was an extremely humbling experience and that evening I wrote in my diary: "I keep thinking this can't continue and yet their warmth and affection seems so genuine I get a lump in my throat. *I pray constantly that I won't let them down.*"

In New York, I did some speech-making to campaign for passage of the economic recovery program. On the second night we went to see Mickey Rooney and Ann Miller, two old friends from Hollywood, in *Sugar Babies*. At the final curtain, Mickey asked the audience to stay in place until we exited, and as we went up the aisle, the audience began singing "America the Beautiful"—more lump-in-throat time.

The next night, we went to the Met to see the Joffrey Ballet. Our son Ron had flown in from the road company for the performance. I think I held my breath for the whole show, but he was great and didn't need any fatherly prayers. He had a grace that reminded me of Fred Astaire, an extra flair that made what he was doing look easy.

When I got back to Washington, the pending and difficult question of how to deal with the growing flood of Japanese car imports at a time when our economy needed every bit of help it could find took center stage and came to a head at a meeting at the White House on March 19. The special task force I'd appointed under Drew Lewis to review the problem wanted to impose mandatory quotas on the Japanese. But several members of the cabinet, including Don Regan, the treasury secretary, and David Stockman, head of the Office of Management and Budget, strongly opposed it. George Shultz, who chaired a volunteer economic advisory committee, was strongly in opposition. They argued that it would violate our commitment to free enterprise and free trade.

I agreed with them but kept quiet. In Washington, I was following the same practice I had followed in Sacramento: I invited all the members of the cabinet to give me their views on all sides of an issue (everything except the "political ramifications" of my decision) and sometimes, as in this case, the result was a heated debate —and if I was leaning a certain way, I tried not to tip my advisors off, to ensure that I'd hear all sides.

As I listened to the debate, I wondered if there might be a way in which we could maintain the integrity of our position in favor of free trade while at the same time doing something to help Detroit and ease the plight of its thousands of laid-off assembly-line workers.

The Japanese weren't playing fair in the trade game. But I knew what quotas might lead to; I didn't want to start an all-out trade war, so I asked if anyone had any suggestions for striking a balance between the two positions. George Bush spoke up:

"We're *all* for free enterprise, but would any of us find fault if Japan announced without any request from us that they were going to *voluntarily* reduce their export of autos to America?"

I knew the Japanese read our newspapers and must know about the sentiment building up in Congress for quotas on their cars; I also knew there must be some apprehension in Tokyo that, once Congress imposed quotas on automobiles, there was a good possibility it might try to limit imports of other Japanese products.

I liked George's idea and told the cabinet I'd heard enough and would make a decision, but didn't tell them what it was. After the meeting, I met privately with Secretary of State Al Haig and told him to call our ambassador in Tokyo, Mike Mansfield, and have him pass the word informally to Japanese Foreign Minister Masayoshi Ito, who was scheduled to make a visit to Washington in a few days, that pressure was building in Congress for passage of a bill establishing mandatory quotas. I told him to suggest that an announcement of a *voluntary* cutback by Japan might head it off.

During this one-on-one meeting with Haig, I was surprised by his mood. He claimed other people in the administration were trying to undercut him on matters of foreign policy, which he said was *his* territory, and he didn't want others interfering with it. He was very upset and angry. As he would do on later occasions, he pounded the table and seemed ready to explode. The intensity of his attitude surprised and worried me, but he was placated when I agreed to meet with him privately three times a week to talk about foreign affairs and I gave him my assurance that no one was about to usurp his role in the administration.

Two nights later, Nancy and I made our first trip to Ford's Theater in Washington to attend a black-tie gala to raise money for support of this historic building. During the performance, I looked up at the presidential box above the stage where Abe Lincoln had been sitting the night he was shot and felt a curious sensation. As you look up there, you can't help but run those events of 1865 through your mind: You imagine the figure of John Wilkes Booth bursting through the door at the rear of the box, shooting the president, then leaping onto the stage and running away before a stunned audience.

It occurred to me that until that night probably no one had ever given much thought to the possibility someone might want to kill the president. As I watched the show, I thought about all the security provided Nancy and me and the children and how different things were now. Looking up at the flag-draped box, though, I thought that even with all the Secret Service protection we now had, it was probably still possible for someone who had enough determination to get close enough to a president to shoot him.

Three days after the night out at Ford's Theater, Foreign Minister Ito of Japan was brought into the Oval Office for a brief meeting to pave the way for a formal state visit later in the spring of Japanese Prime Minister Zenko Suzuki. I told him that our Republican administration firmly opposed import quotas but that strong sentiment was building in Congress among Democrats to impose them.

"I don't know whether I'll be able to stop them," I said. "But I think if you *voluntarily* set a limit on your automobile exports to this country, it would probably head off the bills pending in Congress and there wouldn't be any mandatory quotas."

Not long after the meeting with Foreign Minister Ito, I got a call from Al Haig, who was extremely upset over a decision I'd made naming George Bush as chairman of a special group within the National Security Council that would help me manage affairs during an international crisis. In the past, the president's national security advisor had generally served as chairman of the White House crisis management team. But Haig didn't like or trust National Security Advisor Richard Allen. I had discussed the matter with the top three staff people in the White House, Jim Baker, Ed Meese, and Mike Deaver, and we'd come up with the plan giving the responsibility to George Bush. Not only would that deal with Haig's unhappiness over Allen; I also thought that it was prudent —and important for the country—for the vice-president to play as large a role in the affairs of the administration as possible; I didn't want George, in the words of Nelson Rockefeller, simply to be "standby equipment."

Now Haig was on the phone going through the roof, saying he

didn't want the vice-president to have *anything* to do with international affairs; it was *his* jurisdiction, he said, and he told me he was thinking of resigning. I couldn't understand why he was so upset, and I told him he had nothing to worry about.

I thought he was seeing shadows in a mirror. No one wanted to invade his turf. But early the next morning, I was awakened by a call from Mike Deaver, who said Haig had raised a fuss with the staff the night before over George's new assignment and was threatening to submit his resignation that day.

I invited Haig to the Oval Office at eight forty-five, expecting his offer of resignation and intending to try to talk him out of it. But when he arrived, he was cool-headed and didn't say anything about resigning; instead, he handed me a statement that he wanted me to issue declaring that he alone was in charge of foreign affairs. The statement was much too broad for me to accept, but after he left I drafted a statement of my own, short and simple, that made clear the obvious: that the secretary of state was my primary advisor on foreign affairs.

That seemed to satisfy him, and with the Haig issue behind us, I continued trying to enlist support on Capitol Hill for my economic recovery program; besides the usual schedule of meetings and conferences and telephone calls to congressmen, there was a banquet of television and radio correspondents at which Rich Little did a pretty fair imitation of me holding a press conference; a luncheon honoring members of baseball's Hall of Fame, where I met players like Bob Lemon and Billy Herman whom I'd covered as a sports announcer; and on Saturday, March 28, the annual Gridiron Dinner, where reporters poked fun at presidents, congressmen, and other members of the Washington scene, and I got the chance to poke fun right back.

Sunday was a beautiful spring day and in the morning we went to St. John's Episcopal Church, the house of worship not far from the White House that's called "the President's Church." The choir from the U.S. Naval Academy at Annapolis sang beautifully and looked and sounded so right that I felt everyone in the church that morning must have felt very good about their country.

The main event on my schedule the following day was a speech to the AFL-CIO Building and Construction Trades Conference at the Hilton Hotel in downtown Washington. Although I spent most of that Sunday afternoon working on my speech, I thought a lot about those people I'd seen in church, the future of America, and the "MAD" policy.

The three initials stood for "mutual assured destruction," three deceptively dull words describing our country's only shield against nuclear annihilation. It was the name applied to the strategic policy of both of the world's superpowers. The United States and the Soviet Union each kept a big enough stockpile of nuclear weapons at the ready that, if one attacked, the other would still have enough to annihilate the attacker. It would be like two spiders in a bottle locked in a suicidal fight until both were dead.

As president, I carried no wallet, no money, no driver's license, no keys in my pockets—only secret codes that were capable of bringing about the annihilation of much of the world as we knew it.

On inauguration day, after being briefed a few days earlier on what I was to do if ever it became necessary to unleash American nuclear weapons, I'd taken over the greatest responsibility of my life—of any human being's life. From then on, wherever I went, I carried a small plastic-coated card with me, and a military aide with a very specialized job was always close by. He or she (I was pleased to be able to appoint the first female officer to this position) carried a small bag everyone referred to as "the football." It contained the directives for launching our nuclear weapons in retaliation for a nuclear attack on our country. The plastic-coated card, which I carried in a small pocket in my coat, listed the codes I would issue to the Pentagon confirming that it was actually the president of the United States who was ordering the unleashing of our nuclear weapons.

The decision to launch the weapons was mine alone to make.

We had many contingency plans for responding to a nuclear attack. But everything would happen so fast that I wondered how much planning or reason could be applied in such a crisis. The Russians sometimes kept submarines off our East Coast with nuclear missiles that could turn the White House into a pile of radioactive rubble within six or eight minutes.

Six minutes to decide how to respond to a blip on a radar scope and decide whether to unleash Armageddon! How could anyone apply reason at a time like that?

There were some people in the Pentagon who thought in terms of fighting and *winning* a nuclear war. To me it was simple common sense: A nuclear war couldn't be won by either side. It must never be fought. But how do we go about trying to prevent it and pulling back from this hair-trigger existence?

During the spring of 1981, the arms race was moving ahead at a pell-mell pace based on the MAD policy. Investing a far larger portion of their national wealth on arms than we were, the Soviets were piling new weapon upon new weapon. We couldn't let them get ahead of us—so, in response to the Soviet threat, we were beginning a top-to-bottom modernization of our nuclear forces and getting ready to send a new family of intermediate-range weapons to Europe to help our NATO allies defend themselves against Soviet missiles.

There didn't seem any end to it, no way out of it.

Advocates of the MAD policy believed it had served a purpose: The balance of terror it created, they said, had prevented nuclear war for decades. But as far as I was concerned, the MAD policy was madness. For the first time in history, man had the power to destroy mankind itself. A war between the superpowers would incinerate much of the world and leave what was left of it uninhabitable forever.

There had to be some way to remove this threat of annihilation and give the world a greater chance of survival. That Sunday afternoon, as I went back and forth from these thoughts and working on my speech for Monday, I reflected that in the past, man had been able to devise a defense against every other weapon thrown against him. I wondered if it might be possible to develop a defense against missiles other than the fatalistic acceptance of annihilation that was implicit under the MAD policy. We couldn't continue this nervous standoff forever, I thought; we couldn't lower our guard, but we had to begin the process of peace. As the afternoon of March 29 passed, I spent a lot of time wondering what I could do to get the process started.

42

I PUT ON A BRAND-NEW blue suit for my speech to the Construction Trades Council. But for reasons I'll never know, I took off my best wristwatch before leaving the White House and put on an old one Nancy had given me that I usually wore only when I was doing chores outside at the ranch.

My speech at the Hilton Hotel was not riotously received—I think most of the audience were Democrats—but at least they gave me polite applause.

After the speech, I left the hotel through a side entrance and passed a line of press photographers and TV cameras. I was almost to the car when I heard what sounded like two or three firecrackers over to my left—just a small fluttering sound, *pop, pop, pop.*

I turned and said, "What the hell's that?"

Just then, Jerry Parr, the head of our Secret Service unit, grabbed me by the waist and literally hurled me into the back of the limousine. I landed on my face atop the arm rest across the backseat and Jerry jumped on top of me. When he landed, I felt a pain in my upper back that was unbelievable. It was the most excruciating pain I had ever felt.

"Jerry," I said, "get off, I think you've broken one of my ribs."

"The White House," Jerry told the driver, then scrambled off me and got on the jump seat and the car took off.

I tried to sit up on the edge of the seat and was almost paralyzed by pain. As I was straightening up, I had to cough hard and saw that the palm of my hand was brimming with extremely red, frothy blood.

"You not only broke a rib, I think the rib punctured my lung," I said.

Jerry looked at the bubbles in the frothy blood and told the driver to head for George Washington University Hospital instead of the White House.

By then my handkerchief was sopped with blood and he handed me his. Suddenly, I realized I could barely breathe. No matter how hard I tried, I couldn't get enough air. I was frightened and started to panic a little. I just was not able to inhale enough air.

We pulled up in front of the hospital emergency entrance and I was first out of the limo and into the emergency room. A nurse was coming to meet me and I told her I was having trouble breathing. Then all of a sudden my knees turned rubbery. The next thing I knew I was lying face up on a gurney and my brand-new pin-striped suit was being cut off me, never to be worn again.

The pain near my ribs was still excruciating, but what worried me most was that I still could not get enough air, even after the doctors placed a breathing tube in my throat. Every time I tried to inhale, I seemed to get less air. I remember looking up from the gurney, trying to focus my eyes on the square ceiling tiles, and praying. Then I guess I passed out for a few minutes.

I was lying on the gurney only half-conscious when I realized that someone was holding my hand. It was a soft, feminine hand. I felt it come up and touch mine and then hold on tight to it. It gave me a wonderful feeling. Even now I find it difficult to explain how reassuring, how wonderful, it felt.

It must have been the hand of a nurse kneeling very close to the gurney, but I couldn't see her. I started asking, "Who's holding my hand? . . . Who's holding my hand?" When I didn't hear any response, I said, "Does Nancy know about us?"

Although I tried afterward to learn who the nurse was, I was never able to find her. I had wanted to tell her how much the touch of her hand had meant to me, but I never was able to do that.

Once I opened my eyes and saw Nancy looking down at me.

"Honey," I said, "I forgot to duck," borrowing Jack Dempsey's line to his wife the night he was beaten by Gene Tunney for the heavyweight championship.

Seeing Nancy in the hospital gave me an enormous lift. As long as I live I will never forget the thought that rushed into my head as I looked up into her face. Later I wrote it down in my diary: *"I pray I'll never face a day when she isn't there . . . of all the ways God had blessed me, giving her to me was the greatest—beyond anything I can ever hope to deserve."*

Someone was looking out for us that day.

Most of the doctors who practiced at George Washington University Hospital had been attending a special meeting there that afternoon and were only an elevator ride away from the emergency room. Within a few minutes after I arrived, the room was full of specialists in virtually every medical field. When one of the doctors said they were going to operate on me, I said, "I hope you're a Republican."

He looked at me and said, "Today, Mr. President, we're all Republicans."

I also remember saying, after one of the nurses asked me how I felt, "All in all, I'd rather be in Philadelphia"—the old W. C. Fields line.

For quite a while when I was in the emergency room, I still thought I was there because Jerry Parr had broken my rib and it had punctured my lung. Little by little, though, I learned what had happened and what the situation was: I had a bullet in my lung; Jim Brady, my press secretary, had been shot in the head; Secret Service agent Tim McCarthy had been shot in the chest; policeman Tom Delehanty had been shot in the neck. All of us had been hit by the gun of a young lone assailant who was in police custody.

When Jim Brady, a funny and irreverent man who was as talented and well liked as anyone in the White House, was wheeled by me unconscious on his way to the operating room, someone told me he was hit so badly he probably wouldn't make it, and I quickly said a prayer for him. I didn't feel I could ask God's help to heal Jim, the others, and myself, and at the same time feel hatred for the man who had shot us, so I silently asked God to help him deal with whatever demons had led him to shoot us.

As people began to tell me more about what had happened, I began to realize that when Jerry Parr had thrown his body on me, he was gallantly putting his own life on the line to save mine, and I felt guilty that I'd chewed him out right after it happened. Like Jerry, Tim McCarthy had also bravely put his life on the line for me. Some weeks later I was shown the TV shots of what happened that day. As I was being thrown into the limo, there, facing the camera between me and the gunman, spreadeagling himself to make as big a target as possible, was Tim McCarthy. He was shot right in the chest. Thank heaven he lived.

I thanked God for what He and they had done for me, and while I was waiting to be taken into the operating room, I remembered the trip I had made just the week before to Ford's Theater and the thoughts I'd had while looking up at the flag-draped box where Lincoln had died. Even with all the protection in the world, I'd thought, it was probably impossible to guarantee completely the safety of the president. Now I'd not only benefited from the self-lessness of these two men; God, for some reason, had seen fit to give me his blessing and allow me to live a while longer.

John Hinckley, Jr.'s bullet probably caught me in midair at the same moment I was being thrown into the back of the car by Jerry Parr. After they took it out of me, I saw the bullet. It looked like a nickel that was black on one side; it had been flattened into a small disc and darkened by the paint on the limousine. First the bullet had struck the limousine, then it had ricocheted through the small gap between the body of the car and the door hinges. It hit me under my left arm, where it made a small slit like a knife wound.

I'd always been told that no pain is as excruciating as a broken bone; that's why I thought Jerry had broken my rib when he landed so hard on me. But it wasn't Jerry's weight I felt; according to the doctors, the flattened bullet had hit my rib edgewise, then turned over like a coin, tumbling down through my lung and stopping less than an inch from my heart.

As I said, someone was looking out for me that day.

On several previous occasions when I'd been out in public as president, the Secret Service had made me wear a bulletproof vest under my suit. That day, even though I was going to speak to some die-hard Democrats who didn't think much of my economic recovery program, no one had thought my iron underwear would be necessary because my only exposure was to be a thirty-foot walk to the car.

I never saw Hinckley at the Hilton, only the crowd of reporters outside the hotel. In the hospital, I learned he had gone to a movie, *Taxi Driver,* and fallen in love with an actress in the picture and then begun trailing her around the country, hoping to meet her so he could tell her how he felt. Although I have never seen the movie, I'm told there was a scene in it in which there was a shooting; for some reason Hinckley decided to get a gun and kill somebody to demonstrate his love for the actress.

I was told he'd plotted to kill Jimmy Carter and had actually stalked him, taking his gun to where Carter was going to be—but he never got the chance so he shot me instead. He was a mixed-up young man from a fine family. That day, I asked the Lord to heal him, and to this day, I still do.

After I left the hospital and was back in the White House, I wrote a few words about the shooting in my diary that concluded: "Whatever happens now I owe my life to God and will try to serve him in every way I can."

43

I HAD WONDERFUL CARE at the George Washington University Hospital, for which I will be eternally grateful. But it wasn't long before I was very anxious to get on my feet, go home, and get back to work, and I'm afraid there may have been times when I was not a perfect patient. Once during those first few days, when I was bedded down and fastened to an intravenous apparatus, I had to go to the men's room. I didn't want to trouble the nurses, so I got out of bed and wheeled the intravenous cart with me over to the restroom. When the nurses found out about it, they gave me a scolding, but I persuaded them to let me out of bed more often and pretty soon they were letting me go out into the corridor outside my room and walk around in a little oval to exercise. I was determined that, when I left the hospital, I was going to walk out, and I did.

On April 12, I wrote in my diary: "The first full day at home. I'm not jumping any fences and the routine is still one of blood tests, X-rays, bottles dripping into my arms but I'm home. With the let-up on antibiotics, I'm beginning to have an appetite and food tastes good for the first time."

Incidentally, I *did* take an afternoon nap during the first three or four weeks after I came home from the hospital, but, despite reports to the contrary, that was the first and only time I'd needed one since I was a child.

On April 14, three days after I got home, the space shuttle *Co-*

lumbia returned to earth in triumph after its maiden voyage. The landing touched off tremendous excitement around the country, convincing me more than ever that Americans wanted to feel proud and patriotic again. I watched the landing on television in the Lincoln Bedroom, where they set up a hospital-style bed for my recuperation. While lying there, or relaxing in robe and pajamas in the solarium on the third floor of the White House, I had lots of time to think about the problems our country faced and the things we could do to deal with them.

On the domestic scene, our economic program was beginning to make a little headway in Congress, but I knew we had a fight on our hands, and I'd have to win the support of more Democrats in the House to get it passed. On the international front, I kept recalling those thoughts I'd had on the Sunday before the shooting about the MAD policy. During my watch as president, I thought, there was nothing I wanted more than to lessen the risk of nuclear war. But how do we go about it?

Our relationship with the Soviets was based on "détente," a French word the Russians had interpreted as a freedom to pursue whatever policies of subversion, aggression, and expansionism they wanted anywhere in the world. Every Soviet leader since Lenin, up to and including the present one, Leonid Brezhnev, had said the goal of the Soviet Union was to Communize the world. Except for a brief time-out during World War II, the Russians had been our de facto enemies for almost sixty-five years; all this while, their policies had been consistently and religiously devoted to the single purpose of destroying democracy and imposing Communism.

During the postwar years, America had repeatedly stood up to the threat of Soviet expansionism, going to the far corners of the world—Turkey, Greece, Korea, Southeast Asia, and elsewhere—to defend freedom. It was our policy that this great democracy of ours had a special obligation to help bring freedom to other peoples, as we did after World War II when we helped the new nations that emerged from the colonial past. We spent billions to help the countries ravaged by World War II, including our former enemies, rebuild after the war. We spent more billions to keep American troops stationed in Western Europe and South Korea for the purpose of containing Communism. Sometimes the price of defending freedom was even higher: Many brave Americans made the ultimate sacrifice. America had always been willing to pay the price of defending human liberty.

During the late seventies, I felt our country had begun to abdicate this historical role as the spiritual leader of the Free World and its foremost defender of democracy. Some of our resolve was gone, along with a part of our commitment to uphold the values we cherished.

Just as it had accepted the notion that America was past its prime economically and said our people would have to settle for a future with less, the previous administration for some reason had accepted the notion that America was no longer the world power it had once been, that it had become powerless to shape world events. Consciously or unconsciously, we had sent out a message to the world that Washington was no longer sure of itself, its ideals, or its commitments to our allies, and that it seemed to accept as inevitable the advance of Soviet expansionism, especially in the poor and underdeveloped countries of the world.

I'm not sure what was at the root of this sense of withdrawal; perhaps it was related to the Vietnam War, the energy crisis, and the inflation and other economic problems of the Carter years—or the frustrations endured by the Carter administration over the failure of its policies in Iran. Whatever the reasons, I believed it was senseless, ill-founded, and dangerous for America to withdraw from its role as superpower and leader of the Free World.

Predictably, the Soviets had interpreted our hesitation and reluctance to act and our reduced sense of national self-confidence as a weakness, and had tried to exploit it to the fullest, moving ahead with their agenda to achieve a Communist-dominated world. With the breathtaking events that have occurred in Eastern Europe since then, it can be easy to forget what the world was like in the spring of 1981: The Soviets were more dedicated than ever to achieving Lenin's goal of a Communist world. Under the so-called Brezhnev Doctrine, they claimed the right to support "wars of national liberation" and to suppress, through armed intervention, any challenge to Communist governments anywhere in the world.

We saw the Brezhnev Doctrine in practice around the globe on a daily basis. In El Salvador, Angola, Ethiopia, Cambodia, and elsewhere, the Soviets and their surrogates, Cuba, Nicaragua, Libya, and Syria, were seeking to undermine and destroy non-Communist governments through violent campaigns of subversion and terrorism. In Afghanistan, they were brutally trying to suppress a revolt against Communist rule with tanks and rockets; in Poland, they were responding to the tentative stirrings of a democratic movement with ominous hints of an invasion, the same method they had used to crush brave freedom fighters who had sought to bring democracy to Hungary and Czechoslovakia.

As the foundation of my foreign policy, I decided we had to send as powerful a message as we could to the Russians that we weren't going to stand by anymore while they armed and financed terrorists and subverted democratic governments. Our policy was to be one based on strength and realism. I wanted peace through strength, not peace through a piece of paper.

In my speeches and press conferences, I deliberately set out to say some frank things about the Russians, to let them know there were some new fellows in Washington who had a realistic view of what they were up to and weren't going to let them keep it up. At my first press conference I was asked whether we could trust the Soviet Union, and I said that the answer to that question could be found in the writings of Soviet leaders: It had always been their philosophy that it was moral to lie or cheat for the purpose of advancing Communism. I said they had told us, without meaning to, that they couldn't be trusted. (Much of the press later got it wrong when it claimed I called the Soviets liars and cheaters, failing to point out that I was simply quoting what the Russians themselves had said.)

I wanted to let them know that in attempting to continue their policy of expansionism, they were prolonging the nuclear arms race and keeping the world on the precipice of disaster. I also wanted to send the signal that we weren't going to be deceived by words into thinking they'd changed their stripes: We wanted deeds, not words. And I intended to let them know that we were going to spend whatever it took to stay ahead of them in the arms race. We would never accept second place.

The great dynamic success of capitalism had given us a powerful weapon in our battle against Communism—*money*. The Russians could never win the arms race; we could outspend them forever. Moreover, incentives inherent in the capitalist system had given us an industrial base that meant we had the capacity to maintain a technological edge over them forever.

But in addition to sending out the word that the United States was dealing with the Soviet Union from a new basis of realism, I wanted to let them know that we realized the nuclear standoff was futile and dangerous for all of us and that we had no designs on their territories. They had nothing to fear from us if they behaved themselves. We wanted to reduce the tensions that had led us to the threshold of a nuclear standoff.

It was ridiculous for both nations to continue this costly, open-ended competition to build bigger and better offensive weapons able to annihilate the world. The money we were spending on weapons could be better spent on so many other things. Somewhere in the Kremlin, I thought, there had to be people who realized that the pair of us standing there like two cowboys with guns pointed at each other's heads posed a lethal risk to the survival of the Communist world as well as the Free World. Someone in the Kremlin had to realize that in arming themselves to the teeth, they were aggravating the desperate economic problems in the Soviet Union, which were the greatest evidence of the failure of Communism.

Yet, to be candid, I doubted I'd ever meet anybody like that.

44

NOT LONG AFTER I moved into the White House, Anatoly Dobrynin, the Soviet ambassador in Washington, made some guarded hints to Secretary of State Al Haig indicating that the Russians were interested in reopening East-West talks on controlling nuclear arms. But he said Soviet leaders were unhappy with some of the harsh things I'd said about them. I told Al to inform Dobrynin that my words were intended to convey a message: There was a new management in the White House along with a new realism regarding the Russians, and until they behaved themselves, they could expect more of the same.

I didn't have much faith in Communists or put much stock in their word. Still, it was dangerous to continue the East-West nuclear standoff forever, and I decided that if the Russians wouldn't take the first step, I should.

As I sat in the sun-filled White House solarium in robe and pajamas that spring, waiting for doctors to give me a go-ahead to resume a full work schedule, I wondered how to get the process started. Perhaps having come so close to death made me feel I should do whatever I could in the years God had given me to reduce the threat of nuclear war; perhaps there was a reason I had been spared.

Finally, I decided to write a personal letter to Brezhnev, whom I had met briefly when I was governor and he had come to San Clemente for a meeting with President Nixon. I thought I'd try to convince him that, contrary to Soviet propaganda, America wasn't an "imperialist" nation and we had no designs on any part of the world. I wanted to let him know that we had a realistic view of what the Soviet Union was all about, but also wanted to send a signal to him that we were interested in reducing the threat of nuclear annihilation.

A week after leaving the hospital, I got out a pad of yellow paper and wrote the first draft of a letter to Brezhnev—still not sure I'd send it, but anxious to get some thoughts on paper.

Before the shooting, I had been leaning toward lifting the grain embargo imposed during the Carter administration. It was hurting our farmers more than it was hurting the Russians. I didn't want to make a concession to the Soviets without a quid pro quo, but felt we could lift the embargo and indicate it was a demonstration of our sincerity in wanting to improve Soviet-American relations. It would also demonstrate to our allies that, as the leader of the Free World, we were willing to take the initiative in attempting to reduce Cold War tensions.

Partly because of concerns in West Germany and European countries, where there was growing political sentiment in favor of unilateral disarmament, Al Haig wanted to go to the arms control bargaining table with the Russians fairly soon, but was against an early summit. He opposed conciliatory gestures toward the Russians until they gave us evidence they were willing to behave. As a result, he opposed lifting the grain embargo, saying it would send a wrong message to the Russians. I understood his feelings, but felt the advantages outweighed the disadvantages.

When I told him I was thinking of writing a personal letter to Brezhnev, Al was reluctant to have *me* actually draft it. If I was going to send a letter, he said the State Department should compose it.

That was probably the first indication I had that it wasn't only other members of the cabinet and White House staff whom Al didn't want participating in foreign affairs. As I was to learn over the next year, he didn't even want me as the president to be involved in setting foreign policy—he regarded it as his turf. He didn't want to carry out the president's foreign policy; he wanted to formulate it and carry it out himself.

I had admired Haig very much and respected his performance as commander of NATO, and had selected him as my secretary of state because of this record and his experience in Washington during the Nixon years. But he had a toughness and aggressiveness about protecting his status and turf that caused problems within the administration. On the day I was shot, George Bush was out of town and Haig immediately came to the White House and claimed he was in charge of the country. Even after the vice-president was back in Washington, I was told he maintained that he, not George, should be in charge. I didn't know about this when it was going on. But I heard later that the rest of the cabinet was furious. They said he acted as if he thought he had the right to sit in the Oval Office and believed it was his constitutional right to take over—a position without any legal basis.

In any case, I told Al that, despite his objections, I wanted to lift the grain embargo and that I was going to send a personal letter to Brezhnev aimed at reaching him as a human being, along with a more formal letter letting him know that, despite lifting the grain embargo, the United States had a new attitude of realism toward the Soviet Union. The State Department took my draft of the letter and rewrote it, diluting some of my personal thoughts with stiff diplomatic language that made it more impersonal than I'd wanted. I didn't like what they'd done to it, so I revised their revisions and sent the letter largely as I had originally written it; on April 24, 1981, two letters went out to Brezhnev from me. In the formal message, I questioned "the USSR's unremitting and comprehensive military build up over the past fifteen years, a build up which in our view exceeds purely defensive requirements and carries disturbing implications of a search for military superiority." Putting him on notice that we weren't going to accept any longer the so-called Brezhnev Doctrine, I criticized

> repeated statements by responsible Soviet officials suggesting that the form of a country's political, social and economic system bestows upon the Soviet Union special rights, indeed, duties, to preserve a particular form of government. I must inform you frankly and emphatically that the United States rejects any such declaration as contrary to the charter of the United Nations and other international instruments. Claims of special "rights," however defined, cannot be used to infringe upon the sovereign rights of any country to determine its own political, economic and social institutions.

Alluding to a possible U.S.-Soviet summit, I said it would have to be preceded by "careful preparations and a propitious international climate. I do not believe that these conditions exist at present and so my preference would be for postponing a meeting of such importance to a later day."

This is the text of the handwritten letter I also sent to Moscow:

Mr. President, in writing the attached letter I am reminded of our meeting in San Clemente a decade or so ago. I was Governor of California at the time and you were concluding a series of meetings with President Nixon. Those meetings had captured the imagination of all the world. Never had peace and good will among men seemed closer at hand.

When we met I asked if you were aware that the hopes and aspirations of millions and millions of people throughout the world were dependent on the decisions that would be reached in your meetings.

You took my hand in both of yours and assured me that you were aware of that and that you were dedicated with all your heart and mind to fulfilling those hopes and dreams.

The people of the world still share that hope. Indeed, the peoples of the world, despite differences in racial and ethnic origin, have very much in common. They want the dignity of having some control over their individual destiny. They want to work at the craft or trade of their own choosing and to be fairly rewarded. They want to raise their families in peace without harming anyone or suffering harm themselves. Government exists for their convenience, not the other way around. If they are incapable, as some would have us believe, of self-government, then where among them do we find people who are capable of governing others?

Is it possible that we have permitted ideology, political and economic philosophies, and governmental policies to keep us from considering the very real, everyday problems of peoples? Will the average Soviet family be better off or even aware that the Soviet Union has imposed a government of its own choice on the people of Afghanistan? Is life better for the people of Cuba because the Cuban military dictate who shall govern the people of Angola?

It is often implied that such things have been made necessary because of territorial ambitions of the United States; that we have imperialistic designs and thus constitute a threat to your own security and that of the newly emerging nations. There not only is no evidence to support such a charge, there is solid evidence that the United

States, when it could have dominated the world with no risk to itself, made no effort whatsoever to do so.

When World War II ended, the United States had the only undamaged industrial power in the world. Our military might was at its peak—and we alone had the ultimate weapon; the nuclear weapon, with the unquestioned ability to deliver it anywhere in the world. If we had sought world domination then, who could have opposed us? But the United States followed a different course—one unique in all the history of mankind. We used our power and wealth to rebuild the war-ravaged economies of the world, including those nations who had been our enemies. May I say there is absolutely no substance to charges that the United States is guilty of imperialism or attempts to impose its will on other countries by use of force.

Mr. President, should we not be concerned with eliminating the obstacles which prevent our people from achieving their most cherished goals? And isn't it possible some of these obstacles are born of government objectives which have little to do with the real needs and desires of our people?

It is in this spirit, in the spirit of helping the people of both our nations, that I have lifted the grain embargo. Perhaps this decision will contribute to creating the circumstances which will lead to the meaningful and constructive dialogue which will assist us in fulfilling our joint obligation to find lasting peace.

A few days later, I got an icy reply from Brezhnev. He said he, too, was against making immediate plans for a summit, repudiated everything I'd said about the Soviet Union, blamed the United States for starting and perpetuating the Cold War, and then said we had no business telling the Soviets what they could or could not do anywhere in the world.

So much for my first attempt at personal diplomacy.

Meanwhile, other important items were popping up on my foreign policy plate: After deciding to sell American-made airborne warning and control system aircraft—the AWACS planes—to Saudi Arabia to help with its defenses in the Middle East, we touched off a firestorm of protest from many elements of the American Jewish community that would last for months. And we continued quiet negotiations aimed at deflating the great pressure building up in Congress to slap a quota on Japanese car imports.

On May 1, this policy paid off when Japan announced it was going to voluntarily limit its exports of motor vehicles to this country to 1.68 million a year. As I expected, the announcement defused the momentum in Congress to impose quotas, which could have been the first shot of a serious international trade war.

At noon on the day Japan made the announcement of its export cutback, the Prince of Wales came to the White House for an informal visit prior to a dinner Nancy was planning for him and a few guests the following evening. I liked Prince Charles very much; he'd first won me over years before when I'd seen him interviewed on his twenty-first birthday and a television interviewer kept asking him to say what it was like growing up in a royal household and having a mother who was the queen of England.

"Well," he said, "I don't know, I just call her Mummy."

When the prince arrived in the Oval Office, he was, as usual, charming, full of life, and full of energy. When a White House steward asked him whether he wanted coffee or tea, he asked for tea, and they brought in a tray and set it beside him.

After a few minutes, I noticed the prince was staring rather quizzically down into his cup, and I thought he seemed a little troubled. We kept on talking and it was all very cordial, but I knew something was bothering him, although I couldn't figure it out. He just kept holding his cup up and looking into it, then eventually put it down on the table without drinking anything. All this time, I'd kept eyeing him, trying to determine what was wrong without making him feel uncomfortable. Finally, it dawned on me: The ushers had given him a cup containing a tea bag. I thought, well, maybe he had never seen one before.

After my discovery, I decided to keep quiet and not embarrass him, but I brought it up over dinner the following night and he joked about it. "I just didn't know what to do with the little bag," he said.

45

AFTER THE SHOOTING AT THE HILTON, the Secret Service wouldn't let me go to church as often, and I had to pass up many public events presidents normally attended, like the annual Easter egg hunt on the White House lawn. When I did go out, the Secret Service made me wear my iron underwear more often. It's hard to feel comfortable or well dressed in a bulletproof vest, especially when you're standing beneath a hot sun. But I took their advice.

One of the first things I asked the doctors at George Washington University Hospital after the shooting was whether I'd be able to ride again. They assured me I could. A month after my discharge, they gave their approval for a Memorial Day weekend visit to the ranch and said I could go riding if I took it easy.

After almost a year on the campaign trail, almost five months in Washington, and only a brief visit to the ranch in February, I wondered as we flew across the country if Rancho del Cielo would have lost its old magic. But I needn't have worried. The weather was beautiful and so was the ranch. Its wild scenery and solitude only reminded us how much we loved it and how much we had missed our life in California.

Over the next eight years, the ranch was a sanctuary for us like none other: Every time we lifted away from Andrews Air Force Base aboard Air Force One and headed westward, it began casting a spell over us. I always took some work with me, but at Rancho del Cielo, Nancy and I could put on our boots and old clothes, recharge our batteries, and be reminded of where we had come from. And I always got a few hours on a horse to do some thinking.

On that first trip after the shooting, we rediscovered a freedom we never had anymore in the White House: In the same pattern we usually followed on subsequent trips, we rode in the morning and, after lunch, I cut brush and did other chores; then, after some office work, Nancy and I had dinner by the fire.

Because it was in wild country, the ranch had its share of wildlife; once or twice people have seen bear tracks on the ranch, all of which made some of the Secret Service agents a little nervous. They established several security posts around the ranch, including one up the hill above the house, where an agent could keep an eye on it. One day, an agent came down from this post and his eyes were as wide as saucers. He'd been sitting on his camp stool watching the house when a big mountain lion had strolled past him only a few feet away; he said he just sat still and let it pass.

"Does that happen a lot?" he asked.

"No," I said, "that's a *little* unusual."

I've never liked hunting, simply killing an animal for the pleasure of it, but I have always enjoyed and collected unusual guns; I love target shooting, and have always kept a gun for protection at home. As I had done when I was governor, I sometimes did some target shooting with the Secret Service agents who accompanied us to the ranch, and occasionally managed to amaze them with my marksmanship. We have a small pond on the ranch that sometimes attracts small black snakes, and every now and then, one would stick its head up out of the water for a second or two. After I'd see one, I'd go into the house and come back with a .38 revolver, go into a little crouch, and wait for the next snake to rise up. Then I'd shoot.

Well, since I was thirty feet or more from the lake, the Secret Service agents were shocked that I was able to hit the snake every time. They'd shake their heads and say to each other, "How the hell does he do it?"

What they didn't know was that my pistol was loaded with shells containing bird shot—like a shotgun—instead of a conventional slug. I kept my secret for a while, but finally decided to fess up and tell them about the bird shot.

. . .

On the Sunday after we returned from our Memorial Day trip to Santa Barbara, James J. (Jack) Kilpatrick, the newspaper columnist, invited Nancy and me to his home in Virginia for lunch. The security people gave their okay, and that Sunday afternoon I discovered another of the more enjoyable perquisites of being president.

We lifted off from the South Lawn aboard a Marine helicopter at about noon on a bright, beautiful spring day, and twenty minutes later were landing a couple hundred yards from Jack's home in rural Virginia. He was waiting to meet us, and on the way to the house he pointed out several men who were busily working in a tent.

"Your fellows have been here all week installing your phones," he said.

"What do you mean, my fellows?" I asked.

"They told me they work for the White House and wherever you go, you have to be able to talk to anyone in the world—in case there's an emergency."

It was the first time I'd heard that. Later, I discovered that even a dinner invitation to a friend's home in Washington meant White House phones would have to be installed and operating there when we arrived. But that Sunday morning, it was news to me. As we walked toward the house, Jack told me more about his conversation with the people from "Signal," the White House communications agency. He said he had questioned their boast of being able to reach anyone in the world from the temporary phone setup. According to Jack, they said: "Okay, name someone."

Jack named his son, a marine who was on guard duty at an embassy in Africa. In less than five minutes, he said, they had his son on the line and Jack and his wife got to talk to him.

Then the man from Signal, possibly with a little sense of pride, said: "Anyone else?"

"Yes, I have a son who is a quartermaster on the USS *Pratt*," a destroyer in the Sixth Fleet in the Mediterranean, Jack said.

A few minutes later, however, the Signal people told him that they were unable to reach Jack's other son, and Jack said, "But you said you could reach *anyone anywhere in the world*."

Yes, normally that was true, they said, but the USS *Pratt* was on maneuvers, and as long as the maneuvers were going on, only the president could reach them.

By the time Jack had finished his story, we were inside the big farmhouse and starting to meet the other luncheon guests; among them was the young wife of the quartermaster who was on a destroyer participating in maneuvers somewhere in the Mediterranean. She was a lovely young woman and she mentioned that she hadn't seen her husband in months. I slipped away and went out to the Signal tent and said: "Is it really true that you can call anybody in the world from here, including Quartermaster Kilpatrick on the USS *Pratt?*"

"Oh, yes sir," one said.

"Get him," I said.

I went back to the house and told the young lady she was going to get to talk to her husband. Understandably, she was ecstatic. Although the call didn't come through until after Nancy and I had left the farm, we'd only been back in the White House ten or fifteen minutes when Jack and his daughter-in-law phoned to say she had spoken to her husband and was overjoyed.

A couple of weeks later I received a letter from Quartermaster Kilpatrick. He thanked me for arranging the chance to speak to his wife, and went on to describe what it had been like that day in the Mediterranean. Because of the maneuvers, he said, the air had been full of radio traffic, ships talking to ships, admirals talking to admirals. Suddenly, a voice came over the air and said, "White House calling." Another voice said, "What code is that?"

Then a third voice spoke up: "Maybe that's no code, maybe it's the White House calling."

"Not even Hollywood could have silenced the airwaves as quickly as they were silenced," young Kilpatrick wrote. "Then they came down and found a lowly quartermaster on a tin can and told him he was wanted on the phone."

The young sailor closed his letter by saying, "It was as if God had called the Vatican and asked for an altar boy by name." He signed his letter, "Your altar boy."

There were more letters from him in the years that followed, always with the same sign-off. When Jack told me his son was going to reenlist and was about to be promoted, I arranged for both events to take place in the Oval Office in the presence of his family.

On the Sunday evening after I had arranged for a young wife to speak to her husband in the middle of the Mediterranean, I told Nancy, "You know, some days, this job is more fun than others."

46

D URING THOSE FIRST FEW MONTHS in the White House, there were certain things I wanted to accomplish as quickly as possible. Nothing was more important than getting the tax and spending cuts through Congress. They were essential to pull the nation out of its economic mess and beginning the modernization of our military forces. But I also wanted to appoint a woman to the Supreme Court.

During the campaign, I pledged that "one of my first" nominations to the court would be a woman—but I felt it was long past the time when a woman should be sitting on the highest court in the land and intended to look for the most qualified woman I could find for my *first* nomination to the Supreme Court. We started looking for her during my first month in the White House, long before there was a vacancy to fill. There was no trouble compiling a list of potential candidates; not surprisingly, there were many outstanding female jurists sitting on the nation's courts. In mid-spring, Justice Potter Stewart sent word to us that he wanted to retire at the end of the current term, giving me my opening. I asked William French Smith, the attorney general, to begin narrowing the search for a woman who was up to the challenge.

I knew that judges had a way of going their own way once they were sitting on the bench. Dwight Eisenhower once told me he believed that the biggest mistake he had made as president was appointing Earl Warren as chief justice of the Supreme Court because, in Ike's view, Warren had changed his stripes and turned into a liberal who took it upon himself to rewrite the Constitution. I'd had a similar experience with one of my appointments in California.

Even though you couldn't always be certain how the judges you appointed would act once they put on black robes, I intended to do my best to choose the most responsible and politically neutral jurists I could find.

When I was governor, we'd instituted a system for selecting California judges that I was very proud of—independently canvassing lawyers, judges, and key citizens in a community to select the best-qualified candidate for a judicial opening. In Washington, we couldn't do it that way, because the federal judiciary was so large and covered the whole country. But I asked Bill Smith and Ed Meese to develop within the Justice Department a system for screening potential judges, taking into account input from their peers and applying the same kind of standards we'd used in California. I said I didn't want politics to play any part in the selection, I wanted the *best* man or woman for the job. The only litmus test I wanted, I said, was the assurance of a judge's honesty and judicial integrity. As in California, I wanted judges who would interpret the Constitution, not try to rewrite it.

At a meeting with Bill Smith on June 21, after paring down a list that included several other distinguished women, I made the tentative decision to nominate Sandra Day O'Connor of the Arizona Court of Appeals to the U.S. Supreme Court.

Everything we had learned about her during our months of searching convinced me she was a woman of great legal intellect, fairness, and integrity—the antithesis of an ideological judge, and just what I wanted on the court.

On July 1, I met with her at the White House. She was forthright and convincing, and I had no doubt she was the right woman for the job. I appointed her and she turned out to be everything I hoped for.

In early May, FBI agents implicated a Libyan terrorist in a Chicago murder and we responded by ordering the Libyan government headed by Muammar al-Qaddafi to close its embassy in Washington. Qaddafi was a madman who was becoming an increasing concern not only to Western democracies but also to moderate Arab regimes and the civilized world at large. Through terrorism, he was trying to unify the world of Islam into a single nation of fundamentalists under rigid religious control—a theocracy, like Iran, that was ruled by priests and mullahs administering an ecclesiastical form of justice that in its most radical forms was regarded by many in the West as barbarous. He was seeking to accomplish his goal using Libya's oil wealth, Russian weapons, and terrorism.

Like the Ayatollah Khomeini, the Iranian despot with whom he was allied and often in contact, Qaddafi was an unpredictable fanatic. He believed any act, no matter how vicious or cold-blooded, was justified to further his goals.

Under Bill Casey, whom I had appointed as Director of Central Intelligence, we stepped up covert activities in the region and knew in some detail how the Soviets were supplying arms to Libya and that Qaddafi gave support to a number of non-Libyan terrorist groups around the world. I wanted to let him know that America wasn't going to tolerate it and we'd do whatever it took to protect our interests and the interests of our allies.

My opportunity to do that came at a meeting of the National Security Council in early June when I authorized the Sixth Fleet to conduct maneuvers later that summer in the Gulf of Sidra, a part of the Mediterranean that indents the northern edge of Libya like a huge half moon. Ships and carrier-based planes of the Sixth Fleet had traditionally entered the gulf during annual summer maneuvers, but Qaddafi during the 1970s had begun claiming that it was legally a part of Libya, not international waters, and he had ordered foreign fleets out of the region. That was as if the United States had drawn a line from the tip of Florida to the U.S. mainland and declared the Gulf of Mexico belonged to America.

The Carter administration, during the period when it was trying to bring home the U.S. hostages in Teheran, had canceled the Sixth Fleet's maneuvers in the Gulf of Sidra the previous year. Secretary of Defense Cap Weinberger urged me to resume the annual exercises, because he said if we continued accepting Qaddafi's claim that the gulf was a Libyan lake, we would be accepting a precedent that any nation could claim any patch of water outside the conventional twelve-mile limit and interfere with lawful shipping. I agreed with Cap and gave an order for the maneuvers to proceed in August. Then we'd see how Qaddafi responded to our decision.

On the same Sunday that I decided to appoint Sandra Day O'Connor to the Supreme Court, I had made another decision: Transportation Secretary Drew Lewis came to Camp David that day and told me that the Professional Air Traffic Controllers Organization, whose members manned Federal Aviation Administration airport control towers and radar centers around the country, was threatening to strike the following day because of our refusal to meet its demand for a huge salary increase. Although I had accepted the argument that the unusual pressures and demands in their occupation justified an increase, their demands would have cost taxpayers almost $700 million a year. I told Lewis to advise the union's leaders that, as a former union president, I was probably the best friend his organization ever had in the White House, but I could not countenance an illegal strike nor permit negotiations to take place as long as one was in progress. I hoped the air controllers realized I meant what I said.

PATCO was one of only a handful of national unions that had backed me in the election. By instinct and experience, I supported unions and the rights of workers to organize and bargain collectively; I'd served six terms as president of my own union and had led the Screen Actors Guild in its first strike. I was the first president of the United States who was a lifetime member of an AFL-CIO union. But no president could tolerate an illegal strike by Federal employees. Unions can strike a business and shut it down, but you cannot allow a strike to shut down a vital government service.

Governments are different from private industry. I agreed with Calvin Coolidge, who said, "There is no right to strike against the public safety by anybody, anywhere, at any time."

Congress had passed a law forbidding strikes by government employees, and every member of the controllers' union had signed a sworn affidavit agreeing not to strike. I told Lewis to tell leaders of the union that I expected them to abide by it. After our meeting, there was a brief resumption of negotiations. But on the morning of August 3, after the union's executive board rejected a tentative agreement, more than seventy percent of the FAA's force of nearly seventeen thousand controllers went on strike.

I suppose this was the first real national emergency I faced as president. The strike endangered the safety of thousands of passengers on hundreds of airline flights daily, and threatened more harm to our already troubled economy. But I never had any doubt how to respond to it. That morning, I sent a directive to FAA supervisors and to those controllers who had crossed the picket lines and were at work in the control towers and radar rooms; I instructed them, above all, to maintain the safety of the airways. Flight operations were to be reduced to the level the system could accommodate *safely*. Then I called reporters to the Rose Garden and read a handwritten statement I'd drafted in my study the night before.

Citing the pledge made by controllers never to strike, I said that if they did not return to work within forty-eight hours, their jobs would be terminated. I didn't like disrupting the lives and careers of these professionals, many of whom had spent years serving their country. I don't like firing anybody. But I realized that if they made the decision not to return to work in the full knowledge of what I'd said, then I wasn't firing them, they were giving up their jobs based on their individual decisions.

I think that members of PATCO were poorly served by their leaders. They apparently thought I was bluffing or playing games when I said controllers who didn't honor the no-strike pledge would lose their jobs and not be rehired; and I think they underestimated the courage and energy of those controllers who decided not to go on strike. The airlines and these hard-working FAA employees, as well as the traveling public, went through a difficult period. But as each day passed, there were more planes in the air; we discovered that before the strike, the air traffic control system had about six thousand more controllers than it really needed to operate safely.

Training a new crop of controllers to replace those who chose not to return would take more than two years, but our air traffic control system emerged safer and more efficient than ever.

I didn't think of it in such terms at the time, but I suppose the strike was an important juncture for our new administration. I think it convinced people who might have thought otherwise that I meant what I said. Incidentally, I would have been just as forceful if I thought management had been wrong in that dispute.

47

To GET THE SPENDING and tax cuts we wanted through Congress, we needed the help of a substantial number of Democrats in the House as well as the votes of virtually all the Republicans in both houses of Congress. I spent a lot of time in the spring and early summer of 1981 on the telephone and in meetings trying to build a coalition to get the nation's recovery under way. Reeling from the effects of years of mismanagement, the economy was falling deeper into recession every day. I knew things wouldn't get better until we got the recovery program up and running. I met dozens of times with congressmen from both parties, on Capitol Hill and at the White House, trying to explain what it was we were trying to accomplish and to rebut erroneous reports in the press and fictions about the program being spread by Tip O'Neill.

Sometimes I made a convert, sometimes not. I remember one example of the efficiency of the White House operators: We were approaching an important vote on our proposed budget cuts when I asked to speak to a certain congressman. After quite a delay, I got a call back from him and I said jovially, "Where did we find you?" He said, "New Zealand." I said, "What time is it in New Zealand?" He answered, *"Four o'clock in the morning."* I wanted to hang up and pretend I'd never called him; but instead, after an apology, I proceeded with my pitch. When he got back to Washington, he voted with us.

Opinion polls showed ninety-five percent of the American people were behind the proposed spending cuts and almost as many supported the thirty-percent, three-year tax cut. But Tip O'Neill and other Democratic leaders in Congress used every procedural trick they'd learned in decades on Capitol Hill to block this legislation.

That meant I had to dip into FDR's bag of tricks and take my case to the people.

To his credit, Tip granted my request to speak before a joint session of Congress a week after I left the hospital. I walked in to an unbelievable ovation that went on for several minutes. I explained why I thought tax and budget cuts were essential for ending the economic emergency the nation was facing. At one point, forty or so Democrats stood up and applauded and I felt a shiver go down my spine. I thought to myself: "Boy, that took guts; maybe our economic package has a chance." Later, I joked to someone, "That reception was almost worth getting shot for."

With Tip convinced that I was determined to destroy everything he had worked his entire life for, the Democratic leadership really dug in its heels following that speech. He sent out the word that any Democrat who was even thinking about supporting the tax and budget cuts could expect merciless discipline from the party leadership. And every time he got a chance, he went public and accused me of having horns and trying to destroy the nation. I was never able to convince Tip that I didn't want to deprive the truly needy of the assistance the rest of us owed them; I just wanted to make government programs more efficient and eliminate waste, so that we no longer spent $2 for every $1 of aid we delivered to people.

A few days after my speech to Congress I started to think we might make it. In early May, I wrote in my diary: "More meetings with Congressmen. These Dems are with us on the budget and it's interesting to hear some who've been here ten years or more and say it is their first time to ever be in the Oval Office. We really seem to be putting a coalition together."

The next day we got tangible evidence we were creating the coalition we needed. Sixty-three Democrats defied Tip and voted along with every Republican in the House for the Gramm-Latta budget resolution, the first of a series of congressional actions that slashed billions of dollars in federal spending in 1981. "We never anticipated such a landslide," I wrote in my diary. "We felt we were going to win due to the conservative bloc of Dems, but expected

Republican defections so that we might win by one or two votes. It's been a long time since Republicans had a victory like this."

Joining the Republicans was a group of Democrats who, like Representative Phil Gramm of Texas, called themselves the "boll weevils" and shared our philosophy that government was spending too much of the national wealth and wanted to cut it back. Without their help, we would have never passed the economic recovery program.

As sweet as this initial victory was, we had a long way to go on the two fronts of cutting spending and cutting taxes. I realized I would have to compromise and settle for less than the full thirty-percent, three-year cut I wanted, but got some plums I hadn't expected: In late May, a group of Democrats announced a counter-proposal to our tax plan that rejected the thirty-percent-over-three-years cut, but accepted a smaller cut in personal income tax rates while proposing a reduction in the top rate on unearned income from seventy percent to fifty percent. I'd wanted that in the first place, but figured the Democrats would attack us for pandering to the rich, so we hadn't asked for it in our package. To get on the people's new antitax bandwagon, some Democrats also called for indexing income tax rates, so that rates would decline each year in step with inflation and end "bracket creep." That was something else I wanted but doubted we could get.

I agreed "reluctantly" to give in to their proposals and accept a twenty-five-percent reduction in rates over three years, phased in at five, ten, and ten percent, and hailed it as a great bipartisan solution. "H—l," I wrote in the diary, "it's more than I thought we could get. I'm delighted to get the seventy down to fifty. All we gave up is the first year 10 per cent beginning last Jan. to 5 per cent beginning this October. Instead of 30 per cent over 36 months, it will be 25 per cent over 27 months."

I tried to keep the heat on Congress. I flew to Chicago in early July, ostensibly to speak at a fund-raiser for Governor Jim Thompson, but used my visit to the district of Dan Rostenkowski, chairman of the House Ways and Means Committee, to point out to his constituents that he held the fate of the tax-cut proposals in his palm. I urged them to write to him: "If all of you will join with your neighbors to send the same message to Washington, we'll have that tax cut and we'll have it this year." I was told that the speech generated hundreds of letters to Rostenkowski, who subsequently became something of a conciliatory voice among the Democratic leaders in the House as we approached the finish line in the battle over tax reduction.

Matters started coming to a head shortly after that. In mid-July, Nancy flew to London to attend the wedding of HRH the Prince of Wales and Lady Diana Spencer. "I worry when she's out of sight six minutes," I wrote in my diary that night. "How am I going to hold out for six days? The lights just don't seem as warm and bright without her." But I had lots to keep me busy.

July 27, 1981, was a Monday, the beginning of a pivotal week that would determine whether our program got off the ground or crashed. Almost everyone following the events, from the members of our staff to the Washington press corps, said the battle was too close to call.

Six months earlier, I'd come to Washington to put into practice ideas I'd believed in for decades. Now it was down to a few hours; Congress had two tax programs before it: the administration plan, and one crafted by the Democratic leadership meant to respond to the public clamor for tax relief. That plan proposed a fifteen-percent tax cut over two years, distributed most of the benefits to low-income people, and excluded many of the pump-priming features I felt were needed to encourage business investment and give a jolt to the economy. If the economic recovery plan was to work, I was convinced, Congress had to provide across-the-board relief equally for all Americans for three years. I believed this would create millions of jobs and trigger an economic resurgence.

I knew that, if we were going to get it passed, it wouldn't be enough to make Congress see the light; I had to make 'em feel the heat. That Monday I spent virtually every minute from early in the morning until seven thirty at night on the phone or in meetings with congressmen lobbying for the tax cuts; at eight, I made a televised broadcast to the nation in which I compared the Democrats' tax relief plan with ours and said: "The plain truth is, our choice is not between two plans to reduce taxes; it's between a tax cut or a tax increase." (Under their plan the total taxes paid by Americans would have gone up, not down.) Then I asked the people to make their views known to their elected representatives. The White House switchboard was swamped with calls from around the nation—more than after any speech I had given—and were six-to-one in favor of the administration's tax bill.

As soon as I got up the next day, I was on the phone again making calls to congressmen; most said their phones had been ringing off the wall since the speech with calls in support of the administration tax bill. "Tomorrow is the day," I wrote in my diary before going to bed the night of July 28, "and it's too close to call but there is no doubt the people are with us."

Wednesday, July 29:

> The whole day was given to phone calls to Congressmen except for a half dozen to name ambassadors.
>
> I went from fearing the worst to hope we'd squeak through. As the day went on though some how I got the feeling that something good was happening. Then late afternoon came word the Senate had passed its tax bill [ours] 89 to 11. Then from the House where all the chips were down, we won 238–195. We got 40 Democrat votes. On final passage almost 100 joined the parade making it 330 odd to 107 or thereabouts. This on top of the budget victory is the greatest political win in half a century.
>
> Tip O'Neill and his leadership called me and with complete graciousness congratulated us on our win.
>
> Now we must make it work—and we will.

The economic program I'd brought to Washington six months earlier was now in place. Next on my agenda was realizing another dream I had brought with me: reducing the threat of nuclear war.

48

In early August, a senior admiral came to the White House to brief me and the cabinet about the maneuvers that were scheduled to begin in the Gulf of Sidra later that month. He said Libyan planes were already sporadically harassing our ships and aircraft in the Mediterranean north of the gulf, and it was likely the level of harassment would heighten substantially once the maneuvers began. It was clear he wanted guidance from me on how the navy should react if the Libyan planes fired on our aircraft or vessels or otherwise interfered with their freedom of movement on the high seas.

My response was simple: Whenever our ships or planes were fired upon or otherwise deprived of rights granted sovereign countries in international waters, the navy was to respond in kind. "Any time we send an American anywhere in the world where he or she can be shot at, they have the right to shoot back," I said.

One cabinet member asked: "What about hot pursuit?"

He wanted to know the extent to which our planes should be permitted to pursue Libyan planes if they harassed our aircraft or ships in violation of international law.

The admiral stopped, cleared his throat, and looked over at me, waiting for an answer from me, and suddenly it was very quiet in the room.

"All the way into the hangar," I said.

A smile broke out on the admiral's face, and he said, "Yes sir."

. . .

A few days later, President Anwar Sadat of Egypt came to Washington for a state visit. In the Oval Office, I revealed our plans for the maneuvers; before I could finish, he almost shouted: "Magnificent."

Sadat was a very likable man with both a sense of humor and a sense of dignity, and he had a good grasp of events and personalities in the Middle East. He was a staunch ally of the United States and also a courageous statesman whose efforts to achieve peace with Israel had isolated him from most other Arab nations. As had Jimmy Carter, I regarded him as a giant figure in the Middle East and thought he might hold the key to resolving that region's long and bitter struggle between Arab and Jew.

During his visit, Sadat had other things on his mind besides the difficult task of resolving the Arab-Israeli dispute. Terrorists and radical Muslims who were allied with Qaddafi and Iran's Ayatollah Khomeini in trying to create an Islamic fundamentalist state were trying to subvert his government and were making significant inroads in neighboring Sudan and Chad. The goal of Libya and the fundamentalists, Sadat said, was to remove him and impose a government in Egypt modeled after Iran's fundamentalist regime. The Soviet Union, Sadat said, was working hard to gain influence over the Islamic fundamentalist movement and was using Libya as its surrogate in the region, supplying it with large amounts of arms that Libya transferred to terrorists in the Middle East and elsewhere. In response to indications that Libya was building up hostile forces along its border with Egypt, we had agreed to give limited technical assistance and other support to Egypt if Qaddafi did attack.

I assured him we would continue doing everything we could to help Egypt, and as he left I had a good feeling about the visit. That night, writing in the diary, I said, "I'm encouraged that between us, maybe we can do something about peace in the Middle East."

Two weeks later, on August 20, Qaddafi sent up several of his planes and they fired at two F-14 jets from the USS *Nimitz* that were participating in our naval maneuvers. The incident took place in the Gulf of Sidra about sixty miles off the coast of Libya, well into international waters, and in compliance with my instructions, the F-14's turned on their tails and shot down the two Libyan aircraft.

We'd sent Qaddafi a message: We weren't going to let him claim squatters' rights over a huge area of the Mediterranean in defiance of international law. I also wanted to send a message to others in the world that there was a new management in the White House, and that the United States wasn't going to hesitate any longer to act when its legitimate interests were at stake.

A few days after the incident over the gulf, security people obtained secret information indicating that Qaddafi had advised some of his associates that he intended to have me assassinated. So, it was back into my iron vest whenever I was out in public.

Subsequently, security people obtained what they considered highly credible information that not only I, but George Bush, Cap Weinberger, and Al Haig were targeted by Libyan hit squads that had been smuggled into this country. From then on, security precautions became even more rigid—not only was my iron vest de rigueur, a variety of other steps I can't even now discuss were put in place. One thing I can mention is that whenever we went anywhere by helicopter, the route was selected only minutes before takeoff because of intelligence reports that a Libyan group armed with a heat-seeking missile capable of being launched by hand had entered the country with the intention of shooting down the presidential helicopter, known as Marine One.

Just two months after Nancy and I said good-bye to Anwar and Jehan Sadat at the White House, I was awakened by an early morning call from Al Haig. He told me Sadat had been shot, but was expected to live.

Several hours later we learned he had died instantly, assassinated by Muslim fundamentalists. I had to continue my regular schedule that day, but it was very difficult.

The news had hit Nancy and me like a locomotive: we had spent only a few hours over two days with the Sadats, but felt we had formed a deep and lasting friendship with them. Now, suddenly, this great, kind man filled with warmth and humor was gone; it was an enormous tragedy for the world and a terrible and painful personal loss for us.

A few hours after we got news of Sadat's death, I watched Muammar al-Qaddafi on television. He was almost doing a jig, gloating over Sadat's death while Libyans danced in the streets. We discovered that even before Sadat's death was confirmed, Qaddafi had gone on the radio to call for a holy war on behalf of Islamic fundamentalism—propaganda material tied to Sadat's murder that had to have been prepared before the shots were fired in Cairo. He had to have known in advance that Sadat was going to be assassinated.

As I prayed for Sadat, I tried to repress the hatred I felt for Qaddafi, but I couldn't do it. I despised him for what had happened in Cairo.

With hundreds of Americans living in Libya, there were limitations on what we could do in response to this evil man. Through diplomatic back channels, we sent word to Qaddafi that any acts of terrorism directed against Americans would be considered acts of war and we would respond accordingly.

After the dogfight over the Gulf of Sidra, I hoped he realized I meant what I said.

49

I DECLARED OUR COMMITMENT to reducing the risk of nuclear war and asked the Soviet Union to join us in doing so in a television address from the National Press Club in Washington on November 18, 1981. The address was broadcast live via Worldnet, a worldwide satellite system developed by the director of USIA, Charles Wick. As I made the speech, I couldn't resist an ironic thought: I was talking about peace but wearing a bulletproof vest. Our intelligence agents had been told that a Libyan assassin named Jack was in the country and planning to kill me on the day of the speech. There may have been more security agents than reporters at the National Press Club, and no one was happier about it than I: if Jack was there, he wasn't able to get through the wall of security and pull off his assignment, and I was able to deliver the most important speech on foreign policy I'd ever made.

The principles contained in the speech took shape during months of debate within the administration. Hoping it would be received in Moscow as a sincere effort to begin the process of arms reduction, I called for the elimination of all intermediate-range nuclear force (INF) weapons in Europe by both sides, a proposal that came to be known as the "zero" or "zero-zero" option.

In addition, I invited the Soviet Union to enter with us in new negotiations aimed at reducing our mutual stockpiles of long-range strategic nuclear weapons to equal and verifiable levels. I proposed that, instead of referring to our next round of negotiations as

SALT, for "Strategic Arms Limitation Talks" (the name of the largely futile previous meetings on controlling intercontinental-range nuclear weapons), we adopt a more positive approach and we call them START—for "Strategic Arms *Reduction* Talks."

I also suggested we begin negotiations aimed at bringing conventional forces in Europe down to parity between East and West, a step that was essential if we were to reduce the arsenal of nuclear weapons in Europe.

The journey leading to arms reduction wasn't going to be short or easy. And I knew it had to begin with an *increase* of arms. A few weeks before this speech, I had given the final approval to blueprints for a multibillion-dollar modernization of our strategic forces. In order to assure that we would regain and sustain a military superiority over the Soviet Union, which for a decade had been moving forward with the largest and costliest military buildup in the history of man, we had decided to build one hundred B-1B bombers to replace our deteriorating fleet of B-52 bombers (the B-1's development had been canceled by the Carter administration); to build one hundred new intercontinental-range missiles, the MX Peacekeeper; to deploy new Trident nuclear submarines and develop a new missile to be launched from them; to develop the Stealth bomber, which was to be capable of penetrating Soviet defense radars; and to construct a wide array of new surface ships, fighter aircraft, and space satellites for communications and other military purposes. Over the next few years, many of my critics would claim it was contradictory and even hypocritical to embark on a quest for nuclear peace by building more nuclear weapons. But it was obvious that if we were ever going to get anywhere with the Russians in persuading them to reduce armaments, we had to bargain with them from *strength*, not weakness. If you were going to approach the Russians with a dove of peace in one hand, you had to have a sword in the other.

Most of the time since World War II, we had maintained a lead over the Soviets in nuclear weapons. But during the late 1970s, they had caught up with and exceeded us in a number of critical areas, including the development of unusually powerful ICBMs capable of delivering multiple nuclear warheads and of wreaking enormous devastation over great distances. They had also produced new missile-launching submarines, a vast fleet of modern surface ships, and tens of thousands of tanks and other conventional weapons, all of which had changed the balance of power.

At the time of the Cuban missile crisis in the early 1960s, it had been relatively easy to stand up to the Soviets: Our nuclear weapons outnumbered theirs almost ten to one; the Soviets took their missiles out of Cuba and Khrushchev backed down. But the balance of power had all been changed by the early 1980s. The Soviet Union was building missiles hand over fist, and their nuclear forces outnumbered ours.

During the period of this great Soviet military expansion, we had built no new bombers, developed no new missiles, and the morale, weapons, and readiness of all our military forces had deteriorated. If we were ever going to stop Soviet troublemaking around the world, we'd have to persuade them to sue for peace. And so, as we prepared for new arms control talks, we began the task of undoing the years of neglect of our armed forces.

My proposal of the zero-zero option sprang out of the realities of nuclear politics in Western Europe: In 1979, the Soviets began deploying at a rate of two a week a new three-thousand-mile-range mobile missile with three warheads called the SS-20. It was designed specifically to reach cities in Western Europe from the Soviet Union. In response, our NATO allies asked America to send them nuclear weapons of comparable range that they could hurl back at Moscow if attacked. The Carter administration then initiated development of the Pershing II and the cruise missiles. Parallel with this decision, in what was called the two-track policy, the NATO countries agreed to seek negotiations with the Russians aimed at reducing nuclear weapons in Europe.

Now that I was in office and the American-made INF missiles were being scheduled for shipment to Europe, some European leaders were having doubts about the policy. Whipped up by Soviet propagandists, thousands of Europeans were taking to the streets and protesting the plans to base additional nuclear weapons in Europe, arguing that their presence would cause future nuclear wars to be confined to Europe. (I've often wondered why these antiwar groups got so angry at their own leaders; it was the Soviets who had targeted nuclear weapons at them.)

Helmut Kohl, leader of the opposition party in Germany, told me during a White House visit that the propaganda offensive was becoming highly sophisticated and effective in convincing Europeans that the United States was a bloodthirsty, militaristic nation. This view of America shocked me: We were the most moral and generous people on earth, we'd spent thirty-five years since World War II helping to rebuild the economies of our former allies and enemies, we had gone to the corners of the world in the defense of freedom and democracy, and now we were being cast—effectively, Kohl said—as villains. It was clear we'd have to do a better job of conveying to the world our sense of morality and our commitment to the creation of a peaceful, nuclear-free world.

After considerable discussion with the cabinet and our arms control experts, I decided to propose the zero-zero plan, which was also advocated by the then-chancellor of West Germany, Helmut Schmidt: If the Russians would dismantle their SS-20 missiles and two shorter-range missiles—the SS-4 and SS-5—that they had targeted at Western Europe, I told the Russians, we would scrap plans to install the Pershing II and cruise missiles. Then there would be zero INF weapons in Europe.

Al Haig was not keen about the zero-zero proposal. He felt NATO required the new missiles to counter the Soviet threat, and argued that it did not leave enough room for bargaining with the Russians; he suggested that in offering the zero-zero plan, we should indicate that we would be willing to consider leaving a few INF weapons in Europe on both sides—a "zero-plus" option. Cap Weinberger, on the other hand, was strongly in favor of the zero-zero option; he said it would get the arms control talks moving on a realistic basis and put the Soviets on the defensive in the European propaganda war.

It was one of many instances I faced as president when my policy of encouraging cabinet members to speak frankly and to fight for their points of view put me in the middle. The hardest decisions to make are in those situations where there are good arguments on both sides of a question; as you think out the problem you have to weigh the advantages and disadvantages of the two options against each other. Usually, the debate would rage, the meeting would end, and then I'd say: "I'll make my decision after I've given some more thought to this." Sometimes, I might call another meeting and say I hadn't heard enough from the two sides on the issue and get them into another debate to help me reach a decision. As this was going on, I kept a poker face. Then, after more debate, I'd end the meeting, go away, and make my decision. If a horse was nearby, that always helped in my decision-making, but sometimes I might just stand in the shower or think out a problem at my desk or before going to sleep.

In this instance, I had time to think over my choices while flying cross-country in a unique and very special Boeing 747. Sometimes called the "doomsday plane," it was a windowless jumbo jet, with an interior stuffed with communications equipment, that reminded me of a submarine. During an airborne briefing in the plane, I learned that wherever I was, the doomsday plane was never far away; during a major crisis, I was to go there to keep the government functioning during the onset of a nuclear attack. It was a heady environment for making a decision regarding nuclear arms control.

Al's idea of leading with a flexible proposal had merit, but I'd learned as a union negotiator that it's never smart to show your hole card in advance. If we first announced that our goal was the total elimination of intermediate-range nuclear weapons from Europe and then hinted we might be willing to leave a few, we'd be tipping off the bottom line of our negotiating position before the negotiations even began. I thought our goal should be the total elimination of all INF weapons from Europe, and stating this before the world would be a vivid gesture demonstrating to the Soviets, our allies, the people storming the streets of West Germany, and others that we meant business about wanting to reduce nuclear weapons.

We eventually achieved our goal of zero-zero intermediate-range missiles in Europe. But it took longer than I hoped it would, and it was a lot more difficult than I expected.

50

MY FIRST YEAR in the White House was coming to an end. I had some things to feel good about: The first phase of the largest tax cut in the nation's history had gone into effect, allowing Americans to keep and spend more of the money they earned, and, I hoped, sowing the seeds for a resurgence of the economy. Congress had approved more cuts in federal spending than in any previous year in history while still maintaining a broad safety net for unemployed, disabled, and destitute Americans. The prime interest rate had fallen six points and, thanks in part to a tight money policy (which I supported) on the part of the Federal Reserve Board, inflation was below ten percent for the first time in three years.

We had begun the task, as I promised in my inaugural address, of making government work with us, not over us; stand by our side, not ride on our back. The annual rate of growth of federal spending had been cut almost in half, to 7.5 percent from an average of fourteen percent during the previous three years. Under George Bush, we had begun storming the citadel of unnecessary restrictions that obstructed the workings of our economy, eliminating thousands of pages from the federal bureaucracy's rules and regulations. We had begun to restore to states and cities authority usurped from them by the bureaucracy, broadening the use of "block grants" that gave local teachers and community officials more say over how to spend federal aid—and less say to social engineers on the Potomac who had been setting policies and dictating rules for states and cities under strings-attached "categorical" grants.

On the international front, we had gone back to the bargaining table with the Russians to begin the process of reducing the threat of nuclear war while also beginning the first comprehensive modernization of our strategic and conventional forces in twenty years. By making a military career more attractive, we had begun to draw more of the best and brightest of our young people into the voluntary military forces.

And I think the nation had begun the process of spiritual revival that was so badly needed. It was once again striving to live up to that special vision of America expressed more than three hundred years ago by John Winthrop on the deck of a tiny vessel off the coast of Massachusetts, when he told the pilgrims gathered with him on the edge of the New World that they had the opportunity to create a new civilization based on freedom unlike any other before it, a unique and special "shining city on a hill."

But for all our progress, there was much left to be done.

We were plunging deeper into the nation's worst recession since the 1930s, and the world was still a very dangerous place. Leonid Brezhnev had rebuffed my expressions of hope for a warmer relationship between our countries. In the Middle East, dangerous embers of malevolence and hatred smoldering since biblical times had erupted into savage warfare. In Afghanistan, the Soviets were attempting to subdue winds of freedom with a ruthlessness bordering on barbarity, and in Poland their puppet government was preparing to impose martial law to suppress a growing trade union movement. In a cynical rejection of basic human rights, Soviet leaders, some of them motivated by the same anti-Semitism seen in the murderous Russian pogroms of the past, held thousands of Jews captive, refusing to let them emigrate. And every day there was more evidence that Fidel Castro, the proxy of Moscow, was shipping more arms and Communist "advisors" into Central America, and that Nicaragua was becoming a base camp for Communizing all of Central America.

Nicaragua's Sandinista government had taken power in 1979, after the overthrow of dictator Anastasio Somoza, with pledges to the Nicaraguan people and the Organization of American States that it would replace Somoza's dictatorship with democracy. It promised free elections, a free press, free enterprise, and an independent judiciary. But within weeks of Somoza's overthrow, the Sandinistas had begun replacing one dictatorship with another: They seized television and radio stations and began censoring newspapers and crushing whatever democratic sentiment they encountered as violently and ruthlessly as Somoza had ever done. Meanwhile they allied themselves with Castro, Moscow, and the Eastern bloc.

Once they were in power, the Sandinistas began trying to export their Marxist revolution to neighboring El Salvador and other countries in Central America. They proved themselves masters at propaganda, peddling an image of themselves in Europe and America as kindly men whose democratic reforms were being thwarted by the Great Colossus of the North—us.

Early in my first year in the White House, we launched an initiative aimed at helping Caribbean and Central American countries reverse the great economic and social inequities that made many of them ripe for subversion and revolution. But it was soon apparent it was going to take more than that to stop the Marxist guerrillas financed by Castro and Brezhnev. And while our friends in Mexico and Venezuela had indicated that they would join us in a collaborative effort to resist the advance of Marxism in Latin America, it was becoming apparent that they weren't ready to make the kind of commitment necessary to do the job. The United States would have to meet the challenge largely alone—but without sending our troops across the border. That was an option I never entertained.

Bill Casey and others at the CIA drafted a plan to meet the Communist threat in Central America through a covert program that, over the next few months, would provide for the support of anti-Sandinista Nicaraguans who would try to halt the flow of Soviet-made arms from Cuba to Nicaragua and El Salvador. These men, just a few in the beginning, were the nucleus of Nicaragua's Contra freedom fighters.

A month later, after we went over the program in more detail, I formally approved the plan, hoping that it would halt the advance of Communism seven hundred miles from our border. Only time would tell.

· · ·

As all this was going on, we were witnessing the first fraying of the Iron Curtain, a disenchantment with Soviet Communism in Poland, not realizing then that it was a harbinger of great and historic events to come in Eastern Europe. Brave men and women in Poland had demanded one of the most basic human liberties, the right to organize a trade union in defiance of a government that forbade any instrument of power or influence beyond itself.

When this heroic and spontaneous ground swell on behalf of freedom refused to recede, Poland's Communist leaders had been forced to grant Lech Walesa's Solidarity trade union an inch of freedom, recognizing it as a bona fide representative of the workers, and under more pressure even spoke of introducing a modicum of democratic reform to the Polish Communist Party.

Moscow responded to these acts of insubordination by sending its troops on maneuvers along the Polish border during the spring of 1981. It installed a military regime in Warsaw with orders to halt the liberalization. It also cut off loan credits, thus leaving the Polish economy, already unable to feed its people and nearly in ruin because of the failure of Communism, teetering near the brink of collapse.

As seen from the Oval Office, the events in Poland were thrilling. One of man's most fundamental and implacable yearnings, the desire for freedom, was stirring to life behind the Iron Curtain, the first break in the totalitarian dike of Communism.

I wanted to be sure we did nothing to impede this process and everything we could to spur it along. This was what we had been waiting for since World War II. What was happening in Poland might spread like a contagion throughout Eastern Europe.

But our options were limited and presented us with several dilemmas:

Although we wanted to let the Polish people who were struggling for liberty know that we were behind them, we couldn't send out a false signal (as some say the United States did before the doomed 1956 uprisings in Hungary), leading them to expect us to intervene militarily on their side during a revolution. As much as we might want to help, there were limits on the actions our people would support in Poland, especially if, as was likely, there was a charade in which the Polish government appeared to request intervention by Russian troops.

We wanted to help the hungry of Poland fill their stomachs, yet we didn't want to do anything that would prop up the ailing government and prolong the survival of Communism. We didn't want to keep the Communist government afloat by shoring up its economy, yet if the economy collapsed, the result might be violent popular uprisings that would bring in Soviet tanks and doom the embryonic democratic movement. That summer we supported efforts by U.S. and European banks to negotiate an extension of Poland's international debt payments to avert a collapse of the economy, and agreed to send millions of dollars' worth of food to feed the people of Poland. We were striking a delicate balance.

Almost as soon as I moved into the White House, we began informing Moscow that military intervention by the Soviets in Poland would be resisted by us through every diplomatic means at our disposal. In late spring, after intelligence reports indicated that the Soviets were contemplating an invasion of Poland, I wrote to Brezhnev that the United States and the rest of the Western world would look very unfavorably on such an attack; I said the Soviets could forget any new nuclear arms agreements or better trade relations with us and expect the harshest possible economic sanctions from the United States if they launched an invasion. Brezhnev replied that what was going on in Poland was an internal matter for Poland's puppet government alone to deal with, and the Soviet Union had no interest in the United States attitude about Poland.

After our initial correspondence following my release from the hospital in April, Brezhnev and I had exchanged several other chilly letters in which we expressed an interest in continuing a dialogue between the two of us. But he always refused to abandon the Brezhnev Doctrine (although he didn't call it that), and I kept telling him there was no hope of improving our relations until the Soviet Union stopped pushing its policy of expansionism and trying to subvert democratic governments. As I concluded one letter, "In sum, the United States is more interested in actions which further the cause of world peace than in words."

Poland's brave shipyard workers continued their fight for freedom throughout the fall of 1981, triggering persistent rumors and intelligence reports that the Soviets were considering an invasion, along with continued expressions of our opposition to this possibility. On Sunday, December 13, Poland—and Moscow—finally acted. Without warning, the Polish military government closed the country's borders, shut off communications with the rest of the world, arrested the leaders of Solidarity, and imposed martial law.

The crackdown fell short of the military intervention we had warned against, but our intelligence experts established that the entire exercise had been ordered from and orchestrated by Moscow.

A day or two after the crackdown, Al Haig brought me confidential information that the Polish ambassador in Washington, Romuald Spasowski, wanted to defect immediately. Our people managed to spirit him away before the KGB got to him; the ambassador and his wife, daughter, and son-in-law were taken to a safe place.

Two days later, I wrote in the diary,

[At today's N.S.C. meeting] I took a stand that this may be the last chance in our lifetime to see a change in the Soviet Empire's colonial policy re Eastern Europe. We should take a stand and tell them unless and until martial law is lifted in Poland, the prisoners were released and negotiations resumed between Walesa and the Polish government, we would quarantine the Soviets and Poland with no trade or communications across their borders. Also tell our NATO allies and others to join us in such sanctions or risk an estrangement from us. A TV speech is in the works.

On December 22, Ambassador Spasowski and his wife came to see me in the Oval Office; both had looks of desperation that were mixed with relief. Their faces brightened when I told them I welcomed them to America as genuine Polish patriots. Spasowski said he and his family had been thinking about defecting for several years and had been moving closer and closer to it, then decided to act after the imposition of martial law and crackdown on Solidarity.

It was an emotional meeting for all of us and left me with more disgust than ever for the evil men in the Kremlin who believed they had the right to hold an entire nation in captivity.

Subsequently, I learned Ambassador Spasowski had been condemned to death by the generals who ruled Poland.

· · ·

Later that day, I finished writing my speech to the nation; although it was supposed to have been a Christmas message, I decided to deliver a strong message to the Soviets condemning their action in Poland. "We can't let this revolution against Communism fail without our offering a hand," I wrote in the diary afterward. "We may never have an opportunity like this in our lifetime." Then I wrote a message to Leonid Brezhnev condemning the Soviet role in the crackdown in even harsher language; it was sent over the Washington-Moscow cable "hot line," known in the White House as the "Molink." I said:

> The recent events in Poland clearly are not an "internal matter" and in writing to you, as the head of the Soviet government, I am not misaddressing my communication. Your country has repeatedly intervened in Polish affairs during the months preceding the recent tragic events. . . . Our two countries have had moments of accord and moments of disagreement. But since [the invasion of] Afghanistan nothing has so outraged our public opinion as the pressures and threats which your government has exerted on Poland to stifle the stirrings of freedom. Attempts to suppress the Polish people—either by the Polish army or police acting under Soviet pressure, or through even more direct use of Soviet military force—certainly will not bring about long term stability in Poland and could unleash a process which neither you nor we could fully control.

I said that in our correspondence both of us had expressed a desire for better Soviet-American relations, but that it was being jeopardized by "political terror, mass arrests and bloodshed in Poland . . . the Soviet Union must decide whether we can move ahead with this agenda [of trying to improve relations] or whether we will travel a different path."

On Christmas morning, after we'd opened our gifts around the family tree in the White House, I was handed a reply to my message to Brezhnev, a terse note sent via the Molink claiming it was the United States, not his country, that was interfering in Polish affairs.

"If a frank exchange of opinion between Communist parties and the expressions by them of their opinions to each other is not pleasing to someone in the United States," Brezhnev said, "then, in reply, we must firmly say: That is the business of the parties themselves and only them. And the Polish people do not sit in judgment of others who would force their values on them." Apparently referring to several recent speeches I had made, Brezhnev accused me of "defaming our social and state system, our internal order," a charge to which I pleaded guilty.

Attempts to dictate your will to other states are in gross contradiction to the elementary norms of international law. I would like to say further: they are thoroughly amoral. And no sort of game with words regarding the rights of man can hide this fact. The Soviet Union repudiates the claims of anyone to interfere in the events occurring in Poland. You, Mr. President, hint that if further events in Poland should develop in a manner unsatisfactory to the United States damage will be inflicted along the entire range of Soviet-American relations. But if we are to speak frankly, it is your Administration that has already done enough to disrupt or at the very least undermine everything positive which was achieved at the cost of great effort by previous American administrations in the relations between our countries. Today, unfortunately, little remains of the reciprocal positive political gains which were achieved earlier. . . . One cannot help but notice that the general tone of your letter is not the way in which leaders of such powers as the Soviet Union and the United States should talk with each other, especially considering their power and position in the world and their responsibility for the state of international affairs. That is our opinion.

What a good Christmas present, I thought: I'd made my point to Brezhnev.

In a Christmas Day reply to him, I told Brezhnev we would not intervene in Poland if the Russians did not, and proposed that the Polish people only be given the right of self-determination that had been promised to them by Joseph Stalin himself at the Yalta Conference. At Yalta, I reminded him, Stalin had promised Poland and all the countries of Eastern Europe the right of self-determination, but the Soviets had never granted it to any of them.

Shortly before New Year's Day, we backed up our words with action: I announced that we were imposing sanctions against Poland and the Soviet Union in an expression of our displeasure over the crushing of human rights in Poland. We suspended negotiations on a new long-term grain-sale agreement; banned flights to the

United States by the Soviet airline, Aeroflot; canceled several exchange programs; and imposed an embargo on shipment to the Soviet Union of critical American-made products, including pipe-laying equipment that was to be used in the construction of a trans-Siberian gas pipeline. When I sought the support of our European allies for this policy, I was disappointed. They agreed we should send a signal of disapproval to the Russians, but not if it involved halting work on the pipeline; the reaction of some of our allies suggested that money spoke louder to them than principle. They said they wanted freedom for the Polish people but also wanted to expand trade with the Eastern bloc, and they refused to join our efforts to block work on the new pipeline that was to bring natural gas from Siberia to Western Europe.

As I thought back on that letter I'd sent to Brezhnev after the shooting, I realized I hadn't made much progress with the Russians in reducing Cold War tensions during my first year in office. Although Brezhnev's Christmas message had made it clear that they knew there was a new team in Washington, the Soviets were acting more like international brigands than ever.

Unfortunately, as my first year came to an end, it also appeared we weren't making much progress in curing our economic problems. Like a runaway train that keeps hurtling along the tracks long after its locomotive has lost power, the economy was racing deeper into a recession that was the product of years of mismanagement in Washington, and was depriving millions of Americans of their livelihood. Although the prime interest rate was no longer 21.5 percent as it was in January, it was 15 percent, still too high for an economy badly in need of a jump start. The country had added more than 250,000 new jobs during the year, but the national unemployment rate was 8.4 percent, the highest in six years, and still climbing. In industrial states like Michigan and Pennsylvania, the rate was even higher, and hundreds of factories were being forced to close their gates. New home sales and new car sales were in a tailspin. In all, more than nine million Americans were out of work.

Tip O'Neill used every opportunity he got to lambaste me as a "rich man's president" who cared nothing about the little man, the unemployed, or the poor, and said my economic program was a "cruel hoax." The press wrote that my program had failed, my honeymoon with Congress was over, and I'd have to give up everything I'd fought for during that first year. Public opinion polls showed that a lot of Americans agreed with that; they blamed us, not the Carter administration, for the recession.

My memories of the Great Depression were too personal and too vivid for me not to feel great sadness and compassion for those Americans who were out of work; having experienced those devastating days during the 1930s, I knew what it was like to be deprived of a paycheck and the pride of earning one, to watch the pain on the face of a loved one who had lost a farm or a store.

I prayed a lot during this period, not only for the country and the people who were out of work, but for help and guidance in doing the right thing so that I would be able to justify the faith Americans had placed in my hands the previous November.

In my inaugural address, I'd said America was on the threshold of "a new beginning." We had made the new beginning. Now, I believed, we had to stay the course.

PART THREE

Staying the Course

51

THERE WERE DIFFICULT TIMES AHEAD, both for me and for the country. But I never lost faith in my belief that the tax cuts would unleash a burst of energy that would pull us out of the recession and ignite an economic bonfire.

As I look back on those times now, I realize that the turnaround took a little longer than I expected. But I always expected it to come. I believed the economic recovery program would work because I had faith—faith in those tax cuts and faith in the American people. I felt we were going to solve our problems because we had a secret weapon in the battle: our factory workers, our farmers, our entrepreneurs, and the others among us who I believed would prove once again that the American people were gifted with and propelled by a spirit unique in the world, a spirit tenaciously devoted to solving our problems and bettering our lives, the lives of our children, and our country—and if these forces could be liberated from the restraints imposed on them by government, they'd pull the country out of its tailspin.

As I remarked at a ceremony in 1981 commemorating the two-hundredth anniversary of our victory over the British at Yorktown, "We have economic problems at home and we live in a troubled and violent world. But there is a moral fiber running through our people that makes us more than strong enough to face the tests ahead."

I was right. But it took longer than I wanted, there were a lot of things I wanted I never got, and I had some disappointments along the way.

The economic recovery program was threefold: Cut tax rates, get government regulators out of our way, and reduce government spending. We made progress on the first two, far too little on the third.

We cut about $40 billion in spending from the budget the first year, the biggest reduction ever. But that autumn, as I waited for the effects of the tax cuts to work their way into the economy, I realized how right I'd been when I'd said there wasn't going to be a quick fix to our economic problems: The deficit went up instead of down, and I realized we weren't going to balance the budget by 1984 as I expected. There was an ironic aspect to the situation: Because we had brought down inflation at a faster clip than we anticipated, federal tax revenues were smaller than projected, which made it more difficult to balance the budget.

After a cabinet session on the 1982–83 budget in December 1981, these words in my diary expressed the sense of disappointment I felt:

> We who were going to balance the budget face the biggest budget deficit ever. And yet percentage wise, it will be smaller in relation to G.N.P. We have reduced Carter's 17 per cent spending increase to nine per cent. The recession has added to costs and reduced revenues, however, so even with that reduction in govt. size, we have a large deficit.

A few weeks before our meeting, I invited several of the country's best-known economists to the White House to ask them why they thought the country was falling so deeply into the recession and what could be done to halt the slide. They all gave me a different answer, reminding me of something Harry Truman once said: "Find me a one-armed economist, because every one I know always says, 'Well, on the other hand . . .' "

I mentioned to one of the economists a story about three men who arrived in heaven at the same time. Saint Peter, realizing that he had room for only one newcomer, said that he would give the opening to the man who practiced the oldest profession. One stepped forward and said, "I guess that's me, because I'm a surgeon; we all know the Lord made the earth in six days and then created man, and from Adam's rib he created woman—and that took surgery." But before he could move forward, the second man stepped up and said, "Wait just a minute, I'm an engineer; in those six days before the creation of man, everything was chaos and the Lord had to work six days and six nights to eliminate the chaos; that took engineering." Before Saint Peter could respond, the third man stepped forward and said, "Well, I'm an economist, and where do you think they got all that chaos?"

Thomas Jefferson once said about lawyers: "On every question the lawyers are about equally divided, and were we to act but in cases where no contrary opinion of a lawyer can be had, we should never act." I think you could say the same thing about economists.

One thing was absolutely clear: To reduce the deficit, we'd have to render fat which had worked its way into the federal budget over decades of mismanagement and ill-guided giveaway programs and persuade Congress to stop adding fat to the budget every year. But, just as it became evident that we needed more cuts, the coalition that had come together to pass the twenty-five-percent, three-year tax cut and the Gramm-Latta budget reductions began to disintegrate.

The 1982 congressional elections were less than a year away. Many Democrats who had stuck their necks out and supported these bills returned to the party fold; Tip O'Neill and other Democratic leaders had brought them into line with warnings that they'd lose important committee assignments as well as the party's financial help during the election.

Even many Republicans, conservatives among them, feared a backlash at the polls because of the recession; without the faith I had that the tax cuts would recharge the economy, they began pressing me to raise taxes and increase spending. In short, as some reporters wrote, my honeymoon with Congress seemed over.

We had to withdraw a plan to cut billions of dollars in waste and fraud from the Social Security system—among other abuses, we'd discovered monthly Social Security checks were being sent to eighty-five hundred people who'd been dead an average of eighty-one months—after the Democrats began accusing us of plotting to throw senior citizens to the wolves. (Later on, we worked out a bipartisan program that assured the system's integrity for decades to come.) Then, *The Atlantic Monthly* published an article in which David Stockman, the director of the Office of Management and Budget, was quoted as criticizing the economic recovery program and saying it wasn't going to work. Ed Meese and others on the White House senior staff (as well as Nancy) urged me to ask for Stockman's resignation as a turncoat.

I invited him for lunch at the White House. I ate my meal, he didn't touch his. Stockman offered his resignation, but said that the author of the article was a friend of his who had published comments he had meant to be private; I refused his resignation. Although I do not necessarily regret my decision, he later wrote some things about our economic recovery program that weren't true. In a book, he portrayed himself as someone who had been swimming upstream—sometimes against me—to reduce spending.

During the early months of the administration, Stockman did a good job at the Office of Management and Budget, but he was one of the first on our team to begin clamoring for a tax increase, long before the tax cuts had had a chance to begin working their effect into the economy. Moreover, many times when I suggested that we push Congress to cut spending on a certain program, his response was that it was hopeless—or in his words, "DOA" ("dead on arrival")—on Capitol Hill. Stockman, in fact, was one of those pushing me to abandon my program and raise taxes a few days before Christmas 1981 when I wrote in the diary:

> The recession has worsened, throwing our earlier figures off. Now my team is pushing for a tax increase to help hold down the deficits. I'm being stubborn. I think our tax cuts will produce more revenue by stimulating the economy. I intend to wait and see some results.

During the next three years, I was under almost constant pressure to abandon the economic program. Along the way, I made some compromises: To win congressional approval of additional spending cuts and show the financial community we were serious about reducing the deficit, I made a deal with the congressional Democrats in 1982, agreeing to support a limited loophole-closing tax increase to raise more than $98.3 billion over three years in return for their agreement to cut spending by $280 billion during the same period; later the Democrats reneged on their pledge and we never got those cuts. I also agreed to a slower pace than I wanted for the military modernization program. But with these few exceptions, I was determined to stay the course and did.

Nancy sometimes calls me stubborn. Well, in this case, I *was* stubborn. I thought I was right. It was going to take time for the tax cuts to generate the kind of economic resurgence we needed to bring down interest rates, inflation, and unemployment. I believed we just had to wait it out.

On the domestic front, it was largely a tug of war on this issue that dominated my first term in the White House. I said: Let's wait until the tax and spending cuts have a chance to work their economic magic. The other side said: They aren't working, they aren't going to work, let's raise taxes.

Excerpts from my diary in 1982 will provide a view of the tug of war as I saw it from the Oval Office:

Jan. 11

Republican House leaders came down to the W.H. Except for Jack Kemp they are h—l bent on new taxes and cutting the defense budget. Looks like a heavy year ahead.

Jan. 20

First anniversary [of inauguration]. The day was a tough one. A budget meeting and pressure from everyone to give in to increases in excise taxes . . . I finally gave in but my heart wasn't in it.

Jan. 21

Met with U.S. Chamber of Commerce group. They made an impassioned plea that I not raise any taxes. They were touching a nerve when they said I would look as if I were retreating from my own program. That's exactly how I feel. After meeting, told Ed [Meese], Jim [Baker] and Mike [Deaver] we had to go back to the drawing board. I just can't hold still for the tax increases. We'll go at it again in the morning . . .

Jan. 22

I told our guys I couldn't go for tax increases. If I have to be criticized, I'd rather be criticized for a deficit rather than for backing away from our economic program. Left for Camp David to work on the State of the Union speech . . .

Jan. 26

I wonder if I'll ever get used to addressing the joint session of Congress. I've made a million speeches in every kind of place to every kind of audience. Somehow there's a thing about entering that chamber, goose bumps and a quiver. But it turned out fine. It was well received and I think the speech was a four base hit.

Jan. 28

. . . the press is trying to paint me as now trying to undo the New Deal. I remind them I voted for FDR four times. I'm trying to undo the "Great Society." It was LBJ's war on poverty that led us to our present mess. . . . I hope I'm not getting too optimistic but several economic indicators have turned upward indicating that maybe the recession has bottomed out. The market staged the sharpest rise since last March.

Feb. 22

Lunch on issues. I'm convinced of the need to address the people on our budget and the economy. The press has done a job on us and the polls show its effect. The people are confused about economic program. They've been told it has failed and it's just started.

Feb. 23

Met this a.m. with our [Republican] Congressional leaders. They are really antsy about the deficit and seem determined that we must retreat on our program—taxes and defense spending. Yet they seem reluctant to go for the budget cutting we've asked for. . . .

March 26

Briefing on Soviet economy. They are in very bad shape and if we can cut off their credit they'll have to yell "Uncle" or starve. We had cabinet meetings on our own economy. It is imperative that we get further budget cuts. So far the Dems aren't budging. Our strategy is to move toward a bipartisan agreement on the entitlements, the only real savings must be found there.

March 30

News conference briefing. Family theater. Bunch of Congressmen came in for photos, one from Tampico area brought mementos from my birthplace and a picture that is eerie. The day before election day, Nov. 3, 1980, a photo was taken of a rainbow, the end came down exactly on the building where I was born. . . . Senators Bob Dole and [Russell] Long came up to the house to talk the deficit. I love Sen. Long and he's a Dem. who has been with us all the way, but now he thinks only answer to deficit is a big tax raise. I just can't go along . . .

April 14

Met with our team on the budget discussions. I think we're coming close to a good negotiating position but it requires Cap W. to make a $5 billion cut, plus another $2 billion cut in a cap on salaries which would be applied to all salaries across the board, a 4 per cent increase for each of next three years. He's not happy; neither am I but the stakes are too high to not do it.

April 15

Income tax day. People actually demonstrating against paying their tax and Dem. Congressmen are demanding that we rescind our tax cuts or at least part of them.

April 19

Met with Repub. Congressional leadership. The budget was the subject. I think they are relieved to learn that I'm willing to compromise some in return for a bipartisan program. I called Tip O'Neill. I'm not sure he's ready to give. Tip is truly a New Deal liberal. He honestly believes that we're promoting welfare for the rich.

April 23

. . . the group debating the budget seems unable to arrive at any kind of consensus. If we can't get a bipartisan agreement to act together in the face of the projected deficit, then I take to the air—TV —and there will be blood on the floor.

April 26

. . . at 10:15 addressed 2000 delegates of the U.S. Chambers of Commerce convention. What a shot in the arm. They interrupted me a dozen times or more. I was talking about the budget and our economic program. [Later,] a budget meeting. The gang goes back at it with the Dems tomorrow. I felt they were tiring a lot and the Dems are holding out for more concessions. The Dems are playing games —they want me to rescind the third year of the tax cuts—not in a million years!

April 27

Well, it looks like the three weeks of budget talks got nowhere. The Dems are after a campaign issue and from Tip's words to the press and Jim Wright's, I think it will be that my recovery plan failed [*it hasn't started*]. Well, I'm meeting Tip tomorrow afternoon.

April 28

The big thing today was a meeting with Tip, Howard Bohling, Jim Wright, Jim Baker, Ed Meese, Don Regan and Dave Stockman. The result of my call to Tip. The "gang of 17" had come fairly close together on the budget and revenue package. Their combination of cuts and revenue increases came to $60 billion on the R. side and $35 billion on the D. side. It should have been straight haggling especially since our original budget package called for $101 billion. I didn't try to start bargaining from that figure but started at the $60 billion. Three hours later we'd gotten nowhere. Finally I said I'll split the difference with you and they refused that. Meeting over.

April 29

. . . upstairs to write the speech for tonight's TV broadcast. Got it finished about 5 p.m. Went on at 8 p.m. I hope it gets results . . .

April 30

After the broadcast last night phone calls and wires to W.H. broke all previous records. By 3 p.m., telegrams were 2,723 for 373 against; phone calls, 4,745 for, 1103 against. Met with some of our members of the Gang of 17; they are going to begin putting a budget together in committee.

May 4

. . . [a poll indicated] my speech was to a smaller TV audience than usual; probably due to its last minute nature and no promotion. But people are confused on the whole budget issue and my ratings are way down.

May 5–7

Never got to this journal until today, Friday. Wednesday, things turned up. We got together with Sen. Pete Domenici's budget committee and worked out a compromise budget package. It passed out of committee on a straight 11 to 9 party line vote. It's a good budget and will trim the projected deficits down to $106 billion next year,

$69 billion in 84 and $39 billion in 85. The Dems are screaming and lying like bandits charging us with cutting Social Security; we aren't touching it.

May 11
Dems have come up with a House proposal for budget. It would add $151 billion in taxes and make most if not all its savings . . . in defense.

May 18
It looks as if the Senate is coming together on our budget program and the House is coming close to a compromise agreement.

May 19
Nancy is very depressed about her father's health and understandably so. I want so much to speak to him about faith. He's always been an agnostic; now I think he knows fear for probably the first time in his life. I believe this is a moment when he should turn to God and I want so much to help him do that.

May 20
Ron's birthday. But here a frustrating day, much of it spent on the phone with members of Congress on the budget. Most are going to be with us, but some I talked to are dedicated, they say, to what we're trying to accomplish but they won't vote with us because the budget compromise isn't exactly to their liking. A compromise is never to anyone's liking; it's just the best you can get and contains enough of what you want to justify what you give up.

May 21
My fight has started but it isn't bloody, just messy. I'm on the phone all day calling Congressmen. The Senate is supposed to pass a budget, not too different from what I wanted, tonight. The House has 5 budgets before it, one of which resembles the Senate bill. It's called the Bipartisan Recovery budget. They'll be voted on next Monday; Don Regan called—inflation for the first six months is running 2.8 per cent and for the last year, 8 per cent.

May 22
Last night the Senate budget bill passed 49 to 43. Now it's up to the House where there are seven budgets, only one of which is any

good . . . they'll begin voting on them Monday. Ours first, but then according to the rules . . . even if [ours] passes, [it] will be replaced by the last one to pass.

May 24

I hate Mondays. One of those days with meetings, briefings and interviews overlapping to where I couldn't even read a memo and my desk was full of them. . . . We had a session on sanctions [over the crackdown on freedom in Poland], limiting Soviet credit and the Versailles [economic summit] meeting. There was a lot of talk about not having a set to with our allies. I firmly said to h—l with it. It's time to tell them this is our chance to bring the Soviets into the real world and for them to take a stand with us, shut off credit etc.

May 25–30

Since last Tuesday, it's been Calif. . . . Wednesday through Saturday at the ranch. I called Congressmen re the budget which we lost, but so did the Dems so there is no budget. Rode Thursday, Friday and Saturday. Never saw the sun till Saturday afternoon. . . .

June 22

A day without a break. [Met with] Congressional leadership, maybe that paid off because the House passed the conference budget bill, 211 to 208. . . . Meeting Sens. [Richard] Lugar and [Jake] Garn re bill to subsidize home mortgages. They are both good friends and supporters but I'm afraid I have to veto their bill. . . . Hinckley was found innocent by reason of insanity. . . . Quite an uproar has been created.

June 29

Economic indicators are up, showing the beginning of an upturn. It will be slow and not too robust.

July 12

We announced our go ahead on getting an amendment to the Constitution requiring a balanced budget.

July 21

. . . A really tough problem not yet resolved has to do with defense budget and the projections Dave Stockman must give to Congress re deficits for next five years. Cutting defense sends a message I don't like to allies and enemies alike. But Dave's reports of deficits are too high and send shock waves to the world just when we seem to be gaining ground.

Aug. 4

We won on the Constitutional amendment to balance the budget, 69 to 31. Russell Long gave us the deciding vote. Met with Jack Kemp (alone) and then in leadership meeting. He is adamant that we are wrong on the tax increase. [I had finally approved an increase of $98.3 billion in business and excise taxes over three years in return for a Democratic promise of $280 billion in budget cuts over three years.] He is in fact unreasonable. The tax increase is the price we have to pay to get the budget cuts.

Aug. 6

Well, we won't go to the ranch next Wednesday—the Congress will still be here and probably voting on the tax bill. But the good news is we'll be going a week from Wed. and get an extra week added on until after Labor Day.

Aug. 7

At the W.H. No Camp David. Spent most of day working on a tentative speech re the economy and explaining my support of the tax increase bill. It's a price we have to pay to get more budget cuts.

Aug. 8

Again at W.H. More of Saturday's work plus a long letter I feel I have to write to Loyal. I'm afraid for him. His health is failing badly. [As a young man, Nancy's father had an experience that had made him question his faith in God; I believed strongly in a supreme being and wanted to convince him he was wrong and should see a minister before he died and acknowledge a belief and faith in God, so I could not resist writing and urging him to do so.]

Aug. 9

. . . Nancy in tears when I came home. Her father is back in the hospital. She's going out there Wednesday. I wish I could bear her pain myself . . .

Aug. 10

Most of the day spent in meetings with Congressmen and ladies re the tax bill. We're up against a strange mix, it isn't going to be easy . . .

Aug. 15

Worked on speech. About 30 R. congressmen and women plus our own staff came up for lunch meeting on tax bill, which came out of conference committee at about 2 a.m. Think it was good meeting and some progress made. Back to the speech. Talked to Nancy. She's very low, thinks the end may come to Loyal in next few days. How I wish I could be with her and help her.

Aug. 16

Spent morning phoning business leaders and meeting with Congressmen one on one re the tax bill. . . . tonight did my 20 minute speech on national TV explaining the tax bill and why it should be adopted. The phone calls are coming in almost three to one.

Aug. 17

Best reaction to last night's speech was the market . . . second biggest jump in history, 93 million shares traded, almost a record. Citibank joined the others at 14 per cent prime rate. Housing starts in July reported as going up 34 per cent—savings rate went up to about 7.9 per cent after 10 years of declining.

Aug. 18

Tomorrow is D-Day in the House. Most of the day with Congressmen, in groups and singly. Met with the hard core conservatives in the state dining room. Met with about 20 boll weevils. They are pretty much with me. Then a series of one on ones. Last night or the night before, Nancy says Loyal asked for the chaplain at the hospital in the middle of the night.

Aug. 19

Dr. Loyal died this morning. Nancy wasn't alone, thank heaven. Ron and Doria [Ron's wife] were there. But it seemed awful to be here and not be with her. All day I sat at my desk phoning Congressmen on the tax bill and tonight it passed with 103 Republicans and more than half the Democrats, 225 to 207. Tip O'Neill made a speech to Republicans telling them why they should support me. It seemed strange. Both of us on the same side. The Senate took it up tonight and it won 53 to 47. Again some of our ultra pure conservatives deserted. Now I'm packing to leave for Phoenix and my sweetheart. [The compromise tax package had been passed, but our economic problems weren't over yet by any means.]

Sept. 23

Had an economic rundown in Cabinet. Not bad, not good. One thing sure, the recession has bottomed. Price index for August, .3 of 1 per cent, that would be an annual rate [of inflation] of less than 3.3 per cent.

Oct. 1

Supposed to leave early for Camp David but House was playing games with balanced budget amendment. First they introduced a straight statute which was overwhelmingly defeated as it should have been. Then came the constitutional amendment which required a two thirds vote. It got a sizable majority but failed to make the two thirds. I appeared in the press room and laid it on the House Democratic leadership where the blame properly lies.

Oct. 16–17 Camp David

... Saturday's radio broadcast was on the economy. I cited FDR and said our greatest problem now was fear itself.

Nov. 2

Election day!

I didn't have time to think about the election today. An N.S.C. briefing . . . on the MX, then an N.S.C. meeting . . . then a briefing on our upcoming budget situation. We really are in trouble. Our one time projections, pre-recession, are all out the window and we look at $200 billion deficits if we can't pull some miracles. Speaking of miracles and such the market went up more than 20 points . . .

Election: Lost 25 in House and had to expect that; it could have been worse. Held the Senate 54–46. Millicent Fenwick lost, I'm sorry. But high spot, we won governor and senator in California. Bye bye Brown.

Nov. 3

Did a press appearance in Rose Garden re the election returns. I'm sure they were worried I was so happy. P.M. [Giovanni] Spadolini of Italy arrived. I like him. We had a good meeting and then lunch. . . . Italy has become under him a dependable ally. . . . A lengthy budget meeting. We really face some tough decisions if we are going to reduce the deficits. . . . Meanwhile, the economy continues looking up. Today broke all time record on Wall Street for increase in a single day and all time record high—1065. Credit is given to election results, that Dems did not win enough to change our direction.

Nov. 12
Spent most of the afternoon in another budget meeting. It's going to be a battle but we must make deeper budget cuts.

Nov. 18
Met with Sen. Baker and Rep. Bob Michel. They weren't as upset as I was prepared to see them re the economic situation and the election. Still they predicted tough going for much of what I feel we have to do in view of the continuing unemployment and the projected budget deficits.

Nov. 19
Back to Cabinet meeting on the budget. Our deficits are structural as well as recession-caused. We have a built-in increase in the budget which is automatic; we must deal with it.

Dec. 14
Spent most of the afternoon in a dismal economic briefing about the deficits and the little chance we have of getting further budget cuts. . . .

Maybe it's true, as some people say, that it's always darkest before dawn. Although I didn't realize it, when I wrote those last few entries the country had already begun the longest sustained economic expansion in peacetime history. Economic researchers say the turnaround began in November 1982, exactly one year after the first phase of the three-year, twenty-five-percent tax cut went into effect.

It took another year for the expansion to gain full momentum, but we were on our way: We had started the process of getting government off the backs and out of the pockets of people and business, and they were responding with a burst of economic activity that would bring down unemployment, inflation, and interest rates.

As the economy started to take off, I started joking around the Oval Office: "Do you notice they're not calling it 'Reaganomics' any more?" Until the recovery began, "Reaganomics" had been a term of derision.

I regarded the 1984 presidential election as pivotal—not because I wanted to live in the White House for four more years, but because I believed the gains we'd made during the previous four years were in jeopardy. Although she never brought it up, I think Nancy would have preferred that I not run for reelection in 1984. But I never doubted I would. I wanted to preserve what we had accomplished, and there were a lot of things I still wanted to do that I hadn't been able to do yet. Foremost among them, domestically, were cutting the deficit and balancing the budget.

Although an economic expansion was under way, I thought we could do more to stimulate the economy by making our tax system fairer and simpler. I wanted to persuade Congress to cut more waste out of the budget and continue the process of making government smaller and less intrusive in our lives. I still thought I had a shot at balancing the budget during the next four years.

To me, former Vice-President Walter Mondale, the Democratic presidential nominee in 1984, was another classic tax-and-spend liberal from the *new* school of the Democratic Party—the one that had parted company with its founders, Thomas Jefferson and his friends who believed that the least government was the best government and that "governments are not the masters of the people, but the servants of the people governed." The new school of Democrats thought of government in exactly the opposite way. In 1984, it had become a conglomeration of blocs and special-interest groups, each with narrow special agendas directed at grabbing more of the national wealth for their own interests. Thomas Jefferson's party had become the party of big promises, big government, and big taxes— the bigger the better.

Yet, when I watched Mondale's acceptance speech at the Democratic convention in San Francisco, it almost seemed (with one important exception) that he was trying to sound like a Republican. Apparently sensing that the public was in a conservative mood and fed up with big government, he talked about old-fashioned values and improving the efficiency of government, and promised the people he wanted to do some of the very same things we were already doing—but he made it sound as if he had to do it to cure an economic crisis. Mondale reverted to type once, when he pledged to raise taxes on the rich to reduce the deficit—after being introduced by a millionaire, Senator Edward Kennedy, who had assailed me as a friend of the rich.

Mondale tried to make it sound as if he had undergone a metamorphosis. But I knew that the first thing he'd do as president was revert totally to form and join with Congress in enacting huge tax increases that would abort the recovery and destroy everything we'd spent four years trying to build.

A few days after the Democratic convention ended, I drew an assignment to help officiate at the opening ceremonies of the Summer Olympic Games in Los Angeles. While I was there I sensed a renewed national pride in America that made me feel warm inside. The spiritual rebirth I had hoped for was under way, as vigorous and as robust as the nation's economic turnaround. America was coming back, becoming proud of itself again, becoming confident again about the future. More than ever, I thought, we had to stay the course and not turn back.

After leaving Los Angeles, Nancy and I spent almost two weeks at the ranch, a summer vacation that was the longest uninterrupted time we'd ever spent there. The weather was terrific except for one foggy day, but even that day we had our regular morning ride and I spent every afternoon pruning trees and fixing things around the ranch.

At the time, the papers were full of reports that I was planning to raise taxes if reelected. "They find every excuse to say I'm really hedging," I wrote in my diary one day. "Well d—m it, there will be no new taxes on my watch and Mondale is stuck with his campaign promise to raise the income tax."

After George Bush and I were nominated a second time amid a tumultuous celebration in Dallas, I said in my acceptance speech that voters had their clearest choice between the two national parties in fifty years: Despite the Democrats' attempts to change their tune during their four days beside San Francisco Bay, the choice was between a government of "pessimism, fear, and limits and [one] of hope, confidence, and growth." After the speech, Ray Charles sang "America the Beautiful" and I don't think there was a dry eye in the house.

I believe that someday we are going to have a woman president, possibly during my life, and I've often thought the best way to pave the way for this was to first nominate and elect a woman as vice-president. But I think Mondale made a serious mistake when he picked Geraldine Ferraro as his running mate. In my view, he guessed wrong in deciding to take a congresswoman that almost nobody had ever heard of and try to put her in line for the presidency. We have had many successful woman governors around the country who have demonstrated the potential to serve as president, but he overlooked them. I think if the Republicans had done this with a Jeane Kirkpatrick (our UN representative), for example, there would have been a lot more sense to it. I don't know who among the Democrats might have been a better choice, but it was obvious Mondale picked Geraldine Ferraro simply because he believed there was a "gender gap" where I was concerned and she was a *woman;* I don't think they picked the most electable woman.

As each day of the general election campaign passed, I found myself getting angrier at Mondale, whose basic theme was that I was a liar: He claimed I said I was not going to raise taxes after the election when in fact I really intended to, already had a plan for it. I kept saying I wouldn't raise taxes, but he kept saying I was lying and deceiving the public.

Many of our key supporters said to George Bush and me that we had nothing to worry about from the Mondale-Ferraro challenge because the economy was booming and people always voted their pocketbooks. Inflation was down to 4.6 percent, unemployment had plummeted, interest rates were far below the level of four years before, and opinion polls said I had a solid lead over Mondale.

Well, despite what they said, I told myself I was not going to get overconfident. I have never liked to lose and so I set out to campaign as hard as I could for a second term. By no means did I think of myself as a shoo-in, and throughout that summer and fall I was a little edgy.

In a campaign, I always like to act as if I'm one vote behind; overconfidence is a candidate's worst mistake. I knew anything can happen in an election campaign; it's just as well I did run scared, because in the view of many people, I nearly blew the whole race during my first debate with Mondale that fall.

I wrote in the diary in early October after the debate in Louisville was over:

I have to say I lost. I guess I'd crammed so hard on facts and figures in view of the absolutely dishonest things he'd been saying in the campaign I guess I flattened out; anyway, I didn't feel good about myself. And yet he was never able to rebut any of the facts I presented and kept repeating things that are absolute falsehoods. But the press has been calling him the winner for two days now.

I had spent too many hours poring over briefing books and in skull sessions and mock debates preparing for the encounter, and on the night of the debate, I think I was just overtrained.

I don't think anybody could have retained all the things pumped into my brain during the days leading up to the debate; I goofed a couple of times. Although I don't blame them, in a way I was hurt by people trying to help me: A debate was coming up and everybody around me started saying, "You have to know this . . . you have to know that"; then they fill your head with all sorts of details, technicalities, and statistics as if you were getting ready to take an exam on those topics. Finally, when you're in the debate, you realize you just can't command all that information and still do a good job as a debater.

I don't feel low very often, but I take pride in my public speaking ability—after all, I'm an old performer. The verdict that I'd lost the debate didn't make me feel very happy. A lot of supporters tried to make me feel better afterward. But I knew I'd stumbled two or three times while millions of people were watching, and I was embarrassed.

After Louisville, I had some genuine reasons to feel nervous about the campaign. Several polls taken after the debate indicated that some of my supporters were having doubts about me, and some of the pundits in the press claimed my stumbles proved that I was too old to be president. One White House television correspondent even proclaimed that the Louisville debate had brought to the surface what he called the "senility factor."

A second debate—covering foreign affairs—was scheduled in two weeks in Kansas City, so I had a second chance; another disastrous performance could send Nancy and me packing, headed back to the ranch for good.

I decided I wasn't going to do as much cramming as I had done before the first debate, and it's a good thing I didn't, because something happened at the second debate that I think wouldn't have happened if I had been overtrained. One of the reporters on the panel asked me whether age was going to be a handicap or other factor in the campaign. I suppose it was a polite way of raising the fact that I was seventy-three; and the question alluded, by inference, to my troubles at the previous debate.

My answer to the question just popped off the top of my head. I'd never anticipated it, nor had I thought in advance what my answer might be to such a question. I just said, "I am not going to exploit for political purposes my opponent's youth and inexperience."

Well, the crowd roared and the television cameras flashed a shot of Mondale laughing. I'm sure that if I had been as stuffed with as many facts and figures as I was before the first debate, I wouldn't have been able to come up with that line; your mind just isn't flexible enough if it's saturated with facts because you've been preparing for an examination.

According to the count of some reporters, Mondale took twenty-two tough personal potshots at me during the debate in Kansas City, most of which questioned my capabilities for leadership. But the majority of people watching the debate that night, the reporters wrote, remembered that one line more than any other: I guess my response had satisfied them that I wasn't senile. After my goofs during the previous debate, I think it's possible I sewed up reelection with those fourteen words; I'm not sure. But the incident reminded me once again of how unpredictable, even fleeting things can often make a big difference in life.

Besides the debates, two other things stand out in my memory from the 1984 campaign. One was the enthusiasm of the blue-collar workers—voters traditionally allied with my former associates in the Democratic Party—that I met while stumping the country that summer and fall. While Walter Mondale and Ted Kennedy and Tip O'Neill were forever harping that I was the "rich man's candidate," everywhere I went crowds of working men and working women roared with approval when I asked them whether they thought they were better off than they had been four years earlier; the country was moving again, and they were sharing in the fruits of the economic recovery.

Another thing I will always remember: an outpouring of affection and support from college and university students I never expected. Although there were always a few hecklers on the campuses I visited, they were usually outnumbered by students enthusiastically cheering the policies of the previous four years, and this really took me by surprise: These students in the eighties seemed so different from those that I'd dealt with as governor a decade earlier.

Two days after the Kansas City debate, following a busy schedule of campaigning that began at the University of Oregon and ended with a giant rally on the campus of Ohio State University, I wrote in the diary: "The O.S.U. students were on fire; another small heckler group only added to the fun. By this time I was so in love with young America I was all choked up. For lunch we went to the T.K.E. house, my fraternity. These have been the greatest four days I can remember."

As election day approached, our campaign polls showed that following the second debate I had increased my lead over Mondale substantially. But I was still edgy. What happens, I thought, if my supporters read the polls and decide their vote isn't necessary? I kept pressure on the staff, telling them to work me hard and add as many appearances to the campaign schedule as they could before election day.

Two days before the election, after getting up in Milwaukee and flying to rallies in Minnesota, Missouri, and Chicago, we arrived in Sacramento for a rally the following day. Nancy and I were put up in a suite at the Red Lion Inn that had a bed on an elevated platform. About 3:30 A.M., Nancy got up to get an extra blanket and took a header off the platform that left her with an egg-size lump on the left side of her head.

In the morning, she could hardly walk and I was very frightened for her, but a doctor who saw her said the injury, while painful, would not leave any lasting damage. Still worried, I resumed the campaign schedule. That day I felt a twinge of nostalgia as I spoke as president before a huge crowd that gathered on the steps of the state capitol—the same place where twice I'd been sworn in as governor.

From there, we flew to Southern California for some final campaigning and then our traditional election-night party at the Jorgensen home to await the voters' verdict. Nancy was still badly bruised but feeling better.

While we were having dinner, I was called to the telephone. It was Walter Mondale, conceding.

The next day, with Nancy still sore from her fall, we flew to Rancho del Cielo for three days of rides in the morning and cutting and splitting wood from downed oak trees in the afternoons. It was a happy time. I was feeling high after the election; we had taken forty-nine states and fifty-nine percent of the vote, and I saw the election as approval of what I'd been trying to do and a mandate to continue it.

In the rotunda of the Capitol on a very cold day ten weeks later, I pledged to do that. George Bush and I first took our oaths of office, as required by the Constitution, on Sunday, January 20, in the White House. The formal inaugural ceremonies and parade were scheduled the following day. But on Sunday afternoon, the inaugural committee came to the White House and suggested I cancel the parade and outdoor ceremony because the wind-chill factor the next day was predicted to be twenty degrees below zero or worse; doctors were warning that at that temperature, exposed skin would freeze in about fifteen seconds. We couldn't inflict that on the bandsmen and other people who had come to Washington for the parade, so we canceled it, and just before noon the following day, George and I took our oaths of office a second time before about one thousand people in the Capitol rotunda.

Afterward, at the traditional inaugural lunch with congressmen, Tip O'Neill made a point of telling me privately that he was very much aware of the fact that we had received fifty-nine percent of the vote during the election. I hoped that was a signal he'd be more agreeable the second time around, but it didn't work out that way. As far as he was concerned, it still wasn't six o'clock.

I felt sorry for all those bandsmen who had come to Washington from the fifty states and were deprived by cold weather of a chance to participate in the inaugural parade, so that afternoon Nancy and I helicoptered to a big arena in Maryland where thousands of dis-appointed paraders from all over the nation were gathered in their uniforms and regalia. I got a chance to thank them and they got a chance to play some of the music they'd planned for the parade. We all had fun, and I think it made up for some of their disappointment.

That night, there were eleven inaugural balls. Nancy and I got to all of them and danced a few steps at each.

331

The next day, January 22, it was back to work. On the economic front, my biggest goal for the second term was to make the federal tax code less complicated and less onerous on the Americans who were the real producers in our economy. Tax reform, I thought, would not only accelerate the economic expansion but make our whole system of taxation more fair.

In 1986, after almost two years of haggling with Congress, we got the tax reform bill we wanted.

52

A NUMBER OF THINGS that happened during my watch as president gave me great satisfaction, but I'm probably proudest about the economy. In 1981, no problem the country faced was more serious than the economic crisis—not even the need to modernize our armed forces—because without a recovery, we couldn't afford to do the things necessary to make the country strong again or make a serious effort to lessen the dangers of nuclear war. Nor could America regain confidence in itself and stand tall once again. Nothing was possible unless we made the economy sound again.

The economic expansion that began in October 1982, a year after the first phase of the three-year tax cut went into effect, created more than eighteen million new jobs by the time I left office, the largest increase for a comparable period of time in history. Meanwhile, the percentage of Americans employed at good jobs rose to an all-time high. As I write this, the expansion is in its ninety-second month and still going strong.

The twenty-five-percent tax cut, followed by the Tax Reform Act of 1986, touched off a surge of growth in America that brought down inflation, brought down interest rates, brought down unemployment, and created a cascade of additional tax revenue for government. Realizing that they could keep more of what they earned, people went out and made more money. They used this money to buy more houses, more furniture, more appliances, more cars.

Corporate as well as personal taxes were simplified and reduced to the lowest rate since 1941. Businesses began investing more in plants and equipment, making their workers more competitive. And instead of throwing money into wasteful shelters and tax dodges, individuals and businesses began putting it into productive investments that created growth and new jobs.

Although it didn't bring as much simplification to the tax code as I had hoped, the Tax Reform Act of 1986 reduced the number of personal income tax brackets from fourteen to three, and lowered the top personal tax bracket (which had been seventy percent in 1981) for most Americans to twenty-eight percent, the lowest rate since 1931.

Knowing they could now keep seventy percent of what they earned instead of paying seventy percent of it to the government, the most affluent Americans invested in new projects and new ideas; but contrary to what some of the tax-and-spend liberals have said, tax reform didn't create a windfall for the rich at the expense of the poor; instead, it was the other way around.

Under the new laws, more than eighty percent of Americans paid the lowest tax rate, fifteen percent, or no tax at all; the households of four million lower-income working Americans were excused from paying federal income taxes altogether. Meanwhile, the proportion of personal income taxes paid by the top-earning one percent of Americans increased by more than a third between 1981 and 1987—from 17.9 percent to almost twenty-five percent. During the same period, the tax burden on the poorest half of American taxpayers fell by almost twenty percent—from 7.4 percent of the total to 6.1 percent. More than eighty percent of the increased personal income tax revenues since 1981 have come from taxpayers with incomes of over $100,000 a year, while the amount paid by those earning less than $50,000 dropped by billions of dollars.

By and large, the jobs created during the expansion were *good* jobs: more than ninety percent were full-time jobs; more than half paid salaries of over $20,000, and a large proportion of these were in managerial and professional occupations with a median income of more than $27,000. Many of the best of the new jobs went to women and minorities. During those six years, the median income for American families increased twelve percent, compared with a decline of 10.5 percent during the previous decade. The nation's real gross national product (the value of all goods and services produced in the United States, adjusted for inflation) went up twenty-seven percent; manufacturing production went up thirty-three percent. American workers became more productive each hour they worked and made their employers more competitive in world markets.

We got government out of the way and began the process of giving the economy back to the people, but I don't take credit: The American people did it themselves, responding to incentives inherent in the free enterprise system. I watched in wonder and awe as they responded and excelled and produced. There is no limit to what a proud, free people can achieve.

With the tax cuts of 1981 and the Tax Reform Act of 1986, I'd accomplished a lot of what I'd come to Washington to do.

But, on the other side of the ledger, cutting federal spending and balancing the budget, I was less successful than I wanted to be. This was one of my biggest disappointments as president. I just didn't deliver as much to the people as I'd promised.

I never thought we could cut costs so fast that we'd balance the budget overnight. I knew it would take time. There were too many programs that people based their lives and businesses on; you couldn't pull the rug out from under all of them at once. But I wanted to cut more of the waste that had accumulated in government like flab around the waist of a middle-aged man.

I didn't come to Washington with stars in my eyes, thinking it would be easy. I'd been through the same kind of battle at the state level and knew how difficult it could be. I came to Washington thinking that it was going to be tough, but that it could be done.

Over time, we rendered a lot of fat out of the government; we reduced the size of the bureaucracy and cut the rate at which the government was growing and spending money, and I'm very proud of that. But the vested interests that hold sway over Congress prevented us from cutting spending nearly as much as I had hoped to, or as the country required.

I'd argued for years that if you cut tax rates, government revenues would go up because lower rates would stimulate economic growth. Well, in the first six years after tax rates started coming down in late 1981, the federal government, despite the lower rates, experienced an increase of $375 billion in tax revenues—more than four times greater than the amount projected before the cuts. This was more than enough to pay for our $140 billion military build-up. But, during this same period, Congress increased *spending* by $450 billion. So, we lost our chance to slash the deficit.

Deficits, as I've often said, aren't caused by too little taxing, they are caused by too much spending. Presidents don't create deficits, Congress does. Presidents can't appropriate a dollar of taxpayers' money; only congressmen can—and Congress is susceptible to all sorts of influences that have nothing to do with good government.

Presidents can propose a budget, lobby to get it passed, and do their best to make sure that government agencies under their control within the executive branch don't waste the money appropriated by Congress. They can veto spending bills passed by Congress. But under our system of separation of powers, it is Congress that determines the programs government finances and how much money is appropriated for each of them.

Spending for government "entitlement" programs—money committed by Congress for various programs in past years that is as good as spent before the administration ever gets a shot at writing its budget—accounts for forty-eight percent of federal spending. To many members of Congress, this money is off-limits forever: Once a program gets started, it's virtually impossible to reduce or stop it. Every one of these programs—most of which were born or expanded enormously during the explosive growth of big government in the 1960s and 1970s—develops a powerful constituency in Congress, and a bureaucracy that is dedicated to preserving it. As I once said in a speech, the tendency of government and its programs to grow are about the nearest thing to eternal life we'll ever see on this earth.

Presidents can try to rein in spending through their powers of persuasion, but aside from jawboning members of Congress and taking their case to the people, their running room is limited. Over the years, the majority party in Congress (for fifty-five of the last fifty-nine years the Democrats) has devised a bag of tricks that can be very effective in foiling efforts by the executive branch to contain spending. Congress may write a vital piece of legislation, then tack on a pork-barrel rider that throws billions at the pet project of a narrow special-interest group, knowing the president may be forced to accept something he doesn't want in order to save something he does.

Congress has the power to prevent even as basic a thing as the adoption of a budget for the federal government, and it does so routinely almost every year. Every budget I submitted to Congress outlined spending reductions; if I'd gotten cuts I proposed in 1981, for example, the cumulative deficit between 1982 and 1986 would have been $207 billion less than it was. But I could never get a complete budget passed. Instead, we got a succession of "continuing resolutions" that allowed the government to stay in business and keep on spending money without a formal budget. Meanwhile, Congress, posturing and playing cynical games with the truth, blamed the White House for the deficit, and at the same time slipped costly gifts for special interests into these makeshift spending resolutions, preventing any real progress in cutting the deficit.

When one of these spending resolutions would go through Congress, it would be a foot thick and fourteen hundred pages long. (I once sprained a finger picking up one of these hefty budget resolutions.) I don't believe any congressman on Capitol Hill ever reads all those fourteen hundred pages. The press, which tries to keep an eye on everything in Washington, seldom digs deeply into the process. Yet there are things contained in these budget resolutions that cost taxpayers billions.

Congress put virtually every one of the budgets I drafted on the shelf and sent me a continuing resolution. If I had vetoed it, the government wouldn't have been able to write a paycheck or a Social Security check. The whole government might have ground to a halt, and the baby would have gone out with the bath water. So, they'd have me. I'd have to sign the next continuing resolution and, as a result, I never got the things we were asking for with regard to major cuts in spending and I wasn't able to persuade Congress to balance the budget.

I don't think we'll solve the problem of the deficit until three things happen: We need more discipline on spending in Congress. We need a constitutional amendment *requiring* Congress to balance the budget. And we need to give our presidents a line-item veto.

I think the first American to favor a balanced-federal-budget amendment was the founder of the Democratic Party, Thomas Jefferson. After the Constitutional Convention was over and the Constitution was approved, signed, and ratified, he pointed out a glaring omission: There was no provision to prevent the federal government from borrowing money and going into debt. Times haven't changed; that's still a glaring omission in the Constitution.

In the past fifty-nine years, there have been only eight scattered years in which the budget was balanced. For fifty-one of those years there was a deficit, and, as I pointed out, for fifty-five of those years the Democrats controlled the House of Representatives.

Every year that I was president, I asked Congress for a constitutional amendment that would require the federal government—like any well-run household or business—to balance its budget. But Congress (and I concede there was opposition to it on both sides of the political aisle) wouldn't sit still for this infringement on its spendthrift ways. There was some important progress: The spending limits imposed on Congress by the Gramm-Rudman-Hollings law have helped curb its extravagance. But never underestimate the willingness of congressmen to circumvent their own rules, or the public will, in the pursuit of their enthusiasm to spend other people's money.

I don't put all the blame on Congress. Part of the problem rests with political realities. It's a fact of life that running for political office in this country is very expensive; once in office, few incumbents want to surrender their seats in Congress, so they often turn to the special interests, who want special consideration from them, for the money to finance their campaigns. Then, after the election, they repay the favors—with the taxpayers' money.

That's one of the reasons I think presidents need a line-item veto authority. I had it when I was governor of California, and governors in forty-two other states have it as well. When the state legislature sent me a budget, I could take a blue pencil and reduce spending on individual items to a level taxpayers could afford. If there was something laudable about a piece of legislation, I could sign it but veto features in it that were pure pork. The legislators had the opportunity to override my decision—but none of my 943 vetoes in Sacramento were overturned, because legislators didn't want to publicly defend, under the full scrutiny of voters, their pork-barrel projects or items they had husbanded through their committees because of the influence of campaign donors and special-interest groups.

Until presidents have a line-item veto and there is a constitutional amendment mandating a balanced budget, I think the country is likely to face never-ending deficits piled up by a profligate Congress unable or unwilling to make the hard-nosed decisions necessary to bring down spending to a level the country can afford.

Although I was disappointed that I wasn't able to do more, we still made progress in slowing the growth of government. Despite resistance from Congress and the bureaucracy, and despite continuing population growth, the size of the federal civilian work force declined about five percent during the eight years we were in Washington. Manpower levels in some bureaucracies were cut in half, and while we were cutting the overall federal work force, minority employment went up—it rose twenty-seven percent—and the number of women in professional positions in the federal force went up thirty-four percent.

A lot of the reductions resulted from simply giving government workers the opportunity and tools to operate as efficiently as their counterparts in the private business world. In 1982, I asked J. Peter Grace, chief executive of W. R. Grace & Company and a Democrat, to establish a panel of top businessmen to study federal operations and recommend how we could reduce waste and make the government more efficient. The Grace Commission—also known as the Private Sector Survey on Cost Control—was patterned after that panel of businessmen I'd appointed when I was governor to streamline the government of California. The idea had worked in Sacramento; why not in Washington?

There was lots of ground for his group to cover. As Grace has pointed out, the federal government is the world's largest power producer, insurer, lender, borrower, operator of hospitals, landowner, tenant, holder of grazing land, timber seller, grain owner, warehouse operator, shipowner, and truck-fleet operator. He recruited more than two thousand volunteer businessmen from around the country to review all aspects of federal operations, and produced a report with 2,478 recommendations on how to make those operations more efficient. I think it should be required reading for anyone interested in how the federal government operates.

These volunteers discovered things going on in government that businesses hadn't been doing for a generation. The examples of waste and mismanagement they found are so numerous they could fill a book by themselves, but here are a few examples:

• It cost the Veterans Administration between $100 and $140 to process (not pay) a medical claim—versus $3 to $6 for doing the same thing at private insurance companies.

• The army spent an average of $4.20 on administrative costs to issue a paycheck, versus an average of $1 in private business.

• Although the federal government accounts for about one-quarter of all economic activity in the country, it had no centralized system of management for its financial and accounting operations, resulting in waste, inefficiency, and constant problems of the left hand not knowing what the right hand was doing. There were 132 different payroll systems and 380 different and incompatible accounting systems used by government agencies. The utilization of antiquated cash-flow management techniques instead of modern electronic funds-transfer systems alone cost taxpayers some $2.3 billion a year. Some agencies were still using cardboard checks, which business hadn't used for years.

• Of the seventeen thousand computers used by the federal government, half were so obsolete that their manufacturers refused to service them. The bureaucracy's process for purchasing new computers took an average of more than two years, an interval guaranteed to perpetuate this obsolescence.

• Despite eighty thousand pages of government procurement regulations and twenty thousand additional pages generated every year, federal employees had virtually no incentive to seek the lowest cost for items they purchased for the government, or to find less expensive ways of carrying out any of their duties for government. The incentive to work efficiently and at the least cost, which is found in any well-managed business, simply did not exist in the government.

• While salaries paid many categories of federal civil service workers were at least as high as those of Americans in comparable jobs in private industry, the value of their fringe benefits, on average, was seventy-six percent more than in the private sector.

• Pensions paid federal civilian employees were almost twice as high as those for Americans with comparable jobs in private business.

• Fraud and waste were common in government entitlement programs, amounting in the federal food stamp program alone to at least $1 billion a year—a sum equivalent to the income taxes paid by 450,857 median-income families. The Social Security Administration was found to have made $14.6 billion in erroneous payments in the years 1980–1982.

Of the Grace Commission's 2,478 recommendations, we were able to implement almost 800, which saved taxpayers tens of billions of dollars and kept the deficit from growing even larger than it did. Based on these recommendations and those of other advisory panels, for example, we eliminated seventy-five federal printing offices that we didn't need (and eliminated about half the government's publications, including such best sellers as *How to Buy Eggs*). Just by installing improved accounting and cash-flow management systems in a few agencies to handle the federal government's $2-trillion-a-year cash flow, we earned taxpayers billions of dollars a year in additional interest revenues on the government's money. The number of different computer payroll systems used in government was reduced to fewer than 50 from 132; the number of accounting systems was reduced from 380 to fewer than 250. While the size of the federal bureaucracy was reduced, the application of modern, streamlining administrative procedures brought down the time it took to obtain a Social Security card from forty-nine days to ten; the time to get a passport from forty-three days to ten; and the time to get an export license from seventy-five days to seventeen. The proportion of federal contracts awarded competitively was increased from less than forty percent to fifty-eight percent. The volume of new regulations, listed each day in the *Federal Register,* was reduced by forty-three percent, or an average of 149 pages a day. Overall, the average number of regulations issued by the government during our administration marked a decline of forty-one percent compared with the number issued during the previous administration.

We tried to implement all the Grace Commission's recommendations and those of other advisory groups I appointed with a challenge to give Americans a better payoff for their tax dollars— but many of the proposals needed legislative approval, and various groups that hold sway over Congress kept us from getting all we wanted. Despite this resistance and my disappointment over not doing more, we made progress I'm proud of: In 1980, federal expenditures were growing at an annual rate of more than fourteen percent; by 1987, the rate of growth was down to one percent, and if you factor in inflation, there was a net decrease in spending that year, the first since 1973.

I hope history will look back on the eighties not only as a period of economic recovery and a time when we put the brakes on the growth of government, but as a time of fundamental change for our economy and a resurgence of the American spirit of generosity that touched off an unprecedented outpouring of good deeds. While growing up in Dixon, I came to the conclusion when I was still fairly young that when it came to solving a community's problems, no one was better at it than ordinary people. Whether it was my mother bringing a meal to a family that was down on its luck, my dad canvassing the county in search of work for the jobless, or a group of neighbors getting together to help rebuild a farmer's barn lost in a fire, I witnessed how people helping one another could be a far more effective means of solving a community's problems than government giveaway programs. With that in mind, I created the White House Office of Private Sector Initiatives. Under the direction of Fred Ryan, a Los Angeles attorney, its task was to revitalize the great American spirit of neighbor helping neighbor. Through its efforts, countless Americans joined volunteer programs, and private charitable giving in America more than doubled between 1980 and 1988. The total giving in 1988 was $103.87 billion, compared with $48.73 billion in 1980—a 101.2-percent increase.

The economic crisis of the early 1980s brought hard times for many Americans. I don't undervalue for a moment the suffering they experienced as we fought together to pull the nation out of its worst economic crisis in half a century. For those who lost their farms or businesses or saw their jobs vanish during the recession, life was as bleak as it was for Americans caught up in the economic upheavals of the Great Depression. A lot of those people took the time to write to me, some expressing anger, others compassion and support for me. There was something I found very interesting about many of these letters: Despite the great hardships and suffering they were experiencing, many of the Americans who wrote to me expressed an optimism and faith in the future, a belief that, yes, we were living through a difficult storm, but it would pass. One twenty-seven-year-old mother of three from a small town in Oregon wrote that her husband, a construction worker, had been out of a job for over a year, their family's car had been repossessed, and they had been forced to move in with her grandparents when they couldn't pay their rent any longer. "When we thought all was lost," she wrote, "my grandparents taught us survival skills that they had learned during the Depression. We've learned the art of sewing and quilt making, we've had the pleasures of long winter nights rediscovering our family roots and growing closer; most of all, we're learning the old values, humility and independence that helped to make this country strong." Despite the hardships her family had experienced, she said she wished me well on our economic programs and the administration's efforts to cut government spending, even though it might mean more hardship. "I think it's time," she said, that "we as a country came off our high horses and got back to the business of living with pride and independence. Of living within our means. It's time we started asking, 'What does it cost?' instead of 'how much are the payments?' "

As difficult as it was, I think the period of economic hardship that began during the Carter years and continued until the economic recovery program took hold taught us something about ourselves and our country and, in the end, America emerged stronger than ever. Take American agriculture: For decades, it had been one of the wonders of the world. For most of the postwar period, a relative handful of men and women produced enough food not only for themselves but for the growing population of America and much of the rest of the world. Along the way, though, they became too dependent on handouts and artificial price supports.

Franklin D. Roosevelt first proposed the notion of paying farmers not to plant their land as an emergency measure during the pit of the Depression. But, he said in 1933, the subsidies had to be *temporary:* It was wrong for the government to pay farmers *not* to produce and keep land fallow, FDR said.

Nevertheless, over the decades, largely because of the influence on Congress of farm states and agribusiness, the subsidies became as deeply planted in the Washington firmament as other entitlement giveaway programs. Our government paid farmers billions to grow commodities that were already in excess supply, sometimes with irrigation water subsidized at high cost by the taxpayers; then it paid them not to grow the commodities and spent millions to store the surplus that subsidies had generated. Instead of crops, farmers discovered they could harvest money from the federal pocketbook —that is, money from the pocketbooks of the rest of us. In a way, you can't blame them. It was there to be taken.

Our farmers have always had to deal with the capriciousness of nature—floods, droughts, tornadoes. But in the late 1970s and early 1980s, they also rode a roller coaster of man-made problems: rapid inflation, high interest rates, depressed prices related to the Soviet grain embargo, then rapid disinflation. For many, it was a roller coaster ride to disaster.

Land prices and prices for many commodities rose out of sight during the years of rapid inflation that finally began to ebb in 1981. During this heady period, farmers borrowed billions using the inflated value of their property as collateral. Many overextended themselves, assuming they would be able to repay these big loans with inflated dollars. As inflation came down, however, so did the value of their land and, in some cases, the prices they received for their products. They still had to pay off their loans at double-digit interest rates, and after a while some banks began calling in their notes, pointing out that the land wasn't as valuable as the farmers had once said it was.

Meanwhile, American farmers had new competition. Once, they had had the only game in town and were relied upon to feed a large part of the world. But during the 1960s and 1970s, other countries began developing—often with help from some of our best farmers and agronomists—an agricultural base that was capable not only of feeding their own people but of producing enough grain and other food for export. Many countries, including some of our allies, were not content to let the free market determine prices in the export market; they subsidized farmers to overproduce, glutting the market and bringing down the prices received by our farmers.

Coupled with the growing competition from abroad and droughts and other natural disasters at home, the crippling debt that farmers had taken on caused tens of thousands of them to lose their farms during the early and mid-eighties. Through it all, the farmers who suffered most were those who had been encouraged to overproduce by the billions of dollars available in federal subsidies.

About half of American farmers—fruit and vegetable growers, for example—operate essentially outside the subsidy system. Although they are subject, like all farmers, to the whims of nature, their fortunes are largely determined by their individual decisions: Based on market conditions, they must choose how much land they will plant, how many crops they will produce. Many, if not most, of these farmers prospered during the years of economic pestilence that ravaged the rest of American agriculture.

In the farm crisis of the mid-eighties, we gave farmers more billions than any administration in history. Frankly, I didn't relish giving so much of the taxpayers' money away, especially when we were battling to bring down the deficit. But farmers were facing a real emergency, and since government had produced many of their problems, I believed it had an obligation to help bail out the victims, then to work to return farming to the free market.

We made some progress in dealing with the problems in agriculture: In a bill I signed in 1985, Congress took large amounts of land that had been under the subsidy programs out of production, lowered the per-bushel subsidies farmers received, and offered other incentives that reduced farmers' reliance on subsidies. Together with improvements in the overall economy—reduced unemployment, lower inflation, and lower interest rates—the law helped American agriculture begin a historic turnaround: Within a year of its passage, farm revenues, profits, and exports were on the rise, while the amount of federal subsidies was in decline.

Between 1986 and 1989, subsidies fell from more than $25 billion annually to less than $10 billion. I wish I could have ended farm subsidies altogether—I still feel the answer is unfettered free competition—but, as I learned in Washington, you seldom get everything you want, and I'll settle for the progress we made.

There were other hardships in America during the long recession: In the emerald forests of the Pacific Northwest, loggers and sawmill workers saw thousands of jobs swallowed up by a prolonged slump in housing construction caused by bloated interest rates. In scores of tree-shaded towns in the South, textile mills, often a community's only major employer, shut their doors and furloughed thousands because of slack sales and new competition from abroad. From the industrial states of the Northeast to the dusty mining towns of the West, more jobs disappeared.

This was indeed a very bleak time for many Americans. But sometimes, as my mother said, troubles carry with them the seeds of something better. These were difficult years, but their hardships forced American industry to take a look at itself, and to become leaner, more efficient, more competitive. And thanks to provisions in the tax bills, businesses had new incentives to invest in the future and make their workers more productive.

I remember visiting a huge lumber mill in the state of Washington, which, like many in the region, had been forced by the slump in lumber sales to lay off almost half of its workers. When I visited, the tax cuts and lower interest rates were beginning to stimulate a rise in home sales. The lumber mill was coming back; it had rehired many of its laid-off workers—but they were now producing twenty-five percent more finished lumber per worker than before the recession, thanks to improvements in productivity that the hard times had forced management to think about and introduce.

I saw another example of the resilience of American industry at a motorcycle plant in York, Pennsylvania.

At one time, dozens of American manufacturers made motorcycles, but now only one was left, the Harley Davidson Company. And until the mid-1980s, its future was in doubt, largely because of the growing competition of cheaper motorcycles made in Japan. To preserve the last American motorcycle company, we had imposed temporary tariffs on Japanese motorcycles, making them more expensive in this country. But when I visited the Harley Davidson plant in York in the spring of 1987, company executives informed me that I could cancel the tariffs a year ahead of schedule, because they had made a turnaround and no longer needed protection to compete with the Japanese.

I'd been hearing stories of how American industry was learning to be more competitive, but at the Harley Davidson plant—as I later did in every corner of the country—I saw firsthand what was happening, and it was a thrilling experience. I'd always believed that the vast majority of American workers, whatever their work, have an inherent pride that makes them want to excel, and that when this fund of pride and energy is liberated, we are unbeatable at whatever we do.

We are not a lazy people; we are an innovative, pragmatic, industrious people, and have demonstrated as much time and again during more than two centuries of problem-solving. At the Harley Davidson plant, I was told how managers and assembly-line workers had joined in a team to figure out how they could beat back their competition from Japan. Meeting around a table, production workers and their bosses talked over their jobs. They discussed how they ordered and handled inventory, and how parts were utilized on the assembly line. The workers pitched in and came up with ideas for doing their jobs more efficiently and improving the quality of the products they made. As the workers became more involved in decision-making, the result was a drastic change in operations that made the whole plant more efficient. Also, where the company had once made a single model, it had now developed a family of motorcycles of different sizes to compete with the motorcycles from Japan.

The Harley Davidson workers told me they could now compete with anyone in the world. What a difference, I thought, between a factory worker like that and one in a Communist factory, who is given no choice of a job, just ordered to go there, and given no incentive to make a decent product or excel in any way. The men and women on the Harley Davidson line had a fervor and pride that was uplifting and contagious.

"That's not a factory," I told someone after the visit, "that's a religion."

What I saw at the motorcycle plant and the lumber mill were just samples of a quiet revolution that was going on all over the country.

Few industries complained as much to me or to Congress as our textile industry, which demanded restrictive trade barriers so that it wouldn't have to face such stiff competition from foreign manufacturers. We wouldn't give it the concessions. As a result, the American textile industry undertook its first comprehensive modernization program in decades: Companies closed obsolete plants, built more efficient ones, and installed millions of dollars' worth of modern computer-controlled spinning, weaving, and other equipment that drastically cut production costs and increased productivity for each employee by an average of more than twenty-five percent. Although the demand for unskilled workers in the textile industry declined, there was an upsurge in higher-paying jobs for workers who were given more demanding, more interesting, more responsible, more productive work.

In different ways, much of American industry underwent a similar transformation during the 1980s. Faced with new competition and responding to forces in the free market, our companies went out and made better products and became more efficient at doing it, a transformation borne out by statistics: Between 1982 and 1987, the productivity of American industry increased at an annual rate of more than 4.2 percent, more than one and one-half times the average for the postwar period, while the productivity of individual workers grew by an average of 1.8 percent a year, fifty percent more than the average rate of growth during the seventies.

Adversity made us tougher. New competition made us work harder.

Again, I don't take credit for this. The American people did it. And it wasn't only factory workers and plant managers who brought America back. A lot of our growth during the eighties didn't come from the giants of American industry but from smaller, innovative companies that tapped new markets, often with new products born out of their own ingenuity. Most of those millions of new jobs produced during the economic expansion were created by entrepreneurs—independent businesspeople pursuing one of the oldest of American dreams.

I met a lot of them while I was president, and if ever there was evidence of why Communism failed and capitalism triumphed, it was in the faces of these people. They were the people capitalism was all about. I heard story after story of someone taking an idea to the bank, borrowing, working hard, then experiencing the joy of seeing a business flourish. They were just ordinary Americans who had had an idea or a dream or a longing for economic independence, and they had gone after it. They had taken risks, worked, and realized their goal. Not all of them succeeded, but America gave every one of them the opportunity to fulfill their dream.

One woman I met had graduated from college with plans to become a classical pianist. Then she had developed arthritis in her hands and couldn't play anymore. So, there she was, wondering what she would do with her life. One of her aunts said, "You've always made wonderful brownies, why don't you make some and sell them down at the neighborhood grocery store? At least you'll have some spending money until you find out what you're going to do." Well, she started doing that and before long she was selling more than $1 million worth of brownies a year and had thirty-five employees.

Other Americans I met or corresponded with pursued other unique dreams: A father-and-son team turned family recipes into a $10-million-a-year business making frozen Mexican dinners. In a small town in Illinois, dozens of people lost their jobs when a local factory closed—then, through their own determination and labor, and with a little capital from someone who placed faith in them, they created a thriving metal fabrication business. . . . And they were just a few of the quiet heroes who helped turn around our economy.

As I have often said, governments don't produce economic growth, people do. What government *can* do is encourage Americans to tap their well of ingenuity and unleash their entrepreneurial spirit, then get out of the way.

The tax cuts and the Tax Reform Act allowed people to accumulate money to start new businesses. As the tax laws began to have an effect, people began doing so in record numbers, not only enriching their own lives but adding to the national wealth and helping to send a wave of prosperity across the land.

Reduced interference by the government also helped. Although I wasn't able to eliminate as much governmental red tape as I would have liked, we did manage to reduce government interference in the economy and make available more money for investments in the future.

Then, as I say, Americans did the rest.

349

53

I WAS THE NEW BOY in school when I flew to Ottawa in the summer of 1981 for my first economic summit, the annual meeting of the heads of seven industrialized nations held on a rotating basis in each country. Before leaving, my "sherpas"—that's what they call the specialists and assistants who prepare presidents for international summit meetings—told me the United States was likely to come under fire in Ottawa for our high interest rates, which several of the countries blamed for their own economic troubles. Margaret Thatcher of Great Britain, Pierre Trudeau of Canada, Zenko Suzuki of Japan, Helmut Schmidt of West Germany, François Mitterrand of France, and Giovanni Spadolini of Italy and I had a freewheeling discussion about the state of the world's economy. None of us was very enthusiastic about it. Schmidt, a socialist, was in a particularly gloomy mood. Although Mitterrand suggested our interest rates were contributing to the world's problems by draining off capital from other countries, he didn't find any support around the table. Everyone knew I was new on the job, and when I described the economic recovery program I was trying to get through Congress, they wished me well. I suspect, however, that several of them didn't think much of some of my more radical ideas for cutting taxes and reducing the government's interference in economic affairs.

Two years later, the economic summit convened amid the breathtaking colonial beauty of Williamsburg, Virginia, just as the economic turnaround in the United States was beginning to gain a strong head of steam. It was my turn to serve as chairman, and I was a little edgy. At dinner the first night, the seven of us sat down around a big round table, everyone fell silent, and someone—I believe it was Helmut Kohl, who had replaced Schmidt as chancellor of West Germany—spoke up: *"Tell us about the American miracle."*

He wanted to know how we had managed to turn the tide on both inflation and unemployment while most of the rest of the industrialized world was still gripped by the recession.

Looking at a semicircle of faces, I launched into what I guess was a variation of the speech I'd been making for years. First, I gave them my thoughts about how excessive tax rates take away the incentive to produce, and how lower tax rates, in the end, generate more economic growth and also greater revenue for government. Then I told them what we had done to lower our tax rates, and some of the other things we were trying to do, such as reducing the size of government, eliminating unnecessary regulations and interference in the free market, and turning over to private enterprise some of the functions government had taken over. Everyone around the table just listened in silence as I spoke.

It wasn't long after that that I began reading about a wave of tax cutting in several of their countries. And at subsequent economic summits, several leaders told me they were introducing economic and taxation policies based on ours—not only cutting taxes, but reducing the regulation of business. The next time I'd see them, they'd say the policies were stimulating a turnaround like the one we had had in the United States.

No one did more in this regard than Margaret Thatcher. But I don't claim credit for convincing her of the merits of free enterprise and downsizing government. She was at least as determined as I was to get government out of the pocketbooks and off the backs of the people. From our first meeting, we'd been on the same wavelength. Whenever we saw each other, she usually told me her ability to point to the success of our policies in the United States had made it easier for her to convince Britons the policies had merit. As everyone now knows, her policies touched off a boom that brought great prosperity to the British people. In many ways she accomplished more than we did in returning government-run enterprises to where they belonged—the private sector—and created a model that has since been copied by other countries. I wish we could have done as well on this as she did. Maybe the difference between what a prime minister can accomplish and what a president can do has to do with the fact that a prime minister automatically has a majority in Parliament, and a president can't say the same thing about our Congress. For all of my eight years in office, the opposing party had a majority in our House of Representatives.

Before going to my first economic summit, I'd wondered what it would be like to have the heads of seven nations in the same room: What tensions of ego and status would be at work? As I will explain shortly, we did have occasional conflicts. But, as our first meeting got started, I was surprised to hear the others addressing each other by their first names. When I got my first chance to speak, I said, "My name's Ron . . ."

Although I never asked her about it, I think the idea of addressing the other summit leaders by their first names was Margaret Thatcher's. It did wonders to make the meetings cordial and productive. I was always Ron to the others and I addressed them by their first names.

Once I was no longer the freshman of the group, I went out of my way to tell newcomers about the policy. When the new Japanese prime minister, Yasuhiro Nakasone, came to his first summit, for example, I asked him, "What does your wife call you at home?"

He said, "Yasu."

I said, "Well, Yasu, my name's Ron, and here we all go by our first names."

I liked the idea so much that after the Ottawa meeting, when I met the heads of other nations during their state visits to Washington, I would suggest (unless there was a custom or cultural reason that made it inappropriate) that we go on a first-name basis. It worked wonders in breaking the diplomatic ice. Suddenly, instead of a formal meeting between government officials, you had two *people* sitting across from each other.

Not everything at the Williamsburg summit went as cordially as on that first night when I was asked to explain the "American miracle."

As I've mentioned, in November of 1981 I had made my zero-

zero proposal to eliminate all intermediate-range nuclear weapons from Europe. After that, we reopened negotiations with the Russians in Geneva with the proposal on the table. But now, more than a year later, the talks were deadlocked. The Soviets refused to give up their intermediate-range missiles targeted at European cities and accept parity with NATO. I still believed the only acceptable INF agreement was one eliminating *all* intermediate nuclear missiles from Europe. If they wouldn't give up their missiles, I thought the only way we would persuade them to do it was to proceed with our plans to deploy Pershing II and cruise missiles as a counter to their missiles in Europe.

At the time we met at Williamsburg, the newly developed missiles were almost ready for deployment in Europe. I opened our discussion by reminding the others that the Geneva talks were at an impasse. I thought we had to go ahead and deploy NATO's new weapons on schedule in order to apply pressure on the Soviets to accept zero-zero parity. After a lengthy discussion, we agreed on the principles of a communiqué incorporating this position, and asked our foreign ministers to draw up a statement reaffirming support for the "two-track" policy that included deployment of the new missiles as well as continued negotiations aimed at eliminating intermediate-range weapons from Europe.

Everything was settled, or so it seemed. The next morning, however, François Mitterrand and Pierre Trudeau declared that they couldn't support the statement, and in effect called those of us who favored installing the new missiles warmongers. Obviously, they had gotten together the night before and decided to renege on the previous day's agreement.

Our discussion became very hot, with the two of them entrenched on one side of the argument and the rest of us on the other. I was angry at their turnabout and spoke for twenty minutes straight defending our position.

Because of the disagreement, we were an hour late for lunch. As we left the meeting for the building where lunch was to be served, our group walked together and they walked alone. Neither group spoke to the other throughout lunch. In our afternoon session, we asked our foreign ministers to work on a revised statement that would satisfy Mitterrand and Trudeau but not water down the heart of the communiqué; then we started working on a statement of economic policy endorsing liberalization of trade policies. Once again, from out of the blue, Mitterrand and Trudeau objected.

"I thought at one point Margaret Thatcher was going to order Pierre to go stand in a corner," I recorded in my diary that night. "It was hard to remember [that] we had started the day with a prayer service in the tiny church. Maybe that's what did it because we closed the day with both issues resolved, cordiality restored and no winners or losers."

A year later, there was a similar dispute at the economic summit in London, with Mitterrand and Trudeau again squaring off against the rest of us. Pierre bitterly lit into Margaret, the chairman of the meeting, and told her she was being heavy-handed and undemocratic in dealing with their objections. I was horrified by his rudeness and the insulting way that he spoke to her; but she ignored him, kept her cool, and never skipped a beat. When the session was over, I caught up with her in the hall and said, "Margaret, he had no business talking to you like that, he was way out of line." But she just said very quietly: "Oh, women know when men are being childish."

That night over dinner at Buckingham Palace, Pierre mentioned that he had read someplace that I could recite by heart "The Shooting of Dan McGrew" by the Canadian poet and storyteller Robert W. Service. I'm not sure he really believed I could do it; maybe he just wanted to put me on the spot and see how I'd handle it. Sitting between Pierre and me was the Queen Mother, and as it turned out she was a great fan of that story and one of its characters, "the lady known as Lou." So when she heard what Pierre said, she turned to me and said, "Oh, do you know 'The Shooting of Dan McGrew'?"

I said, well, yes, then she started urging me to say it. She wouldn't let up, and the whole table fell silent waiting to see what I would do. Across the table were Prince Philip and the queen. Everybody was waiting for me. I was on the spot, and so I plunged into reciting that poem I'd memorized when I was a lad back in Dixon, and every time I said "the lady named Lou," the Queen Mother chimed in with me. When we were through, everybody at the table applauded.

All in all, it was a memorable evening.

·   ·   ·

Although there were a few problems at the economic summits, they were, by and large, productive forums for frank discussions of economic issues, which in today's world extend more and more across international boundaries.

One issue that always came up was trade protectionism.

The principles underlying my support of free and fair trade are pretty simple: The operation of the free market is based on the concept that people make a product or produce a service which they hope other people will want to buy. Then, in millions of separate decisions, consumers choose which products and services they want to buy, when they are going to buy them, and how much they are willing to pay for them. Free competition and the law of supply and demand determine the prices and the winners and the losers in the competition. If customers stop buying an enterprise's product because it doesn't match the standards of another product, it's up to that enterprise to improve the product or it will lose its ability to compete.

If consumers in one country are going to be able to buy goods produced in another country, their nation must have income generated by the sale of goods and services abroad. We can't say to them, "We want to sell you something that we make, but don't send us your products."

For the free market to work, everyone has to compete on an equal footing. That way, prices and demand go up or down based on the free choices of people; there are winners and losers under the system of free competition, but consumers are the ultimate benefactors. Free competition produces better products and lower prices. However, when governments fix or control the price, impose quotas, subsidize manufacturers or farmers, or otherwise intervene in the free market with artificial restrictions, it isn't free and it won't work as it is supposed to work.

At all eight of the economic summits I attended, I tried to preach the virtues of free trade. In principle, the other leaders expressed a similar view, and denounced the trade barriers of other nations. But the plain truth was that all of us were protectionist to some extent.

I've mentioned how most countries (including ours) subsidized farmers, resulting in production of more grain and certain other farm commodities than the market can absorb, often depressing export prices to less than the cost of production. Every country (including ours) imposes barriers to free trade that are intended to protect or subsidize particular industries, usually because of domestic political pressure from groups that have a vested interest in limiting competition. Barriers are also sometimes imposed to retaliate against the protectionism of another nation.

When I came to the White House in 1981, I had hopes of making international trade freer and fairer. We made substantial headway: We concluded a bilateral trade agreement with Canada, our largest trading partner, that created the largest open market in the world. We reduced barriers restricting trade with Israel and Mexico and, to a limited extent, with several other countries. In 1986, we and our major trading partners opened a historic round of multinational trade negotiations under the General Agreement on Tariffs and Trade (GATT) aimed at virtually eliminating agricultural subsidies worldwide over a ten-year period (it would have been impossible to move faster without pulling the rug out from under farmers and industries whose livelihoods were geared to existing protectionism).

At each economic summit, I could feel the mood shift more strongly in favor of free trade, although we all realized that as a practical matter there were limits to the pace with which we could disturb the status quo. Even with Japan, with whom we have the greatest imbalance of trade and have had perhaps the most difficult trading relations, we made limited progress: Following Japan's 1981 voluntary cutback of car exports, Prime Minister Nakasone stuck out his political neck to fight for a reduction of barriers to some of our exports, and Japanese manufacturers started building some of their cars in this country.

While I was president, we retaliated against a number of countries, including some of our allies, that imposed trade barriers to our products. But retaliation isn't a solution to the problems of protectionism; it only perpetuates it. Many countries, including Japan, continue to impose barriers that give them an unfair advantage in international trade, and until they become more willing to compete on a level playing field, they can expect protectionist sentiment to grow in this country.

The widening of our international trade deficit during the 1980s was to a large extent a by-product of our country's strong economic recovery. When our economy started to take off at the end of 1982, it expanded much faster than those of our major trading partners; the dollar rose in value, imports became a bargain for Americans, and some American products and services were priced out of foreign markets. The result: a widening trade gap that caused difficult times for many of our manufacturers who relied on exports for a major part of their profits.

Once again, I think this was a situation in which hard times had a good result: Our difficulties accelerated the modernization and restructuring of our industrial base and in the end helped make America more productive and more competitive. After several years of decline, our exports began to surge in 1986, and by 1989 the trade gap had fallen to the lowest level in five years. Our exports continued to surge in 1990; the gap grew narrower, and our exporters more prosperous.

It's true that we now have tougher competitors overseas than we used to have, but America is tougher, too. We've proved that we can respond to competition, as we always have. As a nation we have always thrived on competition, and we always will.

Throughout the eight years of my presidency, no alliance we had was stronger than the one between the United States and the United Kingdom. Not only did Margaret Thatcher and I become personal friends and share a similar philosophy about government; the alliance was strengthened by the long special relationship between our countries born of shared democratic values, common Anglo-Saxon roots, a common language, and a friendship deepened and mellowed by fighting two world wars side by side. The depth of this special relationship made it impossible for us to remain neutral during Britain's war with Argentina over the Falkland Islands in 1982, although it was a conflict in which I had to walk a fine line.

Argentine marines wearing civilian clothes landed on South Georgia Island, a British possession in the South Atlantic about 600 miles east of the Falklands, in late March 1982. At about the same time, our intelligence indicated, Argentina was preparing to invade the Falklands, an archipelago of two hundred or so islands located 250 miles off the coast of Argentina. The islands had been under British rule for nearly a century and a half.

After the landing on South Georgia Island, Margaret Thatcher called me and said that Britain would never submit to a takeover of one of its crown colonies. She asked me to telephone Leopoldo Galtieri, president of the military junta that ruled Argentina, to urge him not to proceed with the invasion and to say that Britain would use whatever force was necessary to keep her colony.

I spoke to Galtieri for about forty minutes, but couldn't budge him: He claimed that the Falklands (which he called the Malvinas), by reasons of history, culture, and proximity, rightfully belonged to Argentina, not to a European colonial power, and that Argentina's national honor was at stake in establishing sovereignty over them.

As we spoke, Argentina's invasion preparations were already under way. The next morning, about one thousand Argentinean troops landed on the Falklands, whose total population was less than two thousand people, most of them of British ancestry. Within a few days, a British Royal Navy armada had steamed toward the Falklands and both sides asked for our help should the dispute come to war.

The leaders of Argentina's military junta were trying to seize the remote islands to save their government. Their domestic political position was precarious because of mounting economic troubles and rumors of grave human-rights abuses in Argentina. Galtieri thought we would side with Argentina because we were neighbors in the Americas and because we had requested the junta's help in fighting Communism in the hemisphere. It was true that I had placed a high priority on improving relations with our Latin neighbors, and Argentina was one of the countries where we had been working hardest to bring about democratic reforms. But the junta misjudged not only Margaret Thatcher's will but the strength of our ties to England and our opposition to armed aggression wherever it occurred, even on the obscure shores of a few rocky islands in the South Atlantic.

Despite some resistance from Jeane Kirkpatrick, our UN representative, who disagreed with our position, we let the junta know privately that, while we would provide military help to neither adversary, our sympathies were on the British side. We were staunch allies of the United Kingdom and supported its right to defend its colony. We also assured Margaret Thatcher that we were fully behind Britain. Publicly, however, I decided it was wisest to mute our reaction while extending the good offices of the United States to see if we could help settle the dispute between mutual friends.

With this in mind, I asked Al Haig to try to mediate the dispute and avert an armed clash. He shuttled between Washington, London, and Buenos Aires for most of the next three weeks, making a valiant effort to avoid a war. Nevertheless, hostilities erupted on the first of May. I think Al had been caught between an immovable object and an irresistible force: Splintered badly and trying to whip up a jingoistic fervor to increase its own sagging popularity, the junta rejected any settlement that stopped short of unquestioned Argentinean sovereignty over the Falklands; Margaret Thatcher was willing to make limited concessions to avoid bloodshed, but was adamant in her determination to defend British interests.

As the Royal Navy sailed toward the Falklands, we learned that Soviet ships were trailing the British vessels and providing intelligence information about the fleet to Argentina via Cuba. We also learned that the Soviets offered to supply low-cost arms to Argentina if war broke out—an offer which, to its credit (and with encouragement from us), the junta refused.

Despite reports to the contrary in *The Washington Post* and elsewhere, we maintained a genuine as well as an official neutrality during this period. Although London utilized one of our military satellites to communicate with its fleet as it headed for the Falklands, this was done under an agreement that had been in effect long before the crisis. We provided no other military assistance to the British. However, once fighting started, after the Argentineans had repeatedly rejected reasonable offers of a settlement, we declared our full support of Britain and provided her with whatever aid we could.

What had been a war of nerves and a battle of words quickly became very bloody: Britain and Argentina each lost warships and planes in the war and, between them, almost one thousand lives.

A few days after hostilities started, the president of a Latin American country told me that he had received a tip from his ambassador in Buenos Aires that the British were preparing to attack military bases on the mainland of Argentina. This would have substantially escalated the level of combat. Our intelligence community confirmed that preparations for such attacks were under way. I called

Margaret Thatcher to say that, while we fully supported Britain's effort to take back the Falklands, we thought it would be dangerous to move the war onto the mainland of South America. Margaret heard me out, but, demonstrating the iron will for which she is famous, she stood firm. I couldn't persuade her to make a commitment not to invade, and for several days we waited for a nighttime attack by British planes on the mainland—one that never came.

In late May, I called Margaret again, this time to suggest a possible settlement that stopped short of Britain scoring a complete victory over Argentina. A total victory was certain to topple Argentina's government, and some of our people believed that this might lead to violence and chaos that would be exploited by leftist guerrillas. But she told me too many British lives had already been lost for Britain to withdraw without total victory, and she convinced me. I understood what she meant.

Before long, British troops reclaimed the Falklands from the over-matched Argentinean forces. President Galtieri was ousted as head of the junta, and the following year democracy came to Argentina with the election of Raúl Alfonsín as president.

Margaret Thatcher, I think, had no choice but to stand up to the generals who cynically squandered the lives of young Argentineans solely to prolong the life of a corrupt and iron-fisted totalitarian government. She did so, I believe, not because, as was speculated in Britain, her government might fall if she did not, but because she believed absolutely in the moral rightness of what she was doing and in her nation's obligation to guarantee the handful of people living in the Falklands the right of self-determination.

After I accepted Al Haig's resignation as secretary of state a few weeks later, he privately blamed it on his inability to mediate a settlement to end the Falklands crisis and avert war. But in truth I thought he did a good job under difficult conditions. The reasons I accepted his resignation went deeper than that.

As I've said, I discovered only a few months into the administration that Al didn't want anyone other than himself, me included, to influence foreign policy while he was secretary of state. He was never shy about asserting this claim. After a briefing on one foreign policy issue during the spring of 1982, I wrote in my diary, "Al

Haig made great good sense on this entire matter. It's amazing how sound he can be on complex international matters but how utterly paranoid with regard to the people he must work with."

I first met Al Haig in the 1970s when he was commander of NATO, and I was greatly struck with him at that time. He was highly respected as the military leader of the Atlantic alliance, and that was why he was my first choice as secretary of state. But the Al Haig who was my secretary of state wasn't the same Al Haig I met when he was at NATO. He was effective in getting our new policy of realism and peace through strength off the ground, but we sometimes disagreed on other things. He never said as much to me, but others told me he had shocked some congressmen by giving them the impression that if it were up to him, he'd deal with some of our problems in Central America and Cuba with a bombing run or an invasion. He and I also differed about Taiwan: I regarded Taiwan as a loyal, democratic, longtime ally to whom we owed unqualified support. Haig and others at the State Department were so eager to improve relations with the People's Republic of China that they pressed me to back away from this pledge of support. I felt we had an obligation to the people of Taiwan, and no one was going to keep us from meeting it.

During that first year, Haig threatened several times to quit, but I talked him out of it. In June of 1982, as the Falklands crisis was coming to an end, he issued the same threat to senior members of the White House staff, claiming they were invading his turf. When he came to the Oval Office the next day, I was prepared to accept his resignation, but he didn't resign; instead, he launched into a bitter attack on the top staff and gave me a bill of particulars listing his complaints, which he asked me to correct. In fact, a few of his grievances were legitimate: One or more people in the White House were trying to do him in with malicious leaks to the press. Still, the jealousies and turf battles had gone too far. Two days later, apparently after he had decided I wasn't going to respond to his demands, he came to my office again, and this time submitted his resignation. I think he was hoping I would not accept it. But when I did, he didn't seem surprised. I had asked the staff to sound out George Shultz about becoming secretary of state; I called him and he accepted.

"This has been a heavy load," I wrote in my diary June 25.

[Went] Up to Camp David where we were in time to see Al read his letter of resignation on TV. I'm told it was his fourth rewrite. Apparently his first was pretty strong, then he thought better of it. I must say it was okay, he gave only one reason and did say there was a disagreement on foreign policy. Actually, the only disagreement was over whether I made policy or the Secretary of State did.

Several years after the Falklands war, we had to face another crisis involving an ally.

In September 1984, Cardinal Jaime Sin, the Catholic prelate in Manila, came to Washington and told me that many Filipino people believed Marcos was responsible for the murder of his political rival, Benigno Aquino. He said there was growing anti-Marcos sentiment among the people that, if unchecked, would fuel the cause of Communist rebels in the Philippines. The cardinal said that he believed Marcos had to go, and I think he was seeking American support for those in Manila who were trying to oust him. I was surprised at the intensity of his remarks but made no commitment.

The future of the Philippines was of great importance to the United States. Our huge military stations there, Clark Air Force Base and the Subic Bay naval base, were among our largest in the world and the anchor of our defense in the western Pacific; and we had had no stronger ally anywhere than Marcos. The February following Cardinal Sin's visit, senior U.S. diplomats in Manila reported that Marcos had developed a serious kidney ailment and was putting in less than two hours a day of work; his wife, Imelda, they said, was keeping people from her husband while making important presidential decisions herself. But they agreed that Marcos still represented our best counterforce to the Communist rebels and that we should maintain our support for him.

Later that year, I began to receive reports from our ambassador in Manila, Stephen Bosworth, that the Communist insurgents in the Philippines were continuing to make political gains and that Marcos was underestimating the effect of his policies on the Filipino people. I asked Senator Paul Laxalt to go to Manila to investigate the reports. He confirmed that substantial public outrage was building against Marcos—the force that later came to be known as "people power." Paul persuaded Marcos to call a presidential election the following February in a gesture to prove to his people—and the world—that he was not a dictator. Corazon Aquino, the widow of Marcos's former rival, then entered the race against Marcos. The question on everybody's mind then became: Would Marcos permit a free and fair election?

While the political campaign for control of the Philippines was getting under way, thousands of miles from Manila there was another example of people power exerting itself: Revolutionary winds were gathering on the Caribbean island of Haiti. For more than a quarter of a century, Haiti had been ruled by father-and-son dictators, the Duvaliers; but now it was on the verge of an explosion. The Haitian people were fed up with the tyranny and poverty the Duvaliers' rule had brought them.

At a National Security Council meeting on February 6, 1986, election eve in Manila, I made two decisions: To rid the Caribbean of a dictator and avoid civil war, we offered to spirit Jean-Claude (Baby Doc) Duvalier, with his family and a group of friends, out of Haiti and fly them on an air force jet to Paris. And I agreed to the terms of a spy swap with the Russians that would grant freedom to a prominent Soviet dissident, Anatoly Scharansky.

Five days later, Scharansky was allowed to emigrate to Israel, and it became apparent we might have to relocate a third person that month—Ferdinand Marcos—to avoid, as we had in Haiti, a bloody civil war. I came to this realization at a meeting with leaders of a congressional delegation that had gone to Manila to determine if Marcos was running a fair election: They said there appeared to be overwhelming evidence of fraud in the balloting.

I asked our roving diplomatic troubleshooter, Phil Habib, to go to Manila. He confirmed that Marcos had stolen the election and that an uprising of Filipinos on behalf of Mrs. Aquino, the legitimate winner, was inevitable. Things then started to move quickly in Manila: Two of the country's top military leaders—Defense Minister Juan Ponce Enrile and Lieutenant General Fidel Ramos—resigned, gave their support to Mrs. Aquino, took control over part of the Philippine military forces, and called on Marcos to quit.

On February 23, while I was at Camp David, I was told that Marcos and a loyal general, Fabian Ver, had amassed a force of tanks and troops to attack army units loyal to Enrile and Ramos. Ver's tanks were turned back by hundreds of thousands of civilians

—but the next time, the result might be huge casualties. I drafted an appeal to Marcos not to use force and helicoptered back to Washington for a Sunday afternoon meeting in the White House Situation Room, a small room in the basement where we convened during serious international crises. Present were George Bush, George Shultz, Cap Weinberger, Don Regan, Phil Habib, Bill Casey, and National Security Advisor John Poindexter, plus specialists from the State Department and other agencies.

We agreed that it was inevitable that Marcos would have to give up power; he no longer had the popular support to remain in office. Mrs. Aquino had won the election fairly, and the people of the Philippines intended to make her president.

Given these facts, the decision I made wasn't difficult, but it wasn't enjoyable, either.

Everyone agreed that we had to do everything possible to avoid bloodshed in Manila; we didn't want to see it come down to a civil war. I also wanted to be sure we did not treat Marcos as shabbily as our country had treated another former ally, the shah of Iran. At the same time, I knew it was important to start off with a good relationship with the new government of the Philippines.

I knew Marcos was a proud man, and how we approached him was the critical thing. I didn't think we should dictate to him; instead, we should lay down the facts and let him make the decision we wanted him to make. I decided that we would offer to fly Marcos and his family out of the Philippines and give them sanctuary in the United States. Based on my understanding of his personality, I told the others that we had to convince him of the hopelessness and inevitability of his situation and persuade him to give up power voluntarily, using the argument that it would avoid a civil war that could destroy much of the country he loved.

Here are excerpts from my diary during that period, beginning with the aforementioned meeting in the Situation Room:

Feb. 23

It was a long meeting with no disagreement but lots of frustration. President Marcos is stubborn and refuses to admit he can no longer govern. I made the point that a message from me must appeal to him on the grounds that if there is violence I'll be helpless to continue support for the Philippines. We must not try to lay down the law. All we can do is send the message . . . and pray.

Feb. 24

The day started at 5:30 a.m. with a call.

The situation in the Philippines is deteriorating. The Marcos family and the Vers left the Palace and went to the airport. Then Gen. Ver apparently talked them out of leaving. Back in the Palace, they went on TV. The president and the general. They got in an argument. The general wanted to launch an attack on the military that has gone over to the anti-Marcos people. The president said No. All this ended sleep for me.

In the office at 9. The staff meeting and N.S.C. were on the same subject. I was approving statements for delivery to the President, pleading for no violence. Then a call from Nancy—what to say to Imelda Marcos who was calling her? At same time I was told Paul Laxalt, George Shultz, John Poindexter and Don R. were coming in about Paul's call to Marcos. We've agreed that he should be told I'm recommending he step down and we'll take the lead in negotiating his safety and offering him sanctuary in the US. He says he wants to live out his life in the Philippines. Well, we'll try to negotiate that. Wound up the day in the dentist's chair. Time for inspection. I passed.

Feb. 25

The call this morning was at 6:45. President Marcos and his family and close circle I was told are in our Clark Air Force Base. We don't know yet his destination but he's said he wants to stay in the Philippines. He has a home in northern Luzon. In the office I was met by George Shultz and the VP, Cap, John, Don, etc. We are ordering our ambassador and others to contact Aquino to see if we could persuade her to accept his staying in the islands with a promise of security.

As the day went on, we learned she wasn't going to do that. He incidentally is quite ill and is bedridden at Clark. By evening we learned his party had left by medivac plane for Guam. He was carried to the plane on a stretcher.

After the Marcoses received sanctuary in Hawaii, they tried several times to contact Nancy and me as well as Paul Laxalt in order to convince us that they were still the president and first lady of the Philippines. But there was nothing we could do. We recognized

Corazon Aquino (whom I came to admire and respect after first being skeptical about whether she had enough determination to fight the Filipino insurgents) as the duly elected president of the Philippines, and had offered all of our help to her.

Ferdinand and Imelda also asked us repeatedly to see if we could arrange for them to live out their lives at the home they owned on Luzon. Marcos sent word that he envisioned himself as a kind of elder statesman. Several times, we asked Mrs. Aquino if she would accept his return to the Philippines if, in exchange, he agreed to surrender the money he was accused of looting from the Filipino treasury; but she was afraid that if he returned to the Philippines, he would try to arouse his former supporters and regain power. Considering the events that occurred later, she was probably right: Marcos hadn't been in Hawaii more than a few days before we started learning of telephone calls to Manila and other points in which he said he regretted leaving the country without a fight and desperately encouraged supporters to conduct a coup aimed at overthrowing Mrs. Aquino and restoring him to power. We also, at one point, foiled an attempt to ship a substantial number of arms to Marcos loyalists in the Philippines.

The Marcoses didn't like their life on Hawaii—most of all, I think, because their presence in the United States made them easy targets for lawsuits by the Aquino government and others. At their request, we asked several countries, including Panama, Spain, Mexico, and others, to take the Marcoses. But no one wanted them.

We spoke to them one last time, by telephone, during a stopover Nancy and I made in Hawaii while we were en route to the Tokyo economic summit in April 1986. They didn't like Hawaii and spoke longingly of a desire to return to the Philippines, where Ferdinand said he wanted to be buried. Even then, I don't think they understood the depth of the feelings against them, not only among the Filipino people but among many Americans because of the corruption that had been rampant in the Philippines. Imelda kept Nancy on the phone for almost an hour. It was uncomfortable for all of us. We couldn't help but remember how well they had lived in Malacañang Palace when we first met them when I was governor —and note how different their lives were now.

For Nancy and me, the telephone call was a final farewell, a sad and bittersweet parting. We never spoke to them again.

Until the day he died in the autumn of 1989, Marcos continued to claim that he was the president of the Philippines and Imelda claimed that she was the first lady.

54

WHILE I WAS PRESIDENT, Nancy and I made trips overseas that left us with memories that will never leave us. In the spring of 1984 it was China. Subsequent events in Tiananmen Square have tempered the enthusiasm generated in us by that trip, but when we went there during that beautiful spring, it seemed events were occurring in China and Poland that were heralding the demise of Communism.

In March of that year, Treasury Secretary Don Regan had come back from a trip to Beijing with an intriguing report: The People's Republic of China was moving slowly but surely toward acceptance of a free enterprise market, and inviting investment by foreign capitalists. Many farm communes were being disbanded, and Chinese farmers were being granted long-term leases and the right to sell their produce for a profit.

Before most of my major foreign trips, the National Security Council prepared a short film that gave me a preview of the places I would be visiting and the people I would be meeting. The film they showed me on the eve of my trip to China confirmed that significant cracks were appearing in the foundations of Chinese-style Communism.

On Easter Sunday, April 22, after a brief visit to Rancho del Cielo, we left for Honolulu on the first leg of the trip. During a two-day stop there, I saw Barry Goldwater, who was stopping over before continuing to Washington after a visit to Taiwan. Barry was upset about my visiting China and made little attempt to hide it. Although I told him I would make it plain to the leaders of the PRC that we would not forsake old friends in order to make new ones, he suspected I was getting ready to give up on Taiwan, and I don't think I convinced him otherwise.

We began our six-day visit to China in Beijing on a cloudy, overcast morning following another overnight stopover on Guam. We drove immediately to the Great Hall of the People for arrival ceremonies and a twenty-one-gun salute, and that night we had the first of a succession of twelve-course dinners. Thanks to some tutoring we'd gotten in Washington, Nancy and I both managed to handle our chopsticks with adequate deftness. We generally heeded advice that Richard Nixon, who'd come to Beijing in 1972, had given us before we left on the trip: Don't ask about the food they serve you at the big banquets, just swallow it. Still, I had difficulty identifying several items on my plate that first night, so I stirred them around in hopes of camouflaging my reluctance to eat them.

The following morning, when I met for breakfast with the staff, we kept noisy music playing loudly on a tape recorder as a precaution against hidden microphones. It was a good thing we did: Later, we found five listening devices hidden in our rooms in the guest-house. One staffer unscrewed a plate over the light switch in his room, discovered a bug, removed it, and took it home as a souvenir.

At my first official meeting with Chinese leaders, a ninety-minute session with Premier Zhao Ziyang, I emphasized that we were not seeking an alliance with China and that we approved of its non-aligned status, but felt that as friends and Pacific Basin neighbors we could contribute jointly to peace and stability in the basin. With that, I think the official part of the visit got off to a good start. Later that day, I addressed a group of Chinese civic leaders; a recording of my speech was subsequently broadcast to the Chinese people—minus several of my lines about the Soviet Union, religion, and the value of a free economy. Then came another meeting with Zhao and several party leaders, where we discussed trade and investment. At this meeting, a small, feisty ideologue tried to lecture me about removing our troops from South Korea. I tried to give it right back to him. If North Korea really wanted to improve relations with us, as he claimed it did, let them stop digging illegal tunnels under the demilitarized buffer zone between the two Koreas, I said.

That night, there was another twelve-course dinner; somehow, the second one went down easier than the first had. By then, I guess I was really heeding Dick Nixon's advice.

The following day was the big event of the trip, my meeting with the top man in China, Chairman Deng Xiaoping. A small man with thick shoulders and dark, impressive eyes, Deng exhibited a playful sense of humor when we met. Nancy had come with me for the formal introduction, and Deng smilingly asked her to come back to China without me someday so he could show it to her. But later, when we got down to business, his smile was gone and he immediately began criticizing the United States for a whole range of supposed sins: our support of Israel, which he claimed made the entire Middle East unstable; our treatment of the developing nations; and our failure to come to terms on a nuclear arms agreement with the Soviets.

As host, he got the first shot. Then it was my turn. I did my best to rebut just about everything he'd said, correcting his facts and figures. Host or not, he'd touched a nerve, so I let him have it. After that, to my surprise, he suddenly started to warm up; his smile came back and he seemed to want to relax and be more cordial. Still, that didn't keep him from bringing up our friendship with Taiwan, which he claimed was an interference with Chinese affairs. I told him that the split between the PRC and Taiwan was a problem to be worked out by the Chinese, but that the United States wanted it worked out peacefully; any attempt at a military solution mounted by his country would damage relations between our countries beyond repair.

By the time we broke for lunch, the intensity of our earlier discussion had faded into a warm and pleasant social event with toasts all around. By then, I think I understood him, and he understood me. After lunch, I picked up Nancy and we left for a visit to the Great Wall, with huge crowds waving to us along the way. Although I'd seen photographs of the Great Wall since childhood, seeing it rise up and disappear over the mountains in both directions was a tremendously emotional experience, one that even now I have trouble fully describing.

During our tour of Beijing, it seemed that everywhere we looked we saw bicycles—all of them black. Virtually all of the cars, I was told, were owned by the government. One family, however, had just been able to buy a personal car, and instead of punishing them, the government broadcast the news on television while we were there. The government seemed to want to make heroes of the family, sending a message to the people: Private property is not all bad. Work hard and save your money and maybe you, too, can own an automobile.

Next came several more days of sightseeing that included a few opportunities to observe the changes going on in China, as well as a fascinating look into its past. We flew to Xian, the ancient capital of China, then drove almost ninety minutes to the tomb of China's first emperor and the site where archaeologists had unearthed hundreds of life-size terra-cotta figures of soldiers standing in ranks, complete with horses and chariots, to guard the tomb. "They know there are more than 7,000 [terra-cotta soldiers] that haven't been uncovered yet," I wrote that evening in my diary: "It is an unforgettable experience. This—plus the drive past villages surrounded by endless wheat fields dotted here and there with burial mounds and relics of China's ancient past—made for a day we'll long remember."

We had asked to visit one of China's new free markets where Chinese farmers and entrepreneurs could sell items for profit in a departure from Communist ideology. At first the Chinese officials said that it would be impractical because of security restrictions, but then they offered to set up a sample market, and Nancy bought several decorations for our Christmas tree and presents for our grandchildren from a young girl there. Nancy's bill came to five yuan, about $2.50. I handed the girl a ten-yuan note, and when she discovered she didn't have any change, she looked around, flustered and embarrassed, searching for help.

I'd been briefed that tipping was not customary in China, but I felt sorry for her as she looked around in panic for help, so I said, "Keep it," and we moved on. But in a few moments she caught up with us and handed me my change, which somehow she had managed to find.

By then, I was the embarrassed one. I realized that, in trying to be helpful to the girl, I'd appeared to be tipping her. I hadn't thought fast enough and had made a faux pas.

After our visit to Xian and a farewell ceremony in Beijing with Chairman Zhao that marked the close of the official part of our visit, we flew to Shanghai, where we toured a factory China was modernizing with the help of U.S. technology, then spoke to students at a Shanghai university (where about half of the faculty members had attended school in America) and I made an address that was televised live in Shanghai. The next day, we went to the Rainbow Bridge commune (in a subtle indication of the changes that were under way in China, the "commune" in its name had recently been changed to "township"), where we visited a private home in which a young couple lived with their small boy and the husband's father and mother. After years of saving money, the husband had built the house himself and the family was very proud of it. We also spoke to several women who worked outdoors in the fields at the commune; under China's new policies, they told us they were allowed to sell in the open market anything they produced that exceeded quotas set by the government, providing them some of the incentive inherent in the free market. From Shanghai, we flew to Fairbanks, Alaska, for an overnight stop and a brief visit with Pope John Paul II, who was on his way to South Korea, and then home to Washington.

During my remaining four and a half years in the White House, I continued to take a great interest in the changes slowly coming to China. It was still a decidedly Communist country, but in encouraging small businesses and freeing farm workers from their collective farms, allowing them to lease the land they had tilled and to share in the profits from it, they were creating entrepreneurs. Whatever they called it, it was the beginning of a free enterprise system —and with it, they increased agricultural productivity in some areas by almost four times.

I don't claim the vision to have foreseen in 1984 all the dramatic changes that came later to the Communist world. But the events in China and Poland made me feel optimistic; they were an exciting glimmer on the horizon, the first public admission in the Communist world that Communism wasn't working . . . a harbinger of its collapse.

Only history can tell us where China will go from here. The Chinese leadership's brutal crackdown on students seeking fundamental democratic rights makes it difficult to chart the future. Those brave students who laid down their lives against the tanks of Tiananmen Square confirmed what I'd always believed: that no totalitarian society can bottle up the instinctive drive of men and women to be free, and that once you give a captive people a little freedom, they'll demand more. Still, as I watched that drama unfold and learned of the students' fate, I couldn't help but wonder if it might not have been better if they had waited and not moved so soon. I understood and sympathized with them, as anyone would, but I knew there were people in their government trying slowly to increase democracy and freedom in China, and the students' revolt, as courageous as it was, might in the long run have made it more difficult for them to carry out what they were trying to do.

As I say, the future is hard to predict in China, although I'm still betting on the triumph there of the tidal wave of freedom that is sweeping across our world.

A few weeks after we got back from China, I left for the economic summit in London, making along the way two unforgettable stopovers.

In Ireland, we helicoptered to the village of Ballyporeen in County Tipperary. It was from here that my great-grandfather, Michael Reagan, had left for America during the middle of the nineteenth century, at a time of great hardship in his homeland. My father had been orphaned before he was six, and neither he nor I had ever known much about Jack's side of the family. But presidents sometimes enjoy pleasant perks, and for the occasion of our visit, the Irish government had dug up our roots and introduced me to them.

In Ballyporeen, a priest showed me the handwritten entry recording the baptism of Michael Reagan in 1829, then we crossed a street to the church where his baptism had taken place. Next, I walked through the town where he grew up, shaking hands with as many people as I could, on the way to a pub that had been named after me. There, I quaffed a beer and was presented with a copy of my family tree researched by Burke's Peerage; it showed that I was distantly related not only to Queen Elizabeth II, but also to John F. Kennedy.

At a reception in the pub, our hosts told me they had invited several of my distant relatives, including one who looked quite a bit like me. I'd often been told about people who supposedly bore a resemblance to me, and I'd never been able to see much similarity. But that day I got a shock: They brought in a man in his middle twenties who caused me to do a double-take. It was amazing how much he and I resembled each other—his eyes and hair, his whole facial structure all resembled mine. Since it had been over a century since my great-grandfather had left Ballyporeen for America, it was an eerie experience.

Coming as the president of the United States to this village where my branch of the Reagan family had been launched, learning that some of my ancestors were buried there in paupers' graves, was a warming and emotional experience. Although I've never been a great one for introspection or dwelling on the past, as I looked down the narrow main street of the little town from which an emigrant named Michael Reagan had set out in pursuit of a dream, I had a flood of thoughts, not only about Michael Reagan, but about his son, my grandfather whom I had never met. I thought of Jack and his Irish stories and the drive he'd always had to get ahead; I thought of my own childhood in Dixon, then leaving that small town for Hollywood and later Washington.

What an incredible country we lived in, where the great-grandson of a poor immigrant from Ballyporeen could become president. I couldn't help but think that maybe Jack would have been proud that day. Never had I wished more that he and Nelle were still alive, so they could have been there with me.

After Ireland and a brief stop in London, we took a helicopter ride over the English Channel to France for ceremonies marking the fortieth anniversary of the D-day invasion of Normandy. The first stop was Pointe du Hoc, where American Rangers, 225 of them, had overcome enormous German resistance and climbed a sheer hundred-foot cliff to gain a critical foothold during the early hours of D day; more than 100 died or were injured during the climb. Sixty-two of the survivors were there for the anniversary; with gray hair and faces weathered by age and life's experiences, they might have been elderly businessmen, and I suppose some of them were; but these were the boys, some of them just starting to shave at the time, who had given so much, had been so brave at the dawn of the assault. On that windswept point for which so much blood had been spilled, I tried to recount the story of their bravery. I think it was an emotional experience for all of us.

Afterward, Nancy and I entered a massive concrete pillbox from which, when dawn broke, German soldiers had first seen the five thousand ships of the invasion fleet. Then we flew to Omaha Beach, which was a heartbreaker—the sight of endless rows of white crosses and stars of David—more than nine thousand of them, and they represented only a portion of the casualties of D day.

President Mitterrand arrived and together we placed wreaths at a memorial, then I gave a speech containing quotes from a letter I'd received a few weeks before from a California woman, Lisa Zanatta Henn, whose father, Private Peter Zanatta, had not yet been twenty when he waded out of a bobbing landing craft in the first wave of invaders at Omaha Beach on June 6, 1944.

In her letter, Lisa said her father always dreamed of returning to Normandy. "Someday, Lis, I'll go back," he said, "I'll go back and I'll see it all again. I'll see the beach, the barricades and the graves. I'll put a flower on the graves of the guys I knew and on the grave of the unknown soldier—all the guys I fought with." But, she said, he had died of cancer a few years earlier without ever fulfilling his dream, and she had written to me to ask if she could attend the anniversary celebration as his representative.

"My father watched many of his friends be killed," she wrote. "I know that he must have died inside a little each time. But his explanation to me was: 'You did what you had to do and you kept on going.'"

All her life, Lisa said, she had heard stories from her father about D day. "He never considered himself or what he had done as anything special," she said. "He was just an ordinary guy, with immigrant Italian parents who never really had enough money. But he was a proud man—proud of his heritage, proud of his country, proud that he had fought in World War II and proud that he lived through D-Day."

We arranged for Lisa and her family to be a part of our delegation and her words, speaking for her father, somehow seemed to speak for all of the men who had risked their lives that morning in the defense of liberty, including those lying beneath the endless horizon of white crosses. "He made me feel the fear of being on that boat waiting to land," I said, quoting Lisa's letter. "I can smell the ocean and feel the seasickness. I can see the looks on his fellow soldiers' faces, the fear, the anguish, the uncertainty of what lay ahead. And when they landed, I can feel the strength and courage of the men who took those first steps through the tide to what must have surely looked like instant death . . ."

After a few minutes, it was all but impossible to go on. My voice began to crack. But I managed to get through it and was glad when I reached the end: "Through the words of his loving daughter, who is here with us today, a D-day veteran has shown us the meaning of this day far better than any presidents can. It is enough for us to say about Private Zanatta and all the men of honor and courage who fought beside him four decades ago: We will always remember. We will always be proud. We will always be prepared, so we may always be free."

Less than a year later, I was speaking at the site of another World War II cemetery in Europe. It was a memorable experience for a different reason.

When I accepted an invitation from Chancellor Helmut Kohl to make a state visit to West Germany following the Bonn economic summit that was scheduled in the spring of 1985, I agreed with him that it would be an appropriate moment for us to mark not only the fortieth anniversary of the end of World War II, but also the beginning of forty years of peace and friendship between two former enemies. After I agreed to the visit, I received an invitation from a German politician who represented a region around Munich to visit Dachau, the infamous Nazi concentration camp located near Munich, during my trip. Since I was to be an official visitor of the federal government, I felt it wasn't up to me to choose my itinerary, so I turned down his invitation. (Subsequently I was told that the letter had come from one of Kohl's rivals, who wanted me to visit his district for his own political reasons.)

When the West German government announced that my projected itinerary would include a stop at a military cemetery at Bitburg, Jewish organizations in our country complained that among the two thousand or so buried there were forty-eight SS storm troopers—something our advance team hadn't known when they agreed to the schedule. The Jewish organizations argued that I should insist on canceling the visit to Bitburg and go instead to Dachau.

Even Nancy was against me this time. Excerpts from my diary will give readers an idea of what my life was like during this period:

April 4–14

During most of the week, the press has had a field day assailing me because I'd accepted Helmut Kohl's invitation to visit a German military cemetery during our visit to Bonn. I had turned down a not-official invite from a West German politician to visit Dachau in his district. All of this was portrayed as being willing to honor former Nazis but trying to forget the Holocaust. Helmut had in mind observing the end of World War II anniversary as the end of hatred and the beginning of friendship and peace that has lasted 40 years. I have repeatedly said we must never forget the Holocaust and remember it so it will never happen again. But some of our Jewish friends are now on the warpath. There is no way I'll back down and run for cover. However, Helmut is upset and thinks this may become such an uproar it will color the whole Economic Summit. He may change the program. We'll wait and see. I still think we were right. Yes. The German soldiers were the enemy and part of the whole Nazi hate era. But we won and we killed those soldiers. What is wrong with saying, "Let's never be enemies again"? Would Helmut be wrong if he visited Arlington Cemetery on one of his US visits?

Today, Walter Annenberg called. His news wire had picked up a *Pravda* story lacing into me about the Jewish slight in my not going to Dachau. I want to respond to *Pravda* and point out that today 40 years after the Holocaust, the Soviets are the only ones officially practicing anti-Semitism.

April 15

. . . a cable arrived from Helmut Kohl and Mike Deaver took off to Germany. Helmut may very well have solved our problem re the Holocaust. The invite I turned down about a visit to Dachau was a private thing. Helmut is making it official. He'll invite me to visit the camp as well as the cemetery. I can accept both now that it's official.

April 16

After lunch with VP, went to E.O.B. [the White House Executive Office Building] to speak to conference on religious liberty. Prior to that we went into my German problem again. The press has the bit in their teeth and are stirring up as much trouble as they can. At the close of my speech I made a statement acknowledging that we had been confused about the Dachau suggestion—that it was part of the official itinerary and that I was going to visit the Bitburg German cemetery *and* a concentration camp.

April 19

A brief signing ceremony opened the day, then we got back to my "Dreyfus" case—the trip to a German cemetery. I told our people . . . there was no way I could back away in the face of the criticism which grows more shrill as the press continues to clamor. Mike Deaver is back and said Kohl was going to phone me. Our ambassador Arthur Burns met several hours with Kohl. Our people want me to suggest a national German war memorial as a substitute for the military cemetery. I said only if it presented no problems for Kohl. The call came while we were meeting. Helmut told me the camp would be Bergen-Belsen, not Dachau. Then he told me my remarks about the dead soldiers being victims of Nazism as the Jews in the Holocaust were, had been well received in Germany. He was emphatic that to cancel the cemetery now would be a disaster in his country and an insult to the German people. I told him I would not cancel.

While I was on the phone to Kohl, the VP was in the room with our gang hearing my end of the call. He wrote me this note:

"Mr. President, I was very proud of your stand. If I can help absorb some heat, send me into battle— It's not easy, but you are right!!

George"

Then we brought in Elie Wiesel, survivor of the Holocaust and several others who were on hand for the Jewish Heritage Week Ceremony in which I was presenting Elie with the Congressional gold medal. I explained the situation to them and made some gains even if later Elie in his prepared remarks implored me not to visit the cemetery. We've invited Elie to accompany me on the trip. He's said yes except that he won't be present at the cemetery.

April 20–21 Camp David

Weather wonderful, in the 80's—swam both days and rode on Saturday. Sunday an early return. Nancy went on to Calif. . . . just for overnight, to see a house. That comes under the heading of looking ahead. Mermie [my daughter Maureen] here for dinner.

April 26
Sen. Metzenbaum along with others . . . got a non-binding resolution passed asking Germany to let me out of the Bitburg cemetery visit. Unfortunately, some of our Republicans went along. Well, I don't want out. I think I am doing what is morally right.

April 27
A day of reading my eyes out, briefing materials for trip. The press is still chewing on the Bitburg visit. I'll just keep on praying.

April 28
More homework. A nice day and lunch on the Truman balcony. Called Jerry Ford to thank him for his words re Bitburg. I'm worried about Nancy. She's uptight about the situation and nothing I can say can wind her down. I'll pray about that too.

April 29
Getaway day. I'm scratching at drafts of some of the 14 speeches I'll be giving in Europe. We had a Cabinet Council meeting, another on the tax simplification plan. We're making some progress. Then a short meeting with our three head negotiators who are home on recess from the Geneva arms talks. Nothing much to report . . .

I hope I'm not being too optimistic but it seems there are a few signs that the Bitburg issue may be turning . . .

9:25 p.m.: A statement to the press before boarding Marine I on our way to Bonn. We tried something new for jet lag. There is a six hour time change so we took off at 10 p.m. AF I Washington time, it was already 4 a.m. Wednesday in Bonn. The flight was seven hours and 25 minutes. We got on board and went right to bed. I won't say we slept well but got a fair amount of shut eye. We also set our clocks to Bonn time, so in effect we were going to bed at 4 a.m. and due to arrive at 11:25 a.m. It worked. We were met by Ambassador and Mrs. Burns and Foreign Minister and Mrs. Genscher. Then we boarded Marine I and helicoptered to Schloss Gymnisch, the castle now used as a guest house by the German government. We had stayed there on our 1982 visit. . . .

As the time for my visit to the cemetery approached, the drumbeat of criticism got more and more strident, some of it implying that my refusal to cancel the trip proved I was anti-Semitic and pro-Nazi. No one, I think, was more unhappy with my determination to go ahead with the visit—she'd call it stubbornness—than Nancy.

Contrary to some of the speculation about her, Nancy only rarely tried to influence me when I was president. But on Bitburg, she let me know her opinion. She is not one to shout or be critical when she disagrees with me. Most of the time, she'll just go over the points she believes in, perhaps during dinner, then say in her quiet voice something like: "Do you think it's really a good idea for you to do that?" or "I don't think I'd say that anymore if I were you. . . ." Whenever she speaks up like that, I know she's trying to protect me; she isn't trying to interfere with how I do my job, she just wants to keep me out of trouble.

I have always valued Nancy's opinion and, frankly, I'm not sure a man could be a good president without a wife who is willing to express her opinions with the frankness that grows out of a solid marriage. In a good marriage, husband and wife are best friends; if you can't trust your wife to be honest with you, whom can you trust? She'll tell you things nobody else will, sometimes things you don't want to hear, but isn't that how it should be? I wouldn't want a wife who sat across from me at dinner mentally disagreeing with me but afraid to speak up and express an opinion. No, Nancy was my best friend and I wanted to know how she felt.

She argued that my visit to the Bitburg cemetery would be offensive to Jews and make me look insensitive to those who had died in the Holocaust. I told her that once I'd accepted the invitation, I could not embarrass Helmut Kohl by canceling the visit. But that wasn't the only reason I refused to cancel.

I didn't think it was right to keep on punishing every German for the Holocaust, including generations not yet born in the time of Hitler. I don't think all Germans deserve to bear the stigma for everything he did. As I mentioned earlier, during the last days of the war, I saw an Army Signal Corps film with searing images of German villagers being taken to death camps near their homes. They were discovering for the first time what Hitler had done. I knew that from the looks of sickening disbelief and disgust on their faces. A lot of Germans never knew what had happened until after the war. Meanwhile, the modern German government has attempted to come to grips with the horrors of Hitler's monstrous crimes by keeping memories of them alive; it has turned former concentration camps into museums of death containing the most horrifying pictures you have ever seen, and encouraged German schoolchildren to visit the museums and look at the pictures.

Here are additional excerpts from my diary that spring, beginning with our arrival in Germany prior to the economic summit.

May 2
The day started with a working breakfast with all our staff, then at 9:35 a.m. Nancy joined us. We helicoptered into Bonn and motored to Villa Harmerschmidt, home of President [Richard] von Weizsacker. Met by him and his wife plus a greeting part of our embassy people and German officials. It was a formal ceremony. [The German president's functions are largely ceremonial.] He and I inspected the troops, etc. Then Nancy left us for her trip to Rome, an audience with the Pope and a schedule that will keep her away until May 4.

The president and I, plus staffs, had a half hour meeting, then we were off to the Federal Chancellery to meet Chancellor Helmut Kohl. He and I had a 45 minute private meeting. I assured him I was not upset by the press furor over my scheduled wreath laying at Bitburg military cemetery. He said I had won the heart of Germany by standing firm on this. . . . Next visitor was President Mitterrand of France. He's still pressing for a formal monetary conference to deal with exchange rates, etc. We've had our ministers and a task force discussing and studying financial matters for two years since the Williamsburg summit. Their report is due in June. I proposed that we wait for that report and then see what further is needed. He's not satisfied with that and wants to tie a monetary meeting to any trade talks. I briefed him also on our Strategic Defense Initiative and sensed a reluctance on his part as to any participation in this. Then it was back to Schloss Gymnisch where I had a meeting with our solid ally Margaret Thatcher. This was a half hour, mainly spent in discussing the upcoming meeting. Back to the helicopter and off to Schloss Augustberg to meet Helmut, attend a reception, which was jammed. [Later] Back in a motorcade and off to Schloss Falkenbust for the Economic Summit dinner meeting. During the course of dinner I told them how successful Nancy's anti-drug session with seventeen other first ladies had been and by the time I finished they picked up on it and we voted to move together on a program of cooperation in dealing with the drug problem.

May 3

The Summit really begins. Let me interject that in all our motoring the streets are lined with people clapping, waving, cheering . . . all, I'm sure, to let me know they don't agree with the continuing sniping about the upcoming visit to Bitburg. The meeting was going pretty well with consensus on most of the points that would wind up in the final statement. Then we came to the matter of an early 86 round of trade talks. President Mitterrand expressed his own opposition to protectionism, but absolutely refused to agree to an early 86 round of trade talks to further reduce or eliminate protectionist measures that presently exist. We're all guilty of some. His big hang up is the fact that France subsidizes its agriculture so they can compete in export trade at lower than world market prices. Couple that with his upcoming election in 86 and you have the story.

We tried everything, wrote and rewrote the clause. The debate grew heated and then he took on the United States as being an interloper in European affairs, etc. The battle went on way past lunch hour. We finally settled for wording that bluntly said most of us felt there should be such a meeting and our ministers would meet in July to lay plans. Lunch came at about 2:30. Our dinner that night was heads of state only. Instead of business we got into story telling. [Canadian Prime Minister] Brian Mulroney started it and I got on with some and a good time was had by all.

May 5

Dawns the day the world has been hearing about for weeks. By 9 a.m. we were on our way to Konrad Adenauer grave site with the Kohls. Our wives put flowers on the grave. The press had only been given an hour's notice on this. We didn't want them claiming we were doing it to soften the criticism on Bitburg. From there we helicoptered to Bergen-Belsen concentration camp. This was an emotional experience. We went through the small museum with the enlarged photos of the horrors there. Then we walked past the mounds planted with heather each being a mass grave for 5000 or more of the people, largely Jews but also many Christians, a number of Catholic priests and gypsies who had been slaughtered there or who were just starved to death. Here I made the speech I hoped would refute the phony charges that had been made. I declared we must *not* forget and we must pledge "never again." Before the day was out there were reports that my talk had been effective. It was carried live on German TV and elsewhere in Europe.

Next stop later in the afternoon was Bitburg. Here the people were jamming the streets—most friendly but some demonstrators. We went to the cemetery and met General [Matthew] Ridgway, 91 years old, last surviving top World War II leader in America and Gen. Steinhoff, a German general who had been shot down in flames and whose face had been rebuilt by an American army doctor at war's end. Kohl and I and the generals walked through the tiny cemetery and then at a monument there the generals placed wreaths. The German "Taps" was played and then in a truly dramatic moment, the two generals clasped hands. There had been no leak to the press that the generals would be there. Then we motored to the air base where both German and American units are based. There were several thousand people, families of the military plus a number of citizens of Bitburg, the mayor, City Council et al. The German military band played our national anthem. Then the American band played theirs. My speech was sort of a sequel to the one at Belsen. It was enthusiastically received and our people thought it turned the issue around. I felt very good. I was told later the two generals sat holding each other's hands. General Ridgway and his wife returned to Bonn with us on AF I. Back in Schloss Gymnisch we got done up for the white tie state dinner. . . . There was a small reception, then into dinner. After dinner, there was a half hour entertainment, chamber music. Well, this was the day—everyone—well, not everyone—but much of the press had predicted would be a disaster.

One of my most memorable moments on that trip didn't occur at the cemetery, but the following day, our last in Germany, when Nancy and I and Helmut Kohl and his wife flew by helicopter to a lovely forested area and then drove up a mountain road to an ancient German castle. Along the way, there were huge crowds of cheering people. When we reached the castle, about ten thousand teenagers were gathered outside. After I said a few words, these young people, gathered on a hillside above me, suddenly broke into music: Ten thousand voices sang "The Star-Spangled Banner" in perfect English. They had spent weeks studying and learning our national anthem for my visit. After they were finished, I just stood there, listening to the echo of their voices in my mind. If I had opened my mouth I wouldn't have been able to say a word.

· · ·

383

I have never regretted not canceling the trip to Bitburg. In the end, I believe my visit to the cemetery and the dramatic and unexpected gesture by two old soldiers from opposing sides of the battlefield helped strengthen our European alliance and heal once and for all many of the lingering wounds of the war.

General Ridgway had volunteered to go with me to Bitburg after the furor had erupted over my plans to visit the cemetery. It was time, said this man who was among the greatest of our warriors, to make peace.

2

The entire Reagan family got together on inauguration day 1985. At left front are Bess and Neil, behind them are Maureen and Dennis, then Michael and Colleen with Ashley Marie, Cameron is with me, then Patti, Nancy, Ron, Doria, Geoffrey and Anne Davis, Dick and Patricia Davis.

23

Preparing a speech on taxes, and, later, a briefing during one of our first major crises in my second term, the hijacking of TWA Flight 847. George Bush is at my right and George Shultz is at my left in the White House Situation Room.

27

Whenever it was possible, George Bush and I had lunch together on Thursdays, when I got a chance to bring him up to date on problems and the administration's current agenda. We looked forward to these private lunches; the White House mess featured Mexican food on Thursdays, since George was from Texas and I was from California.

26

It was a special honor to present the Medal of Freedom to Mother Teresa in 1985.

When Canadian Prime Minister Brian Mulroney and I saw our wives approaching us at the meeting the press called the "Shamrock Summit," I turned to him and said, "We married up," and he agreed.

25

In 1985, Nancy and I
visited West Germany.
We will never forget the
thrill we felt when ten
thousand young people
suddenly began singing
"The Star-Spangled
Banner"—in perfect
English. Chancellor
Helmut Kohl was our
host during the visit; at
the site of the Bergen-
Belsen concentration
camp, I laid a wreath at a
memorial honoring the
victims of Nazism.

9

Margaret Thatcher and I walking together at Camp David in November 1986. We had many mutual problems to discuss. Margaret was more than an ally—she was a friend.

31

32

It was at the Brandenburg Gate in Berlin in June 1987 that I said, "Mr. Gorbachev, tear down this wall." Two years later, this dream would be realized.

A visit with Pope John Paul II in June 1987.

Queen Elizabeth II and I share a love of horses—in fact, she is an excellent horsewoman. We rode together at Windsor Castle.

His Royal Highness the Prince of Wales and Princess Diana
visited Nancy and me in the living room of the family quarters
at the White House.

Nancy and her mother, Deede, shortly before she died. I've never known a closer bond to exist between two people than between Nancy and her mother.

Nancy welcomed back to the White House following her mastectomy in 1987. She was never braver than during this period.

I invited former hostage David Jacobsen to visit the White House after his release from Beirut. He begged the press to back off on its reporting on the other hostages.

A part of the job—meeting the press—this time outdoors on the South Lawn of the White House.

A meeting with General Colin Powell in April 1988, discussing the crisis in the Persian Gulf.

41

In December 1987, Mikhail and Raisa Gorbachev came to Washington for the signing of the INF treaty—the first in history to eliminate an entire class of nuclear weapons. In May of the next year, I went to Moscow and we signed the formal ratification papers. While I was there, I got a chance to speak about the blessings of freedom, democracy, and free enterprise to some of the Soviet Union's future leaders at Moscow State University. Behind me as I spoke (but not visible in this picture) was a huge statue of Lenin.

With our grandchildren, Ashley Marie and Cameron, on the dock at Rancho del Cielo.

45

At Christmastime in 1987, Nancy and I entertained family upstairs at the White House. With us here are (from the left) Dr. Richard Davis, Jon Peterson, Anne Davis Peterson, Geoffrey Davis, and Patricia Davis.

On a winter's day at Camp David with our dog, Rex.

We were just two people going home. Behind us on the steps of the Capitol are the new president of the United States, George Bush, and the new first lady, Barbara Bush. We had just said good-bye to them and were on our way to board the helicopter for our new life as private citizens.

55

ONE OF THE unexpected pleasures of the presidency has nothing to do with economic problems or international crises. It is the opportunity to lend a hand now and then to other human beings.

I was outraged one day in May 1982 when I read in the newspapers about a black family who lived near the University of Maryland. The husband and wife were both employed in a government printing office. They had been harassed and a cross had been burned on their lawn.

I asked our staff to clear my late afternoon schedule. I called Nancy, and she was happy to join me in visiting these victims of intolerance. They were a nice couple with a four-year-old daughter and a grandma, a most gracious lady, living with them. Their home was comfortable and tastefully furnished. We enjoyed our visit and when it was time to leave they saw us to our car. Our motorcade had naturally been noticed, so there was quite a turnout of people from the neighborhood, and our farewells at curbside were warmly applauded by the neighbors. Needless to say, this fine family had no further harassment.

Another time, I read a story in *The New York Times* about a twenty-nine-year-old father of eight who had been out of work for thirteen months during the depths of the recession. He was returning home after applying for a job when an elderly blind man broke his cane and fell to the tracks of the subway. The young man bravely jumped down onto the tracks and rescued him. We found out his telephone number and I called him. I asked if he had gotten the job he had applied for before the incident; he said he was just leaving his home to go back for a second interview. I called the company; at first, the switchboard operator wouldn't believe it was me and refused to let me speak to the manager. But I finally got through. I'm not sure my call had anything to do with it, but the young man got the job.

It was also always a thrill to witness the kindness and generosity of the American people from the vantage point of the Oval Office. You could measure it by the growth of volunteer programs around the country and see it swing into action whenever there was a major flood, a hurricane, or other emergency: Americans would rush in to help other Americans. Countless times, I observed this phenomenon on a smaller scale, too. There was the couple in Connecticut who had adopted twelve children, all as deformed and handicapped babies—the kind of children who unfortunately are frequently victims of infanticide. I called and spoke to the couple and then to all of the children, and I could feel the love and joy in that household radiating over the telephone wires like a burst of sunshine. If there were people who needed proof that God had a purpose for each of us, I thought, let them meet that family.

Once I was asked by a group of children whether I liked being president, and I told them I enjoyed the job very much. There were moments, I said, of great grief. As I've said, the hardest part of the job was having to send young men and women into situations of danger and then having to tell the families of some why they weren't coming back. But, I told them, there were also many moments of great joy, and I enjoyed being president very much.

Part of it, I said, was being able to have my hand on the throttle after so many years of preaching about my views on the problems of government; now I could try to do something about them.

I even enjoyed the give and take of battling Congress—including Tip O'Neill. But it was more than that: Maybe the most fun of all, I told the children, was being able to pick up a phone, after we'd received a letter from someone who had a problem, and telling someone on the staff, "Fix this." That was really a great joy, which will live with me.

I also enjoyed the ceremonial aspects that go with being president. Even after eight years, the experience of walking into a crowded House of Representatives to deliver a speech sent a chill down my spine. Also, nothing thrilled me more than looking up at a wind-blown American flag while listening to a choir sing "The Battle Hymn of the Republic," my favorite song. On overseas trips, I was always moved when I heard our national anthem played at far corners of the world. And I'll never forget standing once in the Vatican after a meeting with Pope John Paul II and hearing a group of Armenian priests singing "America the Beautiful" in as lovely a rendition as I had ever heard it. Nancy and I were both in tears.

There were many, many small moments that made my job fun, such as visiting the modest hideaway of Prime Minister Yasu Nakasone in the woods outside Tokyo and sitting on the floor of this typical Japanese home while we had an authentic Japanese lunch; or landing in a helicopter on the lawn of Windsor Castle for a fairy-tale visit with Queen Elizabeth and the royal family. The highlight of our stay there came when the queen and I went horseback riding together and Nancy and Prince Philip took a horse-drawn carriage ride. I must admit, the queen is quite an accomplished horsewoman. We will always remember our visit to Windsor Castle because of the queen's and Prince Philip's warmth and welcoming hospitality —they could not have been more gracious. When the queen and Prince Philip later visited us at Rancho del Cielo, it was in February, during the middle of our rainy season, and Santa Barbara was being pummeled by a terrible storm. We waited at the ranch for them while they struggled seven miles up a switchback road. At three places the road was cut by streams and their limousines couldn't get through; our people met them with four-wheel-drive cars. They made it up the mountain, but when they got to our home, it was so foggy no one could see more than a few feet. I tried to explain how beautiful the place really was and apologized for the weather, but the queen said, "Yes, if it was *just* dreary, but this is an *adventure."* Despite the gloomy weather, I'm sure Nancy and I were as proud of our ranch as they were of Windsor Castle. Another special moment with the queen and Prince Philip came when Nancy and I were their guests aboard the royal yacht Britannia for our thirty-first wedding anniversary. They made it wonderful with an anniversary cake and an engraved silver box commemorating the occasion. There were toasts and I said, "I know I promised Nancy a lot when we were married, but how can I ever top this?" Attending the wedding of the Prince of Wales to Lady Diana Spencer was an especially memorable moment for Nancy; when she came home, she told me, "Nobody can give a royal wedding like the British." We were both very fond of Prince Charles; he's thoughtful and intelligent and has a keen sense of humor that always made our visits with him enjoyable.

Nancy and I traveled to many countries when I was president, and among our most enjoyable trips were the short ones we made across our nation's northern border. Prime Minister Brian Mulroney of Canada was a valued ally and we became good friends with him and his lovely wife, Mila. And, of course, our get-togethers with Margaret Thatcher and her husband, Dennis, were always special occasions for us as well.

I always enjoyed welcoming foreign leaders to our country, and will always remember one visitor in particular: President Alessandro Pertini of Italy, eighty-four years old, bright, warm, gentlemanly, an Italian patriot who was in love with America. On his way into the White House, he stopped at the marine guard who was holding our flag, reached out, and kissed it.

I never ceased to enjoy reviewing our men and women in uniform and hope I started a new tradition for presidents. As commander in chief, I discovered it was customary for our uniformed men and women to salute whenever they saw me. When I'd walk down the steps of a helicopter, for example, there was always a marine waiting there to salute me. I was told presidents weren't supposed to return salutes, so I didn't, but this made me feel a little uncomfortable. Normally, a person offering a salute waits until it is returned, then brings down his hand. Sometimes, I realized, the soldier, sailor, marine, or airman giving me a salute wasn't sure when he was supposed to lower his hand.

Initially, I nodded and smiled and said hello and thought maybe that would bring down the hand, but usually it didn't. Finally, one night when Nancy and I were attending a concert at the Marine Corps headquarters, I told the commandant of marines, "I know it's customary for the president to receive these salutes, but I was once an officer and realize that you're not supposed to salute when you're in civilian clothes. I think there ought to be a regulation that the president could return a salute inasmuch as he is commander in chief and civilian clothes are his uniform."

"Well, if you did return a salute," the general said, "I don't think anyone would say anything to you about it."

The next time I got a salute, I saluted back. A big grin came over the marine's face, and down came his hand. From then on, I always returned salutes. When George Bush followed me into the White House, I encouraged him to keep up the tradition.

First ladies, I discovered, are one of the taxpayers' biggest bargains; they're unpaid, work full schedules, and are always on the move. From combating drugs to restoring the beauty of the White House to helping me represent our country overseas, Nancy was among the hardest-working of all our first ladies. That this was known and appreciated by many Americans was evident from the thousands of letters we received praising Nancy. But I never understood or got used to the sniping at her, which at times got so bad that she was in tears when I came upstairs at the end of the day.

Here I was the president, and I was unable to stop my own wife from being hurt. It was hard for me to accept that she had to suffer simply because she was married to me. My attitude—and sometimes I'd express it—was: Dammit, you want to pick on someone, pick on me, not her. I'm in this job, not her. Even when Nancy tried to straighten out things with the facts, it often didn't do any good.

During the eight years we lived in the White House, it became a real *home* because Nancy worked to make it that way. I never stopped missing California; I've often said that a Californian (even one transplanted from the Midwest like me) who has to live someplace else lives in a perpetual state of homesickness. California, I like to say, isn't a place, it's a way of life. I once told Margaret Thatcher that her people should have crossed the other ocean to get to this continent; that way the capital of the United States would have been in California. But Nancy made the White House into a wonderful home for us, furnishing it with our things from home, and I felt very comfortable there—it was home. After the drab second-floor Central Hall was restored, we seldom closed the doors opening out from our living room, and the hall became an extension of it. As I sat looking across to the other side of the building, I never failed to remark to myself how magnificent it was.

Nancy wanted to make the state dinners we had at the White House more relaxed, as if guests were attending a dinner party at home. She worked hard to choose an interesting variety of guests, inviting people from the academic world, sports, business, entertainment, and other fields. The routine at these dinners was usually the same: After a private reception upstairs, we would descend the grand staircase with the guests of honor, there'd be a receiving line, then Nancy and I would escort them into the state dining room. If the guest of honor was male and married, I sat with his wife beneath Lincoln's portrait, while Nancy sat across the room with the male guest of honor at her table; that way, the guests on one side of the room would not feel any less important than those on the other side. While dessert was served, a group of army violinists known as the Strolling Strings came into the dining room and played; then I'd give a toast, the guest of honor would respond, and we'd go into the Blue Room for coffee followed by entertainment in the East Room. From there, it was into the foyer where a marine band played dance music.

At our state dinner honoring President Pertini of Italy, the Strolling Strings had begun moving among the tables when I saw one of them, a very pretty young woman, stroll very close to Pertini. Since I'd heard this courtly gentleman still had an eye for a pretty girl, I tried to catch Nancy's eye—she was sitting next to him—and smiled at her. Later on, when we went upstairs after dinner, I asked her whether he'd noticed the pretty girl and explained why I'd been trying to catch her eye.

"You've got to be kidding," she said.

"What do you mean?" I asked.

"By that time," Nancy said, "he had already kissed her hand twice."

At a dinner honoring François Mitterrand, he and his wife and Nancy and I finished the receiving line and the four of us walked from the East Room into the state dining room. As was customary, everyone in the room was to stand until Nancy led François to her table and I led Mrs. Mitterrand to my table at the opposite side of the room.

Nancy and François headed for their table, but Mrs. Mitterrand stood frozen, even after a butler motioned at her that she was to walk toward our table. I whispered, "We're supposed to go over there to the other side." But she wouldn't move. She said something to me very quietly in French, which I didn't understand. Then she repeated it and I shook my head. I still didn't know what she was saying; suddenly an interpreter ran up to us and said, "She's telling you that you're standing on her gown."

Besides making those big state dinners more relaxed, Nancy started holding smaller dinners upstairs for some of our guests, including, among others, Prince Charles and the crown prince of Japan. Usually, we invited thirty or so people to these dinners upstairs in the family dining room. Here the routine was that of a private dinner at home: first, cocktails in the yellow oval room, and then over to the dining room for dinner, with sometimes a little musical entertainment afterward.

Most of the time, I should emphasize, our dinners in the White House were not this fancy, although when there was a state dinner coming up, we'd sometimes go across the hall to the family dining room for a "rehearsal." Nancy liked to have a dry run, to make sure the menu was right for the next guests.

One of the occupational hazards of being president, I learned, is shaking hands. At some receptions in the White House—for members of Congress and their families, the press, and so forth—I'd have to shake as many as one thousand hands a night. Believe it or not, that can leave you with a sore hand.

Another problem: I'm not very good at remembering faces and names. In national politics, you meet so many people around the country that it's impossible to remember them all, and as a result I was always afraid I was going to slight someone. On a campaign trip, I might visit five or six states a day and be introduced to sizable groups of local Republican leaders and other people at each stop. The next time you see them, understandably, they all expect you to remember them.

Sometimes, it was even difficult remembering the names of all the members of the White House staff. There were hundreds of them; I'd be introduced to a new staffer, hear the person's name once, then see him or her around the White House and sometimes feel embarrassed that I couldn't instantly recall the name. I've met so many people in my life that whenever I encounter someone, I have to assume I might have met that person previously. Before committing myself, I sort of look for clues and react accordingly—although sometimes that technique backfires. Once back in my Hollywood days, a man came up to me in the lobby of the Plaza Hotel in New York, stuck out his hand, and said, "You don't know me . . ." So many people did that to me that I just said, "Wait a minute, oh sure I do, I'm just trying to remember. . . ."

He said, "No, you *don't* know me, I just wanted to tell you how much I enjoy your television program."

I don't think I'm alone in having this kind of problem. I've heard about all sorts of tricks people use to deal with it. When Babe Ruth would run into somebody and wasn't sure whether he had met the person before, he would give a friendly smile and say, "Your name . . . I'm trying to remember."

The other person might say, "John," and the Babe would say, "*John*, of course I know, it's your last name I can't remember." If the person said, "Smith," Babe would reverse it and say, "No, I know that, I'd just forgotten your first name."

When I'm in a receiving line, I usually stick out my hand and smile in the expectation that the next person might be someone I've met before, and if the man or woman says, "The last time I saw you we were at . . . ," I'll say, "Oh, yes . . ."

You just have to do something like that to avoid hurting people. On an average day when I was president, I saw about eighty people, ranging from presidents and prime ministers to the newest multiple sclerosis poster child. Some days, there were more than twenty appointments on my schedule, from about nine in the morning until at least five in the afternoon. As the day passes, you have to shift within a few seconds from conducting a meeting about a serious international crisis to greeting the newest Miss America or meeting in the Rose Garden with a group of champion athletes or being photographed during a heart-tugging visit from a disabled child. You get introduced to hundreds of people, hear their names only once, and don't always put together a name with a face in a moment's time.

. . .

For years, I've heard the question: "How could an actor be president?" I've sometimes wondered how you could be president and not be an actor.

When you've been in the profession I was in, you get accustomed to criticism in the press—true and untrue, fair and unfair—and learn to take what you read about yourself and others with a big dose of salt. Gossip columnists and critics become a part of your life. A picture you've made may be panned by a critic and you'll say to yourself, "You know, that's a pretty good movie and the audience likes it." It teaches you that the press isn't always right, and prepares you for criticism in politics; you develop a skepticism about what you read, and take it in stride. That kind of experience helps when you start reading things about yourself as president.

Regarding the press, I've always believed a free press is as vital to America as the Constitution and the Bill of Rights. A probing, responsible press not only keeps the public informed about what's going on in government, it can keep a watchful eye out to uncover corruption, waste, or mismanagement.

But an unfortunate phenomenon took root in Washington after Watergate. Understandably, the press—especially the White House press corps—was skeptical about what it was being told about presidential behavior. Some reporters in Washington became more vigorous in their investigative reporting, convinced that if there was one scandal, there were probably more.

As I have said, a free and aggressive press corps is essential to the health of our democracy. If the press does not tell us, who will? But with that freedom comes a special responsibility to be accurate and fair. The press should remember the great impact its words can have on a person's life. Sadly, the words *questioned about* sometimes translate into *guilty of* in the minds of readers and listeners. That does not mean that reporters shouldn't do their job. It just means they should be careful.

I understand that it is part of the job of the Washington press corps to pin down the president and report to the nation on what is really going on inside the White House. Inevitably, the relationship between the press and the president has adversarial moments. I always regretted those moments, however. We weren't hiding anything, and I was frustrated that I could never convince the press of that.

It bothered me, too, that, from time to time, some in the press seemed anxious to catch me making a mistake. I don't know any human being who hasn't made mistakes or misstatements from time to time; and this is especially likely when a person gives as many speeches and answers as many questions as a president does. Some in the press corps seemed to make a special effort to play "gotcha" with me, especially during a press conference. If they wanted to question our policies or our approach to solving a problem, fine. But isn't it a little petty to point out every time a *t* isn't crossed or an *i* isn't dotted?

Nancy and I never let these moments get in the way of any personal relationships with the press. Every year at Christmastime we hosted a party for the White House press corps, and every summer in Santa Barbara we hosted a barbecue for the press traveling with us. Some of our fondest memories are of meeting the families and friends of the reporters, photographers, and technicians who followed us around the world. Even though we had different roles, there was a very gratifying feeling of shared adventure among us on those occasions.

I don't suppose there is a politician alive today who hasn't had his or her share of rows with the press—that comes with the territory. We may have had our differences from time to time, but we shared some special moments together and I personally liked most of the men and women who covered the White House.

56

EVEN THOUGH I WAS constantly meeting new people and attending public events in the presence of thousands of people, I discovered a surprising dimension to the presidency—a bird-in-a-gilded-cage sense of isolation. More than once during the eight years I lived there, I stood at a window looking out across the big lawn of the White House, through its black iron fence at the people strolling along Pennsylvania Avenue, and found myself envying their freedom. I'd say to myself, "You know, I can't even walk down to the drugstore and look over the magazine rack anymore. Will I ever be able to do it again?"

In 1981, before our first Valentine's Day in Washington, I decided to buy a Valentine for Nancy and told the Secret Service agents that I wanted to leave the White House for a brief shopping excursion. Their response: a chorus of raised eyebrows. But I told them I had been buying a Valentine for Nancy for almost thirty years and didn't want to stop now, so they drove me to a little gift store near the White House and I bought several cards for her.

Unbeknownst to me, Nancy had done the same thing, and we both surprised each other that night with our Valentines.

But that was just about my last shopping expedition outside the White House. It caused such a commotion that I never wanted to do that to a shopkeeper again.

Back in Hollywood, I had learned that having a familiar face can sometimes cause embarrassing attention when you are out in public. When I was governor, Nancy and I learned how security requirements could impose limits on our movements. We'd gotten used to that. But it was nothing compared with life in the White House, especially after the shooting at the Hilton.

No matter what we did or where we went, elaborate security arrangements were required, and usually had to be planned out weeks in advance. Every time we went out, it was in a caravan of five or six cars behind a blizzard of red lights and screaming sirens. Even if the Secret Service allowed us to go to church, we'd arrive there in a siren-screaming motorcade accompanied by legions of reporters and security people. No longer was going to church a pleasant Sunday morning experience, it was a news event: The other people in the church would have to pass through a magnetometer before they could get in; and once we were seated in church, Nancy and I often felt uncomfortable because so many people in the other pews were looking at us instead of listening to the sermon.

Things got worse after we started getting reports of terrorist hit squads. We were told that our going to church might result in an assassination attempt that could cause the deaths of many other people there. Very unhappily, we just had to stop going to church altogether, and we really missed it.

Even inside the White House, our movements were limited. I had to avoid getting too close to certain windows because of the possibility of sharpshooters and, except at a few spots surrounded by hedges or buildings, we couldn't go for a walk on the White House grounds because we would be exposed to buildings from which a gunman might take aim.

I'm really not complaining, though. There were plenty of things to compensate for the freedom we lost, one of the greatest being Camp David—a slice of heaven a half hour's helicopter ride from the White House where we spent many weekends surrounded by 150 acres of beautiful woods.

Pat Nixon told Nancy, "Without Camp David, you'll go stir crazy." Now I can understand what she meant.

As president, the days I hated most were those with nonstop meetings, one after another, with no time in between to collect my thoughts, and with me scheduled to make remarks or give a short speech at each of them. The days I liked best were those Fridays when I could break away a little early, about three or three thirty, and take off for Camp David.

The president's home at Camp David, called Aspen, is a beautiful rustic house with beamed ceilings, wood-paneled walls, and big windows that look out at the forest. Just as we did at Rancho del Cielo, Nancy and I experienced a sense of liberation at Camp David that we never found in Washington. Because the perimeter was guarded, we could just open a door and take a walk. That's a freedom, incidentally, that you don't fully appreciate until you've lost it.

Lyndon Johnson, I'm told, found psychological relief from the isolation of the White House by getting in his Lincoln convertible and driving it at high speed near his ranch in Texas. Once he was pulled over for speeding and the traffic officer came up to his car, realized the driver was the president of the United States, and said, "Oh, my God almighty," to which Lyndon replied, "And don't you forget it." Somebody told me another story about Lyndon that took place out on the South Lawn of the White House. As he was getting ready to leave on a trip, he mistakenly started walking toward the wrong helicopter. A Secret Service man caught up with him and said, "Mr. President, that is your helicopter over there." Lyndon turned around and said, "Son, they're *all* my helicopters."

I usually took a pile of homework and made my weekly radio broadcast during our weekends at Camp David. But there was almost always time to relax in front of a fire with a book. When the weather was right, we'd go swimming; during the summer, we often ate our meals on the patio. There were always a dozen or so members of the White House staff with us, and on Friday and Saturday nights we usually all got together to watch a movie with big baskets of popcorn in front of us.

In a way, it was like a big family that included the camp commander, the Secret Service supervisor, our lead helicopter pilot and my military and communications aides; Mark Weinberg of the press office; Eddie Serrano, our chief steward; Dr. John Hutton and his wife, Barbara; and Jim Kuhn, my personal assistant, and his wife, Carole, who usually brought their two children with them. At first, the movies we watched were new or recent releases from Hollywood. Then I began trying to sandwich in a few older movies from my generation. Before long, the staff, most of whom were relative youngsters, only wanted to see golden oldies; so each Saturday night we'd bring out an old movie featuring stars such as Clark Gable and Barbara Stanwyck, Humphrey Bogart and Jimmy Cagney, and occasionally a couple of actors named Reagan and Davis.

Every month the White House received thousands of letters addressed to the president. A staff of volunteers went through them, and each week chose thirty or so for me to look over. I tried to answer as many as I could during the weekends at Camp David.

The letters covered every topic under the sun, a few less serious than others, as my reply to one from a young man in South Carolina indicates:

Dear Andy:

I'm sorry to be so late in answering your letter, but as you know, I've been in China and found your letter here upon my return.

Your application for disaster relief has been duly noted but I must point out one technical problem; the authority declaring the disaster is supposed to make the request. In this case, your mother.

However, setting that aside, I'll have to point out the larger problem of available funds. This has been a year of disasters: 539 hurricanes as of May 4th and several more since, numerous floods, forest fires, drought in Texas and a number of earthquakes. What I'm getting at is that funds are dangerously low.

May I make a suggestion? This Administration, believing that government has done many things that could better be done by volunteers at the local level, has sponsored a Private Sector Initiatives Program, calling upon people to practice volunteerism in the solving of a number of local problems.

Your situation appears to be a natural. I'm sure your mother was fully justified in proclaiming your room a disaster. Therefore, you are in an excellent position to launch another volunteer program to go along with the more than 3000 already underway in our nation. Congratulations.

Give my best regards to your mother.

Sincerely,
Ronald Reagan

Another was from a minister who lived in a New York suburb who'd received a Republican senatorial fund-raising letter over my signature. A computer, for some reason, had seen fit to send the minister a letter that started, "Dear Mr. God."

"I've asked God for a great many things—particularly since getting this job—but never for a campaign contribution," I wrote to the minister. "Maybe I'll ask for help in correcting a greedy computer. At least the computer has raised its sights considerably; the only other experience of this kind was hearing from a lady whose prize show horse had received such a letter."

When the weather allowed it, we went for a ride at Camp David, and on some weekends we opened the back gate and rode through the lush green national forest surrounding it, following an old road that passed the tumbledown stone ruins of a onetime summer hotel. During the early 1930s, the hotel had been owned by a young woman named Bessie Darling whose boyfriend was a local doctor. One night, according to her maid, who still lived nearby, the doctor, who had been told Bessie was dating someone else, arrived at the hotel and demanded to see the mistress. The maid went upstairs to tell Bessie, who was asleep alone in bed. But the doctor, apparently in a fit of jealousy and expecting to find another man, followed her up the stairs, holding a gun. Bessie got out of bed and reached for a gun she had tucked under her pillow for protection; she had the gun in her hand when her doctor-lover shot her dead in front of the maid. The doctor was arrested and claimed self-defense, but because the gun in Bessie's hand hadn't been cocked and the safety was still on, he was convicted and sent to prison.

During World War II, the old lodge was used as a safe house where President Roosevelt sometimes met secretly with foreign intelligence officers. Later, a fire all but destroyed the lodge and left only a pile of ruins. Everyone joked that the ruins were haunted by the young woman who died there, and every time I passed on a horse, I'd say, "Hi, Bessie."

The one thing I always missed during our weekends at Camp David was a chance to go to church. But I prayed that God would realize that when I was out in the beautiful forest I felt as if I was in His temple.

The ghost of Bessie Darling, incidentally, wasn't the only one we heard about while we were in Washington.

Not long after we moved into the White House, Nancy happened

399

to be in the Lincoln Bedroom on the second floor, and she noticed that one of the pictures on the wall, one that was said to have been a favorite of Abe Lincoln, was turned, hanging crooked. Nancy started to straighten it and a maid who was in the room at the time said, "Oh, he's been here again."

Later, one of the White House butlers said that he had heard music coming from the direction of the piano in the hall, and as he approached, it stopped.

Well, we'd heard the legend that Lincoln's ghost haunted parts of the second floor and took it all with a grain of salt. Then something happened involving our dog, Rex, that nearly made me join the believers.

One night we were sitting in the living room of the family quarters when Rex suddenly stared down the length of the Central Hall toward the other end of the building. His eyes were fixed straight ahead and his ears stood up as straight as two flagpoles.

I looked out and couldn't see anything. Rex started barking loudly and edging slowly down the hall while I kept an eye on him. He got about halfway down the hall and then stopped and seemed to be looking at something in front of him. It made me wonder: Is there something out there I can't see from my angle?

By now, I was really curious, so I went down to where he was and I said, "Come on, Rex, come on back," trying to persuade him to return to the living room. But he just stayed where he was, feet firmly planted, with that same fixed stare in his eyes and still barking. By then, I was down the hall almost to the Lincoln Bedroom, so I turned and went into it. Rex got as far as the door and stopped; he stopped barking and, with a deep growl, started backing away from the door. When I tried to get him to come into the bedroom, he wouldn't, and finally he just ran away from whatever it was that had scared him in the room.

Another time, I was working in my study at the other end of the hall when Rex suddenly got up on his hind legs—I never saw him do that before or since—and started walking around the room upright while he looked up at the ceiling. It was as if he was following something; he circled around my desk, then went to the other side of the room, then left. The next day, I told the Secret Service about what had happened. I'd been told by our intelligence people that at our embassy in Moscow the Russians used electronic beams to try to eavesdrop on our personnel and detect messages and letters printed out on electric typewriters, so I asked if Rex might have been responding to some sort of electronic signals. Our communications experts checked out the room, but they weren't able to find anything unusual—except an infinitesimal hum from a television set left over from Lyndon Johnson's days as president.

It all seemed pretty strange to me, but I should say right here: I'm not claiming that Abe Lincoln's ghost is alive and well in the White House. I don't want to start another myth.

As I've mentioned before, the myth about myself that has always bothered me most is that I am a bigot who somehow surreptitiously condones racial prejudice. By appointing more blacks to important positions in the California government than all the previous governors combined, I managed to dispel that image when I was in Sacramento. But for some reason, this myth stuck to me when I became president.

In Washington, we tried hard to eliminate waste and fraud from all government programs. I wanted to eliminate some programs because I didn't believe the federal government should plan and control programs better left to state and local government; and I argued that *any* quota system based on race, religion, or color is immoral. Because of these policies, many black leaders claimed that, if I wasn't a bigot, at the very least I was unsympathetic to the aspirations of blacks and other minorities.

Neither claim was true, and I think the record shows that. It is true that I opposed quotas in employment, education, and other areas. I consider quotas, whether they favor blacks or whites, men or women, to be a new form of discrimination as bad as the old ones. But our administration filed plenty of cases to correct civil rights abuses—as many as or more than any previous administration in history. Funding for enforcement of civil rights laws went up eighteen percent over my eight years in office. We took the lead in developing new civil rights legislation that strengthened the Fair Housing Act of 1968. And proportionally, blacks benefited more than any other racial group from our economic policies.

There is still too wide a gap between the average income of blacks in our country and that of other Americans. But the gap narrowed substantially during the eighties: Between November 1982 and November 1988, employment of blacks rose twenty-nine percent while the number of black families in the highest income bracket, $50,000 and over, increased nearly eighty-six percent. During this period, more than 2.6 million blacks were added to the civilian labor force, black employment in the nation's highest-paid occupations jumped almost forty percent, and black unemployment fell from 20.2 percent at the beginning of the expansion to slightly more than ten percent.

During the previous administration, per capita income had increased 2.4 percent for whites and one percent for blacks. Between 1982 and 1988, it rose more than fourteen percent for whites and more than eighteen percent for blacks.

Whatever the reasons for the myth that I'm a racist, I blow my top every time I hear it. In 1987, Supreme Court Justice Thurgood Marshall gave a television interview in which he implied I was a racist, the worst in the White House since Herbert Hoover. A meeting was arranged between the two of us.

We spoke for an hour or so upstairs in the family quarters, and I literally told him my life story—how Jack and Nelle had raised me from the time I was a child to believe racial and religious discrimination was the worst sin in the world, how I'd experienced some of it as the son of an Irish Catholic in a Protestant town; how as a sports announcer I'd been among the first in the country to campaign for integration of professional baseball; how I'd tried as governor to open up opportunities for blacks. That night, I think I made a friend.

As the adjutant of my Army Air Corps post during the war, I'd had the responsibility to call the parents of combat cameramen who had been killed in action and tell them their sons wouldn't be returning from the war. I learned then that there is not much you can say to comfort people in such a situation, but you have to try. All I could do was tell them how much they had to be proud of, and that we had to believe God's promise that one day we will all be united with our loved ones.

As president, I frequently had to speak to the families of men and women who had died in the service of their country. Because of what I'd done during the war, it wasn't a new experience; but it was not one I ever got used to, and this responsibility, this weight on my shoulders, felt like a ton of iron.

On a tragic day in January 1986, after my usual staff meetings, I began the morning with a conference with congressional leaders from both parties at which I had a few words with Tip O'Neill over my continuing (and still frustrated) efforts to cut federal spending. Then Alaska Senator Frank Murkowski brought in a family of his constituents he wanted me to meet. Next came a briefing from Larry Speakes, the acting press secretary. I was scheduled to have lunch a few minutes later with the television network anchors prior to the State of the Union address that night. We were in the midst of the briefing when several members of the staff rushed in to tell me the news that the *Challenger* space shuttle had exploded after takeoff a few moments earlier.

We all headed for a television set and, like millions of other Americans that heartbreaking day, we watched the film of the explosion played and replayed and replayed again.

One of the astronauts on that flight, Christa McAuliffe, had come to the White House with other teachers who had wanted to go into space, and I'd announced that she had won the chance. For some reason, this—this added proximity to the tragedy—made it seem even closer and sadder to me.

After postponing the State of the Union speech, I made a five-minute address to the nation expressing our collective grief over the tragedy. I said we would not be deterred but continue to reach out to the heavens: "Nothing ends here; our hopes and our journey continue."

The rest of the day, I had to go on with the balance of my schedule. It became one of the hardest days I ever had to spend in the Oval Office.

The following day, I telephoned the families of the seven astronauts and tried to say things that might give them comfort. Every one of them asked me to do what I could to ensure that the space program continued; they all said that that was what their loved ones would have wanted.

Three days later, as Washington was carpeted with fresh snow, Nancy and I took off from Andrews Air Force Base on a sad journey to the Johnson Spacecraft Center in Houston and a memorial service for the astronauts. It was a very difficult time for everyone, but especially for the families of the astronauts. Nancy and I sat between the wife of Francis Scobee, commander of the *Challenger*'s crew, and the wife of crew member Michael Smith. I found it difficult to say anything. All we could do was hug the families and try to hold back our tears.

The *Challenger* disaster was a catastrophe that bestowed pain and grief on all Americans. But after a lengthy and thorough investigation pinpointed the cause of the explosion, we picked up the space program, the space shuttle flew again, and we launched a new program aimed at establishing a permanent station in space. In time, I'm sure this project will advance not only our knowledge of the universe but the state of American technology as well, and it will ultimately produce an economic payoff, as yet unforeseen, on earth.

Now more than ever, I'm convinced that the seven who died aboard the *Challenger* would want us to continue the space program. At the memorial service, Mrs. Smith handed me a card on which her husband had written a few words by H. G. Wells which he had intended to read from space. They expressed better than I could why the seven astronauts of the *Challenger* had lifted off into a blue sky on the morning of January 28, 1986:

> For man, there is no rest and no ending. He must go on—Conquest beyond Conquest. This little planet and its winds and ways, and all the laws of mind and matter that restrain him. Then the planets about him, and, at last out across the immensity to the stars. . . . And when he has conquered all the depths of space and all the mysteries of time —still he will be but beginning.

PART FOUR

The Middle East, Lebanon, Grenada

57

As every president since World War II has learned, no region of the world presents America with more difficult, more frustrating, or more convoluted problems than the Middle East. It's a region where hate has roots reaching back to the dawn of history. It's a place where the senseless spilling of blood in the name of religious faith has gone on since biblical times, and where modern events are forever being shaped by momentous events of the past, from the Exodus to the Holocaust.

I never had any illusions that it would be easy, but when I came to the White House in 1981 I hoped to build on the peace process in the Middle East that had been started by Jimmy Carter at Camp David, where Egypt and Israel signed a treaty ending their thirty-year state of war. Although we had moments of progress, and at times we managed to bottle up at least temporarily the savagery that forever lies beneath the sands of the Middle East, the region was still an adders' nest of problems when I moved out of the White House eight years later. And along the way it had been the source of some of my administration's most difficult moments.

There are two intertwined conflicts in this cauldron of hate and strife—one over territory, the other over religion. Each has roots centuries old.

At one level, there is the dispute between Arab and Jew over the land called Palestine. More than three thousand years ago, at the time of Abraham and Moses, a great Hebrew civilization blossomed in this corner of the ancient Fertile Crescent and flourished until the Jews were overrun by successive armies of Assyrians, Babylonians, Persians, Greeks, Romans, and Arabs.

During the late nineteenth century, seeking refuge from the anti-Semitism common in much of Europe, some Jews—known as Zionists—began asserting the right to reclaim this ancient territory as a national homeland for Jews. In 1948, as the world mourned the monstrous crimes of the Holocaust, the Zionists achieved their goal and the State of Israel was born. But with the creation of the new homeland for Jews, the Arabs who had been occupying Palestine for centuries became a stateless people—and a volatile and frustrated force eager to reclaim land they considered *their* homeland.

The Arab world declared war on Israel, and three times, in 1948, 1967, and 1973, the tiny new country courageously drove back its enemies. Throughout its brief history, Israel has had to live in a perpetual state of war as the constant target of Palestinian terror, a small country fighting for the acceptance of neighbors sworn to destroy it.

This conflict alone would make the Middle East a tinderbox. But animosity, prejudice, and divisions among the Arabs have made it even more volatile. First, there are nationalistic and political rivalries among Arab tribes that go back centuries and make them a far from cohesive or politically united people. Then there are deep and bitter divisions among the Palestinians. Although the Palestine Liberation Organization, which wants an independent Palestinian state, claims to speak for all Palestinians, it is splintered into rival factions ranging from relatively moderate ones to those led by bloodthirsty fanatics. Moreover, the creation of an independent Palestinian state dominated by the PLO is the last thing the leaders of some Arab countries want, even though they may publicly endorse the idea.

Add to these problems emotionally charged religious differences among the Arab people, as well as between Arabs and non-Arab Muslims in Iran and Afghanistan, who share with the Arabs only the commitment to destroy Israel.

In a schism reaching back centuries, based on differing interpretations of the prophet Muhammad's writings, the Muslim world split into two major factions, the Sunni and the Shia. Then these two groups split, with the Shia splintering into many rival groups, including several radical fundamentalist sects who demand the abolition of secular governments and their replacement by priestly theocracies; to achieve their goals, they have institutionalized murder and terrorism in the name of God, promising followers instant entry into Paradise if they die for their faith or kill an enemy who challenges it. Twice in recent years, America has lost loyal allies in the Middle East, the shah of Iran and Anwar Sadat, at the hands of these fanatics. I don't think you can overstate the importance that the rise of Islamic fundamentalism will have to the rest of the world in the century ahead—especially if, as seems possible, its most fanatical elements get their hands on nuclear and chemical weapons and the means to deliver them against their enemies.

In addition to the conflicts between Arab and Jew and between Muslim and Muslim, there are equally vicious rifts going back centuries between Christian sects, and between Christian sects and Muslim sects, especially in Lebanon. In 1943, the people of this former French colony reached an uneasy accord to share power, with the Christians given the upper hand based on a 1932 census that indicated they were in the majority: The president, who was to appoint the cabinet and prime minister, was to be a Maronite Christian; the prime minister was to be a Sunni Muslim, and the president of the Chamber of Deputies a Shiite Muslim. This agreement, however, did not anticipate a rapid growth after World War II of Lebanon's Muslim population, nor that this would lead to civil war.

The rainbow of ancient antagonisms in the Middle East produced an instability that the Soviet Union spent decades and billions seeking to exploit. To Libya, Syria, and the PLO, Moscow and its allies in the Eastern bloc became eager suppliers of arms that were used not only to keep the Middle East pot boiling but also to foment terrorism in other parts of the world. Under President Hafez el-Assad, Syria had become virtually a Soviet satellite in the Middle East, its army supplied and trained by the Soviets. Russian money, arms, and influence were showing up throughout the region.

During the 1970s and early 1980s, the rapid spread in Iran and elsewhere of the most fanatical varieties of Islamic fundamentalism, with their goal of toppling secular governments and replacing them with theocracies modeled after Iran's, made the Middle East even more unpredictable, giving the Soviets new opportunities to exploit the instability there. In a region whose oil exports were essential to the West, Soviet meddling was something the United States could not tolerate, and all our presidents since World War II, including me, felt an obligation to help reduce the instability and bring about peace.

I've believed many things in my life, but no conviction I've ever held has been stronger than my belief that the United States must ensure the survival of Israel.

The Holocaust, I believe, left America with a moral responsibility to ensure that what had happened to the Jews under Hitler never happens again. We must not let it happen again. The civilized world owes a debt to the people who were the greatest victims of Hitler's madness.

My dedication to the preservation of Israel was as strong when I left the White House as when I arrived there, even though this tiny ally, with whom we share democracy and many other values, was a source of great concern for me while I was president.

My introduction to the high emotions that surround almost everything to do with the Middle East occurred during my first few weeks in Washington. During its final months, the Carter administration had made a tentative decision, but had not yet announced it, to sell Saudi Arabia several airborne warning and control (AWACS) aircraft—flying radar stations that can spot incoming aircraft and missiles and direct the launching of defensive or offensive missiles. Even before inauguration day, Jewish groups in America began pressing me to cancel the sale. When I got to the White House, I ordered a complete review of the proposed sale and decided to go ahead with it because I was told the planes would not materially change the balance of power in the Arab-Israeli conflict. I thought the Arab world would regard it as a gesture showing that we desired to be evenhanded in the Middle East.

Even though Saudi Arabia had opposed the Camp David accords, I thought it was important to strengthen ties with this relatively moderate Arab country, not only because its oil exports were essential to our economy, but because, like Israel, it wanted to resist Soviet expansionism in the region. In some ways, our interests in the Middle East and those of Saudi Arabia coincided. Its oilfields were among the richest in the world, coveted by the Communist world and by neighboring Iran, but protected by a relatively small Saudi military establishment.

The Saudis needed the friendship and, if necessary, the help of a great power in defending their oilfields. We wanted to keep the Soviets out of the region as well as prevent the radical, anti-American Iranian revolution from spreading to Saudi Arabia, with all the implications that could have for our economy. To put it simply, I didn't want Saudi Arabia to become another Iran. Therefore, although I knew we'd never abandon our pledge to ensure the survival of Israel, I believed we ought to pursue a course that convinced the moderate Arabs that we could play fair and that the United States was a credible ally.

Following the previous administration's decision to look on while the shah of Iran was removed from power, I also wanted to send a signal to our allies and to Moscow that the United States supported its friends and intended to exert an influence in the Middle East not just limited to our support of Israel. Moreover, I thought that strengthening ties to moderate Arab nations might help us in the long run to resolve some of the great problems of the Middle East. If we were ever going to be able to bring the warring parties together and negotiate a peace, we had to convince the Arabs that we could be fair. In 1981, the projected AWACS sale became a symbol to moderate Arab countries of our fairness and the strength of our commitment to them. Unfortunately, to Israel and some of its supporters in Congress, the great AWACS battle became, for reasons with no foundation in reality, the symbol of what they perceived as a betrayal of Israel by the United States. They chose to take on the administration over the AWACS sale and created a donnybrook in Congress that I believed we could not afford to lose. I believed it was a battle that *had* to be won to advance the cause of peace in the Middle East. I also knew that if we lost on AWACS, it might undermine our ability to persuade Congress to approve our domestic programs and the rearmament of the Pentagon.

The battle began to heat up just a few days after I moved into the White House, when I started getting calls and visits from the leaders of American Jewish organizations and their supporters in Congress, voicing opposition to the projected sale. By the middle of April, while I was recuperating from the shooting at the Hilton, I was receiving so much flak on the AWACS issue that it was taking up almost as much time as the economic recovery program. One night during April I wrote in my diary:

> I'm disturbed by the reaction and the opposition of so many groups [to my support of the AWACS sale]. First of all it must be plain to them, they've never had a better friend of Israel in the W.H. than they have now. We are striving to bring stability to the Middle East and reduce the threat of a Soviet move in that direction. The basis for such stability must be peace between Israel and the Arab nations. The Saudis are a key to this. If they can follow the course of Egypt the rest might fall in place. The AWACS won't be theirs until 1985. In the meantime, much can be accomplished toward furthering the Camp David format.
>
> We have assured the Israelis we will do whatever is needed to see that any help to the Arab states does not change the balance of power between them and the Arabs.

At the time the AWACS battle was heating up in Congress, so were hostilities in the Middle East. Israel was becoming increasingly concerned over hit-and-run attacks across its borders by PLO terrorists based in Lebanon. And Syrian forces, which had entered Lebanon in 1976 as a part of an Arab "peacekeeping" force and never left, were fighting in central Lebanon's Bekaa Valley with the Phalange, a Christian militia. After Syria started installing Soviet-made surface-to-air missiles in Lebanon, we began hearing reports from Israel that it was weighing the possibility of invading southern Lebanon to attack PLO and Syrian installations it regarded as hostile to northern Israel.

In an effort to head off a new threat to Middle East peace, I asked our country's extraordinary diplomatic troubleshooter, Philip Habib, to come out of retirement and undertake a special mission to Syria, Lebanon, and Israel to see if he could negotiate an agreement that would keep the peace. All through 1981, he worked to avert war in Lebanon, while Palestinian terrorists continued their sporadic forays into Israel, more Soviet-built Syrian missiles were installed within range of key targets in northern Israel, and Israeli commandos engaged their enemies across the border.

In the late spring of that year, Saudi Arabia agreed to help Habib mediate the dispute on the Syrian and PLO side, giving us hope that war could be averted. A miracle worker who never ceased to amaze me, Habib then negotiated a cease-fire that held intermittently through most of the year despite an eruption of anti-Israeli fervor in the Arab world in early June, after the Israelis, flying U.S.–made planes, bombed a nuclear reactor that was under construction in Iraq.

Israeli Prime Minister Menachem Begin, who informed us of the attack only after the fact, said that Israel had acted because of information it had received that the Iraqi plant was to be used to produce fissionable material for nuclear weapons for use against Israel. He said that a French shipment of "hot" uranium had been scheduled to arrive soon and that if he had waited longer, he could not have ordered the bombing because the resultant radiation would have drifted over Baghdad, Iraq's capital.

"I can understand his fear but feel he took the wrong option," I wrote in the diary June 9, 1981.

> He should have told us and the French. We could have done some-thing to remove the threat. However, we are not turning on Israel. That would be an invitation for the Arabs to attack. It's time to raise h—l world wide for a settlement of the Middle East problem. What has happened is the result of fear and suspicion on both sides. We need a real push for a solid peace. . . .
>
> Under the law I have no choice but to ask Congress to investigate and see if there has been a violation of the law regarding use of American-produced planes for offensive purposes. Frankly, if Con-gress should decide that, I'll grant a Presidential waiver. Iraq is tech-nically still at war with Israel and I believe they were preparing to build an atom bomb.

Technically, Israel *had* violated an agreement with us not to use U.S.–made weapons for offensive purposes, and some cabinet members wanted me to lean hard on Israel because it had broken this pledge. We sent a note to the Israeli government criticizing the raid, and delayed shipment of several additional military aircraft as a show of our displeasure; but I sympathized with Begin's motiva-tions and privately believed we should give him the benefit of the doubt. I had no doubt that the Iraqis were trying to develop a nuclear weapon.

Nevertheless, in Saudi Arabia and other Arab countries, the raid ignited an uproar and poured additional fuel on the AWACS bonfire. Pointing out that Israel's planes had trespassed in Saudi airspace en route to Iraq, the Saudis sent word to me that the raid was evidence that Israel posed a threat to all Arab countries and additional proof that they needed the AWACS planes, so that they could be forewarned of an Israeli air raid.

In Congress, the AWACS controversy simmered all summer long before coming to a boil in early fall. According to the rules, the sale of the aircraft could be blocked by a majority vote in both houses of Congress. Israel's supporters already had the votes in the House. The principal battleground would be the Senate, where our party had a slim majority but Israel also had many friends.

Prime Minister Begin arrived in Washington in early September, not long after Congress had passed the tax cuts that were pivotal to our economic recovery program, and suddenly no legislative issue occupied Washington more than the proposed AWACS sale. After a formal arrival ceremony on the South Lawn, Begin and I adjourned to the Oval Office for a get-acquainted chat. I told him I wanted the two of us to be on a first-name basis. Later, we met with our advisors in the Cabinet Room and Begin, as I expected, urged us not to go ahead with sale of the airplanes. At Camp David, he said, Israel had gone more than halfway to meet the Arabs on the road to peace. In exchange for Egypt's agreement that Israel had the right to exist (a concession for which Anwar Sadat had been excommunicated from the Arab League), he had agreed to return the Sinai peninsula—captured by Israel in the 1967 war— to Egypt in April 1982, and to grant autonomy to more than one million Palestinians who were living in the Gaza Strip and on the West Bank of the Jordan River, territory Israel had also captured during the war.

Now, Begin argued, Israel was owed everything the United States could possibly do to preserve its security. I understood his concerns. Israel was a small country virtually surrounded by enemies: It was under pressure from the international community to abide by United Nations Security Council Resolution 242, which called upon Israel to withdraw from all the territories it had claimed after the 1967 war, including the West Bank. Without the West Bank,

Israel was so narrow in places that a cannon shot could be fired all the way across the country.

Begin told me he was fearful of anything that might change the balance of power in the Middle East. But I told him our military people were convinced that the AWACS planes would not materially alter the balance. I repeatedly emphasized that the United States was committed to ensuring Israel's survival and would do nothing to diminish its position of military superiority over the Arabs. I also tried to explain why we needed the participation of moderate Arab countries other than Egypt in efforts to achieve a lasting and secure peace in the Middle East. Writing that night in my diary about my meeting with Begin, I said:

> I told him how strongly we felt it [the AWACS sale] could help bring the Saudis into the peace making process. I assured him we (Israel and US) were allies. That the partnership benefited us as much as it did Israel and that we would not let a risk to Israel to be created. While he didn't give up his objection, he mellowed. By the time the meetings and the state dinner ended, he said this was the warmest reception he'd ever had from a President of the United States. I think we're off to a good start in the difficult business of peace in the Middle East. My own feeling is that it should come through bilateral agreements just as it did with Egypt. That's why we want to start with Saudi Arabia.

Although I felt that our relationship had gotten off to a good start and that I had Begin's confidence that we would do whatever it took to ensure the safety of Israel, I learned that almost immediately after he left the White House, Begin went to Capitol Hill and began lobbying very hard against me, the administration, and the AWACS sale—after he had told me he wouldn't do that.

I didn't like having representatives of a foreign country—*any* foreign country—trying to interfere in what I regarded as our domestic political process and the setting of our foreign policy. I told the State Department to let Begin know that I didn't like it and that he was jeopardizing the close relationship of our countries unless he backed off. Privately, I felt he'd broken his word and I was angry about it. Late the following month, we won the AWACS battle when the Senate narrowly defeated a measure that would have blocked the sale, and we achieved our goal of sending a signal to moderate Arabs that we could be evenhanded—even though Israel, in a message apparently dictated by Begin, denounced the administration for anti-Semitism and betrayal.

During the preceding weeks, I had experienced one of the toughest battles of my eight years in Washington. Israel had very strong friends in Congress. With the exception of two or three votes on our tax and spending cut legislation, I spent more time in one-on-one meetings and on the telephone attempting to win on this measure than on any other. We had begun the month more than twenty votes behind in the Senate; we finally won by a margin of fifty-two to forty-eight.

That was just the first of many problems I'd have involving the Middle East.

58

AFTER THE TRAGIC ASSASSINATION of Anwar Sadat in October 1981, the future of the Middle East became even murkier, while the clouds of war that had hung over Lebanon began to grow darker with each day. Vice-President Hosni Mubarak succeeded Sadat as president of Egypt, inheriting the same situation that had confronted his predecessor: serious domestic economic problems, Egypt's isolation from the Arab world because of the Camp David agreement and its acceptance of Israel's right to exist, and the increasing political ferment in Egypt of fundamentalist Muslims. Mubarak knew firsthand what the pursuit of Sadat's policies had meant for his mentor: He had been sitting near Sadat when Sadat was assassinated. By no means was it certain that he would find it prudent to continue on the same course as Sadat. It seemed possible that he might renounce the Camp David accords once Egypt had reclaimed the Sinai, then rejoin the Arab League, perhaps even reestablish the close ties with the Soviet Union that had prevailed under Sadat's predecessor, Gamal Abdel Nasser.

There was also a strong possibility that Menachem Begin, who was understandably skeptical and uncertain about the new leadership in Cairo and worried by a growing PLO military buildup in Lebanon, would decide that Israel's security was best served by reneging on the Camp David accords and going to war again with the Arabs.

Why were these events, occurring thousands of miles from our shores, important to Americans? Under Leonid Brezhnev, the Soviet Union was eager to exploit any opportunity to expand its influence and supplant the United States as the dominant superpower in this oil-rich and strategically important part of the world. The Middle East was one of those remote but important stages of the world where, during the late twentieth century, a miscalculation or misjudgment could lead to World War III.

We had an irreversible commitment to the survival and territorial integrity of Israel. And, as the leader of the Free World, America had a special responsibility to attempt to end the killings and settle the disputes between peoples whom we regarded as mutual friends and allies.

As a friend of both Israel and the moderate Arab states, I felt the United States had a duty to do this—in fact, we were the *only* nation in a position to serve as middle man in the quest for peace to this troubled region. Virtually all of the key players, except the Palestinian extremists and radical Muslim fundamentalists, were looking to the United States to help find a solution to the problems. Now we had to press ahead and achieve one.

Through the winter and spring of 1981–82, the cease-fire in Lebanon negotiated by Philip Habib remained in effect despite great pressures: sporadic terrorist attacks against Israel by Palestinians; the delivery of more Soviet-made rockets, artillery, and other weapons to Syrian and PLO forces in Lebanon; repeated Israeli strikes on Palestinians in Lebanon; and a general unraveling of law and order in and around Beirut among Syrian, Christian, and Muslim militias, all of whom claimed the right to control Lebanon.

Syria claimed that its ancestral right to the Holy Land preceded that of the biblical Hebrews, and that Lebanon had no right to exist because it was created by France, its former colonial ruler. Syria's long-term goal was to make Lebanon a de facto colony and strip Christians of any political power there.

In December, the seething tensions in the Middle East were exacerbated when Israel announced that it had annexed the strategically important Golan Heights, which it had taken from Syria during the 1967 war; this was a violation of UN Resolution 242. Meanwhile, Israel's continuing establishment of settlements in the occupied territories, in defiance of the resolution as well as of world opinion, poured more fuel onto the fire.

To signal our disapproval of Israel's annexation of the Golan Heights, we shelved a pending agreement that we were working on (a so-called memorandum of understanding) meant to spell out details of a strengthened military partnership between our countries. Begin responded with an angry letter to me arguing that the United States, after Vietnam, had no business telling Israel what was right or wrong. "The people of Israel lived without the memorandum of understanding for 3,700 years, and will continue to live without it for another 3,700 years," he said, refusing to give up the Golan Heights.

As these events were unfolding, we continued to receive what appeared to be credible reports from Israel that Begin, who believed in the biblical maxim of "an eye for an eye," and his defense minister, Ariel Sharon, a bellicose man who seemed to be chomping at the bit to start a war, were preparing for a full-scale invasion of Lebanon against the PLO, waiting only for the slightest provocation to launch it. While I urged Begin to exercise restraint, Habib continued trying to work out the framework for a settlement. We told Israeli leaders we believed they had lost considerable support in the non-Arab world during the previous year because of the attack on the Iraqi nuclear plant, air strikes in Lebanon that had killed noncombatant Palestinians, the annexation of the Golan Heights, and other actions directed against the Arabs. Each time I communicated with them, however, I emphasized my personal commitment and that of the United States to the support of Israel. I supported its right to *defend* itself against attack, but appealed for Israel not to go on the offensive unless it was the victim of a provocation of such magnitude that the world would easily understand its right to retaliate.

Israel's response was, in effect: Mind your own business. It is up to Israel alone to decide what it must do to ensure its survival.

While the situation regarding Lebanon was growing more tense, we tried to establish a solid relationship with the new leadership in Cairo. We sent messages to Mubarak declaring our desire to continue the ties our countries had developed under Sadat, as well as our commitment to continuing the process begun at Camp David. Early in the new year, Mubarak may have decided he wanted to send *us* a message when he accepted an offer from Moscow to assign a team of Russian technical advisors to Cairo to help Egypt's industrial development. It made us wonder if he was planning to revert to a Nasser-style relationship with Moscow. Just as it could be said that some Israeli leaders wanted to exploit the tensions between the United States and the USSR to strengthen our commitment to Israel, I think Mubarak was trying to send a signal that we shouldn't take Egypt for granted, either.

When he arrived in Washington for a get-acquainted state visit in early February 1982, I brought up the new Soviet advisors and he emphasized that Egypt was a staunch American friend and had no intentions of lining up with the Soviets. But it was plain that Egypt, already a big beneficiary of American aid, wanted something more from the United States for this friendship. We had previously negotiated a $1.3 billion arms-sale agreement that was to include a $200 million outright grant; to give Mubarak something to take home as a symbol of his trip's success and evidence of our friendship, we increased the grant to $400 million.

As the time approached for Israel to return the Sinai to Egypt, hostilities between Israel and PLO and Syrian units in Lebanon were heating up, and I continued to wonder if Begin would live up to the Camp David agreements. By then, it was apparent that too little preparation had been done to achieve the goal of granting autonomy to the Palestinians living in the occupied territories as called for under the accords; this part of the agreement would not be completed. But the deadline was approaching for Israel to give up the Sinai, and I expected it to be emotionally traumatic for Begin.

These were occupied territories taken from other countries, yes; but Israel had won the Sinai during a war started by the other countries. In giving it up, Israel would surrender a strategically important buffer between itself and enemies sworn to destroy it; and, it would be giving up territory where Israeli settlers since 1967 had built homes, cultivated farms, built schools, raised families.

Despite political pressure within Israel to abandon the agreement, Begin proved to be a man of his word, and the transfer of the Sinai to Egypt was completed on schedule on April 25, 1982. That morning, I telephoned Mubarak and Begin to congratulate them on this milestone in history and to wish them well in continuing on the road to peace.

My heart went out especially to Begin. I had many difficulties with him while I was president, but he was an Israeli patriot devoted, above all, to the survival of his country. He passionately believed that the ancient lands of the Israelites rightfully belonged to modern Israel. A survivor and near victim of the Holocaust, he knew from personal experience the depth of the hatred and viciousness that can be directed at Jews simply because they are Jews, and he had sworn, he once told me, to assure that no Jew's blood was ever spilled again with impunity.

I could tell from a sadness in his voice that it had been a difficult day for him. I pledged to Begin and to Mubarak that America would continue to do all it could to further the peace process. After my calls, I felt optimistic that we were on our way.

Unfortunately, as soon as the Sinai was returned to Egypt and we began working on settling differences between Israel and Egypt over the question of Palestinian autonomy in the occupied territories, things started unraveling very quickly in Lebanon. The autonomy talks were put on hold and the peace process came to a halt. According to Phil Habib, who had been working night and day to keep the shaky cease-fire alive, radical elements of the PLO opposed to its leader, Yasir Arafat, were trying to destroy the Camp David accords and provoke Israel into attacking Palestinians in Lebanon with terrorist attacks on Israel. This, the radicals believed, would lead to war, rally Arab and Soviet support behind their cause, reduce the influence in the PLO of the more moderate Arafat, and upset whatever prospects remained for continuing the Camp David process.

We tried very hard to persuade Begin and Sharon that these radical Palestinian elements were trying to goad, manipulate, and provoke them into war. They listened, but they did not hear: As far as they were concerned, any act of terrorism by any Palestinian anywhere in the world was a violation of the cease-fire in Lebanon, and they claimed the right to take whatever steps they thought necessary to defend the people of Israel. By early June, when I was getting ready to leave for the Versailles economic summit, it was apparent that Israel had already made the decision to attack in Lebanon and was waiting only for an excuse to deliver the blow.

The invasion began June 5, after Israel responded to the killing of an Israeli diplomat in London with bombing runs on PLO targets in Lebanon; Arafat replied with renewed shelling of Israel. After this prelude, Israel launched a well-organized full-scale invasion of Lebanon, informing us that its only goal was to drive PLO forces twenty-five miles away from Israel's border with Lebanon, to create a buffer that would end the PLO artillery's ability to lob shells at will on Israelis living in Galilee, in northern Israel.

The Israeli invasion provoked an angry reaction from Leonid Brezhnev. In the first in a series of exchanges between us via the Washington-Moscow cable "hot line," Brezhnev accused the United States of, at worst, complicity in the attack and, at least, advance knowledge of it. "The facts indicate," he said, "that the Israeli invasion is a previously planned operation, whose preparations the U.S. must have known about." I responded that while we believed Israel had the right to defend its northern borders, we did not support the invasion of Lebanon. I called his claim of prior knowledge of the invasion "totally without foundation."

"At the same time," I said, "I am compelled to point out that your government bears no little responsibility for the current crisis in the Middle East by its failure to support the Camp David accords and to use your influence on Syria and PLO" to stabilize the situation in Lebanon.

In Paris, I dictated a message to Begin appealing to him to withdraw his forces from Lebanon, and we joined in voting for a UN resolution calling for Israel's withdrawal and a cease-fire. After encountering little resistance north of the border, however, Ariel Sharon's tanks and troops continued their advance, and he apparently decided that Israel now had a historic opportunity to drive the PLO completely from Lebanon. The Israeli Defense Forces moved on Beirut, then expanded the war dramatically—and engaged a new enemy—with attacks on Syrian missile sites in the Bekaa Valley.

What had started (according to Begin and Sharon) as a limited operation designed only to enhance the security of the Israelis who lived near their country's northern border had suddenly been transformed into a campaign to wipe out the PLO and an all-out war between Israel and its archenemy, Syria.

Within just a few days, the advancing Israeli forces had driven thousands of PLO members into civilian neighborhoods in West Beirut, the Muslim section of the city. Meanwhile, superior Israeli pilots had dealt a stunning defeat to the Syrian air force (who were flying Soviet-built MIGs) and had knocked out dozens of Syrian missile sites.

The Israelis were winning the war, but plunging, probably unknowingly, into a quagmire. After forcing the PLO forces to dig in among the civilian population of Beirut, Sharon and Begin would respond with a policy that would stun the senses of many people in the world and bring even greater international condemnation of Israel.

At this point in mid-June, we decided that the best option for ending the bloody conflict was to persuade rival Christian and Muslim factions in Lebanon to get together (something we knew wouldn't be easy, considering their long history of disputes) and jointly disarm the PLO in their country, then order the PLO, Israel, and Syria off their territory, with the international community serving some role in helping to keep the agreement in place.

We decided on this strategy knowing clearly that it wasn't going to be easy to implement. On June 16, I wrote in my diary:

> We're walking a tight rope. Some 6000 armed P.L.O. are holed up in Beirut. Pres. [Elias] Sarkis of Lebanon, can't say openly, but he apparently wants Israel to stay near until the P.L.O. can be disarmed, then he wants to restore the Central government of Lebanon, allow Palestinians to become citizens and get all foreign forces to withdraw from Lebanon. The world is waiting for us to use our muscle and order Israel out. We can't do this if we want to help Sarkis, but we can't explain the situation either. Some days are worse than others.

Five days later, Menachem Begin arrived in Washington at a time when Israeli planes, gunboats, and artillery units had begun attacking the fringes of West Beirut in what appeared to be relentless and indiscriminate bombardment of neighborhoods filled with Lebanese civilians who had absolutely no role in the Israeli–PLO dispute. Israel then cut off water and electricity to these neighborhoods in West Beirut, causing the civilians more hardship.

When we shook hands, it was still "Menachem" and "Ron," but our meeting had none of the glow of our previous meeting. With only our ambassadors present, Begin and I spent almost an hour going head to head: I told him that, no matter how villainous the attack on Israel's diplomat in London had been, it had not given

Israel cause to unleash its brutal attack on Beirut. Begin wouldn't give an inch. He claimed that the invasion was justified by the PLO's shelling of Israeli villages from Lebanon, then he went on the counterattack, protesting a pending U.S. sale of fighter planes to Jordan. When I said I wanted to create "more Egypts"—Arab countries willing to make peace with Israel—he angrily said that was impossible, no other Arab state would do what Egypt had done and recognize Israel.

Underneath his uncompromising and combative mood, however, I suspected Begin wanted to end the fighting. Although Israeli military might was having a crushing effect on its enemies, the Syrians and Palestinians, Israel was paying a high price for this success. The invasion was taking a rising toll of Israeli lives, and I suspected Begin now believed that the pugnacious Sharon had extended his reach too far. He had driven the PLO forces into Beirut, but had failed to anticipate what would happen after he had accomplished that.

After returning to Israel, Begin endorsed the plan we had proposed calling for the elimination of the PLO and all foreign armies from Lebanon, and the Israeli cabinet subsequently surprised me with a suggestion that the United States take the lead in negotiating a pullout by the PLO. Until then, at Israel's urging, we had refused to do any business with the PLO until and unless they agreed to recognize Israel's right to exist, which they had never done.

During the next few weeks, there were off-and-on cease-fires in Lebanon as Habib pushed forward with his negotiations. He encountered new hurdles, however, including PLO demands that some of its members be allowed to remain in Lebanon, and strong resistance from most Arab nations to accepting into their own countries the PLO members who would be evacuated from Lebanon under the plan. Meanwhile, the killing in Beirut continued.

In late June, Brezhnev sent a message complaining that innocent civilians were dying under Israeli bombardment and said our support of Israel was jeopardizing efforts at improving U.S.–Soviet relations. I replied that we were trying to persuade Israel to withdraw and urged him to use Soviet influence to persuade Syria to do the same thing. "I must also point out," I said, "that your expression of concern for the suffering of the people in Lebanon cannot but appear ironic in view of the fact that the Soviet Union has provided immense quantities of weapons to elements which have actually worked to undermine the political stability of Lebanon and provoked Israeli retaliation by attacking Israel's northern territories."

As the Israeli offensive continued, Brezhnev continued blaming us. In mid-July, after one message, I again rejected this claim and informed him that the United States and other Western nations had been requested by Lebanese authorities to create a multinational force to keep the peace in Lebanon. I told him we were considering doing so, but that if we did, it would be as a temporary step and it should not be viewed as a U.S. effort to offset the prevailing East-West balance in the Middle East.

At the end of July, Habib cabled me a hopeful report that he was making progress and was optimistic that an agreement could be reached. Then, however, things started to deteriorate. Although the cease-fire remained technically in place, it was broken regularly by both sides and the situation became very volatile.

By early August, Sharon's forces had virtually encircled Beirut and were unleashing withering attacks on the fringes of West Beirut. After a new complaint from Brezhnev on August 2, I replied: "I hope that the Soviet Union will do nothing to make a resolution of this tragedy more difficult. I may add that although the U.S. government and Israel maintain close and friendly relations, we are not responsible for the actions of the Israeli government, a sovereign state. If the Soviet government has representations to make in this regard, it should communicate with Israeli authorities."

Then, on August 4, two days after I'd met with Israeli Foreign Minister Yitzhak Shamir in the Oval Office and appealed to him in the strongest words I could think of for Israel to use restraint, I was awakened at 6:30 A.M. by my national security advisor. He said that the Israelis had just moved into new positions within West Beirut and were shelling the city with a savage ferocity that was killing more and more civilians. Outraged, Phil Habib telephoned me from Beirut and said that the shelling was so intense and so unrelenting that he was unable to get to meetings he had scheduled to negotiate a settlement of the dispute.

I decided to appeal personally to Begin to stop the fighting and abide by the cease-fire so that Habib could complete his work. I suggested to Begin that if he didn't, he could expect a drastic change in Israel's relationship with the United States. "This disproportionate bombing of West Beirut," my message stated, was exacting "unacceptable human costs and making negotiations impossible." If it continued, I said, it would be impossible for me to defend the proposition that Israel used American-made arms for defensive purposes only. "We must come to the diplomatic table for a solution and not through use of military means," I said. I reminded Begin that only two days earlier George Shultz and I had told Shamir that Habib's negotiations aimed at removing the PLO from Beirut were making progress and were at a critical stage and further attacks could destroy whatever chances of success they had. "Israel's movement of heavy artillery into West Beirut demonstrated that our message to the Foreign Minister fell on deaf ears. There has to be an end to unnecessary bloodshed, particularly among innocent civilians. I insist that a cease fire be reestablished and maintained until the PLO has left Beirut."

Begin's reply the next day stated that Israel's policy in Lebanon was based on two principles: The first was adherence to the agreed-upon cease-fire provided "it is absolute and mutual, neither of which have been respected by the terrorists in and around Beirut; [we] have already counted at least ten cease-fires and all of them broken by the terrorists, while Israel adhered to the rules." Begin said that under no circumstances could he "ask members of the Israeli defense forces, if fired upon, to refrain from defending themselves."

The second principle, Begin said, was achieving a political solution that provided for expulsion of the PLO from Lebanon. He said, however, that Israel had to preserve the choice of a military option because without one it would have no leverage to seek a political solution. The UN resolution calling for its withdrawal and U.S. officials' statements calling on Israel to leave were encouraging the PLO to procrastinate and refuse to leave. As a result, Israel had to keep up military pressure on the PLO. Begin indicated that he had just received a letter from Philip Habib who had told him there was "increasing evidence" the PLO was prepared to negotiate a withdrawal from Beirut, but then muted this expression of confidence by noting that this issue would remain uncertain for twenty-four to forty-eight hours, while PLO leaders reviewed his latest proposal and efforts were made to locate Arab countries willing to accept the PLO leaders and combatants. "Ambassador Habib, with all his energy and good will, did not know whether the P.L.O. is truly serious or not and indicated that he had not yet established satisfactory destinations" for the Palestinian leaders, Begin wrote. "This is the real situation today on Aug. 5 at the time of my writing to you at the end of a 45 day period which were at the disposal of Ambassador Habib to conclude the negotiations aimed at evacuating the terrorist organizations from Beirut and Lebanon which, Mr. President, is your resolve. The security of Israel and the lives of its citizens are at stake."

Once again Begin had told me, in effect, to mind my own business.

Over the next few days, Habib's reports from Beirut still gave me some hope that his tireless negotiations would pay off, despite mounting attacks by Israel that were taking an increasing death toll among the women and children of Beirut. On August 9, Ariel Sharon sent me a cable asking if he could come to Washington the next day to meet on the crisis. He apparently wanted to defend the attack. George Shultz cabled Sharon a message saying that I would not meet with him because I didn't want to undercut Habib, and that Sharon should do his talking with Shultz. The following day, Shimon Peres, the leader of the Israeli opposition, came to the Oval Office for a meeting. I found him less combative and much more reasonable than Begin. He agreed that the Israeli-Arab conflict would never be settled without terms agreeable to all sides regarding political autonomy for the Palestinians and, unlike Begin, he encouraged us to continue befriending Jordan and other moderate Arab states in hopes they could help resolve the Arab-Israeli conflict.

Despite our appeals for restraint, the Israelis on August 12 opened a new and even more brutal attack on civilian neighborhoods in Beirut that sickened me and many others in the White House. This provoked me into an angry demand for an end to the bloodletting. Here are excerpts from my diary:

Aug. 12
Met with the news the Israelis delivered the most devastating bomb and artillery attack Israel on West Beirut lasting 14 hours. Habib cabled—desperate—has basic agreement from all parties but can't arrange details of P.L.O. withdrawal because of the barrage.

King Fahd [of Saudi Arabia] called begging me to do something. I told him I was calling P.M. Begin immediately. And I did. I was angry.

I told him [Begin] it had to stop or our entire future relationship was endangered. I used the word "Holocaust" deliberately and said the symbol of his country was becoming "a picture of a seven month old baby with its arms blown off."

He told me he had ordered the bombing stopped. I asked about the artillery fire. He claimed the P.L.O. had started that and Israeli forces had taken casualties. End of call. Twenty minutes later, he called to tell me he'd ordered an end to the barrage and pleaded for our continued friendship.

The phone calls worked, at least briefly bringing a cessation to the slaughter in Beirut. I had consciously used the word *holocaust* to describe the indiscriminate bombardment of Beirut because I knew it would have a special meaning for Begin.

After the phone calls, Israel reduced the intensity of its bombardment of Beirut—but its ground and air forces then began attacking populated areas in northern Lebanon, apparently with the intent of eradicating PLO strongholds in that region. This put a new monkey wrench in Habib's delicate negotiations with the Palestinians and Syrians.

To reinforce my remarks during the telephone calls, I sent a follow-up letter to Begin the next day:

This message follows our telephone conversation to emphasize the depth of my personal concerns about recent Israeli military actions and their destructive effect; . . . at this crucial moment in Ambassador Habib's mission, when he is only a few days away from working out the final detailed points of his package plan for departure of the P.L.O. from Beirut, Israeli air strikes, shelling and other military moves have stopped progress in the negotiations. I find this incomprehensible and unacceptable. Israel must adhere to an immediate strict cease fire in place. The assurances which we hear from Jerusalem must be borne out by the actions of Israel's defense forces, who must stop these massive eruptions to any provocation. I cannot stress to you enough how seriously I regard this situation. Our entire future relations are at stake if these military eruptions continue . . . the Ambassador must be able to fulfill the last steps in his mission. Israeli military actions of the past several hours may have made further alteration of the package impossible. If this proves to be the case, we will look to Israel to accept it fully so the agony of Beirut will end . . . I cannot accept this new military advance as compatible with pledges of Israeli withdrawal from Lebanon and support for the emergence of a stable Lebanese government. . . .

Begin replied the following day, explaining that he had not responded immediately to my message because his wife had decided not to awaken him when it arrived the night before, as he had been asleep after a long and difficult day. He went on to say that he had always spoken to me with frankness and that he now wanted to tell me how deeply offended he felt by the tone of my letter following the two telephone conversations.

> I would have understood perfectly well were it written after our first talk, in which you voiced anger and in which you also hurt me personally and deeply, especially through the use of the word "Holocaust," of which I know some facts which may be unknown to my fellow man . . . but after the second conversation, you ended it with the words, "Menachem, Shalom." How can I have shalom of mind having now read your written message?

Referring to my assertion that the new Israeli military campaign in northern Lebanon might make impossible further changes in the package being negotiated by Habib, and that Israel therefore would have to accept it as is, Begin said: "We shall not accept any package agreement if we are not fully consulted about the contents before the package is wrapped up." As for the new Israeli offensive, he said:

> Everywhere in Lebanon where our forces are, is related to our determined right to stamp out the scourge of terrorism; it has nothing to do with our resolve to withdraw our forces from Lebanon simultaneously, as Mr. Habib put it to me at his own initiative, with the departure of the foreign Syrian forces.
>
> Sincerely,
> Menachem Begin

During the next two weeks, Habib finally got all sides to agree on our plan, which provided for a new cease-fire, withdrawal of the PLO from Lebanon under international supervision, and the subsequent withdrawal of Syrian and Israeli armies. At the request of Lebanese leaders, I agreed that the United States would send a contingent of marines to Beirut for three or four weeks as part of a multinational peacekeeping force that would help supervise the departure of PLO forces to Tunisia and other countries.

With the shooting stopped, George Shultz and I regarded this moment in the explosive history of the Middle East as a possible golden opportunity to make a fresh start toward achieving a long-term settlement of the region's problems. We decided to offer the framework for a new peace initiative.

As we saw it, any long-term solution must require, first of all, that the Arab world acknowledge Israel's right to exist, and must provide adequate guarantees of Israel's security and the integrity of its borders. It should also provide for completion of the Camp David agreement, granting full autonomy to Palestinians living in the territories taken by Israel in the Six Day War, with free elections and a five-year transition period leading to full self-government; and a freeze by Israel on the establishment of new settlements in the occupied territories during the transition period, when there would be a peaceful and orderly transfer of authority from Israel to the Palestinians.

After its years of war against the PLO, we knew Israel would oppose (as would some Arab countries fearful of a strong Palestinian state) the creation of an independent Palestinian nation next to it on the West Bank and in Gaza. At the same time, we believed that peace would never come to the Middle East as long as the occupied territories remained under the permanent political control of Israel. We believed that the Palestinians living in these areas had to be given freedom, the right of self-determination and self-government, and that the best way of accomplishing this was not through creation of a Palestinian state, but through some sort of political association of these areas with the government of Jordan under which the Palestinians would have self-rule and autonomy, perhaps like an American state.

Thus, we believed that the solution lay in what came to be known as the "land for peace" option: Israel's withdrawal, under provisions of UN Security Council Resolution 242, from Gaza and most of the West Bank and an undivided Jerusalem, in exchange for peace and the Arabs' acceptance of its right to exist. I felt then—and still do—that Israel will never resolve its conflict with the Arabs unless it gives up some of the land won in the 1967 war in return for peace and safe borders, and that so long as Israel continues building new settlements in the occupied territories, a lasting peace will remain extremely difficult to forge.

In my view, Israel wouldn't have to return *all* of the forty-mile-wide stretch of land between the Mediterranean and the West Bank of the Jordan River; there are one or two points along the West Bank near the narrowest portion of Israel's pre-1967 borders that Israel could retain because of its legitimate security concerns—to prevent, for example, hostile artillery from firing into Israel. But without Israel agreeing to "land for peace," I don't think there will ever be peace in the Middle East.

By late August of 1982, with the cease-fire still in place, we had completed work on the details of our new Middle East peace initiative; I planned to announce it in a nationally televised speech on September 1. Several days before that, officials of our administration presented an outline of the plan to the leaders of Saudi Arabia and Jordan. This was part of our long effort to persuade King Hussein to take part in negotiations with Israel. We were never able to get him completely on board. Expecting Begin to look unfavorably on any proposal that called on Israel to give up any part of the West Bank and its claim to all of Jerusalem, I sent a personal letter to him meant to supplement a more detailed briefing on the plan to be given to him by our excellent ambassador in Israel, Samuel Lewis. My letter read in part:

Dear Menachem:
    Much has happened since we last met in Washington in June. We both have been witness to historic events culminating in the departure of the P.L.O. from Beirut and from its dominant position in Lebanese affairs. . . .
    The population in the north of Israel is now secure and I hope it will remain so. I feel there are now opportunities which lie before us with the P.L.O. military weakened and the Soviet Union shown once again to have minimal impact on the truly significant developments in the Middle East.

I have done much soul searching in an effort to determine how to best take advantage of this situation in a way that will promote the interests of both the United States and Israel. I feel now is the appropriate time for the two of us to mount a major new effort in the Camp David peace process . . . history will not forgive us if we fail to do so. . . . We have a unique opportunity to take a major step toward a comprehensive peace which provides for the security of Israel while recognizing the legitimate rights of the Palestinian people. . . .

I have asked Ambassador Lewis to share with you my thoughts on the key issues that must be resolved if we are to achieve genuine peace as Israel and the U.S. so devoutly wish.

I am well aware your view varies considerably from some of my positions. I am convinced, nevertheless, that taken together the positions we are advocating can lead to a just and comprehensive and durable settlement promised by the Camp David framework. . . . Wherever negotiations may lead, I pledge my absolute commitment to Israel's security. . . .

My friend, I am convinced that we are about to embark together on a journey of historic dimensions. I know that the road will not be easy but I am determined to stay the course, confident that the world will judge our efforts as necessary to insure the permanent security of Israel. I take comfort in the fact that you've already traveled a difficult road to a successful destination of peace with Egypt. I will look to you for counsel and sustenance as we work in the cause of peace.

Ron

When Begin realized we were getting ready to go public with the proposal, he requested Ambassador Lewis to ask me to promise to notify Israeli officials at least twenty-four hours before I did. But I responded: "In view of the fact that Israeli officials have already given the media in Israel a version of some parts of my letter to the Prime Minister, I feel I have no choice but to state my views for myself openly and without delay. Therefore I have decided to address the public tonight, Sept. 1."

The Israeli cabinet wasted no time in rejecting my proposal, and Begin's reply to my letter urging serious consideration of the peace initiative was blunt. Here are excerpts from his reply:

Enclosed is a resolution of the Cabinet adopted unanimously. I can elaborate little on it, but I will take a leaf from your book and say that the government of Israel will stand by its decision with total dedication.

I agree that great events have taken place since our meeting in June, but I have a different view of what took place. . . .

On June 6, 1982, Israel's Defense Force entered Lebanon not to conquer territory but to fight and smash the armed bands operating from that country against our land and its citizens.

This, the IDF did. You will remember we could not accept your suggestion that we proclaim a cease fire on Thursday, June 10, because at that time the enemy was still 18 kilometers from Metulla on our northern border. However, 24 hours later, we pushed the enemy northward and on Friday, June 11, we proclaimed a unilateral cease fire rejected by the terrorists so the fighting continued. And on June 27, we suggested all the terrorists leave Beirut, Lebanon, which they eventually did with the important good offices of Ambassador Habib many weeks later.

. . . [in the intervening battles] Israel lost 340 men killed and 2,200 wounded, 100 of them severely. Also in the battles following the rejection of our appeals by the Syrian army not to interfere, the IDF destroyed 405 Soviet Syrian tanks, among them 9 T72's, considered in NATO circles to be invulnerable; we downed 102 Soviet-Syrian MIGs, including one MIG-25, and smashed 21 batteries of SAM6 and SAM8 and SAM9, a deadly weapon. . . .

Yet in your letter to me and in your speech to the American people you did not, Mr. President, even mention the bravery of the Israeli fighters nor the great sacrifices of the Israeli army and people. One could have gotten the impression that Mr. Philip Habib with the help of expeditionary units achieved the results. Mr. President, I was struck by this omission, but to state a fact, I do not complain.

I do protest your omission to consult Israel before your decision to forward your proposals to Jordan and Saudi Arabia, the former an outspoken opponent of the Camp David accords, the latter a complete stranger to and an adversary of those accords. As there was no prior consultation, the U.S. government could have taken the position that the West Bank should be reassociated with Jordan; what some call the West Bank, Mr. President, is Judea and Samaria and the simple historic truth will never change. There are cynics who will deride history; they may continue their derision as they wish, but I will stand by the truth. And the truth is: Millennia ago, there was a Jewish kingdom of Judea and Samaria where our kings knelt to God, where our prophets brought forth a vision of eternal peace, where we developed a rich civilization which we took with us in our hearts and in our minds on our long global trek for over eighteen centuries and with it we came back home.

King Abdullah [of Jordan] by invasion conquered parts of Judea and Samaria in 1948 and in a war of most legitimate self defense in 1967 after having been attacked by King Hussein we liberated with God's help that portion of our homeland. Judea and Samaria will never again be the West Bank of Hashemite Kingdom of Jordan which was created by British colonialism after the French army expelled King Faisal from Damascus.

At Camp David, Begin said that it had been at Israel's initiative that the agreement had been made to grant autonomy to the Palestinian inhabitants of the region over a five-year period, but he said Israel refused to surrender this land.

Security is of paramount importance. Judea and Samaria are mountainous country and two thirds of our population live in the coastal plain dominated by those mountains. From them you can hit every city, every town, each township and village, and last but not least, our principal airport in the plain below.

We used to live penned in eight miles from the seashore and now, Mr. President, you suggest to us in your proposals that we return to almost that same situation.

Mr. President, you declare that you will not support the creation of a Palestinian state in Judea, Samaria, and the Gaza district. The Palestinian state will rise of itself the day Judea and Samaria are given to Jordanian jurisdiction; then in no time, you will have a Soviet base in the heart of the Middle East. Under no circumstances shall we accept such a possibility ever arising which would endanger our very existence. We have chosen for the last two years to call our countries friends and allies; such being the case, a friend does not weaken his friend, an ally does not put an ally in jeopardy; this would be the inevitable consequence for the positions transmitted to me on Aug. 31 to become a reality.

I believe they won't.

For Zion's sake, I will not hold my peace, and for Jerusalem's sake, I will not rest. (Isaiah, chapter 62)

Menachem

In my response to Begin the following day, I said that despite his cabinet's quick rejection of the proposal, even before it had been made public, I remained confident that it "contained the essential elements for achieving a durable peace in the Middle East which takes full account of Israel's security requirements. After further study, I hope you will share that belief with me . . . I want to reiterate once more our commitment and my commitment to the security of Israel and the Israeli people. Security can only be found in the context of a genuine peace constructed upon sound and enduring treaties between Israel and its Arab neighbors."

As the summer of 1982 came to an end, I still felt cautiously optimistic about the future of the Middle East and believed we were going to be able to continue the peace process. In Beirut, the agreement worked out by Habib seemed to be succeeding: Along with troops from France and Italy, our marines had peaceably evacuated more than ten thousand PLO combatants from Beirut and were themselves preparing to leave Lebanon.

Although Begin and his cabinet had rejected the larger peace initiative, Egypt, Saudi Arabia, and Jordan appeared to be responding favorably to it. I thought there was a good chance that in time Israel, once it had evaluated the alternatives and had developed sufficient trust in it, would accept the plan, too. My goal for the remainder of the year was to continue working on Begin. I couldn't help but believe that once the people of Israel, weary from decades of war, understood that our proposal offered the best prospect for a secure peace in the Middle East, they would support them and bring pressure on Begin's government.

I was optimistic then, not realizing that the worst was yet to come in Lebanon.

59

OUR HOPE THAT THE EVACUATION of PLO forces from Lebanon would mark the beginning of a new and comprehensive peace process and a first step toward a final resolution of the great problems bedeviling the Middle East went up in the smoke of a terrorist bomb three weeks after the PLO forces left Beirut.

During the intervening period, we had continued to receive positive signals from moderate Arab countries in response to the peace plan I announced on September 1, and I had continued trying to persuade Menachem Begin to consider its merits. In a letter to Begin September 5, I said that I was hurt by his continuing public castigation of what I regarded as a serious and realistic peace proposal and his public statements suggesting that the United States—and by implication, that I—was betraying the friendship between our countries. I encouraged him to reconsider the proposal. "The moment has come to breathe new life into a process whose success will insure the permanent security of Israel," I said. "I want us to be together on that journey as we move forward in the cause of peace; this is not a time for recriminations. It's rather a time to explore together how best to move beyond the current perplexing stalemate and to seize the opportunity before us."

I restated my commitment and that of the American people to Israel and urged Begin "in the spirit of our enduring friendship" to take a new look at the proposals "as fair and balanced and this initiative as an appropriate means to launch a fresh start in the Camp David process . . ."

On September 14, a terrorist's bomb destroyed a building in Beirut where the president-elect of Lebanon, Bashir Gemayel, was giving a speech. It threw a nation where chaos had been a matter of day-to-day routine for more than a decade into even greater confusion. Israeli forces immediately responded to Gemayel's assassination by moving into West Beirut and, in fierce fighting, engaged members of the Lebanese army and leftist Muslims, including those believed responsible for the bombing.

I'd expected Saturday, September 18, to be a quiet day: Nancy had left on a brief trip on behalf of her war against drugs, and the only event of the day should have been my noon radio broadcast. But, as my diary reminds me, "Unfortunately things changed. In Beirut, Haddad's Christian Phalanges militia entered a Palestine refugee camp and massacred men, women and children. The Israelis did nothing to prevent or halt it. George Shultz and I met and agreed upon a blunt statement which he delivered to the Israeli ambassador. It was a sad day and one which may very well set our peace efforts back."

The incident touched off a new storm of anti-Israeli sentiment, much of it directed at us. Brezhnev sent me a message accusing Israel of perpetrating a "bloody orgy" and implied we were a party to it. In my response, I said, "I share the revulsion of the entire American people for the deplorable events which have recently occurred in Beirut," and added that the Soviet Union shared a responsibility to end the deadly chaos in Lebanon.

The assassination of Bashir Gemayel, just as Philip Habib seemed to be making great progress in bringing the various sides together, changed everything. After that, Israel and Syria both refused to live up to their agreement to leave Lebanon. The hostilities continued and, more than a year later, Beirut became the focal point of the saddest day of my presidency, perhaps the saddest day of my life.

Here are some of the notes I made in my diary during the period immediately after Gemayel's assassination:

Sept. 19

A busy day for N.S.C. State and defense and staff. I attended meeting in the morning re the Beirut massacre. The Israelis did finally attempt to oust the killers. They have proclaimed their outrage. I finally told our group we should go for broke.

Let's tell the people we are at the request of the Lebanese sending the multi-national force back in. Italy has agreed and we believe the French will too. We are asking the Israelis to leave Beirut. We are asking Arabs to intervene and persuade Syrians to leave Lebanon at which time we'll ask Israelis to do likewise. In the meantime, Lebanon will establish a government and the capability of defending itself. No more half way gesture, clear the whole situation while the M.N.F. is on hand to assure order.

George Shultz and Jeane K. were enthusiastic about the idea and apparently there was no disagreement. The wheels are now in motion . . .

Sept. 20

Spent the morning in an NSPG [National Security Planning Group] meeting framing what I would say or rather how I'd say it on TV, what we were going to do in Lebanon. Anyway, at 5 p.m. I said it: all three networks from Oval Office. . . .

Sept. 26

Our Marines were to have landed in Lebanon but now it will be Tuesday. It is Yom Kippur so the Israelis won't be out until Tuesday but they have agreed to withdraw.

Yesterday we lost two officials in Lebanon. They were assigned to the UN as observers. They and an Irish and Finnish officer were in a vehicle on road to Damascus, hit a land mine, all dead.

Sept. 27

Most of my day spent on homework for press conference tomorrow night. It should be free wheeling what with Lebanon and all. Yom Kippur will be over tomorrow. Our troops will probably go ashore Wednesday.

Sept. 28

Cap W. signed order for Marines to go ashore Wednesday a.m. Israelis will withdraw to south of the airport; Marines will be stationed at the airport. . . . Spent afternoon getting ready for press conference. Have just had it and made it through okay. Everyone says "best yet." My favorite answer was to Sam D. [Donaldson] who asked if I didn't think I had done something to do with our economic problems, which I'd been laying on the Dems over the past year. I said: "Oh, my yes, I share the responsibility—I was a Democrat for years."

Sept. 30
The Congress got the 218 names on the discharge petition and brought the "balanced budget" amendment to the floor. I went up to the Capitol to speak to them . . . a sad day, though, one of our Marines in Beirut, Lebanon, stepped on a mine or a part of a cluster bomb that hadn't exploded. We're still getting the details. One, a corporal, named Reagan was killed, the others wounded.

The terrorism and killings continued through the early fall of 1982. Nevertheless, we had a few reasons to be optimistic about the Middle East. Following the murder of Bashir Gemayel, his brother Amin succeeded him as president and pledged to support our efforts to bring peace to the region. He was a modest, able young man devoted to ending the bloody strife that had torn apart his homeland. During a visit to Washington, he urged me to keep the marines in Lebanon while efforts continued to reach a settlement. I agreed.

Meanwhile, several leaders of the Jewish community in America endorsed the September 1 peace initiative, agreeing that it contained the possible seeds for a long-term solution to the Arab-Israeli conflict. Shimon Peres's opposition Labor Party in Israel also endorsed the plan, despite Begin's continuing resistance, and we continued to get positive, if qualified, signs of interest from Arab leaders.

In November, Phil Habib returned to Lebanon to attempt to get the stalled plan for simultaneous withdrawal of Syrian and Israeli forces back on track. He said the situation had deteriorated substantially since Bashir Gemayel's assassination. The Israelis were now adamantly against leaving Beirut because they feared the PLO might then return to Lebanon; the Arab leaders complained that the continuing presence of Israeli forces in Beirut threatened whatever chances our peace initiative had.

In early December, after I made a brief trip to Latin America, Habib and I had lunch in my study. He had made another trip to the Middle East and was very gloomy. He said that he thought the prospects of ending the bloody war in Lebanon were growing worse each day instead of better. As long as the Israelis refused to leave Beirut, he said, the Arabs would cite their refusal as proof that they didn't want peace, and that it was a waste of the Arabs' time to negotiate with Habib. The Middle East was so unpredictable and explosive, Habib said, that time was of the essence: It was essential to consummate the withdrawal of all foreign forces as quickly as possible or we'd lose a historic opportunity for a lasting peace in the Middle East. The longer the process dragged on, the harder it would be to achieve peace because of the growing influence of radical factions within the PLO. While moderate PLO leaders were likely to accept, however grudgingly, the reality of Israel, they were being challenged by PLO factions dominated by hardline terrorists who would never accept it and would fight to the death to prevent it. Unless the Israelis left Lebanon soon and opened the way to a political settlement of the problems, Habib said, the Palestinian extremists would gain credibility among the Palestinian people and strengthen the hand of the radicals and their Islamic allies. If that happened, it was impossible to predict if there would be another solid chance for a long-term settlement of the problems.

I instructed Habib on his return to the Middle East to again tell Begin that Israel's intransigence might cost it its special relationship with America—and I crossed my fingers. King Hussein of Jordan, meanwhile, during a Washington visit, acknowledged that there were two sides to the Israeli-Arab conflict and indicated he was anxious to work with us to achieve a solution all parties could accept. "I really like him," I wrote in the diary after the visit. "He is our hope to lead the Arab side and the P.L.O. in negotiating with the Israelis. He has some problems in order to keep the trust of other Arab states and right now Israel is proving difficult. I told King Hussein that this was a top priority of mine and we'd go all out to bring peace in the Middle East and we'd stand by Jordan. . . ."

While King Hussein went to work on the Syrians, during the winter and early spring of 1982–83 we continued trying to persuade Menachem Begin to withdraw Israeli forces from Lebanon so that work on the broader peace process could resume and members of the multilateral force could go home. But he insisted that

Israel had to keep its troops in Lebanon or risk losing the advantage it had gained over the PLO and Syria in a war that had cost hundreds of Israeli casualties. The Soviets, meanwhile, had responded to Israel's crushing defeat of Syrian military forces and their Soviet-built weapons by sending the Syrians an array of their most modern arms.

We agreed that Israel had reason to be concerned about the safety of Israelis living in towns and villages near its northern border, but Habib, George Shultz, and I constantly reassured Begin that if Israel lived up to its agreement to pull its forces out of Lebanon, the United States would not allow it to be disadvantaged. Begin, however, wouldn't move. This left my Middle East peace initiative in limbo. Meanwhile, Israel added new settlements on the West Bank, which was in continued violation of UN Security Council Resolution 242 and ignored a cornerstone of my peace initiative. Long-term resolution of the Middle East's problems seemed further than ever from our grasp.

There were millions of Palestinians scattered throughout the Middle East, and all of them looked upon Israel and the West Bank (where 1.7 million Palestinians already lived) as their natural homeland. It seemed obvious that we weren't going to find an enduring Middle East peace until the world found a place for these Palestinians. Even though Israel claimed its ancestors' occupancy of the land gave it a right to the land in modern times, the Palestinians exerted an ancestral claim of their own on the West Bank: Their ancestors, too, had lived there for centuries.

During a visit to Washington early in 1983 in which he reiterated his desire to be a strong friend to the United States, President Mubarak of Egypt told me Israel's continuing refusal to leave Lebanon and its establishment of more settlements on the West Bank were inflaming the Arab world and reducing the momentum that had started to build up in favor of the September initiative. If progress wasn't made soon, he said, Israel's intractability would cause the initiative "to simply die on the vine." I agreed. But I also told him that by no means was the guilt all Israel's, and he agreed with me: "He believes [Israel] and the Syrians," I wrote in the diary, "may be playing a game . . . even though they are hostile toward each other, [they may favor] cutting up Lebanon between them."

Many Jews in America as well as in Israel had been shocked by

Sharon's bombardment of Beirut, which was shown so graphically on the world's television screens, as well as by allegations over his failure to halt the massacre by Christian militiamen of hundreds of Palestinians at the Sabra and Shatila refugee camps. They saw the Israeli assault as diametrically opposed to the moral values of their culture, and told me they believed that Begin's and Sharon's policies were contrary to the principles upon which Israel was founded. Many let me know that they supported our peace initiative and wished us well, and a few began speaking out publicly in criticism of Begin and Sharon. I'm sure this was difficult and painful for them because of their devotion to Israel—but they spoke out anyway, because they were anxious to bring a lasting and secure peace to the land they loved. With their help, and by emphasizing to Begin and Sharon that their policies were jeopardizing America's support of Israel, I still hoped to persuade Israel to leave Lebanon. But throughout that long winter and early spring, I continued to get nowhere with Begin. I suspect his resolve was stiffened by his confidence that supporters of Israel in Congress would ensure that the United States would never reduce its support of Israel, as well as by my own oft-stated commitment to always stand by Israel.

In February 1983, after a judicial panel asserted that he had been indirectly responsible for the massacres at the Palestinian refugee camps, Ariel Sharon resigned as Israel's minister of defense and was succeeded by Moshe Arens, the Israeli ambassador in Washington. I hoped this would mark a change in Israeli policies and help get the peace process started again.

When the foreign minister of Lebanon visited Washington that spring, I told him I was more determined than ever that the withdrawal of all foreign troops from Lebanon would resume soon, and that until that happened, our marines would remain in Lebanon. He said that it had been his experience with American presidents that they at first seemed willing to tackle the problems of Lebanon, but that they "advanced so far and then retreated." I told him I didn't have a reverse gear.

In late March—thanks in part, I think, to Moshe Arens—Israel began sending conciliatory signals indicating it was willing to withdraw from Lebanon under reasonable terms. We responded positively to the new attitude, and once again the level of my optimism that we would achieve peace in the Middle East began to rise. But we soon learned, tragically, that there were many people in the Middle East who did not want peace—at least not as long as it entailed the acceptance of Israel's right to exist.

On April 18, Nancy and I were awakened before dawn by a telephone call informing me that a terrorist's car bomb had just exploded at our embassy in Beirut, killing scores of Americans and Lebanese employees. Among the dead were five marine guards and other U.S. personnel, including our top CIA research specialist on the Middle East.

Shiite Muslim fundamentalists from Iran—who our intelligence people had recently learned were meddling in the convoluted affairs of Lebanon in order to further the Islamic revolution—took credit for the barbarous act. "Lord forgive me for the hatred I feel for the humans who can do such a cruel but cowardly deed," I wrote that night in my diary.

Five days later, I was at Andrews Air Force Base when the bodies of sixteen Americans murdered in the bombing came home. My diary entry that night:

> Nancy and I met individually all the families of the deceased. We were both in tears. All I could do was grip their hands. I was too choked up to speak. . . . [Later] home to change clothes and off to the White House correspondents dinner. I was supposed to do a routine of jokes, etc. I couldn't change gears that swiftly. So as not to put a damper on the evening . . . I waited till the last and then asked their pardon for not "singing for my supper" because of our sad journey to Andrews AF Base.

There were many, too many, days like that when I was president. Agonized as all of us were over this tragedy, George Shultz suggested that he go to the Middle East to attempt to breathe new life into the peace process Phil Habib had so ably kept alive for more than a year. Worn out from service above and beyond the call of duty, Habib wanted to resume the retirement from which we had lured him the year before.

Soon after he arrived in the Middle East, George sent me a cable in which he said that he thought all sides in the dispute seemed to be growing anxious to end the killing and destruction; he said he felt a degree of optimism that his mission would succeed.

It did: During two weeks of intensive negotiations, George worked out an agreement under which Israel promised to withdraw from Lebanon simultaneously with Syrian forces, and Lebanon, the second state in the Middle East (after Egypt) to formally recognize the existence of Israel, agreed to the establishment near its southern border of a security zone designed to enhance the protection of northern Israeli settlements.

Once more, we had reason to be hopeful about the future of the Middle East. Then Syria, apparently emboldened by its new late-model Russian arms and thousands of new Soviet "advisors," began sending signals that *it* would not leave Lebanon. This meant that the hard-won agreement between Lebanon and Israel couldn't be implemented, either.

Once again, we called on Jordan and Saudi Arabia, which had good reason to be worried about the growing Soviet presence in Syria as a serious threat to their oilfields, to apply pressure on Syria to leave. I reassured a nervous President Gemayel that we would keep our marines in Lebanon and not abandon his country while we tried to work out a settlement.

George Shultz went back to Lebanon to see if he could accelerate the departure of Syria, but, disappointingly, he found that the Arab world was badly fractured and either unable or unwilling to exert the necessary leverage to get Syria out of Lebanon. He and Robert C. (Bud) McFarlane of the National Security Council, who had taken over Habib's responsibilities as special envoy to the Middle East, tried hard through the summer and early fall of 1983 to persuade Syria to agree to leave, but the situation deteriorated steadily. The Syrian and Israeli forces remained entrenched, while old feuds between Lebanese Christians and Muslims began to erupt in an increasingly bitter civil war.

Meanwhile, new problems surfaced in the Middle East. Apparently deciding to move while much of the world was distracted by events in Lebanon, the region's foremost terrorist, Libya's Muammar Qaddafi—like Syria's president, Hafez al-Assad, a client of Moscow—began making new moves on two of his neighbors in North Africa, Sudan and Chad. France, the former colonial ruler of Chad, sent in troops to fight against the Libyan-backed rebels, and at France's request we sent several AWACS planes and fighter escorts to help keep tabs on Libyan aircraft.

At summer's end, the fighting in Lebanon between rival Christian, Muslim, and Druse militias grew heavier, putting Lebanon's fragile truce and everything we'd been working for there in jeopardy. The civil war spread rapidly, threatening the stability of the Gemayel government and making it uncertain how Israel and Syria would react. Soon, what had been chaos in Beirut became anarchy and then more tragedy. Syrian forces, Iranian Shiite Muslims, and radical members of the PLO began taking sides in the civil war, and fighting expanded; Druse and Muslim snipers started attacking the members of the multinational force as they patrolled Beirut, then began attacking the Beirut airport compound where our marines were housed, killing several of them.

Here are portions of several entries pertaining to the worsening crisis in Lebanon from my diary of September 1983:

Sept. 6
We lost two more Marines last night in Beirut. The civil war is running wild and could result in the collapse of the Gemayel govt. and then stuff would hit the fan. I called the parents of the two Marines—not easy.

Sept. 7
More on Lebanon. We have to show the flag for those Marines. I can't get the idea out of my head that some F-14's off the *Eisenhower* coming in at about 200 feet over the Marines and blowing hell out of a couple of artillery emplacements would be a tonic for the Marines and at the same time would deliver a message to these gun happy Middle East terrorists.

Sept. 8
Our Marine artillery and one ship off shore at Beirut returned fire of Druse artillery in the hills and silenced it. F-14's from the *Eisenhower* had flown a reconnaissance mission. I called the colonel in command. He said morale was high.

Sept. 10
Met with George Shultz. . . . Our main meeting was on Lebanon. The situation is worsening. We may be facing a choice of getting out or enlarging our mission. Chiefs of Staff want to send the *New Jersey*. I'm concerned as to whether that won't have a bad morale effect on our friends in Central America. We're going to move her through the

canal and offshore to the Atlantic before seeing whether she should head for Lebanon.

Sept. 11

N.S.C. is meeting . . . on Lebanon re a new cable from Bud Mc-Farlane. Troops obviously P.L.O. and Syrian have launched a new attack against the Lebanese Army. Our problem is do we expand our mission to aid the Lebanese army with artillery and air support? This could be seen as putting us in the war.

George Shultz, Bill Casey and Jim Baker have just left me at 2 p.m. to get more info on what is happening and where our partners in the M.N.F. [multinational force] stand. Contingent on what they learn I've ordered use of naval gun fire. My reasoning is that this can be explained as protection of our Marines hoping it might signal the Syrians to pull back. I don't think they want a war with us. If it doesn't work then we'll have to decide between pulling out or going to the Congress and making a case for greater involvement. N.S.C. will meet again at 6 p.m.

The meeting [was held and] didn't change anything so I've called for use of Navy fire power and air strikes if needed.

Sept. 12

N.S.C. on Lebanon. Things a little more quiet. A meeting there in Beirut as Gemayel attempts to get a cease fire. The Druse actually allowed the long delayed Red Cross column into the village where 40,000 Christian refugees have been besieged. . . .

Sept. 14

N.S.C.: Saudi Arabia may exert more pressure on Syria. Things are a little suspended in Lebanon . . .

Sept. 19

N.S.C.: Our Navy guns turned loose in support of the Lebanese army fighting to hold a position on a hill overlooking our Marines at the Beirut airport. This still comes under the head of defense. To allow those who have been shelling our marines to take that position would have made the Marine base untenable.

We met later—George Shultz, Cap W, etc., on a compromise we hope Congress will agree to regarding the War Powers Act and Congressional approval of the Marines being in Lebanon. Sen. Baker thinks he can get it through the Senate. Among other things it would settle their presence in Lebanon for 18 months.

Sept. 30

[Latest opinion polls] show I'm up on job rating, the economy. But on foreign policy—Lebanon—I'm way down. The people just don't know why we're there. There is deeply buried isolationist sentiment in our land.

After each marine was killed that September, I telephoned his parents and tried to console them. They were difficult, terrible calls to make. One father asked me: "Are we in Lebanon for any reason worth my son's life?"

I gulped and said, yes, there was. "No words I can say can ever make up for the loss of your son, but perhaps you might find a little comfort in knowing that your son died while he was living up to the finest traditions of his country and the Marine Corps . . . America is a country whose people have always believed we had a special responsibility to try to bring peace and democracy to others in the world. And brave men and women have always been willing to give up their lives in the defense of freedom—and that's what our marines are doing in the Middle East."

Some men, I told another parent, go through life and never find themselves in a position where they are called upon to do one of the tough jobs that have to be done. Some face that moment and fail. But most Americans accept and do the tough jobs because they know there is no one else to do them, and they know in their hearts that they must be done.

Perhaps no words could convince a grieving father that his son had died for a just purpose; yet I firmly believed in what we were doing in Lebanon. And our efforts had seemed to be working, giving time to the Lebanese, the Syrians, and the Israelis to work out a solution to their problems.

Although some Americans, like that father, had doubts about our purpose in Lebanon, I tried to convince them that America had a duty to be there. "The Middle East," I'd say, "is pretty much everybody's business, it's important to all of us." But to have to explain this to those families—and, as I was to learn shortly, this task had only just begun—was very difficult and very, very painful.

While I tried to persuade Congress and grieving parents that the United States had to maintain its peacekeeping role in Lebanon, the civil war went on unrelentingly, with more and more attacks on the airport and the positions of French troops who were assigned to the multinational force. At this time, Bill Clark, who'd been my national security advisor for almost two years, asked to be relieved of his post, and agreed to take on the slower-paced job of secretary of the interior; he was fatigued and wanted a change.

When Jim Baker heard about it, he told me he was getting a little tired of the routine as White House chief of staff and asked me to give him the NSC job. He proposed that Mike Deaver, whom I knew well from our California days, take over his job.

I agreed to this. But then Ed Meese, Bill Clark, Bill Casey, and Cap Weinberger got together and tried to convince me it was a bad idea. Some were not enthusiastic about having Mike, whose job involved overseeing White House political and public relations, become chief of staff. There was also resistance to Jim as national security advisor. I decided to reverse myself and scrap the change. Otherwise, I thought, the result would be friction among the cabinet and the White House staff.

"Jim took it well but Mike was pretty upset," I noted in my diary. "It was an unhappy day all around. An NSPG [National Security Planning Group] meeting on Lebanon. No decisions, just a listing of the problems. Not a pleasant evening what with all the hassle over the N.S.C. spot."

After that, Bill Casey and some of my more conservative supporters began pushing me to give the NSC job to Jeane Kirkpatrick, who was either tired or bored after more than two years at the UN. She had her heart set on the job and told me so. I admired Jeane, but I had noticed there was some bad chemistry between her and George Shultz, so I decided to give the spot to Bud McFarlane.

My decision not to appoint Jim Baker as national security advisor, I suppose, was a turning point for my administration, although I had no idea at the time how significant it would prove to be.

60

O<small>N</small> F<small>RIDAY</small>, October 21, 1983, four days after Bud McFarlane took over his new post at the NSC, Nancy and I flew to Georgia for a golfing weekend at the Augusta National Golf Course with George Shultz, Don Regan, former U.S. Senator Nicholas Brady, and their wives. After the dispute over the NSC job, a series of frustrating meetings over Lebanon, and more battles with the Democrats over the budget, I was looking forward to a couple of days of relaxation, although I hadn't played golf in quite a while and didn't have high hopes for my performance on the links.

Shortly after four o'clock Saturday morning, Nancy and I were awakened by a telephone call from Bud, who was in Augusta as part of the traveling White House support team. He said it was urgent that I meet with him and George Shultz immediately in the living room of the Eisenhower Cottage, where we were staying. This was the cottage Ike always used whenever he was on a golfing vacation at Augusta. In robe and pajamas, I listened to them explain that the Organization of Eastern Caribbean States had asked us to intervene militarily on the island of Grenada, one of their neighbors in the Caribbean located ninety miles north of Venezuela. Via a secure telephone link with Washington, George Bush, serving in his role as head of the White House crisis management team, also participated in this middle-of-the-night conference.

We'd been watching events on Grenada very closely for several days. In a bloody coup the previous week, Grenada's prime minister, Maurice Bishop, a Marxist protégé of Fidel Castro who had invited Cuban workers to Grenada to build a suspiciously huge new airport on the island, had been executed by leftists who were even more radically committed to Marxism than he was. The leaders of Grenada's island neighbors—Jamaica, Barbados, St. Vincent's, St. Lucia, Dominica, and Antigua—told us that under Bishop they had been worried by what appeared to be a large Cuban-sponsored military buildup on Grenada vastly disproportionate to its needs; now, they said, these even more radical Marxists in control of Grenada had launched a murderous reign of terror against their enemies. Unless they were stopped, the Caribbean neighbors said, it was just a matter of time before the Grenadians and Castro moved on *their* countries. They said that they wanted to join together in ousting the Cubans from Grenada before it was too late, but lacked the military wherewithal to do so, and asked us to join with them in dislodging the radicals.

There was one other thing we had to consider: Eight hundred Americans who attended medical school on Grenada, all of them potential hostages.

Under these circumstances, there was only one answer I could give to McFarlane and Shultz and those six countries who asked for our help.

Several days earlier, after the coup and Bishop's execution, I had ordered a flotilla of navy ships that had just left for Lebanon as part of a routine rotation of marines there to make a detour toward Grenada, in case it was needed to evacuate the students. I asked McFarlane how long the Pentagon thought it would need to prepare a rescue mission on Grenada.

He said the Joint Chiefs of Staff believed it could be done in forty-eight hours.

I said, "Do it."

We agreed that the operation would have to be mounted under conditions of the strictest secrecy, so that the Grenadian forces and Cubans on Grenada would not have time to bring in reinforcements or to make a run for the American students at St. George's University Medical School. Cuba was near enough that with forewarning it could send troops to the island in a hurry. If there were any leaks, the result could be war between us and Cuba, which we didn't want, and the taking of hundreds of Americans as hostage.

We decided not to inform anyone in advance about the rescue mission in order to reduce the possibilities of a leak. Grenada had been a British colony for almost two hundred years before it won its independence in 1974, and was still a member of the British Commonwealth. We did not even inform the Britsh beforehand, because I thought it would increase the possibility of a leak at our end and elevate the risk to our students.

Frankly, there was another reason I wanted secrecy. It was what I call the "post-Vietnam syndrome," the resistance of many in Congress to the use of military force abroad for any reason, because of our nation's experience in Vietnam. No rational person ever wants to unleash military force, but I believe there are situations when it is necessary for the United States to do so—especially when the defense of freedom and democracy is involved or the lives and liberty of our citizens are at stake. I understood what Vietnam had meant for the country, but I believed the United States couldn't remain spooked forever by this experience to the point where it refused to stand up and defend its legitimate national security interests. I suspected that, if we told the leaders of Congress about the operation, even under terms of strictest confidentiality, there would be some who would leak it to the press together with the prediction that Grenada was going to become "another Vietnam." We were already running into this phenomenon in our efforts to halt the spread of Communism in Central America, and some congressmen were raising the issue of "another Vietnam" in Lebanon while fighting to restrict the president's constitutional powers as commander in chief.

We couldn't say no to those six small countries who had asked us for help. We'd have no credibility or standing in the Americas if we did. If it ever became known, which I knew it would, that we had turned them down, few of our friends around the world would trust us completely as an ally again.

I knew that if word of the rescue mission leaked out in advance, we'd hear this from some in Congress: "Sure, it's starting small, but once you make that first commitment, Grenada's going to become another Vietnam." Well, that wasn't true. And that's one reason why the rescue operation on Grenada was conducted in total secrecy. We didn't ask anybody, we just did it.

After giving my approval to the operation, I went back to sleep.

After an hour or so, I got up to play golf. As I'd expected, my golf game needed some work. I hadn't played more than four times in the previous three years, and it showed.

When we reached the sixteenth hole, a group of Secret Service agents suddenly surrounded our group, stopped the golf game, and herded us into White House limousines. The situation was this: An armed man had smashed a pickup truck through a nearby gate at the course and taken seven hostages, including two White House assistants, to the pro shop. There he was threatening to kill them unless I agreed to meet with him.

Normally, I wouldn't have made any response to demands by a terrorist. That only encourages more terrorism. But I was told that the gunman was very unbalanced and the lives of the hostages were in imminent danger. I got on the car phone and called the pro shop, and when the phone was answered, I said: "Hello, this is Ronald Reagan . . ."

There was a silence, then the man hung up without saying a word and the phone went dead. We dialed the pro shop again—in fact, four more times—but every time, he hung up on me. He was insisting on speaking to me face to face, which the Secret Service agents wouldn't permit.

While the agents searched the golf course and the woods around it to discover whether the man had any accomplices, they urged me to return immediately to Washington. I vetoed the idea. I was safe and didn't think we should make any sudden moves that would suggest an air of crisis; this might encourage the press to start digging and learn about the Grenada operation. We went back to the Eisenhower Cottage. After a few hours, the gunman released the hostages unharmed and was arrested.

(The second of our two White House aides wasn't actually *released.* He said to the gunman, "Gee, it's hot in here, don't you think a six-pack of beer would be good?" When the gunman agreed with that proposal, our man walked out of the pro shop on an errand to get the beer, never to return.)

That night, our group had a pleasant dinner together. Nancy and I went to bed a little earlier than usual because we were tired after the early morning interruption the night before. At about 2:30 A.M., however, our phone rang again. Again it was Bud McFarlane: He said a suicide bomber had just driven a truckload of dynamite past our sentries and smashed into the marine barracks at the Beirut Airport. According to the first reports, at least one hundred marines had been killed.

There was to be no more sleep for us that night. I got on the phone with the Pentagon to make sure that everything possible was being done to protect the remaining marines in Beirut, then met with George Shultz and Bud for several hours in the same living room where we'd spent much of the night before. As dawn approached, the news from Beirut became grimmer and grimmer. At 6:30 A.M., we went to the airport, boarded Air Force One, and flew to Washington for what was to become a full day of National Security Council meetings in the White House Situation Room. We discussed the bombings and the preparations for the Grenada operation, which was scheduled to get started late that night with the infiltration of commando teams to gather intelligence paving the way for the landing the next day.

On Monday, October 24, the news from Beirut became even more sickening: As rescue workers sifted through the rubble of the barracks and found more bodies, and as some of the critically injured marines died, the full magnitude of the catastrophe became apparent: In all, 241 marines had died as they slept, resting from the duties of trying to keep peace in Lebanon. Two miles away, and two minutes after the blast at the airport, fifty-eight French soldiers, also members of the multinational force, had been killed by a second car bomb.

The evidence indicated that both suicide vehicles were driven by radical Shiite fundamentalists suicidally bent on the pursuit of martyrdom. They were members of the same group responsible for the barbarous bombing of our embassy in Beirut the previous April, a group whose religious leaders promised instant entry to Paradise for killing an enemy of Iran's theocracy.

Nancy and I were in a state of grief, made almost speechless by the magnitude of the loss. But I had to go on with my schedule for the day: an important meeting with our ambassador in Moscow, Arthur Hartman; a visit from the president of Togo; long-scheduled visits to the Oval Office by more than a dozen people arranged by various members of Congress—a Notre Dame coed who had won a science prize for devising an improved method for classifying and determining the age of fossil reptiles, a young blind man who had just walked across the country from Idaho to Maryland to prove handicapped people could do anything they set out to do, several newly appointed ambassadors, and others. I'll never forget how difficult it was trying to pay attention to the things that were very important in the lives of these Americans, while trying to grasp the enormity of the tragedy in Beirut.

At 2:00 P.M., the Joint Chiefs of Staff briefed me on the final details of the Grenada operation, which was scheduled to start at 9:00 P.M. Throughout the day, we continued to worry about leaks that could endanger the students. But this time (for a change) there were no leaks from the White House, the Pentagon, or Congress. It was one secret we managed to keep.

That evening, after our troops were well on their way, I invited members of the congressional leadership—Tip O'Neill, Jim Wright, Robert Byrd, Howard Baker, and Bob Michel, along with Secretary of State George Shultz—to the family quarters in the White House, telling them in advance that the topic we were going to discuss was so secret that they should not even mention to their wives that they were going to the White House. The briefing began shortly after eight, with Cap Weinberger, Bud McFarlane, and the chairman of the Joint Chiefs of Staff, General John Vessey, joining me in disclosing the secret appeal we'd received from Grenada's neighbors, and going over plans for the rescue mission.

Just before nine, I was called out of the briefing to take a call from Margaret Thatcher. As soon as I heard her voice, I knew she was very angry. She said she had just learned about the impending operation (probably from British officials on Grenada) and asked me in the strongest language to call off the operation. Grenada, she reminded me, was part of the British Commonwealth, and the United States had no business interfering in its affairs.

I had intended to call her after the meeting, once the operation was actually under way, but she'd gotten word of it before I had the chance to do so. I told her about the request we'd received from the Organization of Eastern Caribbean States and said I had believed we had to act quickly and covertly because I feared any communication could result in a leak and spoil the advantage of surprise.

She was very adamant and continued to insist that we cancel our landings on Grenada. I couldn't tell her that it had already begun. This troubled me because of our close relationship.

Early the next morning, after more than nineteen hundred army rangers and marines had landed at two points on Grenada, we announced the news of the Grenada rescue operation to the press. Our forces, despite greater-than-expected resistance, quickly gained control of the island's two airports and secured the campus where the American students were. The Marxists and their Cuban puppeteers were defeated. After I received word that the students were safe and the Marxists neutralized, I wrote in my diary: "Success seems to shine on us and I thank the Lord for it. He has really held me in the hollow of His hand."

The price we had to pay to ensure the freedom of Grenada had been high—nineteen American lives and more than one hundred men injured. But the price would have been much higher if the Soviet Union had been allowed to perpetuate this penetration of our hemisphere. It would have only spread from there.

Before the landings, we had been told there were about two hundred Cuban workers on the island assigned to the airport construction project; we suspected that they might have had weapons training as members of the Cuban military reserves. But our troops encountered resistance from more than seven hundred well-trained and well-armed Cuban warriors, the first evidence we got that the Communist influence on Grenada was even greater than we or its neighbors had suspected.

Militarily, we can look back on the operation as a textbook success. When it was going on, though, there were many uncertainties and potential problems, especially regarding the safety of our students; I suspect that none of us who participated in planning the operation slept well the night before.

The Marxists managed to play one dirty trick on us: Atop one hill on the island there was a mental hospital, and near it was a Grenadian army headquarters and barracks. The army installation was one of the legitimate targets for our airplanes. The Marxist thugs took down the flag over their building and raised it over the mental hospital, and as a result planes attacked the hospital until our forces on the ground alerted them to the ruse.

We discovered over the next few days that Grenada was far from the balmy resort island it was depicted as in travel brochures. Even more than we had realized, it was already a Soviet-Cuban bastion in the Caribbean. Grenada's neighbors had been right. We got there just in time. Grenada's new airport, with its nine-thousand-foot runway, had been designed not for tourism as Maurice Bishop claimed, but for refueling and servicing Soviet and Cuban military aircraft. The barracks used by the Cuban "workers" on Grenada contained enough weapons and ammunition to equip thousands of terrorists. In the Cuban embassy, we found hollow walls stuffed with more weapons, plus documents linking Grenada's Marxists to Havana and Moscow, including one letter sent six months before by a Soviet general to the commander of the Grenadian army that boasted Grenada could be proud of itself for becoming the third outpost of Communism in the New World—after Cuba and Nicaragua—and adding that soon there would be a fourth, El Salvador.

Our troops brought back this letter and hundreds of other documents proving that the Soviet Union and Cuba had been bankrolling the Marxists on Grenada as part of a scheme to bring Communism to the entire region. The program was just beginning in Grenada; it was intended to go all the way through the Caribbean and Central America. We took this storehouse of documents to a hangar at Andrews Air Force Base outside Washington and invited the press to examine it. Reporters would have found evidence of everything we were saying. But very few did. Instead, for several days, most of the news commentators focused on claims that the landings on Grenada had been reckless. They said I was trying to turn the Caribbean into "another Vietnam"—until it began to sink in that the American people understood what was happening on Grenada and agreed that the operation had been a necessary step to foil Communist penetration of our hemisphere.

As for the eight hundred American students, I was among many in our country whose eyes got a little misty when I watched their arrival in the United States on television and saw some of them lean down and kiss American soil the moment that they stepped off the airplanes that brought them home. When some of the students later came to the White House and embraced the soldiers who had rescued them, it was quite a sight for a former governor who had once seen college students spit on anyone wearing a military uniform. In my diary entry for that day I remarked that we had had "the most wonderful South Lawn ceremony we've ever had. About 400 of the medical students we rescued on Grenada came here plus 40 military, all of whom had been on Grenada. Four branches of the service . . . it was heartwarming, indeed thrilling to see these young people clasp these men in uniforms to their hearts."

Some of the students told me tender stories, including several who said they had had to hide beneath their beds for more than twenty-four hours while bullets whistled past their windows. Then, they said, they heard a shout: "Okay, you can come on out." They walked down the stairs, because, as one said, they'd just heard the greatest sound they had ever heard: the voice of an army sergeant, who, along with the other young soldiers, then bravely put their own bodies between the students and enemy fire while escorting them to rescue helicopters.

One of the army helicopter pilots later sent me a letter pointing out that Grenada produced half the world's nutmeg. If the Soviets had succeeded in their attempted takeover of the island, he said, they would have controlled much of the world's nutmeg supply. "You can't make an egg nog without nutmeg," he pointed out, "and some people would say you can't have Christmas without an egg nog. The Russians were trying to steal Christmas. We stopped them."

The people of Grenada greeted our soldiers much as the people of France and Italy welcomed our GIs after they liberated them from Nazism at the end of World War II. The Grenadians had been captives of a totalitarian state just as much as the people of Europe. Later, I went to Grenada and experienced a welcome that showed how deeply the Grenadian people felt about our efforts on their behalf. There were no YANKEE GO HOME signs on Grenada, just an outpouring of love and appreciation from tens of thousands of people—most of its population—and banners proclaiming GOD BLESS AMERICA.

I probably never felt better during my presidency than I did that day. I think our decision to stand up to Castro and the brownshirts on Grenada not only stopped the Communists in their tracks in that part of the world but perhaps helped all Americans stand a little taller.

But if that week produced one of the highest of the high points of my eight years in the presidency, the bombing of the marine barracks in Beirut had produced the lowest of the low.

61

On a Friday morning in early November 1983, Nancy and I flew to Camp Lejeune in North Carolina for a service honoring the marines murdered in Lebanon and the American fighting men who lost their lives on Grenada. "It was a dreary day with constant rain which somehow seemed appropriate," I wrote that night in my diary.

> All the ceremonies were outdoors, rain or no rain. It was a moving service and as hard as anything we've ever done. At the end, taps got to both of us. The only indoor part was a receiving line meeting the families of the deceased. They were so wonderful, sometimes widows or mothers would just put their arms around me, their head on my chest, and quietly cry. One little boy eight or nine politely handed me a manila folder saying it was something he'd written about his father. Later when I could read it, I found it was a poem entitled *Loneliness*. We helicoptered back to Cherry Point and there I addressed a crowd of Marines and families. Before leaving Lejeune I spoke briefly to the families I'd met in the line . . . the Lord was with me. The right words came. We flew back to Washington—a few meetings and then to Camp David where it was snowing.

I later corresponded with and spoke again with some of the families who lost loved ones during the barbarous suicide attack in Beirut. Many, God bless them, reached out and tried to help me deal with my grief. I'll share one of the letters I received:

Dear President Reagan:

I am the mother of L/Cpl David Cosner, killed recently in Lebanon.

I want to thank you for your kind letter sharing our grief. I know this was hard for you to do since you think everyone is blaming you for this tragedy. I was very angry at everyone, including you. I was not ready to give David up and I felt it was not *our* country he was keeping peace for.

As the 23rd of Oct. dragged on, I was constantly reminded that I had asked God to watch over him. I knew if he was safe, God was giving him strength to help his fallen buddies, but, if he was dead, I also know he would be at peace in God's arms. This turmoil continued until 9 P.M. The blessed peace and comfort came, telling me he was in his Heavenly Home.

I really believe it was simply David's destiny to have been there.

He was an excellent Marine and therefore had the *choice* of any base in the world. He chose to stay at Camp Lejeune knowing he was going to Lebanon.

He was not sent nor did he have to go. This is why I am telling you this so you will know that David did indeed give his most precious gift to America, very unselfishly, and some good must come of this tragedy.

He left us a beautiful 2½ year old granddaughter, Leanna, and wonderful memories from the 22 years we shared.

I am so proud to be David's mother and I know in time I will get the hugs from him that are denied me now.

I have asked our wonderful town to stand behind you, our chosen leader, so our enemies will know we are strong. One Nation, Under God.

I pray that God will give you the strength to make the right decisions and keep you safe in His protective arms.

Sincerely,
Marva Cosner

After the service at Camp Lejeune, the Secret Service began randomly altering the route of Marine I because of intelligence reports that Islamic terrorists were plotting to fire rockets at the White House helicopter. An informant in Lebanon also reported that Shiite terrorists were planning to kill my daughter Maureen, which led to a strengthening of her Secret Service protection.

In the profound sadness that fell over the whole country in the aftermath of the Beirut bombing, I had to decide what to do next in Lebanon. Not surprisingly, there was new pressure in Congress to leave that country. Although I did my best to explain to the American people why our troops were there, I knew many still didn't understand it.

I believed in—and still believe in—the policy and decisions that originally sent the marines to Lebanon. The purpose of having our troops and those of the other three nations in Beirut was to help keep the peace and to free the Lebanese army to go after the various militias and warlords who were terrorizing the country. We never had the intention of getting involved in Lebanon's civil war.

For a while, our policy seemed to be working. There was genuine peace on the streets of Beirut. One woman wrote to me that for the first time in eight years she was able to send her children to school in Beirut; a young American woman whose fiancé was employed in Lebanon wrote that he said that if it hadn't been for the multinational force, there would have been several massacres of Christians in Lebanon.

Still, as we were learning, the situation in Beirut was much more difficult and complex than we initially believed. The central government of Lebanon that we were trying to help had all but wasted away, weakened by the virtual collapse of the 1943 agreement under which Lebanon gained its independence from France, and which provided the basis for the sharing of power between Christians and Muslims. With Muslim and Christian believers splintered into many competing sects, Lebanon's political landscape had become a clutter of disorder, violence, and mayhem. Our policy was based on the expectation that the Lebanese army would subdue the militias of these rival groups and reestablish the central government's control over the country while the multinational force helped maintain order. But the Lebanese army simply wasn't strong enough to bottle up the centuries of seething sectarian hatred in Lebanon; nor did we realize until it was too late that many members of the Lebanese army had sympathies for one warlord or another and didn't have the will to fight their countrymen, especially those with similar religious beliefs. We also had not recognized that, when our marines took over the responsibility to keep open Beirut's civilian airport, they were placed in possibly the most vulnerable spot in the city, a wide-open space where they were vulnerable to snipers in the surrounding hills. At first, the marines had camped outdoors in tents, but when the sniping and shooting got heavy, their officers decided they would be safer if they slept in a steel-and-concrete building at the airport. These officers hadn't counted on the depravity of a suicide bomber.

The price we had to pay in Beirut was so great, the tragedy at the barracks was so enormous, and the virulent problems of Lebanon were so intractable, that it wasn't possible to continue with the policy that had put our marines in Lebanon without taking a second look at it. Our choices were limited and none of them easy. In the weeks immediately after the bombing, I believed the last thing we should do was turn tail and leave. If we did that, it would say to the terrorists of the world that all it took to change American foreign policy was to murder some Americans.

If we walked away, we'd also be giving up on the moral commitment to Israel that had originally sent our marines to Lebanon. We'd be abandoning all the progress made during almost two years of trying to mediate a settlement in the Middle East. We'd be saying that the sacrifice of those marines had been for nothing. We'd be inviting the Russians to supplant the United States as the most influential superpower in the Middle East. After more than a year of fighting and mounting chaos in Beirut, the biggest winner would be Syria, a Soviet client. Yet, the irrationality of Middle Eastern politics forced us to rethink our policy there.

How do you deal with a people driven by such a religious zeal that they are willing to sacrifice their lives in order to kill an enemy simply because he doesn't worship the same God they do? People who believe that if they do that, they'll go instantly to heaven? In the Iran-Iraq war, radical Islamic fundamentalists sent more than a thousand young boys—teenagers and younger—to their deaths by telling them to charge and detonate land mines—and the boys did so joyously because they believed, "Tonight, we will be in Paradise."

In early November, a new problem cropped up in the Middle East: Iran began threatening to close the Gulf of Hormuz, a vital corridor for the shipment of oil from the Persian Gulf. I said that if they followed through with this threat, it would constitute an illegal interference with navigation of the sea, and we would use force to keep the corridor open. Meanwhile, another development promised to bring change to the Middle East: Menachem Begin, deeply depressed after the death of his beloved wife and apparently devoid of the spirit he once had to continue fighting against Israel's Arab enemies and its serious economic problems, resigned as prime minister.

King Fahd of Saudi Arabia, perhaps thinking American resolve on behalf of Israel might have been diminished by the horrendous human loss in Beirut, approached us with a new peace proposal that he said could end the warfare in Lebanon, and also take Syria out of the Soviet camp and put it in ours. But the proposal would have required us to reduce our commitment to Israel, and I said no thanks.

I still believed that it was essential to continue working with moderate Arabs to find a solution to the Middle East's problem, and that we should make selective sales of American weapons to the moderate Arabs as proof of our friendship. In this I was constantly frustrated, following the AWACS sale, by strong resistance from Israel's supporters in Congress. That undermined our efforts to improve relations with the moderate Arabs. At the same time, I was beginning to have doubts whether the Arab world, with its ancient tribal rivalries, centuries of internecine strife, and almost pathological hatred of Israel, was as serious about supporting our peace efforts in the Middle East as King Fahd of Saudi Arabia and King Hussein of Jordan said they were. I believed these two monarchs were sincere when they said they were applying pressure on Syria to leave Lebanon, as we renewed our efforts to convince the Israelis to leave. But the Arab world was anything but united on this issue—as on many other issues—and I was beginning to wonder how much we could count on it to help us achieve success.

In any case, Israel wouldn't budge; and Syria, with its new Soviet weapons and advisors, was growing more arrogant than ever, and rejected several proposals by the Saudis aimed at getting them out of Lebanon.

Our intelligence experts found it difficult to establish conclusively who was responsible for the attack on the barracks. Although several air strikes were planned against possible culprits, I canceled them because our experts said they were not absolutely sure they were the right targets. I didn't want to kill innocent people. While our intelligence people resumed their efforts to confirm that we had the right targets, Israeli and French forces, convinced they had sufficient information, raided the same Shiite Muslim redoubts in the mountains that we had considered attacking.

When Druse militiamen began a new round of shelling of the marines several weeks after the bombing at the airport, we had to decide whether to ignore it or respond with firepower and escalate our role in the Lebanese war. "We're a divided group," I wrote in my journal after a National Security Council meeting held to discuss the renewed shelling in early December. "I happen to believe taking out a few batteries might give them pause to think. Joint Chiefs believe it might drastically alter our mission and lead to major increases in troops for Lebanon . . ." The next day, I wrote:

A hectic three quarters of a day with contentious staff and cabinet members on both sides of a couple of issues. One with N.S.C. had to do with attacking Syrian targets around Beirut in response to shelling of our Marines. Some wanted to do this whether they were responsible for the shelling or not. I came down on the side of only responding if we knew our target was the source *unless* that target was in a populated area—then take a nearby target if it was of the same organization such as Druse or P.L.O. etc. Fire at Syrians only if they had fired at us.

Then, the Syrians took an action that more or less made our decision for us: Late the next day, a gray and cold Saturday when Nancy and I were at Camp David, Bud McFarlane and Cap Weinberger separately called me with the news that Syria had launched a ground-to-air missile at one of our unarmed reconnaissance planes during a routine sweep over Beirut. Although there was some resistance from Cap and the Joint Chiefs over whether we should retaliate, I told him to give the order for an air strike against the offending antiaircraft batteries.

We had previously let the Syrians know that our reconnaissance operations in support of the marines were only defensive in nature. Our marines were not adversaries in the conflict, and any offensive act directed against them would be replied to. The following morning, more than two dozen navy aircraft carried out the mission.

One crewman was killed and another captured by the Syrians. Our planes subsequently took out almost a dozen Syrian antiaircraft and missile-launching sites, a radar installation, and an ammo dump. When the Syrians fired again at one of our reconnaissance aircraft, I gave the order to fire the sixteen-inch guns of the battleship *New Jersey* on them.

Two days later, we had a new cease-fire in Lebanon, a result, I'm sure, of the pressure of the long guns of the *New Jersey*—but, like almost all the other cease-fires in Beirut, it didn't last long.

Several weeks after the bombing at the barracks, Cap Weinberger sent me a report that he said he was planning to make public. The report blamed the barracks massacre on negligence by the marines' commanding officers in Beirut. However, I wanted to accept full blame for the tragedy.

I was worried about the effects the report would have on families who had lost loved ones in Beirut, and I thought how it would probably spur the press to pillory the marine commanders, who, I believed, had thought they were doing the best they could for their men under difficult conditions, and who in their own hearts had probably already suffered greatly for what had happened. So I took the full responsibility; I was the one who had sent them there.

As 1984 began, it was becoming clearer that the Lebanese army was either unwilling or unable to end the civil war into which we had been dragged reluctantly. It was clear that the war was likely to go on for an extended period of time. As the sniping and shelling of their camp continued, I gave an order to evacuate all the marines to ships anchored off Lebanon. At the end of March, the ships of the Sixth Fleet and the marines who had fought to keep peace in Lebanon moved on to other assignments.

We had to pull out. By then, there was no question about it: Our policy wasn't working. We couldn't stay there and run the risk of another suicide attack on the marines. No one wanted to commit our troops to a full-scale war in the Middle East. But we couldn't remain in Lebanon and be in the war on a halfway basis, leaving our men vulnerable to terrorists with one hand tied behind their backs.

We hadn't committed the marines to Beirut in a snap decision, and we weren't alone. France, Italy, and Britain were also part of the multinational force, and we all thought it was a good plan. And for a while, as I've said, it had been working.

I'm not sure how we could have anticipated the catastrophe at the marine barracks. Perhaps we didn't appreciate fully enough the depth of the hatred and the complexity of the problems that make the Middle East such a jungle. Perhaps the idea of a suicide car bomber committing mass murder to gain instant entry to Paradise was so foreign to our own values and consciousness that it did not create in us the concern for the marines' safety that it should have. Perhaps we should have anticipated that members of the Lebanese military whom we were trying to assist would simply lay down their arms and refuse to fight their own countrymen. In any case, the sending of the marines to Beirut was the source of my greatest regret and my greatest sorrow as president.

Every day since the death of those boys, I have prayed for them and their loved ones.

In the months and the years that followed, our experience in Lebanon led to the adoption by the administration of a set of principles to guide America in the application of military force abroad, and I would recommend it to future presidents. The policy we adopted included these principles:

1. The United States should not commit its forces to military action overseas unless the cause is vital to our national interest.
2. If the decision is made to commit our forces to combat abroad, it must be done with the clear intent and support needed to *win*. It should not be a halfway or tentative commitment, and there must be clearly defined and realistic objectives.
3. Before we commit our troops to combat, there must be reasonable assurance that the cause we are fighting for and the actions we take will have the support of the American people and Congress. (We all felt that the Vietnam War had turned into such a tragedy because military action had been undertaken without sufficient assurances that the American people were behind it.)
4. Even after all these other tests are met, our troops should be committed to combat abroad *only* as a last resort, when no other choice is available.

After the marines left Beirut, we continued a search for peace and a diplomatic solution to the problems in the Middle East. But the war in Lebanon grew even more violent, the Arab-Israeli conflict became more bitter, and the Middle East continued to be a source of problems for me and our country.

PART FIVE

Iran-Contra

62

For eight years the press called me the "Great Communicator." Well, one of my greatest frustrations during those eight years was my inability to communicate to the American people and to Congress the seriousness of the threat we faced in Central America.

In the early 1980s, Soviet Communism was not just another competing economic system run by people who happened to disagree with us about the merits of capitalism and free enterprise: It was a predatory system of absolute, authoritarian rule that had an insatiable appetite for expansion; it was determined to impose tyranny wherever it went, rob people of fundamental human rights, destroy democratic governments, subvert churches and labor unions, turn the courts and the press into instruments of dictatorship, forbid free elections, imprison and execute critics without charge or trial, and reward the few at the top of the monolith with the spoils of corruption and dictatorial rule. In short, it was against everything Americans have stood for for more than two hundred years.

I wasn't the first president concerned about conspiracies and machinations by distant powers in the western hemisphere. Since 1823, when our fifth president enunciated the Monroe Doctrine, the United States has stood firmly against interference by European nations in the affairs of the Americas.

The Soviet Union had violated the Monroe Doctrine and gotten away with it twice, first in Cuba, then in Nicaragua. In 1959, Fidel

Castro had marched into Havana to create a Soviet satellite within ninety miles of our shores. In 1962, John F. Kennedy stood up to Castro and Moscow and blocked the establishment on Cuban soil of a Soviet missile base capable of hurling nuclear weapons at the United States. Nevertheless, twenty years later, Cuba was, in effect, serving the very function that had caused President Kennedy to face off against Khrushchev: It was a de facto base, if needed, for Soviet missile submarines and aircraft capable of delivering nuclear devastation to the United States. We got confirmation of this in 1981, with the arrival in Cuban waters of a Soviet ship designed with a single purpose: to neutralize American efforts to detect Soviet missile submarines near our shores.

I've always thought it was a tragic error for President Kennedy to abandon the Cuban freedom fighters during the 1961 Bay of Pigs invasion. If he hadn't done so, perhaps history would have been much different in Central America. Training of the invasion force, all Cuban refugees, had started under President Eisenhower. The master plan he had approved called for covert American forces to provide air support for the refugees against Castro's tanks, aircraft, and heavy weapons, and to bomb the airport where his military aircraft were based, while the refugees invaded Cuba. Everything was going according to schedule—the Cuban fighting force had landed and our carriers were waiting offshore with the support aircraft—when Adlai Stevenson, our UN representative, came storming down from New York and told President Kennedy: "I have promised the United Nations that we are not going to in any way interfere in Cuba . . ."

After the Cuban freedom fighters had already landed, an order went out to the carriers: Don't send the planes. President Kennedy had been talked into stranding those courageous men on the beach, letting them die or be captured. The least he could have done was to let the planes come in and rescue them.

By the time I got to the White House, Cuba was well entrenched as an advance base for furthering Soviet colonization of the Americas. It had Latin America's largest army, billions of dollars' worth of Soviet arms, and military training centers devoted to the exportation of Communism, terror, and revolution throughout the Caribbean and Central America, not to mention Angola, Mozambique, and Ethiopia.

Twenty years after Castro's victory, Marxism achieved its second triumph in the New World: the Sandinista takeover of Nicaragua. Dictator Anastasio Somoza was brought down by a coalition of Nicaraguans unhappy with his despotic reign; then, as soon as he stepped down, the Sandinistas, the best organized of the groups, moved in and stole the revolution.

Previously, the Nicaraguan rebels had asked the Organization of American States to ask Somoza to step down to end the civil war and the killing. The OAS had asked the rebels what their goals were. Their answer: self-determination for the Nicaraguan people, free elections, free trade unions, a free press, and a constitution patterned after that of the United States. But as soon as Somoza was gone, the Sandinistas imposed rigid military rule and ousted the leaders of the other factions that had fought with them in the revolution—and they announced that their revolution wouldn't stop at Nicaragua's borders.

Now the Soviets had a second satellite in the Americas. If we didn't already have enough proof of their intentions, we captured secret papers on Grenada that documented how the USSR and Cuba were acting in concert to make the Caribbean a Communist lake.

Why did I believe Americans should be concerned by this? Putting aside the Monroe Doctrine and the fact that Americans have always accepted a special responsibility to help others achieve and preserve the democratic freedoms we enjoy, there were reasons of national self-interest that made the events in Central America worth worrying about: Almost half of U.S. exports and imports, including close to half of our essential petroleum imports, traveled through this region. Two out of three ships transiting the Panama Canal carried goods to or from the U.S. Central America was not only a source of imports, but a customer for our products. There was the security of our borders to think about, and the question of our economy's ability to absorb an endless flow of refugees: If Communism prevailed in Latin America, it would end any hope of achieving the social and economic progress needed to bring prosperity to the region; and this would accelerate the flow of illegal immigrants who, propelled by poverty, were already overwhelming welfare agencies and schools in some parts of our nation. There was another reason for us to have concern: Under Castro, Cuba had become not only a satellite of Moscow but a potential jumping off spot for terrorists directed by his cohort and fellow Soviet client, Colonel Qaddafi.

If the Soviet Union and its allies were allowed to continue subverting democracy with terrorism and fomenting so-called "wars of national liberation" in Central America, it wouldn't stop there: It would spread into the continent of South America and north to Mexico. Then, as I was told that Lenin once said: "Once we have Latin America, we won't have to take the United States, the last bastion of capitalism, because it will fall into our outstretched hands like overripe fruit . . ."

During my first few months in the White House, as I've mentioned, our intelligence experts obtained conclusive proof that the Sandinistas were receiving an ever-increasing flow of Soviet and Cuban money and arms, and were in turn supporting guerrillas in El Salvador as well as infiltrating Honduras, Guatemala, and Costa Rica. In late 1981, I authorized Bill Casey to undertake a program of covert operations aimed at cutting the flow of arms to Nicaragua and other Central American countries.

It was obvious that poverty, social inequities, and abuses of human rights would make Latin American countries ripe for revolution from the left or the right. It would take more than our limited covert operation to hold back the tide: The region's future was wavering between Marxism on the one hand and dictatorial rule by the extreme right on the other. The only long-term solution was economic development of these countries, a better standard of living for their people, democratic rule, and more social justice.

In the past, the United States had spent a lot of money on programs aimed at improving the lot of its Latin neighbors, with little success: Our programs had done very little to stimulate entrepreneurship or broaden economic opportunity for the common people. According to one study by the administration, the U.S. provided more than half the funding for the governments of Central America. But we were seeing scant return where it would have counted most: in economic development.

In early 1982, we launched the Caribbean Basin Initiative. Through tax incentives for investments in the region, direct financial aid, technical assistance, reduced trade restrictions, and other steps, we hoped to help our neighbors south of the border help themselves. At about the same time, through quiet diplomacy, I made overtures to Fidel Castro to encourage him to rejoin the orbit of the western hemisphere. I thought Cuba's deepening economic problems and the lure of U.S. trade might persuade him to come over to our side. But he told my emissary, General Vernon Walters, that he wasn't interested—and he continued bankrolling guerrillas in the region.

I *never* considered sending U.S. troops to fight in Latin America. Realizing that neither our people nor those south of the border would want us to use American forces to repel Communist advances, I proposed to Mexico and other Latin countries that we establish joint programs to resist the subversion. They generally gave lip service to my suggestions, but I was never able to get them as aroused about the problem as I was, although I never stopped trying. Hovering over everything, I think, was that old fear of the Great Colossus of the North—the apprehension that we'd try to dictate and dominate Latin American affairs.

After I got into office, I didn't wait for Latin American leaders to make contact, nor was I going to seek them out with another plan for how we could be of help. Other administrations before mine had offered such help, I knew, but without many favorable results. I came into office determined to visit some of our neighbors, but not to propose a plan to resolve their problems. I intended to listen instead of lecture during a trip to Brazil, Colombia, Costa Rica, and Honduras in December 1982. In each country, I was greeted by the head of state, and in each instance that leader would ask me what plan I had in mind for Latin America. My answer to each was: I don't have a plan. I'm here to learn what plan you have. Their surprise was so evident and their reaction so great that I felt a sense of success at each stop. I tried to emphasize that my goal was to help Latin Americans help themselves and that we weren't going to send in the Marines. I must admit, though, that I used every chance I got to say some good things about democracy and free enterprise.

In São Paulo, I told Brazilian leaders that America would rebound from its recession and get its economic house in order: "Somewhere along the way the leaders of the United States forgot how the American growth miracle was created. We substituted government spending for investment to spur productivity; a bulging bureaucracy for private innovation and job creation; transfers of wealth for the creation of wealth, rewards for risk-taking, and hard work; and government subsidies and overregulation for discipline and competition from the magic of the market place." If we were to halt the spread of Marxist revolution in Latin America, I said, the first principle to be embraced was that "mankind will not be ruled, in Thomas Jefferson's words, 'by a favored few.' The second is a pledge to every man, woman, and child: No matter what your background, no matter how low your station in life, there must be no limit on your ability to reach for the stars, to go as far as your God-given talents will take you. Trust the people; believe every human being is capable of greatness, capable of self-government . . . only when people are free to worship, create, and build, only when they are given a personal stake in deciding their destiny and benefiting from their own risks, only then do societies become dynamic, prosperous, progressive, and free."

During his welcoming toast in Bogotá, the president of Colombia made it clear that Colombians didn't like being taken for granted. Privately, he told me that John F. Kennedy had come to his country and raised hopes with promises of economic development that were never fulfilled. This gave me a chance to say that I hadn't come to his country with any promises or any answers, I'd come to ask questions: What were the problems we jointly faced, and how could we solve them? I told him my dream for the new alliance of the countries of the western hemisphere, saying we shared a common heritage of having come to this land from all over the world and that from pole to pole we worshiped the same God. He told me of his poor beginnings and I told him of mine. Then I pointed out that we were now the presidents of our countries, and I said I wanted the same kind of opportunity for everyone in all the Americas. By the time we had the farewell ceremonies at the Bogotá airport, I believe we were real friends. Still, I consistently found that most of the leaders in Latin American countries didn't regard the Communist threat as seriously as I did. Neither, I was to learn, did many members of Congress.

From the outset of our program of covert operations in Central America, my instructions were that everything we did must be done legally. At first, through the CIA, we helped Nicaraguans who had fought with the Sandinistas against Somoza interdict the flow of Russian arms into their country and El Salvador. Initially, this involved mostly the Nicaraguans' use of homemade mines against ships bringing weapons into their country. In time, the CIA began organizing these freedom fighters into the Contras, a military fighting force that, with our aid and support, undertook the task of bringing democracy to Nicaragua in the same way that the freedom fighters who led the American Revolution brought democracy to our people.

The program was directed by Bill Casey, and may have prevented a Communist takeover of El Salvador during the early and mid-1980s, although it didn't take place without causing friction in the cabinet. George Shultz, who was as strongly committed as I was to halting Communism in Central America, and who wholeheartedly supported the Contras, thought Casey (whose efforts had the full support of others in the administration, such as Bill Clark and Ed Meese) was overly inclined to take risks and was, in effect, making foreign policy on his own without input from the State Department; more than once, Shultz threatened to resign because of Casey. I had to bring them together several times, and they worked out most of their differences and I convinced George not to resign.

In late 1982, congressional opposition began to develop against our support of the Contras and the Salvadoran government. It was usually led by Tip O'Neill and his friend and fellow congressman from Massachusetts, Edward P. Boland, then chairman of the House Select Committee on Intelligence. They began battling to limit virtually everything the administration was trying to do in Central America.

In early 1983, I wrote in my diary: "NSPG meeting re El Salvador: We must step up aid or we're going to lose this one . . ." A few days later, another: "Tomorrow we start trying to convince Congress we must have more money for El Salvador. We have an entire plan for bolstering the government forces. This is one we must win." After a meeting with several Republican and Democratic congressmen who had gone to El Salvador to learn what was going on there, I wrote: "Not all had been on our side before they went—they are now. The stories they told all added up to the fact that El Salvador is only the current battlefield. What is going on is a general revolution aimed at all of Central America and, yes, Mexico." After a meeting about Central America with Bill Casey and Bill Clark in June, I wrote, "We're losing if we don't do something soon. Those in Congress who are dribbling out about one quarter of what we ask for and need could be playing politics. They'd like to give enough money to keep us in the game [while] El Salvador bleeds to death. Then they call it my plan and it lost Central America. We have to take this to the people and make them all see what's going on. If the Soviets win in Central America, we lose in Geneva and every place else."

The skirmishes I had with Congress in 1982 and 1983 were minor compared with those that would come later. My battles with Capitol Hill over Central America would continue through my entire presidency.

I never understood the depth of the emotional resistance among some members of Congress to helping the government of El Salvador. Well-intentioned or not, they were in effect furthering Moscow's agenda in Latin America. The United States had begun sending arms and ammunition to help El Salvador resist Marxist guerrillas when Jimmy Carter was president. I decided we should continue it. Yes, it is true there were extreme right-wing outlaw elements in that country, including members of the government security forces, who were guilty of flagrant and grave human-rights abuses, sometimes against innocent Salvadorans. But the brutal pro-Marxist rebels who were slaughtering innocent peasants, burning and pillaging their crops, destroying electrical power lines, and blowing up dams in their campaign to wrest control of the country were infinitely more barbaric. Unable to win the hearts of the people, they were depriving them of food, water, electricity, and the ability to earn a living and feed themselves. Under prodding from us, the Salvadoran government had begun traveling the road to a more democratic society. It had adopted a fairer criminal justice system and free elections. Throughout the early eighties, we applied pressure on the Salvadoran government to rid its military of right-wing extremists. With our backing, El Salvador eventually established the first democratic government in its history under President José Napoleón Duarte.

To me, the seriousness of the problems in Central America was so obvious that we had no choice: Based simply on the difference between right and wrong, it was clear that we should help the people of the region fight the bloodthirsty guerrillas bent on robbing them of freedom.

I rarely lose my temper, but I did experience a minor outburst in the Oval Office when Tip O'Neill was leading one of his crusades to block our program in Central America. I became angry and said: "The Sandinistas have openly proclaimed Communism in their country and their support of Marxist revolutions throughout Central America . . . they're killing and torturing people! Now what the hell does Congress expect me to do about that?"

During the eight years of my presidency, I repeatedly expressed my frustration (and sometimes my downright exasperation) over my difficulties in convincing the American people and Congress of the seriousness of the threat in Central America. The White House staff regularly received the results of polls that measured what Americans thought of administration policies. Time and again, I would speak on television, to a joint session of Congress, or to other audiences about the problems in Central America, and I would hope that the outcome would be an outpouring of support from Americans who would apply the same kind of heat on Congress that helped pass the economic recovery package.

But the polls usually found that large numbers of Americans cared little or not at all about what happened in Central America —in fact, a surprisingly large proportion didn't even know where Nicaragua and El Salvador were located—and, among those who did care, too few cared enough about a Communist penetration of the Americas to apply the kind of pressure I needed on Congress.

Part of this reluctance, I'm sure, was a result of the post-Vietnam syndrome. There was a depth of isolationism in the country that I hadn't seen since the Great Depression. But I think there was also another reason why I couldn't get my message across: The Sandinistas and Salvadoran guerrillas were as effective manipulators of the press and public opinion as anyone I'd ever seen. Portraying themselves as a blend of Abe Lincoln and George Washington, they hired a public relations firm to mount a sophisticated program of propaganda that was the ultimate in hypocrisy. The unelected and despotic government of Nicaragua piously accused us of plotting to

479

overthrow them at the same time that they were using guns and mortars in an attempt to overthrow elected governments in neighboring Central American countries.

This campaign of disinformation succeeded, in my opinion, partly because many reporters simply refused to apply the same standards of journalistic skepticism that they applied to most of the topics they covered. Perhaps after Vietnam, when many reporters cast Uncle Sam in the role of villain, they didn't want to put white hats on the Contra freedom fighters because the U.S. government was supporting them. Or perhaps they decided that it made a better story to report how the "little guys"—the Sandinistas and the Salvadoran rebels—were battling a Goliath from north of the border.

One time, we got information that a Soviet ship that had gone through the Panama Canal and was headed up the west coast of Central America was loaded with arms bound for Nicaragua. I went public with the information because the Sandinistas had always denied that they were getting any Soviet weapons. After I did, the Sandinistas swore up and down that I was wrong, that the ship was carrying only farm equipment; then they announced that they were going to invite the international press corps to the dock when the ship unloaded to prove that I had slandered them. That scared me a bit, and I wondered: Are they going to stop someplace en route and unload the weapons?

Well, the ship pulled into the harbor and the press was invited—the *Cuban* press. Its representatives dutifully reported that the ship was carrying farm equipment, and some of the American papers picked up this story as evidence that I didn't know what I was talking about.

The ship's cargo was helicopter gunships.

There was lots of other evidence available to the press that Nicaragua, like Cuba, had become a headquarters for exporting revolution throughout Latin America. In April 1983, Libya dispatched a plane to Nicaragua supposedly carrying medical supplies; our intelligence learned the plane was carrying a different sort of cargo, and brought this to the attention of authorities in Brazil. When the plane stopped there for refueling, it was searched. Its cargo: tons of arms and explosives bound for the Sandinistas, whose leaders were being quoted almost daily in the press saying that they weren't getting arms from anyone. The Brazilians made sure that the plane didn't continue on to Nicaragua.

Once, Daniel Ortega, *comandante* of the Sandinistas, had come to New York for a UN meeting, and he and his wife had gone home with $3,500 worth of designer sunglasses. Yet he still managed to portray himself, especially in Europe, as a humble peasant who was being harassed and overwhelmed by the American colossus.

On two occasions, clergymen from Central America, former prisoners of the Sandinistas who were unknown to each other, came to Washington and I presented them to the White House press corps. In both cases, their ears had been cut off with bayonets by the Sandinistas, and the throat of one had been slashed; he had barely escaped death. I told their story in front of the television cameras, but it never received the attention I thought it deserved.

When some well-intentioned congressmen began traveling to Nicaragua to learn for themselves what was going on, the Sandinistas began staging guided tours to show off their supposed reforms, showing visitors only what they wanted them to see. Some congressmen, however, including quite a few Democrats, went privately to Nicaragua, did their homework and independent digging, talked to the people, and discovered the truth: that what was being offered to the congressmen on the government's guided tours was a trip past a Potemkin village—a false-fronted democracy, all illusion and no substance—and these congressmen would vote with us on Contra aid.

Others, along with several American clergymen who made the trip, came back bamboozled by the Potemkin villages and the Sandinistas' disinformation machine and described the Sandinistas as heroes. They insisted that the people of Nicaragua were enthusiastic supporters of the Sandinistas. I knew otherwise, but I never could talk some of them out of it.

After Nicaragua's most recent elections, I'd enjoy talking to them now.

63

My BATTLES WITH CONGRESS over Central America went on for almost the entire eight years I was in the White House, and made good grist for the journalistic mill. Understandably, reporters enjoy a good political scrap. But I believe the issues involved in our tug-of-war transcended those of many Washington political battles.

As I have noted before, the Democrats have controlled the House of Representatives for most of the past six decades. In recent years, I think they managed to perpetuate their control of the House less through the popularity of their political beliefs or their voting records than through the enormous powers of congressional incumbency. Because of their opportunities for bestowing political favors, generating publicity, and raising enormous sums of money for reelection campaigns from special interest groups that want favors from them, it is almost impossible, short of a major scandal, for a member of Congress to lose his or her seat involuntarily.

More than ninety-five percent of congressional incumbents who seek reelection every two years are reelected. The dice are loaded in their favor. I don't think this is good for the democratic—with a small *d*—process, nor is it good for America.

Because it's so easy for incumbents to get reelected, and for the majority party to guarantee itself "safe" districts during the reapportionment of electoral districts each decade, the Democrats have managed to keep a lock on the House and usually the Senate. Yet public opinion polls and recent presidential elections show that

Americans have increasingly been embracing Republican principles as many at the top of the Democratic Party have been distancing themselves from the values of mainstream Americans, whom they claim to represent.

With public support for their political point of view declining, giving them less hope of capturing the White House, the Democrats are trying to impose their point of view through the legislative process—principally via the exploitation of their control of Congress and their power over the federal purse strings. In doing so, they have been trespassing increasingly across the invisible boundary established by the separation-of-powers principles inherent in our Constitution.

Unlike members of Congress, the president is elected by *all* the people. He is the chief executive, and his principal responsibility is the security of the nation and its people. I don't claim that he (or someday, she) should be able to do anything he wants to do. But every four years, the American people elect a president following a long campaign that gives them an opportunity to observe him in action, learn his views, test his judgment. The voters then make a choice. They've heard what he (or she) stands for. Then, they bestow their trust upon the winner.

You can't have 535 members of the House and Senate administer foreign policy. If the president doesn't do what the people want him to do, they will let him know it.

I've always believed that when it comes to foreign affairs, both parties must get together at the water's edge. Until the 1970s, that's the way it was: America had a strong tradition of bipartisan consensus in foreign policy that was based on the support of peace, democracy, individual liberty, and the rule of law. Then came a rash of congressional initiatives to limit the president's authority in many fields—trade, human rights, arms sales, foreign assistance, intelligence operations, and the dispatch of troops in time of crisis. In claiming new prerogatives, the Congress has often failed to speak in a single, cohesive, and responsible voice, suggesting to other countries that U.S. foreign policy is in disarray and making it difficult for our diplomats to conduct a coherent policy. I'm not saying there aren't many patriotic and reasonable men and women in Congress, or that they shouldn't fight for principles they believe in. Congress is a partner with the president in foreign affairs as well as domestic matters; wisdom is not limited to the occupant of the White House. But there are some situations in which only the president can and does know all the facts; he should be permitted to *lead* the nation and make decisions based upon what he knows and the trust placed in him by the voters—although I never felt these views should justify overriding or ignoring validly enacted laws.

Too often, in my experience, Congress reminds us that it is a political organism. The central preoccupation of too many of its members is getting reelected; too often, instead of legislative statesmanship, this produces cynical posturing and pandering to the campaign contributors that have the fattest wallets.

In 1984, 1985, and 1986, as Tip O'Neill and his allies intensified their campaign to abandon the Contras, the Nicaraguan freedom fighters began to face shortages of guns and ammunition, sometimes even of food and medical supplies. It didn't help matters when Tip, declaring he was going to retire in 1986, asked fellow Democrats to vote against the Contras as a farewell gift. Now we had the emotional sentiment surrounding a very popular Speaker of the House involved in setting foreign policy.

While I battled with Congress to get support for the Contras reinstated, I felt we had to do everything we legally could to keep the force in existence. I told the staff: We can't break the law, but, within the law, we have to do whatever we can to help the Contras survive.

I knew that there must be among our allies other countries that shared our concern about the threat to democracy in Latin America, and I believed we should communicate to them our strong convictions regarding the importance of tangible international support for the Contras. Several countries responded and extended help—a case of friendly nations believing we all had a stake in fighting for democracy.

I believed, then and now, that the president has the absolute constitutional right and obligation to share such thoughts and goals with leaders of other nations.

At about the same time, churches and various groups around our country began forming committees with the intention of helping the freedom fighters and refugees from the Sandinistas. They were made up of private citizens worried about the threat of Communism in Latin America and about things they had read in papers concerning the misguided actions of Congress.

I didn't want anyone in the administration to engage in active solicitation of contributions from these citizens. But, I said, "there has to be a way to help these private citizens who otherwise wouldn't know how to get help to the Contras or buy the supplies they need; there must be ways we can help or counsel them if somebody says we've raised some money and want to help the Contras; somebody ought to be able to tell them what channel to use." The staff also asked me to thank citizens who had contributed humanitarian assistance to the Contras, and I was happy to do so. But I repeatedly insisted that whatever we did had to be within the law, and I always assumed that my instructions were followed.

While I continued trying to educate the American people and seek their support in persuading Congress to provide badly needed aid to the freedom fighters, dedicated Americans began contributing money and supplies—one woman contributed enough to buy a helicopter—and helped buy advertising to counter the Sandinistas' Madison Avenue disinformation campaign. I regarded them as patriots, people from the grass roots of America who were voluntarily trying to bring to our neighbors in Central America the same kind of freedom we enjoyed in the United States.

It was only later, when the Tower Board and Congress completed their investigations, that I learned that some on the NSC staff had gone farther to help the Contras than I was aware of.

Let me be clear. I wanted the Contras maintained as a force, to the fullest extent that was legal, until I could convince Congress to appropriate new funds for the freedom fighters; but I was distressed by the investigations' conclusions that the NSC staff had been so heavily involved in the Contra operation. Press reports appeared suggesting that the NSC and the CIA had gone beyond limits set by the Boland Amendment, and were conducting what some members of Congress claimed was an illegal war in Nicaragua. When I inquired about this, I was told the reports were inaccurate. I later repeated some of these assurances to the American people, and assured them we had been abiding by the law.

In 1986, an American was shot down over Nicaragua with a plane loaded with supplies bound for the Contras. I read a newspaper account of this incident and asked about the report. I was told that this individual had no affiliation with our government; I told the American people that. Later, of course, I learned that the flight had been a supply mission apparently arranged by people reporting to the NSC. When reports were published about other alleged illegal activities by the U.S. government in Central America, Bill Casey said the articles were wrong or distorted, and I accepted that. I trusted and believed in Casey, who had taken an agency that during the previous administration had become badly demoralized and turned it into one of the world's greatest intelligence services again.

Since then, investigations have suggested that under Casey the CIA did a number of things that were improper, and that it exceeded limits imposed by the Boland Amendment. Because Casey is dead, he cannot defend himself and we may never know the truth —but I do know that, during part of this period, a fatal tumor was growing next to Casey's brain. Respected neurosurgeons have told me that this could have affected his judgment and behavior during the last part of his life.

I knew Oliver North only slightly when he worked for the National Security Council. What impressions I did have of him were favorable. My main recollection of Ollie North, before the Iran-Contra affair erupted, was that he had a good record as a marine officer in Vietnam. Although press reports claimed that he told others that we met together privately many times, I knew little about him personally and never saw very much of him at the White House. I never met with him privately and never had a one-on-one conversation with him until I called him on his last day at the NSC to wish him well. I don't believe he attended more than a handful of meetings where I was present, and then he was always part of a group, in the role of a junior staff member under Bud McFarlane or John Poindexter.

McFarlane, Poindexter, Casey, and, I presume, North knew how deeply I felt about the need for the Contras' survival as a democratic resistance force in Nicaragua. They also knew how frustrated I was over my battles with Congress. Perhaps that knowledge, along with their own belief in the importance of the Contras' survival, their adherence to the code that absolute secrecy is necessary in intelligence operations, and a belief that the NSC was exempt from the Boland Amendment, led them to support the Contras secretly and saw no reason to report this to me.

Even now, we still don't have all the answers.

As president, I was at the helm, so I am the one who is ultimately responsible. But to those who question why I wasn't more aware of what was going on, I would say this: Central America was only one of many things that occupied me at the time. Besides trying to end the recession, we were working on modernization of our military forces, trying to get a new nuclear arms reduction initiative off the ground, trying to cut federal spending, trying to end the fighting in Lebanon and the Middle East—and many other things were on my plate as well. A president simply cannot monitor the day-to-day conduct of all of his subordinates. He must concentrate as much as possible on setting the tone and direction of the administration, establishing broad policies, and selecting good people to implement these policies. Unfortunately, there will occasionally be transgressions; but had I attempted to involve myself in the details of the activities of the NSC staff, I would have been unable to attend to the other wide-ranging issues before me at the time.

64

Two weeks before the bitterly cold weekend in early 1985 when George Bush and I were inaugurated for our second term, Treasury Secretary Don Regan and Jim Baker came to me separately in the Oval Office with a proposal. It was Regan's idea. He said he was growing a little bored with his job as secretary of the treasury and had mentioned this to Jim Baker, who said he was getting tired of his job, after four years, as White House chief of staff. They told me they wanted to swap jobs. After I thought it over, I approved the switch, thinking the enthusiasm both would bring to their new jobs would be good for the administration.

Four days after the inauguration, Don brought me a proposal for making some changes in the White House administrative line of command that he said would streamline operations and simplify the organizational structure. I approved the plan, not realizing how much it would enlarge Regan's powers at the expense of others on the staff, restrict access to me, and lead to problems later on. We agreed that Jim Brady, a witty and courageous man who was still undergoing difficult therapy to overcome the effects of his shooting by John Hinckley, Jr., would keep the title of White House press secretary as long as I was living there.

Over lunch, Don asked me what my principal goals were for the second term. On the domestic front, I said, I wanted to continue our efforts to reduce federal spending and bring down the deficit, to implement tax reform, and to continue the modernization of our

military forces; on the international front, my goals were to negotiate a solid arms reduction agreement with the Soviets, to improve
relations with our Latin neighbors while continuing to resist the
Communist penetration of Central America, and to do the best we
could to unsnarl the continuing mess in the Middle East. At that
point in early 1985, it had been almost a year since the marines had
left Beirut, and the situation in the Middle East was more tangled
and more violent than ever:

• Israeli and Syrian forces still occupied much of Lebanon. With
Soviet aid, the Syrian government had undertaken a massive rearmament program to gain "strategic parity" with Israel. Meanwhile,
taking sides in a dispute between moderate and radical elements of
the Palestine Liberation Organization, Syria had offered refuge to
some of this organization's most fanatical members.
• The Palestinians, who once seemed willing to let moderate Arab
nations, including Saudi Arabia and Jordan, represent their interests whenever negotiations were held on a permanent peace solution, were becoming more independent-minded. The PLO was
demanding a seat at the negotiating table. We knew the Israelis
would climb the wall over that idea.
• The unremitting violence of the Lebanese civil war was devastating what was left of that country, once a glamorous gateway to the
Middle East.
• Our intelligence experts were continuing to uncover new links
between Libya and terrorism around the world.
• In Teheran, the brutal regime of Ayatollah Khomeini was sum-
marily executing hundreds of Iranians and trying to export the
Islamic revolution to neighboring countries.
• There were reports that the ayatollah was in ill health and that
his death was near, raising the possibility of new instability in this
strategic country that the Soviets almost certainly would try to
exploit.
• Stalemated in its war with Iraq, Iran was threatening to block
lawful shipping through the Gulf of Hormuz, and both countries
claimed the right to attack third-country oil tankers that got in the
way of their troops.
• Meanwhile, the pro-Iranian Islamic Jihad and the Iranian-
dominated "Party of God"—the Hizballah, a group of terrorists

based in Syria and trained, equipped, and controlled by Iranian Revolutionary Guards—had embarked on what could only be described as a savage campaign of terrorism against American citizens. We believed that the Hizballah was responsible for the bombings of the marine barracks and of our Beirut embassy in 1983, and for the bombing of our embassy annex there a year later.

Iran's seizure of American hostages in Teheran and America's frustrated response to it had given the barbarian Hizballah an idea. They had turned the systematic kidnapping and torture of innocent Americans into an instrument of war that was meant to persuade us to abandon our policies in the Middle East. At the beginning of 1985, they held five American hostages, including William Buckley, the CIA's station chief in Beirut. Several days into the new year they added a sixth, Father Lawrence Martin Jenco, head of Catholic Relief Services in Lebanon. There would be others.

No problem was more frustrating for me when I was president than trying to get the American hostages home. It was a problem I shared with Jimmy Carter, a problem that confronted me when I entered the White House and that was with me when I left it.

During one of my morning National Security Council briefings on the state of the world someone handed me an album of photographs. At first they looked like ordinary aerial photos of a wilderness. Then I recognized Rancho del Cielo and my horse, El Alamein, and Nancy's horse, No Strings, grazing in a pasture. The photos had been taken by one of our satellites from hundreds of miles out in space. Someone thought I'd enjoy seeing them.

Our space satellites provided invaluable information to us in helping to assess the military strength of other countries. Through use of satellites and other technologies, we had great ability to learn things about nations that were hostile to us. We also had human intelligence agents—brave men and women whose names the American people will never read or hear—who risked their lives and prevented potentially devastating acts of terrorism against our country when I was president. Even now I cannot disclose details of these operations, because it would compromise people still at work.

Yet, as good as our space-age technology was; as great an intelligence service as the CIA became under Bill Casey; as powerful as America was militarily, I learned, as had President Carter, how helpless the head of the most powerful nation on earth can feel when it comes to the seemingly simple task of trying to find and bring home an American citizen held against his will in a distant land.

The terrorists who kidnapped our citizens in Lebanon relocated them frequently, usually at night, keeping them dispersed in different buildings, always on the move. Our intelligence community occasionally had a little success in trying to infiltrate the Middle Eastern terrorist groups, but never enough. There were dozens of these groups that shared a hatred for the United States. Some were splinter groups of splinter groups. It was extremely difficult to pinpoint which particular organization of cutthroats was responsible for a specific terrorist act. Most kept constantly in motion, taking refuge among the civilian populations of cities or hiding out in remote desert or mountain strongholds. Sometimes a group would claim credit for an outrage it hadn't committed; sometimes, two or three groups claimed responsibility for the same atrocity.

Although we never stopped trying to find them, it was very difficult to pinpoint exactly where a hostage was at any given time. Although we created special commando teams trained for the specific mission of rescuing hostages, we couldn't just storm a building where we believed hostages were held, because of the risk that by the time we got to them, the hostages would be dead. Even a rumor or false newspaper report that we were going to try to rescue them might be fatal.

Our hands were tied in other ways. We couldn't negotiate with kidnappers. That would simply encourage terrorists to take more hostages. And as a nation we placed limits on how far we would go to counter terrorism. A few people within the administration wanted to follow Menachem Begin's slogan of "an eye for an eye" and assassinate leaders of the most bloodthirsty groups that had committed terrorism against the United States and its citizens—but this was a game that America couldn't and didn't play. Early in my administration, I signed an order prohibiting direct or indirect involvement in murder during covert operations. This was one reason why the CIA had difficulty infiltrating terrorist groups—many of which required new members, as a show of loyalty, to assassinate an enemy of the organization.

Often, during our searches for terrorists, as after the marine barracks bombing in Beirut, we collected information that gave our experts reasonable confidence—but not absolute certainty—that they knew where the terrorists were located. I vetoed proposals to attack several of these sites. I just didn't want to take the chance that we'd kill innocents. George Shultz and Cap Weinberger concurred in this position. We also knew, of course, that if we did strike a site where we thought the culpable terrorists were encamped, we might harm the American hostages. Our options were few, and I spent many, many hours late at night wondering how we could rescue the hostages, trying to sleep while images of those lonely Americans rolled past in my mind. In May 1985, another face joined the images in this nightly newsreel; David P. Jacobsen, an administrator at the American University in Beirut, became the seventh American hostage held in Lebanon.

As president, as far as I was concerned, I had the duty to get those Americans home.

Almost every morning at my national security briefings, I began by asking the same question: "Any progress on getting the hostages out of Lebanon?"

I still believed that the key to achieving a permanent peace in the Middle East and ending the strife that had led to the taking of the hostages was to get other moderate Arab countries, in addition to Egypt, to help us work out an agreement that provided for the acceptance of Israel's right to exist together with a land-for-peace concession that gave territory and autonomy to the Palestinians. The problems wouldn't go away until we solved the problems of the Palestinians and until the security of Israel was ensured with adequate safeguards.

I was determined to build more bridges to the moderate Arab countries, and emphasized this during separate state visits by King Fahd of Saudi Arabia, President Hosni Mubarak of Egypt, and King Hussein of Jordan during the spring of 1985. All of them promised help in the search for peace in the Middle East. In return, all wanted U.S. weapons and what they considered a more even-handed U.S. policy in the Middle East.

Understandably, Saudi Arabia was vitally concerned about the security of its oil resources. King Hussein, who had been courageous in trying to persuade his Arab neighbors to come to terms with the reality of Israel, told me that, because of antipathy over his efforts to bring about peace, he felt threatened by Syria and its Soviet-equipped army. Both Hussein and King Fahd said they needed advanced U.S. arms for defensive purposes—weapons the Israelis viewed as a threat.

I liked Shimon Peres, the man who succeeded Begin as Israel's prime minister. A statesman who was more realistic about the Middle East than Begin, he recognized that any solution to the region's problems would have to include a resolution of the issue of the Palestinian refugees. Ultimately, I was disappointed by his failure to use his term in office to turn his words of moderation into action —but he was up against stiff resistance in the Knesset, the Israeli legislature, to any accommodation with the Palestinians and moderate Arabs. Although Peres, like Begin, opposed arms sales to Saudi Arabia and Jordan, I found him more understanding than his predecessor of my desire to improve relations with the moderate Arabs—and more willing than many of Israel's lobbyists in this country to consider alternative ideas. Even though our administration won congressional approval in early 1985 to increase substantially financial aid to Israel, the pro-Israel lobby continued to block our efforts to apply a more even-handed policy in the Middle East by persuading Congress to prevent the sale of modern weapons to moderate Arab nations. As a result, I was never able to strengthen our ties to these countries as much as I wanted. Once again it was a case of Congress—a committee of 535—setting foreign policy.

In early June 1985, a new crisis erupted in the Middle East, which I will describe in the words I used to record it at the time:

June 14

Awakened before 7 A.M. with word that a TWA 727 with a full load of mainly American tourists took off from Athens, Greece, and was hijacked to Beirut. As morning went on it took off for Algiers. The hijackers—two armed men with handguns and grenades released 19 women and children. In Algiers the hijackers demanded release of Shiites held in Israeli jails or they would execute the passengers. Again

493

they released another 21 mostly women and children. In early after-noon (here) they were in the air and headed back to Beirut.

June 15

An early call again. The plane has landed in Beirut about 2:20 A.M. their time. They had shot one hostage in the head and dumped his body out on to the runway. In the confusion there where Nabih Berri's Moslem Shiites run the airport, we would learn later that ten more terrorists boarded the plane. Before the night was over they were on their way back to Algiers where they released several Greeks on the plane in a trade for the one Greek who had helped them in Athens and who had been arrested. He went on board and joined his evil cohorts. Another 53 hostages again women were released. We're down now to about 40 men, mostly American, but they then released 10 men. Total on board now, three crew and 30 men . . .

June 16

We all decided after more night and early morning calls we should cancel an appearance I was to make this afternoon and get back here to the W.H. Had an N.S.C. meeting. It's a frustrating situation. We have forces in the area—a specially trained unit, but it couldn't be used in the hostile atmosphere of Beirut.

The demand is still for the Shiites held in Israel. These are people the Israelis intend to release in a few weeks, but they are unwilling to let it appear that they are giving in to hijackers' demands. I suggested there might be a way to do it and turn it around on the hijackers. But we've all decided to wait and hear the outcome of the Israeli cabinet meeting.

June 17

Day started with what's getting to be my regular early call from Bud M [McFarlane]. Nabih Berri has taken the hostages from the hijackers and has them some place in West Beirut.

His price is release of the 760 Shiites held by Israel. Israel is publicly saying they will, but the U.S. at the highest level of govt. must ask them to do it. This of course means that me—not they, would be violating our policy of not negotiating with terrorists. To do so, of course, negotiate with terrorists, is to encourage more terrorism. . . .

June 18

Today Berri released three of the hostages, one was a Greek citizen with an American girl friend and the third an 18 year old Armenian.

... Tonight's press conference went well and I had to walk a tight rope all the way, what with questions about the hijacking ... we had the biggest phone and telegram response yet ... about 74 per cent favorable.

June 19

Only thing new on hijacking was a plane side interview with plane captain through the pilot's window. He confirmed that the three crew members were only ones on plane along with Shiite guards. That captain is quite a guy, absolutely unruffled ...

June 20

We finally settled on availing ourselves of the generous proposal by Algeria to ask that the hostages be turned over to them. A face saver for Nabih Berri. Algeria wants us to find out what Israel would do with the 766 Shiites if there were no hostages left in Lebanon. We would then give the answer to that question to the Algerians who would use it in dealing with Berri. In the meantime, the Israelis are not being helpful. They have gone public with the statement that they would release their prisoners if we asked them to. Well, we can't do that because then we would be rewarding the terrorists and encouraging more terrorism.

June 21

Off to Dallas to address convention of Lions Club International. In Dallas met back stage with several families of the hostages. They are of course uptight and looking for a ray of hope. I tried to provide that plus reassurance that we weren't planning any military actions that could endanger their loved ones. They seemed very grateful and reassured. We are proceeding with a plan to have the Algerians intercede and ask that the hostages be turned over to them. In turn they want to be able to tell Berri that once the hostages are free the Israelis plan to continue returning the Shiites they hold. We were able to get a statement approximating that. [Foreign Minister] Rabin of Israel, by going public with a statement that the U.S. should ask them to release the Shiites, loused things up by establishing a linkage we insist does not exist.

June 24

An NSPG meeting re the Beirut situation. Bill Casey feels we must come up with a fig leaf for Berri or releasing the hostages would cause his assassination by the fanatics. Bill suggested a spokesman approaching him about offering Israel an assurance of safety in South Lebanon for which they would free the 700 plus Shiites they are holding. At the same time I've urged that we approach Assad of Syria to go to Berri and tell him he can be a hero by releasing our people or he can be stubborn and we will begin some actions such as closing down the Beirut airport, closing Lebanon's harbors, etc., until he releases our people. This is all being staffed out now. I can agree to the need for a fig leaf but there also has to be threat of action (nonmilitary).

June 26

N.S.C. and the newest hostage development: a light at the end of the tunnel. Berri (Assad's doing) has offered to let the hostages go to a western country's embassy in Beirut or Syria, supposedly to remain until Israel frees the Shiites it is holding. We prefer Syria and have no intention of letting them be held there. The Israelis are already planning to begin returning their prisoners. We want linkage between what they are doing and the release of the hostages. Berri released one today because of a heart condition. We are really optimistic. I've just learned that Berri owns a couple of markets and some oil stations here in the U.S. We might consider that a pressure point.

June 27

One hostage home and lots of Berri talk about the rest going to the French embassy in Beirut or Damascus. No further word. Berri has said he has no control or influence on the kidnap victims. Qaddafi is talking to Iran and Syria about a joint terrorist war against us . . .

June 28

[Trip to Chicago] . . . meeting with families of some of the hostages and one family of Rev. Jenco, one of the seven kidnap victims. I did my best to inform them of what we're doing. God bless people. When I had to leave, one young man, whose father is a hostage, told me he approved of what we were doing and he agreed we should not make a deal that rewarded the terrorists. . . . The rest applauded him.

Back in Washington 5:15 P.M. We held an NSPG meeting. Word came in that our press had been notified by Syria to be in Damascus the next morning (tomorrow) to see the hostages arrive there. This could be what we are waiting for.

June 29

We learned the hostages minus four had been moved by Red Cross bus to a building a mile southwest of the Beirut airport. I was ready with a statement for the press to be read at 9 A.M. Having breakfast in bed, we turned on TV. There were our hostages still in Beirut, not in Damascus. Apparently neither Mr. Berri or Assad could spring the missing four from the bastardly Hizballah. The hours passed and it became apparent there would be no further movement today.

June 30

Word came that the hostages were going to leave in a Red Cross motorcade for Damascus. It was a long ride. We then were told that celebrations in small villages along their route were delaying them. About a quarter to three our time, they arrived at the Sheraton hotel in Damascus.

Out to George Shultz's home for dinner with George and O'Bie. A very nice and finally relaxed dinner. Before that, however, I spoke to the nation on TV from the Oval Office, then George took questions in the press room. When I spoke our people were just leaving Syrian air space in a military aircraft . . .

Monday, July 1

Awoke with knowledge our people were in Wiesbaden at our air base there. As far as we know now they and some of their families who flew to Germany to meet them will arrive here tomorrow afternoon. Nancy and I plan to meet their plane.

An NSPG meeting to plan strategy now. We are limited because the seven kidnap victims are still being held. I phoned Assad to thank him and to call upon him to work for their release. He's the only one who has any possible influence on the fanatics who did the kidnapping. He got a little feisty and suggested I was threatening to attack Lebanon. I told him nothing of the kind but we were going to do everything we could to bring the murderers of our young men to justice. A full cabinet meeting to report on the whole episode . . .

July 2

. . . Nancy and I went to the grave of Robbie [Navy diver Robert] Stethem, the hostage murder victim. His sister was there. Then we helicoptered to Andrews Air Force Base to meet the returning hostages and their families. It was a nice homecoming ceremony and a heartwarming one.

July 3

A frustrating NSPG meeting re the seven kidnap victims and the matter of Lebanon generally. Some feel we must retaliate. I feel to do so would definitely risk the lives of the 7. We are going to proceed to enlist other nations in closing down the Beirut airport . . . we know the identity of the two hijackers who murdered Robbie Stethem. The problem is how do we get them for trial in U.S. All in all, it's frustrating even though we are overjoyed at our success in getting the hostages back.

Although one American lost his life during the hijacking of TWA Flight 847, thirty-nine others went home safely. After seventeen days, we had gotten them back without making any deals with the terrorists. It had been a close call, and America had reason to rejoice when the hostages were freed. But seven Americans were still captive in Lebanon, and I was determined to bring them home.

65

THE SPREAD OF international terrorism was very much on my mind during the flight I made aboard Marine One to the Bethesda Naval Hospital in Maryland a week and a half after the crisis over TWA Flight 847 finally came to an end. In intervening days, the State Department had sounded out several of our allies about the possibility of joining us in imposing sanctions on countries that harbored international terrorists, but it had found a dry hole: Several of our allies in Western Europe still had close ties to former colonies in the Middle East and didn't want to endanger profitable economic relationships.

I was going to Bethesda for what I expected to be an overnight stay before leaving the following morning, a Saturday, for Camp David.

My father-in-law, a surgeon, had always drummed into me the importance of having a yearly physical exam, which he said enabled doctors to spot a potentially serious problem in its earliest stages and respond to it when it was easiest to lick. In particular, he said people would never get cancer of the colon if they underwent a thorough annual checkup, because it would uncover early symptoms that could be responded to before cancer had a chance to get established and grow. There were two kinds of polyps that grow in the colon, he said, and one of them, if left alone, will develop cancer cells. If this kind of polyp is neglected and the cancer is allowed to grow, the malignant cells may escape and go through the wall of the intestine—and then you have cancer.

Nancy and I had always followed her father's advice and gotten an annual physical. Based on our experience, it's advice that we enthusiastically want to pass on to everyone.

During one of my routine checkups that spring, doctors found a small polyp in my colon. They said that it looked harmless, but they wanted to remove it as a routine precaution. I'd had one removed before, so I knew what to expect.

After a Friday morning spent sipping eighty ounces of a medicinal concoction called Go Lightly, which is designed to clean out your system prior to certain procedures (and which does so with a vengeance), I went to Bethesda on Friday afternoon expecting to leave the following day—but my plans had to be changed. After the doctors removed the small polyp they had previously spotted, they inspected the entire colon and, several inches away, they found a large, flat polyp, the kind that with time can become cancerous. Nancy and I and Dr. John Hutton, a senior White House physician, held a strategy session: Should I go on to Camp David as scheduled, then return to the hospital in a few days and go through the whole business with the Go Lightly again? Or should I stay overnight at the hospital and just get it over with?

I hated Go Lightly, so my decision was easy: "Let's get it over with."

Before they wheeled me into the operating room, I signed a letter invoking the Twenty-fifth Amendment, making George Bush acting president during the time I was incapacitated under anesthesia. They gave me a shot of Pentathol and I awoke several hours later feeling groggy and confused, with an incision that ran up past my navel to my chest, and my body laced by tubes of various dimensions. My stomach felt as if it had really been through something.

The doctors said that the polyp was suspicious, and that they were testing the surrounding lymph nodes; we wouldn't know the prognosis with certainty until Monday, following a biopsy.

Later, when I was fully alert, I signed a letter reclaiming the presidency from George while Nancy began decorating my room with pictures brought from home. Didn't I say she's a nest builder? The pictures made things better, but I was in a lot of discomfort through the weekend and didn't get much sleep. Again remembering W. C. Fields's famous line, I once thought to myself, "All in all, I'd rather be at Camp David."

Wasn't it a coincidence, I thought, that my brother had had virtually the same operation less than two weeks before me?

On Monday, after it was brought over from the White House, I wrote in my diary: "Nancy came with more pictures and brought me up to date on messages, flowers, etc. This morning, though, I went back to sleep and did pretty well until noon. It turns out there were cancer cells in the tissue they are checking. But they swear they got it all. It means, however, I'll have to have annual checks for the next five years.

"Monday night was miserable. I kept waking up and felt I'd had no good sleep at all. Did some walking around."

On Tuesday, Don Regan came by and we did a little office business. Nancy brought in more pictures and hung them on the walls. As always—as she had been for more than thirty years—she was there to unfurl that lovely smile at me when I needed her, looking fresh, radiant, and beautiful. What a lucky man I am.

Soon, Nancy had the walls almost fully covered with framed color photos of the ranch, Camp David, and our family. Outside my room, there were bouquets and flower arrangements sent by well-wishers from around the world. "They really help," I wrote at the time. "I've taken some short walks down the hall. Nancy visited the children's ward and gave them some balloons that were sent and the flowers. The children responded with home made cards. Nancy visited one 13 year old boy and his heart beat went from 70 to 130. Tuesday night was the best for sleeping. All the way through until 5 A.M. . . . ."

By Wednesday, July 17, I felt better, although I still knew I'd been through something. George Bush and Don Regan and other White House staffers came to the hospital to discuss our latest battles with Congress over the budget. Then, in the next entry in my diary, unaware at the time where it would lead to, I recorded an event that was to mark the beginning of what became known as the Iran-Contra affair:

"Miracle of miracles," I wrote, "I had my first food by mouth. A cup of tea. I'm waiting to see what happens. By evening I repeated that menu with good results. The doctor says maybe he'll take the feeding tube out tomorrow. Some strange soundings are coming from some Iranians. Bud M. will be here tomorrow to talk about it. It could be a breakthrough on getting our seven kidnap victims back. Evidently the Iranian economy is disintegrating fast under the strain of war."

Even now, I'm still a little annoyed at how my operation was reported. "The president has cancer," they wrote. In fact, the president *had* cancer. Yes, doctors found an object in my body that was cancerous. But they removed it, and, because they couldn't take any chances that malignant cells might have penetrated beyond the polyp, they also took out a portion of my intestine. But they learned that no cancer cells had entered the rest of my body at all; there was no cancer beyond the polyp, and it was removed. Yes, it was major surgery, but it was a minor situation.

It happened again barely ten days later, shortly after I left Bethesda.

For years, I had had a tiny bump on my nose that I thought was a pimple. When I got home from the hospital, it was a little more inflamed than usual. I blamed it on irritation from the tape that had fastened the tube in my nose at the hospital. When Nancy's dermatologist saw it, he clipped off a little piece, and a biopsy showed that it was a low-level carcinoma—not something to be ignored, but by no means life-threatening.

Once again, however, some of the papers reported that I had cancer. Such carcinomas, the doctors said, are fairly common, a result of spending too much time under the sun. Nancy had had one removed from her upper lip the year before. For me, it was a result of a lifetime spent outdoors. From the day I started those summers working as a lifeguard, I'd enjoyed being outside and getting a tan; I tanned easily and seldom got sunburned. When I got into pictures, I *had* to stay tanned. I couldn't wear makeup, so I was always the first one out under the sun working on a tan. Now, the doctors told me, either I had to stay out of the sun or button up and wear a hat when I did go out. That night I wrote in my diary: "First I have to give up popcorn and now sunbathing." During my colon operation, the surgeons found evidence of diverticulitis, an inflammation of the intestine that can be easily irritated by small particles of food, and they said: No more peanuts and popcorn. I'd been a popcorn fiend since childhood; if I'd had to, I could have lived on popcorn. I often went into the kitchen and cooked it myself. I didn't think I could ever give it up, but now I did.

Three weeks after I left the hospital, the doctors gave their okay for Nancy and me to finish my recuperation at the ranch.

It was more beautiful than ever at Rancho del Cielo, and for almost three weeks we had picture-perfect weather—*too perfect* for certain kinds of pictures: These were days when we might have enjoyed a little fog.

We had always loved our privacy on this piece of ground, but this time out, on our first evening, we turned on a television set and saw ourselves. The networks had found a spot on a mountaintop, up a fire trail, almost three miles away, from which they could aim their cameras at the ranch and keep an eye on us—literally. We didn't like it very much.

As I've said, aside from Camp David, the ranch was the only place where we had any privacy—where we could just go for a walk and be ordinary people. During the previous four years, we'd come to prize that above almost anything. Now the whole world could watch as we walked around the ranch. The lenses were so powerful that they could even see us through the windows of the house!

Nancy got back at them, though. When she knew the cameras were looking down on us, she waved a sign with three little words on it, the slogan of her antidrug campaign: JUST SAY NO.

66

DURING BUD McFARLANE'S visit to Bethesda Naval Hospital and in following meetings, he informed me that representatives of Israel had contacted him secretly to pass on information from a group of moderate, politically influential Iranians. These Iranians, described as disenchanted members of Iran's government, wanted to establish a quiet relationship with U.S. leaders as a prelude to reestablishing formal relations between our countries following the death of the Ayatollah Khomeini. Bud asked my approval to meet with the Iranians to see if it might lead somewhere.

At that time, there were reports worldwide that the ayatollah was extremely ill. Iran's protracted war against Iraq had reached a stalemate, the Iranian economy was in bad shape, and intelligence reports indicated that several factions had formed to jockey for control of Iran after the ayatollah's death. From our point of view, reestablishing a friendly relationship with this strategically located country—while preventing the Soviets from doing the same thing —was very attractive. Under the shah, Iran had played a pivotal role in our efforts to keep an eye on its neighbor, the USSR. We wanted to ensure that the next government in Teheran was moderate and friendly.

Through quiet diplomacy, we had been trying to end the Iran-Iraq war and reduce instability in the Middle East, which we saw as an invitation to Soviet tampering. We had also spent a great deal of time thinking about possible scenarios for Iran's future once Khomeini was gone. Before becoming president, I had visited Iran, a short time before the shah was ousted, and had met many ordinary Iranian citizens in Teheran and in the countryside. They were not like the fanatics who orbited around Khomeini. It didn't surprise me when I was told that there were moderates in the government who wanted to oust the tyrannical theocracy imposed on them by Khomeini and his cohorts. Therefore, Israel's offer to act as an intermediary and help us open a channel to Iran's potential future leaders seemed very interesting.

There was another thing that made Bud's report exciting: The Israelis said that, to demonstrate their sincerity, the Iranian moderates who had made the overtures had offered to persuade the Hizballah terrorists to release our seven hostages. I don't recall feeling at the time that the Israeli government's proposal seemed earth-shattering. We'd already been through some disappointments and seen several promising covert efforts to free the hostages die stillborn because of the problems that always made the Middle East such a challenge. But I wanted to explore any avenue that offered the possibility of getting the hostages out of Lebanon. Okay, I said, we would send a team to Israel to confer with the Israelis who'd offered to act as intermediaries with the Iranian moderates.

And that's how the Iran-Contra affair got started.

After the talks began, the Israelis said the Iranians wanted us to permit Israel to sell a small number of TOW antitank missiles to the moderate Iranians; they said that this would enhance their prestige with the Iranians and demonstrate that they actually had connections with high officials of the United States government. (Until then, nothing had been said about weapons.)

Israel already had a large stock of TOW missiles in its military stockpile. The Israelis requested our permission to ship some of the missiles to the Iranian moderates; then the Iranians would pay for the missiles, and the United States would replenish Israel's stock of missiles—and be paid for them. As Bud outlined the plan, the transaction was to be solely between Israel and the Iranian moderates and would not involve our country, although we would have to waive for Israel our policy prohibiting any transfer of American-made weapons to Iran.

My first reply to this proposal was: No, we don't do business with countries that sponsor terrorism. I told Bud to turn down the proposal.

But then the Israeli officials, urging us to go ahead with the deal, sent information which they said showed that the Iranians they were talking to opposed terrorism and had fought against it. We had great respect for Israel's intelligence abilities relating to matters in the Middle East, and, as a result, we gave their assertions a great deal of credence. I was told that Israeli Prime Minister Shimon Peres was behind the proposal and that the Israelis involved in the secret contacts with Iran were all close to Peres.

By this time, news reports were saying that the ayatollah was so ill and feeble that he might not even live out the week. I didn't need any arm-twisting by Bud to convince me that we ought to try to establish a connection with responsible people who might be the future leaders of Iran. Here was a bona fide opportunity to shape the future in the Middle East, take the initiative, and preempt the Soviets in an important corner of the world. As I've said, we wanted moderates running the Iranian government. I would not have entertained the plan for a second if the Israelis had said they wanted to sell American weapons to the ayatollah or to his militia, which was operated separately from the Iranian army; it did not seem unreasonable that Iranian moderates who opposed the ayatollah's authoritarian regime would ask for weapons in order to strengthen their position and enhance their credibility with Iran's military leaders. Iran's military forces were to some extent independent of the ayatollah. We knew of many cases where factions fighting for control of a country—often trying to introduce democracy to it—had found it necessary to get the country's military on their side.

The truth is, once we had information from Israel that we could trust the people in Iran, I didn't have to think thirty seconds about saying yes to their proposal. What I was saying yes to was the action of another government, Israel. We wouldn't be shipping any weapons to the people in Iran. I was told that the few TOW missiles would not significantly change the balance in Iran's war with Iraq, so I said, okay, we wouldn't stand in the way of this one small shipment from Israel going through to give credibility to the Israelis, allowing them to prove that they were talking with the highest levels of the U.S. government. But I said there was one thing we wanted: The moderate Iranians had to use their influence with the Hizballah and try to get our hostages freed.

Their answer was yes, they would—and could—do it. So I agreed to the plan, which called for release of the hostages on a beach north of Tripoli in September. Israel promised to abort the sale and order their delivery aircraft to turn back with the missiles if it became apparent the hostages were not going to be released.

Only hours after the shipment was made, the Reverend Benjamin Weir, an American who had been held hostage in Beirut for sixteen months, was released. There was a lot of suspense in the White House during the next two days as we waited for the rest of the hostages to be released. We were told their release had been delayed by the terrorists who held them—but that, nevertheless, it was just a matter of time before all six were free. We were disappointed, yes, but we had succeeded in bringing home one of the hostages, and I felt pretty good. Now we all waited for the others to be released.

It was a busy period at the White House: I was getting ready for my first summit meeting with the new Soviet leader, Mikhail Gorbachev; there were important domestic legislative matters to deal with; we were watching events unfold in the Philippines that would lead to the downfall of Ferdinand Marcos; and intelligence people were continuing to get evidence that Libya was financing acts of terrorism—make that wanton murder—in several parts of the world. And the Middle East, seldom quiescent, had heated up again in early October when Israel bombed Arafat's PLO headquarters in Tunis.

The attack killed a number of women and children and touched off threats of reprisals from Palestinian radicals against Israel and the United States. Three days later, the Islamic Jihad announced it had executed one of the hostages—CIA man William Buckley—in retaliation for the attack on Tunis. (Later, we determined that Buckley had probably died from the effects of his captivity several months earlier.) And six days after the attack, four heavily armed Palestinians hijacked the Italian cruise ship *Achille Lauro* in the Mediterranean.

Once again, we had a crisis in the Middle East in which American lives were hanging in the balance. About one hundred passengers and crewmen, at least half of them Americans, were being held hostage on the ship, and the hijackers announced that they would soon begin murdering them, starting with the Americans, unless Israel released fifty Palestinian prisoners who were held in its jails. We spent much of the next forty-eight hours setting in motion a plan to deploy a crack team of navy Seals to assault the *Achille Lauro* and rescue the hostages from the terrorists. It was time, I said, to strike back at the terrorists, even though we all agreed that attacking the ship would be a high-risk operation.

The need for fast action was underlined by the cold-blooded murder of a sixty-nine-year-old American passenger, wheelchair-bound Leon Klinghoffer. After the Palestinians shot him to death, they casually dumped his body at sea.

Although planning for their mission was nearly complete, the team of navy Seals never got the chance to launch the rescue effort. The hijackers, possibly convinced that they had made their point, directed the cruise ship to Port Said in Egypt, where it had been headed before the seizure. There they surrendered to Egyptian officials. Via diplomatic channels, we urgently requested Egypt to turn the hijackers over to U.S. or Italian authorities for prosecution. But President Mubarak announced that they had already been turned over to representatives of the PLO, who had taken them out of Egypt.

The following day, I went to Chicago to make two previously scheduled speeches. While I was there, I was told that the hijackers were still in Egypt, and that an Egyptian airliner was being readied to take the hijackers to Tunisia and a heroes' reception by the PLO. Through intelligence means, we learned exactly when it was scheduled to leave.

As Air Force One left Chicago for the trip back to Washington, I approved a plan calling for U.S. fighter planes to intercept the airliner and force it to land at a U.S. base in the Mediterranean; we would then either bring the hijackers to America or turn them over to Italy for prosecution. "Of course," I wrote in my diary as Air Force One headed east, "we will not attack the plane, just signal it to turn and crowd it a bit."

This time, I thought, we really had a chance to bring some terrorists to justice. Fortunately, I was right.

At almost the same time that Air Force One was landing at Andrews Air Force Base outside Washington, four Navy F-14's from the aircraft carrier *Saratoga* intercepted the Egyptian Boeing 737 that was carrying the hijackers and forced it to land at an air base operated jointly by the United States and Italy on Sicily. After that, I was up half the night on the telephone, monitoring the operation's progress, then its aftermath.

After the airliner landed, our team of navy Seals, who had been rushed to the base on Sicily, tried to arrest the hijackers so that they could be brought to America for trial. But Italian police officials refused and took custody of them. I made a late-night call to Bettino Craxi, the prime minister of Italy, and, citing Klinghoffer's American citizenship, asked him to allow us to fly the hijackers to the United States for prosecution. But he said he didn't have authority to release them; under Italian law, he said, magistrates were independent of the government and the fate of the four men was lawfully in their hands. (I think he was also worried about the political ramifications that he would face if hijackers of an Italian ship were released to us.)

When we broke the news to the press that the hijackers had been caught, I said I hoped the incident had sent a message to terrorists: You can run, but you can't hide. In my diary, I wrote, "Americans as well as friends abroad are standing six inches taller. We're flooded with wires and calls."

In late November, after I came home from the Geneva summit, Bud McFarlane told me he wanted to resign as my national security advisor at the end of the year. After thirty years of working for the government, he said he owed it to his family to spend more time at home. Bud was an eighty-hour-a-week man. I told him he could stay as long as he wanted, but I wouldn't try to talk him out of leaving; I sympathized with his desire to spend more time with his family. As Bud's successor, I appointed his deputy, John Poindexter, who had been in charge of the successful operation that brought down the terrorists who hijacked the *Achille Lauro*.

On December 5, 1985, Bud presided over his last briefing as my national security advisor and John took over. According to my diary, the subject of our meeting that day was "our undercover effort to free our hostages held by terrorists in Lebanon. It's a complex undertaking with only a few of us in on it." Two days later, I wrote this in my diary:

Saturday, Dec. 7—Pearl Harbor Day

Day opened with "Rex" [our new dog, a year-old King Charles spaniel] on our bed. I then had a meeting with Don R, Cap W, Bud M, John P, George S and McMahon of CIA. This has to do with the complex plan which could return our five hostages and help some officials in Iran who want to turn that country from its present course and onto a better relationship with us. It calls for Israel selling some weapons to Iran. As they are delivered in installments by air, our hostages will be released. The weapons will go to the moderate leaders in the army who are essential if there is to be a change to a more stable government. We then sell Israel replacements for the delivered weapons. None of this is a gift. The Iranians pay cash for the weapons —so does Israel.

George Shultz, Cap and Don are opposed. Congress has imposed a law on us that we can't sell Iran weapons or sell any other country weapons for resale to Iran. George also thinks this violates our policy of not paying off terrorists. I claim the weapons are for those who want to change the government of Iran and no ransom is being paid for the hostages. No direct sale would be made by us to Iran but we would be replacing the weapons sold by Israel.

We're at a stalemate. Bud is flying to London where the Israelis and Iranian agents are. Britain has no embargo on selling to Iran. . . . The plan is set for Wednesday.

Dec. 9

Bud is back from London but not in the office yet. His meeting with the Iranians did not achieve its purpose which was to persuade them to free our hostages first and then we'd supply the weapons. Their top man said he believed if he took that proposal to the terrorists they would kill our people.

Dec. 10

Began the day with a meeting, the Dem and Republican Congressional leadership. Spent most of our time on the Gramm Rudman Hollings bill which later in the day I found had made its way out of the conference. Not as good as we would have wanted but still a bill I'll have to sign. Some of the time we talked tax reform. I've done a lot of telephoning all day and still don't know whether it will pass. Bud M back from England and his meeting with the Iranian "go between," [Iranian arms merchant Manucher Ghorbanifar] who turns out to be a devious character. Our plan regarding the hostages is a "no go."

On December 12, our nation got another reminder of the high price we were having to pay for the continuing strife in the Middle East and our efforts to resolve the Arab-Israeli conflict: Nearly 250 American soldiers returning home after six months of duty as members of the international police force posted in the Sinai under the Camp David accords were killed when their plane crashed after a refueling stop in Newfoundland.

Less than three weeks later—two days after Christmas—we got still another reminder: Palestinian terrorists callously sprayed automatic weapons into crowds of passengers at the Rome and Vienna airports, killing twenty people, including an eleven-year-old American girl and four other Americans. Colonel Muammar Qaddafi promptly called the suicide attack a "noble act."

On the body of one of the terrorists was a Tunisian passport. The passport had been taken by Libyan officials from a Tunisian worker at the time he was expelled from Libya. It wasn't hard to figure out where the terrorist had gotten the passport.

I felt we couldn't ignore the mad clown of Tripoli any longer. By now, we had a shelf full of contingency plans designed to express in a concrete way our displeasure with his terrorism—but whatever we did, we had to take into account the presence of nearly one thousand American oil workers in Libya. Qaddafi wouldn't think twice about taking his vengeance on them.

Two of my cabinet members whom I admired most, Cap Weinberger and George Shultz, never got along especially well together. There was always a little chill—a tension—between them. I suspect that it went back to when they were both executives of the Bechtel Corporation in San Francisco. Whatever it was, they didn't see eye to eye on a lot of things. Sometimes, for example, Cap thought that George was too eager to enter into certain arms control agreements with the Soviets and tried to advise me to go more slowly than George favored (I'll get into this later). There were numerous conflicts between them. I don't think this was necessarily bad for the country or for the administration: Every member of the cabinet had to view the problems of the nation and interpret world events from the special vantage point of his or her own job and responsibilities, based in part on the advice of specialists in their respective departments.

Conflicts between the Pentagon and Foggy Bottom were inevitable no matter who ran them, and they didn't start with my administration. I think it is important for presidents to have advisors who offer them different points of view and express disagreement instead of always expressing unanimity. I always encouraged the members of my cabinet to disagree not only with me but with each other.

But while George and Cap disagreed on many topics, they were united on one thing: Almost from the day Bud McFarlane brought us the proposal for arms sales to Iran, they were against it. They warned me against participating in any arrangement that might be interpreted as linking the shipment of arms with efforts to free the hostages. At that meeting on Pearl Harbor Day, 1985, when we considered continuing and possibly even expanding the covert operation begun the previous summer, they made their opposition clear to me forcefully. They didn't argue that the plan involved a swap of arms for hostages, but they contended that if information about it ever leaked out (and George insisted that it would), it would be made to *look* as if we were.

My response to them was that we were *not* trading arms for hostages, nor were we negotiating with terrorists.

"Look," I said, "we all agree we can't pay ransom to the Hizballah to get the hostages. But we are not dealing with the Hizballah, we are not doing a thing for them. We are trying to help some people who are looking forward to becoming the next government of Iran, and they are getting the weapons in return for saying that they are going to try to use their influence to free our hostages. It's the same thing as if one of my children was kidnapped and there was a demand for ransom; sure, I don't believe in ransom because it leads to more kidnapping. But if I find out that there's somebody who has access to the kidnapper and can get my child back without doing anything for the kidnapper, I'd sure do that. And it would be perfectly fitting for me to reward that individual if he got my child back. That's not paying ransom to the kidnappers."

Because of the opposition of Cap and George, I decided to wait. The Pearl Harbor Day meeting ended without me making a decision, although I said I wanted to keep the channels open and asked Bud McFarlane to take the next step and meet again with the principals involved in the negotiations. I told him to say we wanted a dialogue directly with responsible Iranians, and that the Iranians could prove they were responsible by freeing the hostages, but that we would not trade arms for hostages.

When he returned later that month from a meeting with the group in London, Bud told me that they had demanded shipments of additional weapons and had said that if word leaked out about the negotiations and our refusal to send arms, the lives of Iranian moderates involved in the contacts, as well as those of the hostages, would be in jeopardy. Bud said he thought that Ghorbanifar, an expatriate Iranian arms merchant who was the principal middle man in the negotiations, was untrustworthy, and he was blunt in expressing his misgivings about continuing the initiative.

But I felt that there were not many other options—possibly there were no others—open to us for getting the hostages home. I believed we had to explore every road, to do everything we could to get them out of Beirut as well as to develop a relationship with the future leaders of Iran. Despite difficulties, I believed that this group offered the best hope for accomplishing both objectives.

Although I didn't make a decision at that meeting on Pearl Harbor Day, inside I felt that we should proceed with the initiative on a step-by-step basis—cautiously and in compliance with the law—to see where it would lead. As I've said, I felt a heavy weight on my shoulders to get the hostages home. We were coming up to another Christmas season with American citizens held captive far from home, separated from parents, wives, and children, deprived of basic freedoms, and subjected to almost unspeakable living conditions. What American trapped in such circumstances wouldn't have wanted me to do everything I possibly could to set them free? What Americans *not* held captive under such circumstances would not want me to do my utmost to get the hostages home?

It was the president's *duty* to get them home. I didn't want to rest or stop exploring any possible avenue until they were home safe with their families.

As the year came to an end, we spent a few days, as we usually did over New Year's, at the home of former Ambassador Walter Annenberg near Palm Springs, where I played my annual round of golf and closed out the year with this entry in my diary: "Ended 1985 with 18 holes of golf; as usual, I had some enjoyable shots but many more of the other kind . . . then the New Year's party and as always it was great. Of course, hanging over all of this was a cloud we tried to ignore temporarily—the matter of Qaddafi and his connection with the massacres at Rome and Vienna airports. We all feel we must do something, yet there are problems, including 1,000 Americans living and working in the mad clown's country."

67

T HE FIRST FEW WEEKS of 1986 were a blur of tragedy and international crisis. There was the *Challenger* disaster, the fall of Ferdinand Marcos in the Philippines, a new clash with Japan over its restrictions on American imports, new efforts by Congress to starve the Contras, and continuing problems in the Middle East. On January 7, I wrote in the diary: "After quite a session, I finally came down on the side of an executive order bringing Americans and American business home from Libya and canceling relations—trade, etc., with them. At the same time we beef up the Sixth Fleet in the Mediterranean Sea. If Mr. Qaddafi decides not to push another terrorist act, okay, we've been successful with our implied threat. If on the other hand he takes this for weakness and does loose another one, we will have targets in mind and instantly respond with a h—l of a punch. At tonight's press conference, I announce the executive order."

As I've mentioned before, with all the prominence that the Iran-Contra affair has since received, it might seem that all we were thinking about at the White House during that period was the Iran initiative. But it was only one of many, many things that were occupying us at the time. Not only were there major items of foreign policy such as arms control and problems in Nicaragua and the Philippines and visits with various heads of state, but there was a full plate of domestic issues as well, notably the battle to reform taxes and cut the budget deficit, and, of course, the *Challenger* tragedy. On any given day, I was sent dozens of documents to read, and saw an average of eighty people. I set the policy, but I turned over the day-to-day details to the specialists. Amid all the things that went on, I frankly have had trouble remembering many specifics of the day-to-day events and meetings of that period, at least in the degree of detail that subsequent interest in the events has demanded. In this book, I have set out to describe everything I remember about the Iran-Contra affair.

At the same January 7 meeting of the National Security Council at which I approved the executive order involving Libya, John Poindexter and the NSC staff proposed pressing ahead with the Iranian initiative. This meant approving an additional shipment of TOW missiles, but with a new emphasis on negotiating directly with moderate members of the Iranian government rather than with the go-betweens.

In retrospect, I think there were probably always a few questions in my mind about the reliability of the people we were dealing with during the negotiations that began after Bud McFarlane's visit to me at the hospital in the summer of 1985. Several times, they promised that hostages would be released momentarily, and nothing happened. Still, Bill Casey said that the world of covert operations was full of people who were less than angels. The people we were dealing with *had* managed to get out one hostage, and, since we had made our connection with them, there had been no major terrorist acts committed against Americans by the Hizballah.

In early January, I was assured again that Ghorbanifar and company had good connections in Iran. Warts and all, they were our best hope for getting the hostages out, so I decided to proceed with the initiative despite a deep division within the cabinet and staff: Ed Meese, Bill Casey, and especially John Poindexter—who became the principal manager of the initiative after McFarlane retired —argued for going ahead; Cap Weinberger and George Shultz remained very much opposed, with Shultz especially strong in his opposition. They argued forcefully that I was wrong, but I just put my foot down.

I did not think of the operation (and never have) as an "arms-for-hostage" deal, because it wasn't. Cap and George had both had experience in prior administrations. I couldn't ignore their warning that if word about the initiative leaked out, it would be misinterpreted—but I just felt that the opportunities involved justified taking the chance. I didn't expect the plan to fail, but if it did, I was prepared to take the heat.

Through February, we expected the hostages to be released almost on a daily basis, but they didn't come. We pressed harder for direct talks with moderate Iranian officials, always maintaining tight secrecy over the operation because any leaks could threaten the hostages as well as the people we were dealing with in Iran. Meanwhile, we had other matters to deal with in the Middle East.

In March, the Sixth Fleet launched a new round of naval maneuvers in "Qaddafi's lake"—the Gulf of Sidra—and we waited to see what his response would be. Commanders of our flotilla were instructed to cross what Qaddafi called his "line of death"—an imaginary boundary in the high seas more than one hundred miles off the coast of his country (and far beyond the twelve-mile limit set by international law), which Qaddafi claimed delineated Libyan territory. I ordered that, if Libya attacked our aircraft or ships, our forces were to reply in kind, but with a measured and limited response.

Two days after the maneuvers began, Qaddafi's forces fired SAM missiles at several of our carrier-based planes (and missed) and sent several missile-firing boats within the vicinity of our fleet—an act of aggression in international waters. We responded by sinking the Libyan vessels and knocking out the radar installation that had guided the Libyan missiles. After that, our intelligence agencies went on special alert, waiting to learn what Qaddafi's next move would be.

In late March, Nancy and I flew to California to spend a few days at the ranch. While we were there, I was awakened late at night by John Poindexter, who said a terrorist's bomb had just exploded at a disco in West Berlin that was a favorite of U.S. servicemen. An American soldier and a Turkish woman had been killed and more than two hundred other people, including at least fifty American servicemen, had been injured in the blast.

Our investigation of the bombing quickly focused on Libya. Although Qaddafi went on television and condemned it as a senseless act of terrorism against innocent people (which it truly was), in less than a day our intelligence experts established conclusively that there had been conversations regarding the bombing *before* and *after* it occurred between Libyan diplomats in East Berlin and Qaddafi's headquarters in Tripoli. The evidence was irrefutable. Intelligence data provided positive proof that Libya was responsible for the bombing. Our intelligence agencies also obtained information outlining secret plans for additional acts of terrorism by Libya against Americans and people of other countries. Forewarned, they were able to prevent the attacks.

Now that the American oil workers were out of Libya, I knew we had to do something about the crackpot in Tripoli. "He's not only a barbarian, he's flaky," I said at the time. I felt we had no alternative but a military response: As a matter of self-defense, any nation victimized by terrorism has an inherent right to respond with force to deter new acts of terror. I felt we must show Qaddafi that there was a price he would have to pay for that kind of behavior, that we wouldn't let him get away with it. So I asked the Joint Chiefs of Staff for a plan: What can we do that would send the right signal to Qaddafi without harming innocent people?

At an NSC meeting on April 7, 1986, we reviewed maps and photographs of Libya and weighed various options, including strikes at locations in Tripoli that might have resulted in civilian deaths. "I'm holding out for military targets to avoid civilian casualties because we believe a large part of Libya would like to get rid of the colonel," I wrote in my diary that night. Two days later, there was this entry in the diary: "A full—in fact, two full NSC meetings planning targets for retaliation against Qaddafi. Our evidence is complete that he was behind the disco bombing in West Berlin that killed an American sergeant and wounded 50 G.I.'s. We have five specific military targets in mind." On April 10, I wrote, "Another session with Admiral [Joint Chiefs of Staff Chairman William J.] Crowe on potential Libyan targets. I think it will be Monday night. I've sent a long passage to Prime Minister Thatcher explaining in generalities what we're up to. She has replied with a long message pledging support but expressing concern about possible civilian casualties. That's our concern also."

This was one of the times, incidentally—while we were trying to come up with targets that would let us make our point but not hurt innocent people—when I really lost my patience with the press. Through the inevitable leak, several reporters picked up a scent that we might be planning an operation against Qaddafi in response to the disco bombing. In some cases, they got fairly accurate information, and some of their reports virtually announced to Qaddafi that the United States was planning to attack him. We tried to talk them out of revealing these state secrets—as far as I was concerned, maintaining secrecy in a war against terrorism is as crucial as it was during World War II, when the press accepted restrictions on its reporting to safeguard important operations and American lives—but they would have none of it. Every time they got a leak, they ran with it, even though it meant risking human lives.

On April 13, we settled on the principal target: Qaddafi's military headquarters and barracks in Tripoli, which was located well away from civilian targets. Housed in this compound was the intelligence center from which Libya's worldwide program of state-sponsored terrorism was directed.

The attack was not intended to kill Qaddafi; that would have violated our prohibition against assassination. The objective was to let him know that we weren't going to accept his terrorism anymore, and that if he did it again he could expect to hear from us again. It was impossible, however, to know exactly where he would be at the time of the attack. We realized that it was possible, perhaps probable, that he might be at or near the intelligence center when our planes struck.

France and Italy refused to permit our F-111 bombers to cross their air space on the way from a base in England to Tripoli to join carrier-based planes from the Sixth Fleet in the attack. As a result, the F-111's had to detour more than a thousand miles over the Atlantic and the Mediterranean; this would shorten their effective range and, by leaving them with less reserve fuel, would possibly make them more vulnerable during the attack. The refusal upset me, because I believed all civilized nations were in the same boat when it came to resisting terrorism. At least in the case of France, however, economic considerations prevailed: While it publicly condemned terrorism, France conducted a lot of business with Libya and was typically trying to play both sides.

On April 14, the night the attack was scheduled, I briefed congressional leaders on what was about to happen and told them about the intercepted messages that proved Libyan intelligence agents were responsible for the disco bombing. Late that night, sitting at my desk upstairs in the family quarters of the White House, I wrote in my diary: "Well, the attack took place right on the nose 7 P.M. our time. About 11 minutes over the target areas. Preliminary report. All planes withdrew but two of our F-111's are unreported. Maybe it's only radio failure. Maybe they are down. We don't know as of this time. One thing seems sure. It was a success."

During the first twenty-four hours, the White House received 126,000 phone calls—15,000 couldn't get through—in response to the attack, and in the following twenty-four hours, there were 160,000 calls and 16,000 couldn't get through. They were more than seventy percent favorable.

Tragically, one of our missiles went off track during the attack and caused fatalities in a civilian neighborhood. We had intended to strike military targets only, and I deeply regretted the mishap. I was also deeply saddened that two crewmen were shot down and lost, and that another American may have died as a result of the attack: After the bombing, according to reports that we found credible, Qaddafi sought out the terrorists who had kidnapped Peter Kilburn, librarian at the American University in Beirut, and paid them a fortune to ransom him. Then Kilburn and two British hostages (apparently because of Britain's cooperation with us during the raid) were murdered in cold blood.

As tragic as the loss of life was, I don't think they were lives lost in vain: After the attack on Tripoli, we didn't hear much more from Qaddafi's terrorists.

The following month, Bud McFarlane, interrupting his brief retirement, made a secret mission to Teheran. The Israeli go-betweens involved in the Iranian initiative told him that he would meet face-to-face with the moderate Iranians who supposedly wanted to establish a dialogue with the United States. Following the meeting, he was told, the four surviving hostages—Associated Press reporter Terry Anderson, Father Lawrence Jenco, Thomas Sutherland, and David Jacobsen—would be freed.

Bud and a small delegation arrived in Teheran on May 25. According to the plan, the hostages were to be released by the Hizballah no later than May 28. Shortly after his arrival, however, Bud called on a secure communications link and told me that we had been misled by the go-betweens; he had doubts, he said, about the trustworthiness of the Iranians he had met. He later called again and said that they had outrageous demands as a price for the Hizballah's release of our hostages—including Israel's withdrawal from the Golan Heights and South Lebanon and our agreement to ensure that Kuwait released a group of convicted terrorists. When Bud told them the deal was off, they said they wanted to continue negotiating, but in the end, he returned home without the hostages. "It was a heart breaking disappointment for all of us," I wrote in my diary.

68

I N LATE JULY, a short time after the celebration of the hundredth birthday of the Statue of Liberty, Father Lawrence Martin Jenco, former head of Catholic Relief Services in Lebanon, was given his freedom in Beirut. "He's in West Germany on his way home," I wrote in the diary July 26. "The Hizballah sent a video tape out with him on which one of the remaining hostages—[David] Jacobsen dressed me and our govt. down for not lifting a finger to try and get their freedom. This release of Jenco is a delayed step in a plan we've been working on for months. It gives us hope the rest of the plan will take place. We'd about given up on this."

Talk about a roller coaster ride: First, our expectations had soared because of promises by the people we were dealing with that *all* the hostages would be coming home soon; then, our hopes dropped when they didn't deliver and we realized that they had exaggerated their ability to get out the hostages. Then, from Beirut, another hostage would come out.

It was a roller coaster ride, but I still felt good about the Iranian initiative. Apparently risking their lives by dealing with us, the moderates in Teheran had demonstrated a second time that they could deliver. John Poindexter said Father Jenco's release had been arranged by the same Iranians and Israelis who had brought out the Reverend Benjamin Weir from Beirut the previous September, and was a direct result of Bud McFarlane's Iranian mission in May.

He said that the same group expected to arrange the release of all of the hostages shortly. Moreover, he said, there was another encouraging result of our Iranian initiative: Public pronouncements by Iranian officials had been conveying a more conciliatory tone toward the United States.

Not that there weren't problems: The Hizballah kidnappers were trying to become more independent of the Iranian Revolutionary Guards, and were demanding, as a price for releasing the remaining Americans, that the United States exert pressure on Kuwait to free seventeen Shiite terrorists imprisoned in that country after they had bombed the U.S. and French embassies there in 1983. There was no way we could do that. This was something nonnegotiable on our part: We wanted our hostages back, but we couldn't ask another country to go easy on convicted terrorists at the same time that we were asking the world to crack down on terrorism.

Despite this problem and various delays, disappointments, and frustrations, the Iranian initiative seemed to be working—and we were *not* trading arms for hostages. None of the arms we'd shipped to Iran had gone to the terrorists who had kidnapped our citizens.

After Father Jenco's release, Bill Casey and the NSC staff suggested we authorize a small additional shipment of spare missile parts to the Iranian military forces as a demonstration of goodwill and gratitude. If we didn't, Casey said, it was possible that our principal contact in the Iranian government might lose face and even be executed by those in Iran who were opposed to what he was doing. There was also the possibility, he said, that if we didn't give them a show of goodwill, one or more of the remaining three hostages might be killed. I authorized this additional shipment, and we went back to anxiously waiting for the other hostages to be set free.

About this same time, George Shultz came to me and said he wanted to resign; although he had never stopped letting me know that he didn't approve of the Iranian policy, that wasn't his reason: He thought that Cap Weinberger, Bill Casey, and John Poindexter were ganging up on him and pushing foreign policy issues that he opposed behind his back. He felt that I'd lost faith in him. "That isn't true," I wrote in the diary. "As far as I'm concerned, he can stay as long as I'm here." George came to the Oval Office and I told him that we were on the same wavelength and talked him out of resigning. I thank the Lord I did, because he was to be indispensable in our upcoming arms control negotiations with the Soviets.

I don't know what I expected when Father Jenco visited the Oval Office with his family shortly after his release, after a flight from Rome where he had had an audience with the pope. He was a warm man with an impressive gentleness, and very likable—but I was surprised at his reluctance to condemn his captors. I almost sensed he felt sympathy for the Muslims who had held him captive for nineteen months. He didn't seem to want to criticize them, and had no apparent bitterness, making me wonder if it was an example of the "Stockholm syndrome"—when, after a long time together, captives sometimes relate to their captors—or if it was simply his holy nature to forgive even those who had mistreated him.

Father Jenco handed me two letters. The first was a copy of a letter he had written to Pope John Paul II at the request of his captors. It was essentially a condemnation of the West by Shiite Muslims for "exploiting the female body." It also called on the Pope to help the Muslim Shiites—"the poorest of the poor"—who, Jenco said, complained of being denied proper housing, health care, educational opportunities, dignified work, and a voice in government.

Then he gave me a letter addressed to me:

Dear President Reagan:

An hour before I left my last prison, the leader of the group that held us hostage these past months verbally gave me messages to give to His Holiness Pope John Paul II, to you, and the families of Terry Anderson, David Jacobsen and Thomas Sutherland. He also wished me to convey to the Anderson family their condolences on the deaths of Terry Anderson's father and brother and their condolences to Rev. Ben Weir on the tragic death of his daughter in Cairo, Egypt.

The message that I was to give to you was to be confidential and I was to divulge its contents to no one else, but you and the families of the remaining three Americans and ask them to hold this message in strictest confidence. I wish, Mr. President, that I could be a bearer of good news. The message, Mr. President, is: "The condition for the release of Mr. Terry Anderson, Mr. David Jacobsen and Mr. Thomas Sutherland is the release of the seventeen being held in Kuwait. Their lives and the lives of other Americans are dependent on that condition being realized . . . and soon."

They believe that all you have to do, Mr. President, is pick up the phone and call the Emir of Kuwait and tell him to set the 17 free. I wish it were that easy.

One hour prior to that final conversation another leader informed me of the deaths of Terry Anderson's father and brother and of Rev. Ben Weir's daughter. He also said that they killed Mr. William Buckley because he was an evil man, he was the head of the C.I.A. in that region of the world. I personally believe Mr. Buckley died a natural death and my captors want other radical groups to believe they did execute him.

Both leaders asked forgiveness from me for the 19 months of suffering I had to endure; both quoted the final words of Jesus: "Father, forgive them for they know not what they do." Also they expressed their sadness about the kidnappings. They know kidnapping is wrong but they have no other forum to present their cause to the world.

They also asked that the American government's foreign policy in the Middle East be just. Presently, it is one sided: pro-Israel. And not all Arabs are oil millionaires. There are millions of poor Arabs in the Middle East who have legitimate human needs and rights that are denied them.

My captors in those final minutes stressed that they do not want the Syrians to be involved in any negotiations on the release of the other three Americans.

I have given you the message that I gave the Pope in Rome, John Paul II. I do this so that you know its contents. I did not tell them of the condition of the 17 of Kuwait. I am sure they know.

I pray to our dearest God I have recalled well those final conversations and I have honestly conveyed their messages.

Mr. President, there were times I did not have kind and charitable thoughts about my government, my Servite order, my church and the C.R.S. I have asked God's forgiveness for these sinful [thoughts] and ask your forgiveness, too. Thank you for your prayers and all that you have done on our behalf. In the future, I might still get angry— bear with me.

May the God of Abraham, Isaac and Jacob, of Jesus, of Mohammed, our God, answer our prayers, for the release of our fellow Americans . . . still held hostage somewhere.

> With gratitude.
> Father Lawrence Martin Jenco
> Servite

In the weeks after the release of Father Jenco, we had more disappointments—three more Americans were kidnapped in Beirut, not by the same faction of the Hizballah but by another terrorist group. On the plus side, the NSC succeeded in opening up what seemed to be a promising second channel of communication with high-level people in the Iranian government, involving a relative close to one of these officials; this relative seemed to share our concerns about the potential Soviet threat to Iran and wanted to patch up U.S.–Iranian relations. The young man was brought secretly to the United States for talks. Although I didn't meet him, John Poindexter told me that the official had asked his relative to bring him back signed photographs of me and other gifts, including a Christian bible. At John's request, I signed the bible and inscribed what I was told was one of the official's favorite verses.

Early fall 1986 was a busy time for all of us at the White House: Besides completing work on the tax reform act, there was the crisis set off by the arrest of American journalist Nicholas Daniloff in Moscow, my second summit conference with Mikhail Gorbachev, and other matters that kept us hopping, including congressional elections.

In early November, we got new evidence that the Iran initiative was working when a third American hostage, David Jacobsen, was freed in Beirut, and the Muslims who had held him promised to release the last two hostages they were holding within forty-eight hours.

When they released Jacobsen, his captors indicated vaguely that they were responding to unspecified American overtures. I decided that the only way to assure that the other hostages were released, as well as to protect our new channel in Teheran, was to say nothing about it: The United States would publicly keep at arm's length from Jacobsen's release. The day after he was freed—November 3,

1986—as we waited for the release of Anderson and Sutherland, a small magazine in Beirut published a story that asserted that America was trading arms for hostages, and mentioned Bud McFarlane's mission to Beirut in May.

That, of course, ignited a firestorm in the press. Pretty soon every newspaper and television station in America was repeating the same erroneous report—that I not only had traded arms for hostages but had been dealing with the Ayatollah Khomeini.

My diary entry for November 7 read:

> Usual meetings. Discussion of how to handle press who are off on a wild story built on unfounded story originating in Beirut that we bought hostage Jacobsen's freedom with weapons to Iran. We've tried "no comment." I've proposed and our message will be: "We can't and won't answer any questions on this subject because to do so will endanger the lives of those we are trying to help."

I wanted to keep quiet about the events in Iran and Beirut, not because they were something I was ashamed of—getting out three hostages was something I was proud of—but because I didn't want anything to interfere with the impending release of the other hostages or to endanger the Iranians who were helping us. But this was a case when silence did not beget silence.

David Jacobsen came to the White House on November 7 with his family. He was even more upset than I was over the press reports about the hostage negotiations. The situation faced by the other hostages was desperate, he told me, and if the drum beat of publicity continued, the Hizballah would not release Anderson and Sutherland. Then he went with me into the Rose Garden and begged the press to use restraint: "In the name of God, would you please just be responsible and back off?"

But the journalistic firestorm got larger and larger and, in it, I saw our expectations of bringing home Terry Anderson and Thomas Sutherland go up in smoke. It was one of the most unpleasant experiences of my presidency to watch this happen—hoping it would not happen, then accepting the reality that the other hostages weren't going to be coming home. My diary entry on November 10, three days after Jacobsen's visit to the White House, read:

A bright, pretty day. . . . At 11:30 a meeting in Oval Office—Don R., George Shultz, George Bush, Cap W., Bill Casey, Ed Meese, John P. and two of his staff. Subject the press storm charging that we are negotiating with terrorist kidnappers for the release of hostages using sale of arms as ransom. Also that we are violating our own law about arms sales to Iran. They quote as gospel every unnamed source plus such authorities as a Danish sailor who claims to have served on a ship carrying arms from Israel to Iran etc. . . . etc. . . . etc. I ordered a statement to effect we were *not* dealing in ransom, etc., but that we would not respond to charges or questions that could endanger hostage lives or lives of people we are using to make contact with the terrorists.

On November 12, my exasperation over the tenor of the coverage showed up again in this entry in my diary:

This whole irresponsible press bilge about hostages and Iran has gotten totally out of hand. The media looks like it's trying to create another Watergate. I laid down the law in the morning meetings. I want to go public personally and tell the people the truth. We're trying to arrange it for tomorrow.

In a twelve-minute address to the nation the following night, I made public the Iranian initiative and said: "We did not, repeat, did not trade weapons or anything else for hostages, nor will we."

If I thought candor and forthrightness would calm the storm, I was wrong. At a press conference, I tried again to explain what my motivations had been for the initiative and acknowledged that George Shultz and Cap Weinberger had opposed it. "I weighed their views," I said. "I considered the risks of failure and the rewards of success, and I decided to proceed. And the responsibility for the decision and the operation is mine and mine alone. As Mr. Lincoln said of another presidential decision: If it turns out right, the criticism will not matter. If it turns out wrong, ten angels swearing I was right will make no difference."

Although they never said "I told you so," George and Cap had been wise and correct: Whatever the truth of the matter, the Iranian initiative was made to *look* like an arms-for-hostage deal. We learned that the secrecy of our covert operation had first been revealed by an enemy of Rafsanjani's who wanted to embarrass him politically and leaked the story to that paper in Beirut. Except that he told it wrong. He said we were doing business with the *government* of Iran—in other words, the ayatollah himself—and that we were trading arms for hostages. Then our press took it up and printed the same false story—to this day, they still are—that we were doing business with the ayatollah, trading arms for hostages. We weren't. We had never had any contacts with the kidnappers, had seen to it that the defensive weapons that went to Iran never got into the hands of the people who held our hostages. But the press took the word of the Beirut paper over ours.

On November 20, a Thursday, after the furor had been going on for more than two weeks, Don Regan told me that George Shultz, who by then had gone public with his unhappiness over the Iran affair, wanted to see me to lay down an ultimatum: Either I fire John Poindexter, or George would quit. I invited George and Don to the living quarters at the White House that evening to discuss the situation. George, as I'd been warned, was extremely upset and urged me to fire Poindexter. He said Poindexter had misled me and others in the administration about the weapons shipments. Although George didn't threaten to quit, I wrote in the diary: "I fear he may be getting ready to say, 'either someone else is fired or I quit.' I've called a Monday afternoon meeting of him and Don, me and Cap W., Bill Casey, John P. and the VP to get everything about the Iran effort out on the table."

I respected George Shultz as a man of the highest integrity. He made me wonder if there were things about the Iranian initiative I didn't know about. So, early the next day, I asked Attorney General Ed Meese to come to the White House and I told him about George's remarks.

Ed said some of his people in the Justice Department had already found inconsistencies in some of the things we had been saying, based on Poindexter's remarks, about the weapon shipments to Iran. I asked him to conduct an immediate and thorough review of the events to find out exactly what had happened. It was Friday; I asked him to spend the weekend looking into the matter, and to report to me on Monday.

Nancy and I spent the weekend at Camp David, where the weather was crisp and very cold. I spent a good part of Saturday and Sunday watching myself being pilloried on television because of the Iran initiative.

On Monday morning, the Iran affair was the subject of a two-hour meeting in the Situation Room. Afterward, I wrote in my diary: "George Shultz is still stubborn that we shouldn't have sold the arms to Iran. I gave him an argument. All in all, we got everything out on the table."

Then, at four thirty that afternoon, Ed Meese and Don Regan brought me a bombshell: Over the weekend, one of Ed's assistants had discovered a memorandum indicating that Lieutenant Colonel Oliver North, while working with the Iranians to arrange the release of the hostages, had diverted part of the money the Iranians paid for the weapons to support the freedom fighters in Nicaragua —and John Poindexter had known about it.

My first reaction was that Poindexter and North wouldn't do anything like that without telling me—that there had to be a mistake. But Ed said he was sure, there hadn't been a mistake, the memorandum made it clear what had happened.

In recounting this meeting in my diary that night, I used these words to discuss the revelation: "After the meeting in the Situation Room, Ed M. and Don R. told me of a smoking gun. On one of the arms shipments the Iranians had paid Israel a higher purchase price than we were getting. The Israelis put the difference in a secret bank account. Then our Col. North (N.S.C.) gave the money to the 'Contras.' . . . North didn't tell me about this. Worst of all, John P. found out about it and didn't tell me. This may call for resignations."

After an initial reaction of surprise, shock, and disbelief to what Ed Meese had found, I told the cabinet and the White House staff that we were going to do everything we could to get to the bottom of the matter, immediately make public the discovery, and hide nothing. The worst thing we could do was try to cover it up. Early the next morning, I met with the leadership of the Congress—both houses, both parties, in one meeting—to tell them what Ed had found. Then I announced it to the press. Ed took their questions for an hour and we leveled with them, the whole truth. John Poindexter submitted his resignation as national security advisor and Oliver North was relieved of his duties on the NSC staff. Then I went on television to inform the American people what we had discovered. I asked ex-Senator John Tower, former Secretary of State (and former Senator) Edmund Muskie, and former White House National Security Advisor Brent Scowcroft to make a full and independent investigation to determine exactly what had happened. I also asked for the appointment of an independent prosecutor to look into the matter and determine if any laws had been violated.

69

THOSE FIRST MONTHS after the Iran-Contra affair hit the front pages were frustrating for me. For the first time in my life, people didn't believe me. I had told the truth, but they still didn't believe me. While I was unhappy, I never felt depressed about the situation: There wasn't a gloom or "malaise" hanging over the Oval Office, as some writers have suggested. I just went on with my job.

Nancy says I never get depressed, and it's true that I tend to see the positive things in life. In this case, I didn't feel that I had done anything to feel depressed about. There's a difference between having done something wrong and feeling bad about it, on the one hand, and, on the other, having an inner feeling that says you haven't done anything wrong—and that's how I felt. I knew everything I had done was within the law and within the president's powers. But if I wasn't depressed about what was going on, I sure felt frustrated that I couldn't get my message across.

Every autumn, just before Thanksgiving, the president is presented with a huge turkey in celebration of Turkey Day; in 1986, it weighed fifty-eight pounds. What many people don't know is that the president and his family don't sit down and eat this behemoth bird: It's a ceremonial gobbler brought for picture-taking. Then it returns home, possibly to make a return appearance the following year. It's never put in an oven. But that Thanksgiving, which we spent at Rancho del Cielo, I felt I was the one being roasted.

The pundits claimed that the administration was "paralyzed"

and "dead in the water." That wasn't true. We were still proceeding with our domestic and foreign policy programs. We had all kinds of things we were battling for every day. Still, the Iran-Contra hoopla caused a lot of distractions for the administration and, until all the answers were in, I knew there would be a cloud over the White House. Every day there was another "revelation" about the affair. Congressmen were demanding answers, and some were calling for the first special session of Congress since 1948.

I wanted answers, too. I told congressional leaders, who formed two committees to investigate the affair, that I was willing to go along with any effort they felt was necessary to get to the bottom of the problem. I asked them to schedule the hearings as soon as possible, and offered to waive the White House's executive privilege so that Poindexter and North could testify openly and we could all learn the truth. In response to my request, an independent counsel was named to investigate possible criminal violations in the Iran-Contra affair. I brought home our NATO ambassador, David Abshire, to handle the White House's response to the investigations, and directed him to make sure no one in the administration kept any secrets from Congress or the Tower Board. And we sent word to the lawyers representing Oliver North and John Poindexter, who knew what had happened, that I wanted them to tell the entire truth and do nothing to protect me.

As the furor continued, I came under pressure to make personnel changes. Some of this advice came from people who were very close to me, including Nancy, my children, and former political advisors like Mike Deaver and Stu Spencer.

George Shultz had to go, some said, because he'd said publicly that he opposed the Iran initiative. That was something I couldn't conceive of: George was a patriot who had done nothing except express an opinion and stick to his principles. Along with Cap Weinberger, he'd been correct: His prediction about what would happen if the Iran initiative ever became public knowledge had been right on the mark.

A lot of people also wanted me to replace Don Regan. They said he had supported the Iran operation and hadn't been on top of things when it started to get into trouble. But I felt that, whatever blame there might be in the Iran-Contra affair, it wasn't his. Besides, I hadn't needed anyone to push me to accept a proposal to meet with responsible Iranians about the possibility of establishing a relationship with the people who might someday be running the government of Iran.

There was also criticism heaped on Bill Casey, and I was urged to replace him, too. That was something I couldn't do to a man who was fighting for his life against brain cancer.

Mike Deaver urged me to hire a criminal lawyer. He said it was likely I'd have to defend myself against criminal charges, because North or Poindexter might try to blame me for what had happened. I told him I had nothing to hide: I didn't care what anybody said, I hadn't done anything wrong, and didn't want to do anything that could be construed as throwing a roadblock in the way of getting at the truth.

Christmas in Washington that year was a difficult time for all of us. As we waited for the Tower Board to complete its investigation, Nancy, as always, gave me support when I needed it, even though it was an extremely tough period on her and the children. Nancy thought that people had served me badly and wanted me to do something quickly to restore the American people's faith in my honesty. She wanted me to be more critical of North and Poindexter for hiding things from me—but I said that I was the one responsible for the Iran initiative, that we still didn't know all the answers, and that it wouldn't be fair to do that.

On Christmas Day, after spending the previous evening at the home of our friends Charles and Mary Jane Wick, we opened our gifts at the White House. There were phone calls from everyone in the family except Patti and her husband Paul, and my brother and his wife. When I spoke to Ron, I could tell something was troubling him. Two days later, when we were in Los Angeles, I found out what it was. He and Maureen told me they wanted to talk with me alone. Once again, the subject was Iran-Contra. Simply put, they said they were worried about their old man—concerned about the licking I was taking in the press—and urged me to show more anger at the people involved in the affair and fire some of them.

Maureen and Ron were trying to help me. I realized that. But I told them that I thought I was handling things the right way, and that I couldn't fire people just to save my own neck.

· · ·

A few days into the new year, after we'd returned to Washington, I had to go again to Bethesda Naval Hospital, this time for minor prostate surgery. After I was released, my doctors told me to take it easy. I went to work on a light schedule and told the cabinet and staff that the administration had been preoccupied too long with the Iran-Contra crisis and it was time to go forward.

We were still trying to free the hostages in Lebanon, but having little success at it. The situation had grown even worse since our efforts went up in smoke during November: Early in the new year, terrorists seized three American college professors in Beirut. We sent our Delta Force commando team to Cyprus with orders to prepare a rescue effort, but British officials urged us not to proceed with the operation. They said that it would be impossible to maintain secrecy over the raid and even rumors of it might cause the death of the hostages or of British emissary Terry Waite, who was in Beirut trying to free them.

Later, after we had scrubbed the rescue attempt, Waite himself was taken hostage; then still more hostages were seized. "It's a frustrating business," I wrote in my diary January 26, 1987. "You feel like lowering the boom on *someone,* but how do you do it without getting some hostages killed? We need more intelligence on who and where . . ." The next day, the Joint Chiefs of Staff began making a list of targets in Iran for possible retaliation because of the hostage-taking; but we knew that any application of military force could bring harm to the hostages.

I appointed Frank Carlucci, a former CIA official, to succeed John Poindexter as national security advisor, and he appointed as his deputy a brilliant army officer, Lieutenant General Colin Powell. Together, they began tightening the lines of authority inside the NSC, while the State Department took over the portfolio for exploiting any opportunities to reestablish relations with Iran.

Bill Casey's continuing absence from the CIA was causing problems there. Although his doctors said it was unlikely that he could ever return to his job, they said that if we told him that, it would probably set back whatever chances he had for a recovery. That left us with a dilemma. We decided to wait a few weeks; if, as the doctors predicted, he still did not recover enough to go back to the

CIA, I would offer him a job in the cabinet (eventually I offered him the post of counselor to the president, Ed Meese's old job, and he was delighted by it) while we began a quiet search for a successor. I initially favored former Senator Howard Baker, who had a reputation for high integrity and had been an outstanding majority leader in the Senate, or Edward Bennett Williams, the Washington lawyer. Williams wanted the job—but before we could offer it to him, he discovered that he, like Casey, was dying from cancer. Ultimately, we persuaded FBI director William Webster to take the job at CIA, and we found another job for Howard Baker.

It has been reported that I replaced Don Regan as White House chief of staff because I thought he did not do a good job of "protecting" me from political damage during the Iran-Contra problem —but in fact I never felt that way, and Iran-Contra had nothing to do with his replacement. I had appointed Don secretary of the treasury on the advice of some of the members of my old Kitchen Cabinet in California; they'd called him a wizard on economic matters. He had gone on to do an outstanding job at the Treasury Department, especially by helping get tax reform off the ground and in winning Wall Street's support of the economic recovery program; he was one of the strongest advocates in the cabinet for sticking with the economic recovery program after David Stockman and others began urging me to abandon it. But I was to learn that I had created some problems when I appointed him to succeed Jim Baker as White House chief of staff.

As I've mentioned, being president sometimes isolates you from events going on right around you: Many people are reluctant to tell you things that they think might cause you worries; some believe you only want to hear "good" news. Many in the administration were less reluctant to speak up to Nancy about troublesome matters—I guess they knew she had my ear—and I'd discovered long before I got to the White House that she was gifted with a special instinct that helped her understand the motives of some people better than I did. In a way, she gave me an extra set of eyes and ears.

I learned from Nancy and then from others that many people— staff members, cabinet members, and congressional leaders—felt that Don had an oversized ego that made him difficult to deal with. Because of the way he treated people, I was told, morale was bad among the staff. According to some, Don thought of himself as a kind of "deputy president" empowered to make important decisions involving the administration. Although I only found out about it later, he resisted having others see me alone and wouldn't forward letters or documents to me unless he saw them first. In short, he wanted to be the *only* conduit to the Oval Office, in effect making that presidential isolation I just complained about even more complete. Nancy, ever protective of me, had been among the first to urge me to let Don go after the Iran-Contra affair began— although, as I've said, I didn't believe he had done anything to warrant it. But the morale issue was another matter, and I decided to look into it, especially after new problems came up following my surgery in January.

My doctors told me to take it easy for up to six weeks after the operation. Nancy, always a doctor's daughter, wanted me to follow their orders. After I left the hospital, she said she thought Don was pushing me too hard in scheduling public appearances, and at one point she called him about it. He ended the conversation by hanging up on her. That night, in early February, when I came up to the family quarters after work, she was very upset and told me how he had hung up on her. I was troubled by this kind of temperamental outburst, especially toward Nancy, who has always had only my best interests at heart.

By then, many other people in the administration were confirming what Nancy had told me about the morale problem and about Don's efforts to shield me from virtually all opinions other than his own. Once it started, I heard the same thing over and over again: Don required everything to go through him. Just down the hall from the Oval Office, he was in a position to do that. I had always liked Don and enjoyed his Irish humor, but that wasn't the way I wanted to run the store.

Several times during the previous year, Don had told me he wanted to return to private life, and in November he had submitted a letter of resignation. But after the Iran-Contra affair started to heat up, he said he didn't want to leave until it was resolved, because if he did it might appear that he was admitting blame for it. I respected that and asked him to stay. At the same time, aware that he was anxious to leave, I started thinking about a replacement, so I'd be ready whenever he gave the word.

By the middle of February, when the release of the Tower report was only a few days off, the complaints about Don had become a chorus. There were reports that he had claimed Nancy was behind my appointment of Jack Koehler as White House director of communications. (Koehler subsequently withdrew his name from consideration after reports surfaced that he had belonged briefly to the Hitler Youth organization as a ten-year-old boy.) I wrote in my diary February 22: *That does it.* Nancy had never met Koehler and had had nothing to do with his appointment." The next day, after the usual morning staff and NSC meetings, Don came alone into the Oval Office. I let him know I thought it was time for him to leave. We agreed that he would depart after I chose a successor and the Tower Board made its report public.

On February 25, the day before I was to receive the report prior to its public release, I got a surprise: Through an intermediary, I learned that Don had changed his mind. He wanted to remain chief of staff through April, then be appointed chairman of the Federal Reserve Board to succeed Paul Volcker, whose term was scheduled to expire that summer. Don never brought this proposal up to me personally, so I can't confirm whether or not it was true. But I sent word to him that it couldn't be.

The next day, George Bush and Don had lunch. Afterward, I noted in my diary that George said he'd observed "for the first time a side of him [Don] he hadn't seen—an outburst of temper. Finally, [Don] snarled he'd be out of here Monday or Tuesday."

That evening, I asked Paul Laxalt to come to the White House and told him I'd like him to take on the White House job. But he said he might make a run for the presidency and didn't want to take himself out of the running by taking the job. "His candidate," I wrote, "is former Senator Howard Baker. It's not a bad idea. He thinks Howard is looking for a graceful way of getting out of running for president. I'd probably take some lumps from our right wingers, but I can handle that . . ."

The entry for February 26 continued: "VP just came up—another meeting with Don. This time totally different. He says he'll hand in his resignation first thing Monday morning. My prayers have really been answered."

Another prayer was answered later the same day during a telephone conversation with Howard Baker. "Howard was in Florida visiting his grandchildren. When he called back I asked him to take the job. Paul was right. He accepted immediately and is coming to Washington tomorrow . . ."

This diary entry concluded: "Now I'll go on reading the Tower report till I fall asleep . . ."

During our meeting the week before, Don Regan had said he would remain on the job until I found a replacement for him; then I would announce his resignation and the name of his successor and the date of the change. Unfortunately, there was a news leak, and it became public that I intended to replace Don with Howard Baker. The leak was not intentional, and I had not wanted to embarrass Don.

The next thing I knew, Kathy Osborne sent an envelope to me at the residence (it was almost 6:00 P.M.) that contained a single sheet of paper. It said:

I resign as Chief of Staff to the President of the United States.
                                        Donald T. Regan.
                                        Chief of Staff to the
                                        President of the United States

I wrote out the following reply by hand for Kathy to type:

Dear Don:

In accepting your resignation I want you to know how deeply grateful I am for all that you have done for the administration and for the country. As Secretary of the Treasury you planted the seeds for the most far reaching tax reform in our history. As Chief of Staff you worked tirelessly and effectively for the policies and programs we proposed to the Congress.

I know that you stayed on beyond the time you had set for your return to private life and did so because you felt you could be of help in a time of trouble. You were of help and I thank you. Whether on the deck of your beloved boat or on the fairway; in the spirit of our forefathers, may the sun shine warm upon your face, the wind be always at your back and may God hold you in the hollow of His hand.

                                        Sincerely,
                                        Ronald Reagan

After this matter was settled, I began writing a speech to deliver to the nation in conjunction with the public release of the Tower Board's report. While I was working on it, my son Ron flew to Washington from California and, in the privacy of the family quarters, we had a man-to-man talk of a kind we'd never had before. I'll always remember and feel proud and blessed by the sentiment that motivated Ron to make that trip across the country. As I wrote late that night in my diary, "Ron came from the coast to plead with me—out of his love for me—to take forceful action and change the situation [that had caused so much anguish for me and the administration]. I was deeply touched." What a lucky father I am, I thought.

In my speech to the nation on March 4, 1987, I accepted full responsibility for the Iran-Contra affair and then added: "What should happen when you make a mistake is this: You take your knocks, you learn your lessons, and then you move on."

Howard Baker went on to become an outstanding chief of staff, a perfect man for the job—smart, fair, personable, savvy about Washington, a decent man. And Frank Carlucci and Colin Powell went on to revitalize and restore honor to the NSC.

The cloud that descended over my credibility during the Iran-Contra affair undoubtedly affected the fate of some of my legislative goals during my last two years in office. With the Democrats controlling both houses of Congress, it's hard to say how much more we might have accomplished if the crisis hadn't occurred, but clearly it had some impact. Still, we were able to move on once the Tower Board had removed the cloud from over the White House and agreed, as did the congressional investigating committees, with what I had been saying from the beginning: that I had had no knowledge of any diversion of monies to the Contras.

To this day I still believe that the Iran initiative was *not* an effort to swap arms for hostages. But I know it may not look that way to some people.

I still believe that the policy that led us to attempt to open up a channel to moderate Iranians wasn't wrong. Nevertheless, as I said in my speech when the Tower report was made public, mistakes were made in the implementation of this policy. Because I was so concerned with getting the hostages home, I may not have asked enough questions about how the Iranian initiative was being conducted. I trusted our people to obey the law. Unfortunately, an initiative meant to develop a relationship with moderate Iranians and get our hostages home took on a new shape I never expected and was never told about.

Mistakes were made and I tried to rectify them, first by appointing the Tower Board to investigate the events, then by reorganizing the National Security Council to ensure that no one there could ever again take it upon themselves to set foreign policy. In time, my ranking in the public opinion polls rose. But that never made me feel as happy as some people might think it would: It was as if Americans were forgiving me for something I hadn't done.

When it first began to appear that North and Poindexter had done things they hadn't advised me of, my initial reaction was, well, perhaps they thought they were doing the right thing and trying to protect me, and I felt compassion for both of them. I did not know, during those first days following the discovery of the "smoking gun" memo, that North and others at the NSC had spent hours shredding documents. Nor did I have any idea of the full magnitude of how I had been misled.

Before learning these things, I called North, after he had been relieved of his duties at the NSC. During this conversation I referred to him as a national hero; I was thinking about his service in Vietnam. As I've mentioned, I subsequently learned that North had allegedly claimed that he met with me often in the Oval Office and at Camp David, and that we spoke on the phone frequently and there was a private pipeline between the two of us. Well, none of those things were true. The truth is—as he testified before Congress —that I hardly knew him.

I received a lot of pressure from my supporters, starting from the first days after the Iran-Contra story broke and continuing to my last week in the White House, to grant clemency to Oliver North and John Poindexter. I never gave it serious consideration: I felt that if I pardoned them before a trial, there would be a shadow of guilt over them for the rest of their lives and the suspicion of cover-up. I felt that once the legal process had begun, the law had to take its course.

· · ·

As exhaustive as its investigation was, the Tower Board did not answer all the questions about the Iran-Contra affair. It told us that Oliver North appeared to have diverted millions of dollars in "residual" income from the weapons sales to keep the Contras equipped and alive. I've seen speculation that the diversion amounted to as much as $8 million or $12 million. Bud McFarlane testified that North had told him the Contras were benefiting from the sale of arms to the Iranians. But, to this day, after all the trials and ten months of congressional investigations, there are still many details we do not know about the transfer of those weapons and the exchange of money for them—exactly how much money was involved and where it went, for example.

Although the Tower Board said that there was "considerable evidence before it of a diversion of funds to support the Contras," it found "no hard proof" of that. The congressional investigations filled in some of the gaps, but a lot remains unclear.

Bill Casey, John Poindexter, Oliver North, and Bud McFarlane knew that I believed that the survival of the Contras as a democratic resistance force was essential in Nicaragua. I made no secret of that. They also knew that I stood firmly behind the initiative proposed by Israel aimed at freeing the hostages and opening up talks with the future leaders of Iran. But until Ed Meese uncovered North's memorandum, I had not heard a whisper about funds being channeled from the Iranian arms shipments to the Contras—and I would not have approved it if anyone had suggested it to me.

Yes, I believed in helping the Contras; but no one, including presidents, is above the law. The Iranian initiative was secret, but I was assured that everything about it was legal. And one thing about the Iranian initiative will never change: we did bring home three hostages.

But looking back now, with the benefit of hindsight and the Tower Board's report, it appears that, despite Israel's repeated assurances that we were dealing with responsible moderates in Iran, some of those "moderates" may have had links to the Ayatollah Khomeini's government and were trying to obtain weapons under false pretenses. And despite Israel's endorsement of them, we now know that some of the middlemen we were dealing with during the Iran initiative (and who helped us win the freedom of three hostages) behaved at times like bait-and-switch con men: They would make promises, then renege on them, lying to McFarlane, North, Poindexter, and others with the sole intention of profiteering. During this process, apparently, Oliver North and others at the NSC agreed to certain things—such as promising secret U.S. intelligence data to the Iranians for use in their war with Iraq—that I was never told about.

Because of his illness and subsequent death, I never had a chance to learn from Bill Casey what he knew about Iran-Contra. Probably only John Poindexter and Oliver North know all the answers. In this regard, I've often wondered if we didn't move too fast after Ed Meese uncovered the memorandum that disclosed the diversion of funds to the Contras. Ed said that Poindexter and North shouldn't remain in their jobs another day, and Don Regan agreed; he said it would be important to show that we took decisive action as soon as the diversion of funds was discovered.

As a result, on the day that John Poindexter came to the Oval Office to resign, I didn't ask him the questions I now wish I had. If we hadn't acted so quickly, maybe he and North would have told me some of the things that are still a mystery to me after all this time.

If I could do it over again, I would bring both of them into the Oval Office and say, "Okay, John and Ollie, level with me. Tell me what really happened and what it is that you have been hiding from me. Tell me everything."

If I had done that, at least I wouldn't be sitting here, writing this book, still ignorant of some of the things that went on during the Iran-Contra affair.

PART SIX

Arms Control: From Geneva to Reykjavík, Washington to Moscow

70

A CERTAIN AMOUNT OF MYTHOLOGY grew up around the Strategic Defense Initiative, the program I announced in 1983 to develop a defensive shield against nuclear missiles. It wasn't conceived by scientists, although they came on board and contributed greatly to its success.

I came into office with a decided prejudice against our tacit agreement with the Soviet Union regarding nuclear missiles. I'm talking about the MAD policy—"mutual assured destruction"—the idea of deterrence providing safety so long as each of us had the power to destroy the other with nuclear missiles if one of us launched a first strike. Somehow this didn't seem to me to be something that would send you to bed feeling safe. It was like having two westerners standing in a saloon aiming their guns at each other's head—permanently. There had to be a better way.

Early in my first term, I called a meeting of the Joint Chiefs of Staff—our military leaders—and said to them: Every offensive weapon ever invented by man has resulted in the creation of a defense against it; isn't it possible in this age of technology that we could invent a defensive weapon that could intercept nuclear weapons and destroy them as they emerged from their silos?

They looked at each other, then asked if they could huddle for a few moments. Very shortly, they came out of their huddle and said, "Yes, it's an idea worth exploring." My answer was, "Let's do it."

So the SDI was born, and very shortly some in Congress and the press named it "Star Wars."

As the myths grew, one of them was that I had proposed the idea to produce a bargaining chip for use in getting the Soviets to reduce their weaponry. I've had to tell the Soviet leaders a hundred times that the SDI was not a bargaining chip. I've told them I'd share it with others willing to give up their nuclear missiles. We all know how to make the missiles. One day a madman could come along and make the missiles and blackmail all of us—but not if we have a defense against them. My closing line was, "We all got together in 1925 and banned the use of poison gas. But we all kept our gas masks."

Some people may take a different view, but if I had to choose the single most important reason, on the United States' side, for the historic breakthroughs that were to occur during the next five years in the quest for peace and a better relationship with the Soviet Union, I would say it was the Strategic Defense Initiative, along with the overall modernization of our military forces.

But looking back now on the entirety of those eight years I was in Washington, I have to say that the improvements in U.S.-Soviet relations didn't come quickly and they didn't come easily.

As I have mentioned before, the Soviet Union we faced during my first winter in office was guided by a policy of immoral and unbridled expansionism. During that first year, we embarked on a broad program of military renewal to upgrade our land, sea, and air forces and adopted a foreign policy aimed at making it clear to the Soviets that we now viewed them through a prism of reality: We knew what they were up to, we were not going to accept subversion of democratic governments, and we would never accept second place in the arms race.

At the same time, recognizing the futility of the arms race and the hair-trigger risk of annihilation it posed to the world, I tried to send signals to Moscow indicating we were prepared to negotiate a winding down of the arms race if the Soviets were also sincere about it—and proved it with *deeds*.

These policies were linked: Because we now viewed the Soviets through the prism of reality, we knew we would never get anywhere with them at the arms control table if we went there in a position of military inferiority; if we were going to get them to sue for peace, we had to do it from a position of strength.

And, because we viewed them realistically, it was clear that if we did negotiate an arms control agreement with the Soviets, it had to be absolutely verifiable. Agreements couldn't be based on trust alone.

I didn't want the United States ever to have to do what it sometimes had been forced to do in the past: go to the arms control table with the Russians holding better cards and having to beg them to negotiate seriously with an appeal to their better nature. That's why "Peace through Strength" became one of the mottoes of our administration.

And I decided that if we were to participate with the Russians in arms control talks, our goal should be to *reduce* nuclear weapons, not just limit their rate of increase, which is what past nuclear arms control agreements had done.

There is a myth that arms control agreements automatically produce arms reduction. Well, between 1969, when the Strategic Arms Limitation Talks (SALT) began, and the mid-eighties, the Soviets increased their number of strategic nuclear weapons by thousands, and under the limits set by the SALT I and SALT II agreements the number could have reached thousands more.

That might be arms limitation, but it sure wasn't arms reduction.

Looking back at the recent history of the world, I find it amazing how far civilization has retrogressed so quickly. As recently as World War I—granted the rules were violated at times—we had a set of rules of warfare in which armies didn't make war against civilians: Soldiers fought soldiers. Then came World War II and Hitler's philosophy of total war, which meant the bombing not only of soldiers but of factories that produced their rifles, and, if surrounding communities were also hit, that was to be accepted; then, as the war progressed, it became common for the combatants simply to attack civilians as part of military strategy.

By the time the 1980s rolled around, we were placing our entire faith in a weapon whose *fundamental target was the civilian population*.

A nuclear war is aimed at people, no matter how often military men like to say, "No, we only aim to hit other missiles."

One of the first statistics I saw as president was one of the most sobering and startling I'd ever heard. I'll never forget it:

The Pentagon said at least 150 million American lives would be lost in a nuclear war with the Soviet Union—even if we "won."

For Americans who survived such a war, I couldn't imagine what life would be like. The planet would be so poisoned the "survivors" would have no place to live.

Even if a nuclear war did not mean the extinction of mankind, it would certainly mean the end of civilization as we knew it.

No one could "win" a nuclear war. Yet as long as nuclear weapons were in existence, there would always be risks they would be used, and once the first nuclear weapon was unleashed, who knew where it would end?

My dream, then, became a world free of nuclear weapons.

Some of my advisors, including a number at the Pentagon, did not share this dream. They couldn't conceive of it. They said a nuclear-free world was unattainable and it would be dangerous for us even if it were possible; some even claimed nuclear war was "inevitable" and we had to prepare for this reality. They tossed around macabre jargon about "throw weights" and "kill ratios" as if they were talking about baseball scores. But for the eight years I was president I never let my dream of a nuclear-free world fade from my mind.

Since I knew it would be a long and difficult task to rid the world of nuclear weapons, I had this second dream: the creation of a defense against nuclear missiles, so we could change from a policy of assured destruction to one of assured survival.

My deepest hope was that someday our children and our grandchildren could live in a world free of the constant threat of nuclear war.

During my first year in Washington, we reopened arms negotiations with the Russians in Geneva but made virtually no progress, blocked by the refusal of the Soviets to end their subversion of democratic governments, their continuing aggression in Afghanistan and brutal crackdown in Poland, and their resistance to the zero-zero plan I proposed in November 1981 to eliminate intermediate-range missiles from Europe. I viewed the zero-zero proposal as the first step toward the eventual elimination of *all* nuclear weapons from the earth; the Soviets saw it as an attempt by us to reduce the immense Soviet imbalance of nuclear missile power in Europe —which it was.

When the Russians wouldn't agree to remove the SS-20 missiles that they had aimed at European cities, we said we were going to proceed with NATO's plans for us to deploy Pershing II and cruise missiles in Europe in the fall of 1983 to counter the threat of the SS-20s.

Although we had imposed economic sanctions on the Polish government and the Soviet Union following the cruel crackdown in Poland, our European allies, more greatly concerned about their trade relations in Eastern Europe, did not back us with the kind of support needed to make the sanctions as effective as I hoped, causing a temporary, if ultimately forgotten, strain in the Western alliance. Alone, we pressed ahead with the sanctions, although, as I wrote in my diary in early 1982, "The plain truth is: we can't— alone—hurt the Soviets that much. The Soviets, however, will be disturbed at the evidence that their attempt to split us off from our allies have failed." A few days after I wrote this, Anatoly Dobrynin, the longtime Soviet ambassador to the United States, and his wife came to the White House for dinner with other members of the Washington diplomatic corps. "Everything we've heard is true: They are a most likable couple," I wrote. "In fact, so much so you wonder how they can stick with the Soviet system. Truth is, he and his wife are most likable and very much in love with each other after forty years of marriage."

Dobrynin was doubtlessly a dedicated Communist. But I couldn't help liking him as a human being, and if that were possible, I wondered, wasn't it possible the peoples of America and the Soviet Union had a chance to reduce the mistrust that had led us to the nuclear precipice?

This dinner for the diplomatic corps occurred only one day after I had been given a briefing on the astonishing Soviet arms buildup, which left me amazed at its scale, cost, and breadth and the danger it posed to our country. The output of long-range missiles alone was staggering. Several days later, I had another briefing, this time on the Soviet economy. The latest figures provided additional evidence that it was a basket case, and even if I hadn't majored in economics in college, it would have been plain to me that Communism was doomed as a failed economic system. The situation was so bad that if Western countries got together and cut off credits to it, we could bring it to its knees. How could the Soviets afford their huge arms buildup? Perhaps, I mused to myself in March 1982, America should "explore if the time hasn't come to confront the Russians and tell them all the things we could do for them if they'd quit their bad acting and decide to join the civilized world. . . ."

In the spring of 1982, in a speech at a Eureka College reunion marking the fiftieth anniversary of my graduating class, I renewed my invitation to the Soviets to initiate the START (the Strategic Arms Reduction Talks), which we'd put on hold after the Soviets imposed martial law in Poland. At the same time, in speeches at the United Nations and other places, I made it a point to speak with frankness on what I thought of Soviet expansionism. I wanted to remind Leonid Brezhnev that we knew what the Soviets were up to and that we weren't going to stand by and do nothing while they sought world domination; I also tried to send out a signal that the United States intended to support people fighting for their freedom against Communism wherever they were—a policy some writers later described as the "Reagan Doctrine." I felt it was time to speak the truth, not platitudes, even though a lot of liberals and some members of the State Department's Striped Pants Set sometimes didn't like my choice of words. Some congressmen and columnists claimed that I was determined to get us into a nuclear war with the Soviets.

My critics in Congress began chipping away, then slashing away, at the money we needed to rebuild our military forces. Meanwhile, inspired by a similar movement in Europe with roots in Moscow, many well-meaning Americans (as well as some driven solely by sympathies for the other side) began taking to the streets to demand an immediate freeze on the development and deployment of nuclear weapons.

Nuclear freeze had a nice-sounding emotional appeal, but the Russians had such a huge advantage over the United States in large land-based nuclear missiles with multiple warheads that if we agreed to one, we'd have had to meet them at the arms talks as second-class citizens—and if the unthinkable happened, it was possible their arsenal of giant missiles could overwhelm our older, unmodernized, and vulnerable retaliatory forces. Well-meaning or not, the nuclear freeze movement had an agenda that could have been written in Moscow.

In May 1982, I sent a letter to Brezhnev suggesting a resumption of arms control talks at Geneva before the end of June. "As you know," I wrote,

> it is my view that our previous efforts at limiting strategic offensive arms did not adequately meet the standards of reduction, equality and verification. The awesome destructive power of nuclear weapons imposes on our two countries both the practical necessity and the moral imperative to do everything within our power to reduce and even eliminate the possibility of their use in war. This has been the thrust of my country's approach to nuclear arms control for over the past 35 years ... we now stand at another historic juncture in the effort to reduce the threat of nuclear war.

While Brezhnev's response was not cordial, he agreed to new talks. "It is not our fault," he wrote, "that the Strategic Arms Limitation process was interrupted for a long time. . . . The position with which the U.S., judging by your speech of May 9, is approaching the negotiations cannot but cause apprehension and even doubts as to the seriousness of the intentions of the U.S. side."

While I was reading the letter, I jotted down my reactions to his comments in the margin. Next to the sentences above, my comment was: *"He has to be kidding."*

To a remark by Brezhnev that "the 'substantial' reduction the U.S. side is talking about on the basis of the picture it has itself presented would naturally be substantial only for the Soviet side," I wrote: *"Because they have the most."*

"Only one thing," he wrote, "would be the result of such a one sided approach—an upsetting of the existing balance of forces and a break of that very stability which the U.S. side is allegedly so anxious to ensure."

(*"He means 'imbalance,'"* I wrote.)

"There should be no misunderstanding, Mr. President. This is not a realistic position, not the path toward agreement. Besides, as you know, we are not the only ones who hold such a view." (This was apparently a reference to the disarmament movement in Europe.) Brezhnev proposed an immediate freeze on the number of nuclear weapons on both sides. "Such an agreement would, in our view, create favorable conditions for the negotiations and facilitate achieving the objectives therein. I would ask you, Mr. President, carefully to consider this proposal." (My note in the margin: *"I have and it is an apple for an orchard."*) Brezhnev continued: "The Soviet people—and you can take my word for that—will resolutely support such an agreement," to which I wrote in the margin: *"How will they know? They haven't been told the truth for years."* At the bottom of the letter, I wrote: *"He's a barrel of laughs."*

Some of the frank things I was saying about the Soviet Union in the spring of 1982, I was told, caused concern among several of our European allies who had their hands full with the nuclear freeze movement, which was being fired up by demagogues depicting me as a shoot-from-the-hip cowboy aching to pull out my nuclear six-shooter and bring on doomsday.

Partly because of these concerns, when I went in June 1982 to the economic summit in Versailles, I accepted invitations to address the parliaments of Great Britain and West Germany. I wanted to demonstrate that I wasn't flirting with doomsday. I told the Europeans how I felt: A nuclear war cannot be won and must never be fought, but before we could persuade the Russians to take their finger off the trigger, we had to make them realize that there was a boundary beyond which the Free World would not accept criminal behavior by another state—and to do that we had to be able to negotiate with the Russians from a position of strength. "Our military strength is a prerequisite to peace," I said to members of the British Parliament,

> but let it be clear we maintain this strength in the hope it will never be used, for the ultimate determinant in the struggle that's now going on in the world will not be bombs and rockets, but a test of wills and ideas, a trial of spiritual resolve, the values we hold, the beliefs we cherish, the ideals to which we are dedicated.
> . . . If history teaches us anything, it teaches self-delusion in the face of unpleasant facts is folly. We see around us today the marks of our terrible dilemma—predictions of doomsday, antinuclear demonstrations, an arms race in which the West must,

for its own protection, be an unwilling participant. At the same time, we see totalitarian forces in the world who seek subversion and conflict around the globe to further their barbarous assault on the human spirit. What, then, is our course? Must civilization perish in a hail of fiery atoms? Must freedom wither in a quiet, deadening accommodation with totalitarian evil?

The answer, I said, was no.

Time was on the side of the democracies: All over the world there were indications that democracy was on the rise and Communism was near collapse, dying from a terminal disease called tyranny. It could no longer bottle up the energy of the human spirit and man's innate drive to be free, and its collapse was imminent. "The decay of the Soviet experiment should come as no surprise to us," I said.

Wherever the comparisons have been made between free and closed societies—West Germany and East Germany, Austria and Czechoslovakia, Malaysia and Vietnam—it is the democratic countries that are prosperous and responsive to the needs of their people. And one of the simple but overwhelming facts of our time is this: Of all the millions of refugees we've seen in the modern world, their flight is always away from, not toward, the Communist world.

On this trip to Europe I wanted to accomplish something else besides convincing the Europeans I wasn't determined to lead the Western alliance into a nuclear war. When I had entered office, I'd been struck by something that didn't seem right: The democracies were up against an expansionist powerhouse that was trying all over the world to peddle its system, yet we who had the system of government that *worked* were doing nothing to sell our vision of freedom and the kind of system in which the people control government, not the other way around.

So when I spoke before the European parliaments I made the point that while the world's democracies might have differences among ourselves, we were united by the same system of beliefs: a belief in liberty and the rejection of the arbitrary power of the state, a refusal to subordinate the rights of the individual to the state, and the realization that collectivism stifles the best human impulses. The democracies, I suggested, like the Communists, should adopt a policy of expansionism: We should try to help the new countries of Africa and elsewhere embrace democracy and become evangelists worldwide for freedom, individual liberty, representative government, freedom of the press, self-expression, and the rule of law.

> Freedom is not the sole prerogative of a lucky few, but the inalienable and universal right of all human beings. . . . I believe the renewed strength of the democratic movement, complemented by a global campaign for freedom, will strengthen the prospects for arms control and a world at peace.

If the democracies maintained their resolve against Communism and encouraged the expansion of democratic rule, I suggested, the rest was inevitable:

Marxism-Leninism would be tossed on the ash heap of history, like all the other forms of tyranny that preceded it.

71

ALTHOUGH I THINK I convinced many people on that trip to Europe that I wasn't a trigger-happy cowboy, the nuclear freeze movement marched along unfazed through the summer and fall of 1982, while the Democratic majority in Congress tried to kill many of the most important elements of our military modernization program, including the MX missile and B-1 bomber, and our efforts to improve the quality of our all-volunteer army. Attempts to slash the military budget continued even after we began seeing tangible evidence of success. After a briefing by the Joint Chiefs of Staff one day that summer, I wrote of the meeting: "It was inspiring. We've really turned the military around. Morale-wise and every other way." A much greater proportion of military personnel were high school graduates, use of marijuana among the troops was down from fifty percent to sixteen percent, reenlistment rates were soaring, and there was a renewed sense of honor among our military men and women that made them proud to wear a uniform again.

Congressional budget battles and Israel's invasion of Lebanon preoccupied us much of that summer. Meanwhile, the continuing Soviet crackdown on Poland, tensions caused by Brezhnev's effort to hold us responsible for Israel's actions in Lebanon, his refusal to concede that the Soviets were meddling in Third World countries, and other problems prevented any improvement in U.S.-Soviet relations. Former Secretary of State Henry Kissinger urged me to consider imposing a blockade around Nicaragua to send a stronger signal to Moscow that we didn't like what the Soviets were doing in Central America, but a blockade would have been an official act of war. I didn't want a state of war existing between us and Nicaragua—and no one could tell where efforts to blockade Soviet ships bound for Central America might lead.

One afternoon, George Shultz and I invited Ambassador Dobrynin over to the White House. We met in our living quarters and engaged in a discussion about mutual problems. He brought up a Soviet desire to resume negotiations on a long-term grain agreement. I tried to explain to him a problem that we had with the American people and the importance of public opinion in our system:

Americans have a deep feeling for the countries of their ancestry; when people in other nations are persecuted, we can't make concessions to countries that mistreat them. But, I told the ambassador, some act on the part of the Soviets might make it easier for us to resume negotiations, but not as a trade or bargain. I reminded him that a Pentecostalist family had been living for four years in the basement of our embassy in Moscow. If they attempted to set foot off the embassy grounds, they would be arrested. Their crime: belief in their religion and belief in God. I said that in mentioning the Pentecostalists I wasn't trying to negotiate or strike a bargain—just pointing out that a kindness to those people would make it easier for us to do something for his government, and we'd never mention it as an exchange or concession. It wasn't long before the Pentecostalists were in America. A short time later we agreed to resume negotiations on the grain agreement.

Throughout most of 1982, I tried to persuade our European allies to restrict credit to the Soviets and join us in imposing other sanctions aimed at halting construction of the trans-Siberian natural-gas pipeline. I eventually had a little success. I was unable, however, to persuade them to apply as much economic pressure on the Soviet Union as I thought we should to accelerate the demise of Communism; many of our European allies cared more about their economic relationships in Eastern Europe than tightening a knot around the Soviets.

During the late summer and fall of that year, while the streets of U.S. and European cities were filled more and more often with nuclear freeze proponents, Soviet negotiators at Geneva sought to exploit this public sentiment and dug in their heels against the zero-zero proposal, and, simply put, U.S.-Soviet relations remained in a deep freeze.

In September, Secretary of State Shultz met with Soviet Foreign Minister Gromyko, who hinted that Brezhnev might be interested in a summit meeting with me. I told George to advise Gromyko that we agreed in principle with the idea but wanted some good deeds from Moscow first. I wasn't surprised when George got nowhere with Gromyko. Nevertheless, I wondered: How long can the Russians keep on being so belligerent and spending so much on arms when they can't even feed their own people?

At 3:30 A.M. on November 11, Nancy and I were awakened by a telephone call from my national security advisor, who told me Brezhnev had just died. I asked George Bush and George Shultz to attend the funeral along with our ambassador in Moscow, Arthur Hartman.

Before Brezhnev's death, I had decided I was going to announce in the middle of November a lifting of the sanctions on construction of the trans-Siberian pipeline; our major trading partners (those represented at the economic summit) had agreed to impose limited trade and credit restrictions on the Soviets, which meant none of us would subsidize the Soviet economy or the Soviet military expansion by offering preferential trading terms or easy credits, and to restrict the flow of products and technology that would increase Soviet military capabilities.

A portion of my diary entry for November 13, 1982:

> To the Soviet Embassy to sign the condolence book for Pres. Brezhnev. There's a strange feeling in that place—no one smiled, well, that is except Ambassador Dobrynin. Back to the oval office to do the Saturday broadcast. Then an emergency. With all seven nations agreed on a uniform policy on East West trade, something we've been after for a year and a half, we got word that Mitterrand had some objections. My script was written as an announcement of our agreement and that as a result I was lifting the pipeline sanctions. The State Dept. chickened and wanted me to go with a back up script on crime. I put in a call to Mitterrand. He was unavailable. I had in my hand Chancellor Kohl's and Margaret Thatcher's messages of joy about the agreement. I said to hell with changing and did the announcement. Maybe Francois Mitterrand will get the message, and maybe

the striped pants types at State will too . . . now we're off to Chicago for the memorial service to Loyal [my father-in-law] by American College of Surgeons. . . .

On November 15, I wrote:

More flak from Paris but we're not answering. We've told them if they are reneging for any reason about the east west trade agreement take it up with all of us, not just the U.S.

Briefing for the [Helmut] Kohl visit. This will be my fifth meeting with him but now he is chancellor of the Federal Republic of Germany.

We had a full ceremonial on a raw windy day. Our meeting was good. He is entirely different than his predecessor, very warm and outgoing. Mrs. Kohl is the same and very charming.

We did hit it off and I believe we'll have a fine relationship. No state dinner but a dinner for about 40 upstairs in our dining room. They felt very good about that and accepted it as something special.

During the day [a meeting] with John Tower re the MX. No doubt we're going to have trouble—the Dems will try to cancel out the whole system. It will take a full court press to get it. If we don't, I shudder to think what it will do to our arms reduction negotiations in Geneva.

The following week, after reviewing a variety of options about where and how it should be based, I decided to order deployment of the still-under-development MX Peacekeeper long-range intercontinental ballistic missile (ICBM) in underground silos at Warren Air Force Base in Wyoming. I was convinced it was essential to deter a Soviet first strike by assuring that the U.S. retaliatory forces could survive an attack by the Soviets' latest super-ICBMs. On the same day, I sent a message to the new Soviet leadership proposing several confidence-building measures, including suggestions that our two nations agree to notify each other in advance of missile and space tests to remove the mutual surprise and uncertainty that can occur at the sudden appearance of a rocket on a warning screen; that we notify each other before major military exercises, again to reduce surprise and uncertainty in our relationship; and that we upgrade the Washington-Moscow hot line to make it more dependable and rapid. And I also made an address to the nation that day that I hoped would help the people understand why it was so important for us to proceed with the military modernization program—especially the MX, which had created an uproar among liberals and the nuclear freeze crowd—and to explain my hopes for success in Geneva.

"I intend," I told the people, "to search for peace along two parallel paths: deterrence and arms reduction. I believe these are the only paths that offer any real hope for an enduring peace."

Because it described the situation we faced at the time and because several of the issues raised in that speech were so important, I'm including substantial excerpts from it here:

> In spite of a stagnating Soviet economy, Soviet leaders invest twelve to fourteen percent of their country's gross national product in military spending—two to three times the level we invest. I might add that the defense share of our United States federal budget has gone way down . . . in 1962, when John Kennedy was President, forty-six percent, almost half, of the federal budget went to our national defense. In recent years, about one quarter of our budget has gone to defense, while the share for social programs has nearly doubled.
>
> The combination of the Soviets spending more and the United States spending proportionately less changed the military balance and weakened our deterrent. Today, in virtually every measure of military power, the Soviet Union enjoys a decided advantage.
>
> The Soviet Union has deployed a third more land-based intercontinental ballistic missiles than we have. Believe it or not, we froze our number in 1965 and have deployed no additional missiles since then.
>
> The Soviet Union put to sea 60 new ballistic missile submarines in the last fifteen years. Until last year we hadn't commissioned one in that same period. The Soviet Union has built over 200 modern Backfire bombers and is building 30 more a year. For twenty years, the United States has deployed no new strategic bombers. Many of our B-52 bombers are now older than the pilots who fly them.
>
> The Soviet Union now has 600 of the silos considered most threatening by both sides—the intermediate-range missiles based on land. We have none. The United States withdrew its intermediate-range land-based missiles from Europe almost twenty years ago.
>
> The world has also witnessed unprecedented growth in the area of Soviet conventional forces. The Soviets far exceed us in the number of tanks, artillery pieces, aircraft, and ships they produce every year. What is more, when I arrived in this office, I learned that in our own

forces we had planes that couldn't fly and ships that couldn't leave port mainly for lack of spare parts and crew members.

The Soviet military buildup must not be ignored. We've recognized the problem and, together with our allies, we've begun to correct the imbalance. If my defense proposals are passed, it will still take five years before we come close to the Soviet level. Yet the modernization of our strategic and conventional forces will assure that deterrence works and peace prevails.

Our deployed nuclear forces were built before the age of microcircuits. It's not right to ask our young men and women in uniform to maintain and operate such antiques. Many have already given their lives to missile explosions and aircraft accidents caused by the old age of their equipment. We must replace and modernize our forces, and that's why I decided to proceed with the production and deployment of the new ICBM known as the MX. Three earlier presidents worked to develop this missile. Based on the best advice that I could get, I concluded that the MX is the right missile at the right time. . . .

Some may question what modernizing our military has to do with peace. Well, as explained earlier, a secure force keeps others from threatening us, and that keeps the peace. And just as important, it also increases the prospects of reaching significant arms reductions with the Soviets, and that's what we really want. The United States wants deep cuts in the world's arsenal of weapons, but unless we demonstrate the will to rebuild our strength and restore the military balance, the Soviets, since they're so far ahead, have little incentive to negotiate with us. Let me repeat that point because it goes to the heart of our policies: Unless we demonstrate the will to rebuild our strength, the Soviets have little incentive to negotiate. If we hadn't begun to modernize, the Soviet negotiators would know we had nothing to bargain with except talk. They would know we were bluffing without a good hand, because they know what cards we hold just as we know what's in their hand. . . .

We know that one-sided arms control doesn't work. We've tried time and time again to set an example by cutting our own forces in the hope that the Soviets would do likewise. The result has always been that they keep building.

I believe our strategy for peace will succeed. Never before has the United States proposed such a comprehensive program of nuclear arms control. Never in our history have we engaged in so many negotiations with the Soviets to reduce nuclear arms and to find a stable peace. What we are saying to them is this: We will modernize our military in order to keep the balance for peace, but wouldn't it be better if we both simply reduced our arsenals to a much lower level?

Let me begin with the negotiations on the intermediate-range nuclear forces that are currently underway in Geneva. As I said earlier, the most threatening of these forces are the land-based missiles which the Soviet Union now has aimed at Europe, the Middle East, and Asia. In 1972 there were 600 of these missiles. The United States was at zero. In 1977 there were 600. The United States was still at zero. Then the Soviets began deploying powerful new missiles with three warheads and a reach of thousands of miles—the SS-20. Since then the Soviets have added a missile with three warheads every week. Although the Soviet leaders earlier this year declared they'd frozen deployment of this dangerous missile, they have in fact continued deployment.

Last year, on November 18th, I proposed the total, global elimination of all these missiles. I proposed that the United States would deploy no comparable missiles, which are scheduled for late 1983, if the Soviet Union would dismantle theirs. We would follow agreement on the land-based missiles with limits on other intermediate-range systems. The European governments strongly support our initiative. The Soviet Union has thus far shown little inclination to take this major step to zero levels. Yet I believe, and I'm hoping, that as the talks proceed and as we approach the scheduled placement of our new systems in Europe, the Soviet leaders will see the benefits of such a far-reaching agreement. This summer we also began negotiations on strategic arms reductions, the proposal we call START. Here we're talking about intercontinental missiles, the weapons with a longer range than the intermediate-range ones I was just discussing. We're negotiating on the basis of deep reductions. I proposed in May that we cut the number of warheads on these missiles to an equal number, roughly one-third below current levels. I also proposed that we cut the number of missiles themselves to an equal number, about half the current U.S. level. Our proposals would eliminate some 4,700 warheads and some 2,250 missiles. I think that would be quite a service to mankind. . . .

We intend to convince the Soviets it would be in their own best interest to reduce these missiles. We also seek to reduce the total destructive power of these missiles and other elements of United States and Soviet strategic forces. In 1977, when the last administration proposed more limited reductions, the Soviet Union refused even to discuss them. This time their reaction has been quite different. Their opening position is a serious one, and even though it doesn't meet our objective of deep reductions, there's no question we're heading in the right direction. One reason for this change is clear. The Soviet Union knows that we are now serious about our own strategic programs and that they must be prepared to negotiate in earnest.

Through a heavy volume of phone calls and letters to the White House and public opinion polls after the speech, I felt I had convinced millions of Americans that we were on the right track with the Peace through Strength policy, but there was one person I did not convince that night—my daughter Patti.

Unlike many previous presidents and their wives, Nancy and I didn't have small children with us when we lived in the White House. Although they traveled east often, Maureen, Michael, Patti, Ron, and their spouses all had their own lives in California during the eight years I was president. Because of this gap of almost three thousand miles, we didn't see them nearly as often as we wanted to, and that was one of the things Nancy and I missed most while we were in Washington. We usually saw the children (and our grandchildren) at Christmas and Thanksgiving and managed gettogethers at the White House and the ranch. But we missed just being able to pick up the telephone and call the children and say, "Why don't you come over for dinner tonight?"

Like all parents, we had occasional problems with the children. All four children had minds of their own, and in different ways they all were capable of expressing their independence. Ron and Maureen showed that when they demanded I act more decisively about the Iran-Contra situation. I'd always encouraged the children to speak their minds.

I suspect it's never easy for children who grow up in a family with celebrities, and I'm sure that the added prominence that fell on the shoulders of the children after I was elected president didn't make their lives any easier. Ron and Patti at times were especially unhappy about having to submit to round-the-clock Secret Service protection, which became especially tight after the CIA received reports of terrorist attacks planned against me and my family. And the prominence of my job may have exacerbated a problem for Michael. During the years I was president, Mike started having difficulty coming to terms with the fact that he was adopted. Although I'd always given him as much love as the other children, he suddenly found it difficult to live with the fact that he was adopted and felt worthless because of it. His wife, Colleen, tried to convince him he had no reason for this concern, but it really weighed heavily on his mind, and as a result, after I'd call or see him to find out whether I could work out the problem, we had several confrontations in which he accused me of not loving him. Then something happened that was almost a miracle: He decided to write a book about his life that became a catharsis for dealing with the problems that had bothered him. After Mike and Colleen brought their children, Cameron and Ashley, to the ranch for one visit, I wrote in my diary: "It was a new Mike. He's writing a book and it has led to a soul searching about himself which resulted in a confession of how he had done things to all of us and that he now saw himself as he had been and what he wanted to be." Later, when I read his book, I had even more of a fatherly pride in Mike than I had had before: I could almost see a transformation taking place as the book progressed, as if it was begun by an unhappy and rebellious young man and ended by a completely different person who was happy and at peace with himself. Mike described a journey of discovery in which he learned he had rebelled against the knowledge that his biological mother didn't want him and had done things to get even. I've since recommended his book many times as an aid to those who are adopted—it can help them understand themselves and their families.

After Nancy and I were married, Maureen was away at school, so we didn't get to see her as much as we wanted to. When I ran for the presidency, she went out and worked hard campaigning for me, and that meant a great deal to Nancy and me. Once we were in the White House, she stayed with us often because she was co-chairman of the Republican National Committee and we grew even closer. It was wonderful for us to be able to spend so much time together, and we were always delighted when our son-in-law, Dennis, was able to join us during Maureen's visits.

Patti, as I've mentioned, cried over the telephone when Nancy and I called her at school to tell her I'd been elected governor. "Oh, no," she said, "how could you do this to me?" She was only fourteen, but she was a child of the sixties who didn't want a member of the establishment in the family. Later on, Patti came under the influence of people with similar views and, philosophically, at least, I guess I lost her.

As president, I was devoting every effort I could to ending the threat of nuclear war. But Patti was convinced I was doing the opposite. She just didn't believe in me.

I suppose because we both knew where we stood, we generally avoided this topic when I was in the White House. But two weeks after I gave my speech about the MX missile and arms control, she asked me if I would meet with Helen Caldicott, one of the leaders of the nuclear freeze movement. I agreed to Patti's wish and the three of us spent more than an hour discussing the problems of nuclear war. "She seems like a nice, caring person," I wrote afterward in my diary of Dr. Caldicott, "but she is all steamed up and knows an awful lot of things that aren't true. I tried but couldn't get through her fixation. For that matter I couldn't get through to Patti. I'm afraid our daughter has been taken over by that whole gang. . . . "

Patti had told me Dr. Caldicott had promised that if I spoke to her she would say nothing publicly about the conversation. But almost immediately she went public with the details of our meeting.

I still dream and hope for a day when Patti and I will develop a close relationship again.

Nancy and I love her very much, as we do all the children. We've reached out to Patti since I left the White House, but so far she's made it plain to me that she thinks I am wrong and that she is against everything I stand for.

72

AFTER A LONG National Security Council meeting in early 1983 at which we considered possible ways to accelerate progress at the deadlocked arms control negotiations in Geneva, I wrote in my diary: "We'll stick with our zero option plan. Found I was wishing *I* could do the negotiating with the Soviets. . . . "

I felt that if I could ever get in a room alone with one of the top Soviet leaders, there was a chance the two of us could make some progress in easing tensions between our two countries. I have always placed a lot of faith in the simple power of human contact in solving problems.

I had made no progress with Brezhnev. Now there was a new leader in the Kremlin, Yuri Andropov, former head of the KGB. I didn't expect him to be any less of a doctrinaire Communist than Brezhnev, but at least there was a clean slate. I still believed the Soviets had done nothing to merit inviting them to a summit meeting—a lot of confidence-building was necessary first—but I decided to experiment with some personal diplomacy using back channels to the Kremlin, outside the spotlight of publicity, through which both sides could speak frankly without the posturing and attempts at diplomatic face-saving that usually accompanied formal dealings between the United States and the USSR.

For a while, my attempts at quiet diplomacy seemed to be working. Then there was a series of events that made U.S.-Soviet relations go from bad to worse. Meanwhile, I kept trying to win the support of our people and Congress for staying the course on the military modernization program. The Democrats were fighting tooth and nail to repeal virtually all the new programs we had started in 1981: They were fighting to cut defense spending by more than $163 billion over five years, increase social spending by $200 billion, and increase taxes $315 billion, and to win their case they were exploiting some of the public's understandable fears about nuclear war. When several prominent Senate Republicans joined in calling for the abandonment of the Pentagon modernization program partly because of the heavily publicized views of the minority of Americans who were demonstrating in favor of a nuclear freeze, I commented in my diary in early March:

> I'm going to take our case to the people, only this time we are declassifying some of our reports on the Soviets and can tell the people a few frightening facts: We are still dangerously behind the Soviets and getting farther behind.

Besides wanting to get my message across to the people, I wanted to get Andropov's attention.

On March 8, 1983, one day after I made the note above and two days after we bid good-bye to Queen Elizabeth and Prince Philip following their visit to a nearly flooded Rancho del Cielo, I flew to Florida to make a pair of speeches. The first was an address at Walt Disney's EPCOT Center to a group of young people regarding the challenges facing their generation in the future. Next I spoke in Orlando to the annual convention of the National Association of Evangelicals, an organization of ministers.

Clergymen were among those in America who were coming under the strongest pressure to support a nuclear freeze. I wanted to reach them, as well as other Americans who—like my daughter Patti—were being told the path to peace was via a freeze on the development and deployment of nuclear weapons that, if implemented, would leave the Soviets in a position of nuclear superiority over us and amount to an act of unilateral disarmament on the part of the United States and NATO.

Although a lot of liberal pundits jumped on my speech at Orlando and said it showed I was a rhetorical hip-shooter who was recklessly and unconsciously provoking the Soviets into war, I made the "Evil Empire" speech and others like it with malice aforethought; I wanted to remind the Soviets we knew what they were up to.

Here are a few paragraphs from that speech:

During my first press conference as president, in answer to a direct question, I pointed out that, as good Marxist-Leninists, the Soviet leaders have openly and publicly declared that the only morality they recognize is that which will further their cause, which is world revolution. I think I should point out I was only quoting Lenin, their guiding spirit, who said in 1920 that they repudiate all morality that proceeds from supernatural ideas—that's their name for religion— or ideas that are outside class conceptions. Morality is entirely subordinate to the interests of class war. And everything is moral that is necessary for the annihilation of the old, exploiting social order and for uniting the proletariat.

Well, I think the refusal of many influential people to accept this elementary fact of Soviet doctrine illustrates a historical reluctance to see totalitarian powers for what they are. We saw this phenomenon in the 1930s. We see it too often today.

This doesn't mean we should isolate ourselves and refuse to seek an understanding with them. I intend to do everything I can to persuade them of our peaceful intent, to remind them that it was the West that refused to use its nuclear monopoly in the forties and fifties for territorial gain and which now proposes a fifty-percent cut in strategic ballistic missiles and the elimination of an entire class of land-based intermediate-range nuclear missiles.

At the same time, however, they must be made to understand we will never compromise our principles and standards. We will never give away our freedom. We will never abandon our belief in God. And we will never stop searching for a genuine peace. But we can assure none of these things America stands for through the so-called nuclear freeze solutions proposed by some. The truth is that a freeze now would be a very dangerous fraud, for that is merely the illusion of peace. The reality is that we must find peace through strength.

I would agree to a freeze if only we could freeze the Soviets' global desires. A freeze at current levels of weapons would remove any incentive for the Soviets to negotiate seriously in Geneva and virtually end our chances to achieve the major arms reductions which we have proposed. Instead, they would achieve *their* objectives through the freeze. A freeze would reward the Soviet Union for its enormous and unparalleled military buildup. It would prevent the essential and long overdue modernization of United States and allied defenses and would leave our aging forces increasingly vulnerable. And an honest freeze would require extensive prior negotiations on the systems and numbers to be limited and on the measures to ensure effective verification and compliance. And the kind of a freeze that has been suggested would be virtually impossible to verify. Such a major effort would divert us completely from our current negotiations on achieving substantial reductions. . . .

Let us pray for the salvation of all those who live in [the] totalitarian darkness—pray they will discover the joy of knowing God. But until they do, let us be aware that while they preach the supremacy of the state, declare its omnipotence over individual man, and predict its eventual domination of all peoples on the earth, they are the focus of evil in the modern world. . . .

If history teaches anything, it teaches that simpleminded appeasement or wishful thinking about our adversaries is folly. It means the betrayal of our past, the squandering of our freedom. So, I urge you to speak out against those who would place the United States in a position of military and moral inferiority. . . . In your discussions of the nuclear freeze proposals, I urge you to beware the temptation of pride—the temptation of blithely declaring yourselves above it all and label both sides equally at fault, to ignore the facts of history and the aggressive impulses of an evil empire, to simply call the arms race a giant misunderstanding and thereby remove yourself from the struggle between right and wrong and good and evil. . . .

I believe we shall rise to the challenge. I believe that Communism is another sad, bizarre chapter in history whose last pages even now are being written. . . .

As I've said, I wanted to let Andropov know we recognized the Soviets for what they were. Frankly, I think it worked, even though some people—including Nancy—tried persuading me to lower the temperature of my rhetoric. I told Nancy I had a reason for saying those things: I wanted the Russians to know I understood their system and what it stood for.

As I was going around the country speaking about the realities of Soviet policy, the arms reduction negotiations in Geneva were getting nowhere fast. Paul Nitze, our brilliant chief negotiator, said he believed, as I did, that the Soviets wouldn't budge on removing the SS-20 missiles aimed at Europe unless and until we deployed our INF missiles.

Our policy in Geneva continued to be based firmly on this premise. Two weeks after the "Evil Empire" speech, after the Joint Chiefs of Staff returned to me with their collective judgment that development of a shield against nuclear missiles might be feasible, I decided to make public my dream and move ahead with the Strategic Defense Initiative by laying down a challenge to our scientists to solve the formidable technological problems it posed. Here are excerpts from my diary that spring:

March 22
Another day that shouldn't happen. On my desk was a draft of the speech on defense to be delivered tomorrow night on TV. This was one hassled over by N.S.C., State and Defense. Finally I had a crack at it. I did a lot of rewriting. Much of it was to change bureaucratese into people talk. But all day there were meetings, with Congress with our volunteer leaders from the business world, unscheduled meetings having to do with problems and finally a trip to the Capitol Club. . . . During the day speaking to our Congressional Republican leadership and blasted the Dem. budget with the press in attendance. It was a good pitch exposing the ridiculous irresponsibility of the phony budget.

March 23
The big thing today was the 8 p.m. TV speech on all networks about national security. We've been working on the speech for about 72 hours and right down to the deadline. We had a group in for dinner at the W.H. I didn't join them except before dinner a few words of welcome. Nancy and I then dined early upstairs. The group included several former sectys. of state, national security advisors, distinguished nuclear scientists, the chiefs of staff, etc. I did the speech from the Oval Office at 8 and then joined the party for coffee. I guess it was okay, they all praised it to the sky and seemed to think it would be a source of debate for some time to come. I did the bulk of the speech on why our arms buildup was necessary and then finished with a call to the science community to join me in research starting now to develop defensive weapons that would render nuclear missiles obsolete. I made no optimistic forecasts—said it might take 20 years or more but we had to do it. I felt good.

March 24

. . . the reports are in on last night's speech. The biggest return—phone calls, wires, etc., on any speech so far and running heavily in my favor. . . .

March 25

Meeting with speech writers—gave them an idea for Saturday radio; it worked out pretty good. A poll taken before the speech shows I've gained on job approval with regard to the economy, but the drum beat of anti-defense propaganda has reduced my rating on foreign affairs. I'll be interested to see how that holds for a poll after the speech. Did a press availability in the press room. It went well, so the press on TV almost ignored it entirely. . . .

April 6

Learned George Shultz is upset. Thinks N.S.C. is undercutting him on plans he and I discussed for "quiet diplomacy" approach to the Soviets [which led to the release of the Pentecostalist families in Moscow, but] we had a meeting later in day with George and cleared things up I think. Some of the N.S.C. staff are too hard line and don't think any approach should be made to the Soviets. I think I'm hard line and will never appease. But I do want to try to let them see there is a better world if they'll show *by deed* they want to get along with the free world.

I suspect the Soviet leadership found it difficult to comprehend why an American president would be so concerned about public opinion when I sent word through Dobrynin that we might be amenable on the grain agreement if they allowed the Pentecostalists to emigrate: The last thing that leaders of a totalitarian country worry about is public opinion. But Dobrynin knew a great deal about Americans, and I suspect he must have told them that if an American president had said what I'd said, they could expect a positive response. I never told anyone about my conversation with Dobrynin—I didn't know when I might want to try the same approach through quiet diplomacy again.

Later that summer, a second group of Pentecostalists was permitted to leave the embassy and the Soviet Union. In the overall scheme of U.S.-Soviet relations, allowing a handful of Christian believers to leave the Soviet Union was a small event. But in the context of the times I thought it was a hope-giving development, the first time the Soviets had responded to us with a deed instead of words. As I'd learn, though, I was overly optimistic if I thought the Russians were going to change overnight.

73

ALTHOUGH I DON'T THINK I was ever able to convince the American people of the seriousness of the threat we faced from Marxist guerrillas in Central America, I think I succeeded in making my point when I took my case to the public regarding the need to press ahead with modernizing our military forces—Americans valued, above all, the security of their nation. During my speech to the country on March 23, I revealed some recently declassified information about the enormous Soviet arms buildup and previously secret photos documenting the expansion of Soviet military facilities on Cuba. "I know that all of you want peace, and so do I," I said. "I know too that many of you seriously believe that a nuclear freeze would further the cause of peace. But a freeze now would make us less, not more, secure and would raise, not reduce, the risks of war. . . ." I didn't want the United States to be in an arms race, I said, but the Soviet Union had put us in one and our survival as a nation was at stake. After appealing to the American people to tell their congressmen they were behind the military modernization program, I revealed my dream for the Strategic Defense Initiative:

> Let me share with you a vision of the future which offers hope. It is that we embark on a program to counter the awesome Soviet missile threat with measures that are defensive. Let us turn to the

very strengths in technology that spawned our great industrial base and that have given us the quality of life we enjoy today.

What if free people could live secure in the knowledge that their security did not rest upon the threat of instant U.S. retaliation to deter a Soviet attack, that we could intercept and destroy strategic ballistic missiles before they reached our own soil or that of our allies?

I know this is a formidable, technical task, one that may not be accomplished before the end of this century. Yet, current technology has attained a level of sophistication where it's reasonable for us to begin the effort. It will take years, probably decades of effort on many fronts. There will be failures and setbacks, just as there will be successes and breakthroughs. And as we proceed, we must remain constant in preserving the nuclear deterrent and maintaining a solid capability for flexible response. But isn't it worth every investment necessary to free the world from the threat of nuclear war?

. . . Tonight, consistent with our obligations under the ABM [Antiballistic Missile] treaty and recognizing the need for closer consultation with our allies, I'm taking an important first step. I am directing a comprehensive and intensive effort to define a long-term research and development program to begin to achieve our ultimate goal of eliminating the threat posed by strategic nuclear missiles. This could pave the way for arms control measures to eliminate the weapons themselves. We seek neither military superiority nor political advantage. Our only purpose—one all people share—is to search for ways to reduce the danger of nuclear war.

During the spring and summer of 1983, while Yuri Andropov was pursuing the old Soviet agenda of world domination, funding rebel guerrillas, keeping an iron hand on Poland, and, in general, acting like all the other Soviet leaders of the past, the administration won a series of close votes in Congress that kept the MX program and other major elements of the military modernization program alive. And, in a new attempt at quiet diplomacy, I tried to communicate privately with Andropov, hoping, as I had with Brezhnev, to initiate the kind of personal relationship that might lead to better relations between our countries.

Although Andropov and I had exchanged formalities after the death of Brezhnev, his letters were stiff and as cold as a Siberian winter, confined to platitudes and promising "the unbending commitment of the Soviet leadership and the people of the Soviet Union to the course of peace, the elimination of the nuclear threat and development of relations based on mutual benefit and equality with all nations"—while blaming the United States entirely for the arms race.

On July 11, 1983, I sent a handwritten note to Andropov assuring him that the people of the United States were equally dedicated to the cause of peace and elimination of the nuclear threat. Then I asked, Wasn't it time that we took the next step and began trying to implement these goals at the meetings of our arms negotiators in Geneva? "We both share an enormous responsibility for the preservation of stability in the world," I wrote, "and I believe we can fulfill that mandate, but in order to do so, it will require a more active level of exchange than we have heretofore been able to establish. There's much to talk about with regard to the situation in Eastern Europe and South Asia and particularly this hemisphere as well as in such areas as arms control, trade between our two countries, and other ways in which we can expand East-West contacts."

Historically, I wrote, "our predecessors have made better progress when they communicated privately and candidly." I wrote that if he wished to engage in such direct communication, "you will find me ready. I await your reply. Ronald Reagan."

In early August, Andropov responded with a letter that demanded we cancel the deployment that fall of the new NATO missiles and refused to discuss the issues I'd raised in my letter, especially Soviet subversion of Third World countries. On the plus side, he expressed a willingness to communicate with me privately. Here is a portion of his letter:

Dear Mr. President:

Thank you for your personal letter, which was conveyed to me on July 21. I have considered its contents with all seriousness.

I take note with satisfaction the assurances that the U.S. Government shares a devotion to the cause of peace and the elimination of the nuclear threat and strives to build relations with other countries on the basis of mutual benefit and equal rights. The most important thing now, it seems to me, is to attempt to embody these principles in practical issues, to seek and find solutions to existing problems in the spirit of peace and cooperation. I agree with you, Mr. President, that we are obliged to remember the responsibility for maintaining peace and international security which rests on our two countries and their leaders.

Of course, in the present complex situation, it is difficult to count on simple solutions. But I think that if we were to try simply to avoid the most important and difficult issues, we would hardly be able to achieve the results to which, as I understand, we both would like to aspire. . . .

The important thing, of course, is to begin to move forward on issues of limiting and reducing nuclear arms. It is a particularly urgent necessity to prevent a nuclear arms race in Europe, the results of which would be extremely serious. If we can achieve that, I believe that the peoples of our countries and of many other countries will be grateful to us.

We believe that a just, mutually acceptable agreement in Geneva, an agreement on the basis of equality, is still possible. In trying to reach an agreement there, we have already gone very far and have taken decisions which were most difficult for us. After all, the Soviet Union is in fact agreeing (contingent upon reaching parity in appropriate categories of aircraft) to reduce to almost a third the medium-range missiles it has in the European zone. And to reduce them without a reciprocal reduction of missiles on the part of the West. Is this understood and appreciated to a proper degree in Washington? In this regard we want nothing more than a counterbalance to the means which the British and French possess. Is this not an honest and moderate position?

I will tell you, Mr. President, the same thing I told Chancellor Kohl when I met him in Moscow: we believe that we must take advantage of the opportunity, while it exists, to reach a genuinely honest agreement which takes into account the legitimate interests of both the NATO and Warsaw Pact countries so that, instead of increasing medium-range nuclear weapons in Europe, they are significantly, very significantly, reduced. That would permit an enormous improvement of the situation in Europe and in the whole world.

So long as the United States has not begun deploying its missiles in Europe, an agreement is still possible. Moreover, it is our conviction, based on a calculation of basic security factors, that there is room for flexibility on both sides. Insofar as you, too, would like movement in the negotiations—as I infer from your letter—I would be pleased to hear how you envision this in practical terms.

I want to add that we would consider it quite possible to have mutual constructive steps for ending the arms race in other directions as well—for example, as regards strategic nuclear weapons and the use of space—but only on the basis of equality and genuine respect for each other's interests.

Mr. President, you propose a discussion of the situation in various geographic regions and mention certain ones. What is there to be said? We have adequate grounds for expressing our assessment of U.S. policy in the areas you mention and others. But at this time I want to emphasize only one thing: every people, every country, wherever they may be located, should be masters of their fate. They should be given the possibility to live as they wish, and no one has the right to interfere in their internal affairs. In our policy we proceed and continue to proceed from this unshakeable principle which is embodied in the U.N. Charter signed by our countries. If the United States is guided by this principle, then our countries would be able to cooperate on that basis at great benefit to ourselves and to others.

Mr. President, it is not my aim to raise many issues in this letter, but to select those which I consider central. I shall welcome a concrete, businesslike and candid exchange of opinions with you on these and other questions. I agree that the exchange be confidential when the interests of the matter so dictate. For my part I would propose to do this through the Soviet Ambassador in Washington and a person whom you would designate.

Respectfully,
Andropov
August 4, 1983

There was a handwritten postscript at the bottom of Andropov's letter:

I sincerely hope, Mr. President, that you will give serious consideration to the thoughts I have expressed and that you will be able to respond to them in a constructive spirit.

The letter made me more certain than ever that we had to go ahead with plans to deploy the new intermediate-range NATO missiles in Europe, because once that threat was removed, the Soviets wouldn't have any reason to eliminate their INF weapons.

This was my reply to Andropov:

Dear Mr. Chairman:

Thank you for your letter which was conveyed to me on August 5. I have of course given it my most serious attention and welcome the assurances of your commitment to finding solutions to the problems that confront us. I can see that we both recognize the awesome responsibility history has placed on our shoulders to guide the two most powerful countries in the world in this difficult and dangerous period.

I agree with you that, if we are to make progress in our joint endeavor, we cannot bypass important issues merely because they are difficult. I also agree that our attention must be directed above all to the central issue of consolidating security in the world.

In my view, this central issue has three key aspects: first, the vital need for the world to move toward the principle of settling international disputes by peaceful means, without the use or threat of force; second, the urgent need to reduce stocks of weaponry, particularly the most destructive and destabilizing types; and third, the necessity of creating a sufficient level of trust and confidence between us to permit us to reach the first two objectives.

Now it is obviously impossible for us to solve all the many problems in our relationship at the same time. But it also seems to me that we will find it most difficult to solve individual problems, even the most critical ones, in total isolation. To be successful, I believe we must find a way to make steady progress in all three areas simultaneously. Permit me to make a few observations on each in total candor.

On the first, I am pleased that you endorse the principles of the United Nations Charter and that you feel that every people and every country should be master of its fate. I am pleased because I do too, and indeed feel very strongly about this principle, which is absolutely essential for a peaceful world. Since we agree on the principle, the problem must be that we interpret it in different ways, because we do have problems here, and very serious ones at that.

You have asked me to try to understand Moscow's view of some of the critical issues, and I can assure you that I do try. Could I ask in return that you take a look at the world as it appears from Washington? As Commander-in-Chief, I have not a single military unit on combat status. If all national leaders could say the same we would be on our way to a safer world. If each of us determined we would not resort to war as a solution to any problem, arms reduction would be simply and easily achieved. If on the other hand we approach the issue holding to a belief that war is somehow inevitable, then we are doomed to failure. I think that we must find a way either to discuss these problems frankly, or at the very least, to give greater weight to the attitudes of the other party when making fateful decisions. In the end, it really makes no difference whether we reduce these problems by specific understandings or by simply acting so that they are reduced. The essential point is that they must be reduced if we are to give the other important items on our agenda a fair chance of success.

Regarding the second facet of consolidating world security, reducing armaments, I have been pleased by the recent progress in the MBFR [Mutual Balanced Force Reduction talks pertaining to conventional forces] in Vienna. And although serious problems remain, I can assure you of good will on our side in trying to resolve them. I also concur that the two sets of negotiations in Geneva, on strategic arms and intermediate-range nuclear weapons affecting Europe, are central and require our most serious attention. I, too, believe that agreements are possible, and as far as I am concerned, the sooner the better.

I appreciated your explanation of the Soviet position in the INF negotiations in Geneva. I can fully understand that your offer to reduce SS-20 deployments was not an easy one. It is rarely easy to give up something one has. But I think we must view the situation in a broader historical context if we are to find a solution that preserves the security of both sides and yet allows us to lower the level of nuclear arms. Throughout most of the 1970's, our Allies and we felt —and prominent Soviet leaders agreed in numerous public statements—that there was a rough military balance in Europe. But then, in 1977, the Soviet Union started deploying a new class of nuclear weapons with much greater range and overall capability than had existed in Europe. This obviously threatened the balance and led to the December, 1979, NATO decision [to deploy the Pershing II and cruise missiles].

The reason I recount these well-known facts is to explain why the current Soviet proposal does not satisfy our concerns. Of course it is encouraging that you recognize that you need many fewer SS-20's than you have deployed, but a monopoly of a weapons system is a monopoly, whether the numbers are small or large, and that is a feature which we cannot accept. You mentioned the British and French systems, and I understand the point you make. But I really believe that is not a relevant point. Most important, the British and French weapons in question are not at all in the same category as the land-based SS-20, and in addition, the French systems are not committed to the defense of NATO. Now these considerations might conceivably be viewed as secondary if the British and French systems constituted a realistic threat to the Soviet Union. Yet how could you possibly consider them a threat, given the tremendous nuclear arsenal which you possess (and ICBM's which can be targeted on Britain and France)? I simply cannot understand why you feel you must have a "counter-balance" to them, when your Central systems exceed their size by many, many times.

The deployment of American Pershing II's and cruise missiles in Europe in December—if we fail to reach an agreement which makes it unnecessary—also should not be viewed as a threat to the Soviet Union. Their only function would be to balance Soviet systems potentially threatening to Europe, and to ensure that no one in the future could doubt that the security of Western Europe and North America are one and the same. Once again, try to see our point of view. What would be the Soviet reaction if we deployed a new, highly threatening weapon against its allies, and then insisted that you should not balance this with something comparable?

In sum, we must insist that any agreement embody a parity of U.S. and Soviet weapons in this category. I cannot understand why this should be incompatible with the security of the Warsaw Pact. If it is a defensive alliance, this could not be. So we also consider our proposal honest and just, aimed only at balance, not superiority. Obviously the best way to achieve parity is to eliminate this class of weapons altogether. This of course was our original proposal? Could you not take a look at that proposal again? To me it seems fully consistent with Soviet and Warsaw Pact security interests.

You said in your letter that "so long as the United States has not begun deploying missiles in Europe, an agreement is still possible." Well, I think an agreement should be possible right now and I certainly hope that we will have one before December, but if it takes longer, then we must keep trying. And I can assure you that NATO in the future will not hesitate to remove deployed weapons if this should be required by a mutually acceptable agreement.

You asked how I could envision an agreement in practical terms. This is difficult to answer before we agree on basic principles, and parity of U.S. and Soviet systems is one of the most basic for us. Whether parity is the elimination of these intermediate-range weapons altogether or reducing their number, doesn't it follow that we have made peace more likely because neither of us can see an advantage in using those weapons?

As for the third aspect of consolidating world security, improving confidence and trust, there are many matters which require our attention. The successful conclusion of the Madrid conference should be helpful, but only if we all ensure that the decisions made there, and the understandings connected with it, are faithfully implemented. Mr. Chairman, I cannot exaggerate the importance of clarifying any misunderstandings which arise regarding the implementation of prior agreements. For nothing is so destructive of confidence as a perception by one party to an agreement that its provisions are being disregarded by the other. I am sure you will understand that it is in our mutual interest if we call your government's attention to matters in this area which give us concern; I expect you to do the same if any doubts arise on your side. . . .

In accord with the last paragraph of your letter, I shall request Secretary Shultz to be in touch with Ambassador Dobrynin to receive in complete confidence communications you have for me. I would also expect, of course, to convey my thoughts by Ambassador Hartman and would appreciate your designating an appropriate official to deal with him as the need arises. In addition, we may find that occasionally it will be useful to arrange more direct contact, as now.

Respectfully,
Ronald Reagan
August 24, 1983

If the Free World needed any more evidence in the summer of 1983 that it was facing an evil empire, we got it the night of August 31 when a Russian military plane cold-bloodedly shot down a Korean airliner, Flight 007, murdering 269 innocent passengers, including a U.S. congressman and sixty other Americans.

This crime against humanity not only set back my attempt at "quiet diplomacy" with the Kremlin, but put virtually all our efforts to improve Soviet-American relations on hold.

I received word of the tragedy while I was at Rancho del Cielo and shared the revulsion that gripped all of the civilized world at this act of savagery in the skies. At first, the Soviets denied any knowledge of the shoot-down, although we knew from the start exactly what had happened, based on the contents of radio transmissions by the Soviet pilots that were monitored by Japanese air traffic controllers. When Andropov finally admitted that Soviet fighters had downed the jumbo jet, he claimed the massacre was justified because the Korean Air Lines Boeing 747 was flying through Soviet airspace on a "spy mission" for the United States.

I was outraged. After a series of middle-of-the-night conference calls, I cut short my California vacation and returned to Washington, and as soon as we landed I called a special evening meeting of the National Security Council at which we decided to ask our allies to join us in imposing sanctions and demanding reparations for the victims' families.

We determined, based on the circumstances of the incident, that the crew of Flight 007, which originated in New York City and refueled at Anchorage, Alaska, en route to Seoul, apparently set the computer on the plane's automatic pilot system incorrectly, allowing it to stray north into Soviet airspace instead of flying toward Japan. The further they went, the further off course their mistake led them, and the crew was apparently never aware of what had gone wrong. Their transmissions also indicated they had no idea Soviet planes were stalking them high above the North Pacific. Although an American reconnaissance plane based in Alaska had made a regular patrol in the general area (outside Soviet airspace) a few hours earlier, none of our planes were in the area at the time of the incident, and there was absolutely no basis for Andropov's claim that the Korean jetliner was an American reconnaissance aircraft. We knew from the intercepted communications that the Soviet pilots flew near the 747 for two and a half hours under a bright half-moon and it seemed impossible that, based on its size and insignia, they did not realize they were tracking a jumbo-jet commercial airliner. But they shot it down anyway—and Soviet leaders never retreated from the claim that the pilots believed they were shooting at a spy plane.

I called key congressional leaders to the Oval Office on Sunday morning, September 4, and played a tape recording of the voice of one of the Soviet pilots as he said he was arming his plane's air-to-air missile system, locking its radar antenna onto his target, and launching his missile, after which he said: "The target is destroyed."

The next day was Labor Day. I'd planned to spend most of it beside the White House swimming pool. Instead, I spent it in damp swimming trunks sitting on a towel in my study rewriting a speech on the incident sent to me by the White House speech writers. Although I used a few of its paragraphs, I rewrote most of the speech so I could give my unvarnished opinion of the barbarous act and also present verbatim some of the recorded communications of the Soviet pilots before their kill. I wanted to show the American people the utter callousness of this act. Then I changed into a blue suit and delivered my speech to the nation:

"Make no mistake about it," I said,

> this attack was not just against ourselves or the Republic of Korea. This was the Soviet Union against the world and the moral precepts which guide human relations among people everywhere. It was an act of barbarism, born of a society which wantonly disregards individual rights and the value of human life and seeks constantly to expand and dominate other nations. . . . We shouldn't be surprised by such inhuman brutality. Memories come back of Czechoslovakia, Hungary, Poland, the gassing of villages in Afghanistan. If the massacre and their subsequent conduct is intended to intimidate, they have failed in their purpose.

In response to the incident, we imposed new restrictions on U.S. landing rights for Aeroflot, the Soviet airline, and suspended implementation of several bilateral agreements with the Soviet Union. Several conservative columnists took after me, saying that I should have been even tougher on the Russians and that in not doing so I betrayed the conservative cause. But our arms control talks were near the threshold of an important new phase—and while I wanted to call a spade a spade, I didn't want to smother the nuclear arms reduction process before it had a chance to get started.

If anything, the KAL incident demonstrated how close the world had come to the precipice and how much we needed nuclear arms control: If, as some people speculated, the Soviet pilots simply mistook the airliner for a military plane, what kind of imagination did it take to think of a Soviet military man with his finger close to a nuclear push button making an even more tragic mistake?

If mistakes could be made by a fighter pilot, what about a similar miscalculation by the commander of a missile launch crew?

Yet, if somebody made that kind of mistake—or a madman got possession of a nuclear missile—we were defenseless against it. Once a nuclear missile was launched, no one could recall it, and until we got something like the Strategic Defense Initiative system in operation, the world was helpless against nuclear missiles.

Shocked as I was by the ruthless attack on the plane, it gave me an opportunity to remind people of what the atrocity revealed about the Soviet government and its totalitarian way of life.

The shooting down of KAL Flight 007 gave badly needed impetus in Congress to the rearmament program and postponed, at least for a while, attempts to gut our efforts to restore American military might.

A few days after the act of mass murder, George Shultz, who was visibly outraged by its barbarity, met Soviet Foreign Minister Gromyko at a previously scheduled conference in Madrid at which there had been the possibility of arranging a summit conference between me and Andropov sometime in 1984. But Gromyko, whom George described as defensive and discombobulated, refused to admit any Soviet liability for the attack, and what prospects might have existed for a summit evaporated.

Other events that autumn besides the KAL incident made me aware of the need for the world to step back from the nuclear precipice. They also made me more aware than ever of the urgent need for a defense against nuclear missiles. This was part of the entry in my diary October 10, 1983:

Columbus Day. In the morning at Camp D. I ran the tape of the movie ABC is running Nov. 20. It's called "The Day After" in which Lawrence, Kansas, is wiped out in a nuclear war with Russia. It is powerfully done, all $7 million worth. It's very effective and left me greatly depressed. So far they haven't sold any of the 25 ads scheduled and I can see why . . . My own reaction: we have to do all we can to have a deterrent and to see there is never a nuclear war.

Not long after that, there is this entry in my diary:

A most sobering experience with Cap W and Gen. Vessey in the Situation room, a briefing on our complete plan in the event of a nuclear attack.

There are many aspects of the report, which I'd requested of the Pentagon two years earlier, that remain so secret even now that I cannot even begin to discuss them. But, simply put, it was a scenario for a sequence of events that could lead to the end of civilization as we knew it.

In several ways, the sequence of events described in the briefings paralleled those in the ABC movie. Yet there were still some people at the Pentagon who claimed a nuclear war was "winnable." I thought they were crazy. Worse, it appeared there were also Soviet generals who thought in terms of winning a nuclear war.

Several weeks later, convinced we had to do everything possible to develop a defense against the horrible weapons of mass destruction that the atomic age had produced, I gave a go-ahead to speed up research on the Strategic Defense Initiative, noting in the diary:

> Some 50 scientists were persuaded to look at the problem after my March 23, 1983, declaration. They started as skeptics and have wound up enthusiastic. We'll proceed.

A few weeks after the Korean airliner was shot down, the parliaments of Great Britain, Italy, and West Germany reaffirmed their intention to deploy Pershing II and Tomahawk cruise missiles in Europe, and we began hearing rumors the Soviets were going to walk out of the INF negotiations in a bid to court favorable public opinion in Europe. "Some on our side want us to come up with an additional proposal," I wrote in the diary.

> That is a lousy negotiating strategy. It's time for the Soviets to come up with a proposal of their own. We can't keep changing our proposals every time they say "nyet." Ambassador Hartman (Moscow), came by. He confirms what I believe: the Soviets won't really negotiate on arms reductions until we deploy the Pershing II's and go forward with the MX. He also confirms that Andropov is very much out of sight these days.

A few days after I wrote this, the Soviets walked out of the Geneva talks on intermediate-range missiles, and shortly after that, the START discussions on long-range missiles.

They'd left the ballpark, but I didn't think the game was over.

We had just changed the rules of the game. And they didn't like it.

The United States was in its strongest position in two decades to negotiate with the Russians from strength. The American economy was booming. We'd come a long way since the late seventies, when our country was plagued with self-doubt and uncertainty and neglecting our military forces.

In spirit and military strength, America was back, and I figured it would be only a matter of time before the Soviets were back at the table—which reminds me of a story I heard about two Russian generals. One of them said to the other:

"You know, I liked the arms race better when there was only one of us in it."

Now there were two of us in the arms race and the Russians knew it. That's why I expected them to come back to Geneva.

74

THREE YEARS HAD TAUGHT ME something surprising about the Russians: Many people at the top of the Soviet hierarchy were genuinely afraid of America and Americans. Perhaps this shouldn't have surprised me, but it did. In fact, I had difficulty accepting my own conclusion at first. I'd always felt that from our deeds it must be clear to anyone that Americans were a moral people who starting at the birth of our nation had always used our power only as a force of good in the world. After World War II, for example, when we alone had the atomic bomb, we didn't use it for conquest or domination; instead, with the Marshall Plan and General Mac-Arthur's democratic stewardship of Japan, we generously rebuilt the economies of our former enemies.

If anything, we had limitless reasons to be wary of the Red Bear, because from the day it was born on the streets of Russia it was dedicated to consuming the democracies of the world.

During my first years in Washington, I think many of us in the administration took it for granted that the Russians, like ourselves, considered it unthinkable that the United States would launch a first strike against them. But the more experience I had with Soviet leaders and other heads of state who knew them, the more I began to realize that many Soviet officials feared us not only as adversaries but as potential aggressors who might hurl nuclear weapons at them in a first strike; because of this, and perhaps because of a sense of insecurity and paranoia with roots reaching back to the invasions of Russia by Napoleon and Hitler, they had aimed a huge arsenal of nuclear weapons at us.

Well, if that was the case, I was even more anxious to get a top Soviet leader in a room alone and try to convince him we had no designs on the Soviet Union and Russians had nothing to fear from us.

Less than a week before the Soviets walked out of the INF talks in Geneva in November 1983, I decided to make another attempt at communicating with Yuri Andropov outside the normal diplomatic channels. As I remarked in my diary after a meeting with George Shultz at which we agreed to create a small group within the National Security Planning Group with the goal of opening new channels to the Kremlin,

> I feel the Soviets are so defense minded, so paranoid about being attacked that without being in any way soft on them, we ought to tell them no one here has any intention of doing anything like that. What have they got that anyone would want? George is going on ABC right after its big nuclear bomb film Sunday night. It shows why we must keep on doing what we're doing.

Early in the new year, President Mika Spiljak of Yugoslavia came to the White House for lunch and confirmed some of my thoughts. "He's a personable and reasonable man," I wrote afterward.

> I picked his brains about the Soviet Union. He was an ambassador there for a time. He believes that coupled with their expansionist philosophy, they are also insecure and genuinely frightened of us. He also believes that if we opened them up a bit, their leading citizens would get braver about proposing changes in their system. I'm going to pursue this.

Throughout 1984, while my own attitudes about the Soviets were changing a little, there were certain parallels in the situations regarding our economic recovery program and my attempts to get the Russians to the arms control table:

In the economy, the tax cuts had begun to take hold, but there was a lag time before their full impact was felt: The effects were on their way, but weren't there yet.

As a result the economy was still in trouble, and I was under constant pressure—not only from Democrats but from many Republicans and many of my own people in the administration—to throw in the towel and raise taxes.

On the foreign affairs front, we had also adopted new policies—policies of realism and peace through strength—and from the laboratories and factories of the land we were starting to see the first fruits of our military modernization program, a new generation of strategic weapons whose development, I'm sure, was eagerly monitored in Moscow.

The balance in the arms race had already changed and I was certain it was going to get the Russians' attention. But, as with the economy, there was a lag time before the full impact of the new policy was apparent. And there were people who said it wasn't working; there was pressure throughout that year to abandon the policy, forget the MX and peace through strength, and try something new with the Russians—which to many of my critics simply meant appeasement.

As with my economic recovery program, I felt sure the new national security policies—if they were given time—would work. My instructions to our national security team were the same as I'd given to those working for an economic turnaround: Hang tough and stay the course.

The collapse of the Geneva talks understandably worried many in the world who were anxious for the superpowers to begin the process of nuclear disarmament.

As a result, the new year brought calls from people in Europe and the United States to submit to the Soviet demands and suspend deployment of the INF missiles. But along with our chief negotiator at Geneva, Paul Nitze, I believed the last thing we should do was yield to the demands—if we did, we'd not only be reneging on promises to our NATO allies to supply the weapons, we'd be accepting the status quo of a dangerous imbalance of nuclear missiles aimed at the capitals of Europe and be rewarding the Soviets for walking out of the negotiations.

Still, from a propaganda point of view, we were on the defensive. In a speech to the nation televised to many other countries of the world January 16, 1984, we went on the offensive. I said that I was sincere in wanting arms reduction and peace and that despite recent reversals in U.S.-Soviet relations, the United States stood ready to undertake another attempt at negotiating an arms agreement with the Soviets

based on three guiding principles—realism, strength, and dialogue. Realism means we must start with a clear-eyed understanding of the world we live in; we must recognize that we are in a long-term competition with a government that does not share our notions of individual liberties at home and peaceful change abroad. . . .

Strength is essential to negotiate successfully and protect our interests. If we're weak, we can do neither.

I have openly expressed my view of the Soviet system. I don't know why this should come as a surprise to Soviet leaders who've never shied from expressing their view of our system. But that doesn't mean that we can't deal with each other. We don't refuse to talk when the Soviets call us "imperialist aggressors" and worse, or because they cling to the fantasy of a Communist triumph over democracy. The fact that neither of us likes the other system is no reason to refuse to talk. . . .

Deterrence is essential to preserve peace and protect our way of life, but deterrence is not the beginning and end of our policy toward the Soviet Union. We must and will engage the Soviets in a dialogue as serious and constructive as possible—a dialogue that will serve to promote peace in the troubled regions of the world, reduce the level of arms, and build a constructive working relationship.

Neither we nor the Soviet Union can wish away the differences between our two societies and our philosophies, but we should always remember that we do have common interests and the foremost among them is to avoid war and reduce the level of arms.

Twelve days later, I received a harsh letter from Yuri Andropov that again criticized deployment of the INF weapons in Europe and was unyielding on virtually every other aspect of the differences I'd raised regarding the U.S. and Soviet positions at Geneva. Here are a few paragraphs from his very long letter:

If one must state today that the affairs between our two countries are taking on, to put it frankly, an extremely unfavorable shape, then the reason for it is not our policy—we did not and do not want it to be so. . . .

We are prepared to accept very deep reductions both of the strategic and European nuclear weapons. With regard to the latter, even to the point of ridding Europe entirely of medium-range and tactical-range nuclear weapons.

However, the United States has destroyed the very basis on which it was possible to seek an agreement. We have only one view of this step—it is an attempt to upset both the regular and global balance. So we are acting accordingly. It appears that the U.S. side has underestimated our resolve to preserve the military and strategic equilibrium, nothing short of equilibrium.

Let us be frank, Mr. President, there is no way of making things look as if nothing happened. There has been a disruption of the dialogue on the most important questions. A heavy blow has been dealt to the very process of nuclear arms limitation.

Yuri Andropov

Twelve days after Andropov sent me this letter, he died, and soon we had another new man—Konstantin Chernenko—in charge at the Kremlin.

Once again, I felt I had a chance, through quiet diplomacy, to reduce the psychological barriers that divided us. U.S.-Soviet relations were not yet at the point where I thought I should attend Andropov's funeral. George Bush led our delegation to Moscow (which also included Senator Howard Baker) and he returned with the opinion that Chernenko seemed less hard-nosed and abrasive than Andropov. After hearing this, I remarked in my diary:

I have a gut feeling I'd like to talk to him about our problems man to man and see if I could convince him there would be a material benefit to the Soviets if they'd join the family of nations, etc. We don't want to appear anxious which would tempt them to play games and possibly snub us. I have our team considering an invitation to him to be my guest at the opening of the Olympics, July in L.A. Then he and I could have a session together in which we could start the ball rolling for an outright summit on arms reductions, human rights, etc. We'll see.

But the next day a letter arrived from Chernenko that was not the kind to encourage expectations of an early improvement in our relations. After thanking me for sending my condolences to the funeral with the vice-president, Chernenko in no uncertain terms said that he and other members of the Soviet leadership stood by the letter Andropov wrote to me just before his death: The Soviet Union remained unswervingly opposed to NATO deployment of the Pershing II and cruise missiles. These are excerpts from his letter:

> I would like, Mr. President, that you and I have a clear understanding from the very beginning on the central matter of the relations between the USSR and the USA.
>
> We are convinced that it is impossible to begin to correct the present abnormal and, let's face it, dangerous situation and to speak seriously of constructive moves, if there is a continuation of attempts to upset the balance of forces and to gain military advantages to the detriment of the security of the other side, if actions are taken prejudicing the legitimate interests of the other side.
>
> There is another important point which the U.S. leadership must clearly understand: Not only the U.S. has allies and friends, the Soviet Union has them too; and we will be caring for them. . . .
>
> We look at things realistically and have no illusions that it is possible to carry on business in total abstraction from the objective differences which exist between a socialist country and a capitalist country. For instance, our morality does not accept much of what is endemic to the capitalist society and what we consider as unfair to people. Nevertheless, we do not introduce these problems into the sphere of interstate relationships. Just as we believe it is wrong and even dangerous to subordinate our relations to ideological differences.

Chernenko ended his letter on a slightly positive note: The Soviets were "resolute advocates of a serious and meaningful dialogue, a dialogue that would be aimed at searching for common ground, at finding concrete and mutually acceptable solutions in those areas where it proves realistically possible," and improvements in U.S.-Soviet relations were "feasible given the same desire on the United States side."

Despite the rebuff from Moscow, I still felt the time had come to explore holding a summit conference with Chernenko. He was cut from the same cloth as Brezhnev and Andropov—a tough old-line

Communist addicted to Lenin's secular religion of expansionism and world domination, so one thing hadn't changed regarding U.S.-Soviet relations.

But something *else* had changed: I felt we could now go to the summit, for the first time in years, from a position of strength, as this entry in my diary a few days after I received Chernenko's letter indicated:

> I met for the seventh time with the Joint Chiefs of Staff. I had one of the most exciting hours being briefed on where we are as a result of these past three years. Our technology is so superior to what our possible adversaries have and our improvement in training and readiness are inspiring. In all branches, 91 percent of our recruits are high school graduates. Highest level in our history. I wish it were possible for our people to know what has been accomplished but too much of it must remain secret.

Ever since I had seen how they operated during the Depression in Dixon, I'd never put much faith in bureaucracies—and bureaucracies usually played a large role in the conduct of American foreign affairs. Whenever I wanted to send a message to a foreign leader, for example, copies of my message were usually first circulated to a half-dozen or more agencies at the State Department, the Pentagon, the Commerce Department, and elsewhere for comment and suggestions. And often the bureaucrats down the line (I'm sure in good faith) would try to add or change something—whether it was needed or not. The result: often a blurring of my original intentions.

Because arms reduction was so important, I decided in this instance to switch to a more hands-on approach—without help from the bureaucrats.

At a National Security Council meeting in early March, I announced that I had decided to draft a response to Chernenko without asking input from the bureaucracy. From then on, I would consult only with a small group—George Bush, George Shultz, Cap Weinberger, and Bud McFarlane, my national security advisor, in the National Security Planning Group to determine whether we could develop a long-range plan that offered the Russians a series of small steps, and showed that we were sincere about wanting to improve relations as a prelude to a summit and hoped they were, too. These entries from my diary in March summarized some of the developments that were happening then:

March 2
I'm convinced the time has come for me to meet with Chernenko along about July 1. We're going to start with some ministerial level meetings on a number of substantive matters that have been on ice since the KAL 007 shoot down.

March 5
Helmut Kohl, West German chancellor, arrived. We had a good meeting and lunch. He confirmed my belief that the Soviets are motivated at least in part by insecurity and a suspicion that we and our allies mean them harm. They still preserve the tank traps and barbed wire that show how close the Germans got to Moscow before they were stopped. He too thinks I should meet Chernenko.

March 7
George Shultz and I met. Our plans about the Soviet Union are going forward. He is giving Ambassador Dobrynin my letter for delivery to Chernenko.

In the letter to Chernenko, I said I believed it would be advantageous for us to communicate directly and confidentially. I tried to use the old actor's technique of empathy: to imagine the world as seen through another's eyes and try to help my audience see it through my eyes. "I fully appreciate the priority you attach to the security of the Soviet state," I wrote, "particularly in light of the enormous costs shouldered by your people in helping to defeat Nazi Germany." I said it was my understanding that some people in the Soviet Union felt a genuine fear of our country.

"But I cannot understand why our programs can be considered threatening," I wrote. Since 1970, the letter went on, the USSR had developed three new intercontinental ballistic missiles, five new submarine-launched ballistic missiles, and thirteen modernized versions of other Soviet missiles. Yes, we had begun to develop new weapons systems after a long period, but only in response to the Soviet buildup.

As we see it, you claim to be responding to the U.S. program. Yet your new missiles have been deployed years ahead of their U.S. counterparts, not to mention in greater numbers . . . I recognize that neither of us will be able to persuade the other as to who is to blame for the poor state of our relations, nor would it be productive for the two of us to engage in a lengthy debate on the subject. I doubt, however, that we can make progress in reducing the high levels of armaments if either of us is unwilling to take into account the concerns of the other.

As for myself, I am prepared to consider your concerns seriously, even when I have difficulty understanding why they are held. I am willing to explore possible ways to alleviate them. But solutions will elude us if you are unable to approach our discussions in the same spirit, or if you demand concessions as an entry fee for the discussions themselves.

(This was a reference to Moscow's demands that we halt deployment of NATO's new INF missiles before it would return to Geneva.)

Perhaps, America's policies had been misunderstood in Moscow: Contrary to what Soviet leaders might believe, I wrote, the United States

has no desire to threaten the security of the Soviet Union and its allies, nor are we seeking military superiority or to impose our will on others. . . .

Alluding to a remark by Chernenko that it was dangerous for either side to attempt to upset the prevailing balance of forces and gain a military advantage (a veiled reference to the INF missiles), I continued:

I agree that such attempts are dangerous, but many actions of the Soviet Union in recent years would represent just such attempts. I do not intend to debate these matters in this letter because the United States views are well known; I feel we should move beyond mutual recrimination and attempts to assess blame and find concrete steps we can both take to put the relations on a more positive track. . . .

I wrote that all of us involved in arms control discussions must realize we had to hurdle a difficult practical stumbling block before we reached an agreement: For understandable reasons of history and geography, I wrote, the Soviet strategic forces were made up almost exclusively of land-based intercontinental-range missiles while the United States had a three-tiered force of land-, sea-, and air-launched missiles.

Since we were dealing to some extent with apples and oranges, I wrote that reaching an equitable agreement would be hard but not impossible; from our perspective, the most destabilizing aspect of the nuclear arms race was the Soviets' substantial edge over the United States in long-range missiles, but I said we were prepared to discuss trade-offs that acknowledged the differences in our forces and bridged the proposals of both sides. The INF weapons in Europe, I wrote, were obviously a major sticking point in our relations, and if the Soviets had any new ideas on how to deal with the impasse, we would pay attention to them. In the meantime, I suggested we move ahead on other issues, including work on a treaty to ban chemical weapons and begin the development of better communications and procedures to avert miscalculations or misunderstandings that might lead to disaster during an international crisis:

> Mr. General Secretary, following his visit to Moscow, Vice President Bush conveyed to me your message that we should take steps to insure that history recalls us as leaders known to be good, wise and kind. Nothing is more important to me, and we should take steps to bring this about.

Referring to the Soviet decision to allow the Pentecostalist families to emigrate to America, I wrote that I was

> touched by that gesture and in my view, it showed how quiet and sincere efforts could solve even the most sensitive problems in our relationship. Similar humanitarian gestures this year would touch the heart of all Americans. Therefore, I conclude as you did, that a turn toward steady and good relations between our two countries is desirable and feasible and I am determined to do my part in working for that end.
>
> Sincerely,
> Ronald Reagan

At the end of the letter, I wrote a postscript by hand:

P.S. Mr. Chairman. In thinking through this letter, I have reflected at some length on the tragedy and scale of Soviet losses in warfare through the ages. Surely those losses, which are beyond description, must affect your thinking today. I want you to know that neither I nor the American people hold any offensive intentions toward the Soviet people. The truth of that statement is underwritten by the history of our restraint at the time when our virtual monopoly on strategic power provided the means for expansion had we so chosen. We did not then nor shall we now. Our common and urgent purpose must be the translation of this reality into a lasting reduction of tensions between us. I pledge to you my profound commitment to that goal.

75

M oscow's response to this attempt at quiet diplomacy was a cold shoulder: Ambassador Dobrynin told George Shultz the Soviet leadership wasn't interested in a summit and Chernenko's reply stated that he had no interest in pursuing a dialogue without acts of "concrete, weighty substance" on the part of the United States—which to him meant removing the Pershing II and cruise missiles. Here are excerpts from his letter, which, like mine, was seven pages long:

> We have already made it known to the United States before, but since you go back again to the matter of intentions and how they can be perceived, I will express thoughts and illustrate them with specific examples:
>
> If one is to summarize what was on many occasions publicly stated by you and other representatives of your administration, the bottom line will be that the United States would only agree with such a situation where it would be militarily ahead of the USSR. But the point of the matter is that we, however, have not agreed nor do we agree with such a situation. In this respect, we have some experience earned the hard way. The history of our relations, especially the post-war period, has seen quite a few complications too; quite a few attempts were made to exert political, economic as well as military pressure on us.
>
> It appears to be an American idiom to put somebody in someone else's shoes. I ask you, Mr. President, to look at the realities of the international situation from our perspective, and you will see right

from the start that the Soviet Union is encircled by a chain of American military bases.

These bases are full of nuclear weapons. Their mission is well known. They are targeted at us. Nothing like it can be found around your country.

And what about entire regions of the globe being proclaimed as spheres of American vital interest and also made subject to U.S. military presence?

This is done, among other places, at our very doorstep. We, on our part, do not do anything like that. What conclusions should we draw from this as to the intentions of the United States? The conclusions readily present themselves: This course of action is nothing but a hyperatrophied idea of one's interests when the legitimate interests of others are completely ignored. Nothing but an urge to gain, to put it mildly, positions of privilege at the expense of the other side. This course of action is not in line with the course of assuring stability; on the contrary, such a course and policy objectively helps to create and maintain tensions. . . .

That no claims can be laid to the Soviet Union for the fact there is a rough parity between the USSR and the USA and in a wider sense between the members of the Warsaw Treaty and NATO can be disputed by no expert familiar with the state of affairs. The SALT II treaty embodied that fact. It was not the end of the road and we did not think it was. But the merit of the treaty was that, among other things, that it stated, I would say with mathematical precision, the existing strategic balance.

I remind you that it was the Soviet Union that offered to reduce their number to the minimum on the side of the USSR and NATO. And in response, Pershing and cruise missiles appeared in the vicinity of our borders.

What would be your attitude, Mr. President, had something like this happened with respect to the United States? I believe your assessment of the intentions of the other side would have been under the circumstances only one with respect to that other side's approach to negotiations, as well as the substance of its intentions. Even under these circumstances we have displayed utmost restraint. And the response measures we were forced to take as far as their scope and character are concerned, have not gone beyond the limits necessary to neutralize the threat created for us and our allies.

Chernenko went on to write that it was conceivable that our countries might increase cooperation at some levels, but no significant progress on arms control was possible as long as NATO continued deploying the new missiles or the United States continued work on the Strategic Defense Initiative. He also said that the United States had no business raising human rights issues involving the Soviet Union.

> I must point out that the introduction into relations between our two states of solely domestic affairs of our or your country does not serve the purpose of improving these relations if this is our goal. I wish that questions of such nature do not burden our correspondence. . . .

After reading Chernenko's letter, I remarked in the diary: "They are going to be cold and stiff necked for awhile. But we must not become supplicants. We're trying to get agreement on a few lesser matters."

A few weeks later, we got an even plainer signal from the Russians that they weren't in a hurry to improve relations when they announced they were going to boycott the summer olympic games in Los Angeles along with other members of the Soviet bloc—a response to Jimmy Carter's removal of our team from the 1980 games in Moscow following the Soviet invasion of Afghanistan.

George Shultz worked hard, in meetings with Dobrynin and other Soviet officials, through the spring and summer of 1984 to reopen a U.S.-Soviet dialogue, but without much success. As I once observed in my diary that spring: "They are utterly stonewalling us."

Meanwhile, in Congress, Tip O'Neill said he had taken on a moral commitment to block further development of the MX missile, and this, I knew, wouldn't make it any easier for me to convince the Soviets that we were a united country committed to a policy of peace through strength.

Once again, a committee of 535 was trying to set foreign policy.

At the same time, opposition to our new strategic policy toward the Russians continued from small but well-organized and well-publicized antinuclear groups in Europe, and some European leaders, feeling the heat, began expressing doubts about NATO's 1979 decision to deploy the new weapons.

What would I think, I asked myself, if I were a Soviet leader and saw this kind of fractiousness among the leaders of the United

States and the Western alliance? I'd try to exploit it, which is what they did. Seeing the split on our side, the Soviets intensified their propaganda offensive, trying to achieve political and military goals through a public relations campaign that blamed us for the impasse and claimed we were leading the world to the brink of nuclear war —when they had been the party who'd walked away at Geneva.

I asked George Shultz, without retreating in any way from our basic positions, to keep probing for the possibility of a summit.

"I have a gut feeling we should do this," I wrote in my diary after I received another letter from Chernenko in June that repeated many of his earlier points. "His reply to my letter is in hand and it lends support to my idea that while we go on believing, and with some good reason, that the Soviets are plotting against us and mean us harm, maybe they are scared of us and think we are a threat."

The 1984 election was coming up. Several of our Soviet experts told me not to expect any movement from the Russians until after it was over. Our intelligence analysts believed Chernenko and other Soviet leaders had decided not to respond positively to suggestions for a summit because they felt that if they did they would help me get reelected. I have no way of knowing whether that was true, but I wouldn't be surprised if it was.

Over the next few months, we were to learn that to a large extent Chernenko was not as much in control of the Communist Party or the Politburo as Brezhnev or even Andropov, but shared it as spokesman for a kind of consensus leadership at the top of the hierarchy.

Like Andropov, we were told, Chernenko was ill and might not live long. When he appeared in public, he seldom said anything without a script. Another old hard-liner from the Stalin era, Andrei Gromyko, was calling the shots on Soviet foreign relations, and it was at his recommendation that the Soviets boycotted the Olympics.

In the middle of the summer, the Russians told George Shultz that they would be willing to return to the arms control table, but to discuss one item only, what they called the "militarization of space," a reference to our research on the Strategic Defense Initiative.

The Soviets were demanding that we halt work on the SDI just as we were beginning to get indications from our scientists that it might work—and at a time when the Soviets already had missile defense weapons that in some cases were more sophisticated than ours.

When it was time for me to host our annual dinner for the diplomatic corps that summer, my tablemate again was its dean, Anatoly Dobrynin. He confirmed that the Soviets wanted to meet in September in Vienna, but to talk only about space weapons. I told him we'd be in Vienna if they were, but to discuss reducing *all* kinds of nuclear weapons that operated in space, including ballistic missiles. We didn't settle anything, but I got a few things off my chest.

In late July, after stopping in Los Angeles to help open the Olympics, Nancy and I spent two weeks at the ranch, the longest uninterrupted time we'd ever spent there. She was busy planning Patti's wedding, which gave me lots of time to do some thinking on the back of my horse about our impasse with the Soviets, and I came to a decision:

Gromyko usually attended the opening session of the UN General Assembly in New York each September; after talking it over with George Shultz and Bud McFarlane, I decided to invite him to the White House after the UN meeting for a visit and some person-to-person diplomacy. As I wrote in the diary after discussing my idea with George and Bud: "I have a feeling we'll get nowhere with arms reductions while they are as suspicious of our motives as we are of theirs. I believe we need a meeting to see if we can't make them understand we have no designs on them but think they have designs on us. If we could once clear the air maybe reducing arms wouldn't look so impossible to them."

After first indicating he had no interest in my invitation, Gromyko agreed to come to the White House September 28. In the diary, I wrote: "I intend to open up the whole matter of why we don't trust them. Maybe if we can ease the mutual suspicion, arms talks can move better."

Several days before our meeting in Washington, I was scheduled to speak to the General Assembly and I went to work on a speech I hoped would tread a fine line, one reiterating our sense of realism and toughness regarding the Soviets, but not offensive enough to torpedo whatever prospects of success there might be for the meeting with Gromyko. I settled on a direct appeal to the Soviets that, while pointing out our concern for their misbehavior in Afghanistan and other places, requested that they return to the Geneva talks and suggested changes in the format of the negotiations to raise their prospects of success. At a reception the night before my speech, Gromyko and I saw each other briefly in a receiving line, and as I looked into his gray face he reminded me of all the Soviet leaders I'd ever seen or heard about in the past: He was tough, stiff, and unsmiling, with no apparent sense of humor unless he had concealed it somewhere beyond his steely eyes. We kept matters cordial and he reminded me that we had once met in California when I was governor. The next day when I gave my speech, he sat with the Soviet delegation front row center just below the microphone. I tried to catch their eyes several times but they looked right through me and their expressions never changed.

The day before my meeting with Gromyko at the White House, the NSC, by coincidence, scheduled a briefing on Soviet espionage at our embassy in Moscow. I was overwhelmed by what Soviet spies had accomplished, including making high-tech alterations to the typewriters in the embassy that had transmitted to them copies of many top-secret documents typed at the embassy.

This is how I recounted my session with the Soviet foreign minister the next day:

> *Sept. 28*
> The big day—Andrei Gromyko. Meeting held in Oval Office. Five waves of photographers, first time that many. I opened with my monologue and made the point that perhaps both of us felt the other was a threat, then explained by the record we had more reason to feel that way than they did. His opener was about 30 minutes, then we went into dialogue. I had taken notes on his pitch and rebutted with fact and figure a number of his points. I kept emphasizing that we were the two nations that could destroy or save the world. I figured they nurse a grudge that we don't respect them as a super power. All in all, three hours including lunch were I believe well spent. Everyone at our end think he's going home with a pretty clear view of where we stand.

We agreed to the customary step of inviting the foreign minister to a small luncheon in the White House, which was also the practice when a head of state visited. As hostess of the White House, Nancy came to the reception. Before lunch, Gromyko came over to her, took her to the side, and whispered in her ear: "Does your husband believe in peace?" Nancy said, "Yes, of course." And he said, "Then whisper the word *peace* in his ear every night." And she said, "I will, and I'll also whisper it in your ear," and she leaned over and did it. For the first time that day, "Grim Grom," as he had been nicknamed by some, cracked a smile.

Gromyko was convinced of the rightness of the Soviet position, and it was impossible for me not to sense in this frosty old Stalinist the confidence that, despite all its problems, Communism was going to prevail over capitalism and eventually there would be a one-world Communist state. We had three hours of give-and-take. I told him we were willing to go back to the negotiating table, but only if the Soviets indicated a genuine interest in negotiating an equitable and mutually satisfactory agreement. As I'd planned, I also tried to let him know the Soviet Union had nothing to fear from us. But if I scored any points, Gromyko didn't admit it to me. He was as hard as granite. He said both of us were sitting on gigantic piles of nuclear weapons that were getting higher and higher and more and more dangerous, and I agreed. He wouldn't commit himself, but he left me with the impression that the Soviets might consider a return to the bargaining table. However, I think he didn't intend to do anything about that until after our election.

Following our meeting, I began devoting more time to the reelection campaign. I told George Shultz and the others to stick with our policies, and said that if I won the Russians would return to the table in Geneva.

George Shultz and Cap Weinberger were having one of their disputes over policy. Cap was not as interested as George in opening negotiating with the Russians, and some of his advisors at the Pentagon strongly opposed some of my ideas on arms control that George supported, including my hope for eventually eliminating all nuclear weapons from the world. Cap had allies among some of my more conservative political supporters, who let me know they thought Shultz had gone soft on the Russians and they wanted me to fire him—an idea, I told them, that was utter nonsense. Meanwhile, Bud McFarlane, who also sometimes differed with Cap and angered him by claiming the Pentagon could modernize its forces effectively at substantially lower cost than Cap was asking for, sided with George. Bill Casey and Ed Meese lined up in Cap's camp in favoring an even harder line toward the Russians, as this entry from my diary in November reflected: " . . . [the dispute] is so out of hand George sounds like he wants out. I can't let that happen. Actually George is carrying out my policy. I'm going to meet with Cap and Bill and lay it out to them. Won't be fun but has to be done." I didn't disagree with Weinberger that the Russians were an evil force in the world and untrustworthy, but I didn't think that meant we shouldn't talk to them.

As I expected, a few days after the election Gromyko said he wanted to meet with George in Geneva to discuss holding a new round of arms control talks.

George agreed and a meeting was set for January.

Following the election, I also got a very unusual message congratulating me on my reelection: Scrawled by hand in Russian on a tiny piece of tissue paper about half the size of a business card, in characters so small a microscope was almost necessary to read them, the message came from ten women who were imprisoned at a Soviet forced-labor camp.

> Mr. President:
>
> We, women political prisoners of the Soviet Union, congratulate you on your reelection to the spot of President of the USA. We look with hope to your country which is on the road of FREEDOM and respect for HUMAN RIGHTS. We wish you success on this road.

With their message was a poem and a chart that listed a series of hunger strikes these brave women had conducted at their camp in 1983 and 1984 in defiance of a cruel regime that threw people in jail simply because they expressed a belief in freedom or said they wanted to emigrate from Russia for religious reasons. The material had been smuggled out of the camp and then out of Russia and delivered to the offices of Radio Free Europe in Munich. This is a translation of the poem they sent to me:

> On the day of your election
> There we were, in deep dejection,
> In a filthy prison cell

Freezing cold and most unwell.
We did not have books or papers
Warming food or legal status,
Only frigid wind and stars
Through the naked window bars,
Like a breath of Dante's hell
As befits a prison cell.
And while others cast their ballots,
Partied, danced—we sat on pallets,
Vainly guessing (what a chore!)
How much more we had in store
Isolations, deprivations,
And what for?
Then a warder scurried up,
Threatened, lied to shut us up,
But by our calculation
Right across your mighty nation
States like Kansas, Illinois,
Gave us cause for lots of joy.
By "lights out" it was quite clear
You had nothing left to fear.
So we hunkered down to sleep
By the heater (minus heat)
Chilly drafts crept round the cell
And we sighed: We wish you well
Mister President,
The White House,
Coast to coast the USA
And those there, who're still awake
We're not sleeping, just like you,
All in goose-bumps, cold and blue,
Our teeth chattering in sorrow:
"Great October" day tomorrow!

What manner of government, I asked myself, stifled a people's yearnings for freedom by making them prisoners?

During December, I held a series of meetings with the small group within the NSPG that I had delegated to help me in developing strategy for our new talks with the Russians.

Cap, a strong booster of the SDI, said the Russians were almost certainly going to demand that we kill it as the price for holding substantive negotiations. I told the group as emphatically as I could: The Strategic Defense Initiative was not a "bargaining chip" and we were going to stick with it no matter what the Russians wanted.

The SDI might take decades to develop, but what more important mission did we have than finding the means to neutralize the terrible weapons produced by the nuclear age?

I never viewed the SDI as an impenetrable shield—no defense could ever be expected to be one hundred percent effective.

But what made the idea promising was that, if it worked and we then entered an era when the nations of the world agreed to eliminate nuclear weapons, it could serve as a safety valve against cheating—or attacks by lunatics who managed to get their hands on a nuclear missile. And, if we couldn't reach an agreement eliminating nuclear missiles, the system would be able to knock down enough of an enemy's missiles so that if he ever pushed the button to attack, he would be doing so in the knowledge his attack was unable to prevent a devastating retaliatory strike. The SDI held too much potential for the security of mankind to be traded away at the negotiating table, I said.

I said at one meeting that I was getting fed up with the way the Russians were behaving and that too often in the past the United States had accepted flawed agreements with them simply because we couldn't get any other kind of agreement. Afterward, I wrote in the diary: "I made it plain there must be no granting of concessions, one sided, to try to soften up the Soviets . . . we're convinced they want above all to negotiate away our right to seek defensive weapons against ballistic missiles. They fear our technology. I believe such a defense could render nuclear weapons obsolete and thus we could rid the world of that threat. Question is, will they use that to break off the talks and blame us?" A few days later there is this entry in the diary: "We had an N.S.P.G. meeting again on our negotiating posture in the upcoming meeting with Gromyko and the arms talks. I believe the Soviets have agreed to the talks only to head off our research on a strategic defense against nuclear weapons. I stand firm we cannot retreat on that, no matter what they offer." A few days after that, on December 18, I made this entry in my diary: "A meeting with the Joint Chiefs re our military force compared to that of the Soviets. In strategic weapons, when the

Soviets refer to maintaining stability they mean superiority and they have it. More and more I'm thinking the Soviets are preparing to walk out on the talks if we won't give up research on the strategic defense system. I hope I'm wrong. . . ."

Just before Christmas, Margaret Thatcher came to Washington and Nancy and I invited her to Camp David. I met her helicopter in a golf cart and took her to Aspen, our weekend home, before going on to the main conference building, Laurel. She had just had a meeting with an up-and-coming member of the Soviet Politburo named Mikhail Gorbachev who, she said, expressed strong Soviet reservations over the SDI. When she seemed to share some of his misgivings I wondered if the British were concerned about the SDI and my hope of eliminating nuclear weapons because of fears that without the American nuclear shield the Soviets' superiority in conventional weapons would pose a threat to Western Europe. I assured Margaret we were simply embarking on a long-term research effort, not making a commitment to deploy the SDI; obviously, I said, it would be some time before we knew it would work as we hoped.

During this period in late 1984, we had another problem in the arms control arena to deal with: Until that time, both the Soviet Union and the United States had agreed to abide voluntarily by the expired SALT I treaty limiting nuclear weapons as well as by the SALT II treaty, which, because of the Soviet invasion of Afghanistan, had never been ratified by our Senate.

Cap thought we should stop living up to the treaties because of evidence indicating strongly that the Soviets were violating them, although the agreements were written so ambiguously that it was doubtful we could prove violations. The Russians were erecting elaborate new radar near the town of Krasnoyarsk in Siberia, for example, that our scientists were convinced was designed specifically for a defensive system against U.S. missiles—a treaty violation. The Russians claimed the radar station was meant only for tracking space satellites. Although we believed that wasn't so, the treaty language was so loosely written that a violation was difficult to prove.

In early January 1985, while George Bush and I were getting ready for our second inaugural, George Shultz met with Gromyko in Geneva and they agreed to a resumption of arms control talks; when we rejected the Soviets' insistence that the talks be limited to questions of space defense, Gromyko agreed they would also involve offensive nuclear missiles. After additional wrangling, a date and place were set for the resumption—March 12 in Geneva, fifteen months after the Soviets had walked out of the previous negotiations.

Here are a few excerpts from my diary that month:

March 4

Our 33rd anniversary. Other than that it was another Monday morning. Why do they always seem different than other days?

Met with the new Secretary General of O.E.C.D. [Organization for Economic Cooperation and Development]—Jean-Claude Paye. It was a brief but pleasant meeting. He is all for urging European members of O.E.C.D. to take steps to free up their economies, etc., so as to catch up with our economic recovery.

We had an N.S.C. meeting with our arms talks leaders looking at various options for how we wanted to deal with the Soviets. It's a very complicated business. I urged one decision on them—that we open the talks with a *concession*. Surprise! Since they have publicly stated they want to see nuclear weapons eliminated entirely, I told our people to open by saying we would accept their goal.

Nancy came to the Oval Office for lunch and we cut an anniversary cake and had a few of the immediate staff share in it. That was the extent of our celebration except that at dinner we opened a 1911 bottle of Chateau Margaux.

March 7

Lunch with Tip O'Neill. . . . Tip surprised me—he won't make an issue of MX but will not personally vote for it. He says it's a matter of conscience; having the MX he says will provoke a Russian nuclear attack. He can't respond when asked how we can remain defenseless and let the Soviets have thousands of missiles aimed at us. Big event was meeting with Politburo member Vladimir Shcherbitsky. He had Ambassador Dobrynin and a couple of others with him. I had George Shultz, Bud M, Don Regan and a couple of others with me. He and I went round and round. His was the usual diatribe that we are the destabilizing force, threatening them. It was almost a repeat of the Gromyko debate except that we got right down to arguing. I think he'll go home knowing that we are ready for negotiations but we d—m well aren't going to let our guard down or hold still while they continue to build up their offensive forces.

March 8

A large breakfast with members of Senate and House teams who are going to Geneva for opening of arms talks plus our negotiators. There seemed to be a feeling of unity even including Senator Ted Kennedy. Then over to the Roosevelt Room and we had formal send off . . . then it was off to Bethesda Naval Hospital for my annual check up. I'm so healthy I had a hard time not acting smug.

March 11

Awakened at 4 a.m. to be told Chernenko is dead. My mind turned to whether I should attend the funeral. My gut instinct said no. Got to the office at 9. George Shultz had some arguments that I should. He lost. I don't think his heart was really in it. George Bush is in Geneva. He'll go and George Shultz will join him leaving tonight.

Word has been received that Gorbachev has been named head man in the Soviet Union.

So, once again, there was a new man in the Kremlin. "How am I supposed to get anyplace with the Russians," I asked Nancy, "if they keep dying on me?"

76

I DECIDED NOT TO WASTE any time in trying to get to know the new Soviet leader. When George Bush went to Moscow for Konstantin Chernenko's funeral, he took an invitation from me to Gorbachev for a summit conference in the United States. "You can be assured of my personal commitment to working with you and the rest of the Soviet leadership in serious negotiations," I wrote. "In that spirit, I would like you to visit me in Washington at your earliest convenient opportunity. I recognize that arriving at an early answer may not be possible. But I want you to know that I look forward to a meeting that could yield results of benefit to both our countries and to the international community as a whole."

Gorbachev replied two weeks later. In doing so, he completed the first round of a correspondence between us that was to last for years and encompass scores of letters. As I look back on them now, I realize those first letters marked the cautious beginning on both sides of what was to become the foundation of not only a better relationship between our countries but a friendship between two men.

Gorbachev thanked me for sending George to the funeral and expressed less hostility than I'd come to expect from Soviet leaders. He said he was amenable to holding a summit, but not necessarily in Washington. Overall, his letter was encouraging. Except for some formalities, here is the complete text of his letter:

Our countries are different by their social systems, by the ideologies dominant in them—but we believe that this should not be a reason for animosity. Each social system has the right to life, and it should prove its advantages not by force, not by military means, but on the path of peaceful competition with the other system. And all people have the right to go the way they have chosen themselves, without anybody imposing his will on them from outside, interfering in their internal affairs. We believe that this is the only just and healthy basis for relations among states. For our part, we have always striven to build our relations with the United States, as well as with other countries, precisely in this manner. Besides, Soviet leadership is convinced that our two countries have one common interest uniting them beyond any doubt: not to let things come to the outbreak of nuclear war which would inevitably have catastrophic consequences for both sides. And both sides would be well advised to recall this more often in making their policy.

I am convinced that given such approach to the business at hand, on the basis of a reasonable account of the realities of today's world and treating with a due respect the rights and legitimate interests of the other side, we could do quite a bit to benefit the peoples of our countries, as well as the whole world having embarked upon the road of a real improvement of relations.

It appears to us that it is important first of all to start conducting business in such a manner that both we ourselves and others can see and feel that both countries are not aiming at deepening their differences and whipping up animosity, but rather, are making their policy looking to the prospect of revitalizing the situation and a peaceful, calm development. This would help create an atmosphere of greater trust between our countries. It is not an easy task, and I would say, a delicate one. For trust is a specially sensitive thing, keenly receptive to both deeds and words. It will not be enhanced if, for example, one were to talk as if in two languages; one for private contacts, and the other as they say, for the audience.

The development of relations could well proceed through finding practical solutions between a number of problems of mutual interest. As I understand it, you also speak in favor of such a way.

We believe that this should be done across the entire range of problems, both international and bilateral. Any problem can be solved, of course, only on a mutually acceptable basis, which means finding reasonable compromises, the main criteria being neither side should claim some special rights for itself or advantages, both on subjects between the two of them and in international affairs.

No matter how important the questions involved in our relations or affecting them in this or that matter might be, the central priority area is that of security. The negotiations under way in Geneva require the foremost attention of the two of us. Obviously we will have to turn again and again to the questions under discussion there. At this point I do not intend to comment on what is going on at the talks—they have just started. I shall say though, that some statements which were made and are being made in your country will, with regard to the talks, cause concern.

I would like you to know and appreciate the seriousness of our approach to the negotiations, our firm desire to work through positive results there. We will invariably adhere to the agreement on the subject and objectives of those negotiations. The fact that we were able to agree on this in January is already a big achievement and it should be treated with care.

I hope, Mr. President, that you will feel from this letter that the Soviet leadership, including myself personally, intends to act vigorously as to find common ways to improving relations between our countries.

I think that it is also clear from my letter that we attach great importance to contacts at the highest level. For this reason I have a positive attitude to the idea you expressed about holding a personal meeting between us. And, it would seem that such a meeting should not necessarily be concluded by signing some major documents, though agreements on certain issues of mutual interest, if they were worked out by that time, could well be formalized during the meeting. The main thing is that it should be a meeting to search for mutual understanding on the basis of equality and account of legitimate interests of each other.

As to a venue for the meeting, I thank you for the invitation to visit Washington. But let us agree that we shall return again to the question of the place and time for the meeting.

M. Gorbachev
March 24, 1985

I can't claim that I believed from the start that Mikhail Gorbachev was going to be a *different* sort of Soviet leader.

Instead, as this note in my diary five weeks after he became general secretary of the Communist Party indicates, I was wary:

"Met with our Ambassador to the Soviet Union, Art Hartman.

He confirms what I believe, that Gorbachev will be as tough as any of their leaders. If he wasn't a confirmed ideologue, he never would have been chosen by the Politburo."

We'd have to be as tough as ever in dealing with the Soviets, I told George Shultz and others in the National Security Planning Group who were helping me coordinate our effort to improve relations with them, but I said we should work hard to establish channels directly between Gorbachev and me through quiet diplomacy—as I put it in the diary, "to lean on the Soviets one on one, not in the papers."

The ball was now in his court regarding a summit. I'd given him an invitation.

The new round of arms negotiations got under way in Geneva, while I kept pressing Congress to approve the MX program so we could keep pressure on Moscow and make Gorbachev see the wisdom of bargaining in good faith. It took a lot of phone calls and meetings with congressmen, but in several close votes we beat back attempts to kill the MX, including a crucial 217-to-210 victory in the House.

In late March, I was awakened shortly after dawn by Bud McFarlane, who said Major Arthur D. Nicholson, Jr., a thirty-seven-year-old Army officer, one of fourteen U.S. military men based in East Germany, had been shot by a Soviet guard as he was legally reconnoitering border facilities in that country. It was all but wanton murder. The guard continued shooting after the officer fell, pinning down an American sergeant who might have gotten to Major Nicholson to administer first aid; by the time Soviet medics arrived an hour later, the major was dead. A few days later, Tip O'Neill and Bob Michel, the Republican leader in the House, were scheduled to lead a bipartisan Congressional group to the Soviet Union to meet Gorbachev. I gave them my blessing, plus a letter for Gorbachev in which I protested the killing of Major Nicholson and the continuing Soviet backing of insurgents in Third World countries. Here are excerpts from my letter:

I believe that new opportunities are now opening up in U.S.-Soviet relations. We must take advantage of them. You know my view that there are such opportunities in every area of our relations, including humanitarian, regional, bilateral and arms control issues. In improving stability, there is no more important issue than the arms control talks we have jointly undertaken in Geneva. Our negotiators have very flexible instructions to work with your negotiators in drafting agreements which can lead to radical reductions and toward our common goal, elimination of nuclear weapons. . . .

In seizing new opportunities, we must also take care to avoid situations which can seriously damage our relations. In addition to the personal tragedy of this brave officer, this act seems to many in our country to be only the latest example of a Soviet military action which threatens to undo our best efforts to fashion a sustainable, more constructive relationship for the long term.

I want you to know it is also a matter of personal importance to me that we take steps to prevent the recurrence of this tragedy and I hope you will do all in your power to prevent such actions in the future.

As you know, I look forward to meeting you personally at a mutually convenient time. Together I am confident that we can provide the important political impetus you mentioned in your last letter for moving toward a more constructive and stable relation between our two countries.

Let me close by affirming the value I place on our correspondence. I will be replying in greater detail to your last letter. I hope we can continue to speak frankly in future letters as we attempt to build stronger relations between ourselves and between our two countries.

Sincerely,
Ronald Reagan
April 4, 1985

Subsequently, the Soviet Union issued a statement saying it had ordered its sentries in East Germany not to use deadly force against Americans, an encouraging signal from the Kremlin. But almost at the same time Gorbachev met with Daniel Ortega and promised the Sandinistas continued Soviet financial support; we announced a U.S. trade embargo against Nicaragua. In May, Secretary of Commerce Mac Baldrige went to Moscow to discuss possible expansion of trade between our countries. I decided to use his trip as an opportunity to remind Gorbachev that while we were still hopeful of improved relations, we expected good deeds from Moscow before there could be a genuine thaw in our relationship—deeds ranging from permitting Soviet Jews and persecuted Christians to emigrate to ending Soviet interference in Central America. In a message Mac carried to Gorbachev for me, I said: "While I believe there is some action we can take now to facilitate trade, I doubt that there can be a fundamental change in our trade relationship without parallel improvements in other aspects of our relationship."

About this same time, George Shultz told me he was tired and wanted to resign before the summer was over. I told him that from the time he took over as secretary of state, I never envisioned anyone but him serving me in that job. Although I said I didn't have the heart to lean on him if he really wanted to go, I also said I really needed him, especially to look after our new approach to the Soviets. I think I convinced him how important he was to our hopes of improving relations with the Russians, and shortly before he left Washington for a meeting with Andrei Gromyko in Helsinki, George agreed to stay on the job. I asked him to suggest to Gromyko the possibility of a summit in mid-November in Washington and, if a subsequent meeting were held, a commitment to hold it in Moscow. If the Soviets insisted on a neutral locale for our first meeting, I suggested Geneva.

In a ten-page reply to my previous letter sent to me in early June, Gorbachev confirmed my intuition that he was going to be tough to deal with, and also my suspicion that he shared many of the misconceptions of his predecessors about America. Still, Gorbachev's letter indicated that he took the question of improving our relations and reducing the threat of a nuclear war as seriously as I did. Addressing some of the complaints I'd raised about Soviet adventurism in Central America and other parts of the world, Gorbachev wrote:

> . . . with regard to third world countries, we impose neither our ideology, nor our social system on anybody. And do not ascribe to us what does not exist. If the question is to be raised without diplomatic contrivances as to who contributes to the international law and order and who acts in a different direction, then it appears that it is precisely the U.S. that turns out to be on the side of the groupings working against legitimate governments. And what about direct pressure on the governments whose policy does not suit the U.S.? There are enough examples of both on various continents. . . .

I think a lot about the shape the affairs between our countries can take. I even more firmly believe in a point I made in my previous letter: an improvement in the relationship between the USSR and the U.S. is possible. There is objective ground for this.

Of course, our countries are different. This fact cannot be changed. There is also another fact, however: when the leaders of both countries, as the experience of the past shows, found in themselves enough wisdom and realism to overcome bias caused by the differences in social systems, in ideologies, we cooperated successfully, did quite a few useful things both for our peoples and for all peoples.

Of course, differences and different views remained, but it was our interaction that was the determining factor and it opened up peaceful vistas. . . .

As to the assertions that the USSR is allegedly engaged in a "large research program in the area of strategic defense," as the Americans put it, apples are confused with oranges. The Soviet Union does nothing that would contravene the ABM treaty, does not develop attack space weapons.

Mr. President, I would like to hope that you will have another close look at the problem of non-militarization of space and its interrelationship with solving the problem of nuclear weapons and from that angle, at the prospects for the Geneva negotiations. . . .

Gorbachev proposed that both our countries continue voluntary compliance with the SALT treaties, impose a moratorium on nuclear weapons testing, ban space weapons, negotiate a reduction of conventional forces in Central Europe, and continue the process I had suggested of assisting each other in trying to see events through each other's eyes:

One of the sources of tensions in the relations between the USSR and the U.S. is a difference in the assessment of what is going on in the world. It seems that the American side frequently ignores the in-depth causes of events and does not take fully into account the fact that today a great number of states operate—and most actively, too—in world politics, each with its own face and interests. All this immensely complicates the general picture. A correct understanding of the world helps avoid serious mistakes and miscalculations.

Without saying so, Gorbachev implied that the Soviets would like to extricate themselves from the war in Afghanistan and urged us to convince the Pakistanis not to support the Afghan rebels. If we did, it would be a "positive signal" from the U.S. side.

> Some kind of movement seems to be discernible in the area of strictly bilateral relations between our countries. You, evidently, have noticed that we support this trend. However, there should be no misunderstanding concerning the fact that we do not intend and will not conduct any negotiations relating to human rights in the Soviet Union. We, as any other sovereign state, have regarded and will regard, these questions in accordance with our existing laws and regulations. Let us proceed, Mr. President, proceed from this in order not to aggravate adversely our relations. The development of our ties can be based only on mutual interest, equality and mutual benefit, respect for the rights and legitimate interests of each other . . . we live in a time when people shaping the policy of the USSR and the U.S. must necessarily meet, have contacts with each other. To speak in broad terms, we stand for building vigorously a bridge to mutual understanding and cooperation and for developing trust.

Gorbachev then asserted that he had a positive attitude about holding a summit conference between the two of us:

> As to the place for holding it, I understand that there are motives which make you prefer the meeting to be held in the U.S. But I have no less weighty motives due to which, taking into account the present state of Soviet-American affairs, this variant is unrealistic. . . . Important international problems are involved and we should use the time to search for possible agreements which could be reached for the meeting. For our part, we are entirely for this.

About the same time Gorbachev was drafting this letter, a new hurdle appeared in the road leading to improved U.S.-Soviet relations: The unratified but voluntarily adhered-to SALT II treaty was scheduled to expire December 31 at the same time that some of our new weapons developed under the strategic modernization program were scheduled to come on line. If we put them into service, we'd have to remove older weapons to stay within the SALT limits.

Should we continue conducting our policies within these restrictions even though we knew the Soviets were cheating on them?

The point of decision on the issue was to come later in the year with the launching of our first new Trident missile-firing submarine; if we continued abiding by SALT II, we would have to scrap an older Poseidon submarine that had missiles of lesser capabilities.

I had always had great doubts about the SALT treaties. Cap Weinberger shared this view. Because he was convinced the Russians were violating the treaties, he wanted to go ahead and deploy the Trident submarines but not remove the Poseidon subs from service; on this some of my conservative supporters expressed a similar view. They believed America would look foolish continuing to adhere to the SALT limits in the face of Soviet cheating. On the other hand, the State Department, the Joint Chiefs of Staff, and some of our arms control negotiators said it was better for us to apply restraint and continue abiding by the limits because, they argued, we had little to gain militarily by not doing so, the Russians had lived up to the most important provisions of the treaties that limited offensive weapons, and it would be a red flag to them and those in the world who were hoping for a slowing of the arms race.

Although all of us agreed the Soviets were cheating on the SALT limits, we knew it might be difficult to prove it before the court of world opinion because of ambiguities in the treaties.

For the moment, I decided on a policy of guarded and cautious restraint, as these entries of my diary during June 1985 indicate:

June 4

An N.S.C. meeting about what to do about the SALT II treaty provisions we and the Soviets are pledged to observe but on which they are cheating. Come Sept., under our agreement we'd have to dismantle a Poseidon missile submarine. I was again presented five options with no consensus on any of them. Our allies want us to continue observing SALT II. I must have an answer before Monday . . .

June 6

I made my decision on the SALT II matter. We will continue to practice restraint on the building of nuclear weapons. That restraint will keep us generally within the frame work of the SALT II but only commensurate with the Soviets' observance of the SALT II restraints and for only as long as the Soviets abide by SALT II restraints.

June 10

. . . today we told Congress and the world what we intended doing about SALT II. Apparently my decision was right—at least I'm being called a statesman by both the left and right.

A few days later, I got a tough letter from Gorbachev in which he attacked our deployment of the Pershing II and cruise missiles in Europe as well as the qualifications I'd expressed in announcing the decision to continue abiding by the SALT limitations (I had reserved the right to change my mind if we became further convinced of Soviet violations).

Mr. President, your version of the past and present state of affairs cannot stand comparison with the facts . . . the United States crossed a dangerous threshold when it preferred to cast aside the practicality of the SALT treaty instead of taking up, as was envisaged, the resolution of those issues that were dealt with . . . it is no secret the U.S. wanted to do so, so it could deploy cruise missiles. The U.S. sought to sharply tilt in its favor the fine-tuned balance of interests underlying the agreement. Now you see, I believe, that it did not work out that way. We too are deploying cruise missiles, which we had proposed to ban. But even now we are prepared to come to an agreement on such a ban, should the U.S., taking a realistic position, agree to take such an important step.

The U.S. deployment in Western Europe of new missile systems designed to perform strategic missions is a clear circumvention, that is, noncompliance by the American side with regard to the SALT II treaty. In this, Mr. President, we see an attempt by the United States to gain a virtual monopoly on the use of weapons in a situation for which our country has no analogs. I know [the need] on your side . . . for some regional balance and sometimes control. But even in that case, it is incomprehensible why the U.S. refuses to resolve this issue in a manner which would establish in the zone of Europe a balance of medium-range missiles, whereby the USSR would not have more missiles and warheads on them than there are currently in the possession of England and France. Such a formula would not infringe upon anyone's interest, whereas the distortion caused by the American missiles in Europe is not a balance at all. . . . I would like you to have a clear understanding of the fact that, in practice, strategic parity between our countries will be maintained. We cannot envisage now nor can we permit a different situation. The question, however, is at what level parity will be maintained—at a decreasing or an increasing one. We are for the former, for the reduction in the level of strategic confrontation. Your government, by all indications, favors the latter, evidently hoping that at some stage the U.S. will ultimately succeed in getting ahead. This is the essence of the current situation. Should one be surprised, then, that we are conducting negotiations, yet the process of practical arms limitations remains suspended? It would probably not be too great a misfortune if this process simply remained frozen. But even this is not the case. The "Star Wars" program—I must tell you this, Mr. President—already at this stage is seriously undermining stability. We strongly advise you to halt this sharply destabilizing and dangerous program while things have not gone too far. If the situation in this area is not corrected, we shall have no choice but to take steps required by our security and that of our allies . . . the SALT II treaty is an important element of the strategic equilibrium and one should clearly understand its role as well as the fact that, according to the well known expression, one can't have one's pie and eat it too.

Your approach is determined by the fact that the strategic programs being carried out by the United States are about to collide with the limitations established by the SALT II treaty, and the choice is being made not in favor of these programs. And this cannot be disavowed or concealed, to put it bluntly, by unseemly attempts to accuse the Soviet Union of all mortal sins. [The United States has criticized] imaginary Soviet violations of the SALT agreement and their publication did not and cannot serve any useful purpose if one is guided by the task of preserving and continuing the process of arms limitations. Why mince words, the objective is quite different: to cast aspersions on the policy of the Soviet Union in general, to sow distrust towards it and to create an artificial pretext for an accelerated and uncontrolled arms race. All this became evident to us long ago.

M. Gorbachev

We were both speaking with frankness. But we were talking. Although Gorbachev refused to come to Washington for a summit, he agreed to meet me in Geneva in November.

77

DURING THE SAME VISIT to my bedside at Bethesda Naval Hospital on July 18, 1985, at which he informed me a group of Iranian moderates wanted to open a dialogue with American officials leading to possible improvement in our relations and release of our hostages in Beirut, Bud McFarlane told me Mikhail Gorbachev had sent word endorsing a proposal I'd made suggesting that before the summit the two of us continue our direct and private communications. "We tried to get such a thing with his predecessors and couldn't make it," I mentioned in the diary. "I gave the word to proceed."

Meanwhile, we were starting to see indications of other changes in the Kremlin—although we still didn't know yet what they signified.

Two weeks earlier, Gorbachev had arranged for Andrei Gromyko to be designated president of the USSR, a purely ceremonial job that ended Gromyko's twenty-eight-year career as foreign minister.

His successor was Eduard A. Shevardnadze, a Communist Party official from the Soviet republic of Georgia about whom we knew relatively little. In late July, George Shultz flew to Finland to meet Shevardnadze and make arrangements for the upcoming summit. Calling from Helsinki on a secure phone, George told me his instinctive reaction to the new Soviet foreign minister was positive: He was tough, but less hostile and more personable than Gromyko.

After the plans for the summit were announced, I told the White House staff and cabinet to do nothing that would raise expectations of great progress at the meeting in Geneva.

George Shultz said it would be a success if the only thing that came out of it was an agreement to hold another summit. As far as I was concerned, I wanted to size up Gorbachev and let him know I was serious about reducing the nuclear threat. "Let's paint with a broad brush and not give the press specifics as to our agenda," I said.

As this was going on, Gorbachev and I continued our correspondence, much of it repetitive as both of us let the other side know where we stood.

This is a portion of one letter I received from Gorbachev in September 1985 that summarized the Soviet view of the United States before the meeting in Geneva:

Dear Mr. President:

I would like to communicate some thoughts and considerations and continue the correspondence between us, specifically with the view to our forthcoming personal meeting. I assume that both of us take this meeting very seriously and are thoroughly preparing for it. The range of problems which we are to discuss has been fairly clearly delineated. They are all very important.

Of course the differences between our two countries are not minor and our approaches to many fundamental issues are different. All this is true, but at the same time, the reality is such that our nations have to coexist whether we like each other or not. If things ever come to a military confrontation, it would be catastrophic for our countries and for the world as a whole. Judging by what you have said, Mr. President, you also regard a military conflict between the USSR and USA as inadmissible.

Since, then, in other words, preventing nuclear war and removing the threat of war is our mutual and, for that matter, primary interest, it is imperative, I believe, to use it as the main lever which can help to bring cardinal changes in the nature of the relationship between our nations, to make it constructive and stable and thus contribute to the improvement of the international climate in general. It is this central component of our relations that should be put to work in the period left before the November meeting, during the Summit itself and afterwards.

We are convinced that there are considerable opportunities in this regard. My meeting with you may serve as a good catalyst for their realization. It seems that we could indeed reach a clear understanding on the inadmissibility of nuclear war, on the fact that there could be no winners in such a war, and we could resolutely speak out against seeking military superiority and against attempts to infringe upon the legitimate security interests of the other side. At the same time we are convinced that a mutual understanding of this kind should be organically complemented by a clearly expressed intention of the sides to take actions of a material nature in terms of the limitation in reduction of weapons, of terminating the arms race on earth and preventing it in space. It is such an understanding that would be an expression of the determination of the two sides to move in the direction of removing threat of war. Given an agreement on this central issue it would be easier for us to find mutual understanding and solutions of other problems. What specific measures should receive priority? Naturally, those relating to the solution of the complex of questions concerning nuclear and space arms. An agreement on nonmilitarization of space is the only road to the most radical reductions of nuclear arms. We favor following this road unswervingly and are determined to search for mutually acceptable solutions. I think that in this field both sides should act energetically and not postpone decisions. It would be good to be able to count on having obtained some positive results by the time of my meeting with you.

In connection with certain thoughts contained in your letter of July 27th of this year, I would note that on several occasions we have explicitly expressed our views on the American program of developing space attack weapons and a large scale antiballistic missile system. It is based not on emotions or subjective views, but on facts and realistic assessments.

Implementation of this program will not solve the problem of nuclear arms, it will only aggravate it, and have the most negative consequences for the whole process of the limitation and reduction of nuclear arms. On the other hand, quite a lot could be done through parallel or joint efforts of our countries to slow the arms race and bring it to a halt, above all in the main arena—the nuclear one. It is indeed for this and no other purpose that we have taken a number of unilateral, practical steps.

Mr. President, both you and I understand perfectly well the importance of conducting nuclear explosions from the standpoint of the effectiveness of existing nuclear weapons and the development of new types of nuclear weapons. Consequently, termination of nuclear tests would be a step in the opposite direction. This is what guided our decision to stop all nuclear explosions and appeal to the U.S. to join us in this. Please look at this issue without preconceived notions. It is quite clear that at the present level of nuclear arms our countries possess, a mutual termination of nuclear tests would not hurt either of them.

Therefore, if there is a true desire to halt the nuclear arms race, then there can be no objections to a mutual moratorium, and the benefit it brings would be great. But the continuation of nuclear tests —albeit in the presence of somebody's observers—would be nothing else but the same arms race. The U.S. still has time to make the right decision. Imagine how much it would mean and not only for Soviet-American relations but a moratorium on nuclear tests, of course, is still not a radical solution to the problem of preventing nuclear war.

In order to accomplish that, it is necessary to solve the whole complex of inter-related matters which are the subject of the talks between our delegations in Geneva. It is quite obvious that in the final analysis the outcome of these talks will be decisive in determining whether we shall succeed in stopping the arms race and eliminating nuclear weapons in general. Regrettably, the state of affairs at the Geneva talks gives rise to serious concern.

We should very thoroughly and from every angle, once again examine what could be done there. And I want to propose to you the following formula: the two sides agree to a complete ban on space attack weapons and a truly radical reduction, say by 50%, of their corresponding nuclear arms.

In other words, we propose a practical solution of the tasks which were agreed upon as objectives of the Geneva negotiations—not only will the nuclear arms race be terminated, but the level of nuclear confrontation would be drastically reduced, and at the same time an arms race in space would be prevented. As a result, strategic stability would be strengthened greatly and mutual trust would grow significantly. Such a step by the USSR and the U.S. would, I believe, be an incentive for other powers possessing nuclear arms to participate in nuclear disarmament, which you pointed out as important in one of your letters. We view things realistically and realize that such a radical solution would require time and effort. Nonetheless, we are convinced that this problem can be solved. The first thing that is needed is to have our political approaches coincide in their essence.

Secondly, given such coincidence, it is important to agree on practical measures which facilitate the achievement of these goals, including a halt in the development of space attack weapons and a freeze of nuclear arsenals at their present quantitative levels, with a prohibition of the development of new kinds and types of nuclear weapons.

In addition, major practical measures would include the removal from alert status of and dismantling of an agreed number of strategic weapons . . . and mutually undertaking to refrain from the employment of any nuclear weapons in countries which are now nuclear free, in undertaking not to increase nuclear weapons stock piles and not to replace nuclear weapons with new ones in countries where such weapons are deployed.

Naturally, the issue of medium range nuclear weapons in Europe also requires resolution. I would like to emphasize once again, the Soviet Union favors a radical solution whereby, as we proposed in Geneva, the USSR would retain in the European zone no more weapons of this type, using warheads as a unit of count, than Britain and France possess. . . .

In proposing practical measures concerning arms limitation in disarmament we [agree] that they should be accompanied by relevant agreed verification measures. In some cases it would be national technical means, in other cases, when it is really necessary, the latter could be used in conjunction with bilateral and international procedures.

I have not attempted to give an exhaustive list of measures to limit arms and relax military tensions. There could be other measures as well. We would listen with interest to the proposals of the U.S. side on this score. The main thing is for both sides to be ready to act in a constructive way in order to build up a useful foundation, which, if possible, might also be included in the Summit meeting.

Mr. President, for obvious reasons, I have paid particular attention to central issues facing our countries. But, of course, we do not belittle the importance of regional problems and bilateral matters. I assume that these questions will be thoroughly discussed by E.M. Shevardnadze and G. Shultz with a view to bringing our positions closer and, better still, finding practical solutions wherever possible.

We hope that in the course of the meetings which our Minister of Foreign Affairs will have with you and the Secretary of State, as well as through active work at the Geneva talks, in Stockholm and Vienna, and by means of exchanges through diplomatic channels, it will be possible in the time left before my meeting with you to create a situation making for a truly productive meeting.

We believe that the outcome of this preparatory work as well as the results of my discussions with you at the meeting itself could be reflected in an appropriate joint document. If you agree, it would be worthwhile, I think, to ask our Ministers to determine how work on such a final document would be best organized.

Sincerely yours,
M. Gorbachev
September 12, 1985

After an NSPG meeting a few days before Shevardnadze brought this letter to Washington, I made this note in my diary: "Made a decision we would *not* trade away our program of research—SDI —for a promise of Soviet reduction in nuclear arms."

Cap Weinberger strongly believed we should resist all Soviet efforts to limit research on the Strategic Defense Initiative. Our scientists and engineers, he said, were making great progress and becoming more optimistic each day that it would be possible to solve the enormously difficult problems of pinpointing missiles rising from their silos and shooting them down from space.

Cap said what made him especially angry was that the Russians were whining about our research on the SDI while they had been conducting similar research of their own for more than twenty years. Even though I agreed entirely with Cap on this one, I sometimes had to ask him to mute his most critical public comments about the Soviets and turned him down when he wanted me to speak more harshly toward the Russians than I thought was prudent at a time we were trying to improve relations with them.

In fact, once we'd agreed to hold a summit, I made a conscious decision to tone down my rhetoric to avoid goading Gorbachev with remarks about the "evil empire."

During this period, Cap and George Shultz were often at odds (this was when Bud McFarlane, who also had considerable friction with Cap, started bringing them together at weekly breakfasts to iron out differences) over how to deal with the Russians, as this entry in my diary on September 11, 1985, reflected: ". . . met with George Shultz about summit. I sense he and Bud feel 'Defense' is going to be uncooperative and not want to settle anything with the Soviets. I can't agree on that. One thing I do know is, I won't trade our SDI off for some Soviet offer of weapon reductions. . . . Got fitted for a new bulletproof raincoat and went home."

After Eduard Shevardnadze came to Washington with the letter from Gorbachev, to make preparations for the summit, I subsequently saw him briefly at the United Nations in New York and noted afterward in my diary: "He's a personable fellow, but we had our differences. My goal was to send him back to Gorbachev with a message that I really meant 'arms reductions'; for the first time, they talked *real* verification procedures. Now I have to decide how to respond to Gorbachev's letter to me."

After an NSPG meeting at which various options were discussed on how to respond to Gorbachev's proposal for a fifty-percent reduction in nuclear weapons—the same proposal I'd made in 1983—I wrote:

"My idea is that we undermine their propaganda plan by offering a counter proposal which stresses our acceptance of some of their figures, such as a 50 percent cut in weapons and a total of 6000 warheads, etc. Those are pretty much like what we've already proposed."

Here are excerpts from my reply to Gorbachev's letter, which summarized much of our position on the eve of the meeting in Geneva:

Dear Mr. General Secretary:

As I told Foreign Minister Shevardnadze in New York October 24, I have given careful consideration to your letter dated September 12. The issues you raised are important ones, the ideas you have put forward are in many ways interesting, and I have wanted to study them thoroughly before replying.

Many of the specific points you addressed in your letter have been or will be dealt with by our delegations in the Geneva arms control negotiations or by our foreign ministers. In this letter, I will therefore focus on what I consider the most significant issues you have raised.

You suggested in your letter that we might reach an understanding on the inadmissibility of nuclear war and other general principles which should guide us. Foreign Minister Shevardnadze has since proposed specific language for our consideration. As I have repeatedly made clear, it is indeed my view that a nuclear war cannot be won and must never be fought. I therefore have instructed Secretary Shultz to discuss this matter with Foreign Minister Shevardnadze in their meetings next week.

As we address this and other elements which figure in any document we may issue in Geneva, I believe it is important to give the most careful consideration to our words. Experience of the past has been that overly vague or rhetorical language has led to expectations which, given the competitive aspect of our relationship to which you referred in your letter, cannot be sustained.

If we are to avoid subsequent misunderstanding and disillusionment, our own achievements should be clear and based on concrete achievements. I am convinced there is substantial common ground on the range of areas that we have been discussing in connection with our forthcoming meeting and I would hope that this common ground can be expanded during our meeting in Geneva. Secretary Shultz will be prepared to discuss all your ideas in concrete terms while he is in Moscow. I believe you will find that we are indeed prepared to go our fair share of the way to insure that our meeting is a productive one.

I do, however, want to address your response to the proposals we have previously made in the Geneva arms control talks, which were foreshadowed in your letter and which your delegation subsequently tabled in Geneva. We have been assessing your counterproposal over the past month. As I stated in my address to the United Nations on Oct. 24, I believe that within it there are seeds which we should nurture and that in the coming weeks we should seek to establish a genuine process of give and take.

In order to foster such a process, I have approved a new and comprehensive proposal designed to build upon the positive elements of your counterproposal and bridge the positions of our two sides. I have asked our negotiators to extend the current round to permit your experts to achieve a full understanding of our approach. This new proposal deals with all three areas under discussion in the Geneva negotiations. Its essence is a proposal for radical and stabilizing reductions in strategic offensive arms and a separate agreement on intermediate range missile systems, both of which bridge U.S. and Soviet ideas. We also propose that both sides provide assurances that their strategic defense programs are and will remain in full accord with the ABM treaty. Such assurances assume a resolution of our current differences over compliance with the treaty.

In the area of strategic arms, the United States agrees with the objective of a fifty per cent reduction of strategic offensive forces. Our proposal builds on this, applying the fifty per cent principle in a manner that is both equitable and can enhance stability. In the area of intermediate range nuclear forces, we have also looked for elements that we find in common. While I continue to firmly believe that the best outcome would be the complete elimination of intermediate range missiles on both sides, in our new proposal we have also moved in your direction. In defense and space, we must begin now to establish a framework for a cooperative transition to more reliance on defenses and we would like to see a more developed dialogue on how such a transition could be jointly undertaken. We have designed our approach to provide for a mutually acceptable resolution of the range of nuclear and space arms issues; to take account of the interrelationship between the offense and the defense; and to address those concerns that you and your negotiators have described as of great importance to you. I am convinced that this new proposal can provide the basis for immediate and genuine progress on the numerous and complex issues facing us in the nuclear and space area and I look forward to discussing it with you in Geneva later this month.

We will also have the opportunity in Geneva to discuss the other areas which make up our relationship. Much work remains to be done if we are to be able to announce specific progress on regional and bilateral issues. I hope that Secretary Shultz's Moscow visit will be a stimulus to rapid progress in the weeks ahead.

In conclusion, may I say once more that I am looking forward to our meeting and I sincerely hope we will be able to set our countries on a less confrontational and more cooperative course in the years ahead. I will personally spare no effort to bring this about.

Sincerely,
Ronald Reagan
Oct. 31, 1985

In early November, George Shultz met in Moscow with Gorbachev for four hours to go over the issues we were to consider at Geneva. Gorbachev, he said, wasn't going to be a pushover. "Apparently not much progress," I wrote after I spoke to George on the secure phone from Moscow. "Gorbachev is adamant we must cave in on SDI. Well, this will be a case of an irresistible force meeting an immovable object."

Privately, I had made a decision: I was going to offer to share SDI technology with the Soviets. This, I thought, should convince them it would never be a threat to them.

After returning to Washington from his meeting with Gorbachev, George said he was convinced Gorbachev was an intelligent man who was sure of himself, had a good sense of humor, and seemed to be fully in charge in the Soviet Union. But he said Gorbachev seemed to be filled with anti-American, anticapitalist propaganda —he believed, for example, along with other falsehoods about us, that Americans hated the Soviets because our arms manufacturers controlled our economy and stirred the people up with anti-Soviet propaganda, all for the purpose of keeping the arms race alive.

Well, I thought, in Geneva I'll have to get him in a room alone and set him straight.

78

On the eve of our flight to Geneva, I made an address to the nation in which I said we were at a special moment in history, with a unique opportunity to set the course of peace through the twenty-first century, and I really felt that way. It was my hope and purpose that at Geneva Mikhail Gorbachev and I would begin a process that our successors and the peoples of our countries would continue after we were gone. The American goal at Geneva, I said, was not only to avoid war, but to strengthen peace; not only to prevent confrontation, but to begin the process of removing the sources of tension that produced confrontation; not to paper over our differences, but to acknowledge and address them realistically; to encourage talk not only between our leaders and diplomats, but between the people of our countries: "Since the dawn of the nuclear age, every American president has sought to limit and end the dangerous competition in nuclear arms. I have no higher priority than to finally realize that dream."

In going to Geneva, I was also planning to live by an old Russian adage:

Dovorey no provorey.

Trust, but verify.

We left Andrews Air Force Base aboard Air Force One shortly after eight o'clock in the morning on November 16, 1985. Just before takeoff, we got word that the Soviets had allowed several of their citizens who were married to Americans to join their spouses in the United States. One wife hadn't seen her American husband in eleven years. During some of my attempts at quiet diplomacy, I'd suggested we'd look favorably on such a decision to reunify these divided families and I took the Soviet decision as a positive signal before the summit.

In Geneva, we drove to our temporary home, la Maison de Saussure, a beautiful villa on Lake Geneva loaned to us by Prince Karim, Aga Khan, and his wife for the duration of the summit. The view from our window looking out across the villa's sweeping formal gardens and lake was spectacular.

The next day, we toured Villa Fleur d'Eau, a twenty-room château where our first meetings were to take place, then Nancy and I walked down to the lakeshore boat house where I had decided to invite Gorbachev for a chat. She agreed it was a perfect spot for the private meeting I wanted with him.

Usually at summit conferences, the real work is done in advance by diplomats and specialists on each side who, based on guidance from their superiors, do the spadework and work out any agreements that are to be signed at the meeting, after which the top leaders come in and preside over the formalities.

Starting with Brezhnev, I'd dreamed of personally going one-on-one with a Soviet leader because I thought we might be able to accomplish things our countries' diplomats couldn't do because they didn't have the authority. Putting that another way, I felt that if you got the top people negotiating and talking at a summit and then the two of you came out arm in arm saying, "We've agreed to this," the bureaucrats wouldn't be able to louse up the agreement. Until Gorbachev, I never got an opportunity to try out my idea. Now I had my chance.

Neither Nancy nor I slept very well as we waited for the meetings to begin, but I never felt tired. The juices were flowing. I wanted to get started. In a very real sense, preparations for the summit had begun five years earlier, when we began strengthening our economy, restoring our national will, and rebuilding our defenses. I felt ready.

On the morning of November 19, I was waiting for Gorbachev at Villa Fleur d'Eau. When I was told his car had arrived, I hurried out to the porch and walked down several steps to greet him. He was dressed in a heavy topcoat and wearing a hat; I was hatless and in a suit. Why the press made a point of the fact that he was bundled up and I wasn't, I don't know—I suppose this was only one measure of the enormous attention being paid to the summit— but for whatever reason, the reporters who were keeping score gave me credit for winning the first round at the summit because I looked more casual than he did. (I hadn't planned it that way; the next time we were outdoors, I was wearing a topcoat—I didn't want to rub it in.)

As we shook hands for the first time, I had to admit—as Margaret Thatcher and Prime Minister Brian Mulroney of Canada predicted I would—that there was something likable about Gorbachev. There was warmth in his face and his style, not the coldness bordering on hatred I'd seen in most senior Soviet officials I'd met until then.

Our first session was scheduled to be a fifteen-minute one-on-one, get-acquainted meeting. It lasted almost an hour and we managed to break the ice, then joined the plenary meeting where each of us was backed up by a team of specialists and experts. I gave the floor to Gorbachev first and he went into a long pitch arguing that Americans had no reasons to mistrust the Soviets and that we should apply no preconditions to our discussions. As George Shultz had predicted, Gorbachev said he believed American munitions makers were the principal obstacle to peace on the American side: They were our ruling class, he suggested, and they kept our people fired up against the Soviets simply because they wanted to sell more weapons. Then he took off on U.S. think tanks that he said tried to do the same thing, and he complained that the United States had declared zones of special interest around the world while attacking the USSR for doing the same thing.

Finally it was my turn and I took Gorbachev through the long history of Soviet aggression, citing chapter and verse of the Soviet Union's policy of expansionism from 1917 onward. I wanted to explain why the Free World had good reason to put up its guard against the Soviet bloc.

As we broke for lunch, I assured Gorbachev he could have the floor next to rebut me, and he used it, arguing again that we had no reason to be suspicious of the Soviets—they were peace-loving and good citizens. When it was my turn to make a rebuttal, I cited more reasons for our skepticism about the Soviets such as the Soviet betrayal of Stalin's promise at Yalta to hold free elections in the nations of Eastern Europe after World War II.

After I finished my rebuttal, our arms control experts were given the floor, and it was during this pause that I suggested to Gorbachev that the two of us walk down to the boat house for a breath of fresh air and a talk. He leaped out of his chair almost before I finished.

The fire was roaring when we got to the cottage and sat down across from each other in stuffed chairs beside the hearth. I had considered suggesting to him that we go on a first-name basis, as our group did at economic summits, but our experts had told me he wasn't likely to appreciate such a gesture of informality at our first meeting, and so I addressed him as "Mr. General Secretary."

It was during the first moments of this fireside chat that I said I thought the two of us were in a unique situation. Here we were, I said, two men who had been born in obscure rural hamlets in the middle of our respective countries, each of us poor and from humble beginnings. Now we were the leaders of our countries and probably the only two men in the world who could bring about World War III.

At the same time, I said, we were possibly the only two men in the world who might be able to bring peace to the world.

I said I thought we owed it to the world to use the opportunity that had been presented us to work at building the kind of human trust and confidence in each other that could lead to genuine peace.

I watched as Gorbachev listened to the translation of my words, and he seemed to nod in agreement.

As our conversation continued beside the blazing fire, he convinced me I had been right to suspect there was a deep-seated fear of the United States and its nuclear arsenal among Soviet leaders. I tried to dispel this vision. After World War II, I pointed out, we had a monopoly on nuclear weapons, but had not used them for aggression or to exert our influence because America was not an expansionist country. We had no designs on any people or any nation; we had built our force of nuclear missiles only to deter a Soviet attack. Then we began debating the Strategic Defense Initiative; he was adamant and so was I.

I told him it was a research project to develop a nonnuclear defense that was permitted under our ABM treaty, and that if it led to an operational defensive system against missiles, it would change the world.

I said it would be years before we knew whether it was practical or not, but *if* it was, the United States would sit down with other countries to discuss how it would be used, open its laboratories to the Soviets, and offer the fruits of its research to all countries, so the entire world could enjoy security against a nuclear holocaust.

The choice we faced, I said as I wound up, was either an agreement to reduce arms or a continuation of the arms race, "and I have to tell you if it's an arms race, you must know it's an arms race you can't win, because we're not going to allow you to maintain this superiority over us."

After more than an hour, Gorbachev and I decided it was probably time for us to rejoin the others, so we began walking up the path to the main building.

Midway in our walk, in the center of a parking lot, I stopped him and, because of a hunch that the time was right to do so, I invited Gorbachev to Washington for another summit.

He not only accepted but invited me to come to Moscow for a third summit. Neither of us mentioned this to the others when we sat down, but after the session ended, when I told the members of our team that Gorbachev and I had already agreed to hold two more summits, they almost went through the ceiling in surprise.

On our second day at Geneva, Gorbachev hosted the formal meeting at the Soviet mission, and he took me into a small room for a reprise of the private meeting we'd had the day before—just the two of us and our interpreters.

Years before, when I'd sat across the bargaining table from the executives who ran the Hollywood studios, I'd learned a few lessons about negotiating: You're unlikely to ever get *all* you want; you'll probably get more of what you want if you don't issue ultimatums and leave your adversary room to maneuver; you shouldn't back your adversary into a corner, embarrass him, or humiliate him; and sometimes the easiest way to get some things done is for the top people to do them alone and in private.

I decided at my next private meeting with Gorbachev to give him a list of the names of people who we knew wanted to leave the Soviet Union in search of freedom but who had been denied permission to do so. One was a pianist, Vladimir Feltsman, whom my son Ron had met in Russia. Ron had been very impressed by his talent and his unfortunate situation. Feltsman, who is Jewish, had stated in public that he wanted to emigrate to Israel. As soon as he did so, a Moscow radio announcer he knew told him he was ordered not to play his records on the air anymore; his records were taken from the stores; and he was no longer permitted to play with major orchestras in Moscow but was sent, if he was given any work at all, to the provinces to play. I mentioned the cases of Feltsman and others I'd heard about to Gorbachev and said I thought I would have a better chance of getting support for some of the things we might agree on in the future, such as increased trade, if his country eased some of its restrictions on ethnic and minority groups.

Gorbachev is an intelligent man and a good listener. He didn't comment on my remarks, but launched into criticism of the United States, saying, in effect, that I had no place talking about human rights in the Soviet Union because Americans lived under far worse conditions than Soviet citizens. He quoted statements by some of our more extreme feminists who claimed American women were downtrodden and argued that we treated blacks like slaves.

The "most basic human right," he said, "is everyone's right to a job." In the Soviet Union, everyone had a job—and that couldn't be said for the United States. (He didn't say that the Soviet people couldn't choose their jobs, that they had to do whatever the government told them to do—if they were handed a broom, they started sweeping.)

It seemed clear Gorbachev believed propaganda about us that he had probably heard all his life. In some things he said there was a grain of truth, but a lot of the "facts" he came armed with and cited so authoritatively about America—such as those about the treatment of blacks in the South—were long out of date, and he didn't know, for example, about the vast improvements we'd made in race relations. "Things have changed," I said, and told him what I had done in California as governor, appointing to policy-making and executive positions more blacks than all the previous governors put together. I spoke about the dynamic energy of capitalism and said it provided an opportunity to all Americans to work, apply themselves, and get ahead; whenever I alluded to the economic problems that by contrast were hounding his country, Gorbachev emphasized that he believed in the Communist system, but he seemed to say mistakes had been made in running it and he was trying to correct them. He was an eloquent debater as well as a good listener, and despite our disagreements, our conversations never turned hostile—he stood his ground and I stood mine.

Later that day, at a plenary session with both our delegations, we went head-to-head again on the Strategic Defense Initiative. Gorbachev, without saying it in so many words, suggested that when I'd made my offer to share our SDI research and open our laboratories to the Soviets so they could see that the SDI was not designed for offensive purposes, I was lying.

No country would do that, he insisted, judging others by his own country. He seemed convinced that I wanted to get a leg up on the Soviets in the arms race and to use the SDI as a cover for an offensive first-strike capability against the Soviet Union. Once again, he was as adamant as I was, and neither of us retreated from our positions.

When I brought up the Soviet invasion of Afghanistan, Gorbachev responded that he had known nothing about it personally until he heard a radio broadcast, suggesting that it was a war he had no responsibility—and little enthusiasm—for.

I let him know that, whatever its roots, the people of America regarded Soviet aggression in Afghanistan as an example of a giant country trying to impose its will on a tiny one.

That evening it was our turn to host dinner and I saw, as I had the night before when the Soviets had entertained us, that Gorbachev could be warm and outgoing in a social setting even though several hours earlier we'd had sharp differences of opinion; maybe there was a little of Tip O'Neill in him. He could tell jokes about himself and even about his country, and I grew to like him more.

During our final business session earlier in the day, Gorbachev and I had discussed language for a joint statement that was to be issued at the close of the summit and that would make note of our mutual commitment to seek a fifty-percent cut in nuclear weapons and include references to several new cultural and diplomatic exchanges. Then, as I wrote in my diary, "we cut short the meeting and our teams went to work on the statement. He and I and the interpreters went into a small room and wound up telling stories." He asked a few questions about Hollywood, and we discovered we had had a few similar experiences dealing with our respective bureaucracies. We chatted for almost an hour, just the two of us, and then the two teams came in to show us a number of things they'd agreed on and several they were still working on. Then we broke up, so he and I could get ready for a reception hosted by the Swiss president.

After the reception Nancy and I hosted a dinner for the Gorbachevs at the villa we were using as our temporary home in Geneva. After dinner, we adjourned to the living room for coffee and conversation. Shortly after we were seated, senior officials from both sides, who had been in a different building working on the statement, came in and said they were at loggerheads over the language for the final document. The Soviets wanted to change something that had already been agreed upon. George Shultz was quite angry at this last-minute change. He pointed at the Soviet official responsible for the problem and said directly to General Secretary Gorbachev: "Mr. General Secretary, this man is not keeping the agreement you and President Reagan reached earlier today, and if we don't reach an agreement it will be his fault." Without batting an eye, Gorbachev turned to his man and said, "Do it the way we discussed," providing more evidence that he was a man who was sure of himself and his power.

When Nancy and I returned to our bedroom after dinner, I took one look at a glass aquarium in the room and said, "Oh, lordy."

The children who normally lived in the house had asked me to feed their goldfish. I'd done it, but one of the fish was dead. Maybe I hadn't fed the fish enough food, or maybe I had fed it too much. Whatever the reason, it had died on my watch and I felt responsible for it. I asked our staff to put the dead fish into a box and take it to a pet store in Geneva to see whether they could find one exactly like it. Luckily, they found two that matched, and I put them in the tank and wrote a letter to the children to let them know what had happened.

The next day, Gorbachev and I released our statement, and Nancy and I returned to Washington via Brussels, where I briefed NATO ministers on the summit.

As we flew home I felt good: Gorbachev was tough and convinced Communism was superior to capitalism, but after almost five years I'd finally met a Soviet leader I could talk to.

It didn't occur to me then, but later on I was to remember something else about Gorbachev at Geneva: Not once during our private sessions or at the plenary meetings did he express support for the old Marxist-Leninist goal of a one-world Communist state or the Brezhnev Doctrine of Soviet expansionism. He was the first Soviet leader I knew of who hadn't done that.

As soon as we got home, after going without sleep for almost twenty-four hours, I addressed a joint session of Congress. I reported that we had made a good start at improving relations with the Soviets and that my experience at Geneva gave me hope for the future. "I can't claim that we had a meeting of the minds on such fundamentals as ideology or national purpose," I said, "but we understand each other better and that's a key to peace . . . we have a long way to go, but we're heading in the right direction. . . . "

I think the enthusiastic cheering and stomping in the chamber of the House of Representatives that night as I delivered my report from Geneva spoke for all peoples of the world who shared a hope for lasting peace in the nuclear age.

Afterward, I wrote in my diary: "I haven't gotten such a reception since I was shot."

We had made a start but, as we were to learn, some of the euphoria was premature.

79

THREE DAYS AFTER we returned from Geneva, George Shultz said again that he wanted to resign; he was just burned out from the intensity of the job, and I suppose he may have been growing tired of his differences with Cap Weinberger. As I had previously, I said I wanted him to remain as long as I was in the White House but I wouldn't try to talk him out of leaving. Once again, George proved himself a patriot: Rather than leave just as we were getting ready to press forward to continue the momentum begun at Geneva, he said he would remain on the job, and during the next three years he proved again and again that he was one of the finest and most distinguished secretaries of state in the history of our country.

A week after we returned from Geneva, I sent a handwritten letter to Gorbachev in which I tried to continue the process begun at the fireside summit and to overcome his resistance to the Strategic Defense Initiative:

Dear General Secretary Gorbachev:

Now that we are both home and facing the task of leading our countries into a more constructive relationship with each other, I wanted to waste no time in giving you some of my initial thoughts on our meetings. Though I will be sending shortly, in a more formal and official manner, a more detailed commentary on our discussions, there are some things I would like to convey very personally and very privately.

First, I want you to know that I found our meetings of great value. We had agreed to speak frankly, and we did. As a result, I came away from the meeting with a better understanding of your attitudes. I hope you also understand mine a little better. Obviously there are many things on which we disagree and we disagree very fundamentally. But, if I understand you correctly, you, too, are determined to take steps to see that our nations manage their relationship in a peaceful fashion. If this is the case, then this is one point on which we are in total agreement—and it is after all the most fundamental one of all.

As for our substantial differences, let me offer a thought or two of my own.

Regarding strategic defense and its relation to the reduction of offensive nuclear weapons, I was struck by your conviction that the American program is somehow designed to secure a strategic advantage or even to permit a first strike capability. I also noted your concern that research and testing in the area could be a cover for developing and placing offensive weapons in space.

As I told you, neither of these concerns is warranted. But I can understand, as you explained so eloquently, that there are matters that cannot be taken on faith. Both of us must cope with what the other side is doing and judge these implications for the security of our own country. I do not ask you to take my assurances on faith.

However, the truth is that the United States has no intention of using its strategic defense program to gain any advantage and there is no development under way to create space-based weapons.

Our goal is to eliminate any possibility of a first strike from either side. This being the case, we should be able to find a way, in practical terms, to relieve the concerns you have expressed.

For example, could our negotiators, when they resume work in January, discuss frankly and specifically what sort of future development each of us would find threatening? Neither of us, it seems, wants to see offensive weapons, particularly weapons of mass destruction, deployed in space. Should we not attempt to define what sort of systems have that potential and then try to find verifiable ways to prevent their development?

And can't our negotiators deal more frankly and openly with the question of how to eliminate a first strike potential on both sides? Your military now has an advantage in this area—a three to one advantage in warheads that can destroy hardened targets with little warning. That is obviously alarming to us and explains many of the efforts we are making in our modernization program. You may feel perhaps that the U.S. has some advantage in other categories. If so, let's insist that our negotiators face up to these issues and find a way to improve the security of both countries by agreeing on appropriately balanced reductions. If you are as sincere as I am in not seeking to secure or preserve one-sided advantages, we will find a solution to these problems.

Regarding another key issue we discussed, that of regional conflicts, I can assure you that the United States does not believe that the Soviet Union is the cause of all the world's ills. We do believe, however, that your country has exploited and worsened local tensions and conflicts by militarizing them and, indeed, intervening directly and indirectly in struggles arising out of local causes. While we both will doubtless continue to support our friends, we must find a way to do so without use of armed force. This is the crux of the point I tried to make.

One of the most significant steps in lowering tensions in the world —and tensions in U.S.-Soviet relations—would be a decision on your part to withdraw your forces from Afghanistan. I gave careful attention to your comments on this issue at Geneva and am encouraged by your statement that you feel political reconciliation is possible.

I want you to know that I am prepared to cooperate in any reasonable way to facilitate such a withdrawal and that I understand that it must be done in a manner which does not damage Soviet security. During our meetings, I mentioned one idea which I thought might be helpful and I will welcome any further suggestions you may have.

These are only two of the key issues on our current agenda. I will soon send some thoughts on others. I believe that we should act promptly to build the momentum our meeting initiated.

In Geneva I found our private sessions particularly useful. Both of us have advisers and assistants, but, you know, in the final analysis, the responsibility to preserve peace and increase cooperation is ours. Our people look to us for leadership and nobody can provide it if we don't. But we won't be very effective leaders unless we can rise above the specific but secondary concerns that preoccupy our respective bureaucracies and give our governments a strong push in the right direction.

So what I want to say finally is that we should make the most of the time before we meet again to find some specific and significant steps that would give meaning to our commitment to peace and arms reductions. Why not set a goal—privately, just between the two of us —to find a practical way to solve critical issues—the two I have mentioned—by the time we meet in Washington?

Please convey regards from Nancy and me to Mrs. Gorbachev. We genuinely enjoyed meeting you in Geneva and are already looking forward to showing you something of our country next year.

Sincerely yours,
Ronald Reagan
November 28, 1985

A week or so later, I sent a second letter to Moscow that was delivered to Gorbachev by Commerce Secretary Mac Baldrige, who was on another trade mission. This time, I raised other issues I felt had to be dealt with before we could achieve normal relations. They included, I said,

the broad question of emigration, whether of members of such groups as Jews, Armenians and others, or of some internationally known individuals. In both categories, we are talking about quite poignant cases. The young pianist I mentioned to you falls into the category of someone whose requests to emigrate have been refused. The political importance of resolving such well known cases as the Sakharovs, Scharansky and Yuri Orlov cannot be overestimated. We are not interested in exploiting these cases. Their resolution will permit greater prominence for other issues in our relationship . . . the issues I have laid out in this letter are serious ones. Progress here would provide an enormous impetus to the resolution of other outstanding problems. Lack of progress will only hold us back.

I also raised the issue of Afghanistan and the Soviet support of Qaddafi.

It is hard to reconcile Soviet interest in restraint in this region with the provision of advanced weapons to a leader whose reckless behavior is a major danger to regional stability. Because we view this development with utmost seriousness, I was disappointed to see that the Soviet response to our presentation failed to address the transfer of [recently shipped advance] weapons to Libya. Our ministers and experts should address this vital matter, since it raises the prospect of dangerous incidents that I hope you want to avoid as much as we do. If you agree, both Angola and Libya are additional subjects which Secretary Shultz and Foreign Minister Shevardnadze might take up in their next meeting.

645

In a Christmas Eve reply to my letter dated November 28, Gorbachev said that he appreciated its personal and handwritten nature and that he was pleased that at Geneva we had managed to

> overcome a serious psychological barrier which for a long time has hindered a dialogue worthy of the leaders of the USSR and the USA.
>
> I also have the feeling now that we can set aside our differences and get down to the heart of the matter—we can set a specific agenda for discussing in the upcoming years how to straighten out Soviet-American relations. . . . I agree with you, Mr. President: In the final analysis, no one besides us can do this.

Then, he launched into an explanation of his country's opposition to "space-strike weapons"—the Strategic Defense Initiative—that I thought was seriously flawed.

He said the Soviet opposition was based on a conviction that such weapons could be used both for defensive and offensive purposes.

"You have said, Mr. President, that the U.S. has no intention of using the SDI program for achieving military superiority," Gorbachev wrote.

> I am sure that you personally could not have any such intention. But, we agree that it is the duty of the leaders of both sides to evaluate the actions of the other in the area of the creation of new types of weapons not in terms of intentions, but rather in terms of the potential capability which might be achieved due to the creation of a new weapon. Viewing the SDI program from such a position the Soviet leadership inevitably arrives at one conclusion: in the current actual conditions, the "space shield" is needed only by the side which is preparing for a first (preemptive) strike. For the side which does not proceed from this notion, the need for such a weapon does not arise. Indeed, space-strike weapons are all global weapons. The space-strike weapons being developed in the U.S. are kinetic energy and long range directed energy systems with a range of several thousand miles and are capable of great destructive power. As both our experts and scientists confirm, these weapons are capable of destroying in space as well as from space within a very short time in great quantities and selectively objects which are thousands of miles away and I stress, thousands of miles away, and [with] a capability to destroy the other

side's monitoring, navigation, communication and other space systems by striking from guided space weapons.

Gorbachev's letter continued:

In essence, the use of this weapon can only be considered as a means to "blind" and take the other side by surprise and to interfere with its capability to respond to a nuclear attack. Moreover, once this weapon is created the process of improving it will begin, giving it ever increasing combat characteristics. Such is the law of the development of any weapons. How, Mr. President, should the Soviet Union respond in this situation? I would like to repeat what I said in Geneva. The USSR simply cannot and will not accept the situation of the U.S. realization of the SDI program and then to reduce nuclear weapons. To provide for its security, come what may, we will be forced to develop and perfect strategic nuclear forces to increase their ability to neutralize the American "space shield." At the same time, we would be forced to develop our own space weapons, including those for national ballistic missile defense. Apparently the U.S., for its part, would adopt other kinds of measures. As a result, we would not be able to break out of this vicious circle, and in the final analysis, from the whirlpool of the ever spiraling arms race. The end results of such action inimical to our people and all of mankind would be unspeakable.

I am convinced that the only rational way is not to do this. From all points of view, the right path for our countries is to prevent an arms race in space and halt it on earth. Moreover, it is necessary to negotiate under equal and mutually acceptable conditions.

In addition to objecting to the SDI program, Gorbachev disputed my view that the Soviets' huge stockpile of long-range land-based missiles gave them superiority in the nuclear race; American Trident submarine-launched missiles, he said, allowed us to launch a surprise attack on the Soviets with much less warning time than their land-based missiles, and therefore they provided a threat to the Soviet Union exceeding that posed by Soviet missiles against the United States. And, he asked:

How can the Soviet Union view the Pershing II missiles deployed in Europe with their high accuracy and short flight time to USSR targets as anything else but first strike weapons? Please forgive me for being concerned with technical details in a personal letter of this kind, but, really, this is a vitally important situation and it simply cannot be avoided. Believe me, Mr. President, we have a real and extremely serious concern over U.S. nuclear weapons. You speak of mutual concerns. The solution of this problem is only possible through consideration and calculations of the sum total of the corresponding weapons on both sides.

Then Gorbachev gave his reaction to what I'd said about "regional conflicts," a euphemism to describe Soviet adventurism in Third World countries.

Let's, he said,

see the world as it is. Both of us offer such assistance. Why apply a double standard here that Soviet aid is a source of tension and American assistance is good will? Better to be guided by objective criteria. The Soviet Union will help lawful governments which ask us for aid because they have been and are being subjected to external armed interference. But the U.S., and such are the facts, inspires action against governments and arms anti-social, and in essence, terrorist groups. Looking at the matter objectively, it is specifically such external interference which creates regional tension and conflict situations. Were there no such activities, I am sure tensions would be reduced and the prospects for political settlements will become much better and more realistic.

Unfortunately, developments are proceeding in another direction. Take for example, the unprecedented pressure and terror to which the government of Nicaragua, which has been lawfully elected, has been subjected. I will be frank—the things the U.S. has done lately make us wary. It seems that just now a shift [in U.S. policies] is exacerbating regional problems. Such an approach does not facilitate finding a common language and complicates the search for political solutions.

With regard to Afghanistan, one gets the impression that the United States side intentionally fails to notice the open door leading to a political settlement. Now there is even a working formula for such a settlement. It's important not to hinder the negotiations in progress but to help them along. In that event a fair settlement will definitely be found.

Mr. President, I would like for you to view my letter as another one of our "fireside chats." I would sincerely like not only to keep the warmth of our Geneva meetings but also move further in the development of our dialogue. I look at correspondence with you as the most important channel in preparing for our meeting in Washington. There are only a few days before the New Year and I would like to convey to you and your spouse our warmest wishes.

M. Gorbachev
December 24, 1985

A few days into the new year, George Shultz began discussing with Ambassador Dobrynin the details for the next summit and we issued an invitation for Gorbachev to come to Washington in late June.

We got no reply to the invitation, although Gorbachev responded to my letter regarding human rights in the Soviet Union by saying these issues were of concern to no one except the Soviet Union:

Dear Mr. President:

Your letter of December 7, transmitted through Secretary Baldrige, addressed questions on which we had a rather thorough discussion in Geneva. At that time, I outlined in detail our approach to these questions, and, it seemed to me, you took in what was said with certain understanding.

It is hardly necessary to repeat, that the questions involved pertain to the internal competence of our state and that they are resolved in strict conformity with the laws. I would like only to point out, the Soviet laws do not create impediments when decisions are taken on the questions of departure from the USSR by Soviet citizens who have legal grounds for that . . . the existing laws are obligatory to everybody—both to those who apply to leave and those who consider exit applications. Such is the essence of our law and order and nobody is entitled to violate it—whether under any pressure or without it. I should think that should be understood in the U.S. We, of course, take into account, that due to various circumstances, divided families appear, which live partially in the USSR and partially in the USA. Only in the past five years there have been over 400 marriages between Soviet and American citizens. The overwhelming majority of those marriages—to be precise, more than 95 per cent—encountered no problems in regard to the reunification of the spouses and to living together. Yes, there are exceptions, and we have frankly and repeatedly told you what they are about. But generally, and I want to stress it once again, questions of this kind are resolved by us on the basis of humanism and taking into account the interests of the people concerned.

I share your desire to channel a relationship between our countries to a more constructive course. And the brakes are being put on this process in no way due to the existence of the cases of such sort—though I do not tend to belittle their importance from the point of view of the lives of individual persons—but because of the attempts to blow them out of proportion in the general balance of Soviet-American relations. The key issues in this area are awaiting their resolution.

I would like to note in passing: as it can be seen, the continuing attempts by the American side to tie up trade and economic relations with questions of a different nature will bring no benefit. It is high time to take a realistic look at this whole issue from the position of today, rather than yesterday.

It would seem that much will now depend on how accurately we are going to follow jointly the real priorities in our relations, if we wish to bring about their tangible normalization already in the near future. I think, the chances are not bad here.

Sincerely,
M. Gorbachev
January 11, 1986

Four days later Gorbachev sent me still another letter. Several hours before I received it, he made it public in Moscow. (Three weeks earlier, he'd written me that he valued the *private* nature of our confidential correspondence.)

This latest letter was clearly meant for propaganda.

He said the Soviet Union wanted to eliminate all INF weapons from Europe, in effect accepting my 1982 zero-zero proposal for intermediate-range missiles in Europe while trying to make it appear that it was a Soviet idea; he proposed a moratorium on nuclear weapons testing; and he called for the elimination of *all* nuclear weapons by both sides by the end of 1999—but *only if* the United States renounced "the development, testing and deployment of space-strike weapons," a reference to SDI.

It was propaganda, yes, but we couldn't ignore it.

"Gorbachev surprisingly is calling for an arms reduction plan which will rid the world of nuclear weapons by the year 2000," I wrote in my diary January 15. "Of course, he has a couple of zingers in there which we'll have to work around. But at the very least it is a h—l of a propaganda move. We'd be hard put to explain how we could turn it down." I made this entry in my diary only a few days later: ". . . over to the Oval Office for staff and N.S.C. meetings and then five Afghan children were brought in. They were mere babies. But all victims of Soviet bombings. One little girl with her face virtually destroyed. Three with one arm each and one without one leg. I'd like to send the photos to Gen. Secretary Gorbachev."

Although I agreed with the goals of Gorbachev's proposal, there were enormous problems to be solved before we could work out an agreement that was equitable and verifiable and airtight in preserving our security. Great problems were posed in reaching an agreement not only by the differences between the Soviets' huge force of land-based missiles and our three-pronged force of land-, sea-, and air-launched missiles, but by the great size of the Warsaw Pact countries' conventional forces in Europe, which dwarfed those of NATO; by French and English nuclear missiles that the Soviets regarded as a threat to them but on which we were in no position to negotiate restrictions; and by Soviet intermediate-range missiles that were aimed at Europe from Asia.

And, while a truly secure and verifiable U.S.-Soviet agreement eliminating nuclear weapons by the year 2000 was something I wanted, too, what about the Qaddafis of the world, or a lunatic who got his hands on an A-bomb?

The Strategic Defense Initiative, if it proved practical, would give us the insurance we needed even after we had banned nuclear weapons—and on this, I decided, Gorbachev was up against an immovable object.

This is part of the entry in my diary for February 4, 1986:

NSPG time in the situation room re Gorbachev's proposal to eliminate nuclear arms. Some wanted to tag it a publicity stunt. I said no. Let's say we share their overall goals and now want to work out the details. If it is a publicity stunt this will be revealed by them. I also propose that we announce we are going forward with SDI but if research reveals a defense against missiles is possible, we'll work out how it can be used to protect the whole world not just us.

Two days later, I sent another handwritten letter to Gorbachev, replying to both his Christmas Eve letter and his mid-January proposal. After chiding him for making public his letter to me, I said I was pleased we were approaching a common ground on the intermediate-range missiles and I hoped remaining problems dealing with verification of an INF agreement could be worked out shortly. I wrote that I agreed with him that we had to make decisions not on the basis of each other's assurances or intentions but with a cold-eyed regard for the capabilities of both sides.

Nevertheless, I do not understand the reasoning behind your conclusion that only a country preparing a disarming first strike would be interested in defenses against ballistic missiles. If such defenses prove feasible in the future, they could facilitate further reductions of nuclear weapons by creating a feeling of confidence that national security could be preserved without them.

Of course, as I have said before, I recognize that adding defensive systems to an arsenal replete with weapons with a disarming first strike capability could under some conditions be destabilizing. That is why we are proposing that both sides concentrate first on reducing those weapons which can deliver a disarming first strike. Certainly, if neither of our countries has forces suitable for a first strike, neither need fear that defenses against ballistic missiles would make a first strike strategy possible.

I also do not understand your statement that what you call "space-strike weapons" are "all-purpose" weapons. As I understand it, the sort of directed energy and kinetic devices both our countries are investigating in the context of ballistic missile defenses are potentially most effective against point targets moving at high velocity in space. They would be ill suited for mass destruction on earth. If one were planning to strike earth targets from space, it does not seem rational to resort to such expensive and exotic techniques; the destructiveness can never approach that of the nuclear weapons in our hands today. Nuclear weapons are the real problem.

Mr. General Secretary, in the spirit of candor which is essential to effective communication, I want to add another point: you speak often of space-strike weapons and your representatives have defined these as weapons which can strike targets in space from earth and its atmosphere and weapons in space that can strike targets in space or on earth.

What country has such weapons? The answer is only one: the

Soviet Union. Your ABM system deployed around Moscow can strike targets beyond the atmosphere and has been tested in that mode.

Your co-orbital anti-satellite weapon is designed to destroy satellites. Furthermore, the Soviet Union began research in defenses utilizing directed energy before the United States did and seems well along in research (and incidentally, some testing outside laboratories) of lasers and other forms of directed energy. I do not point this out in reproach or suggest these activities are in violation of agreements, but if we were to follow your logic to the effect that what you call space-strike weapons would only be developed by a country planning a first strike, what would we think?

We see the Soviet Union devoting enormous resources to defensive systems, an effort which antedates by many years our own effort, and we see a Soviet Union which has built up its counterforce weapons in numbers far greater than our own. If the only reason to develop defensive weapons is to make a disarming strike possible, then clearly we should have been more concerned than we have been.

We *are* concerned, and deeply so, but not because you are developing, and, unlike us, deploying defensive weaponry, we are concerned that the Soviet Union for some reason has chosen to deploy a much larger number of weapons suitable for a disarming first strike than has the United States. There may be reasons for this other than seeking a first strike advantage, but we too must look at capabilities rather than intentions and we feel certain you have an advantage in this area.

Frankly, Mr. General Secretary, you have been misinformed if your specialists say that the missiles on our Trident submarines have a capability to destroy hardened missile silos, a capability your SS-18 definitely has. Current Trident missiles lack the capabilities for such a role; they could be used only to retaliate. Nor is the Pershing II, which cannot even reach most Soviet strategic weapons, a potential first strike weapon. Its short flight time is not substantially different than that of the more capable and much more numerous SS-20's aimed at our European allies whom we are pledged to defend and most of whom have no nuclear capability of their own.

Our forces have very limited capability to strike Soviet silos. We're improving this capability only because we cannot accept this situation in which the Soviet Union holds such a clear advantage in counter force weaponry.

Even if we are to complete all planned deployments in the absence of an accord which limits them they will not match the number of Soviet weapons with a first strike capability. I feel that because the specialists disagree in some areas, let's arrange for them to meet and discuss their concern. A frank discussion of the respective assessments and reasons could perhaps clear up these misunderstandings, which are not based on fact.

In any event we have both agreed to the principle of a fifty per cent reduction of nuclear arms. Implementing that agreement is surely the first task of our negotiators at Geneva.

Let me stress once again that we are willing to reduce the weapon systems which the Soviet Union finds threatening so long as the Soviet Union will reduce those which pose a special threat to the United States and its allies. . . .

So far as defensive systems are concerned, I would reiterate what I wrote to you before: if your concern is that such systems may be used to permit a first strike strategy, or as a cover for basing weapons of mass destruction in space, then there must be practical ways to prevent such possibilities.

Of course, I have in mind not general assurances but concrete verifiable means that both sides can rely on to avoid those contingencies. Neither of which is part of U.S. strategy or planning. I honestly believe that we can find a solution to this problem if we approach it in a practical fashion rather than debating generalities. I would like nothing more by our next meeting than to have found acceptable ways to solve the problem. But I believe it will require two things: accelerating negotiations to reach agreement on the way to reduce offensive weapons by fifty per cent and discussion of concrete ways to insure that any future development of defensive systems cannot be used as a cover for a first strike strategy or for basing weapons of mass destruction in space. Aside from these broader issues, I believe recent proposals bring settlement of intermediate range missiles closer and there are improved measures in several areas.

Regarding regional conflicts, I see that our respective analyses of the causes are incompatible. I see little point in continuing to debate the matter, on which we are bound to disagree. I suggest we simply look at the current situation in pragmatic terms. I think it would show two very important facts. The Soviet Union is engaged in a war in another country and the United States is not. And furthermore, this war is unlikely to bring any benefit to the Soviet Union, so why is it continued? Certainly not because of the United States. Even if we wished we do not have the power to induce thousands of people to take up arms against a well trained foreign army equipped with the most modern weapons. And neither we nor any other country other than the Soviet Union has the power to stop that war. But who can tell the people of another country they should not fight for their motherland, for their independence and for their national dignity? I hope there is an open door to a just political settlement. Of course, we support you in that process and hope that it will take a practical and realistic turn.

However, 1985 was marked by an intensification of conflict. I hope this is not what the future holds. If you really want to withdraw from Afghanistan, you'll have my cooperation in every reasonable way. We've no desire to exploit a Soviet military withdrawal from Afghanistan to the detriment of Soviet interests. But the fighting can only be ended by the withdrawal of Soviet troops, the return of Afghan refugees to their country and the restoration of a genuinely sovereign non-aligned state. Such result would have an immediate positive effect on U.S.-Soviet relations and would help clear the way to progress in many other areas. . . .

The problems of superpower military involvement in local disputes are not limited to Afghanistan. Recent actions by the Soviet Union are most discouraging. What are we to make of your sharply increased military support of a local dictator who has declared a war of terrorism against much of the rest of the world and against the United States in particular? [I was referring to Qaddafi, whose responsibility for airport bombings in Rome and Vienna we had just established.] How can one take Soviet declarations of opposition to terrorism seriously when confronted with such action? And more importantly are we to conclude that the Soviet Union is so reckless in seeking to extend its influence in the world that it will place its prestige (and even the lives of some of its citizens) at the mercy of a mentally unbalanced local despot?

You have made accusations about U.S. policy which I cannot accept. My purpose here, however, is not to debate, but search for a way out of the pattern by which one of us becomes involved, directly or indirectly, in military disputes and then stimulates the reaction of the other, so that which should be of local concern is turned into a Soviet-American confrontation.

As I have said, I believe it is the Soviet Union which has acted without restraint to that respect, and the Soviet Union says it is the United States. An agreement as to who is to blame is not necessary to find a solution. We must find a way to terminate the military involvement, direct and indirect, of both our countries in these disputes and avoid spreading such involvement. . . .

This is the goal of the proposal I made last October and I want to encourage the parties to the conflict to find political solutions while both our countries support the process by agreeing to terminate the flow of weapons and war material into the area of conflict.

There are many points upon which we still disagree and we will probably never reach agreement on some of them. Nevertheless, I'm convinced the critical problems can be solved if we approach them in a proper manner.

I have the feeling we are gradually finding some additional points upon which we can agree and I hope that by concentrating on practical solutions we can give greater momentum to the process.

I feel we have to speed up the negotiating process if it is to occur and I hope you will instruct your delegation in Geneva, as I have instructed ours, to roll up their sleeves and get seriously to work.

When you announced to the public the ideas contained in your letter of January 14, I made a statement welcoming them. Our study of that message will shortly be completed and when it is I will be responding specifically to the points you made in it. Nancy joins me in saying our best regards to you and your wife.

> Sincerely,
> Ronald Reagan
> February 6, 1986

Two weeks later, on Presidents' Day, while Nancy was away on a speaking trip in Texas, I decided to try again and sent Gorbachev a seven-page, handwritten letter with a set of new proposals that I hoped would bring the still-deadlocked Geneva talks off dead center while responding to his proposals. Below are excerpts from this letter:

I am encouraged that you have suggested steps leading toward a world free from nuclear weapons, even though my view regarding the steps necessary differs from yours in certain respects. However, having agreed on the objective and on the need for taking concrete steps to reach that goal, it should be easier to resolve differences in our viewpoints as to what these steps should be. Our initial moves are of course the essential ones to start this process and therefore I believe we should focus our negotiating efforts on them. Of course, if we are to move toward a world in which the eventual elimination of nuclear weapons will be possible, there must be far greater trust and confidence between our two countries than exist at present. We cannot simply wave away the suspicion and misunderstandings which have developed over the past four decades between our two countries. The process of reducing and eventually eliminating nuclear weapons can by itself nurture greater confidence and trust. But there will be many in my country, and I believe in yours, who will question the wisdom of eliminating nuclear weapons—which both sides see as the ultimate guarantor of their security—if they see the other's conduct as threatening.

This meant, I said, that if we were going to make progress on arms control we had to develop effective verification arrangements and make progress on nonnuclear military issues, regional problems, and human rights.

The process of eliminating nuclear arms is liable to prove fragile indeed unless we can deal with our competition in a peaceful and responsible way.

As you know, the United States and its allies must rely today on nuclear weapons to deter conventional as well as nuclear conflict. This is due in large part to the significant imbalance that currently exists between the conventional forces of NATO and the Warsaw Pact. As a result, it would be necessary as we reduce nuclear weapons towards zero, that we concurrently engage in a process of strengthening the stability of the overall East-West security balance, with particular emphasis on redressing existing conventional imbalances, strengthening confidence-building measures and accomplishing a verifiable global ban on chemical weapons. . . .

In the defense and space area, your proposal was ambiguous with regard to strategic defense research. I continue to believe that limits on research could be counter-productive and, in any case, could not be verified; therefore, they must not be included in an agreement. Beyond research, as I suggested in Geneva, if there were no nuclear missiles, then there might also be no need for defenses against them. What I am convinced is that some nonnuclear defenses could make a vital contribution to security and stability. With respect to nuclear testing, I believe that so long as we rely on nuclear weapons as an element of deterrence, we must continue to test in order to assure their continued safety, security and reliability. However, as I wrote to you in December, I see no reason why we should not consider the matter of nuclear testing as we move forward on other arms control subjects. I suggested that we establish a bilateral dialogue aimed at constructive steps in this field. I remain hopeful you will take up this offer. . . .

Then I listed what I thought of as a sweeping package of new proposals aimed at reducing nuclear, conventional, and chemical weapons; in the strategic area, it called for a reduction of warheads on strategic ballistic missiles on both sides to forty-five hundred and the number of ALCMs (air-launched cruise missiles) on heavy bombers to fifteen hundred,

resulting in a total number of no more than 6000 such warheads on strategic nuclear delivery vehicles . . . in the INF area, by 1987, both the United States and the Soviet Union would limit their LRINF [longrange intermediate nuclear force] missile deployments in Europe to no more than 140 launchers each (this is in line with my proposal for a staged reduction of weapons) with the Soviet Union making concurrent proportionate reductions in Asia. Within the following year, both sides would further reduce the number of launchers remaining in Europe and Asia by 50 per cent. Finally, both sides would move to the total elimination of this category of weapons by the end of 1989.

Our proposal also called for broad cutbacks in conventional forces in Europe.

I hope that this concept provides a mutually acceptable route to a goal all the world shares. The goal would be to complete the process as soon as the conditions for a nonnuclear world have been achieved. . . .

Let me conclude by agreeing with you that we should work constructively before your visit to the United States to prepare concrete agreements on the full range of issues we discussed at Geneva. Neither of us has illusions about the major problems which remain between our two countries, but I want to assure you that I am determined to work with you energetically in finding practical solutions to these problems. I agree with you that we should use our correspondence as a most important channel of communication in preparing for your visit.

Nancy and I would like to extend to you, Mrs. Gorbachev and

your family our best wishes. It is our hope this year will bring significant progress toward our mutual goal of building a better relationship between our two countries, and a safer world.

Sincerely,
Ronald Reagan
Feb. 22, 1986

80

AT THE START of 1986, we were getting more and more evidence that the Soviet economy was in dire shape. It made me believe that, if nothing else, the Soviet economic tailspin would force Mikhail Gorbachev to come around on an arms reduction agreement we both could live with. If we didn't deviate from our policies, I was convinced it would happen.

Gorbachev was trying to turn things around but not having an easy time of it. Looking at the situation from his viewpoint, I knew he had to be giving high priority to reducing the vast amounts of rubles the Soviets were spending on weapons. He had to be losing some sleep over the vitality of our economy, which was booming after pulling out of the recession, and he must have realized more than ever that we could outspend him as long as the Soviets insisted on prolonging the arms race.

That spring and summer, I had to make three important decisions that affected our relations with the Soviets:

In March, Tip O'Neill and some of his loyalists in Congress, responding to suggestions by Gorbachev that we join the Soviets in a moratorium on nuclear testing, mustered an effort to persuade the American people to pressure me to halt underground testing of nuclear weapons.

Because of security requirements, I couldn't at the time explain the real purpose of these tests: Although Tip and the others claimed their purpose was to create bigger and better weapons of mass destruction, the real purpose was to test the reliability of our existing weapons and the extent to which they could be trusted to survive the burst of radiation that would be unleashed in an enemy nuclear attack.

I gave the order to continue the tests.

The second decision I faced was whether to continue abiding by terms of the SALT II treaty despite repeated Soviet cheating on its restrictions. We knew of dozens of violations of the SALT and ABM treaties, including the Krasnoyarsk radar, which we knew incontrovertibly was intended for use in an antimissile defense. On the question of whether to continue abiding by SALT, Cap Weinberger and George Shultz were divided once again: George favored restraint and abiding by the agreement, believing there was little to gain by not doing so at a time when we were trying to improve relations with the Soviets. "Others, including Cap," I wrote in my diary after a meeting of the National Security Planning Group in March, "want to give it up. I'm inclined to vote for replacing that informal agreement with our arms reduction proposal now in Geneva: Tell the Soviets we can have a real reduction in weapons or an arms race, but we're not going to sit by and watch them keep on fudging."

To many liberals in Congress, the SALT II treaty, even though it was unratified, had a symbolic importance. It represented one of the few times the superpowers had reached agreement to limit nuclear arms. I understood this symbolic significance. But the treaty was full of holes the Russians were exploiting, and after a while I began saying publicly that because of the Soviet cheating we might end our policy of voluntary restraint—unless there was more evidence the Soviets were applying restraint, too.

In early April, Anatoly Dobrynin, after being appointed secretary of the Politburo and head of foreign affairs for the Communist Party's Central Committee in Moscow, and thus becoming a key adviser to Gorbachev, came to see me. He said Gorbachev was unhappy with my decision to continue nuclear testing and with reports that we might end our restraint in observing the SALT II treaty, and as a result he did not think the time was right yet to set a date for our summit in Washington. I considered this Soviet game-playing. After the meeting I wrote in my diary: "My feeling is the summit will take place, if not in June or July, sometime after the election."

Here are portions of a letter Dobrynin brought to me from Gorbachev:

I would like to share with you some of my general observations that I have, and surely, you must have your own, regarding the state and prospects of the relationship between our two countries. I believe, in doing so, one has to use as a point of departure our meeting in Geneva where we both assumed certain obligations.

I think our assessments of that meeting coincide: it was necessary and useful, it introduced a certain stabilizing element to the relations between the USSR and the USA and to the world situation in general. It was only natural that it also generated no small hopes for the future.

More than four months have passed since the Geneva meeting. We ask ourselves: what is the reason for things not going the way they, it would seem, should have gone? Where is the real turn for the better? We, within the Soviet leadership, regarded the Geneva meeting as a call for translating understandings of principle reached there into specific actions with a view to giving an impetus to our relations and to building up their positive dynamics. And we have been doing just that after Geneva.

With this in mind, we have put forward a wide-ranging and concrete program of measures concerning the limitation and reduction of arms and disarmament. It is from the standpoint of new approaches to seeking mutually acceptable solutions that the Soviet delegations have acted in Geneva, Vienna and Stockholm.

What were the actions of the USA? One has to state, unfortunately, that so far the positions have not been brought closer together so that it would open up a real prospect for reaching agreements. I will not go into details or make judgments of the U.S. positions here. But there is one point I would like to make. One gathers the impressions that all too frequently attempts are being made to portray our initiatives as propaganda, as a desire to score high points in public opinion or as a wish to put the other side into an awkward position. We did not and do not harbor such designs. After all, our initiatives can be easily tested for their practicality. Our goal is to reach agreement, to find solutions to problems which concern the USSR, the USA and actually all other countries. I have especially focused on this matter so as to ensure a correct, unbiased and businesslike treatment of our proposals. I'm sure that it will make it easier to reach agreement.

Now what has been taking place in the meantime outside the negotiations? Of course, each of us has his own view of the policies of the other side. But here again, has the Soviet Union done anything in foreign affairs or bilateral relations that would contribute to mounting tensions or be detrimental to the legitimate interests of the USA? I can say clearly: No, there has been nothing of that sort. On the other hand, we hear increasingly vehement philippics addressed to the USSR and are also witnessing quite a few actions directly aimed against our interest, and to put it frankly, against our relations becoming more stable and constructive. All this builds suspicion as regards to the U.S. policy and surely, creates no favorable backdrop for the summit meeting. I am saying it with no ambiguity in order to avoid in this regard any uncertainties or misunderstanding that only one side should exercise restraint and display a positive attitude. Our relations take shape not in a vacuum . . . The calmer the atmosphere, the easier it is to solve issues which are of equal concern to both sides.

The issues have to be solved—there is no doubt about it. And above all, this bears on the area of security. You are familiar with our proposals, they cover all the most important aspects. At the same time I would like specifically to draw your attention to the fact that we do not say: All or nothing at all. We are in favor of moving forward step by step and we outline certain possibilities in this regard, particularly, at the negotiations on nuclear and space arms.

We maintained a serious and balanced approach to the problem of ending nuclear tests. One would not want to lose hope that we shall succeed in finding a practical solution to this issue in the way the world expects us to do. It is hardly necessary to point out the importance of this matter as it is. The solution thereof carries with it also a great positive political potential. . . .

It was a desire that we work together in the cessation of nuclear tests and set a good example to all nuclear powers that motivated my recent proposal for both of us to meet specifically on this issue at one of the European capitals. Have another look at this proposal, Mr. President, in a broad political context. I repeat, what is meant here is a specific, single purpose meeting. Such a meeting, of course, would not be a substitute for the new major meeting that we agreed upon in Geneva.

I do very serious thinking with regard to the latter, first of all with a view to make that meeting truly meaningful and substantial, so that it should enable us to move closer to putting into practice the fundamental understandings reached in Geneva. As you know, I have mentioned some of the questions pertaining to the area of security which are worthwhile working on in preparing for our meeting. I reaffirm that we are ready to seek here solutions in a most serious way, which would be mutually acceptable and not detrimental to the security of either side. Given the mutual will it would also be possible to ascertain other possibilities for agreement in the context of the forthcoming meeting both in the area of space and nuclear arms and on the issues described in other fora. To be sure, we also have things to discuss as far as regional matters are concerned.

I assume that you are also working on all these questions and in subsequent correspondence we will be able in a more specific and substantive way to compare our mutual preliminary ideas for the purpose of bringing the positions closer together. Obviously, this joint work, including the preparations for our meeting, will benefit from the exchanges of views at other levels and particularly from forthcoming contacts between our Foreign Minister and your Secretary of State. I will be looking forward with interest to hearing from you.

Sincerely,
M. Gorbachev
April 2, 1986

After our air strikes on Libya two weeks later, a Soviet spokesman described Qaddafi as a heroic and innocent victim of our supposed aggression, and Eduard Shevardnadze canceled a meeting with George Shultz at which they were to choose a date for the summit.

The tragic accident at the Soviet nuclear reactor at Chernobyl occurred later that month. I sent Gorbachev a letter conveying our sympathies along with my disappointment over cancellation of the Shultz-Shevardnadze meeting. Excerpts from my letter:

We have made a good faith effort to set in motion the serious, high-level discussions necessary to prepare for a meeting between us. I regret that it has not been possible to begin them. While there have been positive steps in some areas, we have lost a full six months in dealing with the issues which most merit our personal attention. I hope you will agree that it is time to concentrate on the agenda set forth in Geneva last November. I am prepared to do my part. As I have said, I am eager to achieve tangible practical results at our next meeting. I agree with you that an atmosphere conducive to progress is important. The suggestions I have made, which took careful account of your comments to me on the issues, sought to find a mutually acceptable approach to some of the key issues.

The atmosphere of our relationship is also affected, of course, by what the two of us say privately. The approach I intend to take in my public statements is to reaffirm my strong personal commitment to achieving concrete progress in all the areas of our relationship during the remaining years of my Administration.

Mr. General Secretary, our recent history provides ample evidence that if you wait for an ideal moment to try to resolve our differences, we are unlikely to resolve anything. We should take advantage of it since it is a time of historic and possibly unique potential. Let us not lose it for lack of effort.

A few days later, I announced that as long as the Soviets continued cheating on the SALT II treaty, the United States no longer felt bound by it. Frankly, I was just tired of living by the rules and having the other side violate them. At the same time, I continued a policy of moderation in my public statements about the Soviets and I said I believed Gorbachev was sincere in wanting to end the threat of nuclear war.

Then I made my third important decision: In late July, I sent a sweeping new arms reduction proposal to Gorbachev based on ideas that had been developed during weeks of debate within the administration.

It called for both sides to scrap *all* ballistic missiles while continuing research on missile defensive systems, and it said that if these systems proved feasible they would be shared with all nations once all nuclear missiles had been scrapped. "If and when such research should indicate such a defense weapon is possible," I wrote in my diary, "both of us would observe tests [of the new system] and we would agree jointly that deployment must follow elimination of all ICBM's and then the defense be made available to all."

During the discussions in which the proposal was hammered out, some of our arms control and State Department experts wanted me to hint to the Soviets that we might be willing to trade the SDI for greater Soviet concessions on offensive weapons.

Cap Weinberger, the chief evangelist, after me, of the Strategic

Defense Initiative, said that if the Soviets heard about this split in the administration and decided I was wavering on the SDI, it would send the wrong signals to Moscow and weaken our bargaining position. I think he was also worried that I might be persuaded by those advocating possible concessions on the SDI, but he needn't have worried. I was committed to the search for an alternative to the MAD policy and said it as emphatically and as often as I could, privately and publicly: *The SDI is not a bargaining chip*.

George Shultz said it was questionable that development and testing of the SDI was permissible under the 1972 ABM treaty with the Soviets that the Senate had ratified and therefore was the law of the land. Cap argued for a broader interpretation of the treaty that, according to his experts, allowed us to develop and test certain elements of the system.

As these portions of my diary indicate, I sided with Cap:

> *July 17*
> . . . a big N.S.C. meeting on my letter to Gorbachev. Cap and George Shultz differ on some elements, such as what to say about the ABM treaty. On this I'm closer to Cap. I want to propose a new treaty for what we do if and when SDI research looks like we have a practical system.

> *July 18*
> Well, we finally came up with a letter to Gorbachev that I can sign. In fact, it's a good one and should open the door to some real arms negotiations if he is really interested.

While I was waiting for Gorbachev to respond to my new arms reduction initiative, KGB agents seized and imprisoned a Moscow correspondent for *U.S. News & World Report*, Nicholas Daniloff, and accused him of spying for the United States—shortly after we had arrested a Soviet spy in the United States.

The accusation was ridiculous. The circumstances of his arrest were virtually identical to those under which four other Americans had been seized in Moscow in the past after we'd arrested KGB agents in the United States—innocent Americans were arrested, then offered in exchange for the Soviet agents.

The following comments in my diary reflect my feelings on the incident:

Sept. 4

I called George Shultz re our man Daniloff in the Soviet Union. I asked his opinion of my thought that perhaps I should communicate directly with Gorbachev and tell him Daniloff was not working for our govt. At about 5 p.m. I signed such a message. . . .

Sept. 7

. . . word came the Soviets were going to officially charge Daniloff with espionage. Gorbachev's response to my letter was arrogant and rejected my statement that Daniloff was no spy. I'm mad as hell. Had a conference call with George Shultz, John Poindexter, Don Regan. Decision was to wait until Tuesday in Washington where we could explain our course of action. This whole thing follows the pattern: We catch a spy as we have this time and the Soviets grab an American —*any* American and frame him so they can demand a trade of prisoners.

Sept. 9

Meeting, George S., John P., Don R. and myself re the Daniloff case. We are going to try to get him released to our Ambassador pending trial. We'll offer the same here with their spy. If it's possible we'll do something of an exchange but only if they'll release some dissidents like Sakharov. Once we have him back, I propose we kick a half hundred of their UN KGB agents out of the country. There can't be a repeat of this hostage taking. . . .

Sept. 10

George Shultz gave me word that Soviet Ambassador Dobrynin brought an offer to turn Daniloff over to our ambassador if we'd do the same with their spy. I told him to do it. I think it's very important to get our guy out of their jail and away from that four hours a day interrogation.

Sept. 11

It was a short night and a long day. The usual meeting with Don R. and the v.p. and then the N.S.C. briefing. John P. was hesitant about the Daniloff deal with us holding out for more. Since it's only a move pending the trials I reiterated my stand on getting him out of jail. . . .

Sept. 12

. . . an NSPG meeting re Daniloff. We have agreed to turn [Gennadi] Zakharov [the Soviet spy] over to the Soviet ambassador pending trial and they will deliver Daniloff to our ambassador. This does not mean a trade. This we will not do. Their man is a spy caught red handed and Daniloff is a hostage. . . .

Sept. 15

A hastily called meeting with John P. and Don R. to agree on our approach to Gorbachev if Daniloff is not turned over to me at once. We are going to tell him 25 KGB members on their UN staff to get out of the country. . . .

Sept. 17

The press is obsessed with the Daniloff affair and determined to paint all of us as caving in to the Soviets which they of course say is the worst way to deal with them. The simple truth is we've offered no deal and are playing hard ball all the way. . . . [In the afternoon] an N.S.C. meeting getting ready for the Soviet foreign minister's visit and how we treat the Daniloff problem with him. We've notified the Soviet U. we're sending 25 of their UN staff home. All are KGB agents.

Sept. 18

. . . During the day we were receiving bulletins about the Daniloff case. Gorbachev has gone on TV to declare our man is definitely a spy. I have told him in writing twice he is not. Shevardnadze has arrived to meet with George Shultz. Whether I see him or not is up in the air. Gen. Sec. of UN has stated our action in ordering 25 of UN Soviet staff out of the country is against UN charter. He'd better be careful, if we cut off UN allowance they might be out of business. Back to the W.H. and so to bed. . . .

Last night Sen. confirmed my two Supreme Court nominees, Rehnquist and Scalia.

The next day, George Shultz brought Soviet Foreign Minister Eduard Shevardnadze to the White House to deliver a reply from Gorbachev to my letter. When Shevardnadze arrived in the Oval Office, he discovered he didn't have the letter and had left it by mistake at the Soviet embassy. Several KGB agents who were traveling with him left and when they returned half an hour later with the letter they started to enter the Oval Office. Our Secret Service agents said, "Well, no, you can't do that, we don't allow KGB agents to walk into the Oval Office," and they let out a protest.

Finally, after considerable commotion (I learned later), there was a compromise: The Soviet interpreter was called over to the door of the Oval Office and a KGB agent handed him the letter, and the interpreter handed it to Shevardnadze, who handed it to me.

During the delay, Shevardnadze had explained to me the essence of Gorbachev's message: He wanted to meet me in London or Iceland the following month to see if the two of us could accelerate the arms control process before our meeting in Washington. Afterward, I wrote in my diary:

> I opted for Iceland. This would be preparatory to a Summit. I'm agreeable to that but made it plain we wanted Daniloff returned to us before anything took place. I let the F.M. know I was angry and that I resented their charges that Daniloff was a spy after I had personally given my word that he wasn't. I gave him a little run down on the difference between our two systems and told him they couldn't understand the importance we place on the individual because they don't have any such feeling.
>
> I enjoyed being angry.

Besides inviting me to an impromptu summit, Gorbachev's letter indicated he had little interest in the arms control initiative to which we had devoted so much effort in July. This is a portion of the letter:

> After we received your letter of July 25, 1986, which has been given careful consideration, certain developments and incidents of a negative nature have taken place. This is yet another indication of how sensitive relations between the USSR and the United States are and how important it is for the top leaders of the two countries to keep them constantly within view and exert a stabilizing influence whenever the amplitude of their fluctuations becomes threatening.
>
> Among such incidents—of the kind that have happened before and that, presumably, no one can be guaranteed against in the future—is the case of Zakharov and Daniloff. It requires a calm examination, investigation and a search for mutually acceptable solutions. However, the U.S. side has unduly dramatized that incident. A massive hostile campaign has been launched against our country, which has been taken up at the higher levels of the United States administration and Congress. It is as if a pretext was deliberately sought to aggravate Soviet-American relations to increase tension.

A question then arises: what about the atmosphere so needed for the normal course of negotiations and certainly for preparing and holding the summit meeting?

Since the Geneva meeting, the Soviet Union has been doing a great deal to ensure that the atmosphere is favorable and that negotiations make possible practical preparations for our new meeting.

On the major issue of limiting and reducing arms—nuclear, chemical and conventional—we have undertaken intensive efforts in a search for concrete solutions aimed at radically reducing the level of military confrontation in a context of equivalent security.

However, Mr. President, in the spirit of candidness which is coming to characterize our dialogue, I have to tell you that the overall character of U.S. actions in international affairs, the position on which its representatives insist at negotiations and consultations, and the content of your letter all give rise to grave and disturbing thoughts. One has to conclude that, in effect, no start has been made in implementing the agreements which we reached in Geneva on improving Soviet-American relations, accelerating the negotiations on nuclear and space arms and renouncing attempts to secure military superiority. . . .

Both in letters and publicly we have made known our views as to the causes of such developments, and for my part, I do not want to repeat here our assessment of the situation.

First of all, a conclusion comes to mind:

Is the U.S. leadership at all prepared and really willing to seek agreements which would lead to the termination of the arms race and to genuine disarmament? It is a fact, after all, that despite vigorous efforts by the Soviet side we have still not moved an inch closer to an agreement on arms reduction.

Having studied your letter and proposals contained therein, I began to think where they would lead in terms of seeking solutions.

First. You are proposing that we should agree that the ABM treaty continue existing for another five to seven years, while activities to destroy it would go ahead. Thus, instead of making headway, there would be something that complicates even what has been achieved.

We have proposed that any work on anti-missile systems be confined to laboratories. In response, we witness attempts to justify the development of space weapons and their testing at test sites, and declarations made in advance, of the intention to start in five to seven years deploying large scale ABM systems and thus to nullify the treaty. It is of course fully understood that we will not agree to that. We see here a bypass route to securing military superiority.

I trust, Mr. President, you will recall our discussions of this subject in Geneva. At that time, I said that should the United States rush with weapons in space, we would not help it. We would do our utmost to devalue such efforts and make them futile. You may rest assured that we have every means to achieve this and should the need arise, we shall use these means. We favor the strengthening of the ABM treaty regime. This is precisely the reason for our position that work should be confined to laboratories and that the treaty should be strictly observed for a period of up to fifteen years. Should this be the case, it would be possible—and this is our proposal—to agree on significant reductions in strategic offensive arms. We are prepared to do this without delay and it would thereby be demonstrated in practice that neither side seeks military superiority.

Second. As far as medium range missiles are concerned, the Soviet Union has proposed an optimum solution—complete elimination of U.S. and Soviet missiles in Europe. We have also agreed to an interim option—and that, without taking into account the modernization of British and French nuclear systems.

Following our well known steps towards accommodation, the issue of verification would seem no longer to be an obstacle. Yet, the U.S. side has now "discovered" another obstacle, namely Soviet medium range missiles in Asia. Nevertheless, I believe that here, as well, a mutually acceptable formula can be found and I am ready to propose one . . .

Third. The attitude of the United States to the moratorium on nuclear testing is a matter of deep disappointment—and not only in the Soviet Union. The United States administration is making every effort to [delay consideration of] this key problem, to subsume it in talk of other issues. You are aware of my views in this regard: the attitude of a country to the cessation of nuclear testing is the touchstone of its policy in the field of disarmament and international security—and indeed in safeguarding peace in general.

Arguments to the effect that nuclear testing is needed to insure reliability of nuclear arsenals are untenable. Today there are other methods to insure this, without nuclear explosions. After all, the United States does not test devices with yields in excess of 150 to 200 kilotons, although 70 per cent of the U.S. nuclear arsenal—in our case the percentage is not smaller—consist of weapons with yields exceeding that threshold. Modern science combined with a political willingness to agree to any adequate verification measures, including on-site inspections, ensure effective verification of the absence of nuclear explosions. So here, too, there is room for mutually acceptable solutions.

I have addressed specifically three questions, which, in my opinion, are of greatest importance. They are the ones to which positive solutions are expected from the USSR and the USA. They are a matter of concern to the whole world, they are being discussed everywhere. Naturally, we are in favor of productive discussions of other major issues as well, such as reductions of armed forces and conventional armaments, a chemical weapons ban, regional problems and humanitarian questions. Here, too, common approaches and cooperation should be sought. Yet, the three questions mentioned above remain the key ones.

But in almost a year since Geneva, there has been no movement on these issues. Upon reflection and after having given thought to your last letter, I have come to the conclusion that the negotiations need a major impulse; otherwise, they would continue to mark time while creating only the appearance of preparations for our meeting on American soil.

They will lead nowhere unless you and I intervene personally. I am convinced that we shall be able to find solutions, and I am prepared to discuss with you in a substantive way all possible approaches to them and identify such steps as would make it possible—after prompt follow up by appropriate government agencies—to make my visit to the United States a really productive and fruitful one. This is exactly what the entire world is expecting from a second meeting between the leaders of the Soviet Union and the United States. I look forward to an early reply.

Respectfully,
M. Gorbachev
Sept. 15, 1986

I told Shevardnadze I wouldn't respond to Gorbachev's proposal until Daniloff was free, and in a speech to the UN General Assembly the following week, I said some strong things about his arrest as well as Soviet activities in Afghanistan and elsewhere. I half expected the Communist delegations to walk out, but none did. Meanwhile, the tug-of-war over Daniloff continued, as I recorded in these excerpts from the diary:

Sept. 24

George Shultz and Shevardnadze at the UN still dickering about Daniloff. It's getting more apparent that it's the Soviets who are blinking. We're getting closer. The Soviets don't call him a spy anymore. They refer to him as an "American citizen."

Sept. 25

. . . George Shultz [called from New York] about Daniloff and meetings with Shevardnadze; a deal cooking would have Daniloff free—and Zakharov free in exchange for [Yuri] Orlov and others if possible. I think we'll have to settle for Orlov but I recommend only if Orlov comes home as Z. leaves. The Soviets want Z. first and then Orlov about 15 days later. Of course we hold fast that the 25 KGB agents leave the UN and go home. . . .

Sept. 26

High spot was swearing in of Chief Justice Rehnquist and Justice Scalia in the East Room. After lunch meeting with George S., Cap W. and Bill Casey plus our White House people, Don R., John P., etc. It was a sum up of where we stand in the negotiations between George and Shevardnadze. The difference between us is their desire to make it look like a trade for Daniloff and their spy Zakharov. We'll trade Zakharov but for Soviet dissidents. We settled on our bottom line points beyond which we won't budge. Then we picked up Nancy and helicoptered to Ft. Meade for the opening of the new National Security Agency complex. I spoke to the NSA employees. Then we helicoptered to Camp David and topped the day with a swim.

Sept. 29

Didn't sleep at all well last night. I need my roommate. (Nancy is gone.) Into the office for a brief meeting before taking off for some politicking. George Shultz has won the day. Mr. and Mrs. Daniloff will be on their way home before the morning is over. That will be announced. Then tomorrow George will announce that Zakharov will be found guilty and sent to Russia on probation so long as he never returns to the U.S. and Orlov and his wife will be freed to leave the Soviet Union in one week.

Then I'll announce a meeting with Gorbachev in Iceland Oct. 10, 11, 12.

Sept. 30

A hectic day. Arrived at the office about 10:05 and was rushed into the press room to announce the Iceland meeting Oct. 11 and 12.

George Shultz had just done the announcement about Zakharov and Orlov. Already it's plain the press is going to believe I gave in and the trade was Daniloff for Zakharov. By the end of the day the network anchors were laying into me for having given up. . . . Daniloff has arrived in Washington. I'll see him tomorrow afternoon. Zakharov is on his way home to Russia.

In the final analysis, we stood our ground and the Soviets blinked, but (and this brought more complaints from my conservative supporters) we also applied restraint in order not to torpedo prospects for the summit.

I don't believe the crisis over Daniloff's seizure ever brought either of us close to canceling the summit in Reykjavík. I think both Gorbachev and I felt the stakes were too high and acted cautiously to avoid torpedoing in advance whatever prospects we had of success in Iceland.

81

AT REYKJAVÍK, my hopes for a nuclear-free world soared briefly, then fell during one of the longest, most disappointing—and ultimately angriest—days of my presidency. Our meeting spot in Iceland was a waterfront home overlooking the Atlantic. Gorbachev and I first met alone briefly with our interpreters, then he said he wanted to bring in George Shultz and Shevardnadze and that's the way it went for the rest of the two days—through ten hours of negotiations among the four of us.

Gorbachev tried to limit our discussion to arms control. But I led off by raising again the Soviet Union's refusal to let its citizens emigrate because of their religion or to allow the reunification of divided families. I brought up Afghanistan and the continuing Soviet subversion of Third World countries, to which he listened but did not respond. I had brought along a list of twelve hundred Jews who wanted out of Russia and handed it to him and said once again that Soviet human rights policies were impeding the improvement of our relationship. I also asked him why the Soviets had reneged on a commitment to buy six million tons of U.S. grain; he said they couldn't afford it because of falling oil prices, which meant fewer Soviet dollars for wheat.

Then, for a day and a half, Gorbachev and I made progress on arms reduction that even now seems breathtaking.

On the first day he accepted in principle our zero-zero proposal for the elimination of nuclear missiles in Europe and my proposal, made the previous July, for the elimination of *all* ballistic missiles over ten years.

As the day wore on, I began to wonder whether the Chernobyl accident and a fire that had occurred aboard a Soviet nuclear submarine just a few days before our meeting was behind Gorbachev's new eagerness to discuss abolishing nuclear weapons. The radiation emitted at Chernobyl had made it impossible for thousands of people to live in their homes, yet it had been less than the amount of radiation released by a single nuclear warhead; as we talked, I wondered: Has Chernobyl made Gorbachev think about the effects of a missile with ten nuclear warheads?

He and I had at it all afternoon. I proposed that in the first phase of our plan to eliminate our nuclear weapons each of us would scrap fifty percent of our missiles while continuing research on a missile defense system. If and when the SDI reached the point at which it could be tested, the United States would permit Soviet observers at the tests, and if the tests demonstrated that the system was effective, and once we had scrapped fifty percent of our missiles, each of us would destroy the balance of our missiles and both countries would share all SDI technology. At the ten-year point, when all ballistic missiles were eliminated, each of us would deploy the SDI system simultaneously.

When Gorbachev registered objections to the SDI, I said we would abide by the ABM treaty and agree not to deploy the system unilaterally for ten years.

At the end of a long day, George Shultz suggested that we give the notes we had made during the meeting to our teams so they could put in writing what had been agreed to and what sticking points remained. They went to work and kept at it through the night, until six-thirty the next morning. George and I were very excited.

The following day, a Sunday, we had scheduled a half day of meetings, ending at noon. We agreed we were in accord on the account of Saturday's agreements drafted by our teams of specialists, then began a second round of negotiations.

In addition to nuclear missiles, we said we would try to reduce and eventually eliminate other nuclear weapons as well, including bombers, and Gorbachev pledged his commitment to strong and mutually acceptable verification procedures.

When I said we couldn't eliminate tactical battlefield nuclear weapons in Europe because they constituted NATO's principal deterrent against an invasion by the much larger Warsaw Pact conventional forces, Gorbachev volunteered drastic reductions in their conventional forces; this was something which we'd always considered a prerequisite to a nuclear arms reduction agreement, but never expected to get in Iceland.

George and I couldn't believe what was happening. We were getting amazing agreements. As the day went on I felt something momentous was occurring.

Our noon deadline came and went. We ignored the clock and kept on working, the four of us and our interpreters in that room above the sea.

As evening approached, I thought to myself: Look what we have accomplished—we have negotiated the most massive weapons reductions in history. I thought we were in complete agreement and were going to achieve something remarkable.

Then, after everything had been decided, or so I thought, Gorbachev threw us a curve. With a smile on his face, he said:

"This all depends, of course, on you giving up SDI."

I couldn't believe it and blew my top.

"I've said again and again the SDI wasn't a bargaining chip. I've told you, if we find out that the SDI is practical and feasible, we'll make that information known to you and everyone else so that nuclear weapons can be made obsolete. Now, with all we have accomplished here, you do this and throw in this roadblock and everything is out the window.

"There is no way we are going to give up research to find a defense weapon against nuclear missiles," I said. It had been the Strategic Defense Initiative that had brought the Soviet Union to Geneva and Reykjavík. I wasn't going to renege on my promises to the American people not to surrender the SDI.

We knew from intelligence information that the Soviets were secretly researching a missile defense system similar to the SDI; their technology was inferior to ours, but if we stopped work on the SDI and they continued work on their system, it meant we might wake up one morning to learn they alone had a defense against missiles. We couldn't afford that. The SDI was an insurance policy to guarantee that the Soviets kept the commitments Gorbachev and I were making at Reykjavík. We had had enough experience with Soviet treaty violations to know that kind of insurance was necessary.

"If you are willing to abolish nuclear weapons," I asked Gorbachev, "why are you so anxious to get rid of a defense against nuclear weapons? A nonnuclear defensive system like the SDI threatens no one."

From the American vantage point, I said, it looked as if the Soviets didn't want us to proceed with the SDI because the United States was ahead in this technology and they were trying to catch up.

To prove we had no intention of using the SDI offensively or as a shield during a first strike, I repeated my offer once again to open our laboratories and make the system available to all the world; I said it was to be a defense for the entire world that would make nuclear weapons obsolete and speed the day when nations had enough confidence in their security to give up such weapons.

"We all know how to make nuclear weapons," I said. "Even if we all agree that we are never going to use them, down the way there could be another Hitler who could end up with nuclear weapons."

Research on the SDI would probably take years, and the time could be used to complete and implement agreements phasing out nuclear weapons. Then I told him my story about gas masks and how after World War I the nations of the world promised never to use poison gas again in a war. "We went through World War II and nobody used poison gas—but we all kept our gas masks.

"Who knows what kind of madman might come along after we're gone? We live in a world where governments change; in your own country, there already have been four leaders during my term. I believe you mean it when you say you want peace, but there could be a change. It's the same thing on the other side: I think you know I want peace, but you also know I will not be in a position to personally keep the promises I've made to you. That's why we need insurance that our agreements eliminating nuclear weapons will be kept in the future.

"If you think I'm soft in the head in wanting to give the SDI technology, think of this: Suppose we were at the point of deploying the SDI system and we alone had it; our research is done but it is going to take months, maybe years, to deploy. We are also sitting with a great arsenal of nuclear weapons and the world knows it; we'd realize it might seem very tempting for them to push the button on their weapons before our defense is installed because of a fear we'd soon be able to blackmail the world.

"When the time comes to deploy SDI, the United States would have no rational choice but to avoid this situation by making the system available to all countries, so they know we wouldn't have the power to blackmail them. We're not being altruistic. There's a reason why we are willing to share this defense once we have it."

Gorbachev heard the translation of my remarks, but he wasn't listening.

He wouldn't budge from his position. He just sat there smiling and then he said he still didn't believe me when I said the United States would make the SDI available to other countries.

I was getting angrier and angrier.

I realized he had brought me to Iceland with one purpose: to kill the Strategic Defense Initiative. He must have known from the beginning he was going to bring it up at the last minute.

"The meeting is over," I said. "Let's go, George, we're leaving."

When we reached our cars before leaving Reykjavík, Gorbachev said, "I don't know what else I could have done." I said, "I do. You could have said yes." In my diary that night, I wrote,

> He wanted language that would have killed SDI. The price was high but I wouldn't sell and that's how the day ended. All our people thought I'd done exactly right. I'd pledged I wouldn't give away SDI and I didn't, but that meant no deal on any of the arms reductions. He tried to act jovial but I was mad and showed it. Well, the ball is now in his court and I'm convinced he'll come around when he sees how the world is reacting.

I was very disappointed—and *very* angry.

When I flew home to Washington, the reception I got showed the American people were behind me. They didn't want to surrender the SDI.

82

I N EARLY JUNE 1987, after the economic summit in Venice, Nancy and I flew to West Berlin where we were reminded again of the vast gulf between our system and that of the Communists. I was reminded of the Marshall Plan and how America spent billions after World War II helping rebuild the shattered economies of Europe, including those of two of our former enemies, and I wondered what other nation on earth would have done that. I saw an exhibit honoring the courageous pilots—three of whom I met—who had kept the city alive during the Berlin Airlift. And then I saw the Berlin Wall, as stark a symbol as anyone could ever expect to see of the contrast between two different political systems: on one side, people held captive by a failed and corrupt totalitarian government, on the other, freedom, enterprise, prosperity.

I had accepted an invitation to speak to an outdoor gathering at the Brandenburg Gate at the dividing line between West Berlin and East Berlin. Before it was my turn to speak, I met with my West German hosts in a government building not far from the wall. From the window, I could see the graffiti and prodemocracy slogans scrawled on liberty's side of the wall and, across the wall, a government building in East Berlin where I was told there was long-distance monitoring apparatus that could eavesdrop on our conversations.

"Watch what you say," one German official said. Well, when I heard that, I went out to a landing that was even closer to the building and began sounding off about what I thought of a government that penned in its people like farm animals.

I can't remember exactly what I said, but I may have used a little profanity in expressing my opinion of Communism, hoping I would be heard. (Because I wear a hearing aid, I'd been told in Washington I was even more vulnerable than other people to electronic eavesdropping. Hearing aids can be "bugged" by radio waves directed at them from afar and then repeat conversations taking place in the room; because of this, my hearing aid had gone through a special "debugging" process.)

From this building, we went to the Brandenburg Gate, where tens of thousands of Berliners were gathered. Because it contains thoughts I feel strongly about, I'm going to quote portions of the speech I gave that day, June 12, 1987:

> Behind me stands a wall that encircles the free sectors of this city, part of a vast system of barriers that divides the entire continent of Europe.
>
> From the Baltic, south, those barriers cut across Germany in a gash of barbed wire, concrete, dog runs, and guard towers. Farther south, there may be no visible, no obvious wall. But there remain armed guards and checkpoints all the same—still a restriction on the right to travel, still an instrument to impose upon ordinary men and women the will of a totalitarian state. Yet it is here in Berlin where the wall emerges most clearly; here, cutting across your city, where the news photo and the television screen have imprinted this brutal division of a continent upon the mind of the world. Standing before the Brandenburg Gate, every man is a German, separated from his fellow men. Every man is a Berliner, forced to look upon a scar. . . .
>
> As long as this gate is closed, as long as this scar of a wall is permitted to stand, it is not the German question alone that remains open, but the question of freedom for all mankind. Yet I do not come here to lament. For I find in Berlin a message of hope, even in the shadow of this wall, a message of triumph.
>
> In this season of spring in 1945, the people of Berlin emerged from their air-raid shelters to find devastation. Thousands of miles away, the people of the United States reached out to help. And in 1947 Secretary of State—as you've been told—George Marshall announced the creation of what would become known as the Marshall

Plan. Speaking precisely forty years ago this month, he said: "Our policy is directed not against any country or doctrine, but against hunger, poverty, desperation, and chaos."

. . . In the West, [the American dream of prosperity for all] became real. Japan rose from ruin to become an economic giant. Italy, France, Belgium—virtually every nation in Western Europe saw political and economic rebirth. . . . In West Germany and here in Berlin, there took place an economic miracle. . . . [Your] leaders understood the practical importance of liberty—that just as truth can flourish only when the journalist is given freedom of speech, so prosperity can come about only when the farmer and businessman enjoy economic freedom. The German leaders reduced tariffs, expanded free trade, lowered taxes. From 1950 to 1960 alone, the standard of living in West Germany and Berlin doubled.

Where four decades ago there was rubble, today in West Berlin there is the greatest industrial output of any city in Germany—busy office blocks, fine homes and apartments, proud avenues, and the spreading lawns of parkland. Where a city's culture seemed to have been destroyed, today there are two great universities, orchestras and an opera, countless theaters, and museums. Where there was want, today there's abundance—food, clothing, automobiles—the wonderful goods of the Ku'damm. From devastation, from utter ruin, you Berliners have, in freedom, rebuilt a city that once again ranks as one of the greatest on earth. . . .

In the 1950s, Khrushchev predicted: "We will bury you." But in the West today, we see a free world that has achieved a level of prosperity and well-being unprecedented in all human history. In the Communist world, we see failure, technological backwardness, declining standards of health, even want of the most basic kind—too little food. Even today, the Soviet Union still cannot feed itself. After these four decades, then, there stands before the entire world one great and inescapable conclusion: Freedom leads to prosperity. Freedom replaces the ancient hatreds among the nations with comity and peace. Freedom is the victor. And now the Soviets themselves may, in a limited way, be coming to understand the importance of freedom. We hear much from Moscow about a new policy of reform and openness. Some political prisoners have been released. Certain foreign news broadcasts are no longer being jammed. Some economic enterprises have been permitted to operate with greater freedom from state control.

Are these the beginnings of profound changes in the Soviet state? Or are they token gestures, intended to raise false hopes in the West, or to strengthen the Soviet system without changing it? We welcome change and openness; for we believe that freedom and security go together, that the advance of human liberty can only strengthen the cause of world peace. There is one sign the Soviets can make that would be unmistakable, that would advance dramatically the cause of freedom and peace.

Then I said:

General Secretary Gorbachev, if you seek peace, if you seek prosperity for the Soviet Union and Eastern Europe, if you seek liberalization: Come here to this gate! Mr. Gorbachev, open this gate! Mr. Gorbachev, tear down this wall!

Standing so near the Berlin Wall, seeing it in substance as well as for what it symbolized, I felt an anger well up in me, and I am sure this anger was reflected in my voice when I said those words.

I never dreamed that in less than three years the wall would come down and a six-thousand-pound section of it would be sent to me for my presidential library.

I tell the story of this speech here as a reminder that, with all the changes that have occurred in their nation and Eastern Europe since then, in the spring of 1987 we were still facing a lot of uncertainty regarding the Soviets: Gorbachev had announced his new programs of *perestroika* and *glasnost* and it was evident something was up in the Soviet Union, but we still didn't know what it was.

It would be more than a year after I walked out on Gorbachev at Reykjavík before the warming of U.S.-Soviet relations that began at Geneva would resume. But that is not to say important changes were not occurring in relations between our countries.

Despite a perception by some that the Reykjavík summit was a failure, I think history will show it was a major turning point in the quest for a safe and secure world.

During those ten hours of discussions among four men in a room overlooking the sea, we agreed on the basic terms for what fourteen months later would become the INF agreement—a treaty that for the first time in history provided for the elimination of an entire class of nuclear weapons; we created a framework for the START agreement to reduce long-range strategic missiles on each side as well as for agreements on reduction of chemical weapons and conventional forces, while preserving our right to develop the Strategic Defense Initiative.

In the same way that I think the Soviets returned to the negotiating table at Geneva only because we refused to halt deployment of NATO's intermediate-range missiles during the fall of 1983, I think Gorbachev was ready to talk the next time we met in Washington because we had walked out on him at Reykjavík and gone ahead with the SDI program.

But during those fourteen months, progress didn't come easily. Gorbachev continued his resistance to the SDI throughout 1987. And not all of the obstacles to continuing the momentum started at Geneva originated in Moscow.

The months following the Reykjavík summit were very busy: There was the Iran-Contra affair and various changes in the White House staff that followed it; there were more problems between Israel and its Arab neighbors; there were continuing battles with Congress over support for the Contras; there were attempts by Iran and Iraq to close the Persian Gulf to shipping, while we were determined to keep the sea lanes open; and there was the tragic attack by Iraqi planes on the USS *Stark*.

In Congress, there were new efforts by the Democrats to cut the military programs that were essential to continuing our policy of peace through strength that had brought the Soviets to the arms control table. And at the Pentagon, there were a few misgivings about my dream of a nuclear-free world. The Joint Chiefs of Staff, while behind our efforts to negotiate new arms control agreements, said that we would require nuclear missiles for the foreseeable future because of the need to offset the Soviet bloc's huge imbalance of conventional forces in Europe and an unwillingness by Congress to approve bigger budgets. (Among other realities of the nuclear age, the cost of maintaining nuclear deterrent forces is far less than the salary and upkeep for conventional armies.) Eventually, based on their advice, we proposed, instead of aiming for a fifty-percent cut in ICBMs over five years, that it should be seven years, and the Russians concurred.

Meanwhile, some of my more radical conservative supporters protested that in negotiating with the Russians I was plotting to trade away our country's future security. I assured them we wouldn't sign any agreements that placed us at a disadvantage, but still got lots of flak from them—many of whom, I was convinced, thought we had to prepare for nuclear war because it was "inevitable." (I sometimes wondered how *they* would have reacted to a visit to Chernobyl.) Cap Weinberger was strongly against the vision Gorbachev and I shared at Reykjavík calling for the elimination of all nuclear missiles. I told Cap I was going to push for it despite his opposition. But on one thing Cap and I did agree: Throughout that spring and summer, he and George Shultz still disagreed about how we should interpret the ABM treaty and about the pace at which we should develop and deploy—if it proved practical—the hardware produced in the Strategic Defensive Initiative. George continued favoring a narrow interpretation of the treaty, which would have disallowed the testing of certain components; he and Frank Carlucci, my new national security advisor, suggested Cap was overly optimistic in his projections about how soon scientists and engineers would be able to solve the technical problems involved in developing the SDI. I sided with Cap, deciding that our best policy was to stay tough, to proceed with research and testing of the SDI system, to determine if it would work, and, if it did, to begin deploying it in phases starting in 1993. I also thought we should stick to the broad (and entirely legal) interpretation of the treaty advocated by Cap, while still pushing for an agreement to ban nuclear weapons.

In Geneva, reaching agreement on the specific terms for the INF treaty had proved very difficult even though Gorbachev and I had agreed on the zero-zero concept. One obstacle, for example, involved West Germany: Helmut Kohl was worried that if NATO eliminated all INF weapons without a parallel increase in NATO conventional forces, West Germany might become too vulnerable to an invasion by the Warsaw Pact; the only remaining nuclear deterrent would be missiles with ranges of less than three hundred miles that, if used, because of their short range, would inevitably harm German citizens. He wanted to eliminate these short-range missiles, too. At the Venice economic summit, he and Margaret Thatcher argued for hours at one of our dinners over this issue; Margaret believed that if the INF missiles (whose range was from three hundred to thirty-three hundred miles) were removed from

Europe, missiles with ranges of less than three hundred miles had to remain in place because they would be all that remained to deter aggression against Western Europe by the Warsaw Pact countries. I sided with Helmut on this issue and agreed with him that the shorter-range missiles should go.

Then, Gorbachev placed another obstacle involving West Germany in the path of the INF treaty. His negotiators at Geneva said agreement on the treaty was contingent upon Kohl eliminating seventy-two older-model Pershing 1A missile launchers. I said we couldn't negotiate for a third country, but suggested privately to Helmut that he volunteer to eliminate these missiles in the interest of disarmament.

As the pages of the calendar were turning in 1987, so were the pages of history. We were seeing more and more evidence that Gorbachev was serious about introducing major economic and political reforms in the Soviet Union. There would be the first free elections in the Soviet Union; there was official encouragement to entrepreneurs to establish businesses in the Soviet Union; and, on the seventieth anniversary of the Russian Revolution, Gorbachev made a blistering attack on Stalin, opening the way for a new freedom to examine the Soviet past and its mistakes.

There were tentative indications that "quiet diplomacy" was working with Gorbachev: Although neither he nor I discussed it publicly, some of the people whose names were on the lists I'd given him of people who we knew wanted to leave the Soviet Union began receiving exit permits. In August, George Shultz woke me early one morning to tell me Vladimir Feltsman, the concert pianist whom Ron had met in Moscow, was in Vienna with his wife and child. A few weeks later Feltsman arrived in the United States and Nancy decided we should give him a send-off with a concert at the White House. I'll always remember the passion with which he played his first selection: It was "The Star-Spangled Banner," and, as you can imagine, there were plenty of tears in the East Room at that moment. A few days after that, I had another visitor: former Soviet high school physics teacher and poet Irina Ratushinskaya, author of the scribbled poem that had been smuggled to me in 1984 from the Soviet gulag where she was imprisoned for "anti-Soviet agitation and propaganda." She had been permitted to leave Russia. I discovered she was living in Chicago and invited her to the White House.

Although Soviet troops were still fighting in Afghanistan and the Soviets were still supporting guerrillas in Central America and elsewhere, we were at last seeing real deeds from Moscow.

Still, almost two years after Gorbachev had accepted my invitation to Washington, he was refusing to set a date for our next summit, largely because of the dispute over the SDI, which continued through the summer and into the fall of 1987. He kept insisting that we must surrender our right to conduct research on space-based missile defenses, and I kept insisting we wouldn't do that.

As the projected date for a summit kept sliding, some of the pundits began predicting there wouldn't be another U.S.-Soviet summit until I was out of office. But I felt that Gorbachev was serious about wanting a summit and that he was simply trying to hold out for all the concessions he could get. I suspect he thought the resistance of some Democrats in Congress to the Strategic Defense Initiative, as well as my problems during the Iran-Contra affair, might persuade me to buckle under to his demands on the SDI. But I knew we could afford to wait. Perhaps Gorbachev didn't realize that one of the surest ways to strengthen support for something in the United States was for a Soviet leader to attack it.

In mid-September, Foreign Minister Shevardnadze came to Washington for another discussion of the still-substantial hurdles that remained regarding the language and verification procedures for the INF treaty. He brought with him another letter to me from Gorbachev. Here are excerpts from it:

Dear Mr. President:

I think you and I were right when last October we arrived at what was virtually a concurring view that our meeting in Reykjavik had been an important landmark along the path toward specific and urgently needed measures to genuinely reduce nuclear arms. Over the past several months, the Soviet Union and the United States have made substantial headway in that direction. Today, our two countries stand on the threshold of an important agreement which would bring about—for the first time in history—an actual reduction in nuclear arsenals. Nuclear disarmament being the exceptionally complex mat-

687

ter that it is, the important thing is to take a first step, to clear the psychological barrier which stands between the deeply rooted idea that security hinges on nuclear weapons and an objective perception of the realities of the nuclear world. Then the conclusion is inevitable that genuine security can only be achieved through genuine disarmament.

We have come very close to that point, and the question is now whether we will take that first step which the peoples of the world are so eagerly awaiting. This is precisely what I would like to discuss at greater length in this letter, being fully aware that not too much time remains for the preparations for the agreement between us. The Reykjavik understandings gave us a chance to reach agreement. We are facing the dilemma of either rapidly completing an agreement on intermediate and shorter range missiles or missing the chance to reach an accord, which, as a result of joint efforts, has almost entirely taken shape. It would probably be superfluous to say that the Soviet Union prefers the first option. In addition to our basic commitment to the goal of abolishing nuclear weapons, which is the point of departure for our policy, we also proceed from the belief that at this juncture of time there appears to be a convergence of the lines of interest of the United States, the Soviet Union, Europe and the rest of the world. If we fail to take advantage of such a favorable confluence of circumstances, those lines will diverge, and who knows when they might converge again. Then we would risk losing time and momentum, with the inevitable consequences of the further militarization of the earth and the extension of the arms race into space. In this context, I agree with the thought you expressed that "the opportunity before us is too great to let pass by." To use an American phrase, the Soviet Union has gone its mile towards a fair agreement, and even more than a mile. Of course, I am far from asserting that the U.S. side has done nothing to advance the work on intermediate and shorter range missiles. We could not have come to the point when the treaty is within reach had the United States not made steps in our direction. And yet, there is still no answer to the question why Washington has hardened its stance in upholding a number of positions which are clearly one-sided and, I would say, contrived. I would ask you once again to weigh carefully all the factors involved and convey to me your final decision on whether the agreement is to be concluded now or postponed, or even set aside. It is time you and I took a firm stand on this matter.

I further request that you give further thought to the recent important evolution in our positions on intermediate and shorter range missiles, which in effect assures accord. We are ready to conclude an agreement under which neither the United States nor the Soviet Union would have any missiles in those categories.

I have to say that we are proposing to you a solution which in important aspects is virtually identical with proposals that were, at various points, put forward by the U.S. side. For that reason in particular, there should be no barriers to reaching an agreement, and the artificial obstacles erected by the U.S. delegation should naturally disappear, which, as I understand, will be facilitated by the decision of the FRG [Federal Republic of Germany] government not to modernize the West German Pershing 1A missiles and to eliminate them. Of course, we have no intention to interfere in U.S.-alliance relations, including those with the FRG. However, the question of what happens to the U.S. warheads intended for the West German missiles needs to be clarified. We are proposing fair and equitable terms for an agreement. Let me say very candidly and without diplomatic niceties: we have in effect opened up the reserves of our position in order to facilitate an agreement. Our position is clear and honest: we call for the total elimination of the entire class of missiles with ranges between 500 and 5500 kilometers and of all warheads for those missiles. The fate of an agreement on intermediate and shorter range missiles depends entirely on the U.S. leadership and on your personal willingness, Mr. President, to conclude a deal. As far as our approach, it will be constructive, you can count on that.

If we assume that the U.S. side, proceeding from considerations of equivalent security, will go ahead with the conclusion of the treaty— and this is what we hope is going to happen—then there is no doubt this will impart a strong impetus to bringing our positions closer together in a very real way on other questions in the nuclear and space area, which are even more important for the security of the USSR and the USA and with which you and I have come to grips after Reykjavik.

What I have in mind specifically are the issues of strategic offensive arms in space. Those are the key elements of security, and our stake in reaching agreement on them is certainly not at all diminished by the fact we have made headway on intermediate and short range missiles. What is more, it is this area that is pivotal to the U.S.-Soviet strategic relationship, and hence to the entire course of military-strategic developments in the world. At the negotiations in Geneva on those questions, the delegations, as you know, have started drafting an agreed text of a treaty on strategic offensive arms. The Soviet side is seeking to speed up, to the maximum possible extent, progress in this work and shows its readiness to accommodate the other side and to seek compromise solutions. To reach agreement, however, a reciprocal readiness for compromise is of course required on the part of the United States.

Things are not as good with regard to working out agreement on the ABM treaty regime, on preventing the extension of the arms race into space. Whereas we have submitted a constructive draft agreement that takes into account the U.S. attitude to the question of research on strategic defense, the U.S. side continues to take a rigid stand. However, without finding a mutually acceptable solution to the space problem it will be impossible to reach final agreement on radically reducing strategic offensive arms, which is what you and I spoke about in both Geneva and Reykjavik.

If we are to be guided by a desire to find a fair solution to both these organically interrelated problems, issues relating to space can be resolved. The Soviet Union is ready to make additional efforts to that end, but it is clear this cannot be done through our efforts alone, if attempts to secure unilateral advantages are not abandoned.

I propose, Mr. President, that necessary steps be taken, in Geneva and through other channels, particularly at a high level in order to speed up the pace of negotiations, so that full scale agreements could be reached within the next few months both on the radical reduction of strategic offensive arms and ensuring strict observance of the ABM treaty . . . if all those efforts were crowned with success, we would be able to provide a firm basis for a stable and forward-moving development not just of the Soviet-U.S. relationship but of international relations as a whole for many years ahead.

We would leave behind what was, frankly, a complicated stretch in world politics, and you and I would crown in a befitting manner the process of interaction on the central issues of security which began in Geneva. . . .

Does it not seem paradoxical to you, Mr. President, that we have been able to bring our positions substantially closer together in an area where the nerve knots of our security are located, and yet we have been unable so far to find a common language on another important aspect—namely, regional conflicts? Not only do they exacerbate the international situation, they often bring our relations to a pitch of high tension. In the meantime, in the regions concerned— whether in Asia, which is increasingly moving to the forefront of international politics, the Near East or Central America—encouraging changes are now under way, reflecting a search for a peaceful settlement. I have in mind, in particular, the growing desire for national reconciliation. This should be given careful attention and I believe encouragement and support. As you can see, the Soviet leadership once again reaffirms its strong intention to build Soviet-U.S. relations in a constructive and business-like spirit. Time may flow particularly fast for those relations, and we should treat it as something extremely precious. We are in favor of making full use of Eduard A. Shevardnadze's visit to Washington to find practical solutions to key problems. In the current situation, this visit assumes increased importance. Our Foreign Minister is ready for detailed discussions with U.S. leaders on all questions, including ways of reaching agreement on problems under discussion in Geneva and the prospects and possible options for developing contacts at the summit level. He has all necessary authority with regard to that. I want to emphasize, as before, I am personally in favor of actively pursuing a business-like and constructive dialogue with you.

Sincerely,
M. Gorbachev
September 15, 1987

Once again I told Shevardnadze to tell Gorbachev we weren't going to give in on the SDI. While we didn't solve all of our problems during his visit, I think it was a turning point. We kept alive the process of trying to improve relations and he and George Shultz signed an agreement establishing crisis centers in each country that were designated to reduce the danger of an accidental war between us. Moreover, there was a new atmosphere in our dealings with the Soviets. I commented in my diary after Shevardnadze left: "They were good meetings, free of the hostility we used to see even if we were disagreeing on some things."

As Gorbachev's letter indicated, our Geneva negotiators, with concurrence by West German leaders, were moving close to a compromise regarding Germany's older Pershing missiles. Over the next few weeks, the compromise, which was ultimately pivotal to reaching agreement on the INF treaty, was completed. Under the compromise, Germany's older Pershing missiles were excluded from the U.S.-Soviet agreement, but West Germany agreed to remove them once the agreement took effect—and we agreed to remove and destroy the U.S.-controlled nuclear warheads installed in these missiles.

Even after this compromise, Gorbachev refused to set a date for a summit. He was waiting me out, still expecting me, I suspect, to cave in on the SDI because of the continuing furor over the Iran-Contra affair.

I sent word to him through George Shultz that I wasn't budging on the SDI, and so the impasse continued into the first weeks of autumn.

83

O N OCTOBER 19, 1987, the stock market, after a record run-up, had the largest one-day collapse of prices since 1914. It was in many ways a crisis for the country. But I confess this was a period of time in which I was more concerned about the possibility of an even greater tragedy in my own life than I was about the stock market.

On a Monday afternoon early that month, Dr. John Hutton of the White House medical staff came to the Oval Office and told me he wanted to give me some news about Nancy: During one of her regular mammogram checkups at Bethesda, doctors had detected what appeared to be a possible tumor in her left breast; a biopsy was necessary to determine if it was malignant. If it *was* malignant, she would have to have an operation. Afterward, John told Nancy I reacted to the news with an expression he would never forget. "I think the president," he told her, "has always believed that nothing would ever happen to you."

He was right.

When I came up to the family quarters, I kissed Nancy and felt a tension in her body that I knew from long experience indicated she was very worried. "I wish I could erase the worry which she feels," I wrote that night in my diary.

But this was another one of those instances that reminded me of human limitations: For all the powers of the president of the United

States, there are some situations that made me feel helpless and very humble.

All I could do was pray—and I did a lot of praying for Nancy during the next few weeks.

The next ten days may have been the longest ten days of our lives. Nancy continued her full schedule of responsibilities, refusing to cancel commitments in her campaign against drugs and the foster grandparent program that were dear to her heart. While we waited it out, I had to battle Congress for approval of my nominee to the Supreme Court, Robert Bork, and then the stock market turned unusually volatile, prompting this comment in my diary October 16: "I'm concerned about the money supply. Has Fed been too tight? Alan [Greenspan, chairman of the Federal Reserve] doesn't agree and believes this is only an overdue correction." (In hindsight, I think the stock market crashed principally because it was simply overpriced; investors suddenly realized the prices were too high.)

The same night, I flew with Nancy to Bethesda, where she was bedded down on the eve of her surgery. I returned to the White House, but was restless much of the night. I got up at six the next morning to fly to the hospital, but heavy fog made it unsafe for the helicopter, so we had to drive and I was late; I got there only in time to kiss Nancy and watch her being wheeled on a gurney down a hallway into the operating room.

Nancy's brother, Dick, had come from Philadelphia to be with us, and the two of us tried to busy ourselves with newspapers to make the time pass, but it didn't work. Then, with no news, we adjourned to a small dining area and were eating breakfast when I looked up and saw John Hutton and Dr. Ollie Beahrs of the Mayo Clinic approach us.

Their faces telegraphed the news that they were about to give me:

Nancy had a malignancy and she and her doctors decided on a mastectomy.

I know how desperately Nancy had hoped this would not be the case and I couldn't reply to them. I just dropped my head and cried. After they left, I remained at the table, motionless and unable to speak. Then I felt an arm around my shoulders and heard a few quiet, comforting words. They were spoken by Paula Trivette, one of the four military nurses assigned to the White House and, like all of them, a warm and wonderful human being. With her words and her arm on my shoulder she was trying to comfort me. I learned later that John Hutton had suggested she do it; she stepped in and was truly an angel of mercy. I can't recall her exact words but they lifted me from the pit I was in and kept me out of it.

In the early afternoon, I was able to visit Nancy in the recovery room. She was asleep when Dick and I got there. Suddenly, as we were standing by her bed, there was a little movement of her body. Her eyes didn't open, but I heard a tiny voice say, "My breast is gone."

Barely conscious because of her anesthesia, Nancy somehow had sensed we were there. She was devastated by the loss of her breast —not because she was worried about herself, but because she was worried about me and how I would feel about her as a woman.

"It doesn't matter," I said. "I love *you.*" Then I leaned over and kissed her softly, and repeated that it made no difference to me. But seeing that sadness in her eyes, it was all I could do to avoid breaking up again.

Two days later, the stock market took its plunge. But stock market or no stock market, it was mainly Nancy, not Wall Street, I worried about—and, as thousands of letters and calls to the White House indicated, she was in the hearts and minds of many Americans during that period, too.

As ever, Nancy had been a brave woman.

The doctors had told her that she had two choices for the removal of the tumor: She could have a lumpectomy or a mastectomy. After listening to them, she chose a mastectomy because she realized she wouldn't be able to perform her duties as first lady if she had to undergo the radiation that would be required after a lumpectomy, and, at her age, she thought it was best.

Later, during talks to women about the importance of having mammograms, she would also tell them that this was a personal choice every woman had to make for herself.

Very soon, we learned Nancy would have to plumb the depths of her courage again.

I had just finished an interview with five foreign television reporters on October 26 when my secretary, Kathy Osborne, came into the office and said she had just been told by Elaine Crispen,

Nancy's press secretary, that Nancy's mother, Edith Davis, had died in Phoenix.

I canceled the rest of my schedule and took the elevator upstairs to see Nancy on what I knew would be a heartbreaking mission. Although she was making a good recovery, Nancy was still bedridden and weak from her surgery. On my way up to the family quarters, I saw Dr. Hutton and told him what had happened, and he went with me so he would be there when I broke the news to Nancy. She was talking to Ron when I came in but put the phone down when she saw us. Perhaps she had feared the worst.

It was extremely difficult for her because I have never known any family with such a close bond between mother and child as there was in Nancy's family. Nancy worshiped her mother and seldom a day passed when they did not talk on the phone. I worshiped her too. Like Nancy, she lit up a room when she walked into it. Deede was a remarkable, warm, and loving woman. From the time I met her, I could never tell another mother-in-law joke.

As I knew she would, Nancy took the news very hard.

At nine the next morning, we left for Phoenix. A half hour before we left, I had a conference call with George Shultz and others that I described this way in my diary:

"*The Soviets blinked.* Shevardnadze, speaking for Gorbachev, is arriving Thursday for meetings on INF and plans for the Summit."

Although it was obvious I would have to be in Washington during the next few days to meet with Shevardnadze now that the Soviets were ready to talk seriously about setting a date for the summit, I couldn't let Nancy make that sad trip to Phoenix alone, so I flew there with her, then returned to Washington later in the day.

After landing in Arizona, we drove first to the mortuary. Seeing her mother was too much for Nancy. She broke down sobbing and began speaking to her mother, telling her how much she loved her and how much she meant to her. I had never seen Nancy in such pain. I held her and said that her mother knew how she felt but that she was no longer with her body. While I am sure I comforted Nancy a little, nothing I could say or do could bring Deede back, and once again I felt helpless against the limitations imposed on all men: I was president of the United States but there was nothing I could do to bring happiness to my wife at a time when she desperately needed it. All I could do was stand beside her, hold her, pray, and try to soak up some of the pain she was feeling.

Then, after promising to return in three days for the funeral, I had to leave Nancy to deal with her grief alone, so that I could return to Washington for Shevardnadze's visit. When Nancy asked me to give a eulogy, I said: "I wanted to do that, but I didn't want to push myself."

Back in Washington, we cleared away the last obstacles to the INF treaty and then announced the date for the summit. This is a portion of the entry in my diary for October 30, 1987:

> Shevardnadze brought me a letter from Gorbachev. It was states-manlike and indicated a real desire for us to work out any differences. The outcome of the letter and meetings was a Summit to start here Dec. 7. Purpose to sign INF agreement and set in motion the START treaty to reduce ICBM's by 50 per cent and to finalize that at a summit in Moscow next spring. On that note of optimism we lifted off the South Lawn for Andrews Air Force Base . . . for Phoenix and Deede's funeral.

Everyone in the family came to the funeral in Phoenix except Patti. Her absence added to the hurt Nancy felt during this month of almost nonstop pain.

Although Nancy would never get over the loss of her mother, the funeral went a long way toward helping her deal with her grief—she saw how much so many people loved Deede, and I think she realized Deede had joined her husband in heaven.

Perhaps I considered the letter Shevardnadze had brought from Gorbachev "statesmanlike" because he had accepted our position on several key points: Although he said he wanted to discuss space defense (i.e., the SDI) in Washington, he dropped his insistence that we had to accept limits on SDI development as a prerequisite to signing the INF treaty, discussing the START treaty, or setting an agenda for our next summit in Moscow.

With the language of the INF treaty now settled, he said he hoped we could agree on the principles for the START agreement during his visit in Washington, then sign it when I came to Moscow. In addition, he appeared to back away from his previous insistence that the ABM treaty be strengthened, insisting only that it be observed and that we make a ten-year commitment not to withdraw from the treaty.

Mikhail and Raisa Gorbachev pulled up to the White House on the morning of December 8 in a large Russian-made limousine. After the customary welcoming ceremonies, he and I and our interpreters went to the Oval Office and, as I reflected later in the diary, had "a good rousing meeting." I brought up Soviet human rights abuses again: I said we were pleased that some Soviet Jews were being allowed to leave the Soviet Union, but felt more should be allowed to emigrate. As he had at Geneva and Reykjavík, Gorbachev bristled when he heard the translation of my remarks on Soviet human rights abuses.

He replied that he was not the accused standing in a dock and I was not a prosecutor, and that I had no right to bring up domestic matters of the Soviet Union. In fact, he said, a proposal then current in Washington to build a fence along the Mexican border was as bad as anything the Soviets had ever done.

I replied that the fence was meant to stop illegal immigration by people who wanted to join our society because it offered democratic and economic opportunities—that was hardly the same thing as building the Berlin Wall, which imprisoned people in a social system they didn't want to be part of.

"Americans have fewer human rights than the Soviet people," Gorbachev persisted. "What about your people who sleep in the streets and all your unemployed? Where are their human rights?"

"Yes," I said, "but are you aware that we have something in this country called unemployment insurance, that when a man loses his job, for a certain period of time he continues to receive payment?"

Gorbachev asked:

"What happens when he comes to the end of that period and still doesn't have a job?"

"Well," I said, "then we have another program. We call it welfare. They become eligible for that if they still can't get a job."

He'd never heard of unemployment or welfare benefits before.

We didn't come to any agreement on this issue, but I enjoyed the debate and I think he did, too. We agreed to disagree. After that, we signed the INF treaty. I was proud to be part of a genuinely historic moment, something I'd been striving for since 1981, and I was very happy.

Before the signing, Gorbachev and I each made brief remarks. "We can only hope," I said,

> that this history-making agreement will not be an end in itself but the beginning of a working relationship that will enable us to tackle the other urgent issues before us: strategic offensive nuclear weapons, the balance of conventional forces in Europe, the destructive and tragic regional conflicts that beset so many parts of our globe, and respect for the human and natural rights God has granted to all men.

Not only did the INF treaty provide for the elimination of an entire class of nuclear weapons, I said, it contained teeth to assure compliance. "We have listened to the wisdom of an old Russian maxim:

"*Dovorey no provorey*—trust, but verify."

"You repeat that at every meeting," Gorbachev said, to which I said, "I like it."

Gorbachev then made some remarks I agreed with:

> For everyone, and, above all, for our two great powers, the treaty whose text is on this table offers a big chance at last to get onto the road leading away from the threat of catastrophe. It is our duty to take full advantage of that chance and move together toward a nuclear-free world, which holds out for our children and grandchildren and for their children and grandchildren the promise of a fulfilling and happy life without fear and without a senseless waste of resources on weapons of destruction . . . may December 8, 1987, become a date that will be inscribed in the history books, a date that will mark the watershed separating the era of a mounting risk of nuclear war from the era of a demilitarization of human life.

Under the INF agreement, more than fifteen hundred deployed Soviet nuclear warheads would be removed and all Soviet ground-launched intermediate-range missiles in Europe, including the SS-20s, would be destroyed; on the U.S. side, all Pershing II and ground-launched cruise missiles, with some four hundred deployed warheads, would be destroyed, plus backup missiles on both sides.

As part of the agreement, each nation was permitted to make on-site inspections in the other country to verify compliance with the agreement.

It was the first time in history that any nations had ever agreed not only to stand down but to *destroy* nuclear missiles.

The next day, Gorbachev came back to the White House and we agreed that our next goal was to achieve a fifty-percent reduction of strategic missiles on both sides. On this "morning after," I think we both felt as if we'd participated in something important, and we relaxed a little. I told him I'd been collecting stories about the Russians; although there were quite a few I'd heard that I *couldn't* tell him, I told him one about an American and a Russian who were arguing about the respective merits of their countries. The American said, "Look, in my country I can walk into the Oval Office and I can pound on the president's desk and say, 'Mr. President, I don't like the way you are running the country,'" to which the Russian said, "I can do that, too." The American said, "You can?" and his friend said:

"Sure, I can go into the Kremlin and pound on the General Secretary's desk and say, 'Mr. General Secretary, I don't like the way President Reagan is running his country.'"

The interpreter translated the joke, and when he got to the punch line, Gorbachev howled.

Then I told him about an order that had gone out to traffic policemen in Moscow stating that, in the future, anyone caught speeding would be given a traffic ticket, no matter how important he might be. One day, I said, the General Secretary was leaving his home in the country and, discovering he was late for a meeting in the Kremlin, he told his driver: "Here, you get in the backseat and I'll drive."

Down the road, they passed two motorcycle policemen and one of them took after the car. A few minutes later, he rejoined the other policeman, who asked him, "Did you give him a ticket?"

"No," the traffic cop said.

"Why not? We were told that no matter who it was we were supposed to issue a ticket."

"No, this guy was too important," his friend said.

"Who was it?"

His friend said:

"I don't know. I couldn't recognize him, but his driver was Gorbachev."

He howled again.

During the remainder of his visit, our teams met literally around the clock and made substantial progress in defining the principles for the START agreement Gorbachev and I wanted to sign in Moscow in the spring, although we both knew serious problems remained, particularly the question of how sea-launched nuclear cruise missiles were to fit into the agreement. Among all nuclear missiles, they were the hardest to count and verify—from space, it was virtually impossible for satellites to determine whether a seaborne missile launcher would fire nuclear warheads or conventional warheads.

Just before noon the next day, Gorbachev returned a final time to the White House for more work on the START treaty. When this meeting was over and the two of us were walking to lunch, I told him there was one thing he could do that would go a long way toward improving U.S.-Soviet relations: He could end the shipment of Soviet military weapons to Nicaragua.

As we walked across the White House lawn under gray, threatening clouds that later turned to rain, Gorbachev told me he would do that.

Forty minutes behind schedule, the summit came to an end as Nancy and I said good-bye to the Gorbachevs under a light rain. "Well, at last it's over," I wrote in the diary that night. "They've departed and I think the whole thing was the best summit we've ever had with the Soviet Union."

84

On January 25, 1988, in my eighth State of the Union address, I said I hoped during my final year in office to complete the START agreement so that the Soviet Union and the United States could begin reducing the number of nuclear warheads we aimed at each other. We came close, but not close enough.

I thought the state of the union was pretty good that night and said so before a joint session of Congress: The country was strong, our economy prosperous, our spirits high.

Across the country, employment was at a record level; government spending, taxes, and inflation were falling; militarily, we were second to no nation on earth; and, above all, Americans felt good about their country and good about themselves.

Then, after pointing with pride to what Americans had accomplished, I took extra pride in pointing to one member of the audience: I thanked Nancy for what she had accomplished in her war against illegal drugs, but in my heart, I was really trying to say, "Thank you, Nancy, for *everything;* thank you for lighting up my life for almost forty years."

A few days before I gave the State of the Union speech, I read *Perestroika,* the book by Mikhail Gorbachev that outlined his goals for restructuring the Soviet economy.

Although he didn't describe it as such, it was a bill of particulars condemning the workings of Communism, and it was as damning as anything ever written about Communism in the West. It was an epitaph: Capitalism had triumphed over Communism.

The rapid changes we were then beginning to see in the domestic life of the Soviet Union under *perestroika* and *glasnost* were not the only developments that gave the Free World reason to feel optimistic at the start of 1988:

Gorbachev would soon announce his decision to pull out of Afghanistan after eight years of a brutal war. In Poland, a people stubbornly determined to rid itself of tyranny was rising up in a final historic upwelling of freedom that would mark the beginning of the end for the Soviet empire—and yes, it was an evil empire.

Before long, the Berlin Wall would crack and then crumble and the captive nations of Europe would enter a new era of freedom.

All around the world, in a reverse of what people once called the domino theory, the forces of Communism were in retreat; the world was saying, to paraphrase a onetime fellow traveler:

"We have seen the future, and it doesn't work."

In Nicaragua, despite the risky and shortsighted resistance of many in Congress to supporting the Contras, the Sandinistas had lost the battle for the soul of their country, and before many months would pass, freedom and democracy would prevail and the corrupt Sandinista *comandantes* in designer glasses would be thrown out of office.

In dozens of other countries, from Latin America to the Philippine Islands, there was a stunning renaissance of democracy and economic freedom. In 1981, fewer than a third of the people in the Americas were living under democracies. By 1988, this figure was ninety percent. Emulating our efforts to put more freedom in the free market, many democracies around the world were waging war on excess regulation, high taxes, and oversize and domineering central governments, unloosing economic forces for the good of all their citizens.

That's not to say there weren't still many problems in the world at the start of 1988.

While we were negotiating an agreement with the Soviets to reduce nuclear arms, the capability to produce nuclear weapons was continuing to spread to other countries—according to some reports, to Pakistan, Taiwan, Israel, and possibly other nations. China had entered the business of exporting missiles, offering nations the potential to send nuclear or chemical weapons over great distances.

In Panama, although we tried many different approaches over several months during the spring of 1988, I was unable to persuade Manuel Noriega to end his corrupt dictatorship peacefully. After I was gone, the situation continued to deteriorate. President Bush decided the safety of Americans living in Panama required us to help the people of Panama end his criminal rule and bring him to justice on drug charges in the United States. I agree wholeheartedly with what he did.

In 1988, the Middle East was as much a snake pit of problems as it was when I unpacked my bags in Washington in 1981.

Although our air attack on Libya had silenced some of the state-sponsored terrorism directed from Tripoli, the forces of radical Islamic fundamentalism were on the march there and elsewhere in the Middle East; Colonel Qaddafi had begun a crash program to develop chemical weapons to advance his revolution, with all that meant to a world that had good reason to worry about the next move by this unpredictable clown. The bloody Iran-Iraq war was still raging and, after Iran attacked U.S. vessels that were keeping the Persian Gulf open to lawful navigation, we had to respond in kind. Lebanon was more hopelessly mired than ever in the senseless, bloody, sectarian violence of civil war, and Israel and its Arab neighbors remained at each other's throats.

George Shultz worked hard through much of the spring of 1988 on a new effort to bring peace to the region by offering the help of the United States in arranging an international conference to deal with the Palestinian problem. But despite appeals from him and me, Israeli Prime Minister Yitzhak Shamir refused to join in the effort, while the PLO and some of its Arab allies became more uncompromising than ever. George was unable to bring the parties together, ending our last initiative at bringing peace to the area. My support of Israel was as strong as ever: On the fortieth anniversary of its founding we restated our pledge to its security, and I repeatedly assured Shamir of our support. At the same time, I was still trying to strengthen U.S. ties with the moderate Arab nations in the belief that their cooperation could help produce a lasting solution to the deep-seated problems in the region. But whenever I tried to implement a more evenhanded U.S. policy by meeting their requests for advanced arms, I was thwarted by the friends of Israel in Congress, and some of the Arab nations began turning to China and other countries for arms. The continuing construction of Israeli settlements in the occupied Arab territories and, later, Israel's stern efforts to suppress Arab uprisings in the territories made peace in the Middle East seem more remote than ever. For eight years, I gave high priority to bringing lasting peace to the Middle East, but in the end it eluded me, as it had eluded other American presidents before me.

Mikhail Gorbachev and I hoped to sign the START treaty when I went to Moscow in late May. Although our experts worked on it through the spring, they couldn't resolve the remaining questions, particularly those involving sea- and air-launched cruise missiles. The experts said they remained hopeful that the hurdles could be overcome before I left office, but we wouldn't be able to sign the START treaty in Moscow.

Nancy and I arrived in the Soviet Union on May 29, 1988. During a stopover in Finland, we learned that the Senate had overwhelmingly ratified the INF treaty after weeks of brinkmanship that made it uncertain Gorbachev and I could complete the ratification papers while I was in Moscow.

This was my first visit to the Soviet Union, but my fourth meeting with Gorbachev and perhaps the most memorable, partly because for the first time I also got to meet and shake hands with ordinary Soviet people.

At our first session alone, Gorbachev again expressed his desire for increased U.S.-Soviet trade. I was ready for him. I'd thought about what I was going to say when he brought up the issue: One reason we have trouble increasing trade with your country, I said, was that many members of Congress as well as many other Americans oppose it because of what they consider Soviet human rights abuses.

I brought up a thought that had been expressed to me in a letter from a recent immigrant to America: Americans, he said, come from every corner of the world, but once they are in America, they are assimilated in a way that is unique in the world. An immigrant can live in France, he said, but not become a Frenchman; he can live in Germany but not become a German; he can live in Japan but not become a Japanese; but anyone from any part of the world can come to America and become an American. "Our people have diverse backgrounds," I told Gorbachev, "but they are united when they see any people discriminated against simply because of their ethnic origin or religious belief." Then I raised an issue that had been on my mind for a long time: religious freedom in the Soviet Union. "This isn't something I'm suggesting we negotiate," I told him, "just an idea. I'm not trying to tell you how to run your country, but I realize you are probably concerned that if you allow too many of the Jews who want to emigrate from the Soviet Union to leave, there'll be a 'brain drain,' a loss of skilled people from your economy. [According to estimates I'd seen, something like four hundred thousand to five hundred thousand Jews wanted to leave the Soviet Union.] I can see where this could present problems. These people are part of your society and many of them must have important jobs. But did it ever occur to you, on this whole question of human rights, that maybe if these Jews were permitted to worship as they want to and teach their children the Hebrew language, that maybe they wouldn't want to leave the Soviet Union?

"That's how our country was started, by people who were not allowed to worship as they wished in their homeland, so they came to our shores, a wilderness across the Atlantic, and founded our nation. I'm sure a lot of your people who are asking to leave wouldn't want to leave if they had freedom of religion. They say they want to leave, but they're Russians. I know they must love their country as much as other Russians do, so perhaps if they were allowed to reopen their synagogues and worship as they want to, they might decide that they wouldn't have to leave and there wouldn't be that problem of a brain drain."

I said Americans were very encouraged by the changes occurring in the Soviet Union and hoped the changes would soon be institutionalized as laws under the Soviet system. And, for all the changes that Gorbachev had made, I said, wouldn't it be a good idea to tear down the Berlin Wall? Nothing in the West symbolized the differences between it and the Soviet Union more than the wall, I said; its removal would be seen as a gesture symbolizing that the Soviet Union wanted to join the broader community of nations.

Well, Gorbachev listened and seemed to take in my opinions;

from his expression I knew he didn't like some of the things I was saying, but he didn't try to say anything harsh in rebuttal. Whether my words had any impact or not I don't know, but after that the Soviet government began allowing more churches and synagogues to reopen and, of course, in time, the wall came tumbling down.

Looking back now, it's clear that there was a chemistry between Gorbachev and me that produced something very close to a friendship. He was a tough, hard bargainer. He was a Russian patriot who loved his country. We could—and did—debate from opposite sides of the ideological spectrum. But there was a chemistry that kept our conversations on a man-to-man basis, without hate or hostility. I liked Gorbachev even though he was a dedicated Communist and I was a confirmed capitalist. But he was different from the Communists who had preceded him to the top of the Kremlin hierarchy. Before him, every one had vowed to pursue the Marxist commitment to a one-world Communist state; he was the first not to push Soviet expansionism, the first to agree to destroy nuclear weapons, the first to suggest a free market and to support open elections and freedom of expression.

When Gorbachev came into power in March 1985, I believe, he would have continued on the same path as his predecessors *if* Communism had been working, but it wasn't.

When I met him the first time in the fall of that year, he made it plain he believed wholeheartedly in the Communist system of government. I inferred from his remarks that he thought Communism had been managed poorly and it was his intention to change its management.

I can only speculate as to why he ultimately decided to abandon many of the fundamental tenets of Communism along with the empire that Joe Stalin had seized in Eastern Europe at the end of World War II.

Perhaps the metamorphosis started when he was still a young man, working his way up the inefficient and corrupt Communist bureaucracy and witnessing the brutality of the Stalin regime. Then, I think that when he reached the top of the hierarchy he discovered how bad things really were and realized that he had to make changes in a hurry, before there was so much chaos in the Soviet Union nothing would be worth saving.

From my own experience, I know there are some aspects about governing a nation you can't fully appreciate until you actually have your hands on the controls, and I think he probably discovered that, too. Perhaps it took something like discovering that the three percent of Soviet agricultural land cultivated by private, profit-making farmers produced forty percent of the meat in his country. Perhaps the robust recovery of the American and Western European economies following the recession of the early eighties— while the Communist economies went nowhere—convinced him that the central planning and bureaucratic control of the Soviet economy, as he wrote in *Perestroika,* sapped the people's incentive to produce and excel.

Seventy years of Communism had bankrupted the Soviet Union economically and spiritually. Gorbachev must have realized it could no longer support or control Stalin's totalitarian colonial empire; the survival of the Soviet Union was more important to him. He must have looked at the economic disaster his country was facing and concluded that it couldn't continue spending so much of its wealth on weapons and an arms race that—as I told him at Geneva —we would never let his country win. I'm convinced the tragedy at Chernobyl a year after Gorbachev took office also affected him and made him try harder to resolve Soviet differences with the West. And I think in our meetings I might have helped him understand why we considered the Soviet Union and its policy of expansionism a threat to us. I might have helped him see that the Soviet Union had less to fear from the West than he thought, and that the Soviet empire in Eastern Europe wasn't needed for the security of the Soviet Union.

Whatever his reasons, Gorbachev had the intelligence to admit Communism was not working, the courage to battle for change, and, ultimately, the wisdom to introduce the beginnings of democracy, individual freedom, and free enterprise.

As I said at the Brandenburg Gate in 1987, the Soviet Union faced a choice: Either it made fundamental changes or it became obsolete.

Gorbachev saw the handwriting on the Wall and opted for change.

· · ·

During our first session at the Moscow summit, he and I pledged again to do our best during my last months in office to complete the START treaty and parallel agreements to reduce chemical weapons and conventional forces in Europe, although I emphasized that no agreement on long-range missiles was possible until the Soviets dismantled the huge radar installation they were building at Krasnoyarsk in violation of the ABM treaty. Despite our differences, it was not a contentious meeting. Even though I raised my pet concerns about human rights and religious freedom, Gorbachev didn't bristle as he had in the past. "It was a good session and a nice way to launch the summit," I wrote that evening in my diary.

After my session with Gorbachev, Nancy and I wanted to go out on the streets of Moscow and meet some Muscovites. Our son Ron had told us about Arbat Street, which was lined with shops and artists displaying their work. "It was amazing how quickly the street was jammed curb to curb with people—warm, friendly people who couldn't have been more affectionate," I wrote later in my diary. "In addition to our Secret Service, the KGB was on hand, and I've never seen such brutal manhandling as they did on their own people who were in no way getting out of hand." Boy, what a reminder that I was in a Communist country; *perestroika* or not, some things hadn't changed.

But perhaps the deepest impression I had during this experience and other meetings with Soviet citizens was that they were generally indistinguishable from people I had seen all my life on countless streets in America. They were simply ordinary people who longed, I am sure, for the same things that Americans did: peace, love, security, a better life for themselves and their children. On the streets of Moscow, looking into thousands of faces, I was reminded once again that it's not people who make war, but governments— and people deserve governments that fight for peace in the nuclear age.

The following day, during another meeting with Gorbachev, we agreed that we had both begun our relationship with misconceptions about the other, and that it had taken these one-on-one sessions to build trust and understanding. That, I thought to myself, was what I'd been trying to do since I sent my first letter to Brezhnev in 1981 a few weeks after I was shot.

That evening, the Gorbachevs invited us to dinner at their home in the wooded countryside outside Moscow. For a description of that evening, I'll rely on a memo written to me by Secretary Shultz:

Memorandum for: The President

From: George P. Shultz

While the memory is still fresh, I want to record for you my thoughts on the remarkable evening you, Nancy, O'Bie, and I had with the Gorbachevs and Shevardnadzes. The dinner at the Tsarist palace they styled a dacha was an historic occasion between our two countries and deserves to be recorded for posterity.

My first impression was of the liveliness of the conversation and the easy conviviality of the evening. Gorbachev seemed determined to match you joke for joke and even Raisa told a couple to spice up the conversation. There were hardly any lingering signs of rancor from the tough conversation of the morning or of any desire to return to old arguments. Indeed, the Gorbachevs and Shevardnadzes went out of their way to make it a pleasurable evening. It appeared they would have been happy to prolong it even longer than they did.

I was struck by how deeply affected Gorbachev appeared to be by the Chernobyl accident. He commented that it was a great tragedy which cost the Soviet Union billions of rubles and had only been barely overcome through the tireless efforts of an enormous number of people. Gorbachev noted with seemingly genuine horror the devastation that would occur if nuclear power plants became targets in a conventional war much less a full nuclear exchange. Gorbachev agreed that Chernobyl was a "Final Warning" as Dr. [Robert] Gale had called it in his book. It was obvious from that evening that Chernobyl has left a strong anti-nuclear streak in Gorbachev's thinking.

Gorbachev showed open pride in your accomplishments together, mentioning that the INF treaty was an accomplishment for the entire world. While the Gorbachevs commented on the good press coverage of the Moscow Summit in our two countries and around the world, they betrayed some frustration at Western media stories on them personally. Gorbachev registered an interest in more discussions with us on regional issues, and his joke about dressing a Brazilian soccer team like Georgians so their Armenian opponents would get fired up was an ironic reference to his major nationality problems at home.

Finally, both the Gorbachevs revealed something of themselves during the evening. Evidently true lovers of the ballet, they recalled fondly how they had watched standing from the upper balconies in their student days. Gorbachev noted that his only two connections with religion had been his baptism which he could not remember and a recent meeting with Soviet church leaders. His comment that he had never used his law degree brought out a strong defense of his successes in life from Raisa. She also remarked to you on the responsibilities and burdens of leadership. Both expressed a confident sense of national pride in their descriptions of the variety of the Soviet Union, remarks which came across to me as genuine and not overbearing.

In sum, Mr. President, the evening was a fitting climax to your four summits with General Secretary Gorbachev. O'Bie and I were honored to take part.

There were many high points of our visit to Moscow, one of them being when I stopped the car so Nancy and I could take a walk in Red Square at midnight, on the way back from dinner at the Gorbachevs' dacha. Gorbachev and I had been there earlier in the day, when we chatted informally with a group of Muscovites, and I was so taken with it that I wanted to take Nancy there. Another high point was a night at the Bolshoi Ballet with the Gorbachevs. From the moment we walked into that famous hall, we were overwhelmed by its beauty. Resplendent in gold and red, richly detailed and elegant, the magnificence of the hall was surpassed only by the grace and elegance of the dancers. I knew the world was changing when we stood with the Gorbachevs in our box, with the Soviet flag on one side and ours on the other, and "The Star-Spangled Banner" was played. To hear that song, which embodies everything our country stands for, so stirringly played by a Soviet orchestra, was an emotional moment that is indescribable. Around us were our respective teams of advisors, experts and aides —but for a few moments, at least, official business was far from our minds as we were treated to a performance by one of the world's truly great cultural institutions.

After we returned to Washington, I sent a letter to Gorbachev thanking him for his hospitality and expressing pleasure at the evolution of our relationship. In his reply, Gorbachev agreed: "Indeed, along with significant political results, our meetings in Moscow have been given an encouraging human dimension—not only in terms of our personal liking for each other, but also in terms of warmer relations between our peoples and their more correct perception of each other. The importance of all this transcends even the U.S.-Soviet dialogue."

85

F OR MORE THAN THIRTY YEARS, I'd been preaching about freedom and liberty. During my visit to Moscow, I was given a chance to do something I never dreamed I would do: Gorbachev let me lecture to some of the brightest young people of Moscow—among them some of the future leaders of the Soviet Union—about the blessings of democracy and individual freedom and free enterprise.

On what was for me an extraordinary day I never thought possible, I tried in a few minutes at Moscow State University to summarize a philosophy that had guided me most of my life.

Many countries of the world, I said, had constitutions, but in almost every case they were documents in which governments told their people what they could do. The United States had a constitution, I said, that was different from all the others because in it the people tell their government what *it* can do. Its three most important words are "We the people," its most important principle, freedom. Then I said something about the great economic engine that had made America what it was.

"The explorers of the modern era," I told the students,

are the entrepreneurs, men with vision, with the courage to take risks and faith enough to brave the unknown. These entrepreneurs and their small enterprises are responsible for almost all the economic growth in the United States. They are the prime movers of the technological revolution. In fact, one of the largest personal computer firms in the United States was started by two college students, no older than you, in the garage behind their home. Some people, even in my own country, look at the riot of experiment that is the free market and see only waste. What of all the entrepreneurs that fail? Well, many do, particularly the successful ones; often several times. And if you ask them the secret of their success, they'll tell you it's all that they learned in their struggles along the way; yes, it's what they learned from failing. Like an athlete in competition or a scholar in pursuit of the truth, experience is the greatest teacher. And that's why it's so hard for government planners, no matter how sophisticated, to ever substitute for millions of individuals working night and day to make their dreams come true. . . .

We Americans make no secret of our belief in freedom. In fact, it's something of a national pastime. . . . Freedom is the right to question and change the established way of doing things. It is the continuing revolution of the marketplace. It is the understanding that allows us to recognize shortcomings and seek solutions. It is the right to put forth an idea, scoffed at by the experts, and watch it catch fire among the people. It is the right to dream—to follow your dream or stick to your conscience, even if you're the only one in a sea of doubters.

Freedom is the recognition that no single person, no single authority or government has a monopoly on the truth, but that every individual life is infinitely precious, that every one of us put on this world has been put there for a reason and has something to offer. . . .

Your generation is living in one of the most exciting, hopeful times in Soviet history. It is a time when the first breath of freedom stirs the air and the heart beats to the accelerated rhythm of hope, when the accumulated spiritual energies of a long silence yearn to break free. I am reminded of the famous passage near the end of Gogol's *Dead Souls*. Comparing his nation to a speeding troika, Gogol asks what will be its destination. But he writes, "There was no answer save the bell pouring forth marvelous sound."

We do not know what the conclusion will be of this journey, but we're hopeful that the promise of reform will be fulfilled. In this Moscow spring, this May 1988, we may be allowed that hope: that freedom, like the fresh green sapling planted over Tolstoi's grave, will blossom forth at last in the rich fertile soil of your people and culture. We may be allowed to hope that the marvelous sound of a new openness will keep rising through, ringing through, leading to a new world of reconciliation, friendship, and peace.

One of my regrets as president is that I was never able to take Mikhail Gorbachev on a trip across our country: I wanted to take him up in a helicopter and show him how Americans lived.

"You choose the route," I was going to say. "I don't want you to think we're showing you a Potemkin Village. We'll go where you want to go . . ."

Then, from the air I would have pointed out an ordinary factory and showed him its parking lot filled with workers' cars, then we'd fly over a residential neighborhood and I'd tell him that's where those workers lived—in homes with lawns and backyards, perhaps with a second car or a boat in the driveway, not the concrete rabbit warrens I'd seen in Moscow—and say:

"They not only live there, they *own* that property."

I even dreamed of landing the helicopter in one of those neighborhoods and inviting Gorbachev to walk down the street with me, and I'd say, "Pick any home you want; we'll knock on the door and you can ask the people how they live and what they think of our system."

The greatness of America, of course, doesn't lie in its houses and cars and material riches.

Democracy triumphed in the cold war because it was a battle of values—between one system that gave preeminence to the state and another that gave preeminence to the individual and freedom.

Not long ago, I was told about an incident that illustrated this difference: An American scholar, on his way to the airport before a flight to the Soviet Union, got into a conversation with his cab driver, a young man who said that he was still getting his education. The scholar asked, "When you finish your schooling, what do you want to be, what do you want to do?" The young man answered, "I haven't decided yet." After the scholar arrived at the airport in Moscow, his cab driver was also a young man who happened to mention he was still getting his education, and the scholar, who spoke Russian, asked, "When you finish your schooling, what do you want to be, what do you want to do?" The young man answered: "They haven't told me yet."

The battle of ideas and values between East and West isn't over —far from it. In dealing with the Soviet Union, we must remain vigilant and strong. I'll say it one more time: "*Dovorey no provorey* —trust, but verify."

There will be bumps in the road. But after talking with these bright young people in Moscow and seeing what was happening in their country, I couldn't help but feel optimistic: We were at the threshold of a new era in the political and economic history of the world.

I can't wait to see where it will lead us.

After my trip to Moscow, our teams continued work on the START treaty, but there were too many mountains to climb—not only the complex problems of reaching agreement on how to verify cutbacks in sea-launched and other missiles but the continuing refusal of the Soviet Union to destroy the huge radar station it was building at Krasnoyarsk, twenty-one hundred miles east of Moscow.

By early September, four months before I was scheduled to move out of the White House, it had become apparent that we weren't going to resolve the remaining problems on the START agreement before I left office. Gorbachev sent me a letter that expressed his regrets and looked back on the journey the two of us had traveled together:

Dear Mr. President:

I take advantage of the visit by Minister of Foreign Affairs Eduard A. Shevardnadze to Washington in order to continue our private discussions.

In one of our conversations in Moscow, it was suggested that we might have a chance to meet once again this year to sign a treaty on drastic reductions in strategic offensive arms in the context of compliance with the ABM treaty. Regrettably, this goal that both of us share has been set back in time, although I continue to think it can still be attained, even if beyond this year.

I take some consolation in the awareness that still in effect is our agreement to do the utmost in the remaining months of your presidency to insure the continuity and consistency of the fundamental course that we have chosen. As I recall, you said you would do your best to preserve the constructive spirit of our dialogue, and I replied that in that respect our intentions were quite identical. And so they are indeed, which is a source of great hope for our two peoples.

Four months have gone by since the summit talks in Moscow—a short period of time given the dynamic and profound developments in international affairs and those that fill the political calendar in the Soviet Union and the United States. Still, a great deal has been accomplished in putting into effect the jointly agreed platform for the further advancement of Soviet-U.S. relations. For the first time in history, nuclear missiles have been destroyed . . . nuclear disarmament is becoming an established and routine practice.

In several regions of the world, a process of political settlement of conflicts and national reconciliation has got under way. The human dimension of our relations, to which we have agreed to give special attention, is becoming richer. Ordinary Soviet people continue to discover America for themselves, marching across it on a peace walk, and right now, as you are reading this letter, another public meeting between Soviet and U.S. citizens is being held in Tbilisi.

Someone might object that in the past, say in the 1930's or 1970's, Soviet-U.S. relations also had their upturns. I would think, however, that the current stage in our interaction is distinguished by several significant features. The four summit meetings over the past three years have laid good ground work for our dialogue and raised it to a qualitatively new level. And, as you know, from high ground it is easier to see the path we have covered, the problems of the day, and the prospects that emerge.

A unique arrangement for practical interaction has been established, which is supported by fundamental political affirmations and, at the same time, filled with tangible content. This has been facilitated by the principal approach on which we agreed already in Geneva, i.e. realism, a clearer awareness of the essence of our differences, and a focus on active search for possible areas where our national interests may coincide. Thus, we gave ourselves a serious intellectual challenge —to view our differences and diversities not as a reason for permanent confrontation but as a motivation for intensive dialogue, mutual appreciation and enrichment.

Overall, we have been able to achieve fairly good results, to start a transition from confrontation to a policy of accommodation. And this is, probably, not just a result of a frank and constructive personal relationship, although obviously personal rapport is not the least important thing in politics. Paraphrasing a favorite phrase of yours, I would say that talking to each other, people learn more about each other.

And yet, the main thing that made our common new policy a success is, above all, the fact that it reflects a gradually emerging balance of national interests, which we have been able in some measure to implement. We feel, in particular, that it is favorable to the development of new approaches, of new political thinking, first of all in our two countries—but also elsewhere. The experience of even the past few months indicates that increasing numbers of third world countries are beginning to readjust to our positive interactions, associating with it their interest and policies.

Ironic as it may sound, it is our view that the strength of what we have been able to accomplish owes quite a lot to how hard it was to do.

It is probably not by a mere chance that the jointly devised general course in the development of Soviet-U.S. relations is now enjoying broad based support in our two countries. So far, as we know, both of your possible successors support, among other things, the key objectives of concluding a treaty on 50 per cent cutbacks in Soviet and U.S. strategic arsenals. In the Soviet leadership, too, there is a consensus on this. And yet, it has not been possible to bring the Geneva negotiations to fruition, a fact about which I feel some unhappiness. It is our impression we have to tango alone, as if our partner has taken a break.

In another letter to you, I have already addressed the matter which you raised in your letter of August 12 regarding compliance with the ABM treaty. I think you would agree with me that it would be unforgivable if our mutual complaints of violations of the ABM treaty resulted in undermining what we have been able to accomplish to rectify Soviet-U.S. relations through the efforts of both sides. I would like Eduard Shevardnadze's visit to the United States and his talks with you and Secretary Shultz to result in reviving truly joint efforts to achieve deep cuts in strategic offensive arms. Our minister has the authority to seek rapid progress on the basis of reciprocity in this exceptionally important area.

Today, the process of nuclear disarmament is objectively interrelated with the issues of deep reductions, and the elimination of asymmetries in imbalances in conventional arms and complete prohibition of chemical weapons. In these areas, too, there is a good chance of making headway toward agreements.

I am confident, Mr. President, that you and I can make a further contribution to the emerging process of settlement of regional conflicts, particularly to a consistent and honest compliance with the first accords that have already been concluded there.

In Moscow we also reinforced the foundation for a dynamic development of our bilateral relations and helped to open up new channels for communication between Soviet and American people, including young people and artists. All these good endeavors should be given practical effect, and we stand ready to do so. I am aware of your deep personal interest in questions of human rights. For me, too, it is a priority issue. We seem to have agreed that these problems require an in-depth consideration and a clear understanding of the true situation in both the United States and the Soviet Union. Traffic along this two-way street has begun and I hope that it will be intense.

Our relationship is a dynamic stream and you and I are working together to widen it. A stream cannot be slowed down, it can only be blocked or diverted. But that would not be in our interests. Politics, of course, is the art of the possible. But it is only by working and maintaining a dynamic dialogue that we will put into effect what we have made possible, and will make possible tomorrow what is yet impossible today.

Sincerely,
Mikhail Gorbachev
September 20, 1988

A year later, Gorbachev announced that the Krasnoyarsk radar station would be dismantled. A month after that, Foreign Minister Shevardnadze, in a public apology, said the facility, an earth station "equal in size to the Egyptian pyramids," represented, "to put it bluntly, a violation of the ABM treaty," and in the same speech, he apologized for the Soviet invasion of Afghanistan.

That fall, I went back on the campaign trail—this time, stumping the nation for George Bush and Dan Quayle. I wanted to do all I could to see that the policies we'd set in motion in 1981 would continue. During the primaries, I'd had to follow the Eleventh Commandment and remain neutral. But once George won the nomination, I did all I could to help him get elected. I knew George would be a great president.

After the Moscow summit, I saw Gorbachev one more time while I was president.

In December 1988—less than six weeks before Nancy and I were to leave the White House—he came to New York to make a speech to the United Nations at which he announced substantial cuts in the conventional forces of the Warsaw Pact.

Since I had last seen him, there had been more signs of change in the Soviet Union and its disintegrating empire: What had started as a trickle of refuseniks allowed to leave the Soviet Union was becoming a stream; the relentless Soviet expansionism in the Third World seemed to be waning; Cuba, under a U.S.-mediated settlement and apparently under pressure from Moscow, had agreed to remove its troops from Angola; Vietnam would soon begin pulling its forces from Cambodia; Moscow was no longer bankrolling the insatiable appetite of Syria's Hafez Assad for Soviet arms and had stopped jamming the broadcasts of Radio Liberty and Radio Free Europe.

When Gorbachev came to New York, I was concerned for his safety.

Soviet officials had expressed concern that if he visited the United States there might be an attempt on his life from the streets of New York.

Before we could respond and say Gorbachev was looked on favorably by most Americans and we didn't think he faced a danger in our country, we were told their concern was based not on fears that an American would try to assassinate him, but that while he was out of the Soviet Union there would be a coup attempt in Moscow—and as part of it, someone from the Eastern bloc would try to kill him and make it look as if an American had done it. I do not know to what extent the Soviet concern was warranted, but it didn't take a great deal of logic to imagine that Gorbachev had enemies in the Communist world. Our security people were put on alert, but as far as I know no attempts were made on Gorbachev's life while he was in New York. I've still worried about him: How hard and fast can he push his reforms without risking his life?

After our reunion in New York, I wrote this in my diary: "The meeting was a tremendous success. A better attitude than at any of our previous meetings. Gorbachev sounded as if he saw us as partners making a better world."

Gorbachev, George Bush, and I met privately with our interpreters on Governors Island in New York Harbor, then joined a small group of officials from both countries for lunch, where I enjoyed watching, now almost an outsider, as Gorbachev and George started to get to know each other. I felt good about it: They seemed to have a rapport that encouraged optimism for the future.

In fact, after another year and a half of hard negotiations, they would come to terms on a number of agreements, including the first phase of the START treaty based on the principles Gorbachev,

George Shultz, Eduard Shevardnadze, and I worked out in 1986 in that room overlooking the sea in Reykjavík.

At one point during lunch, Gorbachev mentioned that George Bush had been a navy flier and George Shultz, who was also there, had been a marine. He joked that he felt outnumbered by American military men. He hadn't mentioned me, so I said, "Just a minute here, you've been dealing with one all the time," and he laughed.

Then the three of us went down to the waterfront where George and I showed Gorbachev the Statue of Liberty and the New York City skyline. George then left us alone and Gorbachev and I went down to a dock to say our good-byes.

We recalled some of the things that we'd said during our first meeting at Geneva about the importance of building trust between our countries and agreed that we had come a long way since then.

Gorbachev said he regretted that I couldn't stay on and finish the job, and I have to admit there was a part of me that wanted to do that. But I had enormous faith in George Bush, and I knew the country was in good hands.

The next five weeks passed quickly—lots of packing, my farewell address, a succession of parties, and various final decisions.

Despite appeals from their supporters, and despite my own sympathies, I reaffirmed my decision not to give presidential pardons to John Poindexter, Bud McFarlane, and Oliver North. I still felt the law had to be allowed to take its course.

This was an especially emotional time for Nancy and me. For eight years, the White House had been our home. From around the nation, members of the White House staff and others in the administration had come to Washington to be part of our team, and we had become like a family. Now it was time to move on and we all felt sadness about it.

I've always thought of the presidency as an institution of which presidents are granted only temporary custody; now my custody was coming to an end and the hardest part was having to say goodbye to those who had helped me carry out my responsibilities and had always been there to help us in difficult personal times.

During the final week, many of these talented and hard-working people came to the East Room for one final good-bye. Nancy tried to thank everyone for a lovely enameled box that had been given to her, but couldn't get through. I managed a little better, but not much. As I looked into the faces of those gathered there, I couldn't help but think about what they had sacrificed on our behalf. So many late nights in the office, so many weekends at work away from home, pagers going off at all hours, meals skipped, telephone calls in the middle of the night, vacations abruptly canceled, toddlers' birthday parties missed, and so much more. In the eight years, we had experienced virtually all of life's highs and lows. We had been through it all together, and now it was time to say good-bye. How I wanted to say to each one how deeply Nancy and I appreciated them and how much their work had meant to us. We tried to do some of that as we left the East Room, but when the band started playing "Auld Lang Syne" we couldn't say much of anything.

On January 20, I got up earlier than usual and did some last-minute puttering in my study, then went over to the Oval Office.

Alone in the office, I wrote a note to George Bush and stuck it in the top drawer of the desk that in a few hours would become his. I wrote the note on a little pad of paper with a printed heading: DON'T LET THE TURKEYS GET YOU DOWN. It said:

Dear George

You'll have moments when you want to use this particular stationery. Well, go for it.

George, I treasure the memories we share and wish you all the very best. You'll be in my prayers. God bless you and Barbara. I'll miss our Thursday lunches.

Ron

All the members of my staff had submitted their resignations effective January 19, so I didn't expect anyone else to come into the Oval Office that morning. But Ken Duberstein, who had replaced Howard Baker as my chief of staff, came in at our regular meeting time, and so did my national security advisor, Colin Powell, who gave me my last national security briefing:

"Mr. President," he said, "the world is quiet today."

As he had so many times over the eight years, Mark Weinberg of the press office then brought in a group of photographers for one last photo.

They left, and I was alone again in the Oval Office. I got up and started to walk out. When I was halfway through the door, I turned around and took one last look at the Oval Office. Then I was gone.

I walked back to the family quarters, where soon it was time for Nancy and me to say good-bye to the White House staff who had looked after us for eight years, everyone from the ushers and gardeners to the plumbers and chefs.

A few minutes later, George and Barbara Bush and Dan and Marilyn Quayle arrived at the White House, along with the congressional leaders who were going to escort us to the inauguration.

At eleven, we left for the Capitol and a ride up Pennsylvania Avenue. At noon, George Bush was inaugurated as the forty-first president of the United States. After he finished his inaugural address and our part in the ceremonies was over, George and Barbara walked Nancy and me under the great dome of the Capitol to where a helicopter was waiting east of the building. And from there we headed home.

Epilogue

The helicopter door closed and we lifted off. Without telling us he was going to do it, the pilot made a turn and circled the Capitol. Beneath us was the spectacular panorama that had been our neighborhood: the Washington Monument, the Lincoln and Jefferson memorials, and now the bands and floats of the inaugural parade —and, everywhere on this day, huge crowds. Everything pointed to the marvel of our system of government and the ease with which it exercised the peaceful transition of power.

But then the pilot reduced the circle and took us lower. We were circling the White House. There it was, complete with its sweep of green lawn and sparkling fountains. I said: "Look, honey, there's our little shack."

I find it hard to describe my feeling. It was entirely different from the way it was back in those days when I'd looked on the building with such a feeling of awe. Now I was looking at what had been our home for eight years. We were familiar with every room and hallway and had the warmest memories of our life in that beautiful, historic mansion. Now we were saying good-bye. We kept looking back until it was out of sight. As we came in to Andrews for our landing we saw a large military detachment, an equally large civilian crowd, and a military band awaiting us. It was a farewell in which I reviewed the troops, then shook hands with each of them. The band played the National Anthem and we boarded the airplane that for eight years had been Air Force One.

Here again we were filled with memories. We had literally been around the world more than once in that plane and had covered our nation many times. As we stepped aboard for the last time, I noticed how much things seemed just the way they had always been for the past eight years—Jim Kuhn was in my small compartment to talk about the arrival ceremony we would have in California; Ken Duberstein, M. B. Oglesby, and Stu Spencer were conferring in the lounge; Fred Ryan was working on the schedule; Kathy Osborne and Dottie Dellinger were at their typewriters; Dr. John Hutton was warning about the evils of smoking; Elaine Crispen, Jane Erkenbeck, and Jack Courtemanche were talking to Nancy; Jim Hooley was on the phone to the advance man at our next stop; Mark Weinberg was briefing the press photographers on what to expect at Los Angeles International Airport; Pete Souza was snapping pictures; and Bill Plante, Bob Abernathy, Gene Randall, Lou Cannon, Sam Donaldson, Dale Nelson, Lee May, Tom Ferraro, and Jerry O'Leary were in the press section predicting what I would say in my remarks when we touched down. We were joined on the flight by some staff family members: Genny and Genevieve Ryan (Genevieve was born almost a month later, which makes her the youngest passenger ever to be aboard a presidential airplane), Sydney Duberstein, Susan Wing (M. B. Oglesby's wife), Carole Kuhn, and Shelley Osborne (Kathy's daughter).

But one person was notably absent: the military aide, the person who, since twelve noon on January 20, 1981, had been at my side with the information I would need in the event of a nuclear strike. Today that officer was with the new president.

Today there would be no last-minute changes in a speech text.

There would be no conferences with the national security advisor, or air-to-ground telephone calls to cabinet members. No legislation would be signed, no press conferences would be held in the back section, no meetings with advisors in the staff section. Today I could take time to look out the windows of the airplane at the breathtaking beauty of our land—the emerald hills of Appalachia, the farms and small towns of the Midwest, the granite peaks of the Rockies, the rugged deserts of the Southwest, and, finally, the great metropolitan panorama of Southern California. It truly is "America, the Beautiful," and God has, indeed, "shed His grace on thee." I looked at the houses below and wondered about the people in those houses. Were they better off than they were eight years ago? I hoped so.

And yet as I reflected on what we had accomplished, I had a sense of incompleteness—that there was still work to be done. We need a constitutional amendment to require a balanced budget. Congressional redistricting has become a national disgrace and needs to be cleaned up. The president needs a line-item veto to cut out unnecessary spending.

I said earlier that in Hollywood if you didn't sing or dance, you became an after-dinner speaker. I didn't learn to sing or dance in Washington, so I was thinking about my plans to be back out there on the speaking circuit, trying to get the people to pressure their representatives to take action on these issues.

Just then there was a quiet knock on the door of our cabin and I was reminded that we were taking our last ride aboard what had been Air Force One. We were told there was a gathering of all of those on board—staff, press, and Secret Service—a chance to say good-bye before we landed. There were warm handshakes, tearful embraces, and lots of picture-taking. Finally, champagne was poured and glasses were raised. "Mission accomplished, Mr. President," someone called out, "mission accomplished."

Not yet, I thought to myself, not yet.

Index